THE
BILL JAMES
BASEBALL
ABSTRACT
1987

Also by Bill James
The Bill James Historical Abstract

THE BILL JAMES BASEBALL ABSTRACT 1987

Bill James

Ballantine Books   •   New York

All rights reserved under International and Pan-American Copyright
Conventions. Published in the United States by Ballantine Books, a division
of Random House, Inc., New York, and simultaneously in Canada by
Random House of Canada Limited, Toronto, Canada.

Library of Congress Catalog Card Number: 86-91560
ISBN 345-34180-5

Cover design by James R. Harris
Photo by Don Banks

Manufactured in the United States of America

First Edition: April 1987

10 9 8 7 6 5 4 3 2 1

DEDICATION

This book is dedicated to the sales force of Ballantine Books, including:

Lee Anderson
Chris Barnard
Barry Bloom
Mark Bloomfield
Stan Cohen
Jackye Colleran
Ian Doherty
Dick Efthim
Peter Gilman
Bruce Goodis
Kevis Haas
Randy Hickernell
Sue Hughes
James Jester
Alice Kesterson
Linda LaFrance
Karyn Mauldin
Michael Murphy
Mark Mutchler

Judy Nosel
Beth O'Connor
John Ortiz
Bill Parker
David Phethean
Peter Plishka
Art Polczynski
Cathy Procopio
Sandy Siegle
Sarah Simons
Lilia Smith
Carol Springer
Johanna Steinberg
Cate Sullivan
Cissy Tiernan
Sharon Valenta
Jack Werstein
Tierney Whipp

ACKNOWLEDGMENTS

A few years ago, Ballantine Books sent me out into the trenches to meet with and work with a few of their field representatives. I was supposed to be out there meeting route drivers and selling books, and I'm afraid it was a waste of their money on that account because I'm not any salesman. But the trip was a revelation to me, to get out there and meet all of these quiet, anonymous people who, without my knowing anything about it, had been for years working on my behalf, selling my book to distributors, bookstores, even supermarkets. Realizing how naïve I really was about the book business, I was nonetheless shocked to get out and discover that my book does not simply zip off the presses and on to the best-seller lists by itself, as I had always kind of assumed, but is carefully lifted step by step along the sales staircase. And as a bonus, I learned more about the nuts and bolts of the book business in those couple of weeks than I have otherwise in all the years I've been doing this.

So I thought I would dedicate a book to those guys sometime, and here it is.

In the past, my beloved wife, Susie, has been a nine-month-a-year artist and a three-month-a-year baseball researcher. Well, we've got a baby now, wonderful little girl, but as you can imagine, there's been a reallocation of time, and in the process I'm afraid Susie's own life has been squeezed pretty hard. I solemnly promise, Suzie, to spend all next summer just watching that baby grow and letting you get back to your studio, but I wanted to say here how much I appreciate your letting me work day and night these last four months. I appreciate not only your time and your effort and your patience and your work as a statistician, secretary, and work organizer, but your sacrifice of your own interests to the 24-hour-a-day demands of Rachel and me.

I have a terrific agent in Liz Dahransoff and an indulgent editor in Peter Gethers, who are both much appreciated. I appreciate all of the people who wrote letters and comments, which are included herein, and the people of *Project Scoresheet*, whom we shall deal with one by one in the other book. I should mention D, T, B, S, I, the S and LF, TB, TrB, CB, DJ, GLC, and I; you all know who you are. Thanks.

CONTENTS

INTRODUCTION METHODS, ESSAYS

INTRODUCTION

All right, who is Bill James, and why does he have two books out this spring?

In 1914 there was a pitcher named Bill James who went 26–7 with the Boston Braves, helped them whip up a World Championship. He has nothing to do with this book. Then there was William James, who wrote *Varieties of Religious Experience* and probably several other things—but who remembers them—and he has nothing to do with the book, either.

I'm Bill James, and the first thing I need to do is explain about the two books. This is the *Baseball Abstract*, which I have been doing every year since 1977. The general purpose of the *Abstract* is to line up a few hundred questions that baseball people are discussing and try to find the evidence that relates to them. In the years of doing this I have felt keenly the need to have access to the accounts of each and every major league game. To obtain those accounts I started an organization called *Project Scoresheet*, which now includes a few hundred people who score baseball games and send the figures to Chicago, where they are scratched into a computer and printed out in a standard form and sent back to the people who are interested in them.

Now I'll talk about the economics of it and the competition and all that in a moment, but when we assembled all of those scoresheets it was pretty apparent that there was too much information on them to run it all in the *Abstract*. With access to the scoresheets, we could figure out how each and every player had hit in game situations—with the bases empty, with men on base, in the late innings of close games, etc. We could figure out what percentage of each player's RBI had come when the game was close, and what percentage had occurred after the game was decided. We could look at how each player had hit when facing groundball pitchers and when facing flyball pitchers. We could look at how each player had hit against finesse pitchers and against power pitchers. We could look at how each player had hit across the calendar.

We could look at how many bases were stolen against each pitcher, and how many runners were caught stealing when he was pitching. We could look at how players had done against left-handed and right-handed pitchers. We could look at that information over a period of years, trying to distinguish the short-term flukes from the true performance variables.

We could do all of that—but we couldn't do it in this book. Thus was born *The Great American Baseball Stat Book*, also with my name on the cover, and also available from the same publisher. There is some overlap in the information of the two books, but there are several distinctions. Let me clarify:

1) With the exception of a letter here or a short article there, I write all of this book. I didn't personally write that much of *The Great American Baseball Stat Book*.

I had a lot to do with the other book. I helped to decide what would be in the book, in both the broad outlines and the details. I made up the title.

I wrote the introduction and some of the player comments. I helped with the research, and I helped organize *Project Scoresheet* itself. But most of it was written by other people (which was another reason for doing that book: there are a lot of people other than me who have interesting ideas about the things that I discuss here, and there is a limit to how much of their material I can use in this book).

2) The other book contains much, much more raw statistical information than does this one—and, for that matter, much more than any other baseball statistics book has ever contained. We broke down the record more ways than it has ever been broken down before, and then we looked at those breakdowns over one-year and three-year periods to make the categories meaningful.

3) In this book, I use analytical methods to look at the issues of the game. Rather than speculating about whether someone might get 3,000 hits in his career, I have a method to look at the question. And, rather than arguing about who should be in the Hall of Fame, I have a method to predict whether or not a likely player *will* go in the Hall of Fame. Rather than relying solely on subjective judgments of value, I use analytical methods to assess value.

Those methods are mine. (I mean, other people are welcome to use them, but they don't ofen choose to.) They're in this book.

4) We did something in the other book that I felt strongly needed to be done. There are several reference books around that present player records year by year over the player's career. All of these books, in my opinion, have allowed themselves to get dangerously out of date. Almost anyone would agree that double plays are an important part of the game, but no source tells you how many times each player has grounded into a double play, except in the most recent year. Nobody gives you a year-by-year record of Rickey Henderson's caught stealing, or a year-by-year record of Don Baylor's being hit by a pitch, or a year-by-year record of Wally Backman's sacrifice bunts. There is no systematic record of sacrifice flies or intentional walks drawn or on-base percentage. Most of those publications don't even carry strikeouts and walks, for heaven's sake. There is no reason for that, except for the intransigence and laziness of the people who publish those books. So we decided, while we were doing *The Great American Baseball Stat Book,* to assemble and provide that information.

5) This book is sometimes challenging, occasionally abstruse or difficult to figure. I don't intend it to be that way: I'm just a confusing writer. The other book probably will have an article or two which might be difficult to understand, but in the main it is closer to the surface.

6) Most of this book discusses *issues* and is organized by *teams*. Most of the other book discusses *players* and is organized by players.

7) A certain amount of this book is personal. It's not just that I talk about my baby girl and my wife and my Royals, but that most of what I write reflects my attitude not only about the subject but about stuff in general. I tell jokes. I swear. I relate the lessons of baseball to the lessons of my own life. I write about the philosophy of baseball and science. I mean, I know very well that a lot of people don't like it and aren't interested in my opinions, but if you don't you don't have to read it. If you're offended by what I write or the way I write, I'm sorry but I'm not going to change to accommodate you.

The other book, being written and edited by a large number of different people, is not personal. Like most sportswriters, these people do care about offending you. The book is factual, not speculative. The book is more accurate and less argumentative. The book is more interested in being informative, and less in being funny.

The distinction is clear in my mind now: I hope it is in yours. There is some overlap between the statistical information in the two books, which is unfortunate, but it has to be there for a couple of years.

Let me back off and take this one from the top. I didn't start this publication as a resource book. It wasn't my original intention to gather and make available information about hitting against left-handed and right-handed pitching, batting at home and on the road, that sort of thing. I have always been interested in *issues,* not in *details*.

But a command of the details is essential to a command of the issues. You can't figure out what the platoon advantage means in baseball unless you have the data and can study it. I started gathering and presenting that data simply because nobody else was doing it. I'm a lousy statistician. I'm impatient, sloppy and easily bored with statistics. I really don't *care* whether Rickey Henderson hit .235 or .238 in Yankee Stadium and don't know what difference it makes, and that is a sane attitude for a baseball fan but a lousy attitude for a statistician. Had there been an Elias *Analyst* or any similar book when I began my book, I would have been very happy to let them have that market.

But there wasn't any such reference, and I wanted the data, and I wanted to make a living as a writer. To assemble and provide that information was something that I saw I could do to add value to my book.

So I started doing it, and the book has been a terrific success. Because the book has been successful, there have been other people who have decided there must be money in it after all so let's publish a book, too. If the public wants baseball statistics, the thinking goes, hell, we can produce more statistics than James can. While *I* see the *Abstract* as being a book about the relationship between baseball statistics and the issues that baseball people are discussing, other people just see it as being a book of baseball statistics.

Now, while I would have been perfectly happy for somebody else to have published all the data years ago, I am not all that thrilled to have people trying to push me out of the market that I have established. But the *Abstract* cannot be all things to all people. It can be a book about the philosophy and theory of sports and all that crap, or it can be a statistical reference book. With the information that is now available it is no longer possible—unless I give up what *I* see as being the essential elements of the book—for the *Abstract* to be the *best* statistical reference about the game. And that's why it was necessary to create the other book—to stay ahead of the market insofar as statistical evidence is concerned.

At the same time, there are many readers who have come to depend on the *Abstract* for certain reference material—what do people hit against right-handed and left-handed pitchers, etc.—and it would not be fair to those people to simply drop that information and tell them to go buy the other book. I wouldn't do that. And so, for a few years, there will be an area of overlap between the two books. It's time for me to start getting out of the business of rounding up and selling statistics, and I couldn't be happier about that. Directly and indirectly, I have made a great deal of information permanently available to the public, and I'm happy about that. It served its purpose in my career, but it's time to move on. (It will be a great relief not to have to try to beat information out of the San Diego Padres anymore. The Padres always like to pretend that they won't send us information because they don't think we should have it, but we suspect that the real reason is that nobody in the organization knows anything.)

As I write this I haven't seen all of *The Great American Baseball Stat Book*. In what I have seen, there's a lot of good stuff. *Project Scoresheet* is a loose organization of nobody-knows-exactly-how-many scorers who keep track of every major league game and make sure somebody is scoring it. John and Sue Dewan run the organization and do a terrific job of it. They keep track of the games and make sure that somebody enters each game into the computer. They supervised the design of the software by which each game is entered. They constructed the volunteer network to get the work done. They supervised the design of the software to print out any of several kinds of box scores—a traditional box score to check against the other sources and account-form box scores so you can tell what actually happened. They organized the effort to check each box score for errors. They developed the software to compile the statistics from those accounts. Once in a while, they go out for pizza.

Anyway, you got a couple hundred people seriously involved, not counting the marginal help. Most of those people pitched in on *The Great American Baseball Stat Book,* and there is a lot of talent in the group, as there would be in any group that size. After the introduction and the player register (the year-by-year records), there is a section of 260 one-page articles on players, one page to a player. There is a 400-word comment about the player and then the data chart. I'm the editor for the player comments of one division, the American League West. We've got lawyers and mailmen and college professors who are also baseball fans—and very knowledgeable fans—playing at being sportswriters. Their results are sometimes delightful, and consistently informative. I mean, I write player comments every year, but there's no way I can know as much about José Canseco as the fans in Oakland do *and* as much about Cal Ripken as the fans in Baltimore *and* as much about Billy Doran as the fans in Houston. The player comments are a mix of the short statistical notes of the *Analyst* and the observations of *The Scouting Report,* with occasional bursts of the off-the-wall comments of the *Abstract.* I think you'll like it.

The final section of *The Great American Baseball Stat Book* will be a collection of essays by some of these same writers and some others. The idea for this section was to provide a place for people to do sabermetric research or essays or whatever it was that they wanted to do, so long as it made some sense and/or was entertaining. It's an opportunity for the people who might want to be the next Bill James to show off their stuff.

Incidentally, we still need help in the project, and we will always need help. We need people to score games. We have enough people involved now that there's no great load on any one individual; all you have to do is learn our scoring system, which is simple, and score a baseball game once in a while. If you contact John Dewan (write: P.O. Box 46074, Chicago, Illinois; or phone: 312–774–3798), he'll put you in touch with your team captain. For some reason, we have a lot of trouble getting scorers in some places, most notably the Los Angeles area, St. Louis, and Dallas. The Dodgers, Padres, and Angels are the three teams for which we have the most trouble getting scoresheets.

Well, I didn't mean to do a sales pitch for the other book or for the organization; I just wanted you to understand basically what *The Great American Baseball Stat Book* was so that you could make an informed decision about whether or not you wanted to try it. I know what we should do—we should take one page out of that book and reproduce it here, so people can study what the information would be. I'd tell you about this book, but you already bought it, right? We'll stick in the odd page here, and then get to work.

Ed Correa
Texas Rangers

It is appropriate that the baby-faced Rangers had the youngest player in the majors in 1986. He was 15 days shy of his twentieth birthday when he won his first game in a Ranger uniform. Actually, Kid Correa is a remarkably mature player both physically and emotionally. The native Puerto Rican has made a splendid adjustment to life in the States. His command of English as his second language is astounding, and he handles himself like a veteran on the post-game shows. Physically he is a bull of a young man. José Guzman is three years older but looks far younger than Correa. The rookie ended up with 189 strikeouts to lead the team. That also was a club record for a rookie, as were his 12 wins. He led all 1986 rookie pitchers in innings (202 1/3) as well as in strikeouts. With Bobby Witt striking out 174, the Rangers became the first team in history to have two rookie pitchers over 150 strikeouts in the same season. Edwin's 7.43 hit average was good enough to rank sixth in

the league. His only real weakness was his control, a common problem with young pitchers. In a game in May he walked eight batters. He finished with a 5.60 walk average and even managed to throw more wild pitches than Charlie Hough. Between the minors, majors, and winter ball, Correa threw almost 250 innings in 1985. He started to drag a little in the middle of the 1986 season but bounced back strong after being given a little more rest. In his last four starts he had a 0.55 ERA and struck out 38 in 32 2/3 innings (10.47 per 9 IP). There may be another benefit to the Rangers' super trade with the White Sox. Ed has a younger brother back in Puerto Rico who all the scouts are drooling over. Puerto Rican ballplayers are not part of the amateur draft. They sign with who they choose, and it looks like Kid Correa II would like to team up with his brother as a Texas Ranger.

—Craig Wright

1986: Power, Groundball												1985: Power, Flyball											1984: Did not play	
	1986 SEASON											**THREE YEARS (84 – 86)**													
	G	IP	H	BB	SO	SB	CS	W	L	S	ERA	G	IP	H	BB	SO	SB	CS	W	L	S	ERA			
Totals	32	202.1	167	126	189	35	9	12	14	0	4.23	37	212.2	178	137	199	35	9	13	14	0	4.36			
							At Home and on the Road																		
Home	13	83.2	64	41	89	13	4	6	6	0	3.98	16	91.0	71	48	97	13	4	7	6	0	3.96			
Road	19	118.2	103	85	100	22	5	6	8	0	4.40	21	121.2	107	89	102	22	5	6	8	0	4.66			
							During the Day and at Night																		
Day	5	35.0	25	28	34	9	3	2	2	0	3.09	6	40.0	29	34	40	9	3	3	2	0	3.15			
Night	27	167.1	142	98	155	26	6	10	12	0	4.46	31	172.2	149	103	159	26	6	10	12	0	4.64			
							On Grass and on Turf																		
Grass	26	164.0	129	103	153	24	8	11	10	0	4.06	30	173.1	139	114	163	24	8	12	10	0	4.26			
Turf	6	38.1	38	23	36	11	1	1	4	0	4.93	7	39.1	39	23	36	11	1	1	4	0	4.81			
							By Month																		
April	4	25.1	22	13	21	4	0	1	2	0	4.62	4	25.1	22	13	21	4	0	1	2	0	4.62			
May	5	37.2	23	26	37	6	3	2	1	0	1.67	5	37.2	23	26	37	6	3	2	1	0	1.67			
June	6	38.2	35	20	35	5	2	2	3	0	5.59	6	38.2	35	20	35	5	2	2	3	0	5.59			
July	5	25.2	27	18	29	5	1	1	3	0	6.66	5	25.2	27	18	29	5	1	1	3	0	6.66			
August	5	27.0	30	23	18	6	1	2	2	0	6.67	5	27.0	30	23	18	6	1	2	2	0	6.67			
Sept/Oct	7	48.0	30	26	49	9	2	4	3	0	2.25	12	58.1	41	37	59	9	2	5	3	0	3.09			

vs. Opponent Batters																									
	1986 SEASON											**THREE YEARS (84 – 86)**													
	Ave.	OBP	SLG	AB	H	2B	3B	HR	RBI	BB	SO	Ave.	OBP	SLG	AB	H	2B	3B	HR	RBI	BB	SO			
Totals	.223	.336	.324	750	167	29	1	15	84	126	189	.225	.341	.333	790	178	32	1	17	89	137	199			
						Pitching vs. Left and Right-handed Batters																			
Left	.224	.327	.290	397	89	15	1	3	35	61	88	.226	.330	.299	411	93	16	1	4	36	64	91			
Right	.221	.345	.363	353	78	14	0	12	49	65	101	.224	.352	.369	379	85	16	0	13	53	73	108			
							Situational																		
Bases Empty	.202	.326	.290	410	83	13	1	7	7	75	103	.204	.332	.300	427	87	15	1	8	8	82	107			
Leadoff	.230	.354	.303	178	41	7	0	2	2	34	39	.227	.359	.303	185	42	8	0	2	2	38	40			
Not Leadoff	.181	.304	.280	232	42	6	1	5	5	41	64	.186	.311	.298	242	45	7	1	6	6	44	67			
Runners On	.247	.348	.365	340	84	16	0	8	77	51	86	.251	.351	.372	363	91	17	0	9	81	55	92			
First Base Only	.317	.396	.488	123	39	6	0	5	12	14	26	.313	.391	.493	134	42	6	0	6	14	15	30			
Scoring Position	.207	.322	.295	217	45	10	0	3	65	37	60	.214	.330	.301	229	49	11	0	3	67	40	62			
Late Innings, Close	.154	.267	.231	52	8	1	0	1	3	6	12	.154	.267	.231	52	8	1	0	1	3	6	12			

RBI/Opportunities						
Scoring Position	54 / 305	(18%)		56 / 328	(17%)	
Scoring Position, 2 Out	27 / 140	(19%)		27 / 149	(18%)	
On Third, Less than 2 Out	17 / 45	(38%)		18 / 50	(36%)	
RBI in close games / RBI Total	65 / 84	(77%)		66 / 89	(74%)	

MEANINGFUL AND MEANINGLESS STATISTICS

Wins and losses are the sun around which baseball statistics revolve. I get asked a lot about meaningful and meaningless statistics. "Bill," they will ask—"One thing I wanted to ask our guest"—"what's the most meaningless statistic in baseball? What are some of the most important?" My general answer is that the first and most serious mistake people make in talking about baseball statistics is that of trying to sort them into "meaningful" and "meaningless" statistics.

The categories don't fit. Statistics aren't "meaningful" and "meaningless"; that's just a way of cutting down the amount of information that you have to deal with. All player statistics in baseball, without any exception that I am aware of, are flawed; they are all subject to outside influences. There is no statistic that is a pure statement of any ability, not dependent on the context in any way. *All baseball statistics are compiled in the context of specific situations, and thus all statistics reflect those situations as well as the individual skills of the player.* Thus no statistic is 100% "meaningful." There is no such thing as a baseball statistic which can be taken without a grain of salt.

At the same time, all baseball statistics, with very minor exceptions, bear some relationship to some baseball ability. The importance of any baseball statistic depends ultimately upon the relationship it bears to the win column. That relationship is never easy to see. This book is, among other things, about that relationship.

I am not aware of any baseball statistic that is produced at random. I am not aware of any baseball statistic that has no correlation to winning percentage, be it a positive or a negative correlation. *All baseball statistics are in one way or another related to wins and losses; thus no statistic is 100% meaningless.* If a baseball statistic is meaningless to you, that is simply because you don't know what it means.

Still, declaring this statistic or that one to be "absolutely meaningless" is a popular hobby for baseball fans and writers; it is, to borrow from a later essay, a statistical form of logical telescoping. I get letters every week telling me why won-lost records of pitchers are meaningless, or why saves or game-winning RBI are meaningless. The problem with this is that, when you declare one category to be meaningless, you are left to rely that much more heavily on the ones remaining. And they ain't perfect either.

In evaluating a starting pitcher, for instance, there are two primary things that one ordinarily relies on—his won-lost record, and his ERA. Most anybody does; when you know that a pitcher is 17–11 or 11–17 and has an ERA of 3.04 or 4.03, you feel that you know how effective he has been. Now, if you say that won-lost records are meaningless because they depend on who the player plays for and how many runs he scores (which they do) then you're left judging the pitcher essentially by his ERA—which is, in fact, also subject to outside influences. When people say that one statistic is meaningless, what they are really saying is that they have learned to see the distortions in that statistic—but haven't yet learned to see the distortions in the alternatives.

In learning to understand baseball one needs to learn to deal with both the positives and the negatives of each type of information, and to learn to see through the distortions of statistics just as one learns to see through the distortions of media judgments or the distortions of history. In this article, I'm going to try to deal with the difficult question of how much weight can be put on various statistics, to deal with it not by sorting them into "meaningful" and "meaningless" stats, but by looking at the degree to which each statistic can be made to carry weight.

First off, we need to make a quick list of the categories we will be evaluating here in the first phase of this article. There are 40 basic categories of a hitting, pitching, or fielding record, which we will look at first. In this case we are considering only one-year totals; later, we'll consider how the career figure might differ from that one year. Those 40 are, alphabetically, but in groups:

BATTERS—19 Categories
At Bats
Caught Stealing (Stolen Base Percentage)
Doubles
Games Played
Game Winning RBI
Grounded Into Double Plays
Hits (Batting Average)
Hit By Pitch
Home Runs
On Base Percentage
Runs Scored
Runs Batted In

Sacrifice Flies
Sacrifice Hits
Stolen Bases
Strikeouts
Total Bases (Slugging Average)
Triples
Walks

PITCHERS—15 Categories
Balks
Complete Games
Earned Runs Allowed (Earned Run Average)
Hits Allowed (Hits Per Nine Innings)
Hit Batsmen
Home Runs Allowed
Innings Pitched
Runs Allowed (Runs Allowed Average)
Sacrifice Hits Allowed
Sacrifice Flies Allowed
Saves
Shutouts
Strikeouts
Walks Allowed
Won/Lost Record

FIELDERS—6 Categories
Assists (Assists Per Game)
Double Plays (or Double Plays Per Game)
Errors (Fielding Average)
Passed Balls
Putouts (Putouts Per Game)
Range Factor

Let's look at the underlying question. What is it that makes a baseball statistic valuable?

In the 1978 *Baseball Abstract*, I suggested five rules for evaluating a proposed statistic. Those were:

1. Never divide A by B unless there is a damn good reason why A should be divided by B.

2. Any statistic which is never surprising is never interesting. Any statistic which is consistently surprising is probably wrong.

3. No amount of statistical evidence will make a statement invulnerable to the laws of common sense.

4. The final test of any statistic is whether or not it correlates with winning.

5. Any statistic the meaning of which can be expressed in understandable terms in a common English sentence is greatly to be preferred, other things being equal, to one which cannot.

Looking back on these rules, I realize that something has changed in the last nine years. These rules were proposed in an environment in which what I call "freak-show statistics" were proliferating. Almost every month, the *Baseball Digest* or some contributor to *The Sporting News* would propose some new method of evaluating ballplayers. These methods often added doubles, batting average, and outfield assists together willy-nilly, without any apparent pattern or purpose but accompanied by an impassioned argument usually amounting to the contention that this method rated highly all of the people whom the author thought were good ballplayers. The "Sisler statistic," a haphazard jumble of pitching categories, was one of the few examples to receive enough attention that you might remember it now.

Thus, the rules that I proposed then were designed to help the reader distinguish among these Rube Goldberg statistics. What has happened since is that, with the success of the *Abstract* and the other books that have followed, this entire genre of statistics has more or less died (or at least *had* more or less died before I revived it by introducing several off-the-wall statistics in the 1987 *Baseball Abstract*). As information about batting against right-handed and left-handed pitchers and at home and on the road has become available, along with information on many other aspects of player performance, the freak show statistics have been squeezed out. It is not that it is no longer true that one should not divide A by B unless there is a damn good reason A should be divided by B, but that it is no longer necessary to say it; the discussion has moved past that. The baseball statistics of today tend to do what I suggested a decade ago they should do: either focus on specific skills and try to find ways to measure them, or else put them together in ways which make sense and accomplish a specified purpose.

There I was suggesting criteria for a *proposed new* statistic: here I am evaluating (first of all) just the basic numbers—wins and losses, saves, ERA, strikeouts and walks, home runs, RBI, that sort of thing. Later we'll get into the survivors among the evaluative stats.

I would suggest now that there are four basic criteria by which statistics can be judged. Those are:

1) Importance
2) Reliability
3) Ease of comprehension
4) Construction

I'll rate each of the first three on a ten-point scale, and then much later in the article we'll introduce the fourth. Although there is a ten-point scale for each, the first three will *not* have equal impact on the final "stat value score."

I. CATEGORY IMPORTANCE

By *importance* or *significance*, I mean primarily this: does it correlate with winning? Rule number four above, and the first sentence of the article. Whether it is a statistic, a skill, a personality trait, or an organizational pattern we still ask the same essential question: *Is it a characteristic of winning teams to do this?* How often do winning teams do this? Why do winning teams do this? When do winning teams do this? Do winning teams do it better than losing teams? Do they do it more often than losing teams?

A "ten" in this category is a statistic that directly measures the ability to win. Among the basic player stats, there is only one ten in this respect, that being the **Pitcher's Won-Lost Record.** Other stats obliquely—but nothing else directly—measure the ability to win.

Winning games in baseball consists of three parts—scoring runs, preventing runs, and putting the two together in a desirable combination. A **Pitcher's ERA** is a nine—it directly measures his ability to prevent runs. Later on, some of the manufactured statistics will be scored as nines on the offensive side.

An eight in this category would be a statistic that measures one of the major components of one of those three factors. That is, since putting runs on the scoreboard consists of two parts—scoring runs and driving them in— **Runs Scored** and **RBI** are both eights. Or, to look at the same thing a bit differently, run creation consists of two parts, getting runners on base and advancing them. Thus, on base percentage and slugging percentage (which measures the ability to advance runners) are both eights.

A seven in this category is a statistic that does not sum up one of the two or three essential elements of run creation or prevention, but that measures one of the primary skills that goes into those. For example, the ability to hit home runs is not the same as the ability to drive in runs, which would be an eight, but it is *one of the major components* of the ability to drive in runs. Thus, **Home Runs** are a seven.

Batting Average is also a seven, and one could make a good argument that it should be an eight. The argument is this: Batting average does not directly measure either of the two essential elements of offense, but it *contributes heavily to both*. Batting average is one of the two major parts of on-base percentage—walks being the other—but it is also one of the two major parts of slugging percentage—isolated power being the other. As run creation (and thus offensive ability) can be separated into runs scored and runs batted in or into on-base percentage and slugging percentage, it can also be separated into batting average and secondary average.

Against this argument is the fact that the correlation of team batting average and team runs scored is just not high enough to justify considering batting average on the same level as on-base percentage or slugging percentage. The score that any stat receives in this area is largely determined by the correlation between the category and team wins, as well as the correlation to team runs scored or allowed. If that correlation is high, the score will be high; if it isn't, the score in the significance category won't be. On a team level, the number of home runs hit has a higher correlation with team wins than does batting average.

Well, we shouldn't get too carried away with that. We can only see the correlations clearly on a team level, but the significance of a statistic as measured on a team level can be very different from what we are really interested in, which is the significance on an individual level. This can be true for any of many reasons. Team at bats have a fairly high correlation with team wins, the reason for that being that a good hitting team takes longer to be put out than a poor hitting team, hence has more team at bats. A good hitting team has lots of at bats, but to conclude from this that a player who has a lot of at bats must therefore be a good hitter would be nincompoopery. A different example would be wild pitches: There is a fairly strong negative correlation between wild pitches and wins—but that doesn't mean that the wild pitches are all that costly. The wild pitches themselves are fairly trivial, except that it is not characteristic of a good pitching staff to throw them. A wild pitch is to a wild pitcher what a wart is to a cancer; it's not that anybody cares about having the wart except that it's a symptom of the cancer. There can be all kinds of relationships between an accomplishment and wins, other than the cause-and-effect relationship in which we are interested.

Anyway, I'm going to leave batting average at seven.

I should explain that, in inquiring about the significance of a statistical category, we are inquiring only about those things that are recorded in this category, and not about the significance of the underlying traits which create the tendency. A pitcher who hits a lot of batters with pitches might do so because he likes to pitch inside or he might do so because he is wild, but when we ask about the significance of hit batsmen for a pitcher, we are not asking about the importance of pitching inside or about the importance of being wild, only about the impact of hitting batters with pitches. Or when we ask about the importance of stolen bases, we are not interested in the value of speed, which creates stolen bases. We are interested in the stolen bases themselves. In these cases the distinction is fairly clear; in other cases it is not clear at all. While it may prove to be a rule more honored in the breach than in the observance, we will try to steer clear of confusing statistics with the skills which create those statistics.

A six in this category is a statistic that measures a still important, though less central, aspect of run creation or prevention. Let's run the scores for everything, and then I'll explain the rest later:

Ten: Won-Lost Record.
Nines: Earned Runs Allowed (Earned Run Average), Runs Allowed (Runs Allowed Average).
Eights: On-Base Percentage, Total Bases (Slugging Average), Runs Scored, Runs Batted In, Saves.

Sevens: Hits (Batting Average), Hits Allowed (Hits Per Nine Innings), Home Runs, Range Factor.

Sixes: Doubles, Game Winning RBI, Double Plays turned on defense, Double Plays Grounded Into, Pitchers Walks Allowed, Batter's Walks, Home Runs Allowed.

Fives: Triples, Putouts (Putouts Per Game), Assists (Assists Per Game), Innings Pitched, Games, At Bats, Strikeouts By Pitchers.

Four: Errors (Fielding Percentage).

Threes: Caught Stealing (Stolen Base Percentage), Shutouts.

Twos: Stolen Bases, Balks, Complete Games, Sacrifice Flies, Sacrifice Flies Allowed, Hit By Pitch, Passed Balls.

Ones: Sacrifice Hits, Sacrifice Hits Allowed, Strikeouts By Hitters, Hit Batsmen.

Saves rate an eight because they bear such a close relationship to wins. We mentioned three basic elements of winning—scoring runs, preventing runs, and putting the two together in desirable combinations. Having someone to stop the other team at the critical moment is *one of the most basic elements* of putting runs and opposition runs together in a desirable way, hence an eight.

Range Factor is the only one of my own statistics that is evaluated in this group. Range Factor (successful plays made per game) is such a basic computation that it is closer to straight information than it is to one of my funny formulas. It is sort of my term and my refinement of a standard category, total chances per game.

There's little room for argument about the importance of the trait; defensive mobility is one of the three or four most basic attributes of any player. A .220 hitter can play in the majors if he is mobile enough on defense; a .280 hitter can't if he is extremely immobile. While many people would argue about the reliability of the measurement, certainly few would doubt that the amount of ground a fielder covers is very important, whether or not it can be accurately measured. If one player makes 150 plays a year that another player would not make, then that would make defensive range a hell of a lot more important than batting average (since no player gets 150 hits in a season that another player would not get).

My thinking about **Game Winning RBI** is that it is an attempt to measure something that is relatively essential to putting runs and opposition runs together, that being the ability to get timely hits. Let's assume for the moment that such an ability exists (that is, let us assume that the deviations in performance which occur in this area are a function of ability, rather than a function of chance). How important is it? Fairly important, though not as important as some announcers might tell you. A team that scores 650 runs and allows 750 runs will have a losing record about 97% of the time, which is to say that the ability to win games by getting *timely* runs, as opposed to getting abundant runs, is a relatively minor factor—but there is that 3% chance. A team which scores as many runs as it allows will, on rare occasion, finish 90–72 or 72–90 because they do or don't get timely hits. That still leaves timeliness as much less important than simple offensive or defensive ability, but far from trivial. I'll call that ability a six, mean-

ing that it is less important than stuff like hitting homers and hitting for average.

Walks—walks taken, walks given—I rated at six. It could be argued that a pitcher's control is one of the central elements of his ability to keep people off base, which is true, except. Walks are not, one for one, as damaging as hits. The correlation of walks to runs, again, is (while quite strong) not strong enough to justify considering walks to be on the same level of importance as batting average and home runs.

Doubles have a good correlation with team wins; actually, their correlation is about the same as that of team batting average and team home runs. I think, however, that that is an indicative, rather than a causative, relationship (that is, good teams tend to hit doubles, rather than hitting doubles wins ballgames.) Since the standard deviation of doubles (per team) is only about 25, intuition tells you that 25 doubles can't have the same impact as 30 home runs. Doubles are also a six.

Another six are **Home Runs Allowed.** Home runs are a seven offensively and a six defensively because they are more of a hitter's trait than a pitcher's (that is, the hitter is a larger determinant of when a home run occurs than is the pitcher), so that the correlation of home runs hit with wins is stronger than the correlation of home runs allowed with losses.

Though, as discussed later, the correlation to wins is diminished by a cross-correlation, the ability to turn (or avoid) a **Double Play** is certainly a tremendously significant factor in many innings, and an important variable among teams. Of course, the defensive responsibility for double plays rests largely on two players, the shortstop and second baseman. The number of double plays turned is thus a much more "significant" factor in evaluating those players than it is for the team as a whole.

Strikeouts I split, giving one score from an offensive standpoint and a different one from a defensive (or pitching) standpoint. This is because it is not really a characteristic of poor hitting teams or poor hitters to strike out more than good hitting players or teams (in fact, the correlation between team wins and batter's strikeouts is positive; on the whole, teams that strike out a lot score more runs and win more games than teams that strike out seldom). It's not that it is good to strike out, but if you do it lowers your batting average and you have that held against you, and at that it is still not especially characteristic of people with poor batting averages to strike out a lot: Rafael Santana strikes out less than Keith Hernandez. On the other hand, it *is* very much characteristic of good pitchers (and good teams) to gather strikeouts. Batters tend to strike out as a function of their batting style and as a function of the risks that they take, rather than as a function of their ability, whereas pitcher's strikeouts tend to be a function of ability.

Of course, some people will tell you that strikeouts are important because, with a runner on base, the strikeout freezes the runner, whereas a groundout or a flyout can advance the runner. On the one hand, this is an essentially trivial advantage—despite Gene Mauch's insistence that you can, the reality is that no team creates very many runs by making outs—and, on the other hand, it ignores the fact that while a strikeout won't move a runner from first to second it also won't move him from first back into the dugout. In many cases, probably *most* cases, the strikeout is actually *preferable* to any other out with a man on base, because it doesn't result in a double play. The strikeout might be less preferred than a flyout, but it certainly should be much more preferred than a groundout.

Putouts Per Game and **Assists Per Game** are the elements of range factor, hence naturally go about two notches below them, at five.

Triples are less significant than doubles simply because there are many fewer of them. Triples have less to do with determining who wins than do doubles not because triples are less important than doubles, but because they are less common. Triples are also a five.

Below that you get the things which a) don't happen very often, hence are of limited importance; or b) are not characteristic of winning (or losing) teams; or c) are only incidentally characteristic of winning or losing teams. Like **Fielding Average** . . . fielding average, despite its arbitrary nature, does correlate with winning. However, the difference between the best and worst players at most positions is just a handful of plays—only occasionally as many as a dozen—so that the impact range of the ability is comparatively minor.

Stolen Bases we'll argue about later, but the simple fact is that it is not a characteristic of good teams or good offenses to steal lots of bases. In most cases it's just irrelevant: in the rare case of a player who steals a hundred bases and is seldom caught stealing, there is an offensive impact in the same range of magnitude as the impact of Don Baylor's being hit by a pitch (that is, it has to be considered in evaluating that particular player, although it is not very meaningful in the larger scheme of things).

To clarify something that you probably could figure out yourself if you cared, "HB" or "**Hit Batsmen**" is a pitcher's category, indicating how many times he plunked somebody with a pitch; "HBP" or "**Hit By Pitch**" is a hitter's category, indicating how many times he was the plunkee. Both leagues use the HB abbreviation for hit batsmen, but for hit by pitch, the batter's stat, the National League uses HP and the American League uses HB. *The Sporting News* also uses HB and HP, like the National League, but all sensible people use HB and HBP because you can keep them straight that way. Anyway, HB is rated one and HBP is at two because, in today's baseball, it is much more of a batter's tendency. Although there probably is somebody, I don't think I could name an active pitcher who tends to hit a lot of batters with pitches.

I could have scored **Sacrifice Bunts** at half a point, but decided that was more in the nature of an insult than an evaluation. A sacrifice bunt is a pretty neutral event, a sort of offensive delaying action. A sacrifice bunt total is worth about as much as a count of how many times the batter stepped out of the box.

Finally, what is the "significance," the importance, of the opportunity columns—the **Games Played, Innings Pitched, At Bats,** that sort of thing. What do they tell us?

What these columns tell us is whether or not the guy is good enough to play. Although it divides the world into a dark/light universe (those who are good enough to play and those who aren't, with the intermediate stage of those who are good enough to play some of the time), this is basic information. It could be argued that if a player has good stats but never acquires much playing time—Lee Lacy, let's say—then that "game limitation" is telling us something. It's describing his role with the team. If you have a player without good hitting stats who plays 160 games a year, the game column is telling you that his glove is valued. If he plays 120 games a year and hits .320, maybe the games are telling you he doesn't hit left-handers. Maybe they're telling you he is injury prone. Acknowledging freely that in this case we are violating our rule about confusing the value of the accomplishment with the value of the traits that create it, I think the games, at bats and innings should be considered significant, if somewhat unreliable, evidence about the overall quality of the player. I'll list them all at five.

II. RELIABILITY

By *reliability* or *integrity,* I mean the extent to which the statistic truly reflects the ability. What outside influences are there on this accomplishment? How many things are there, *other than the player's own ability,* that might cause him to do well in this category? What illusions are there in this category?

A ten in this category would be a statistic that was not subject to any influences other than the ability of the player. As I said earlier, I am not aware of any such statistic.

A nine would be a statistic that was relatively free of illusion—that was subject, let us say, to only one minor extraneous influence, or two very minor influences.

Strikeouts are a nine. The only outside influence that I know of on strikeouts is the visibility in the park in which the player or pitcher performs. At the margin, let's say in the case where two pitchers are competing for the league lead in strikeouts, this can be a reasonably significant consideration. Probably the most extreme case is Exposition Stadium in Montreal, where the visibility for the hitter is terrible, but there are other poor visibility parks, such as Shea Stadium, Candlestick, the Kingdome, the Metrodome, County Stadium in Milwaukee, and Comiskey. The pitchers and hitters who play in these parks will always have an edge when it comes to leading the league in strikeouts.

On the other end, you have Busch Stadium, Royals Stadium, Wrigley Field, and Cincinnati's Riverfront, where a terrific hitting background reduces strikeouts, thus making strikeout-prone hitters more effective, and strikeout-prone pitchers less effective. These effects are not dramatic unless compounded by other elements; one might guess that a pitcher who strikes out 200 men in 250 innings in Montreal might get 170 in St. Louis. It's a distorting influence, but it's the most minor type of illusion to which any category is subject.

The effect of visibility on **Walks** drawn may be even more minor than that on strikeouts, but then for walks there are other park considerations. A power hitter will probably draw more walks when playing in a home-run park than when playing in Busch Stadium, simply because there is less fear for the pitcher to be guided by. Some hitters—George Brett for example—draw quite a few semi-intentional walks that they wouldn't draw if the man coming up behind them was a better hitter. It's a minor thing, but I'll leave walks/walks allowed at nine, as well as their cousin, hit by pitch/hit batsmen.

An eight would be a statistic that was subject to one *major* outside influence. **Batting Average** is an eight. The only important illusion in batting average is the park in which the player plays. I would state the difference this way, that whereas it is still possible for a pitcher to lead the league in strikeouts no matter what park he pitches in, it is extremely difficult for a hitter to lead the league in hitting unless he plays in a park that is conducive to so doing. Well, it can happen—Tim Raines and Al Oliver have proved that, leading the NL in batting in Montreal.

Visibility is important, but visibility is only one of many facets of a ballpark that cause the batting average in that park to go up or down. To name a few others, roughly in order of importance, there are:

1) Dimensions.
2) Surface (Artificial or Grass Turf, with variations in both types).
3) Climate (Batters do not hit well in cold weather).
4) Altitude (The ball travels much better at high altitudes).
5) The amount of foul territory.

In naming those six, we haven't named half of the factors that can effect the batting average in a park, but we have probably named the major ones. (Then there's always the announcers favorite bugaboo, the height of the mound. They *measure* the mounds, Jack. They measure them all the time. The mounds are all the same height.)

Anyway, combining these, it makes a big, big difference. You're not going to see very many people winning the batting crown while playing in Candlestick Park or Dodger Stadium or the Oakland Coliseum. I mean, if the Cub players hit 35 to 50 points better *as a team* in Wrigley Field than on the road, which they often do, while the Giants hit 20 or 30 points worse in Candlestick than on the road, that makes it pretty tough for a player in San Francisco to contend for the batting title. It is probably about seven to ten times more difficult to hit .300 in Oakland than it is in Fenway Park. (That is to say that, given the same players playing for both teams, there would probably be seven to ten times as many .300 hitters in Fenway as in Oakland.) So almost all batting titles are won by the players playing in a few parks.

While batting average is subject to a very large illusion from the park, the other illusions are fairly inconsequential. A player's batting average can be hurt or helped by the manual orientation of his team—that is, if he is a left-handed hitter on a team that sees a lot of left-handed pitchers, that could hurt his average. It was always said about Duke Snider that he received a break because the Dodgers were so deadly against left-handed pitchers that he rarely had to face one, hence had the platoon advantage almost all the time. Compared to some of the illusions to which statistics are prey, that one's pretty near nothing. Some people like to say that the hitters coming up ahead and behind you can make you a better or worse hitter, but I don't believe that amounts to anything, and most good hitters don't believe it, either.

Oh—I should discuss changes over time. When I said that the ballpark is almost the only thing that effects the integrity of batting average, some of you probably thought about the changes in batting average over time, that in 1930 it was probably 40 or 50 times easier to hit .300 than it was in 1968. Sure, that's a problem. I'm not deducting for that because changes over time effect almost everything. The standards for home runs are a lot different now than they were in the fifties, when most major league teams had at least one fence within 320 feet of home plate. Night baseball changed the standards for strikeouts, artificial turf changed the standards for triples and stolen bases . . . everything changes over time (except wins and losses). So let's just say, rather than knocking everything down one or two, that we are talking about *today's* statistics.

Almost everything is also subject to the park influence, but the effects are variable. Some things you might not think about—like stolen bases—but the park still plays a role. People run faster on artificial turf than they do on grass, so stolen-base percentages are higher. That's a minor effect; I'll put **Caught Stealing/Stolen Base Percentage** at nine. Stolen base *totals,* however, are subject to more influences. The change in percentage effects the willingness to run, and also, of course, you can't steal if you're not on base, so if the park changes your batting average, it changes your stolen base total. A home run park reduces stolen base attempts sharply because nobody wants to steal second when you are looking for a two-run homer. I'll subtract one point for the two of those and another because stolen base totals are subject to managerial whims, and **Stolen Bases** stands as a seven, which is only to say that stolen base totals are, in general, a fairly accurate statement of the player's ability to steal bases.

Runs, RBI, Slugging Percentage—they're all heavily subject to park illusions. The only thing that really *isn't* subject to a park illusion is, again, the won/lost record. There is one win and one loss in every game in every park.

The number of **Hits Allowed** by a pitcher (hits per nine innings) is subject to his defense as well as to the park, so we'll move that down to seven. **On-Base Percentage** is an eight, **Slugging Percentage** an eight; these things are pretty clean except for the park influence.

I am trying, you see, to go down two for each major

distraction in the statistic, and down one for each minor one. **Home Runs/Home Runs Allowed** we'll make an eight, although the park influence in that case could be a little larger. **Doubles** are an eight, **Triples** a seven. There are two reasons for triples being lower here. One is the problem of scale; no category can be reliable on less than 20 "trials" a year. Also triples, being an extreme test, are the *most* subject to park illusions of any category. It was commented upon last year that Mariano Duncan hit nine triples in spring training and none in the season, but what you have to understand is that *you just don't hit triples in Dodger Stadium.* The small outfield area and the slow turf just don't produce triples. In 1985 the Cardinals hit 36 triples in Busch Stadium, whereas the Dodgers hit only four in LA. But when the same teams went on the road, the Dodgers actually hit more triples than the Cardinals, 24–23.

Runs Scored and **RBI** are fully subject to the park illusion (minus two), but also subject to influence from two kinds of offensive context. Obviously, you're not going to drive in as many runs when hitting after Bob Boone as you are when following Rickey Henderson (minus one). Even if you have exactly the same hitters coming up behind you and ahead of you, where you are in the order still has an easily measurable impact on runs scored and RBI, since a leadoff hitter bats many more times with nobody out and nobody on than a third or fourth place hitter, and bats many more times period than an eighth place hitter. Minus one for that, and runs scored/RBI are at six.

Grounded Into Double Plays (GIDP) are about like RBI—subject to park and offensive context illusions. They're a six.

From a defensive standpoint, the problem with double plays is more acute. While the ability to turn a **Double Play** is no doubt important, the problem with DP statistics is that the teams that are best at turning the double play and the teams that turn the most double plays are often not the same teams. The correlation of double plays turned with wins is very weak, because the teams that turn the most double plays are the teams that have the most enemies on base to begin with. DP totals are sort of like the FBI's reports of drugs seized or the immigration services records for the number of illegal aliens deported. If the FBI seizes $4 billion worth of cocaine in Miami and 28 cents worth in Springfield, Illinois, this should not be taken as evidence that drug enforcement in Miami is more effective than it is in Springfield. Similarly, if the Chicago Cubs turn . . . well, you know this stuff.

In addition to park illusions and opportunity illusions, double play totals are subject to variation from pitching staffs. Some staffs simply throw a lot more ground balls than other staffs. That's three major and two minor illusions; double plays turned can be rated only a five on the reliability scale.

A pitcher's **Runs Allowed** (Run Average), in addition to the park illusion, is subject to every nuance and whim of defense, the combined effect of which can make the difference between John Tudor past and John Tudor present. Or Bob Ojeda; you know that story, too. That's the point, you see, that *if the statistic changes when the cir-cumstances change, then the statistic is not reliable.* To the degree to which the statistic changes with the circumstances, the statistic reflects the circumstances rather than the ability, and is unreliable.

Anyway, runs allowed are subject to park and defense. The defensive distortion *can* be enormous; still, I'm going to score run average at seven. It is my belief that, while the defense can help, the pitcher has got to be considered basically responsible for keeping the other team off the scoreboard. Some pitchers—sinkerball pitchers, control pitchers—are no doubt captives of their defense. Still, I think that, in the ordinary case, a pitcher who can get people out for one team probably could get them out for another.

Earned Run Average I will allow, generously, the same value. What ERA does is to introduce one bias—scorer's judgment—while attempting not very successfully to remove another bias—defensive support. Of course, ERA *doesn't* adjust for defensive support: if the second baseman can't turn the double play, the catcher can't throw and the left fielder can't move, the pitcher is still held accountable for their deficiencies. The pitcher is only let off the hook if somebody drops the ball or throws it away. ERA only purports to adjust for one relatively minor attribute of defensive support, and, because of inconsistent scoring, doesn't even do that very well.

Fielding Average (errors) are subject to two major illusions. The park bias, again, is larger than most people would imagine. There are some parks, like Candlestick and Jack Murphy Stadium in San Diego, that just breed errors. Bad hops that aren't quite bad enough to be ruled hits are common. Wind currents force the player to move his glove one foot in the last 20 feet of the ball's flight, and if he just misses you've got an error. When we combine that with the arbitrary nature of scoring decisions (could you believe some of those rulings in Fenway during the playoff?), we've got a ten, minus two, minus two, which is six.

With respect to **Range Factors,** park illusions exist but are less serious. It is true that ballparks influence the number of plays available; a left fielder in Fenway Park or a center fielder in Dodger Stadium will have fewer opportunities because of the small space of the area that he patrols. The Oakland outfielders consistently handle more fly balls than almost anybody else. The park illusion is less powerful with respect to range factors (minus one as opposed to minus two or minus three) because the 27-out nature of the game causes one team to total up about the same as another, wiping out most of the park differences. This, of course, is a mixed blessing, replacing one bias with another, for the same 27-out limit thus distorts the statistic; an entire team of good fielders will make only a few more plays than a team of poor fielders (although the team of good fielders actually will have a slightly higher collective range factor. Different teams do *not* have the same number of putouts and assists, and a good defensive team *will* have more than a poor one. Putouts and assists do correlate with team wins).

Another outside influence on range factor is the pitching staff behind which the fielder works. A ground-ball staff will cause an infielder to have more chances; a flyball staff helps the outfield. A left-handed staff gives extra chances to the third baseman. That's another "minus one," which makes range factor a seven. Then there's the problem of partial games in the field, which is something you have to keep in mind when reviewing them; a defensive replacement won't get a reliable reading because of his three-inning "games." What that is, really, is just an oversight in the statistics, the failure to maintain the obviously needed category of defensive innings. I'll leave it at seven because that may already be too low. I've got range factor lower than batting average and home runs—but if you checked what happened to players who changed teams, I think you'd find that their batting averages and power stats probably changed more (hence were shown to be more dependent on the circumstances) than their range factors.

Essentially the same level of reliability attaches to the components of range factor—**Putouts Per Game,** and **Assists Per Game.** One amazingly popular belief is that, for an infielder, assists per game are more reliable as an indicator of range than putouts per game or range factor. Putouts are often the result of force plays, these people will tell you, and balls caught in the air are usually just routine pop-ups. I regard this as one of those bizarre beliefs to which people can fall prey if they play a lot of APBA but never actually watch the games. I find it incomprehensible that anybody could watch Billy Doran or Shawon Dunston or Frank White play two or three games, and pay attention to what they are seeing, and still believe that putouts are mostly routine plays. Among outstanding plays by middle infielders, I would estimate that 75–80% are on balls hit in the air, and thus are scored as putouts. In fact, it is the *assists* that are usually on routine plays, and the putouts that primarily define the fielder's range. While it is true that putouts often occur on force plays, and this creates a good deal of noise in the data (love that expression), this merely tends to even the scales between the two. I think it's ridiculous to throw out infielder's putouts.

The whole range factor is probably a little more reliable than either of the two components, because the data is larger and the bias of a ground ball or fly ball staff tends to balance out when the two are combined. I'll make putouts/game and assists/game a six.

Outfielder's Assists totals, however, have to be given a somewhat lower berth. Outfielder's assist totals generally indicate his throwing ability, which they do with some reliability over time. Single-season assist totals can be tremendously misleading simply because the data is so small that it is unstable. You have probably heard that some people get extra outfield assists because their arms are so weak that they get plenty of opportunities to throw at passing baserunners, and I think that can happen. I'd peg the reliability of outfielder's assists in a single season as an indicator of throwing ability at only three.

Around the midpoint, we have an array of categories which combine individual abilities more or less in equal parts with the reflection of managerial decisions. These include **Sacrifice Hits** (four), **Complete Games** (five) and **Shutouts** thrown (four). Sacrifice hits tell you more about whether the manager likes to bunt than about whether the player is a good bunter, so sac hits are four; sacrifice hits allowed by a pitcher are not subject to this bias and so are

at six. I figure complete games are about half stamina and half managerial preference, so these are listed at five. Shutouts reflect park illusions (minus two) and, requiring the complete game, managerial preference to a more minor extent (minus one). However, the data sample is *really* tiny—the norm is below two—plus, like triples, shutouts are an extreme test for the tendency of the park, so they'll be listed at four.

One category that I don't know what the hell to do with is **Balks.** If balks are considered to be a reflection of the ability to hold runners, they fail the test; the league leader in balks is often a pitcher who also leads in runners picked off, the unofficial half of the stat pair. Steve Carlton in a good year used to commit five or seven balks and pick ten or twelve men off first base, which is a tremendous trade. But other pitchers just commit balks out of inexperience or poor concentration, so if the category systematically indicates anything, I don't know what. On the other hand, it does seem to be unusually free of illusions, since one can balk about as easily in one park as in another, and about as easily for a good team as for a bad one. I'll list balks as a neutral five, and you can change it if you have a better idea.

Below five, you get statistics that might be said to be not only *influenced* by the conditions under which the player plays, but actually *created* by those conditions, as much or more than they are created by the player's own skills. Among these categories, the most prominent is the pitcher's **Won-Lost** record.

Some people put a lot of stock in a won-lost record. Over a period of years, you should. In one year, you can't. There are always people around who will tell you that if Dave Dravecky only goes 9–11 despite his 3.07 ERA, he can't be a good pitcher. He didn't pitch well when it counted. He pitched just well enough to lose. The truth is that if Dave Dravecky only goes 9–11, that doesn't mean monopoly to a groundhog.

There are simply too many outside influences. The offense of the team—a massive outside influence. The defensive support. The help out of the bullpen. I mean, *ballparks* are a large factor effecting the integrity of a category, but you only play at home half of the time, so that in most areas the range of the impact is 10–20%. In winning percentage, it may be 50%, the difference between a .600 and a .400 team—and the pitcher has got that same team behind him, home or road, day or night, rain or shine.

Yet an even bigger variable than that is random luck. The most naive assumption about won-lost records, and the place where the most people go astray, is to think that run support will even out over the course of the long season. It takes many, many seasons for run support to even out between pitchers on the same team. I've figured offensive support for pitchers for more than ten years now. In some cases, I'm still waiting for it to even out. In a season, it's just not uncommon for one pitcher to get the support of five and a quarter runs a game, while his teammate (who may be a better hitter) struggles along with three and a half. The differences aren't just a matter of one explosion; they're caused by one pitcher having five or more runs to work with twenty-two times, while his teammate has five or more runs ten or twelve times in as many starts.

It happens all the time—and every time it happens, the result goes directly into the won-lost column.

If two people roll a dice twenty-five or thirty times and count anything four or above as a win, three as a loss, will the wins and losses even out, in those twenty-five or thirty trials? Of course not. After a hundred rolls—the equivalent of three to four seasons—there might still be huge differences between them. So why would anyone think that a pitcher's luck would even out in twenty-five or thirty trials?

If you take a .500 pitcher and give him thirty decisions, the chance that he will win twenty or more games by random luck is 5%. For a .525 pitcher, the chance is 8%. In other words, it's not that unusual. It happened one year ago to Tom Browning. It's not so unusual that it can't happen two or even three times in a row. But whenever it happens, it's always going to be written that the pitcher has an *ability to win*. He pitches well when the game is on the line. He can smell a victory. But a year later, when the pitcher (usually) returns to .500, it will always be written that he has lost his confidence, or he has lost his concentration at key moments of the game, or he has lost something intangible, or he has lost command of his slider—when in reality he has lost nothing except his luck.

The won-lost record is so revered among baseball men that, until a few years ago, the pitcher with the best won-lost record would almost automatically win the Cy Young Award, even when it was obvious that his won-lost record was not representative of his pitching. The most egregious examples in recent years were Steve Stone in 1980 and Pete Vuckovich in 1982, pitchers who were somewhat better than average but had terrific luck. Each had the best offensive support in the majors. It's a little better now. Progress has been made.

Another way to demonstrate the essentially unstable nature of won-lost performance is revealed in the unusual fact that Earned Run Average actually predicts won-lost performance better than won-lost performance predicts itself. Ordinarily, the best predictor of future performance in any area is past performance in the same category. Nothing predicts how many doubles a player will hit in 1987 as well as the number of doubles he has hit in the past. The same is generally true of every statistic—but not of wins and losses. Run a test. Find all the cases in 1986 in which two pitchers on the same team split the advantages, one with a better won-lost record, but the other with a better ERA. (For example, in 1986 Danny Cox was 12–13 but with a 2.90 ERA; teammate Bob Forsch was 14–10 but with a 3.25 ERA.) If the won-lost record was truly an indicator of an ability to win, one would expect to find that ability carried through into 1987. The ones with the better won-lost records would continue to win more often. Follow them in 1987, and you'll find that they don't. The pitchers who had the better ERAs in 1986 will, in 1987, have not only better ERAs but better won-lost records as well. Even if you controlled the study so that there was a large difference in won-lost record but a very small difference in ERA, you would still find, over time, that the pitchers with better ERAs were more successful in the following seasons.

Winning percentage, as I said, is the only category that is immune to park influences, and the only category in which the norm does not change over time. But if you put Zane Smith (8–16) and Rick Reuschel (9–16) on good teams, they might win. Even on bad teams next year, they might win—pitching no better than they pitched in 1986. The stat simply does not reliably indicate the ability of the individual. So I rate won-lost record, on the reliability scale, a four.

Saves rate higher, on the integrity scale, than wins and losses. You know the argument—how can the save mean anything when a pitcher is credited with a save in an 11–2 game. Nobody ever asks how wins and losses can mean anything when a pitcher is credited with "winning" an 11–10 game. The irony is that saves are singled out for attack precisely because the category does attempt to protect itself. Saves are carefully defined so that a pitcher cannot be credited with a save unless (a) he pitches well (b) in a meaningful situation. This definition occasionally, but very occasionally, fails on one count or the other. When the definition fails, the people who write letters to the editor will seize on the oddball "undeserved save" in a lopsided game, and use that game as an example, literally for years. But "wins" and "losses" make only the most passing effort to protect themselves, requiring five innings for a win, so that the undeserved wins and undeserved losses are an everyday occurrence. Every day, some pitcher gives up five runs in six innings but gets a win, while somebody else loses on an error in the top of the ninth. Because this is so common it is as accepted as gravity.

Still, saves are heavily influenced by outside factors. It is harder to pick up saves for a bad team (although Quisenberry in 1983 did save forty-five games for a team with a losing record). The way in which a pitcher is used has a great deal to do with his save total (Donnie Moore wasn't saving many games for Atlanta). I can't see clearly whether saves should be a six or a seven, so I'll put them at six and a half.

In the same general class of statistics are **Game-Winning RBI.** GW RBI are subject to all the same illusions to which RBI are subject, which starts them out at six. In addition, the number of game-winners a player gets depends heavily on how often the team wins, a major distortion, which cuts them down to four. In addition, the alleged game-winning hit, while it is always a hit of considerable significance, is often not the key hit of the game. (The faults of game-winning hits along this line are much exaggerated, in the same way as the faults of saves. New statistics are routinely subjected to scrutiny that the established categories could never survive). Anyway, that leaves us at three—and that's not even deducting anything for the fact that GW RBI are trying to measure an ability that probably doesn't exist.

People are fascinated by "payoff statistics," statistics like wins, saves, and RBI that measure who delivers the goods at the end of the production line. Game-winning RBI are a doomed attempt to single out of the "payoff" category that which *really* pays off, the juiciest heart of the juiciest melon. The problem is that one run simply does not win a game, no matter which run you choose. The one run wins a game only in conjunction with the other runs, which win only in conjunction with the pitching and defense. In most cases, the game-winning "hit" only puts a run on the scoreboard because it works together with another hit. This statistic, more than any other, denies, resists the team nature of the game, imagining a statistical solipsism in which a lonesome player wins games in his own little universe with one swing of the bat. Baseball fans have largely ignored the category because they instinctively know that it don't work that way.

"**Passed Balls**" we will peg even lower, at two, regarding them as essentially a creation of circumstances, the usual circumstance being a knuckle-ball pitcher.

The opportunity counts—**At Bats, Games Played, and Innings Pitched**—we could consider to be merely statements of the conditions, rather than performance categories, and hence score them at one. I decided earlier, however, to consider opportunity counts to be indicators of whether the guy was good enough to play, and as such we need to ask instead to what flaws this indicator is liable. On the one hand, you've got a big problem with the teams—a guy who is good enough to play for San Diego ain't necessarily good enough to play for the Mets. You've got the prejudice or predisposition of the manager; Vince Coleman sure as hell couldn't play for Earl Weaver. Remembering that we are evaluating *one-season* stats, we have to allow for the "memory" of the category; a guy can play for one or two years, like Cecil Cooper, because he

used to be good. I'd say they're about a four as to integrity.

Let's see, we haven't hit **Sacrifice Flies** and **Sacrifice Flies** allowed. Are the number of sacrifice flies a player hits a reliable indicator of his ability to hit sacrifice flies? First of all there's a problem of scale; sac fly totals aren't large enough for the data to be stable. The park will affect them a little—a team in a park with a big outfield area will hit more sacrifice flies than a team in a small park. For the individual, there's an immense deviation in opportunities. Tommy Herr batted 64 times in 1985 with runners on third and less than two out; a leadoff man might see that situation only 15 or 20 times a year. So combining one really massive outside influence with two minor problems, I'd rate the reliability of sacrifice fly data a four for hitters, a six for pitchers. Of course, pitchers are subject to their outfielders' throwing arms, but combining the fact that they go repeatedly through the order (thus eliminating most of the opportunity bias), and that a starting pitcher faces a hitter almost twice as many times as a hitter faces a pitcher (thus reducing the problem of scale), I think that's justified. Also, sacrifice flies are very useful for telling you whether the guy is a ground-ball or fly-ball pitcher.

III. Intelligibility

By *ease of comprehension* or *intelligibility*, what I mean is "Can the average baseball fan make sense of this information?" This is related to Rule number five above: Can what this category says be explained in simple terms in an English sentence? Are there common standards with reference by which this information can be understood?

Although scored on the same ten-point scale, this category has much less effective weight than the two before, because most stats will be scored as nine or ten. The basic stats—batting average, home runs, RBI, won-lost record—those will all be scored tens. Well, let's list them:

Tens: At Bats, Doubles, Games Played, Hits (Batting Average), Home Runs, Runs Scored, Triples, Runs Batted In, Stolen Bases, Caught Stealing (Stolen Base Percentage), Earned Runs Allowed (Earned Run Average), Strikeouts (By Pitchers), Walks Allowed, Won-Lost Record, Complete Games, Shutouts, Saves, and Innings Pitched.

In these eighteen areas, there exist commonly held standards which make the accomplishment meaningful. There are "magic numbers," like .300 and 200 strikeouts, which enable us to store and appreciate subtle distinctions in the stat. The next four categories are ones which a few years ago would have had to be considered nines (that is, less generally understood), but which are now moving rapidly toward the "ten" level, and hence are listed at nine and a half:

Nine and a Half: Strikeouts (by Batters), Walks

Taken (By Batters), On Base Percentage, Total Bases (Slugging Average).

A nine is something like "Sacrifice Flies." Everybody knows what a sacrifice fly is, or failing that it easily can be explained, but few people know what the standards are. If I were to ask, "Is the record for home runs in a season more or less than 50? Is the career record more or less than 500?", you would all know the answers to those questions. But if I asked, "Is the record for sacrifice flies in a season more or less than 25? Is the record for Sac Flies in a career more or less than 250?", many or even most of you would *not* know the answers. So the category receives a nine, rather than a ten, because the standards by which it is interpreted are less commonly understood.

You might think that, if *you* know what the standards are, it is irrelevant to you whether the average fan does or doesn't. But even so, there is a difference. You probably know how many home runs Hank Aaron hit in a typical year. If I asked "How many home runs did Hank Aaron hit in 1963?" I would guess that at least 40% of you would know. There are thousands of home run totals which are embedded in your memory. But, even if you know *some* sacrifice fly data—enough to have a frame of reference— you won't have the same data bank to draw on to compare sacrifice fly data. You *don't* know how many sac flies Aaron hit in 1963. So it's not the same.

The other categories in this group are all listed at nine. Nines: Game Winning RBI, Grounded Into Double Plays,

Hit By Pitch, Intentional Walks, Sacrifice Flies, Sacrifice Hits, Runs Allowed (Run Average), Hits Allowed (Hits Per Nine Innings), Home Runs Allowed, Sacrifice Hits Allowed, Sacrifice Flies Allowed, Hit Batsmen, Balks, Fielding Average, Putouts (Putouts Per Game), Assists (Assists Per Game), Range Factor, Double Plays Per Game and Passed Balls.

All of those lack commonly understood standards for evaluation. In some cases such as the defensive categories, the development of those standards is obstructed by the multiplicity of the positions. The fielding records of a third baseman look just like those of a shortstop, superficially, but what would be an exceptional range factor for a third baseman—say, 3.7—would be terrible for a shortstop,

and what would be a good fielding percentage for a third baseman—say, .965—would not be considered good at any other infield position. The need to develop different norms at each position slows down the growth of understanding. In other areas, like sacrifice hits allowed, norms haven't developed largely because nobody cares what the data is.

An eight would be a category that lacked a clear or precise definitional meaning; a seven would be a category that would be confusing even if you tried to make sense of it. Many of the old *Baseball Digest* freakshow stats might score at seven or even less, but none of the things that we look at here will score down that low.

IV. PUTTING THE ELEMENTS TOGETHER

When we put these three elements together, we'll have what we call the "stat value" score. But how should we do that?

If the value of the stat was dependent on its cumulative impact in these three areas—in other words, if the "significance" of a stat was not diminished by the illusions to which it was subject—then we would simply add them up. But the strength of the stat is, like the strength of a chain, dependent on the weakest link. If the stat is subject to so many illusions that it doesn't measure the skill accurately, it means little that what is supposedly being measured is tremendously important. If what the stat is telling you is impossible to understand, then the "importance" and "reliability" of the stat are lost; information which you can't understand has no value. So we'll put them together as a chain, by multiplication. If the stat scored 10/10/10, the Stat Value score would be ten times ten times ten, or one thousand. The perfect, ultimate stat would score 1000. If the stat scored 9/4/9, the Stat Value would be 324.

THE TEN MOST MEANINGFUL (BASIC) STATS IN BASEBALL

630	1.	Earned Run Average (9/7/10)
608	2.	On Base Percentage (8/8/9.5)
608		Total Bases or Slugging Percentage (8/8/9.5)
560	4.	Batting Average (7/8/10)
560		Home Runs (7/8/10)
540	6.	Pitcher's Walks (6/9/10)
520	7.	Saves (8/6.5/10)
513	8.	Batter's Walks (6/9/9.5)
480	9.	Runs Batted In (8/6/10)
480		Runs Scored (8/6/10)

The best basic stat in baseball is a starting pitcher's ERA. While the stat is less reliable for a reliever—maybe I should have made an adjustment for this, but it seemed awkward to consider ERA to be two different stats—

Earned Run Average is the only basic statistic in baseball that does a reasonably accurate job of summing up the total effectiveness of a player.

For a hitter, there are two statistics that stand above the others. Those are on-base percentage and slugging percentage. Those two statistics, almost without any aid from any other category, will tell you how many runs a team will score, and thus will tell you how effective an offensive player has been. There isn't anything else that has the same degree of importance and reliability.

Television, with it's need to condense, likes to reduce each player to three statistics—home runs, runs batted in, and batting average. It's not a bad choice; all three are among the ten best statistics in the game. I rate home runs and batting average—the basic elements of on-base percentage and slugging percentage—in a tie for fourth, and RBI in a tie for ninth. RBI and runs scored are, like ERA, a summation of the basic effectiveness of an offensive player. They rate lower than ERA because, like slugging and on-base percentage, each measures only half of the job—runs batted in have to be taken together with runs scored, also tied for ninth—and lower than slugging and on-base percentage because they are more subject to illusions of context. But they are still among the best of stats.

As power is one of the most basic elements of a hitter's effectiveness, control is one of the most basic elements of a pitcher's effectiveness. A pitcher's control record, rated sixth, is, by consensus, one of the most important statistical categories. The walk is a bomb that explodes both ways; as a pitcher can cause an inning to explode by giving a walk, so a hitter can cause an inning to explode by taking a walk—and actually, the hitter's patience, and not the pitcher's control, is the strongest determinant of when a walk occurs.

And pitcher's saves, maligned as they have been, are a reasonably accurate statement of the ability to fill a key role on a team. They rate seventh.

TEN OTHER BASIC STATS WHICH ARE ALSO VERY IMPORTANT

567 1. Pitcher's Runs Allowed or Runs Per Nine Innings (9/7/9)
480 2. Doubles (6/8/10)
450 3. Pitcher's Strikeouts (5/9/10)
441 4. Pitcher's Hits Allowed or Hits Per Nine Innings (7/7/9)
441   Range Factor (7/7/9)
432 6. Home Runs Allowed (6/8/9)
400 7. A Pitcher's Won/Lost Record (10/4/10)
350 8. Triples (5/7/10)
324 9. Grounded Into Double Play (6/6/9)
270 10. Stolen Base Percentage or Caught Stealing (3/9/10)

Those of you who are paying careful attention may have noticed that in drawing up the top ten, I cheated. A pitcher's runs allowed average, which scores at 567, actually should rank fourth, but it is primarily a duplication of the more common earned run average, which rates first, so I decided to give it the score that it deserves but just kick it out of the top ten, rather than including two measures of the same thing. It's worth knowing, and in some cases it does contribute information not contained in the ERA.

I also made an arbitrary decision to include RBI and runs scored in the top ten, although the number of doubles hit actually has the same score. On the other end, I included stolen base percentage rather than some other stats which had the same score because of my belief that a good stolen base percentage may have indicative significance. I don't know, but it seems to me that a lot of times a good stolen base percentage indicates a good percentage player in other ways, a good all-around baserunner or a player who shows good judgment in the field, whereas a guy who steals eight bases and gets caught twelve times is often (not always, certainly) a player who takes stupid chances on the bases and takes risks in the field that aren't well calculated. But then, sometimes a low stolen base percentage just indicates that the manager likes to hit and run. Or sometimes it goes to one of those players who has good speed but doesn't get a good jump on the pitcher, but people keep telling him he ought to steal more bases so he keeps trying. As Freud said, sometimes a cigar is just a cigar; and, incidentally, I should have observed before that stolen base percentage is only reliable if the player attempts to steal a few bases; it doesn't become reliable on seven trials.

TEN STATISTICS WHICH ARE WORTH KNOWING, AND WHICH CAN BE SIGNIFICANT IN SOME CASES

270 1. Double Plays Per Game By a Fielder (6/5/9)
270   Putouts Per Game (5/6/9)
270   Assists Per Game (5/6/9)
216 4. Fielding Percentage (4/6/9)
200 5. Games Played (5/4/10)
       At Bats (5/4/10)
       Innings Pitched (5/4/10)
162 8. Game Winning RBI (6/3/9)
       Hit By Pitch (2/9/9)
140 10. Stolen Bases (2/7/10)

Double plays turned, as mentioned, are a significant stat only for infielders, and then only with a consideration of the context—still, in the case of a Glenn Hubbard or a Bobby Grich, a thing very much worth knowing. Putouts per game and assists per game are occasionally useful in diagnosing a defense, looking at where the balls are hit, etc. Fielding percentage is interesting in the extreme case, where you have a player who makes so many errors that he just can't handle the position to which he is assigned. In the case of a Dale Sveum, a Lonnie Smith, a Rafael Ramirez, it's a significant stat; in most cases it doesn't really tell you much.

Games played, innings and at bats are worth considering in a case where what they're trying to tell you is at odds with the rest of the statistical package, like Alfredo Griffin a few years ago or Wes Covington. Game-winning RBI will, in a few odd cases like Jack Clark in 1982, actually call to your attention the fact that a player has had a year in which he delivered an unusual number of game-breaking hits. Hit by pitch counts, while of no real interest most of the time, are quite significant in a case like Don Baylor or Chet Lemon, where the player may score a hundred runs in his career after catching a pitch on the shoulder. Stolen base counts are significant in the case of a Vince Coleman or Rickey Henderson, who might add 15 runs a year to his team by extraordinary success at stealing bases.

Though not listed separately, assists totals for outfielders (outfielders assists per game) would score at 135, on 5/3/9. They, too, are sometimes very useful, in the case of a Jesse Barfield or a Roberto Clemente, but they have been known to tell fibs or half-truths on occasion.

TEN STATISTICS TO WHICH I WOULDN'T RECOMMEND THAT YOU PAY TOO MUCH ATTENTION

120 1. Shutouts (3/4/10)
108 2. Sacrifice Flies Allowed (2/6/9)
100 3. Complete Games (2/5/10)
90 4. Balks (2/5/9)
85 5. Batter's Strikeouts (1/9/9.5)
81 6. Hit Batsmen (1/9/9)
72 7. Sacrifice Flies (2/4/9)
54 8. Sacrifice Hits Allowed (1/6/9)
36 9. Passed Balls (2/2/9)
36 10. Sacrifice Hits (1/4/9)

Enough said.

MODIFICATIONS FOR CAREER STATISTICS

To this point, we have been discussing single-season totals only. In talking about career statistics, the general rules are that:

1) The "significance" or "importance" of the stat remains the same. The question of whether or not a tendency is related to winning is the same whether you are considering one year or a career total.

2) The "reliability" or "integrity" of most stats increases when career totals are considered. The nagging concern about unreliability due to small sample sizes virtually disappears in the consideration of career totals. Since few players play for one team or in one park over the course of their entire careers, the illusions resulting from park influences tend to diminish somewhat, although by no means do they disappear. Other illusions of context, such as distortions created by the hitters ahead of and behind the player, tend to diminish greatly when career totals are considered. In general, reliability increases over time.

3) The "intelligibility" of some statistics is reduced for career totals, since in some cases single-season standards have no meaningful career equivalents. Our array of magic numbers for single-season stats is much larger than those we can draw on to interpret careers.

The second point is the most major among these, since changing the third score from ten to nine or nine and a half wouldn't dramatically alter the evaluation of the stats. One important exception to the rule about reliability increasing for career stats is that, in comparing single-season stats, one is usually comparing contemporaries, and thus players for whom changing standards over time are not a problem. But in comparing career stats, one may often be comparing similar players from different eras, like Mel Ott and Al Kaline or Bobby Grich and Bobby Doerr. When you do this, it is important to remember that the norms in one era may be radically different from those of another—and thus that the statistical comparison may not be reliable in this way. Being a .300 hitter in the twenties didn't mean much, since most of the outfielders of the twenties were .300 hitters.

While I'm not going to recount and recalculate point by point all the stats, there are two categories that are not particularly meaningful for a single season, but that do become extremely meaningful in looking at the career as a whole. Those are games played (for a hitter), and won-lost record (for a pitcher).

Let's review the two main reasons that won-lost record cannot be considered reliable for a single season. Number one, there is a blinding illusion of luck, which is accentuated by the positive/negative nature of the statistic, revolving around relatively tight norms. Over the course of a career, the luck still doesn't even out, but it does become a minor consideration. Number two, the won-lost record is subject to huge influence from the quality of the team. This effect, while remaining significant, becomes over time a less over-riding concern; a pitcher does not ordinarily work his entire career with the support of very good or very poor teams.

Meanwhile, as mentioned before, in career statistics there is a special concern for the influence of changing standards over time. While the norms in wins and losses do change a little bit (they changed a lot before 1920), won-lost records are the most nearly immune to changing standards over time, since they remain anchored at a norm of .500. This unique advantage, combined with the fact that won-lost records are virtually immune to park illusions, leaves us with a statistic which, over enough time, in comparison to stats which are subject to these two distortions, must be considered as quite reliable. I rate the reliability of won-lost records as a career statistic at eight. That gives the statistic, for careers, a stat value score of 800 (10/8/10)—the highest of any basic category.

This leads us to another point. You remember what I rated highest as a single-season stat? ERA—the other basic pitcher's stats.

I get letters a few times a year talking about the differences between pitching stats and hitting stats. Generally, the letter reads something like this: "Batter's statistics gives us specific counts of how often the batter does something, and thus give us a specific description of the batter's skills. Unfortunately, pitcher's stats don't do the same thing. They don't tell us how many doubles or triples the pitcher allows, or how many bases are stolen against him or how many double plays are turned behind him. This is too bad, because we need this kind of specific information about pitchers, just as we need it about hitters."

Well, yes, it would be nice to have specific performance categories against pitchers; one of the many contributions of *The Great American Baseball Stat Book* will be to make a great deal of that information available. But in general, pitcher's stats do a much *more* effective, not less effective, job of describing the pitcher's abilities. The basic pitcher's stats *summarize* his effectiveness, evaluating his performance in terms of runs per out and in terms of wins. Unfortunately, no basic statistics do the same thing for hitters. A great deal of the work that I have done has been in attempting to do for hitter's records exactly what the won-lost record and ERA accomplish for pitchers—state the impact in terms of runs and in terms of wins.

This is far from a trivial distinction: it has massive impact on the way that people perceive players and their abilities. Because of the evaluative nature of pitcher's stats, it is very, very difficult for a lousy pitcher to stay in the league. If a pitcher has an ERA of 5.15 and a record of 6–12, he's going to have to fight for his job the next year, because people will see immediately that he isn't effective. If he pitches that way for three or four years, he doesn't have a chance. *Because of the nature of his statistics, a pitcher can't fool anybody for very long.*

On the other hand, it is quite possible for a poor player—a poor hitter even at a key offensive position—to stay around and keep his job in the major leagues, simply because there is no one statistic which is going to tell on him. If the player does reasonably well in the basic columns, maybe even excels in some flashy statistic like batting average or stolen bases, it may take a long, long time for baseball decision-makers to figure out that the player is not productive on balance.

One classic example would be Omar Moreno. Omar *looks* like a ballplayer; he is trim and strong and fast and throws fairly well. He just doesn't produce. Oh, his batting average is sort of OK, and he steals a few bases, but he has no power and never draws a walk, so that in the context of the outs that he makes, the runs that he scores and the runs that he drives in are puny. In terms of runs scored and driven in, he was a far worse offensive player last year than Mike Heath, driven out of St. Louis because of his low batting average. And this isn't new—Moreno *hasn't* been an effective offensive player for many years. If the people making decisions about him would simply look at the number of outs that he makes, and look at the production they were getting on a per-out basis, and translate the per-out basis to per-inning (3 outs) or per-game (27 outs) . . . well, Moreno would have been out of the major leagues five years ago. Instead, he signed a multi-million-dollar contract.

That can't happen to a pitcher. A pitcher has an ERA.

Another example would be Steve Garvey, the San Diego Padres' glamorous first baseman. Steve Garvey was once a productive player, from 1974 through 1980 with the Dodgers, when he hit over .300 with over 100 RBI a year. Even at that time, the entire picture of Garvey's effectiveness was not as impressive as that suggested by his triple-crown statistics. His failure to draw walks gave him a modest on-base percentage, despite the .300 average, and his power was just medium range, so that he never had a slugging percentage that was among the best in the league. Still, Garvey was a good player at that time.

That was a long, long time ago. For the last six years Garvey has been a very poor player. His ability to drive in runs remains his strongest attribute, yet even in that respect he is no more than an average hitter. His on-base percentage, one of the two most important offensive statistics for any player, is just terrible—actually worse than that of most players with batting averages of .220 or .230. His ratio of runs scored to outs made is awful. He plays a position at which offensive talent is comparatively plentiful; there are many young sluggers around who can't get playing time because they can't play any position except first base. He is not a good defensive player. Although he doesn't make errors, his complete lack of a throwing arm makes him unable to execute many of the plays that other first basemen can make. His weaknesses greatly outweigh his strengths—which is to say that he is losing many more ballgames for the Padres than he is winning.

The fact that Garvey continues to play, despite this balance, is once again testimony to the simple fact that no basic batting statistics state the relationship between the player's positives and negatives. If baseball people would simply look at the ratio between the runs scored and driven in and the outs made, they would understand immediately that Garvey is one of the least productive first basemen in the major leagues.

That can't happen to a pitcher. A pitcher has a won-lost record.

The other statistic which is much more valuable as a career statistic than as a season statistic is games played. Few people realize it, but there may be no other single statistical category which does as good a job of defining productive players.

The reliability of games played as an indicator of the quality of play increases substantially for career totals as opposed to single-season totals. There are still illusions due to unequal opportunities and due to managerial preferences or misjudgments, but it's unlikely that a player could play in the major leagues for 15 years just because some manager liked him enough to turn a blind eye to his weaknesses. At some point, the continuation of the career must rest on ability, so that the reliability of games as an indicator of quality increases from four to more like seven. Which is not unusual; other categories would show even larger increases in reliability.

What *is* unusual about games is that, in addition to increased reliability, games played also acquire a unique significance. Where do I start this . . . suppose that you make a list of the major league players who have played the most games. The top ten men would be Pete Rose (3,562), Carl Yastrzemski (3,308), Hank Aaron (3,298), Ty Cobb (3,034), Stan Musial (3,026), Willie Mays (2,992), Rusty Staub (2,951), Brooks Robinson (2,896), Al Kaline (2,834), and Eddie Collins (2,826). What do those ten men have in common? Only one thing: They were all outstanding players, all great players with the exception of Staub.

Now, why is that? Why couldn't it happen that someone who was just an ordinary player could get a break early, play 150 games at age 20, and just hang around until he plays as many games as these men?

It couldn't happen because no player's level of ability is constant over a period of 20 years or more. Every player takes a while to reach his peak, and begins to decline after some point. *For a player to play regularly for 20 years in the major leagues, he has to be a player of such quality that he even before he reaches his peak, and even after he has lost perhaps 40% of his peak ability, he is still good enough to play regularly in the major leagues.* Thus, the length of the player's career is an excellent indicator of his ability.

To state this graphically, first imagine a line graph describing a player's ability to play baseball over the course of his entire life, beginning at birth, when he can't play the game at all, and ending at death, when he can't play it again. Between those two points, his ability looks something like this:

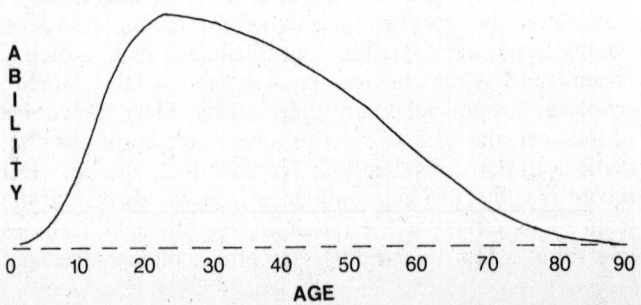

There is relatively little difference in the rising and falling pattern for any two human beings. Some people, who aren't major league players, would peak at age 18; other people, who aren't major league players either, wouldn't get in shape until age 45. But the great majority of major league players would peak in their late twenties, with the greatest number peaking at age 27. While it would not be truly unusual for a player to peak in his early twenties or early thirties, these deviations are relatively trivial over the course of the 70- or 90-year span. It is very, very rare for a player to reach his peak in his late thirties; the frequency of players being better in their late thirties than in their late twenties is much, much less than one in one hundred—and even that would be a fairly minor deviation from the normal pattern.

Second, imagine that an object—a baseball, let us assume—is thrown into the air, and that we graph the height that the baseball reaches across a period of several seconds. The graph would look somewhat similar:

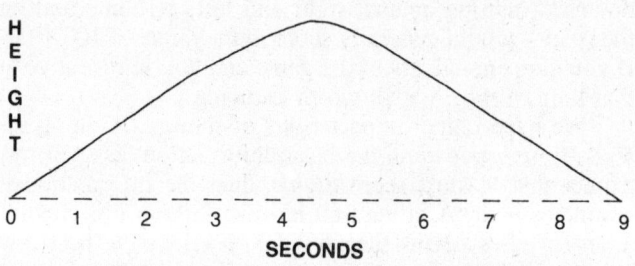

In the first case, most of the graph is invisible; we can't really measure a player's ability to play baseball at age 8 or at age 63, because he probably isn't playing in any league that we could find records of or figure out what to do with them if we could. The only portion of this graph that shows up as a major league record is the highest portion of it, so that the graph of his major league record (in one dimension) would look something like this:

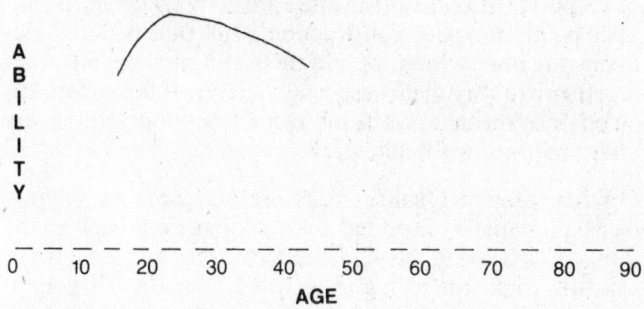

On this graph, the player's *level of greatest ability* is represented by *the highest point of the line*. The player's *time of service in the major leagues* is represented by *the length of the line exceeding a minimum height,* the height needed to be able to play in the major leagues.

The graph of the thrown baseball *over the period in which it is at least 70 feet in the air* would look much the same:

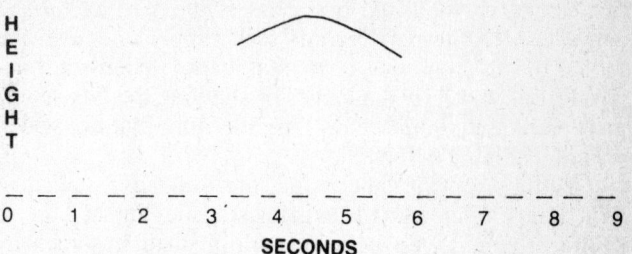

Now it is easy to see that, in the case of the baseball, the greatest height to which the ball rises (the height of the line at its highest point) and the length of time which the ball stayed more than 70 feet in the air (hence, the length of the line on the graph above) would be very highly correlated—in fact, virtually perfectly correlated, since there would almost no other factors affecting the length of the line, other than the height to which the ball was thrown. In the case of the ballplayer, the correlation is less perfect, because the "gravity" of aging is less precise than the gravity of the earth. Still, there is a very strong correlation between the height to which the player ascends, and the length of time that he remains over the minimum needed to play in the major leagues. The idea that a player could remain as a major league regular for a long period of time *without* being a great player is like the idea of a thrown baseball reaching 71 feet and just hanging in the air. It just doesn't happen.

So the number of games played in the major leagues is an excellent, excellent indicator of the quality of play. If you chose at random two groups of twenty players, one group of players playing 1500 or more games in the major leagues, and the other being lifetime .300 hitters, which do you think would likely be the better players? I'll guarantee you: the players playing 1500 or more games would be far better. A random assortment of .300 hitters would include some guys who went 8 for 26 in their major league careers, some guys who were reserve outfielders in the 1890s or the 1920s, when batting averages were extremely high, and a few guys like Fatty Fothergill and Eddie Wilson who could hit but were hopeless in the field. But the guys playing 1500 or more games would almost all be good ballplayers.

Games played were scored before at five (significance), four (reliability) and ten (intelligibility). They increase in reliability to about seven, which is not unusual, but they also acquire this unique significance, which boosts them to about eight on that scale. The new score: 8/7/10, or 560—making career games played into one of the best, most meaningful basic statistics in the game.

BEYOND THE BASICS

Beyond the basic statistics, the proposed "new" statistics can be divided into two classes, those being *ratings* and *records*. The new records seek simply to extend the record of the game into uncharted areas. Records are derived from watching the games or studying the box scores and extracting some new, specific information which wasn't available before.

Ratings, on the other hand, are evaluative statistics, which most often take the existing statistics and add them, subtract them, divide them and multiply them in some way so as to arrive at a statement of their impact.

We have different expectations of these two categories of statistics. New records, since they seek to provide us with information on things that we can only speculate otherwise, usually focus on specific skills or player attributes. How well does the player hit on artificial turf? How well does he hit left-handers? Does this pitcher get mostly ground balls or fly balls? Although none of this stuff is as important as the basic questions like how many home runs does he hit and what's his average, it is all part of the patchwork of information which is needed to guess along with the game, and as such it is generally considered useful and beneficial if it would score in the range of 100–400 by our stat evaluation process. Batting against left-handed pitching, for example, would score about 3/6/10, or 180 (that is, of less significance than the basic totals but important in some cases, not real reliable on a one-year basis but fairly reliable if looked at over two or three years, and perfectly understandable). That puts the information in the "occasionally worth knowing" category. It is good for that information to be out there in the public's hands.

I'm not going to score proposed new records one by one, but I will say in general that the best new records here are the things which could be described as "statistical oversights," things that should have been counted all along, but weren't. These would include:

Save Opportunities. Obviously save opportunities should have been defined and recorded when saves were first introduced. We are just now getting around to correcting the oversight.

Inherited Runners. Inherited runners who score, inherited runners left on the bases. The methods of charging runs scored entirely to the pitcher who puts the man on base is just obsolete; it was something that worked alright at the time the rule was made (1910) but hasn't really worked very well for many years. The development of the modern relief role obviously requires an accounting for the disposition of inherited runners.

Holds. The development of a new relief role requires, I suppose, a new statistic to evaluate the performance.

Stolen Bases Allowed. Stolen bases against catchers, stolen bases against pitchers. All plays have an offensive and a defensive aspect. When the league started counting stolen bases, they should have resolved to keep track of them as defensive accomplishments, as well as the offensive accomplishments. They didn't, but we're getting around to that now.

Runners Picked Off First Base. Same thing.

Baserunning Errors. The "disappearing outs" in the game's statistics. Players who make outs on the base paths have, in the main, escaped notice. From a selfish standpoint, a player should try to stretch any long single into a double, because if he makes it he gets credit for a double, but if he doesn't the record doesn't show anything. That's not right; a gamble should not be without its risks.

These sorts of new statistics would generally score in the range of 200 to 400 by our method. The "breakdowns"—batting against right and left, at home and on the road—would generally score in the range of 100–300. If you care enough about the game and you're receptive to that kind of info, it's all worth knowing.

We have higher expectations of ratings. A rating intends to *improve upon* the basic information; as such, we expect that it must score *higher* than the information it competes with. A rating of a hitter's skill isn't of any use unless it rises *above* the 560–600 level of the best raw statistics. Think about the counts of "quality starts." What are they trying to do? They're trying to *improve on* won and lost records, to provide a *better* record of how many times the pitcher pitches well. So in order to have value, the stat must be better than that which it is a refinement of.

Before I get into the evaluation of new ratings, I should explain about the fourth category, *construction*. The *construction* of a rating is an evaluation of whether or not the rating puts the elements together in a sensible way. The evaluation of the statistic's construction is a minor thing, added in to the score as a plus or minus a maximum of 25 points after the other three are combined. We'll subtract points for poor construction if the stat puts the elements together wrong, or add them if it puts the elements together in a way that is especially clever. If the stat makes an obvious mistake, we'll subtract a few points; if it nicely dodges a trap, we'll add a few.

Quality Starts: Quality starts are Vin Scully's favorite baseball statistic, invented by a sportswriter back east I think. In assessing the significance of the stat, we have to ask first what it is trying to measure. What it is trying to measure is *how often the pitcher pitches well*. Pitching well consistently would be a major element of run prevention, and thus would score, on the "significance" scale, at eight.

The ground on which quality starts are often assailed by the letters-to-the-editor types is that of reliability. This argument, best expressed by Moss Klein in the April 28, 1986, *Sporting News* is that "quality starts isn't a quality stat. . . . A quality start is defined as pitching six or more innings and allowing three or less runs. That means a pitcher can turn in a "quality start" every time and have a 4.50 ERA (six innings, three runs). Does a 4.50 ERA represent quality?"

To me, that line of reasoning is not very damaging. It's not a realistic situation; in order to have a 4.50 ERA with all quality starts, you would have to pitch exactly six innings in every start and allow exactly three runs. If you averaged six and a third innings and 2.8 runs an outing, which would be keeping an average extraordinarily close to the margins, your ERA would be in the high threes.

You can do that to any statistic. If every game that a pitcher pitched was won by a score of 9–7, you could get the hell beat out of you and go 40–0. If every RBI that you had was on a ground ball to short in a 16–0 game, you could hit .000 on the season and drive in 195 runs. The fact that one can contrive a situation in which the statistic would be meaningless does not mean that it *is* meaningless. As a practical matter, I doubt that any pitcher had an ERA higher than 3.20 in his quality starts.

There are real problems with the stat. It tends to discriminate against a durable pitcher, and tends to be more favorable than it really should be to a pitcher of the type that used to be called a seven-inning pitcher (for you younger fans, as recently as the sixties a sportswriter would call a pitcher he didn't think could win a "seven-inning pitcher." The expression is obsolete now). In addition, quality starts are subject to the illusions of ERA—seven innings and four runs in Dodger Stadium probably isn't going to get you a win, but seven innings and four runs with the wind blowing out at Wrigley is a heck of a performance. Since ERA is a seven on reliability, I'd score the reliability of the statistic a six.

As to ease of comprehension, I see no reason that it shouldn't be a ten. It's easy to understand what the results mean, easy to understand the definition. I'd evaluate quality starts at 8/6/10, or 480—better than won-lost records, but not the best thing you can come up with to evaluate a pitcher by.

Total Average: The product of the fertile mind of Thomas Boswell, possibly America's finest baseball writer, Total Average attempts to sum up the total effectiveness of an offensive player. As such, it attempts to measure the player's success in one of the key elements of the game, and rates a nine on significance, as will all of the following statistics, which will be attempting to measure the same thing.

As to the question of to what extent the measurement truly represents the ability, total average is somewhat difficult to assess. Its correlation with runs scored on a team level, while lower than that of runs created or linear weights, is still quite high, higher than any of the basic statistics. I'd score it an eight.

Total average is not difficult to understand, not a complicated concept or formula. It can't rate a "ten," because there aren't the very detailed standards that make basic stats instantly meaningful. You don't instantly know, or at least I don't, what an .857 total average would mean in the way that you would know what a .278 batting average would mean. So I'd peg total average at 9/8/9, or 648—well into the range in which ratings have value.

Runs Produced: Runs produced were invented by Spiro Agnew, and attempt to measure the same thing. The "formula," of course, is runs + RBI − home runs (Spiro never was too complex). The major illusions to which they are prey are the illusions to which Runs Scored and RBI are prey, and thus the stat scores six on reliability, as do runs scored and RBI.

On "intelligibility" I'll score runs produced a nine, since they are closely enough related to run and RBI standards to draw some benefit from the common acceptance of those categories.

The runs produced method makes a silly mistake, in subtracting the home runs. All runs are counted at two—the run scored and the run batted in—except home runs, which are only counted one. This is an obvious construction error in the statistic, and I'll subtract 15 points for that, scoring the rating 9/6/9.5, or 513, which becomes 498 with the penalty.

Runs scored and RBI, by themselves, score 480. Runs produced are an attempt to improve on that, making runs and RBI one superstat. But the loss in intelligibility which occurs when you throw aside the basic standards, plus the construction error, leave runs produced really no better than just having runs scored and RBI counts.

Linear Weights: Linear weights, devised by my friend Pete Palmer, are another way of summing up the offensive worth of a hitter (nine in importance). The formulas aren't perfect, but they are immune to most outside influences and are even so designed that they can remove distortions such as park effects; I'll score them eight and a half on reliability.

Linear weights state their outcomes in terms of runs above or below the league average, a simple concept which is difficult to misunderstand but at the same time a little bit limiting, in that sometimes runs above or below average is not what you need to know. I'll score them nine and a half on intelligibility, which puts the method at 9/8.5/9.5, or 727. That's the highest rating given to a statistic yet except career won/lost records.

On Base + Slugging: On base plus slugging, which also comes from the work of Pete and Dick Cramer, is a sort of short-form evaluation of a hitter.

I'm not big on on base plus slugging. Its accuracy is not quite that of linear weights, but it is high—higher than total average, for example. The correlation between on base + slugging and runs scored is higher than the correlation between total average and runs scored. I'll put it at eight and a quarter.

But the sum of the two isn't quite as easy to make sense of as are linear weights. There are no commonly recognized standards; if you asked me if .825 is "outstanding" or merely "excellent," I wouldn't know. Linear weights are scored at nine and a half on intelligibility, as are the individual elements of this stat, on base percentage and slugging percentage, so I'd place this one about nine.

And the statistic is put together wrong. I mean, it isn't that getting on base creates runs and slugging creates runs and so if you put them together you get runs, but that the two create runs when they work together. They shouldn't be *added* together, they should be *multiplied*. A team with a .400 on-base percentage and a .400 slugging percentage would score more runs than a team with .350 and .450, although both would add up to .800. So I'm going to take off a ten-point construction penalty, and evaluate on base plus slugging at (9/8.25/9) − 10, or 658. It's about as valuable a statistic as total average.

RABS and TIBS: Rabs (runs per at bat) and Tibs (teammates batted in, which is RBI-HR) were developed for use in a Bay Area draft league, and are promoted at annual SABR conventions by Richard Zitrin. Richard is so likeable that nobody (including me) exactly wants to come out and tell him that his idea is not poised to take the baseball world by storm, and his enthusiasm for the brainchild is sometimes infectious.

The biggest problem with Rabs and Tibs is that they not only do not attempt to remove the biases and illusions inherent in runs scored and runs batted in, but rather exalt those illusions, promoting them as sacred insights. Bill Buckner is put forward not as a lucky stiff who happens to hit behind Wade Boggs in the best hitter's park in the American League, but as one of the great Tibbers of all time. Runs Scored and RBI rate at six in reliability, and Rabs and Tibs can't move any higher.

The standards of accomplishment in this area are very meaningful to Richard and his buddies, as any category would become if you talked about it daily, but they don't have the inherently intelligible form of linear weights or runs created. One of the pair is stated as a ratio and the other as a cumulative accomplishment, which to Richard seems a great advantage of the method but which complicates the comprehension of the standards for anybody else. I'll peg them at nine on intelligibility, which I think is pretty generous.

But then Rabs and Tibs, like runs produced, make the ridiculous decision to give only half credit to home-run hitters, and there's a 15-point construction penalty for that error (of course, if they didn't subtract home runs from RBI they'd just have RBI), and we have a total rating, for the rating, of (9/6/9) − 15, or 471. That's a pretty marginal position when you consider that just the basic triple crown stats are in the range of 480 to 560.

MY OWN MENAGERIE

The final category of baseball statistics that I will discuss here, mostly for the benefit of those of you who haven't bought the *Abstract* in previous years—are the ones that I have developed myself. It wouldn't be appropriate for me to evaluate my own statistics in competition with other people's methods, so let me just say that obviously I have developed my methods and statistics to accomplish the things that I think are important to accomplish, and have developed them in the way that seems to me to optimize the benefits. I certainly believe that all of the statistics below are very meaningful, but just as certainly I don't believe that any of my own statistics should rate at 1,000 or anything like that.

Rather than discussing what the formulas are in this part of the book, I'll talk about what the statistics are intended to accomplish. In the appendix, I'll explain exactly what the formulas are.

Runs Created: Runs created is my way of evaluating a hitter. There are several versions of the runs-created formula, one designed to accommodate almost any data set.

The runs-created formulas attempt to take the "category stats" for a hitter and estimate the number of runs for the team that probably resulted from these accomplishments. Runs-created estimates are one-to-one equivalent to RBI or runs scored. As driving in 100 runs is an outstanding accomplishment, so creating 100 runs is an outstanding accomplishment. The formulas are designed so that they estimate accurately the number of runs a team will score, and thus each team has about the same number of runs created as runs scored.

Compared to something like runs produced, I would much prefer to use runs created because runs scored and runs driven in are so subject to illusions of context that the individual totals cannot be said to be individual accomplishments. I would prefer to base an evaluation as much as possible on what the individual has accomplished for the team, rather than on what the team has accomplished for the player.

Compared to, say, total average, there are three reasons that I would prefer to use the basic runs-created method. First of all, it's easier to figure. Total average has eight elements (or more if sacrifice data is used) and requires seven mathematical computations (five additions, one subtraction, one division). The basic runs-created method has four elements and requires four computations (two additions, one multiplication, one division). Second, runs created is more accurate. Any system is going to have times when it is wrong, when it says that Team A should have a better offense than Team B when Team B has actually scored more runs. But no matter how you study the correlation, runs created have a higher correlation with team runs scored and with team wins than does total average.

And third, the outcome is more meaningful. Anything you measure in baseball ultimately has to be expressed in the form of runs. When you figure out exactly how good a defensive player somebody is, what you are figuring is how many runs he saves. To estimate what the won-lost impact is, you have to work through runs. Other things being equal, it is much better to have an output expressed in real-world terms rather than along a scale which has only internal meaning.

Compared to linear weights, the advantages are more

subtle. Pete feels that his method is the most accurate that has been devised. It is the most accurate, if you use Pete's method of figuring accuracy. If you use my method of figuring accuracy, runs created is more accurate.

Second, I think it is preferable to have a number of runs created, rather than a number of runs created above or below the league norm.

Offensive Winning Percentage: Offensive winning percentage attempts to place runs created in context—in the context of the number of outs made, in the context of the offense and defense of the team, etc. A normal offensive winning percentage is .500. Anything about .500 is above average, and anything below .500 is below average.

Defensive Winning Percentage: Defensive winning percentages attempt to evaluate defensive statistics. A normal defensive winning percentage is .50. Anything above .50 is above normal, etc.

Approximate Value: The value approximation method attempts to deal with all accomplishments by players at any position—pitchers, middle infielders, whatever—and state their value on a common scale in the simplest possible form. Its purpose is to make it possible to compare *groups of player seasons;* in evaluating a single season it does not deliver spectacular accuracy. A better explanation is in the next article.

There are two value approximation methods in use in this book, for which I will apologize. It isn't my intention to promulgate an unwieldy number of different formulas to figure approximate value, as I have with runs created, but I radically revised the method this year, making it more consistent but harder to figure. I did this because I thought I would get the information in this year's book computerized, so that the extra computation time wouldn't make any difference, but then my new computer broke down during the *Abstract* crunch, and I was back figuring value approximations by the old method. The new system is used in the article on rookies, but the old one is used elsewhere. The values are equivalent; it's just a case of using a newer and better system for individuals to get to the same group totals.

Power/Speed Number: Combines home runs and stolen bases into a single number. A player who hits 30 homers and steals 30 bases will have a power/speed number of 30.0, but the player has to do *both* things to rate well. A player who hit 10 homers and stole 50 bases would have a power/speed number of 16.7.

Secondary Average: Secondary average is a way of stating quickly and in a familiar frame of reference the impact of a player's secondary offensive skills—that is, those not reflected in his batting average. The elements of secondary average are power, strike zone judgment, and stolen bases. An average secondary average is about the same as an average batting average, but secondary averages range all the way from around .100 up over .500. Rickey Henderson and Mike Schmidt have usually had the highest secondary averages in baseball, but in 1986 it was the new kid from Cincinnati.

Defensive Efficiency Record: The defensive efficiency record is a team statistic, which attempts to answer this question: when a ball is put into play against this team, how often does the team turn that ball into an out?

Isolated Power: Isolated power is the difference between batting average and slugging percentage.

Established Performance Levels: Established performance levels reflect the levels of performance that a player has *established* that he can reach. There are established performance levels in each category—Wade Boggs has established performance levels of 107 runs, 217 hits, 43 doubles, 8 homers, etc. Kirby Puckett does *not* have an established performance level of 30 homers, nor does Roger Clemens have an established performance level of 24 wins. To reach those levels, they need to continue to produce at that level for two or three years.

There are different ways of figuring established performance levels, and I'm liable to use any of them. One of my basic theories about baseball stats is that if a thing is real, you have to be able to measure it in different ways and see about the same thing. If the thing that is being measured is defined by the precise formula that you use, then you're just looking at an illusion or an image, not a real object.

The Favorite Toy: The favorite toy is not a statistic, but a process that I go through to estimate a player's chance of accomplishing some particular, very difficult goal. I estimate that Dave Parker has a 6% chance of getting 3,000 hits in his career.

The Brock6 System: The Brock6 system is a set of several hundred interlocking formulas that attempts to project the normal expectation for the rest of a player's career.

In the ten years that I've been doing this book, I've developed dozens of other statistical methods and God knows how many other statistics. If I use any of the others, and I'm sure I will somewhere, I'll try to explain what they are at the time.

ROOKIES

CONTENTS

CHAPTER ONE
The Greatest Rookie Crops of All Time

One of the major stories of the 1986 baseball season was the emergence of a superb rookie crop, certainly the most impressive collection of rookies to surface in at least ten years. "I recently read with mild amusement," wrote Bill Conlin in the August 11 *Sporting News,* "that it was possible that the rookies crop of 1986 could be the *greatest* ever."

Mr. Conlin, as you might surmise, doesn't feel that it should be considered the greatest ever; he argues for the 1948 National League crop, which contained Gil Hodges, Duke Snider, and Roy Campanella of the Dodgers, Alvin Dark of the Giants, Richie Ashburn, Robin Roberts, and Curt Simmons of the Phillies, and Ted Kluszewski of Cincinnati.

While Mr. Conlin's argument has considerable merit, as we shall see later, there is in this analysis an obvious bias, in that we now have a full view of the accomplishments of Duke Snider, Roy Campanella, et al., while we can see only a tiny corner of what will eventually be done by Danny Tartabull and Cory Snyder. If you're going to compare what Danny Tartabull did *as a rookie* to what Duke Snider did *throughout his career,* obviously the 1986 rookie crop doesn't stand a chance.

If you compare what was accomplished *by the players as rookies,* you get a rather different picture. As a rookie in 1948, Duke Snider played in 53 games and hit .244. We can safely say, I think, that Danny Tartabull had a more impressive rookie season. As a rookie in 1948, Gil Hodges hit .249 with 11 homers in almost 500 at bats; Pete Incaviglia, we can safely say, had a better rookie year. Roy Campanella was probably the most impressive of the Dodger rookies that year, because of his obvious defensive skills—but he played just 83 games and hit .258 with 9 homers. Cory Snyder, we can safely say, had a better rookie season. Ted Kluszewski, as a rookie in 1948, hit .274 with 12 homers and 57 RBI; Jose Canseco would seem to cover that one with some margin of safety. Robin Roberts, as a rookie in 1948, was 7–9; Edwin Correa had a better rookie year. Curt Simmons, as a rookie n 1948, went 7–13 with a 4.87 ERA, which would put him approximately in a class with Juan Nieves or Jose Guzman. Alvin Dark had a fine rookie season, hitting .322 with 3 homers and playing championship shortstop—but was it a better year than Wally Joyner had in 1986? Compared by what they did as rookies, the 1986 American League class is, in fact, far, far ahead of the 1948 National League.

But was it, in fact, the greatest rookie crop ever? Was it one of the greatest ever? Where does it rank? As. Mr. Conlin said, "The great thing about baseball is that if you pore through the record books, you probably can top the vintage N.L. crop of 1948." It happens to be my job to do that—to pore through the record books until I find the one rookie crop that tops all of the others. This is one question about rookies: what were the greatest crops ever. There are many others: What *team* in what season produced the greatest rookie output? What league? What seasons produced the megastars, the Babe Ruths and Ty Cobbs? What was the *worst* rookie crop of all time? Do the seasons that produce the most awesome rookies, like 1986, also produce the most long-term stars, like 1948? How often does a Hall of Famer come up?

In looking over the rookie crop, what clues are there that will help you distinguish between those destined for greatness and those destined to flame out? How much difference does the player's age make? How much difference does his speed make? Should you pay any attention to his strikeout-to-walk ratio? Does it make any difference whether he is black or white?

The 1986 rookie explosion forces all of these questions to the fore, and in this article we will attempt to answer them.

First we need to make a point of order and establish our definition of a rookie. The point of order is the one that I already discussed. In talking about the greatest rookie crops of all time, we are talking about two things, **eventual distinction,** meaning what the players did over the course of their careers, and **rookie performance.** Obviously, we can't yet discuss the 1986 rookie crop in the former context. I'll establish a method to deal with the first set of questions, and a method to deal with the second set of questions, and I'll try not to mix them up.

The definition of a rookie is complicated by the fact that there has been no consistent definition over time; many people who were not considered rookies when they had their first full seasons, or at least were not eligible for Rookie-of-the-Year awards, must be considered rookies by today's standards. The definition of who is and is not a rookie has been changed at least three times since 1947, maybe more. When Vada Pinson had his sensational first season in 1959, he was not considered technically a rookie—but he was obviously a rookie by modern standards, having less prior playing time and less prior roster time than José Canseco in 1986. No definition holds across time.

In my first set of studies below, every major league player must be assigned to some rookie class, even if, like Steve Balboni, he really had no "rookie" year. So no definition of a rookie is entirely successful, but the definition I used is this: a player is considered eligible to be a rookie until he has played in 50 games, has 150 plate appearances, has pitched in 15 games or has pitched 45 innings in the major leagues. His rookie season is the season in which he reaches one of those goals, unless this would cause him to be considered a rookie in a season in which he had less playing time than in a previous season. Three examples, all tough cases:

DUKE SNIDER

Year	G	AB	HR	RBI	Avg.
1947	40	83	0	5	.241
1948	53	160	5	21	.244
1949	146	552	23	92	.292

Snider was considered eligible for rookie status in both 1947 and 1948, but not 1949. He reached the 50 games and 150 plate appearances in 1948, so that is his rookie season.

SANDY KOUFAX

Year	G	IP	W–L	ERA
1955	12	42	2–2	3.02
1956	16	59	2–4	4.91
1957	34	104	5–4	3.88

Koufax, a bonus baby, sat on the bench a large part of the 1955 season, so by the standards of his time of ours he would not have been considered eligible for the 1956 Rookie-of-the-Year award, had his performance merited it. However, he pitched so little in 1955 that for purposes of this study, we're considering him a 1956 rookie.

STEVE BALBONI

Year	G	AB	HR	RBI	Avg.
1981	4	7	0	2	.286
1982	33	107	2	4	.187
1983	32	86	5	17	.233

Balboni was considered eligible for rookie designation in any of these three seasons, and would ordinarily have been put in the 1983 rookie class. However, this would mean that he had more playing time in a season *before* he was a rookie than he did in his rookie year—so he was put in the 1982 group.

OK, these are oddball cases; 98% of the time there's no problem figuring out when the guy was a rookie. Let's get to it.

To study the issue of which seasons produced the most rookies who became players of distinction, I devised a method of evaluating the rookie crop by counting the number of outstanding accomplishments by the players in each group, and then simplifying the counts by grouping them. I started by counting the number of times every major league player coming up since 1900 had 200 or more hits, drove in or scored 100 runs, hit 30 or more homers or led the league in a positive category (runs, hits,

doubles, triples, homers, walks, stolen bases or batting average). Pitchers were evaluated by counting seasons of 18 or more wins, seasons of 200 or more strikeouts, etc. There was also credit given for MVP or Cy Young Awards and for long careers; I don't want to digress into the details of the method here, but a full accounting is given in the appendix to this article. It's quite a bit like the value approximation method except that whereas the value approximation method evaluates all accomplishments, this method—let's call it the star value system—ignores ordinary accomplishments, and bases evaluations only on those accomplishments which are characteristic of stars, of outstanding players.

The logic is that those seasons that produce the most rookies of distinction must also produce the most rookies who have accomplishments of distinction. By counting the number of times each player did these things (got 100 RBI, won the batting title, etc.), all major league players coming up since 1900 were evaluated and placed in one of six groups:

The "FIVES" are the all-time greats, the players who kick open the doors of Cooperstown and barge in like TV cops at a drug bust. These are the players who routinely glide past the standards of excellence which have been outlined. Alphabetically, the first five players who are designated fives are Hank Aaron, Grover Cleveland Alexander, Ty Cobb, Steve Carlton, and Joe DiMaggio.

The "FOURS" are the players who are still major stars—still, in most cases, clearly of Hall of Fame calibre. These players have brilliant careers, often over a long period of time. After DiMaggio in the alphabet, the first five players who are designated fours are Rollie Fingers, Whitey Ford, Frankie Frisch, Bob Gibson and Goose Goslin.

The "THREES" are the players who could be described as "marginal Hall of Fame candidates." These players are unquestionably of star quality, but their stars are not as brilliant or as durable as those of the higher echelons. Whereas the "fives" who are power hitters hit 30 homers and drive in 100 runs even in their off seasons and the fours who are power hitters hit 30 homers and drive in 100 runs in all of their good seasons, the threes might be players who rise to that level intermittently throughout good careers. These are players who will go in the Hall of Fame if they get some breaks, if they're at the top of the three group or for some reason are perceived as being. Following Goslin in the alphabet, the first five players who are designated threes are Dick Groat, Ron Guidry, Stan Hack, Chick Hafey and Jesse Haines.

With respect to Guidry, the first active player listed, we will point out quickly—it should be obvious—that in a "counting" evaluation, a player's total mounts up throughout his career. If Guidry pitches well, his total will continue to rise, so that he could be reclassified a four. The system measures career value; it starts at zero and can only go up.

The "TWOS" are the players who could be said to be "very good ballplayers" or to have "some of the characteristics of a star." Some of the twos are players who are big stars but only for three or four years; others are players who play a long time and contribute, but never really acquire the lustre that would project them as Hall of Fame candidates. "Minor stars," we'll call them. Following Jesse Haines in the alphabet, the first five players who are designated twos are Mel Harder, Tommy Harper, Toby Harrah, Jeff Heath and Jim Hegan.

The "ONES" are the players who could be described as "good ballplayers," sometimes generously but in the main accurately. They are not stars, or if they are then their stardom lasts only for a season or two before fading. These players qualify by scoring 100 runs in a season, maybe a few times but maybe only once, or by leading their league in stolen bases, or by playing 1100 or more games in the major leagues. Pitchers can qualify by winning 90 or more games, saving 140 or more, or perhaps leading the league in complete games or shutouts. Usually these players have a modest collection of such credentials. Following Jim Hegan in the alphabet, the first five players who are designated as ones are Ken Heintzleman, Woody Held, Tommy Helms, Rollie Hemsley, and Solly Hemus. Though not stars, these are men who contribute, men of a type essential to playing winning baseball.

Players who do not fall into any of these groups are not registered in this study. Players who do not fall in any of these groups are players who never drive in or score 100 runs, never hit 30 homers, never lead the league in any basic category, never have 200 hits. They play less than 1,100 major league games (about seven seasons worth), and less than 1,000 at a key defensive position. Though some of them do turn in two or three good seasons and could as well be included in the survey as not, these are players who either have limited ability or "fail to reach their potential," passing out of the game leaving only a scattered memory. Their personal accomplishments, though significant in isolation, are of such a magnitude that their exclusion is not deemed to damage an evaluation of the rookie crop of which they are a part. Following Hemus in the alphabet, the first five players who are not considered eligible for rank in the study are Bill Henderson, Dave Henderson, Ed Henderson, Hardie Henderson, and Steve Henderson. Dave Henderson's lack of classification is merely his current status; he is almost certain to earn designation at least as a one.

Among the thousands of players who have played major league baseball in this century, an estimated 82–86% are not classified in this study. Of the 1,615 players who are classified, 1,011 (63%) are in group one. Three-hundred fifty-four (354), or 22%, are considered minor stars, or twos. One hundred seventy-six (176), or 11%, are in group three, the "marginal Hall of Fame candidates." Group four contains 48 major stars, or 3% of those good enough to be included in the study. Twenty-six of the 1,615 players, or between one and two percent, are ranked as the all-time greats. A quick chart:

Unclassified	8,400 Approx.
(1) Good Players	1,011
(2) Minor Stars	354
(3) Marginal Hall of Famers	176
(4) Major Stars	48
(5) All-Time Greats	26

We have, then, a list of how many good ballplayers, how many stars, etc., were rookies in each league in each season of this century. It's not quite a diagram of exactly how strong each rookie class is, but it's about as close as you're likely to come. Let's run the totals for one year of interest—let's say, 1951:

1951 American League
Mickey Mantle (5)
Jackie Jensen (3)
Minnie Minoso (3)
Pete Runnels (2)
Jim Busby (1)
Charlie Maxwell (1)
Gil McDougald (1)
Harry Simpson (1)
George Zuverink (1)

1951 National League
Willie Mays (5)
Johnny Logan (2)
Roy McMillan (2)
Frank Thomas (2)
Bob Friend (2)
Smokey Burgess (1)
Solly Hemus (1)
Clem Labine (1)
Turk Lown (1)
Chet Nichols (1)

Mantle in the American League and Mays in the National hed up rookie crops including other MVPs, batting champions, and defensive wizards. In looking at one rookie collection without looking at the context provided by the other seasons, one might be tempted to say, "Wow. Mantle and Mays in the same year, plus two other guys who were awfully good and might eventually get into the Hall of Fame themselves. That's got to be one of the best rookie seasons ever."

It isn't. It was a good year for rookies; it wasn't a great one. 1948, 1954 and 1956 were better, looking at the crop as a whole. A few notes:

Almost every season produces at least one rookie of Hall of Fame calibre. Between 1900 and 1962 there were only nine seasons which produced no rookies who eventually went into the Hall of Fame—and three or four of those nine produced players who are extremely likely to be elected in time.

The rookie crops which produced no Hall of Famers were 1906, 1934, 1935, 1943, 1945, 1949, 1953, 1958, and 1961. While the first three of those are probably permanently locked out (the strongest candidates are Jack Coombs, Dolph Camilli and Phil Cavaretta, respectively), as you get closer to the present the candidates become stronger. The 1943 rookie crop, though thinned by the war, contains a real diamond in Allie Reynolds, whose career was brilliant if a little short for Cooperstown. The 1945 crop contained Red Schoendienst, an outstanding infielder who I think is worthy of recognition and may eventually receive it. Nellie Fox was a rookie in 1949; his election waits only on his renewed eligibility. In 1953 there were three viable candidates, in Harvey Kuenn, Junior Gilliam, and Elroy Face; I'd bet on at least one of the three to make it eventually. The top candidate from 1958, Orlando Cepeda, messed up his shot with a bad knee and a jail term, but the 1961 crop contained two certain future selections, in Carl Yastrzemski and Billy Williams.

Going forward from there you get the same picture—Pete Rose, Willie Stargell, and Gaylord Perry in 1963; no shoo-ins but six viable candidates in 1964; Jim Palmer, Catfish Hunter, Steve Carlton, and Joe Morgan in 1965; Don Sutton in 1966; Rod Carew and Tom Seaver in 1967; Johnny Bench and Reggie Jackson in 1968; etc.

Looking at the picture as it eventually will be, then, less than one season in ten produces no Hall of Famers. So saying that a season produces a Hall of Fame rookie or produces two or three Hall of Fame rookies . . . well, that's really nothing.

About three players are elected to the Hall of Fame each year. Since there are as many years of election as there are years of entry (rookie years), it follows that there must be about three rookie Hall of Famers in an average season. It also follows, in the same way, that in an average rookie crop there are 2.00 MVP Awards, 2.00 Batting titles, 2.00 Home Run crowns, etc. The strength of the 1951 crop can be seen in that it produced six MVP awards (three for Mantle, two for Mays and one for Jensen) and four batting titles (two for Pete Runnels, one each for Mantle and Mays). But it produced no Cy Young award winners, and the six MVPs is not a record. And the 1982 rookies have already amassed five batting titles.

Who are the highest-rated stars in this study who are not in the Hall of Fame? Of the 26 "fives" of this century, 22 are eligible for the Hall of Fame, and all twenty-two have been selected. The four not yet eligible are Rose, Schmidt, Seaver and Carlton.

Among the 48 "fours" in history, only two players are eligible for the Hall of Fame and have not been selected. Those two are Hal Newhouser, whose statistical accomplishments are usually discounted somewhat because his best years were during the War, and Billy Williams, who will be elected very soon (this is written in November, in case that becomes relevant).

There are five seasons in history which have produced two All-Time greats, two fives in our survey. The 1925 season saw the emergence of Lou Gehrig, almost certainly the greatest first baseman of all time, and Lefty Grove, in my opinion the greatest pitcher of all time—both in the American League. The 1927 season produced Jimmie Foxx of Philadelphia and Mel Ott of New York, both teenagers who began to earn some playing time that summer after sitting next to their managers and watching for a year. The 1936 American League season electrified the nation with the emergence of two super-kids who did not disappoint in subsequent years, the twenty-one-year-old Joe DiMaggio and the seventeen-year-old Bobby Feller. Mantle and Mays came up in 1951, and the National League in 1956 produced Sandy Koufax and Frank Robinson, although the classification of Koufax as a rookie in 1956 is somewhat arbitrary.

Since we've got ten of them out of the way, let's run a list of the rest of the 26 players classified by our method as the All-Time greats, and the years of their emergence:

1901—Christy Mathewson
1905—Ty Cobb

1907—Walter Johnson
1911—Grover Cleveland Alexander
1915—Babe Ruth
1916—Rogers Hornsby
1924—Al Simmons
1926—Charlie Gehringer
1939—Ted Williams
1942—Stan Musial
1946—Warren Spahn
1954—Hank Aaron
1963—Pete Rose
1965—Steve Carlton
1967—Tom Seaver
1973—Mike Schmidt

Those may not be your selections as the 26 greatest players of all time, and they wouldn't be mine, either, but you'd probably have to agree with at least 20 of them, and I preferred an objective list to just making my own judgments. There are, of course, many players who have come up since 1973 who are working on reclassification and could wind up as "fives"; Don Mattingly, in particular, is hustling in that direction.

What are the greatest one-team rookie crops of all time? There are about seven candidates.

The **1924 New York Giants** came up with three Hall of Famers, in Bill Terry, Freddi Lindstrom, and Hack Wilson. (As rookies, the three were not impressive. Terry and Lindstrom were used sparingly and didn't hit. Wilson hit .295 in 107 games as a rookie but then played so poorly that he was benched in 1925.)

Despite the three Hall of Famers, the class isn't a handsdown winner. Terry was a great player, essentially the Cecil Cooper of his time, but I wouldn't have voted for Hack Wilson for the Hall Fame (almost nobody who saw him play *did* vote for him, after all), and Lindstrom's election was a joke. It was a good rookie crop.

The **1909 Boston Red Sox** came up with two Hall of Fame outfielders, in Tris Speaker and Harry Hooper, plus Smokey Joe Wood and Ray Collins, another good pitcher.

The **1926 Pittsburgh Pirates** were the only team to come up with two major stars in one year, in Paul Waner and Joe Cronin. The Pirates ruined their good fortune by shipping Cronin out to the bushes without giving him a full shot.

Actually, that's a little misleading. The **1925 Philadelphia Athletics** introduced, in addition to Lefty Grove, Mickey Cochrane, who is classified here a three, but is probably better described as a major star than a marginal Hall of Fame candidate.

The **1958 San Francisco Giants** produced the unequalled total of six good ballplayers—Orlando Cepeda (a marginal Hall of Famer on the basis strictly of his record), Felipe Alou and Leon Wagner (minor stars), and Jim Davenport, Willie Kirkland and Eddie Fisher (good players). The first three were outstanding hitters with power; Davenport was a Gold Glove third baseman and a good hitter, Kirkland hit over 20 homers a year for four straight years and Eddie Fisher was a fine knuckle-balling reliever from 1962–1971, appearing in 82 games with a 15–7 mark and 24 saves in 1965. There are a good many eight-team leagues which did not produce as much talent as the 1958 Giants, and I took notice of only one other team which came up with even five good players in one season, although in that case one of them was a lot better than Orlando Cepeda.

The only all-time great who emerged in a class with other top rookies was Stan Musial, who was one of five good players to come up with the **1942 St. Louis Cardinals;** the others were Murry Dickson (two), Whitey Kurowski (one), Harry Walker (one), and Johnny Beazley (one).

Still, as the greatest one-team crop of rookies ever, I choose the **Dodgers in 1948.** Granted, Duke Snider's being listed as a 1948 rookie is pretty arbitrary but still better than listing him in any other year. Behind the Duke, there's Roy Campanella. Behind Campy, there's Gil Hodges. Behind Hodges, there's Carl Erskine. Those four men were the backbone of the Boys of Summer, and it says here that no other team can match that 1–2–3–4 punch for one team in one year.

Which season produced the most rookie Hall of Famers? The 1924 and 1925 seasons produced six Hall of Famers each; no other season has produced more than four. However, this is as much a reflection of the Hall of Fame's bias toward the glory-hitting late twenties as it is evidence of outstanding talent. The 1924 season saw the emergence of Al Simmons (a legitimate Hall of Famer), Bill Terry (a legitimate Hall of Famer, I suppose), Ted Lyons (about as good a pitcher as Tommy John), Kiki Cuyler (a fine player but not anybody who should be in the Hall of Fame; comparable to Willie Wilson), Hack Wilson (cough, ahem), and Freddie Lindstrom (gag).

The 1925 Hall of Famers were a better lot, with three players often cited as the best at their positions (Gehrig, Grove, and Cochrane). The other three Hall of Famers were Red Ruffing (comparable to Ferguson Jenkins, but probably not quite as good), Earle Combs (a little better than Mickey Rivers) and Chick Hafey (would fall about midway between George Foster and Ellis Valentine.)

Which one league in one season produced the most talent? Score two points for Bill Conlin. It was the National League in 1948, by a knockout. I talked about the Dodgers, but the Phillies rookie crop, which I didn't mention then because I didn't want to give this one away, was also one of the top three of all time: Robin Roberts (a four), Richie Ashburn (three), Granny Hamner (two) and Curt Simmons (two). The 1948 Dodgers outpoint them only 12–11.

Let's outline our statistical method here. I designed this basically so that the points can just be added together. You may be tempted to think that a five is worth more than five ones, or worth more than two twos and a one, and you might be right but I wouldn't want to bet on it, either. Let's take an average five—say, Bob Feller. Bobby Murcer is a two, meaning that he's not quite up to Hall of Fame calibre. Dave McNally, a 184-game winner, is a "two" because 184-game winners don't usually make the Hall of Fame. Pick a one at random—say, Phil Garner. Would you trade Murcer *and* McNally *and* Garner to get Bob Feller? I don't know, but I know for sure that if you had those

three players in your lineup and playing for you, you'd think about it for a long time before you gave them up for anybody, up to and including Babe Ruth.

Would you trade Vida Blue (three) *and* Amos Otis (two) to get Stan Musial? You might do it, but it wouldn't be a lopsided trade. Would you trade Don Demeter *and* Jim O'Toole *and* Jose Pagan *and* Johnny Edwards, all "good players," for Willie McCovey, a four. You might, but from 1961 through 1964 any team in baseball would have been delighted to have added those four players and given up McCovey.

With larger groups this ratio becomes confused, because a team would never trade four fives—four all-time greats—for twenty ones. You'd never trade Stan Musial, Ted Williams, Willie Mays, and Lefty Grove for twenty guys like Jim Busby or indeed for 150 guys like Jim Busby, because on the one hand if you had four guys like that you could clinch the pennant in February, and on the other hand you can't use 150 players. But that's an artificial situation, because since you can't use 150 good players they aren't really 150 good players, but thirteen good players and 137 guys on the bench. The realistic situation is that good ballplayers are always in short supply and hence have value, and nobody has ever had more than two players of prime quality on one team.

Anyway, while there are obviously variations in the quality of players in each group, and while there are a few cases in which a player is listed as a three when you'd rather he was a four or a two or something, I feel that if you simply total up the players in a group, you do arrive at meaningful values. It is quite reasonable to say that a 20-point collection of star talent has the value of four Stan Musials or five Willie McCoveys or seven Mickey Loliches (almost) or ten Bill Whites or twenty Don Moneys, understanding that some of the Don Moneys would be better than Don Money and some of the Don Moneys would not be as good as Don Money.

By this addition, the 1948 National League rookie crop produced 33 units of star value—the equivalent of eleven Mickey Loliches. A normal league/season produces about 1.8 units of star value per team, or about 15 for an 8-team league. No other season prior to the 1961 expansion produced as many as 30, and even with expansion the total of 33 units has never been topped, although it will be soon. The National League's complete rookie crop in 1948:

Duke Snider (4)
Robin Roberts (4)
Richie Ashburn (3)
Roy Campanella (3)
Gil Hodges (3)
Ted Kluszewski (3)
Alvin Dark (2)
Granny Hamner (2)
Carl Erskine (2)
Curt Simmons (2)
Whitey Lockman (1)
Don Mueller (1)
Vern Bickford (1)
Bob Rush (1)
Herm Wehmeier (1)

I agree with all of the classifications except that Roy Campanella should probably be a four, despite his short career, and Alvin Dark could be a three. An All-Star team would have to move Gil Hodges back to third base, where he'd be a liability, but they'd still win any league with C-Campy, 1B-Kluszewski, 2B-Hamner, 3B-Hodges, SS-Dark, LF-Snider, CF-Ashburn, RF-Mueller, rotation of Roberts, Erskine, Simmons and Bickford. Altogether, it makes 15 good players, 33 units of star value and three Hall of Famers working on five (Ashburn and Hodges)—the best one-league rookie crop ever.

If you buy the point-total method of evaluating one-team crops, the top six would be:

1. 1948 Dodgers (12)
2. 1948 Phillies (11)
3. 1942 Cardinals (10)
   1958 Giants (10)
   1924 Giants (10)
   1909 Red Sox (10)

So unless I missed one somewhere, one could say that the two greatest rookie crops of all time both appeared in the same league in the same season—quite a remarkable concentration of talent.

What was the worst rookie crop for a league?

The American League in the war-shortened 1917 season produced only one player of note, a Ray Burris—type pitcher named Allen Sothoron who died in St. Louis in 1939. The American League in 1945 produced only two players of note, Cass Michaels and Boo Ferris (both ones). Among the peacetime seasons, the 1933 National League produced the fewest players of note, with two, but one of them was Joe Medwick, so the group total is five. The 1941 National League produced only three players of note and a group total of four—Howie Pollett (two), Danny Murtaugh (one) and Ace Adams (one).

Ok, stop stalling, James. **What was the best rookie season of all time,** in terms of what the players eventually produced? In a surprisingly easy decision, the greatest rookie crop of all time, considering both leagues, was that of 1913. Amazingly, the season achieved this level of distinction not only without any Babe Ruths or Willie Mayses, but without any Paul Waners or Willie Stargells as well, with no fives and no fours. You'll probably find that hard to believe and so would I if I didn't know better—but the 1913 rookie crop was not only larger and deeper and richer than any other crop, but so much larger and deeper and richer than any other crop that, despite twinges of regret over the absence of major stars, it must be granted the championship.

The season was tremendously strong in both the American and National Leagues. The American League produced only one Hall of Famer, and that a marginal one in **Ray Schalk.** But look at the rest of the crop:

Bobby Veach, a Tiger outfielder, led the American League in RBI three times by 1918, then hit .355 in 1919, .338 with 16 homers and 128 RBI in 1921 and a .327 with 126 RBI in 1922.

Jack Fournier, White Sox first baseman, wrested the American League slugging championship from Ty Cobb

in 1915, then, after a career crisis, reemerged as a superb slugging first baseman for the Dodgers in the twenties.

Wally Schang, Athletics catcher, was probably a better player than the Hall of Famer, Schalk. He played 19 years and caught for seven league championship teams.

Bullet Joe Bush went 26–7 with the Yankees in 1922 and won 194 games in a 17-year career.

Hooks Dauss established and still holds the Detroit Tiger record for career wins, with 221 (or 223, depending on source.) His won-lost logs include 18–15, 24–13, 19–12, 17–14, 21–9, 21–13 and 16–11.

Dutch Leonard posted a record 1.01 ERA in 1915 and won 139 games in his 11-year career.

Bob Shawkey went 16–8, 24–14, 20–11, 20–13, 18–12, 20–12, 16–11 and 16–11, won 196 games total, pitched in five World Series and led the American League in ERA in 1920.

Ray Chapman was the outstanding shortstop in baseball for the rest of the decade, probably on course for the Hall of Fame when killed by a pitch in 1920.

Rube Foster was the top pitcher for the World Champion Red Sox in 1915.

Reb Russell went 22–16 for the White Sox as a rookie, later 18–11 and 15–5. Switching to the outfield after an arm injury, he drove in 75 runs in 60 games for the Pirates in 1922.

I've mentioned eleven players here; the American League crop also included Babe Borton, Doc Lavan, Nemo Leibold, Fritz Maisel, Fred Anderson, Nick Cullop, Earl Moseley and Al Schulz. That's just the American League half–19 good players, including eight minor stars or better. The total "star value" is 29—the highest of any league prior to expansion except for the champion, the 1948 National League. No other league prior to 1964 produced more than 16 good players, with the average being about nine.

There are two other leagues prior to expansion which produced exactly 16 good players—the National League in 1928, and the Natoinal League in 1913. That's the same season—a total of 35 good players produced in the two leagues, almost twice the normal number. I'll look more at who the National League players were in a moment, but first just look at the number, 35. It's way out in front among the years 1900–1963. These are the top ten:

Year	Good Players	Star Value
1913	35	56
1962	28	44
1928	28	41
1954	28	40
1909	26	41
1934	26	41
1914	26	38
1961	25	40
1942	25	37
1912	25	35

If it was a close call, I'd ignore the point-count and say, "Well, no matter how many good-to-outstanding pitchers they produced, I can't go with a season which didn't produce *any* big stars." But first of all, no other season is close to 1913 in terms of the number of good players produced. And second, of those seasons which were closest, none could match it, let alone exceed it, in terms of quality. For while the 1913 season produced no fours or fives, it produced a disproportionate share of twos—minor stars—and threes—marginal Hall of Fame candidates—so that the average quality of those 35 players is, actually, quite good. The average quality of the thirty-five 1913 products is **higher** than the average quality of any other productive pre-expansion season.

The 29 "star points" produced by the American League in 1913 was the highest pre-expansion AL total; the 27 star points produced by the National League in 1913 was the second-highest, trailing only the 1948 campaign. (Well, 1924 also produced 27).

Like the AL, the National League produced only one Hall of Famer, that being the less-than-overwhelmingly qualified **Rabbit Maranville,** the 23-year glove man. But backing up Maranville are:

Wilbur Cooper, a 216-game winner in the National League who from 1917 through 1924 went 17–11, 19–14, 19–13, 24–15, 22–14, 23–14, 17–19 and 20–14.

George Burns, the premier leadoff man in baseball over the next ten years. Burns led the NL in runs scored five times, in walks six times and in stolen bases twice, hitting regularly around .300.

Cy Williams, who led the National League in home runs four times, including in 1927 when he was 39 years old. Had the so-called "lively ball" era arrived three or four years earlier, Williams would unquestionably be in the Hall of Fame.

Heine Groh, of the famous bottle bat, National League leader at various times in hits, doubles, walks and runs scored, and hero of the 1922 World Series.

Bill Doak, 20–6 with a league-leading 1.72 ERA in 1914, 20–12 in 1920, league leader in winning percentage and ERA in 1921, winner of 170 games total.

Dick Rudolph, 27–10 with the Miracle Braves, and the other **Bill James,** 26–7 with the same team. Rudolph had some other good years; James didn't.

Casey Stengel, a good outfielder with the Dodgers and later an outstanding platoon player.

That's nine players; the other seven were Al Demaree, Tommy Griffith, Les Mann, Chief Johnson, Erskine Mayer, Gene Packard, and Pol Perritt.

Altogether, the season produced 15 "minor stars" or higher designation. No other season produced more than 13. The total of 35 good players was never surpassed when there were 16 teams, not surpassed in 1961 when there were 18, never surpassed when there were 20, never surpassed when there were 24. Finally in 1977, when there were 26 major league teams, there was a class of 37 good-quality rookies.

As to why this happened—why there was this explosion of rookies at that time—I would suggest that it was mostly just coincidence but point out that the effect of the coincidence was exaggerated by two factors. First, the 1913 season was the height of the free minors. From about 1905 through 1913, the number of minor league teams operating increased greatly. Although I have never seen a count, I'm fairly sure that there were more minor leagues operating in 1913 than in any other year, even in the late thirties or early fifties. In 1914 baseball attendance de-

clined dramatically, and many (maybe even most) of the small minor leagues collapsed. Thus the 1913 rookie crop was the fruit of a burgeoning plant which would soon be cut back, while the 1913 players, once established, would face less job competition from the withered minors.

Second, throughout baseball history, career length increases whenever salaries increase. After 1920 baseball salaries went up sharply, thus providing a strong incentive for players to continue in the profession as long as possible. As happened in the late seventies, the number of older players shot up dramatically in just a few years. The 1913 rookies were among those players who stayed around into the late twenties.

After 1913, picking the top rookie crops becomes tougher. I pick the top six as, in order, 1913, 1924, 1965, 1948, 1973, and 1956. A few details:

The 1924 crop is distinguished by the six Hall of Famers listed before (Terry, Cuyler, Lindstrom, H. Wilson, Simmons and Lyons), as well as five fine pitchers (Ray Kremer, Guy Bush, Red Lucas, Firpo Marberry, and Earl Whitehill) and two excellent middle infielders (Glenn Wright and Maxie Bishop.) Altogether, 13 star-quality or better players, 22 good players and 45 points of star value.

The 1965 crop contributed a formidable starting rotation of Jim Palmer, Steve Carlton, Catfish Hunter, and Phil Niekro, backed up by Tug McGraw in the bullpen and Jim Lonborg and Rudy May for long relief. Oddly, not one of those seven pitchers made much of an impression as a rookie. Carlton was 0–0 in fifteen relief appearances, Palmer 5–4 and Hunter 8–8 in limited work and Niekro 2–3. At least those guys broke even; Lonborg was 9–17, Rudy May 4–9 and McGraw 2–7. The top non-pitchers were Joe Morgan (four; should be five), Tony Perez (three), and Paul Blair, Willie Horton, and Don Kessinger (all twos). That's 12 star-quality or better players, among a total of 32 good players for 55 points of star value. (In the rankings I discounted these totals somewhat as an adjustment for expansion.)

Had the National League crop of 1948 received any real support from the American League, that season would rank higher than fourth. The 1948 American League crop was good quality but very thin, listing only six players: Larry Doby (three), Billy Pierce (three), Billy Goodman (two), Gene Bearden (one), Ned Garver (one), and Bob Porterfield (one). Only Doby in right field and Pierce as a starter could crack the National League All-Rookie team, given before, but they are enough to make that outfit probably the strongest rookie All-Star team that could be chosen from any season. The stats on 1948: Thirteen players of star quality, 21 good players and 44 units of star value.

The 1973 rookie crew, like that of 1965, did not look particularly impressive at the time. The American League rookie of the year was Al Bumbry, a part-time player, and the National League's was Gary Matthews, probably a little below-average as Rookies of the Year go. But as time has passed and players have developed it has emerged as one of the greatest crops of all time—and when the final records are in the book, it may very well have to be ranked as the greatest ever. Mike Schmidt, a third baseman who hit .196 in 132 games as a rookie, has gone on to become the greatest third baseman in the history of the game. An unspectacular 22-year-old outfielder who played 54 games for the Pirates that summer has gone on to compile a career that, except for a three year time-out for drugs, would probably rank right beside Schmidt's. I mean, of course, Dave Parker. Another giant NL outfielder who came up and had a very similar record as a rookie (56 games, .277) has now driven in 100 runs five straight times, in addition to which he runs well, throws extremely well and is a good outfielder; that, of course, is Dave Winfield. Yet another rookie right fielder who hit just .223 in 1973 has gone on to have a career in the same group, that being Dwight Evans. A teammate of Evans who hit just .238 that summer didn't emerge as a regular until five years later: Cecil Cooper. That's five players of at least marginal Hall of Fame quality. Ten other players qualify as minor stars: Darrell Porter, Frank White, Gorman Thomas, Bob Boone, Ron Cey, Davey Lopes, Gary Matthews, Randy Jones, J. R. Richard, and Steve Rogers. Most of these players are still active and still could be reclassified upward in time, as well as Charlie Hough, now classified a one but in the prime of a knuckle-baller's life. In the end, they might well force us to mark the 1973 season as the greatest emergence of rookies in the history of the game. For now, 32 good players, 15 stars, 54 points of star value.

The 1956 season, on the other hand, saw the emergence of two dramatic rookies who went on to win Hall of Fame status. Frank Robinson went from 38 homers as a 20-year-old rookie to two MVP awards; Luis Aparicio, AL Rookie of the year, also developed and endured. When these are joined by Don Drysdale, Rocky Colavito, Bill Mazeroski, Bill White, and Lindy McDaniel, they form an impressive rookie list. When you add Harmon Killebrew and Sandy Koufax, who are listed as rookies in 1956 because they have to be listed somewhere, you've got one of the greatest sets of rookies anywhere: 22 players, 9 stars, 42 points of star value.

A few notes about other rookie crews. The best rookie crop of 1900–1909 was that of 1909, which included Tris Speaker, Home Run Baker, Donie Bush, Harry Hooper, Jack Quinn, Joe Wood, Rube Marquard, Bob Bescher, and Babe Adams. The 1915 crop, which contained Babe Ruth was strong but not awesome; Ruth was backed by George Sisler, Carl Mays, and Dave Bancroft. The 1928 crop was large and good, but contained only two players of Hall of Fame calibre, Chuck Klein and Carl Hubbell. The 1929 crop, sometimes cited as one of the strongest, was actually a rather weak group in terms of eventual output. The 1939 group, led by Ted Williams and Lou Boudreau, was good.

The 1954 rookie crop is an interesting one, in that it was huge (28 good players) and had terrific front-line quality, led by Hank Aaron, Ernie Banks, and Al Kaline. But the problem there is a serious lack of second-line stars; the only two worth mentioning are Frank Bolling and Camilo Pascual. Otherwise the year is distinguished by an exceptionally long list of Joe Cunninghams and Don Hoaks.

The 1963 National League crop was terrific (Rose, Stargell, Gaylord Perry, Staub, Wynn), but the American League support was not strong. The 1970 crop was exceptionally large in the NL (20 good players), but exceptionally small in the American League (5 players), and contained no major stars in either league (Blyleven might be reclassified as a four, but not yet.) The 1977 crop was the largest ever in terms of good players (37), but the quality has yet to impress by historic standards and probably never will; 1977 Rookies of the Year Eddie Murray and Andre Dawson remain the best, with Jack Morris their primary help.

Finally, the "hot new candidate." The hot new candidate is 1982. While it will be a long, long time until the group can be firmly evaluated, consider this: the average rookie crop produces two batting titles. Wade Boggs has won three, Willie McGee one and Tony Gwynn one, a total of five so far for the 1982 rookie class. While the average crop will win two MVP awards, the 1982 crew has already won three: Cal Ripken, Ryne Sandberg and Willie McGee. The big names are magnificently supported by, among others, Jesse Barfield, Brett Butler, Johnny Ray, Frank Viola, Kent Hrbek, Steve Sax, Gary Gaetti, Steve Balboni and Von Hayes. Atlee Hammaker and Alejandro Pena contributed ERA titles to the class before blowing their arms out. While it is true that we might overrate this class because these players are right now in their prime, the 1982 class has already surpassed every other class back to 1977 and is gaining rapidly on everything back to 1973. If Boggs, Ripken, Sandberg, and Barfield keep on keeping on . . . well, they're going to finish well up the list.

CHAPTER TWO
Outstanding Performances by Rookies as Rookies

That completes my studies concerning the eventual distinction earned by a class of rookies. From now on, when I talk about what a rookie class did, I will be talking about what they did *as rookies,* in their rookie seasons. I will be talking about 1948 and 1986 on even grounds, so to speak.

With respect to these questions, my research is less comprehensive. I started with a data base which contained *all rookies who played in 100 or more games (as rookies) between 1950 and 1975.* I wanted the group to be far enough back from the present that we would be able to look at what the players did in their careers, essential for trying to figure out what is meaningful and what isn't in the rookie season. I chose the 1950 and 1975 markers because, apart from being a quarter-century apart, both were outstanding rookie seasons, the 1950 campaign introducing Walt Dropo (34 homers, 144 RBI and .322), Al Rosen (37 homers, 116 RBI) and Luke Easter (28 homers, 107 RBI) and the 1975 campaign being the only one in which a rookie won the MVP award (Fred Lynn, pushed to the wire by Jim Rice).

This group was enlarged upon several times.

After seeing Bill Conlin's comment about the 1948 season, I pushed the start of the study back to 1948.

After apologizing to the readers a certain number of times because a study ignored pitchers, I made up a database which included *all rookie pitchers winning nine or more games or saving fifteen or more games* during the same period (1948–1975).

After apologizing a few more times about the exclusion of rookies who made a profound impact although appearing in less than 100 games, like Willie McCovey in 1959 and Cesar Cedeno in 1970, I made up a database which included all rookies during the period whom I judged to have made a significant impact although appearing in less than 100 games.

Altogether, 666 rookies were included in the various studies, 464 "rookie regulars" in the basic group (on which the most detailed studies will be based), 174 rookie pitchers, and 28 in the supplemental group. Before I get into the dry, serious analysis which is sure to follow here, let me make a few random comments based on the research.

Distribution of Rookies by Years

The 1969 season (with four expansion teams) had the most qualifying rookies, 38. The 1968 season had the fewest, 11. The 1954 season had the most rookies of any pre-expansion season, 35.

An average pre-expansion season had 20 rookies, or one and a quarter per team. The post-expansion per-team average was almost exactly the same (1.23 per team per season).

Distribution of Rookies by Teams

The Chicago Cubs and Boston Red Sox had the most rookie/regulars during the 1948–1975 period, with 45 apiece; they were followed by the Giants and Phillies (42 each) and the Cardinals (40). A total of 45 rookies in 28 years is 1.6 rookies per season, as opposed to the 1.25 norm.

The Montreal Expos had the fewest rookie regulars, 10, but of course they were in existence only for the last seven years of the study. Among the established teams, the Detroit Tigers used by far the fewest rookies during the period, with only 21 qualifying rookies in the 28 years; they were followed by the Yankees (25), the Braves (26) and the Reds (also 26).

Distribution of Rookies by Age

The youngest rookie in the study was, of course, Robin Yount, 18 years old when he played shortstop for the Brewers in 1974 (a gutsy managerial move for which Del Crandall is never given the credit due him). The oldest rookie in the study was Luke Easter, 34 years old when his break came with the Indians in 1950.

The most common age for rookies are 22 and 23. Sixty percent of rookies (399 or 366) are between 21 and 24 years of age, and 86% (575 of 666) are between 20 and 26.

The full age spectrum looks like this:

Age:	18	19	20	21	22	23	24	25	26	27	28	29	30–34
Rookies:	1	12	51	81	103	117	98	72	53	34	22	13	9

Distribution of Rookies by Position

The distribution of rookies by position clearly reflects the defensive spectrum which has been outlined annually in the *Baseball Abstract*. There were more rookies playing center field than any other position other than pitcher (76); shortstops were the second most common (66). The reason this happens, of course, is that some players start out at those positions and drift over time to the less demanding positions. Bob Allison, George Altman, Jose Cruz, and Tommie Davis, to name just four, all started out as center fielders. Failing to invoke comparisons with Richie Ashburn, they were shifted to less demanding locations.

There were many fewer rookie/regular catchers (42) than players at any other position. The other five positions all had between 60 and 63 rookies in the study.

Distribution of Rookies by Race

The study included 58 Latin American rookies (9%), 116 Black rookies (18%) and 492 "white" rookies. Actually, the study contained a few Canadians, the odd Greek, Pole, Jew, or Indian; all taken together there weren't ten of them, and they were all counted as "white."

Only 11 of the 174 rookie pitchers were black.

Distribution of Rookies by Sex

All 666 rookies were considered male.

One odd thing that I noticed in the study was . . .

In 1952 the top three teams in the National League had three very similar rookies. The League champion Dodgers had a 28-year-old, right-handed rookie reliever named Joe Black, who went 15–4 with a 2.15 ERA in 58 games. The second place New York Giants had a 28-year-old, right-handed reliever named Hoyt Wilhelm; Hoyt went 15–3 with a 2.43 ERA in 71 games. And the third place St. Louis Cardinals had a 27-year-old, right-handed rookie reliever named Eddie Yuhas, who went 12–2 with a 2.73 ERA in 54 games.

Everybody knows Wilhelm; he's in the Hall of Fame. Any real baseball fan remembers Joe Black; he was the Rookie of the Year and a Brooklyn Dodger to boot. But did you ever hear of Eddie Yuhas? He did almost the same thing as the other two in that memorable season, but he's been totally forgotten.

The Cardinal Center Fielders

Between the retirement of Terry Moore in 1948 and the emergence of Curt Flood in 1961, the Cardinals changed center fielders every year, with most of the regulars being rookies—yet with the exception of one or two years, it could not really be said that the Cardinals ever had a poor center fielder. After Enos Slaughter played center field late in 1948, the Cardinals in 1949 gave the job to a 26-year-old pinch runner named Chuck Diering. Diering was a fine fielder and hit a respectable .263, but he had no power, so when the Cardinals came up a game short in 1949 they put a rookie named Bill Howerton in left field and moved Stan Musial to center.

Howerton hit OK but he was pushing 30 and didn't seem to have much of a future, so in 1951 the Cardinals traded him to Pittsburgh and, imagining themselves to be making a pennant charge, purchased a veteran center fielder named Peanuts Lowrey. Lowrey hit .303 in 1951, but he was well past 30 and had lost a step in the field, so in 1952 the Cards flipped Musial back to center and put Lowrey in left. Foreseeably, Musial didn't provide the 1952 Cardinals with championship quality defense in center, and Lowrey didn't provide them with championship quality offense in left, so in 1953 the Cardinals put a rookie in center field, in Rip Repulski.

Repulski hit fairly well (.275 with 15 homers) but wasn't born to play center field, so in 1954 he shifted to left and the Cardinals put another rookie, Wally Moon, in center feld. Moon hit .304 and scored 106 runs, winning the Rookie of the Year award over a few people like Ernie Banks and Hank Aaron, but the Cardinals had a dismal year. So in 1955 the Cardinals traded Enos Slaughter to the Yankees for another rookie outfielder, Bill Virdon, who could run rings around Wally and Rip in center field. Though the Cardinals, now playing an outfield of Repulski, Moon and Virdon, had an even more miserable season (seventh place), Virdon hit .281 with 17 homers and became the second straight Cardinal center fielder to win the Rookie of the Year award.

Early in the 1956 season, however, Virdon developed a problem with his vision and stopped hitting for awhile, so the Cardinals traded him to Pittsburgh for a miserable little outfielder named Bobby Del Greco, who became the Cardinal center fielder for the 1956 season. Del Greco was a decent center fielder but no hitter, so he was dealt to Chicago and in 1957 the Cardinals attempted to solve their center field problem by relocating Ken Boyer, a fine young third baseman, and playing a rookie named Eddie Kasko at third base. Kasko was decent and Boyer led National League outfielders in fielding percentage at .996. The Cardinals finished second behind Milwaukee. Still, Boyer had a sub-par season with the bat, by his own standards, and was regarded as being more valuable at third base, plus the Cardinal shortstop, Alvin Dark, was getting up in years, so in 1958 the Cardinals shifted Boyer to third and Kasko to short, making a trade with Cincinnati to acquire a talented 20-year-old named Curt Flood.

Flood was a superb center fielder, posting a 3.03 range factor with 18 outfield assists in 120 games, but his .261 batting average with 10 homers was considered a disappointment. That winter the Cardinals traded Wally Moon to the Dodgers to acquire another outfielder, Gino Cimoli, who had played well as a left fielder for the Dodgers in 1957 before dropping off in 1958. Cimoli played center for the Cardinals in 1959, hitting .279 with 40 doubles, but as a center fielder his range was a liability, and the Cardinals had the worst ERA in the league. In 1960 the Cardinals reluctantly returned Curt Flood to center field, but had him sharing the position with Charlie James, Leon Wagner, John Glenn, Ellis Burton, Don Landrum, and for at least a few innings Walt Moryn and Joe Cunningham. Oh, I forgot to mention Bill White—Bill White played center for the Cardinals for almost three weeks. For the first two months of the 1961 season Flood sat on the bench and the job belonged to Landrum, James, and Carl Warwick, until Solly Hemus was fired as manager on July 6, 1961, and was replaced by Johnny Keane. Keane announced in his first hours as manager that Curt Flood would be the Cardinal center fielder—putting an end to thirteen unlucky years of constant shuffling at the position.

Yet the odd thing was that, looking at the thirteen years as a whole, it wasn't that the Cardinals couldn't solve the problem, but that they solved it time and time and time again, only to abandon the solution and reopen the wound. Granted, Stan Musial and Enos Slaughter weren't true center fielders—but there were six National League teams that would have been delighted to have them there. There wasn't anything really wrong with the outfield of Howerton, Musial, and Slaughter. Wally Moon, as a young man, was an OK solution to the center field problem; you could love the bat and live with the defense. Bill Virdon was a fine center fielder; you could love the defense and live with the bat. Ken Boyer would have been one of the best in the league in center field if he'd had time to work into it. Curt Flood was just wasting away for three years while the Cardinals lost games they should have won. Even Repulski and Cimoli weren't the worst in the league, at least giving the Cardinals a bat in the spot. Among all the solutions to the problem, only Del Greco was really poor. Many of the players that the Cardinals looked at in center field, like Leon Wagner, were players who could have helped them at some other position.

During these 13 years, the Cardinal farm system was tremendously productive—yet the team wasted the last two-thirds of Stan Musial's career in faltering, directionless hyperactivity, never slowing down to look more than a week ahead. They played baseball like Jimmy Carter conducted foreign policy, always reacting; reacting to one problem by creating another one, always trying to catch up with their last mistake.

Let's get back to work.

Introduction to Value Approximation Method

The basic method that we will be using to evaluate rookie seasons, and eventually to evaluate how the 1986 rookie crop stacks up against those of other years, will be the value approximation method.

The value approximation method is a method which is used to evaluate *groups of seasons*. The method begins by reducing all of the things that a player does in a season—all of the hits, the doubles, the triples, the wins and losses for a pitcher, the range factor—into one number. It was originally intended that an average regular player in an average season would score about 10; in practice an average player might score at 10 *if he plays 162 games* or very close to it. The number 10 represents the *weight:* of the player's contributions, and thus represents his value in the sense that weight represents value, which is to say sometimes very well and other times not so well. A 15- or 16-point season is always a great season, without exception just as 15 ounces of gold are always valuable regardless of what is made of the gold. But, just as a 120-pound man can be a gymnast or a cancer victim (that is, can have a small but great body or a large but wasted body), a 6-point season for a pitcher can be a season in which he pitches brilliantly for a third of the year, like Mel Stottlemyre in 1964 (9–3, 2.06 ERA in 96 innings), or it can be a season in which a pitcher pitches all year without doing anything great, like Arnold Portocarrero in 1954 (9–18, 4.06 ERA in 248 innings). If the player plays well the ratio of Approximate Value to playing time will be higher, but it is not possible to play regularly without acquiring *some* approximate value points.

The scale of approximate values, expressed in English, would go something like this:

17 Strong MVP candidate
16 MVP candidate
15 Definite All-Star, marginal MVP candidate
14 Probable All-Star
13 Marginal All-Star
12 Very fine season; All-Star "candidate"
11 Above average player playing every day
    Excellent player missing 20–30 games
10 Average player playing every day
    Outstanding platoon player
 9 Average season for a regular
    Good production for platoon player or injury season
 8 Fair season for a regular
    Excellent figure for player playing 100–120 games
 7 Poor season for a regular
    Good productivity from pitcher making 20–25 starts
 6 Very Poor season for a regular
    Typical performance for player playing 100–120 games
 5 Undistinguished part-time player
    Decent middle reliever in 40 games might place here
 4 Part-time player
    Player making favorable impression in 40–50 games
 3 Unimpressive in limited playing time
    Fair performance in 12–15 starts or 25 relief games
 2 Very limited playing time over season
    Player making good impression in September
 1 Plays very little, contributes on occasion
    Typical September call-up in 60–70 at bats
 0 Plays little and does nothing special
    Plays well in less than 10 games

Because we are dealing with just one figure for each player, we can evaluate a group of unlike sessions—some pitchers, some outfielders, some part-timers, etc—by simply adding together the "weight" of their accomplishment.

While you do, of course, have to use some discretion in evaluating groups of players in this way, the advantage of the method is that it enables us to deal with larger groups of accomplishments than we can assess accurately just by staring at them. When I first introduced the value approximation method in the 1980 *Baseball Abstract,* I explained the advantages this way:

The purpose of this [is] not directly to create knowledge or to broaden or improve [your] knowledge of the players involved; it [is] instead to take that knowledge and understanding that [you] already have and to store it. In evaluating any one season the system [is] unmistakably less precise, often less accurate than other forms of analysis, including subjective judgment. But while I could judge any one season more accurately than the system, I was—and anyone would be—quite incapable of making a series of 40 or 50 such judgments, stacking them up mentally one atop the other and assessing their total "size" or "weight." The advantage of the (Value Approximation Method) is that it can—40, or 50, or 5000. The parallel, I suppose, would be that if somebody handed you a brick, you could probably guess its weight within a few ounces. But if somebody handed you a building, you would know only that it weighed considerably more than you could lift. Large amounts of talent, like buildings, overpower one's ability to hold them in mind, and thus make it impossible for us to assess accurately their weight.

Unlike most offensive indicators, which have several hundred possible degrees of excellence to assign to a season, the [value approximation method] attempts to be no more precise than language. A 16-point season could be called "superstar," others described as "excellent," "all-star," "good to excellent," "good," "above average," "solid," or whatever. But if you were to start applying those words to, let us say, 1000 seasons, how far could you go before your standards became eroded and uncertain? Let's see, did I call that last .280 season "fair to good" or just "fair." Would I trade this 10–12 pitcher for that .245 hitting shortstop even up? Well, this season is a little better than that one, which was "fair," so it must be "fair to good." But wait a minute, he's only .020 better than that guy, who was "weak."

The value approximation method never becomes confused; it churns through reams and thousands of players without ever losing perspective. The value approximation method evaluates records, and not ballplayers, and as such it lacks any knowledge of timing, clutch ability, baserunning judgment, mental lapses, leadership ability, winning spirit, or throwing to the right base. But if the method evaluates talent without regard to deeper insights, it also evaluates talent without regard to favoritism, press clippings, self-promotion, overexposure or a lack of exposure, or any of the other greater forms of ignorance. It is perhaps not such a bad trade. It is just the facts, reduced into a spare adjective and the adjective into a number, stated, weighted and approximated in the simplest possible form.

We will use this simplest possible summation to evaluate each rookie between 1948 and 1975, and thus to evaluate the rookie classes therein.

In the process of doing this study, I became dissatisfied with the value approximation method that I was using. That is, it wasn't that I didn't feel that it was the right method to use to study the issue—it is the right method—but that the rules used to arrive at the "weight" for each player were not as accurate as I would have liked them to be. And so, for the first time since I developed the method in 1977, I thoroughly revised the method used.

The old method worked by "cutoffs" or "magic numbers"; if you hit .300 and slugged .500, that would be three points for batting average and three for slugging percentage. But if you hit .299 and slugged .499, that was two points in each category. This occasionally created troubling situations in which players would be misevaluated because they just missed or just skimmed over a number of cut-off points.

I've always known this and always been somewhat troubled by it, but I have resisted changing the method for two reasons. One is that, since the method is used to evaluate groups of hundreds of seasons, it is necessary to keep the method simple enough that the work of performing the calculations does not become oppressive. The second is that, having done many studies using the method over a period of nearly a decade, I was afraid that a switch in the method would wipe out the "book," the backlog of value approximations which are already known.

I solved this problem by devising the new method so that there was a one-to-one relationship with the old one. That is, a 10-point approximate value by the new method means exactly the same thing as a 10-point season by the old method. A group of seasons will have almost exactly the same total no matter which method they are evaluated by, so that old-style and new-style value approximations can be used together. We just use the new style approximation when we have it, and the old-style when we don't.

The other thing that has changed is the arrival of the modern personal computer. Within a year, I believe that there will be available to anybody who wants to have it a database of player records which is considerably larger and more comprehensive than the *Macmillan Encyclopedia*. When that happens, the "calculation load" becomes no problem.

So I did what some people have been trying to tell me to do for years, and revised the method. The new method will be explained in *Not of Any General Interest*; it still isn't perfect, but there are many fewer cases in which a player has a value approximation that is out of line with that of comparable players.

Who the Rookies Are

Let's start by looking at the Rookies of the Year. One way to demonstrate the working of the system is to compare a list of the players who were chosen Rookie of the Year with a list of the players who have the highest approximate value among rookies eligible for the award. The list below gives the rookie with the highest approximate value for each league in each year from 1948 through 1975.

	National League	*American League*
1948	Alvin Dark (13)	Gene Bearden (15)
	Whitey Lockman (13)	
1949	Don Newcombe (13)	Roy Sievers (13)
		Alex Kellner (13)
1950	Sam Jethroe (13)	Al Rosen (16)
1951	Randy Jackson (12)	Minnie Minoso (12)
1952	Joe Black (13)	Bob Nieman (11)
		Jim Rivera (11)
		Harry Byrd (11)
1953	Harvey Haddix (15)	Harvey Kuenn (15)
1954	Wally Moon (15)	Bill Tuttle (12)
		Bob Grim (12)

National League	American League
1955 Bill Virdon (10)	Herb Score (12)
	Ken Boyer (10)
1956 Frank Robinson (15)	Luis Aparicio (11)
1957 Jack Sanford (13)	Frank Malzone (13)
1958 Orlando Cepeda (12)	Albie Pearson (10)
1959 Vada Pinson (17)	Bob Allison (12)
1960 Pancho Herrara (10)	Ron Hansen (14)
1961 Dick Howser (13)	Billy Williams (11)
Chuck Schilling (13)	
1962 Tom Tresh (15)	Ken Hubbs (11)
1963 Jimmie Hall (14)	Pete Rose (10)
Gary Peters (14)	Ron Hunt (10)
1964 Dick Allen (16)	Tony Oliva (16)
1965 Joe Morgan (12)	Curt Blefray (11)
Frank Linzy (12)	Willie Horton (11)
1966 Tommie Agee (14)	Sonny Jackson (13)
1967 Dick Hughes (12)	Reggie Smith (12)
1968 Johnny Bench (14)	Stan Bahnsen (13)
Jerry Koosman (14)	
1969 Ted Sizemore (11)	Bill Melton (13)
Larry Hisle (11)	
1970 Billy Grabarkewitz (15)	Thurman Munson (11)
	Ray Fosse (11)
1971 Willie Montanez (12)	Bill Parsons (9)
1972 Jon Matlack (12)	Carlton Fisk (12)
1973 Gary Matthews (13)	Pedro Garcia (11)
	Doc Medich (11)
1974 Bake McBride (14)	Bucky Dent (11)
1975 John Montefusco (12)	Fred Lynn (17)

In this period there were 55 Rookie of the Year awards, one in 1948 and two each year from 1949 through 1975. Among those 55 awards:

There are 26 cases in which the player with the highest approximate value won the award.

There are ten cases in which there was a tie between two or more players with the same approximate value, and the award was given to one of the players with the highest approximate value.

There were six cases in which the player with the highest approximate value was not eligible for the Rookie of the Year award according to the definition of a rookie in use at that time. In all of these cases except one (the National League in 1959) the award went to the eligible player with the highest approximate value. Those awards were:

1950 American League: Al Rosen led the AL with 37 homers, drove in 116 runs and played a strong third base, but was ineligible for the award after playing 35 previous games. Had he been eligible, it would have made for an interesting contest with Walt Dropo, who had even better offensive stats (34 homers and 144 RBI, .322) but was a moose at first base. Dropo (AV 14) won over a still-exceptional field including Whitey Ford (9–1), Irv Noren (98 RBI) and Luke Easter.

1951 National League: Randy Jackson of Chicago had the highest AV of any rookie, 12, but was not eligible for the Award after playing in 34 games the previous year. In truth, he probably would not have won the award anyway.

His stats were quite similar to those of Willie Mays, whose AV was 11 (Jackson: 16 homers, 76 RBI, .275; Mays: 20 homers, 68 RBI, .274), and Mays probably would have won the award even if Jackson had been eligible.

1957 American League: Frank Malzone drove in 103 runs for the Red Sox and had an approximate value of 13, but was ineligible because he had played 33 games in previous seasons, so Tony Kubek won the award in a virtually unanimous ballot (23 of 24). The chance that Malzone would have won the award had he been eligible can perhaps be seen in the fact that there was a special hearing of his position by the BBWAA board of directors, who ruled that no exception was to be made and that Malzone was not eligible for the award. One writer insisted on voting for Malzone anyway, depriving Kubek of unanimous recognition.

1959 National League: Vada Pinson, a 20-year-old center fielder for the Cincinnati Reds, had one of two 17-point seasons by a rookie during the period of the study. Fred Lynn in 1975 had the other. Oddly, the two seasons were quite similar. Pinson hit .316 with 47 doubles, 9 triples and 20 homers; Lynn hit .331 with 47 doubles, 7 triples and 21 homers. Both men led the league in runs scored, Lynn with 103 and Pinson with 131. Their strikeout/walk ratios were similar, 98–55 for Pinson and 90–62 for Lynn. Lynn drove in more runs, 105–84, while Pinson stole more bases, 21–10. Both men were outstanding defensive center fielders.

Pinson, however, was not eligible for the award, so it was voted unanimously to Willie McCovey, who joined the Giants in time to play 52 magnificent games. Though McCovey's approximate value was actually lower than that of two other NL rookies (Joe Koppe and George Altman), the voters obviously figured that 52 games of slugging .656 was more impressive than a full season of decent but undistinguished play. Pinson outpointed McCovey 11–1 in voting for the MVP Award, for which both were eligible.

1969 American League: Lou Piniella (11 homers, 68 RBI, .282) won the Rookie of the Year award although Bill Melton had better stats (23 homers, 87 RBI, .255) and a higher approximate value (13–10). Melton was apparently not eligible for the award after playing 34 games in 1968.

1970 National League: Billy Grabarkewitz had an excellent season for the Dodgers, hitting .289 with 17 homers, 84 RBI, 95 walks, 19 stolen bases and 92 runs scored. Grabarkewitz, who was a fine fielder at that time, hurt his arm in spring training in 1971 and could no longer play third base, after which he mysteriously stopped hitting. Anyway, he was ineligible for the award after playing 34 games in 1969, so the award fell to Carl Morton, an 18-game winner for the Expos whose AV (13) was the highest among the eligibles.

Note the odd pattern: of the six players who were denied Rookie of the Year awards because they had played just a little too much the previous year, five were third basemen, and all five of those third basemen had played 33 to 35 games in previous seasons.

There are thirteen cases in which there is an actual conflict between the rookie of the year as selected by the BBWAA, and the rookie with the most value as seen by the value approximation method. In most of those cases, it can easily be seen that the writers voted wisely, picking up on some difference between the players which is not apparent in the statistics. In most cases they selected the player who would eventually achieve greater status in the baseball world. In several cases they chose players who had played well in 125 or fewer games over players who reached a slightly higher value approximation in significantly more playing time. In only three cases did the writers clearly blow it—picking Gil McDougald over Minnie Minoso in 1951, Don Schwall over several better players in 1961 and Jim Lefebvre over Joe Morgan in 1965. These are the votes which went against the player with the highest approximate value:

1948 Alvin Dark (13) over Gene Bearden (15)

Bearden went 20–7 with a league-leading 2.43 ERA, pacing Cleveland to the Worlds Championship. For good measure he threw a shutout game in three of the World Series and saved the sixth and final game for Bob Lemon. Alvin Dark hit .322 to top an exceptional National League crop, leading Boston to the NL pennant.

1951 American: Gil McDougald (10) over Minnie Minoso (12)

Helped by playing in New York and on a pennant winner, McDougald won a close 13–11 vote.

1953 National: Junior Gilliam (14) beat Harvey Haddix (15).

Haddix, 20–9, would have been a deserving recipient of the award—but certainly no more so than was Gilliam.

1960 National: Frank Howard (8) over Pancho Herrara (10).

The two men had similar skills and similar stats. The writers correctly chose Howard, who started the season in the minors, on the basis of potential.

1961 American League:

In a wildly split vote that defies justification, Don Schwall (approximate value: 10) won out over several better players, including Dick Howser, Chuck Schilling, Ken Hunt, Carl Yastrzemski and Jake Wood. There is no defending the vote; Schwall had walked 110 men in 179 innings and picked up a 15–7 mark mostly on luck, but backed into the award with 7 of 20 votes when the three better infielders (Howser, Schilling, and Wood) split the vote.

1965 National: Jim Lefebvre (10) over Joe Morgan (12)

1966 National: Tommie Helms (10) over Sonny Jackson (13)

1967 National: Tom Seaver (11) over Dick Hughes (12)

All 20 votes went to right-handed starting pitchers—eleven votes for Seaver (16–13, 2.76 ERA), six for Hughes (16–6, 2.68) and three for Gary Nolan (14–8, 2.58).

1967 American: Rod Carew (10) over Reggie Smith (12)

1971 American: Chris Chambliss (6) over Bill Parsons (9)

1971 National: Earl Williams (11) over Willie Montanez (12)

1973 American: Al Bumbry (8) over Pedro Garcia (11)

1974 American: Mike Hargrove (8) over Bucky Dent (11)

The essential points that I am making are one) that it is not the purpose of the value approximation method to recognize *potential* or *playing a key role in a pennant race* or those human qualities which might lead to greater eventual success, but only to summarize neatly the accomplishments of the players; and two) that there is a very substantial degree of agreement between value as seen by writers or any other observers and value as seen by the value approximation method. It isn't the value *precision* method; it isn't necessary that we agree with it in *every* case, that it *never* evaluate the players differently than we might evaluate them. It is necessary only that the system be reasonable, consistent, and fair, that we never be confronted with a situation in which the system has failed to recognize major accomplishments or has given a high value to a season of nonaccomplishment.

Rookie All-Star Teams

An All-Star team of the rookies in the 28-year period, if chosen by approximate value, includes Johnny Bench, c, 1968 (approximate value: 14), Walt Dropo, 1b, 1950 (14), Junior Gilliam, 2b, 1953 (14), Al Rosen, 1953 or Dick Allen, 1964, 3b, (16), Harvey Kuenn, 1953 or Tom Tresh, 1962, ss (15), Fred Lynn, 1975, lf (17), Vada Pinson, 1959, cf (17), and Tony Oliva, 1964, rf (16). The starting rotation would be Gene Bearden, 1948 (15), Harvey Haddix, 1953 (15), Gary Peters, 1963 (14), and Jerry Koosman, 1968 (14) with either Dick Radatz, 1962 (14) or Bob Lee, 1964 (14) in the bullpen. (My ordinary rule in choosing All-Star teams is to choose four starting pitchers including at least one left-hander and at least one right-hander. This unit consists of four left-handers; however, since all four left-handers are clearly better qualified than any right-handed starter during the period, and since there are several right-handed starters with an approximate value of 13, hence a many-sided tie, I decided to go with the four lefties.) Using runs created to break the ties, the stats for the rookie All-Star team follow:

Pos		Runs	Hits	2B	3B	HR	RBI	SB	Avg.
C	Bench	67	155	40	2	15	82	1	.275
1B	Dropo	101	180	28	8	34	144	0	.322
2B	Gilliam	125	168	31	17	6	63	21	.271
3B	D Allene	125	201	38	13	29	91	3	.318
SS	Tresh	94	178	26	5	20	93	4	.286
LF	Lynn	103	175	47	7	21	105	10	.331
CF	Pinson	131	205	47	9	20	84	21	.316
RF	Oliva	109	217	43	9	32	94	12	.323

Pos		G	IP	W–L	Pct.	SO	BB	ERA
SP	Bearden	37	230	20–7	.741	80	106	2.43
SP	Haddix	36	253	20–9	.690	163	69	3.06
SP	Peters	41	243	19–8	.704	189	56	2.33
SP	Koosman	35	264	19–12	.613	178	69	2.08
RP	Radatz	62	125	9–6	.600	144	40	2.23
RP	Lee	64	137	6–5	.545	111	58	1.51

Radatz had 24 Saves and Lee had 19. We'd lead off with Gilliam, who drew 100 walks, and bat Lynn or Pinson second, whichever one would give us the platoon advantage. Then we'd get to the power core (Allen, Oliva, Dropo), use the other of Pinson or Lynn and finish off with Tresh and Bench. I figure most of the games would be over with by the third inning.

Outstanding Rookies for Each Team

The outstanding rookie for each team in the period 1948–1975 is listed below:

Baltimore (StL)	Ron Hansen, 1960 (14)
Boston	Fred Lynn, 1975 (17)
Cleveland	Al Rosen, 1950 (16)
Detroit	Harvey Kuenn, 1953 (15)
Milwaukee	Pedro Garcia, 1973 (11)
Yankees	Tom Tresh, 1962 (15)
California	Bob Lee, 1964 (14)
White Sox	Tommie Agee, 1966 (14)
	Gary Peters, 1963 (14)
Royals	Lou Piniella, 1969 (10)
	Dennis Leonard, 1975 (10)
Minnesota (Wash)	Tony Oliva, 1964 (16)
Athletics	Alex Kellner, 1949 (13)
	Dick Howser, 1961 (13)
	Ed Charles, 1962 (13)
New Senators	Del Unser, 1968 (11)
Cubs	Ernie Banks, 1954 (13)
Montreal	Carl Morton, 1970 (13)
New York	Jerry Kossman, 1968 (14)
Philadelphia	Dick Allen, 1964 (16)
Pittsburgh	Bob Chesnes, 1948 (10)
Cardinals	Harvey Haddix, 1953 (15)
	Wally Moon, 1954 (15)
Braves	Alvin Dark, 1948 (13)
	Sam Jethroe, 1950 (13)
Cincinnati	Vada Pinson, 1959 (17)
Houston	Sonny Jackson, 1966 (13)
	Greg Gross, 1974 (13)
Los Angeles	Billy Grabarkewitz, 1970 (15)
San Diego	Dave Campbell, 1970 (10)
Giants	Whitey Lockman, 1948 (13)
	Jim Ray Hart, 1964 (13)

Probably the outstanding rookie who has not been selected in these lists is Frank Robinson, who blasted 38 home runs and scored 122 runs as a 20-year-old rookie for Cincinnati in 1956. Robby's approximate value is 15, which would put him on the list if he had played for 19 of the 24 teams above. Unfortunately, he played for 19 of the 24 teams above. Unfortunately, he played for one of the other five, and by value approximations is in the shadow of his good friend Vada Pinson—who, ironically, played most of his career in Robinson's shadow. You might think that it is hard to leave a 20-year-old rookie who hits 38 home runs and plays well otherwise off of any list, but look carefully at the comparison. Pinson scored more runs (131–122) and drove in more (84–83), giving a basic indication that he was a slightly more effective offensive player. Pinson had more hits, hit more doubles and more triples. Pinson hit for a higher average and stole more

bases. Pinson played a more demanding defensive position (center field as opposed to left) and was a more outstanding defensive player at the position he played. Pinson created an estimated 122 runs, as opposed to 115 for Robinson, although Robby does have a narrow 7.1 to 6.9 edge in runs created per game. As great as Robinson was, his 18-homer advantage is his only significant edge over Pinson—and it doesn't outweigh Pinson's extra positives.

Outstanding Rookies Selected By Age

Selected by age, the outstanding rookies of the period were:

18	Robin Yount, 1975 (5)
19	Wally Bunker, 1964 (13)
20	Vada Pinson, 1959 (17)
21	Whitey Lockman, 1948 (13)
	Sonny Jackson, 1966 (13)
	Greg Gross, 1974 (13)
22	Dick Allen, 1964 (16)
23	Fred Lynn, 1975 (17)
24	Wally Moon, 1954 (15)
	Tom Tresh, 1962 (15)
	Billy Grabarkewitz, 1970 (15)
25	Irv Noren, 1950 (14)
	Jimmie Hall, 1963 (14)
	Bake McBride, 1974 (14)
	Dick Radatz, 1962 (14)
	Jerry Koosman, 1968 (14)
26	Al Rosen, 1950 (16)
27	Gene Bearden, 1948 (15)
	Harvey Haddix, 1953 (15)
28	Sam Jethroe, 1950 (13)
	Joe Black, 1952 (13)
	Jack Sanford, 1957 (13)
29	Dick Hughes, 1967 (12)
30	Jim Dyck, 1952 (11)
31	Monte Irvin, 1950 (7)
32	Hector Rodriguez, 1952 (7)
33	Al Heist, 1961 (5)
	Don Lang, 1948 (5)
34	Luke Easter, 1950 (13)

Future Development Among Outstanding Rookies

One of the things that you should have gathered in reviewing these lists is a sense of how often outstanding rookies do develop into great players. Among non-pitchers, there are many outstanding rookies who do develop their skills further and will eventually be listed among the all-time greats. I'd say, as a generalization, that outstanding rookies will eventually be sorted into three almost equal groups:

About one-third will turn in brilliant careers, establishing themselves as strong Hall of Fame candidates.

About one-third will be decent ballplayers, good ballplayers, without really progressing from the point at which they entered the league.

About one-third will be definite disappointments, fading out of the league without making much of a mark, perhaps never even repeating their outstanding rookie seasons.

To date, only five Rookies of the Year have been elected to the Hall of Fame—Jackie Robinson (1947), Willie Mays (1951 N), Frank Robinson (1956 N), Luis Aparicio (1956 A), and Willie McCovey (1959 N). There have been 76 recipients of the award. However, many more of those 76 will be eventually elected, perhaps as many as 25 to 30. Pete Rose, Rod Carew, Johnny Bench, Billy Williams, and Tom Seaver are certain selections; that's ten. Dwight Gooden, Cal Ripken, Eddie Murray, Fernando Valenzuela, and Lou Whitaker are still amassing credentials at a terrific rate. Many other former Rookies of the Year either are viable Hall of Fame candidates (Al Dark, Harvey Kuenn, Jim Gilliam, Orlando Cepeda, Frank Howard, Tony Oliva, Dick Allen, Thurman Munson, Carlton Fisk) or are still around and still assembling their dossiers (Fred Lynn, Andre Dawson, Bob Horner, Steve Sax, Darryl Strawberry, Alvin Davis, Alfredo Griffin, Ozzie Guillen, Vince Coleman). It is likely that 20 to 30 of the first 76 Rookies of the Year will one day enter the Hall of Fame.

On the other hand, Walt Dropo, after driving in 144 runs in 1950, never again drove in 100. Joe Charboneau, rookie of the year in 1980, never again approached his 1980 performance. Kene Hubbs was killed in a plane crash before having a chance to fulfill his potential. Ron Hansen never repeated his outstanding rookie season of 1960. Earl Williams, Tommie Agee, Tom Tresh, and Bake McBride never bettered their rookie campaigns, and drifted out of baseball within a few years. Fewer than a third of the top (non-pitching) rookies will meet this fate, but not much less.

Between those two groups there are the Bumbrys, the Sieverses, the Chamblisses and Piniellas—players who play, who contribute, who make All-Star teams in their good years. About a third of Rookies of the Year will be in this class.

Later on, we'll take a look at some of the ways that you can get a line on what a player's chances are to develop, what the likelihood is that he will disappoint.

That's for non-pitchers. **For a pitcher, there is virtually no relationship between outstanding performance as a rookie and eventually attaining star status.** Whereas about 35% of outstanding rookie non-pitchers will eventually go into the Hall of Fame, for pitchers the percentage is probably no higher than 10%. Consider:

As a rookie in 1948, Robin Roberts was 7–9.

His teammate Curt Simmons was 7–13 with a 4.87 ERA.

As a rookie in 1952, Lew Burdette was 6–11 with a 3.61 ERA.

As a rookie in 1955, Jim Bunning was 3–5 with a 6.35 ERA.

As a rookie in 1956, Sandy Koufax was 2–4 with a 4.91 ERA. His teammate Don Drysdale was 5–5.

As a rookie in 1959, Bob Gibson was 3–5 with a 3.33 ERA.

As a rookie in 1960, Jim Kaat was 1–5 with a 5.58 ERA.

As a rookie in 1963, Gaylord Perry was 1–6 with a 4.03 ERA.

As a rookie in 1964, Tommy John was 2–9.

As a rookie in 1965, Jim Palmer was 5–4 with a 3.72 ERA.

As a rookie in 1965, Steve Carlton had no decisions.

As a rookie in 1966, Ferguson Jenkins was 6–8.

As a rookie in 1968, Nolan Ryan was 6–9.

As a rookie in 1969, Rollie Fingers was 6–7 with a 3.71 ERA.

Or, on the other hand:

There were four rookie pitchers in the period who won 20 games. Gene Bearden in 1948 was 20–7. He never won more than eight games again. Alex Kellner was 20–12 in 1949. His second best season was 1952, when he was 12–14. Harvey Haddix was 20–9 in 1953. He won 18 as a sophomore in 1954, but then never again won more than 13. Bob Grim in 1954 was 20–6. He never again won more than 12.

Among the four rookies who won 20 games, there was a total of one more season in which they won more than 13 games.

Joe Black, a rookie sensation in 1952, never again had more than six wins or an ERA below 4.00.

Don Schwall, 15–7 in 1961, never again won in double figures.

Harry Byrd, rookie of the year in 1952, lost 20 games with a 5.51 ERA the next year, and was never effective again.

Wally Bunker, 19–5 as a 19-year-old rookie in 1964, never had a comparable season.

Among all the rookies in our study, there were only three who had both outstanding rookie years and outstanding careers. Those three were Hoyt Wilhelm (1952), Don Sutton (1966), and Tom Seaver (1967). Three or four others had good careers after strong rookie seasons—Don Newcombe, Jerry Koosman, Gary Peters, Jack Sanford, Jim Perry. They are the exception, rather than the rule.

If you are in a rotisserie league or an APBA league that drafts players for their careers, this is a very important thing for you to consider. So before you try to apply this, you'll probably want to look at whether or not this rule holds in the time periods before and after the 1948–1975 study. Its seems obvious that it does. Make up your own list of the ten greatest pitchers of all time, and check how they performed as rookies. The only two you will find who had brilliant rookie seasons are Seaver and Alexander. Cy Young was 9–7 was a rookie, Walter Johnson 5–9, Lefty Grove 10–13, Warren Spahn 8–5, Carl Hubbell 10–6, Bob Feller 5–3.

Look at the greatest pitchers at this moment. Sure, Valenzuela and Gooden are exceptions, Righetti too, but they are the exceptions of recent history as well. Jack Morris impressed hardly anybody as a rookie in 1978 (3–5, 4.33 ERA). Mike Scott as a rookie in 1979 was 1–3, 5.37 ERA. Roger Clemens, while pitching a couple of terrific games, was 9–4 with a 4.32 ERA—hardly Wally Bunker stats. Mike Witt as a rookie was 8–9, 3.28 ERA. Higuera did pitch well as a rookie a year ago.

Look at the rookies who have had outstanding seasons since 1975, other than Dwight, Dave, and Fernando. Remember the 1976 rookies of the year, Mark Fidrych in the AL and a tie between Butch Metzger and Pat Zachry in the NL?

As to why this happens, I might suggest that it can be explained by the conjunction of two facts. One is that pitching places a tremendous strain on a pitcher's arm.

The other is that a pitcher's arm is not mature before the age of 23 to 26.

I'll write more about this in the Dwight Gooden comment, but a young pitcher who is too successful too soon will, in many cases, tend to be destroyed by the strain that this puts on his arm. Many of the rookie pitchers who were big winners, like Tom Browning a year ago, were older rookies who arrived in the majors representing finished products—as opposed to rookie non-pitchers, who tend to represent raw ability.

The more we learn about baseball, the more we appreciate Earl Weaver. Remember Earl's comment about rookie pitchers in *Weaver on Strategy?* It was called Weaver's Eighth Law: The best place for a rookie is long relief. "I believe young pitchers have to serve an apprenticeship," said Weaver, "both for their own good and for the good of the team."

Analyzing the Best Rookie Crops

OK, now that we've established the method and looked at the best rookies of the period, let's get to the questions that we couldn't have answered just as well without the method. What are the best seasons for rookies within the period? How many good rookies does an average season produce? How many good rookies does a team produce per year? How many *really* good rookies does a typical season produce? What kind of season does it normally take to win the Rookie of the Year award? What is the most "Rookie of the Year" type seasons that any league has produced? What is the best rookie crop for a single team?

The Strongest and Weakest Award Winners

Any rookie with an approximate value of 15 or higher could be described as an "unusually strong" rookie. On the other hand, any rookie of the year with an approximate value of less than nine could be described as a "weaker than normal" rookie of the year. The chart below summarizes the unusually strong and unusually weak rookies of the year from 1947 to the present, not counting the strike year:

UNUSUALLY STRONG

Player (AV)	HR	RBI	Avg.
Fred Lynn, 1975 (17)	21	105	.331
Dick Allen, 1964 (16)	29	91	.318
Tony Oliva, 1964 (16)	32	94	.323
Harvey Kuenn, 1953 (15)	2	48	.308
Wally Moon, 1954 (15)	12	76	.304
Frank Robinson, 1956 (15)	38	83	.290
Tom Tresh, 1962 (15)	20	93	.286

UNUSUALLY WEAK

Player (AV)	HR	RBI	Avg.
Willie McCovey, 1959 (5)	13	38	.354
Chris Chambliss, 1971 (6)	9	48	.275
Bob Horner, 1978 (6)	23	63	.266
Frank Howard, 1960 (8)	23	77	.268
Al Bumbry, 1973 (8)	7	34	.337
Mike Hargrove, 1974 (8)	4	66	.323
John Castino, 1979 (8)	5	52	.285

Also Steve Howe, a pitcher, won in 1980 with an approximate value of 8. Of the "unusually weak" group, three of the first four started the season in the minor leagues, the other being Horner who wasn't signed until mid-season. McCovey wasn't called up until July 30. Bumbry, Hargrove, and Castino were in the majors all year, but platooned a good part of the year, Bumbry batting 356 times, Hargrove 415 and Castino 393. They were all perceived as being players whose abilities were greater than were reflected in the short-season totals, and so were granted the award—but it is also true that none of them was up against Fred Lynn. The stiffest competition beaten back by any of these men was Ozzie Smith in 1978, and Ozzie should have won the award anyway.

McCovey played in less than one-half as many games as any other (non-pitching) rookie of the year except Bob Horner. McCovey played 52, Horner 89, all others over a hundred.

How Many Outstanding Rookies Are There in a Normal Year?

For rookies in general, as opposed to Rookie of the Year candidates, we should consider any player with an approximate value of eight or above to be a "contributing rookie." Such a player is ordinarily not a rookie of the year candidate, but he might be considered to be one in a weak year for rookies, or if he is an outstanding prospect who reaches the 8 level in limited playing time, like Cory Snyder in 1986.

A player with an approximate value of 10 or higher could be considered a "rookie of the year candidate," while a player with an approximate value of 12 or more could be described as a *strong* rookie of the year candidate," or as a player who would win the award in many seasons.

During the period of the study, an average season produced:

Three rookies (2.8, actually) who were strong rookie of the year candidates.

Three more rookies (3.3) who were viable rookie of the year candidates in the absence of anyone better.

Five more rookies (4.7) who contributed quite significantly to their teams.

That's a total of 11 contributing rookies in a normal season, or .575 per team.

In most seasons, the Award winner has an approximate value of 10 to 12.

The Best Rookie Crop of the Period

Were we to go strictly by the total approximate value of all of the rookies in the group we would have to appoint the 1954 rookie class as the best of the 1948–1975 period. The 1954 rookie crop included 35 players who either played in 100 games (22 players), won 9 or saved 15 games (11 pitchers) or made a a significant contribution while playing in less than 100 games (2 players). The total approximate value for these 35 players was 273 points, the highest of any season in the 1948–1975 period.

The award winners for the 1954 season were Bob Grim, a 20-game winner with the Yankees (approximate value: 12) and Wally Moon of the Cardinals (approximate value: 15). An All-Star team of the 1954 rookies is shown below:

Pos	Player (AV)	Runs	2B	3B	HR	RBI	Avg.
C	Bill Sarni (9)	40	18	4	9	70	.300
1B	Vic Power (7)	36	17	5	8	38	.255
2B	Gene Baker (11)	68	32	5	13	61	.275
3B	Jim Finigan (11)	57	25	6	7	51	.302
SS	Ernie Banks (13)	70	19	7	19	79	.275
LF	Wally Moon (15)	106	29	9	12	76	.304
CF	Bill Tuttle (12)	64	20	11	7	58	.266
RF	Hank Aaron (8)	58	27	6	13	69	.280

		G	IP	W–L	SO	ERA
SP	Bob Grim (12)	37	199	20–6	108	3.26
SP	Gene Conley (10)	28	194	14–9	113	2.97
SP	F. Sullivan (10)	36	206	15–12	124	3.15
SP	Jack Harshman (9)	35	177	14–8	134	2.95
SP	B. Lawrence (9)	35	159	15–6	72	3.74

Tuttle's approximate value was boosted to 12 by exceptional defensive stats in center field, including 18 assists, which is why I put him in center and moved Moon to left.

That's a good team, but it's not a pennant winner. There's no reliever, and there's no power core. There is no true leadoff man. The starting rotation lacks an anchor, with Grim winning eight games in relief and pitching less than 200 innings.

In this study as in the earlier one, which looked at the *eventual distinction* earned by the rookies, the 1954 rookie crop is notable more because of its great size than its great achievements. The front-line quality of the crop is good, much better than average, but Wally Moon's price seems a little steep at 15. Even if you accept that figure at face value, the front-line quality of the group is not as strong as in some other seasons. There were eight 1954 rookies who had an AV of 10 or more, whereas there had been nine such rookies in both 1952 and 1953, though there were no more than nine in any season. The 1954 group was good, but not the greatest rookie class of the period.

The second-highest approximate value total of any season belongs to the rookies of 1969, in which there were 38 qualifying rookies with a total approximate value of 258. However, the 1969 season is like 1954 only much more so. The addition of four expansion teams created an enormous rookie crop, but a crop which not only is indistinguished, but which actually is rather weak.

The next serious candidate for outstanding rookie crop of the period was that of 1962, when 31 rookies had a total AV of 235, third highest in the period. The front-line players of 1962 are stronger than those of 1954:

1962	1954
Player (AV)	Player (AV)
Tom Tresh (15)	Wally Moon (15)
Dick Radatz (14)	Ernie Banks (13)
Ed Charles (13)	Bill Tuttle (12)
Rich Rollins (13)	Bob Grim (12)
Bernie Allen (12)	Gene Baker (11)
Dean Chance (12)	Jim Finigan (11)
Bob Rodgers (12)	Gene Conley (10)
Ken Hubbs (11)	Frank Sullivan (10)

The 1962 rookie All-Star team would have a formidable infield, but weak starting pitching and only one good out-

fielder, in Many Jiminez. Oddly, the best player among the 1962 rookies was an outfielder, Lou Brock, who was regarded at the time as a disappointment (AV: 6). The 1962 crew wouldn't win the pennant, either.

The team that *might* win the pennant would be the 1964 rookie All-Stars. An All-Star team of the 1964 rookies would include:

Pos	Player (AV)	Runs	2B	3B	HR	RBI	Avg.
C	Mike Brumley (7)	36	19	2	2	35	.244
1B	Jim Hart (13)	71	15	6	31	81	.286
2B	Dick Green (8)	48	14	5	11	37	.264
3B	Dick Allen (16)	125	38	13	29	91	.318
SS	Jimmy Stewart (7)	59	17	0	3	33	.253
LF	Rico Carty (11)	72	28	4	22	88	.330
CF	Tony Oliva (16)	109	43	9	32	94	.323
RF	Conigliaro (7)	69	21	2	24	52	.290

		G	IP	W–L	SO	ERA
SP	WallyBunker (13)	29	214	19–5	96	2.69
SP	Luis Tiant (7)	19	127	10–4	105	2.83
SP	Mel Stottlemyre (6)	13	96	9–3	49	2.06
SP	Wade Blasingame (5)	28	117	9–5	70	4.23
RP	Rob Lee (14)	64	137	6–5	111	1.51
RP	Sammy Ellis (11)	52	123	10–3	125	2.58

In forming this All-Star team, I moved Jim Ray Hart from third to first and shifted Tony Oliva from right field to center. I think he could have covered it at the time. I also chose Dick Green (AV:8) over Bobby Knoop (AV: 9) or Don Buford (AV: 7) at second base and Tony Conigliaro (AV: 7) over Sam Bowens (AV: 10) in right field.

The All-Star team isn't perfect. The catching isn't strong, although Brumley is backed up by Jerry Grote, and the starting pitching would have to struggle by with Buster Narum (9–15) and John O'Donoghue (10–14) until Tiant and Stottlemyre are called up. The defense up the middle is just fair.

It is still the strongest rookie All-Star team of any season within the study—and probably the strongest rookie All-Star of any year, ever.

Only four rookies in the 28-year study had 200 hits. Two of them did it in 1964. The 1948–1975 leaders in basic runs created as a rookie were:

Dick Allen, 1964	135
Tony Oliva, 1964	133
Vada Pinson, 1959	122
Walt Dropo, 1950	121
Fred Lynn, 1975	120

The 1964 season was *not* a hitter's year; the league batting averages were .254 and .247. Yet remarkably, a third rookie slugger that year, also combining batting average and power, created more runs per game (or per out) than either Allen or Oliva. That would be Rico Carty, who, with a .330 average and 22 homers in 455 at bats, created 8.01 runs per 25 outs—the most of any player in the study except Bernie Carbo, 1970 (8.99), Fred Lynn (8.51) and Walt Dropo (also 8.01). And, of course, McCovey in 52 games (10.68).

Behind these front three, the talent continues to impress. Tony Conigliaro, a 19-year-old kid, hit .290 with tremendous power; no other 19-year-old in the study had as good a year with the bat. Wally Bunker, another 19-year-old, had a 19–5 won-lost record, making him the outstanding teenager in the study. Bob Lee ranks with Radatz as the outstanding relief pitcher in the study. Mel Stottlemyre, called up in late July, played a decisive role in the pennant race, won by the Yankees by a single game. Luis Tiant pitched equally well for a non-contender.

How often does a rookie hit .286 with 31 homers? Jim Ray Hart did that. How often does a rookie reliever pitch as well as Sammy Ellis? Perhaps one year in three.

In 1964 Sam Bowens hit .263 with 22 homers and 71 RBI. No one was impressed. The next spring he went into a slump and lost his job to Curt Blefray. Blefray posted almost identical stats—.260, 22 homers and 70 RBI. He won the Rookie of the Year award.

Dick Green, an exceptional defensive second baseman, hit .264 with 11 homers. Players of that calibre have won the award. Bob Chance of Cleveland drove in 75 runs in 390 at bats. Billy Cowan of the Cubs played regularly and hit 19 home runs. Wonderful Willie Smith, a rookie pitcher with the Angels, was used as a pinch hitter a few times early in the year, and succeeded so convincingly that he was converted to the outfield, where he got 359 bats in before the season was out, hitting .301 with 11 homers.

There were at least a dozen other rookies that year who, in the context of an ordinary cropful of rookies, would draw some consideration in the award voting, and yet I must say this: I was surprised, in doing this study, that the 1964 rookies didn't stand out more than they did. I really thought, when I started the study, that the 1964 rookie crop would dominate the field, that no other season would be close to it. It was the best, but it's a close call. There is room for reasonable disagreement. I'm surprised by that.

The outstanding rookie seasons of the period, in order, were 1964, 1962, 1950, 1975, and 1954. The 1964, '62 and '54 seasons we covered. The 1950 season had 14 contributing rookies (approximate value of 8 or more); the 14 were Gus Bell, Chico Carrasquel, Walt Dropo, Luke Easter, Monte Irvin, Sam Jethroe, Irv Noren, Al Rosen, Bill Serena, Wayne Terwilliger, Don Lenhardt, Whitey Ford, Bob Hooper, and Bob Miller. No other season prior to expansion had as many—and the top three or four men, as mentioned before, were terrific. The second-line support wasn't as good, plus we are counting as rookies here at least four players who were not considered rookies at the time.

The 1975 class, of course, included Fred Lynn and Jim Rice, and was also large—17 contributing rookies. An All-Star team would include catcher Gary Carter (9), second baseman Manny Trillo (11), third baseman Larry Parrish (9), and outfielders Jim Rice (12), Fred Lynn (17), and Dan Ford (9), with pitchers John Montefusco (12), Dennis Eckersley (10), Dennis Leonard (10) and Jim Hughes (10) backed up by Rawley Eastwick (10). Only Lynn and Rice presented knockout credentials, but the others all played well enough to establish themselves.

The Worst Rookie Crops

Within the 28 years, the worst rookie years were, in order, 1968, 1959, 1956, and 1957.

The striking thing here is that the 1956 season, which

was one of the greatest ever in terms of what it eventually produced, was one of the weakest ever in terms of what they did as rookies; basically, it was the two Hall of Famers (F Robby and Little Looie) and little else. Of the other outstanding rookies of that season, none really had a "rookie" year. Drysdale and Koufax watched a lot, as did Killebrew. Mazeroski wasn't called up until mid-season and wasn't great when he did arrive.

This brings up a question: Are the seasons which produce the rookies who make a big impact, like 1986, also going to be the seasons which produce the most rookies of eventual distinction? Can we expect that in twenty years we can look back and say, "Wow, that 1986 season sure did produce a bunch of fine players, didn't it?"

The answer, in the main, is no, we cannot expect to say that. There probably is a correlation of some sort between the output of a group of rookies as rookies and the output of the group over time. But it's not a strong relationship. Examples:

The 1948 season was eventually distinguished, among other things, by it's power hitters (Hodges, Kluszewski, Snider, Doby). But *as rookies,* none of those men hit more than 14 home runs, and no rookie that season hit more than 18.

The 1973 season, here as in the other study, was huge (19 contributing rookies), but whereas in the long run it is one of the five best crops ever, in its first look it was so devoid of front-line credentials that it doesn't rate serious consideration. No one from the season really had what you would call a *good* rookie-of-the-year season.

The 1964 season, the best of the lot in terms of rookie impact, produced no certain Hall of Famers, and probably produced less long-term value than either 1963 or 1965.

So, while the 1986 season *might* be remembered as a year which saw the emergence of a large number of great players, I wouldn't want to put a lot of money on it.

The Best One-League Rookie Crop

The American League in 1962, by far. The top seven rookies from that season were all American Leaguers and all classed as "strong Rookie of the Year candidates" (that is, approximate value of 12 or more). No other league produced more than five players with an AV of 12 or more.

How the 1986 Rookies Rate

The 1986 rookie crop was a large one and a good one. By the standards of history, it was nothing special on either count.

I am writing this in November and the National League has not yet released their official stats, so I am making a few estimates, and the approximate values for a few players may be different than will be listed in other parts of the book. These differences will not effect the evaluation of the rookie crop.

In the 1986 season there were 38 rookies who either played in a hundred or more games (21 players), won 9 games or saved 15 (16 pitchers) or made an undeniable impact without actually playing in 100 games (1 player). The total approximate value for those 38 players was 273 points AV.

Compared to the 1948–1975 era and without adjusting for expansion, this would rank the 1986 rookie crop as the equal of the largest:

Year	Rookies	Total AV
1954	35	273
1986	**38**	**273**
1969	38	258
1973	31	239
1962	31	235

However, remembering that we now have 26 teams as opposed to 16 in 1954, the 1986 rookie crop is not exceptionally large. An average season introduces 1.25 qualifying rookies per team. In 1986 there were 1.46 per team. In 1954 there were 2.19 per team.

The question of front-line quality if, of course, one which requires the use of some subjective judgment; still, the 1986 rookie crop was clearly not the equal of the best rookie seasons of the 1948–1975 period, and probably would not have been one of the top five rookie seasons had it occurred during that period.

Let's start by making the comparisons to 1950, since 1950 was the most comparable year (that is, the season in which the outstanding rookies were of a comparable type). In 1986 there was Jose Canseco, who was terrific; in 1950 there was Walt Dropo:

	Runs	2B	3B	HR	RBI	Avg.
Dropo	101	28	8	34	144	.322
Canseco	85	29	1	33	117	.240

Obviously, Dropo had a better year. Dropo's year was evaluated at 14. Canseco is evaluated at 12. In reality, it isn't that close.

In 1986, Pete Incaviglia had a big year. For 1950, the comparable player would be Luke Easter:

	Runs	2B	3B	HR	RBI	Avg.
Easter	96	20	4	28	107	.280
Incaviglia	82	21	2	30	88	.250

Again, there is an obvious advantage for the 1950 player, Luke Easter. The value approximation method measures that advantage at 13–10.

In 1986, Danny Tartabull drove in 96 runs for the Mariners. Let's compare him to Irv Noren of the 1950 campaign.

	Runs	2B	3B	HR	RBI	Avg.
Noren	80	27	10	14	98	.295
Tartabull	76	25	6	25	96	.270

Despite Tartabull's advantage in power, this comparison shows that the two players were comparable offensively, with Noren driving in and scoring more runs. What the comparison does not show is that Noren had tremendous defensive statistics in center field, fielding .984, leading the league with 20 assists and posting a 3.11 range factor. Tartabull started the season at second base, was moved to the outfield and had defensive problems, posting a .953 fielding percentage and a 1.62 range factor, with 7 assists.

Noren must be given the edge. The Value Approximation method assesses that difference at 14–10, which is probably a little too large.

Wally Joyner had a fine year as a rookie in 1986. Let's compare him to Al Rosen:

	Runs	2B	3B	HR	RBI	Avg.
Rosen	100	23	4	37	116	.287
Joyner	82	27	3	22	100	.290

Joyner was a good defensive first baseman. Rosen was a good defensive third baseman. You can make it what you will. The Value Approximation Method makes it Rosen, 16 to 12.

Now granted, the 1950 season was an even better hitter's year than 1986, and that biases the evaluations, but it wasn't that much better. Rosen's 37 homers led the American League. Dropo's 144 RBI tied for the American League lead. It seems obvious that, as impressive as the rookie sluggers were, those in 1950 were better.

If you focus on the rest of the rookie crop, the 1986 season probably would rate the edge. The 1950 season did not produce a rookie pitcher who had a season like Todd Worrell or Mark Eichorn, who are seen by the value approximation method as being the best of the 1986 rookies. But comparing the rookie classes from the top, it seems clear that the 1950 class is superior:

1950	1986
Al Rosen (16)	Todd Worrell (14)
Walt Dropo (14)	Mark Eichorn (13)
Irv Noren (14)	José Canseco (12)
Luke Easter (13)	Wally Joyner (12)
Sam Jethroe (13)	Robby Thompson (12)
C. Carrasquel (12)	P. Incaviglia (10)
Don Lenhardt (10)	Danny Tartabull (10)
Monte Irvin (10)	Cory Snider (8)
Whitey Ford (8)	Bruce Ruffin (8)
Gus Bell (8)	Kevin Mitchell (8)

Both years could go on supplying "eights" for quite some time, but I think the advantage of the 1950 season is apparent. And when you consider that in 1950 there were only 16 teams, as opposed to 26 now, and when you remember that the 1950 season was just the third-best rookie crop of the 1948–1975 period . . . well, I don't think there's any basis for argument.

The 1986 season was a very good year for rookies—very good, but no better than that. Not excellent, and certainly not one of the best ever.

The 1986 Rookie of the Year Race

The 1986 *American League* season was one in which the Rookie of the Year as voted by the sportswriters and the rookie with the largest value as seen by the value approximation method were not the same. The writers picked José Canseco as the best; the value approximation method evaluates Mark Eichorn at 13, Canseco and Joyner at 12. The question naturally occurs of whether the figures for Canseco and Joyner should perhaps be higher, which could make the 1986 crop look better in the historical comparisons.

It would be very inappropriate to argue that the value approximation method has "proven" or has "shown" that Eichorn was superior; it is not the purpose of the value approximation method to do anything of the sort. It is the purpose of the value approximation method only to recognize what is apparent in the statistics, and to store that knowledge in such a way as to allow the comparisons of groups of seasons, as we have been doing here. When the value approximation method and contemporary observations disagree about an individual comparison, we should in most cases be willing to heed the observations.

In this particular case, I would humbly submit that the value approximation method is right: Mark Eichorn *should* have been the American League's Rookie of the Year.

What I think happened here is that Eichorn got buried behind a developing story. Canseco was a big story even before the 1986 baseball season arrived. The Minor League Player of the Year in 1985, he had arrived in Oakland in September of that season with bat a'blazin'; he hit .302 and slugged .490 in 29 games.

Then Wally Joyner came along, and he was the star of the winter league, and they handed him Carew's job. Both started out hot; Joyner had 16 homers and 41 RBI by the end of May, and you couldn't help but project him out to finish in the forties in home runs with God knows how many RBI. Canseco, holding up his part of the story, was hitting in the .270s with about the same astonishing power totals by the end of May—15 homers and 46 RBI, in addition to which he was putting on a daily show in batting practice which had people talking about Hank Aaron and Jim Rice and Mickey Mantle. In terms not favorable to the elders.

For some time after, riding these torrid starts, it seemed realistic to talk about the season as being the greatest rookie year ever—assuming that the performances held up. As late as August, Canseco seemed likely to drive in 130 to 140 runs, while Joyner was hitting well over .300 with power. There was a lot of talk about Ted Williams' rookie record of 145 RBI.

And so the contest between these two rookie Titans, supplemented by two more in Incaviglia and Tartabull, became one of the big stories of the 1986 season. By the end of July we had read about José Canseco's biceps and José Canseco's childhood and Wally Joyner's admiration for Dale Murphy and Wally World and Wally's little spat with a reporter in Cleveland, while Mark Eichorn, though pitching well all year, hardly existed beneath the banners.

But that's not what they ultimately did. *After the terms of the discussion had been defined,* after the Rookie of the Year debate had developed into Wally Joyner against José Canseco, Wally Joyner *didn't* hit 40 homers; he ultimately hit the rather unremarkable total of 22, with a .290 average. José Canseco *didn't* drive in 140 runs; he drove in 117, with 175 strikeouts dragging his average down to a miserable .240. For a player with very little defensive value, it simply is not a tremendously impressive season unless you put a great weight on the RBI column.

The value approximation method puts very little weight on the RBI column, and I can certainly understand why someone would wish to consider it more heavily, and to assign Canseco a value higher than 12 (and Dropo a value higher than 14). It still seems to me that if you step back and look at what they did, what Mark Eichorn did is more impressive than what either Canseco or Joyner did.

Eichorn pitched 69 games and 157 innings. That's an awfully impressive workload for a reliever, isn't it? How many relievers carry that kind of a load for a full season? Eichorn struck out 166 men in those 157 innings. That's awfully good. He walked only 31 men unintentionally (14 intentionally). That's awfully good, both the control ratio and the strikeout-to-walk ratio. His ERA was 1.72, which speaks for itself. He surrendered only 105 hits in 157 innings, a ratio that Dwight Gooden has never approached. He won 14 games and lost only 6.

There aren't any termites in Eichorn's foundation—no .240 average, no 175 strikeouts, no league-leading 14 errors with 4 outfield assists (Canseco's totals). Toronto didn't win, but Eichorn helped greatly to stabilize the pitching staff and put the Blue Jays back in the race. I think that if you look at the whole package, rather than just at the first two months, if you look at the whole package, rather than just the first couple of stats you see, you'll agree with the value approximation method that Mark Eichorn was the best rookie in the American League.

A Final Word About the 1986 Rookie Crop

Defense. The Achilles' heel of the 1986 rookie crop: Defense.

Perhaps the value approximation method puts too much emphasis on defense. I don't think so, but what the hell; I'll consider the possibility. I'll consider that possibility if you'll consider this one: that the defensive accomplishments of the 1986 rookies were miniscule.

There are four basic kinds of defensive value. Those are:

1) The ability to play a key defensive position, like shortstop, second base, center fielder or catcher, at which talent is always in short supply and where consequently the aggregate offensive performance is less.

2) Range, which is the ability to maximize opportunities at the position assigned, and which is measured by range factor.

3) Reliability, which is the ability to make the plays a player at the position is expected to make, and which is measured by fielding percentage or errors.

4) Specialty skills, such as the ability to turn the double play or a strong throwing arm.

In an ordinary rookie crop, there is a mix of offensive and defensive skills—slugging first basemen, yes, but also some sprightly shortstops or a swift center fielder or two.

The 1986 rookie crop, particularly in the AL, was all offense. Sure, there was Andy Allanson and Lombardozzi, but among the players who really did something, the players who really define the class, none played a key defensive position, and the overall defensive characteristics of the group are—it would not be accurate to say anything else—absolutely terrible. Wally Joyner is a first baseman, but at least he is a pretty good first baseman. Well, he was second in the league in errors (15), but he is mobile and alert—but he does play the defensive position at which there are the most candidates. The defensive performance of the three outfielders was bad, worse, and worst. Canseco was bad—a .958 fielding percentage, 2.08 range and four assists. Tartabull was worse—a .953 percentage, 1.63 range and 7 assists. But Incaviglia, a born DH, was the worst—a .921 fielding percentage, a 1.43 range factor with six assists. Not since Greg Luzinski have I seen a fielding line like that.

The public realized early in 1986 that we had a group of players who shared an outstanding strength. In large part because of the simple fact that hitting statistics are in the paper every week while defensive statistics are not, there was very little recognition of the fact that these players also shared a weakness.

Somewhat redeeming this is Cory Snyder and his much-heralded throwing arm. But even there, I wonder. Snyder can't play a key "up the middle" defensive position, although he could probably make it at third base. He doesn't have any speed. The throwing arm is his weapon, his badge.

Is his arm really that good? Snyder played 74 games in the outfield, and had only four outfield assists. Now, I will grant you that outfield assists are not terribly reliable, and it takes a lot more than 74 games for them to acquire what reliability they do have, but I still find that a little strange. Ordinarily a rookie with a good arm will pile up a lot of assists when he first comes into the league because the opposition will want to test him, see how he throws in a combat situation. Roberto Clemente as a rookie threw out 18 runners in 118 games. Jesse Barfield as a rookie threw out 15 runners in 137 games.

Cory Snyder may well have the arm that I've read about; I'm not saying he doesn't. But I saw him play three or four times live last year, and he didn't make any throws that impressed me. Until he impresses me, or until he throws out some runners, I ain't signing that petition.

Three of the National League rookies, Barry Bonds, Kurt Stillwell and Robby Thompson, did have significant defensive value.

Is the Quality of Rookie Seasons Declining?

Overall, definitely not; there are as many contributing rookies and as many rookie of the year candidates in the last few years as there have ever been. There are, *as there have always been,* a few players who can come right out of college or even sometimes high school and play major league ball.

There are many players now who are called up in mid-season, taking a cut out of their "rookie" seasons—but that has been the case since the fifties. I don't think there are any more now.

At the very top levels, looking at the 28 years of the study and at what has happened since, it does appear that the number of truly outstanding rookie seasons is declining. A 15-point season is an MVP-candidate season, in 1986 just as it was in 1950. There were 12 such seasons during the study, but there were only two after 1964, and there have been none since the period of the study ended eleven years ago.

Twenty-win seasons by rookie pitchers were once an almost annual occurrence; there were such seasons in 1948, 1949, 1953, and 1954. There has been only one since, in 1985.

A decline in the top-level rookie seasons would imply that it is tougher to come out of the minors and star at the highest level, and that would imply that either the quality of the play in the minors has declined, or that the quality of the play in the majors has improved, or both. I suspect that it may be both.

I think it is unfortunate that the minor leagues have lost their pyramid shape, and attained basically the form of a tube—that is, that whereas the one major league team used to have two AAA teams and three or four AA teams and there were a large number of affiliated and unaffiliated teams at the lower levels, an organization now tends to have one major league team served by one AAA team, one AA team, one or two A league teams and one or two rookie league team. I think that that can't help but make the minor leagues less competitive, that whereas a player used to advance against competition, advance by being better than the others at his level, he now must advance against attrition within the tube, advancing most often on the front office judgment of his "potential." I don't think that is healthy.

But at the same time, I feel that, for other reasons, the quality of play at the major league level is probably the best that it has been in many years. The improved training methods and the improved salary structure have kept veterans in the game, making the competition for jobs more intense, but at the same time preserving and incorporating into each game the knowledge and experience of those veterans. So I think it is harder for a rookie to break in spectacularly now, and that it will remain so until the veterans of the pre-salary inflation era pass out of the game. And it may or may not be that what we saw in 1986 was the first stage of that passage.

CHAPTER THREE
Evaluating a Rookie

The third chapter of this article will focus on this question: When you look at a rookie, how do you evaluate his chances of developing into a star? What are the variables that indicate a potential for growth? How much weight should you put on which factors?

It will be noted that of course many of the most important factors to consider in this light are things that cannot be studied systematically. Does the player hustle? It is my belief that there is limited short-term value to a "hustling" player, the kind of guy who runs into walls or tries to take an extra base on a single. The extra bases the guy takes will probably be negated by the times that he gets thrown out trying, and running into walls is a stupid way to waste your ability. Nonetheless, I do believe that (short of self-destructive behavior) a player who hustles on the field will, over a period of time, "stretch his skills" so that he becomes a better player than he ought to be. You look at Brian Downing, at Pete Rose or Hal McRae, and you see players who became better players than they should have been because the things that they pushed themselves to do one day became part of their skills the next day.

Does the player tend to put on weight? Does he conduct himself in a manner consistent with stardom? I remember when Joe Charboneau came up and caught the public's fancy, my reaction to him was "I just can't reconcile this personality with that of a superstar." Hank Aaron didn't open beer bottles with his eye sockets. Joe DeMaggio didn't drink beer through his nose.

There might have been a couple, but there have been very few "zany" superstars in baseball. Almost without exception, great ballplayers are players who want to draw attention by what they accomplish on the field, and who are uncomfortable with any attention which comes to them from their behavior. Probably the least suitable personality for a baseball star among the 1986 rookies was that of Charlie Kerfeld, the chubby Houston reliever with the off-the-wall sense of humor. He may *attain* stardom, but if he does he'll blow out of it in a couple of years.

These are important things to consider, and they cannot be systematically studied. At the same time, there are things that can be systematically studied, and which are also important indicators of success. How much difference is there between the career expectation for a 20-year-old rookie and a 22-year-old rookie of the same ability? How much difference is there between the expected growth of a catcher and an outfielder of the same hitting ability? How much difference is there between a rookie who possesses speed and a comparable hitter who does not run well? Is

strikeout-to-walk ratio an indicator of probable development? How much weight should you put on what? The following sections of the article will deal with those issues and others like them.

Similarity Scores

The primary method that we will use in analyzing these questions is that of forming comparable groups by the use of similarity scores. Similarity scores, introduced in the 1986 *Baseball Abstract,* are a method by which two players are compared. If the two players were identical in all aspects of similarity considered (which never happens), their similarity score would be 1,000; for every difference between them, points are subtracted from 1,000. If one player hits .300 and the other player hits .299, that's one point off. If one player hits 20 home runs and the other hits 21, that's two points off. If one player is 23 years old and the other is 25, there's an appropriate subtraction for that.

Using this method, we will attempt to define groups of players who are identical in every respect except the one that is under study. The traditional form in which theories about baseball are stated is that of "Other things being equal." "Other things being equal," I think that a pitcher who is over seven feet tall will be more durable than one who is under five feet 8 inches. Other things being equal, most major league managers would rather have a player who has speed than one who has power.

In reality, of course, other things are never equal, but the method of similarity scores allows us to form groups which approach that condition. If you compare George Altman as a rookie in 1959 and Sixto Lezcano as a rookie in 1975, you find that they have extremely similar totals:

	G	AB	R	H	2B	3B	HR	RBI	SB	Avg.
Altman	135	420	54	103	14	4	12	47	1	.245
Lezcano	134	429	55	106	19	3	11	43	5	.247

Both men were center fielders, but there were distinct differences between them—Lezcano was 21 years old whereas Altman was 26, Lezcano was Latin whereas Altman was Black, Altman was five inches taller, etc. In addition, there were the individual differences in desire, intelligence, throwing ability, etc.

Suppose, however, that we focus on *one* of those differences, such as the age difference, and select *groups* of players who have extremely similar statistics in each case, but one of whom is always 26 years old and the other of whom is in each case 21. In forming the groups, it is likely that all of the incidental characteristics of the players—the height, the differences in throwing arm, intelligence, and color—would tend to balance out. At the same time, since in one case you would select a player who hit two more home runs at 26 and in the next a player who hit three more at 21, the small differences in the batting records of the players will tend to become, in the aggregate, truly minuscule. You wind up with a group of 20 to 50 21-year-olds and the same number of 26-year-olds who have virtually identical batting statistics and quite similar incidental characteristics, so that the difference in age is, if not the *only* difference between the groups, certainly very much the *largest* difference between them. In this way, we are able to focus on and evaluate the importance of one distinction in a relatively sterile environment.

The exact method of similarity scores will be explained somewhere if I remember to do it, but the details of the method are not what make it work. "Similarity" is not an absolute; those elements of similarity that are important in one case may not be so important in the next. It is necessary to adjust the method so that it adapts to the needs of each study.

Only a tiny portion of all players who are compared will have the degree of similarity which makes them suitable for the study, but we have enough players in the database here to make the concept work. There are 47 21-year-old non-pitchers in the study, and 36 26-year-olds, so that (although these are two of the smaller groups) there are 1,692 potential comparisons, of which 32 are acceptable comparisons. By contrast, there are 80 22-year-olds and 86 23-year-olds in the studies, so that there are 6,880 possible comparisons, of which 70 comparisons are usable.

Normally, 1 to 2 percent of potential comparisons are suitable for a study. One of the problems is what to do about duplications; that is, George Altman is comparable to Sixto Lezcano at age 21, but also comparable to Rick Monday at 21. Do we use him as a comparison for both players?

Lezcano is comparable not only to Altman but also to three or four other players. Sometimes you get groups of players, all of whom are very comparable to all of the others. If you try to use all of the acceptable comparisons, you wind up with much larger groups but groups that might contain a dozen or more Rick Mondays on one end and seven George Altman's on the other. On the other hand, if you only use each player once, you will wind up excluding from the study players for whom there are very good comparisons.

My solution to this problem was to restrict the study to a single use on one end but allow duplications on the other end. This prevents the "clusters" in which the same players enter the study repeatedly from forming, and as a practical matter you never get the players on the uncontrolled end being used as comparables more than two or three times, so that their impact on a group that is usually 30 or more is not enormous. It's not a perfect solution, but I thought it was the best I could find.

In practice, no matter what you do you still have "leakage" or "contamination" of the study groups. If you simply tried to compare a group of players on good teams to a group of players on poor teams, you would find that the former would last longer simply because they were better players. We are trying, by this method, to "seal out" the other factors, and study the effects of only this one factor. But in fact, you do get leakage; no matter what you do the players on the good teams will still be somewhat better players than those on the poor teams. If you could set the standards of comparison high enough, you could seal out any differences, but baseball history just isn't large enough to enable us to find the nearly perfect comparisons that we need.

In studying "durability" or "development," as we are doing here, the most serious kind of leakage is *quality leakage,* because the quality of play is the primary determinant of how long a player will last. But there is also "power leakage" (as, for example, when a group of first basemen is compared to a group of shortstops), "speed leakage" and leakage of almost any other trait into one study or another. The leakage is ordinarily 2 to 7% of the difference—that is, if one group of players would ordinarily hit 500 home runs more than another group, they might hit 10 to 35 more even in a controlled study.

Comparisons Between Age Groups

Suppose that you have a 20-year-old player and a 21-year-old player of the same ability as hitters; let's say that each hits about .265 with ten home runs. How much difference is there in the expected career home run totals for the two players?

As best I can estimate, the 20-year-old player can be expected to hit about 61% more home runs in his career. That's right—61%. If you expected that figure to be so high, then you can probably skip this section and go on to the comparisons between positions. If you find the difference to be shocking, you might want to study this section, and see if I can convince you that that is a realistic estimate, and not just a fluke of some sort.

For obvious and non-obvious reasons, we start by comparing comparable hitters at different ages. We start by comparing ages because we know what the pattern of the data ought to be across an entire spectrum. When comparing 21-year-olds and 26-year-olds of the same ability, we know who probably will have better careers, and thus we will be alerted if the method in use doesn't work. We start by measuring differences between ages because those differences are a big item effecting the expectation for a player, and so we need to evaluate the impact of age so that we can adjust for it in the other studies.

In trying to figure out how much a player will develop, probably the one most important factor to consider, other than the player's ability, is his age. Every year is important. If you compare a 20-year-old rookie and a 25-year-old rookie of exactly the same ability, the 20-year-old rookie can be expected to play almost three times as many games in the major leagues. A 20-year-old rookie can be expected to hit about four times as many home runs as a 20-five-year-old rookie of the same ability.

Let's look at the 20-year-olds and 25-year-olds in some detail:

As a 20-year-old rookie in 1954, Hank Aaron hit .280 with 13 homers and 69 RBI. As a 25-year-old rookie in 1955, Gene Green had very similar stats, .281 with 13 homers and 55 RBI in a few less at bats. Aaron, as you know, hit 755 home runs in his career. Green hit 46.

As a 20-year-old rookie in 1972, Buddy Bell hit .255 with 9 home runs and 36 RBI. As a 25-year-old rookie in 1966, Chuck Harrison had very similar stats, .256 with 9 homers and 52 RBI. Buddy Bell has now hit 177 home runs in the major leagues, and will probably hit many more. Chuck Harrison hit 17.

As a 20-year-old rookie in 1968, Johnny Bench hit .275 with 15 home runs and 82 RBI. As a 25-year-old rookie in 1951, Randy Jackson had similar stats—.275 with 16 homers and 76 RBI. Johnny Bench hit 389 home runs in his career. Jackson hit 103.

As a 20-year-old rookie in 1951, Willie Mays hit .274 with 20 homers and 68 RBI. As a 25-year-old rookie in 1964, Sam Bowens had similar stats—.263 with 22 homers and 71 RBI. Willie Mays, as you know, hit 660 home runs in his career. Sam Bowens hit 45.

As a 20-year-old rookie in 1961, Joe Torre hit .278 with 10 homers and 42 RBI. As a 25-year-old rookie in 1952, Clint Courtney had somewhat similar stats, hitting .286 with 5 homers and 50 runs batted in. Joe Torre hit 252 home runs in his career. Courtney hit only 38.

As a 20-year-old rookie in 1962, Boog Powell hit .243 with 15 homers and 53 RBI. As a 25-year-old rookie in 1964, Billy Cowan hit .241 with 19 homers and 50 RBI. Boog Powell hit 339 home runs in his career. Billy Cowan hit 40.

Sometimes the difference doesn't show up in power as much as in other areas. As a 20-year-old rookie in 1958, Curt Flood hit .261 with 10 homers and 41 RBI. As a 25-year-old rookie in 1962, Ted Savage had similar stats—.266 with 7 homers and 39 RBI. Flood developed. Savage didn't.

Altogether, I found 28 sets of comparable 20-year-old and 25-year-old hitters. In only one case (Bob Boone versus Curt Flood) did the 25-year-old subsequently play more major league games. The 28 20-year-olds played 65,630 major league games. The 28 25-year-olds played only 22,843.

The 28 20-year-olds hit 10,083 major league home runs. The 28 25-year-olds, who hit just as well as rookies, hit only 1,700 major league home runs—a ratio of 5.93–1. (I should explain—there were a few still-active players, like Buddy Bell, who were included in the study. For those players, I used the Brock7 career projection system to estimate their completed career totals, and used these estimates to represent their final career stats. So when I say that a group of players "hit" 1,719 home runs, what I actually mean is that they have hit or are projected to hit 1,719 home runs. But since the study includes no rookies who have come up since 1975, we're just filling in the tail ends of a few careers; the projections are much less than 1% of the totals shown.)

OK, you may say, I'll buy that there is a big difference between a 25-year-old rookie, two years away from his prime, and a 20-year-old rookie, who may have seven years to develop his skills. But how can there be such a large difference between a 20-year-old and a 21-year-old?

Before we discuss how there can be such a large difference between the two groups, let's first of all look at a little of the evidence which says that there is. In this case

I'll just run names; you can look them up yourself to see what the rookie stats are

20-Year-Old	21-Year-Old
Hank Aaron	Gus Bell
Buddy Bell	Sixto Lezcano
Johnny Bench	Greg Luzinski
Curt Flood	Jim Spencer
Tony Kubek	Tim McCarver
Willie Mays	Curt Blefray
Rick Manning	George Brett
Joe Torre	Gus Bell
Boog Powell	Rick Monday

Yes, it's true that Mays, a fleet defensive center fielder, is compared to Curt Blefray, a less-than-fleet right fielder—but then it is also true that going the other way Rick Monday, a fleet defensive center fielder, is compared to Boog Powell. (By the way, Rick Monday when he was signed by the A's was proclaimed by the Kansas City front office to be the fastest player in baseball. Anybody remember that?) Yes, it is true that Tony Kubek, an outfielder as a rookie, is compared to a catcher, but then going the other way there is also an outfielder compared to a catcher (in fact, two of them.) *From what you could tell as rookies, these players would have seemed to be about even*. The 20-year-olds averaged .272 with 22 doubles, 3 triples and 11 homers, scoring 55 runs and driving in 52; the 21-year-olds averaged .270 with 20 doubles, 6 triples and 11 homers, scoring 55 runs and driving in 53.

But over the course of their careers, the 20-year-olds accomplished much more. In the complete study, there were 23 matched sets of 20-year-old and 21-year-old players. The 20-year-olds played 28% more games (49,863 to 38,815), scored 49% more runs (25,808 to 17, 292)—and hit 66% more home runs (6,735 to 4,047). The 61% figure given earlier is actually smaller than the figure derived by direct comparison; an explanation of how the 61% figure is derived will be included in the appendix to the article.

The studies of comparable rookies by age covered the ages 20 to 28; in summarizing that data, I stated the home run potential of a 20-year-old at "1000," and the home run potential of a player at any other age as a three-digit figure. I made such estimates for games played, doubles, triples, home runs, etc. For home runs, the line looks like this:

Age 20:	1000
Age 21:	623
Age 22:	465
Age 23:	369
Age 24:	303
Age 25:	252
Age 26:	210
Age 27:	177
Age 28:	150

You can compare the expected home run development of a 23-year-old and a 25-year-old (or any other two ages) by just dividing the 23-year-old figure by the 25-year-old figure. For 23 vs. 25, that's 369 divided by 252, so 23 year olds have a 46% advantage.

The advantage of 20-year-olds as compared to 21-

year-olds is derived not only from the direct comparison of 20-year-olds to 21-year-olds, but also from comparisons of players at each age to every other age. If you compare 20-year-olds to comparable 25-year-olds and 21-year-olds to comparable 25-year-olds, the advantage of the 20-year-olds will be about 60% greater.

We are basing all of these studies on a group of only 24 20-year-old regulars; it is not absolutely clear that what is true of those 24 players would be true of another 24 20-year-old rookies if you had them. But it is absolutely clear that the 20-year-old rookies in the 1948–1975 period, as a group, showed tremendous growth from the point at which they began. It isn't that they *always* displayed growth as hitters; in fact, there were several among the 24 who never advanced as hitters from the point at which they entered the league. This list would include Rick Manning, Dalton Jones, Jack Heideman, Bob Didier, and Ken Hubbs. In other cases, such as Frank Robinson, Vada Pinson, and Orlando Cepeda, the players were tremendous hitters at the age of 20 and became somewhat better, but not all that much.

But of the 24 players, fully half showed tremendous growth as hitters relative to the point at which they entered the league. In addition to Aaron, Buddy Bell, Torre, Boog Powell, Mays, Flood, and Bench, mentioned before, one should consider Eddie Mathews, Roberto Clemente, Ron Fairly and Bob Bailey. Mathews grew from his .242, 25-homer performance as a rookie to be one of the games great power hitters. As a 20-year-old rookie in 1955, Roberto Clemente hit just .255 with 5 homers and 47 RBI. You know what kind of hitter he became. Fairly and Bailey, who seemed overmatched as 20-year-olds, went on to become good enough hitters that they were able to stay in the major leagues for a long time. John Bateman, who hit just .210 as a rookie in 1963, three years later hit .279 with 17 homers and 70 RBI, although he never had another season as good.

No other group of players—as a group—showed anything like comparable growth. That is why the figures for 20-year-olds are so high.

But if the difference between 20-year-olds and 21-year-olds is tremendous, there are still many 21-year-olds who also show outstanding growth, enough so that the 21-year-olds also tower over the 22-year-olds. George Brett, a fair hitter as a 21-year-old rookie, went on to become a great hitter. Gus Bell, Gary Carter, Tommy Davis, Willie Davis, Bill Freehan, Larry Parrish, Carl Yastrzemski, Sixto Lezcano, Bill Buckner, Dwight Evans, Joe Morgan, and Greg Luzinski all came up at age 21, and all showed tremendous growth as hitters in subsequent years. They don't represent as large a percentage of their group and their subsequent development is not quite as dramatic—yet it certainly is true that 21-year-old rookies on many occasions will develop into far better hitters than they seem to be as rookies.

I would estimate the percentages as shown in the chart below. The first column shows the percentage of players at that age who show dramatic future development. The second column shows the percentage who show some future development, and the third column the percentage who show no future development:

	Dramatic	Some	None
Age 20:	50%	25%	25%
Age 21:	33%	33%	33%
Age 22:	22%	40%	38%
Age 23:	15%	42%	43%
Age 24:	10%	40%	50%
Age 25:	7%	30%	63%
Age 26:	4%	20%	76%
Age 27:	2%	10%	88%

At 27, I'm speculating. There were 18 27-year-old rookie non-pitchers in the 1948–1975 period. Only two of them, Chuck Hinton and Davey Lopes, ever had a better season than they had as rookies. In neither case could you really say that the growth was "dramatic," although in the case of Lopes you could certainly say that he has surprised a lot of people, including me.

At younger and older ages, there aren't enough rookies to form a study, there being only four teenaged rookies in the period who played regularly. However, it should be noted that three of the four showed *very* dramatic growth as hitters. Al Kaline, Robin Yount, and Rusty Staub all became incomparably better hitters than they were in their first seasons in the big time; the fourth was Tony Conigliaro.

A group of 20-year-old players will hit about 61% more career homers than a group of comparable 21-year-olds.

A group of 21-year-old players will hit about 36% more career homers than a group of comparable 22-year-olds.

A group of 22-year-old players will hit about 26% more career homers than a group of comparable 23-year-olds.

A group of 23-year-old players will hit about 22% more career homers than a group of comparable 24-year-olds.

From there on, the percentage advantage appears to stabilize at about 20% per year.

Comparisons by Age Based on Other Categories

The advantage of the younger player, if measured in terms of home runs, is larger than it is if measured in any other category. Home runs are the *most* effected; games played, which tend to be a nonlinear consequence of productivity, are the *least* effected. A comparison of the age advantage if based on various categories is shown below:

	20	21	22	23	24	25	26	27	28
Home Runs	1000	623	465	369	303	252	210	177	150
Games Played	1000	782	625	501	402	354	313	272	231
Stolen Bases	1000	762	613	490	382	334	282	223	215
Hits	1000	760	623	487	371	331	261	217	197
Walks Drawn	1000	756	590	465	361	304	246	219	215

A 20-year-old player can be expected to play about 26% more major league games than a comparable 21-year-old, 60% more than a comparable 22-year-old, about twice as many as a comparable 23-year-old, 2.5 times as many as a comparable 24-year-old, about 2.8 times as many as a comparable 25-year-old, 3.2 times as many as a comparable 26-year-old, 3.7 times as many as a comparable 27-year-old, and 4.3 times as many as a comparable 28-year-old.

How Can the Age Difference Be So Large?

Let us consider for a moment why the advantage of the younger players is as large as it is. How can that be? How can a 20-year-old rookie be expected to hit almost twice as many home runs as a 22-year-old rookie of exactly the same ability?

Suppose that you assume that there is a "function of growth or decline" which measures changes in player value over age. Let us suppose that a player's value in his rookie season is measured by the number "105." We don't need to know exactly what that 105 measures—maybe it means the guy is 5% better than an average player. 105 represents his value.

Let us suppose that the player's value in the next season will tend to be predicted (understanding of course that there will be individual variations) by the function (value times 27.5 divided by age). If the rookie is 24 years old, his value at 25 will tend to be predicted by ($105 \times 27.5/25$), which would calculate at about 116.

This function suggests itself because it causes value to rise until the age of 27, stablilize for a few years and then decline with increasing speed as the player reaches his thirties. That, of course, is exactly what happens.

The value of our player (who started at a value of 105 at age 24 and went to 116 at age 25) would continue to rise, up to 122 at age 26, and 124 at age 27. Then the value would start to slip, to 122 at age 28, to 116 at 29, to 106 at age 30. Then it would begin to slip faster, to 94 at 31, to 81 at 32.

We will assume, to complete the model, that a player will continue to play as long as his value is above 90, but will be forced out at mid-season in the first year in which his value is below 90 (that is to say, as soon as he establishes himself as below-average and then starts to slip further, he's out.) The value of 81 at 32 is divided in half for the last season, and becomes 41. The line representing his value over age is:

Age	24	25	26	27	28	29	30	31	32
Value	105	116	122	124	122	116	106	94	41

Suppose, however, that he had started out one year earlier, at age 23:

Age		23	24	25	26	27	28	29	30	31	32	33
Value A			105	116	122	124	122	116	106	94	41	
Value B		105	120	132	140	143	140	133	122	108	93	39

Because he started at 23 rather than 24, he would have an extra year of growth. *Because the ability to grow in value declines with age, the extra year of growth that he gains will be a year in which he gains more than in any other year.* Because he has an extra year of growth, and because that extra year of growth is his *best* year of growth, he will reach a peak which is 16% higher than he would have had he started one year later. Because he reaches a higher peak, it takes longer for the years to catch up with him, and he stays in the league for an extra year.

Suppose that he had started another year earlier, at 22:

Age		22	23	24	25	26	27	28	29	30	31	32	33	34
Value A			105	116	122	124	122	116	106	94	41			
Value C		105	126	144	158	167	170	167	159	146	129	111	92	38

The sum of the yearly values of the first player, who started at age 24, would be 947. The values for the second player, who started out at 23, would total 1,275. The values for the third player, who started out at 22, would total 1,712—80% more than that of a player starting out at the same point two years later.

A full pyramid of values for players starting at the same point from ages 20 to 28 is given in the chart at the bottom of the page.

The player who reaches the level of 105 by the age of 20 goes on to reach a peak value of 279—31% higher than any other age—simply by virtue of that one extra year of growth, which is a stronger year of growth than anyone else has. The total value of the seasons for the players starting at each age are given below:

Age 20:	3240
Age 21:	2329
Age 22:	1712
Age 23:	1275
Age 24:	947
Age 25:	685
Age 26:	549
Age 27:	435
Age 28:	337

Those value ratios are, in a loose way, extremely consistent with the ratios of actual accomplishments. We measured the ratio of games played by 20-year-olds as op-

20	21	22	23	24	25	26	27	28	29	30	31	32	33	34	35	36
								105	100	91	41					
							105	103	98	90	40					
						105	107	105	100	91	41					
					105	111	113	111	105	97	43					
				105	116	122	124	122	116	106	94	41				
			105	120	132	140	143	140	133	122	108	93	39			
		105	126	144	158	167	170	167	159	146	129	111	92	38		
	105	131	157	180	198	209	213	209	198	182	161	139	116	93	37	
105	138	172	206	235	259	274	279	274	260	238	211	182	151	122	96	37
20	21	22	23	24	25	26	27	28	29	30	31	32	33	34	35	36

posed to comparable 21-year-olds at 1000 to 782. We measured the ratio of home runs by 20-year-olds compared to 21-year-olds at 1,000 to 623. The value ratio in the model is 3240-2329, which would be 1,000 to 702.

The "formula" for growth, or the "growth function," is probably an individual function, different for each player. Exactly what it is in a collective sense, I wouldn't claim to know. We do know, however, that the value of almost any group of players that you can define reaches a peak at age 27 and declines after that. That means that whatever the growth function is, it has to increase value up to the age of 27, and decrease it after that. In the model here, I used (value times 27.5 divided by age), but you could also use something like (value times 37.5 divided by [age plus ten]). That makes the cycle of growth and decline more moderate—but it makes comparatively little difference in how the relative values of different ages will stack up. You can make it (value time 47.5 divided by [age plus twenty]), and it will still show essentially the same thing.

Whatever the growth function is, it has to increase value up to the age of 27. That means that a player who starts at 20 has seven years to grow in—40% more than if he had started at 22. Whatever the growth function is, the growth in the earlier years has got to be stronger than the growth in the later years. Any other pattern would violate not only the known facts of baseball records, but our common knowledge about growth and development, applying to everything from babies to corporations. That means that the growth in those extra two years has got to be larger than the growth in the latter five, and that means that the advantage of the 20-year-old has got to be much more than 40%. And that means that the player who reaches a given point of ability two years earlier has got to be expected to reach a much higher peak of ability. And that means that he has got to be expected to stay in the majors longer.

So, in a sense, is it not inevitable that a 20-year-old player *must* be expected to accomplish dramatically more than a comparable 22-year-old?

As to why the advantage in home runs is larger than in any other category, that is rather easier to explain with our model. It is an obvious and established fact that, as a player ages, the ratio between his power and his total value tends to rise. That is, power increases somewhat longer and declines somewhat more slowly than do most other baseball-related skills. While speed and reflexes tend to decline almost from the beginning of a player's career, strength tends to increase at least until the age of 25, and does not decline significantly until past 30.

Suppose that our player, who has a value of 105, hits 10 home runs. The ratio between his home runs and his value, then, is .095 (10 divided by 105). Suppose that this ratio rises by just .003 per season—up to .098 in his second year, up to .101 in his third year, etc.

Because this process will continue for a longer period of time for the younger player than for the player coming up at 24 or 25, his ratio—we are assuming that the players we are comparing are identical as rookies, remember—his ratio of power to total value will rise higher. The .003 annual rise in power/value ratio seems modest, yet using that assumption the 20-year-old in our model would, if he hit 10 home runs as a rookie, figure to hit 381 in his career.

That is 47% more than he would figure to hit if he hit 10 home runs at age 21 (267), and 281% more than he would hit if he had started at age 24 (100).

So the tremendous advantage that 20- and 21-year-old players have in our comparative studies isn't unrealistic. Moderate-sized advantages, iteratively applied, can grow to have very large effects on group totals. That, in all likelihood, is what happens in real life.

A few words in closing. The known facts are these:

1) Most major league players reach the majors at age 22 or later. Seventy-eight percent of rookies in our study were 22 years of age or older, and sixty-three percent were 23 or older.

2) The great majority of major stars reach the majors at age 22 or earlier. If you draw up a random list of 20 (non-pitchers) who are big stars and check them out, you'll probably find that 19 of the 20 reached the majors at age 22 or younger.

3) That means that, sampling older and younger rookies, the percentage of those who are destined to become major stars must be dramatically higher at the earlier ages.

4) The *performance* of the younger rookies is not dramatically better (in fact, it isn't better at all).

I ain't no logic professor, but that seems to mean that:

5) If the performance of a 21-year-old and a 23-year-old rookie is just the same, the 21-year-old has a dramatically better chance to become a major star.

In the appendix to this article, there are lists of comparable players (20-year-olds to 22-year-olds, etc.). These lists cover only 15–20% of the comparisons, but you can look them over if you'd like to get a sense of who compares to who as a rookie. These were selected at random, and I didn't check to see if they reflected the patterns of the larger data, but I'm sure they would.

Development Effects of Defensive Positions

Catchers

The second basic thing that we need to study, just so we'll know how to adjust for it in future studies, is the effect that playing a defensive position like catcher or second base has on the development and durability of a player. As I considered 20-year-olds to be the "full expectation standard" in the other study, I'll treat outfielders as the standard among positions.

What most baseball people would assume is that catchers, as hitters, would show less development than players at other positions. The "strain" of catching—for want of a better term for the succession of endless great and small injuries that have always been the fate of a catcher—tends not only to shorten a catcher's career (Johnny Bench, after all, is 19 months younger than Reggie Jackson), but also in many cases to impede his development as a hitter. But how much?

Studying the effects of position on development as a hitter is much more complex than studying the effects of aging. Ages fall into a neat spectrum, one after another. The data always makes sense and always reflects the linear arrangement. Postion relationships have all sorts of complicating secondary considerations. To begin with, the studies here have to make an immediate distinction between catchers who can hit and those who can't. We'll start with those who can hit.

Assuming that the player can hit, a rookie catcher:

• Will lose 17% of his career games when compared to an outfielder.

• Will lose about 30% of his career when compared to a middle infielder.

• Will lose 32% of his career when compared to a first baseman.

I compared 40 rookie catchers (some duplications) to 40 rookie outfielders with very similar batting records (no duplications). This study was limited to those players creating at least 4.25 runs per 25 outs. Having studied the effects of aging, a control was put in the study to consider each year of difference in age to be a strong "dissimilarity," so that in almost every case (if not every case) the two players compared were within one year of being the same age. The 40 outfielders played 54,688 major league games. The 40 catchers, with the same hitting ability as rookies, played 45,574—17% fewer. (Turning it around, if the catchers played 17% fewer, that means that the outfielders played 20% more.)

Perhaps more surprisingly, most of this difference did not come in the form of shortened careers from injuries, but came about because the catchers by and large did not display comparable development as hitters. The outfielders played 20% more games, but hit 44% more home runs (5978-4150). The outfielders scored 49% more runs (24,997-16,698), had 33% more hits (stop running the numbers, James; nobody cares what they are, anyway) and drove in 31% more runs. The outfielders hit 68% more triples and 34% more doubles. The outfielders had a career batting average of .277. The catchers, who hit just as well as rookies, hit .264.

In 28 of the 40 cases, the outfielder was more successful as a major-league hitter than was the comparable catcher—and Joe Torre, moved to another position in mid-career, represented three of the counter-examples. A few cases:

As a 23-year-old rookie in 1961, Jim Pagliaroni hit .242 for the Boston Red Sox with 16 homers and 58 RBI in 376 at bats. There happened to be three rookie outfielders in the study with somewhat similar stats. Willie Stargell, also 23 years old in his rookie year, hit .243 with 11 homers and 47 RBI in 304 at bats. George Foster, 22 years old, hit .241 with 13 homers and 58 RBI in 473 at bats. Roger Maris, 22 years old, hit .235 with 14 homers and 51 RBI in 358 at bats.

While Stargell, Foster, and Maris all went on to become feared power hitters, hitting over a thousand home runs among them and all carrying off MVP trophies, Pagliaroni played a hundred games in his career in only two other seasons, his best being 1965 when he hit .268 with 17 homers and 65 RBI.

As a 22-year-old rookie outfielder in 1950, Joe Adcock hit .293 with 8 homers and 55 RBI, slugging .406. As a 23-year-old rookie catcher in 1952, Sammy White had similar stats, hitting .281 with 10 homers and 49 RBI, slugging .423. While Adcock continued to develop as a hitter until reaching 38 homers and 108 RBI (separate seasons), White reached only 14 homers and 75 RBI. Adcock played 1,959 major league games, While 1,043. Adcock

hit 336 home runs, White 66. Their career batting averages were almost exactly the group totals: .277 for Adcock, .262 for White.

As a 22-year-old rookie catcher in 1971, Earl Williams hit .260 with 33 homers and 87 RBI, slugging .491. As a 22-year-old rookie outfielder in 1965, Willie Horton had a similar year, hitting .273 with 29 homers and 104 RBI, slugging .490.

Williams never had as good a year again, finishing his career with 889 games played, 138 homers, and a .247 average. Horton went on to have a career which is extremely similar to Adcock's—2,028 games, .273 average, and 325 homers.

As a 22-year-old rookie in 1974, Barry Foote hit .262 with 11 homers and 60 RBI. As a 22-year-old rookie in 1972, Garry Maddox had similar stats, .266 with 12 homers and 58 RBI. As a 21-year-old rookie in 1967, Rick Monday had similar stats (to Foote's)—.251 with 14 homers and 58 RBI.

Foote, derailed by constant injuries, had only one other major-league season as good. Both Monday and Maddox developed as hitters and played almost 2,000 games in the major leagues. Their major league totals are below:

	Games	HR	RBI	Avg.
Foote	687	57	230	.230
Maddox	1749	117	754	.284
Monday	1986	241	775	.263

I want to note here that all of the catchers we have mentioned were big men—all 6'3" or 6'4" and weighing 200 to 225. They all failed to develop as power hitters. I'll get back to that later.

There are counter-examples, of course, although they are less numerous and less dramatic. Manny Jiminez had similar batting stats as a rookie to Thurman Munson. Danny Walton had similar batting stats as a rookie to Darrell Porter. Munson and Porter, catchers, had better subsequent development as hitters.

Joe Torre, a catcher, had similar batting stats as a rookie to Tommy Davis, Curt Flood, Gus Bell, and Henry Aaron, and played more career games than any of them except Aaron. However, Torre is as much an illustration of the general case as of the exception, since his career was foundering when he was catching, and he revived sharply, winning a batting title and an MVP award, after moving to third base. Also, while he played more games and was probably a better hitter than Davis, Flood, or Bell, he didn't play *many* more games and wasn't *much* better; those guys were pretty good, too. If you add in Aaron the average goes way up. Torre probably accomplished significantly less as a major league hitter than he would have accomplished had he not started out as a catcher.

The comparisons of catchers to middle infielders who can hit are small; I turned up only three comparisons to second basemen and three to shortstops. This data shows a big advantage for the middle infielders, but it is so limited I'll skip it and go on to the first baseman.

The comparisons of catchers to first basemen showed the career advantage for a first baseman to be even larger than that for an outfielder. I found 12 comparisons between catchers and first basemen creating more than 4.25 runs per game. In ten of the twelve cases, the first baseman played more major league games. As a group, the first baseman played 47% more games (which is to say that the catchers played 32% fewer games), hit more than twice as many home runs, and hit for a career batting average 18 points higher (.278-.260). A couple of comps:

As a 22-year-old rookie in 1969, Al Oliver hit .285 with 17 homers and 70 RBI. As a 23-year-old rookie in 1970, Ray Fosse had similar, slightly better stats—.307 with 18 and 61. Al Oliver had 2743 major league hits and a .303 average. Ray Fosse, hammered repeatedly by foul tips and reruns of his famous collision with Pete Rose, had 758 hits and a .256 career average.

In 1951, a 24-year-old rookie catcher for the Detroit Tigers hit 8 homers, drove in 37 runs, and averaged .260. In 1974, a 24-year-old first baseman for the Cubs hit 10 homers, drove in 46 runs, and averaged .261. The catcher was a guy named Joe Ginsburg. The first baseman was Andre Thornton.

The first basemen compared to catchers did better than the outfielders, although in a direct comparison the career expectation for first basemen was much better. As to why this happened, my first thought was that it might be just the small data sample. That's a good possibility, but another one is this: that in comparing catchers to outfielders, we tended to select slow outfielders, such as Stargell, Adcock, Foster and Willie Horton, thus selecting for a condition that would be a liability for an outfielder, though not so much for a catcher or a first baseman. Thus, *unless* the outfielder developed dramatically as a hitter, his career could be untimely aborted.

That's one of the complications that you get into when comparing players at different positions. Here's another one, a more major one. While the career expectation *for a catcher who can hit* is substantially less than for a comparable hitter at any other position, the career expectation for a poor hitter is substantially *greater* at catcher than at any other position.

I ran the position comparisons in two groups, for players creating more than 4.25 runs per 25 outs, and less than 4.25 runs per 25 outs. A catcher who creates fewer than 4.25 runs per 25 outs can be expected to play 10% more games than an outfielder with the same batting stats as a rookie. Comparing a rookie catcher who doesn't hit and a rookie first baseman who doesn't hit, the catcher can be expected to play 37% more games in his career (although still hitting 17% fewer home runs and for an average 10 points lower, .259–.249).

The reason for this, obviously, is that if you hit .250 with no power as an outfielder, nobody is going to have a job for you except maybe the Royals. The injuries that befall catchers create a constant shortage of talent at the position, which enables a catcher who might hit .230–.250 to latch onto a job. So the career expectation for a light-hitting catcher is substantially greater than it is for a comparable hitter at any other position, including shortstop. (Actually, it's 41% greater than it is for a shortstop. You have to understand that, since organizations are always looking first for athletes and good athletes start out at shortstop, there are more young shortstops around than

there are young players at any other position—but fewer good ones.) Anyway, that's the kind of complication you don't get into when studying ages, since a guy who is 21 one year will be 22 the next. A .265-hitting catcher is more valuable than a .265-hitting left fielder—but a .265-hitting 21-year-old is no more valuable at the time than a .265-hitting 26-year-old.

There is an important point to be made out of this rather unsurprising study. The point is this: that *if a player can hit,* and if he *isn't* an outstanding defensive catcher, he probably should be moved to another position. How much of a career-shortening effect there is is somewhat random; it might be a great deal in one case, such as Ray Fosse, and not so much in another. But let's look at the catchers listed above—Pagliaroni, Sammy White, Earl Williams, Barry Foote, Ray Fosse. Sammy White was a good defensive catcher, so in his case maybe the organization did what was in their best interest, even if not in the best interest of the player. *Somebody's* got to catch. Fosse was a good defensive catcher, so you can just put that one in the random chance category and say that the Indians took a reasonable gamble in keeping him as a catcher, and it just didn't happen to work out. He could just as easily have turned out to be Carlton Fisk. Maybe you could put Foote in the same class, although he wasn't quite as good a player.

But Earl Williams and Jim Pagliaroni? Pagliaroni was never a good defensive catcher. Can't we all see, with the benefit of hindsight, that it would have been a better idea to put Pagliaroni in left field or at first base, and give him the opportunity to develop into a true slugger? Maybe he wouldn't have developed anyway, but I think there's a very realistic chance that, given the opportunity, Pagliaroni would have developed into a slugger comparable to Maris, Foster or Stargell. His teams traded that chance in to get a little bit of an offensive edge at catcher, giving up defense in the bargain.

The case of Williams is even stranger; Williams had the tools to be a good defensive catcher, but apparently didn't want to do it. But just as it was a good idea to keep Gary Carter at catcher because Carter really wanted to do it, wouldn't it have been a better idea to let Earl Williams do what *he* really wanted to do—move to left field and work on becoming one of the game's great sluggers? Instead, his offensive talent was wasted in an on-going battle with his managers over whether or not he should catch.

Perhaps the clearest case for the argument that an outstanding offensive prospect should not be used as a catcher unless he has good defensive tools is Ted Simmons. Unlike Williams, Simmons was willing to catch, but just never did have good equipment for the position. His arm wasn't exceptionally strong, and, with his knees being unnaturally low to the ground, he never was real quick about coming out of the crouch.

But the man could hit. By making Simmons a catcher, the Cardinals almost certainly prevented Simmons from becoming as great a hitter as he would have been at another position. He was a heckuva hitter anyway, but (like most catchers) he never led the league in anything. He'd have been a better hitter as an outfielder. At the same time, the Cardinals

1) Shortened his productive period as a hitter,

2) Exposed him to constant criticism about his defensive play, and

3) Went through an entire decade without a quality defensive catcher.

In that decade, they never won the pennant, and rarely contended. It says here that if the Cardinals had made Ted Simmons a third baseman when he was 22 years old, Simmons would have had a lot better career—and the Cardinals would have had a lot better chance to win the pennant. Instead, they waited until he was 31 and set in his ways when Whitey Herzog finally recognized that the Cardinals would be better off with him at another position; he resisted, and was lost to the organization.

Comparing a catcher and an outfielder or first baseman, the relationship of career expectation to offensive ability varies along a line something like this:

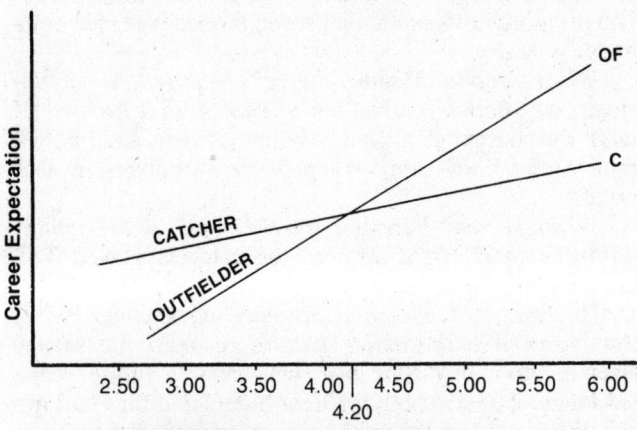

RUNS CREATED PER GAME

For an outfielder, hitting ability and career games played are *very* highly correlated, since how well you hit is the primary determinant of how long you play. But for a catcher, the correlation is much less, since there is always a place for you to play, and the number of games that you can play is limited mostly by how long it takes for the bumps and bruises to destroy you. So the better hitter a man is, the more his team gives up by putting him at catcher; conversely, the worse hitter he is, the more they gain and the more he gains if they can successfully convert him into a catcher.

One final note: If you look at Earl Williams, Pagliaroni, Barry Foote, and some of the other catchers that I've named whose careers degenerated quickly after promising starts, one thing that strikes you is their size. They were huge men. If you look at the catchers who have caught the most games in baseball history, one thing that strikes you is that they're *not* that big. Boone is good-sized (6'2", 202), and so is Fisk (6'2", now listed at 217), but they're at the upper boundary. Most of the most durable catchers in baseball history (Jim Sundberg, Bill Dickey, Yogi Berra, Al Lopez, Rick Ferrell, Ted Simmons) weighed no more than 185 pounds. Johnny Bench was 6'1" and a little under 200, Gabby Hartnett and Jim Hegan about the same. The biggest catcher around today, Lance Parrish, seems to be almost through as a catcher after catching just 1,039 games.

There is a tendency to associate size and durability. You look at Lance Parrish and think that a big guy like that can take the punishment, can take the home-plate collisions. But one of the real killers of the profession is the getting in and out of the crouch. The extra size is just putting extra pressure on his knees and on his back. If you want a catcher to last over a long period of years, you're probably better off looking for somebody more the size of Don Slaught or Scott Bradley.

As a generalization, a good-hitting player loses 25–30% of his career and 40–50% of his career production if he is a catcher. A great-hitting catcher loses more than that. A poor hitter gains 25–30% more games by being able to catch.

Second Basemen

In the comment concerning Juan Samuel in the 1985 *Baseball Abstract,* I reviewed the fates of a large number of young second basemen (particularly those who had trouble turning the double play), and reached this conclusion among others:

Doing the study, I came to an appreciation of the wisdom of [the] decision . . . to get Pete Rose out of the middle of the infield before he got hurt. There were just so many young second basemen who came up and hit well and fielded well, but who didn't become the players that they might have been because their progress was continually set back a pace or two by injuries—major injuries, minor injuries, all kinds of injuries . . . I have been skeptical about Samuel's superstar potential; and I still am. I think that, absent injury, he'll be very good; I don't think he'll be great.

But if he is great, I think he's more likely to be a great center fielder. I don't think he'll be a great second baseman.

Since then, Samuel has had a good year, leaving me somewhat impressed, and a not-so-good year, leaving me about back where I started. I still think he's going to be a good player, but not a great player, and I still think he'd have a better chance at a less demanding position.

Anyway, the point was that, at that time, I had become convinced that second basemen, as a group, suffered significant loss of offensive development due to the types of injuries intrinsic to the position—like catchers, but without the publicity. I talked about this with Tom Reich, who very strongly agreed with me, it being something that he had thought about many times in the course of representing players, and with Craig Wright, who admires Juan Samuel, and didn't think that Samuel was likely to suffer any real loss in value from playing the position.

With the database created here, we are now able to study the issue. Though occasionally contradictory, **the data in the main would suggest that second basemen do suffer very serious impairment of their development as offensive players due to the stress of their defensive position.** Since outfielders are our standard (and also the best study here), let's start with second basemen compared to outfielders.

When second basemen who hit well were compared to outfielders with very similar batting records, I found nine acceptable comparisons. In six of those nine situations, the outfielder had a longer and better career. In two of the three exceptions, what happened was that the outfielder stopped hitting in his second year, and washed out of the league. The third comparison was that Red Carew (21 years old, .292 average, 8 homers and 51 RBI) did develop more as a hitter than Gus Bell (21 years old, .282 average, 8 homers and 53 RBI). On the other hand, Ron Hunt as a rookie had a batting record comparable to Carl Yastrzemski.

As a group, the outfielders played 43% more games, scored 74% more runs, drove in 92% more runs, and hit 3.2 times as many home runs. Although it is a small study, it tends to suggest that there is a very significant impairment of development for the second basemen.

When second baseman who created less than 4.25 runs per 25 outs were compared to outfielders with very similar batting records, we had a large data sample, and a very surprising result.

There were 86 sets of comparable second basemen and outfielders. One would expect that, since second basemen are not expected to hit as much as outfielders, the second basemen would have an advantage when studying players who don't hit well as rookies (although, since I set the break at 4.25, there are some pretty decent hitters in this group). In fact, the outfielders played more major league games in 53 of 86 comparisons. As a group:

- The outfielders played 27% more career games.
- The outfielders had 32% more hits.
- The outfielders outhit the second basemen, .267-.253.
- The outfielders stole more than twice as many bases.
- The outfielders had 42% more RBI.
- The outfielders hit 82% more home runs.

Let's list a few of the second basemen and outfielders who had comparable records as rookies:

Dick Green and Don Baylor
Pedro Garcia and George Foster
Dalton Jones and Paul Blair
Jim Lefebvre and Reggie Smith
Rob Andrews and Al Cowens
Granny Hamner and Roberto Clemente
Frank Bolling and Roy White
Wayne Terwilliger and Jim Hickman

In all of these cases, the outfielder dramatically outperformed the second baseman as a major league hitter. In only two cases did the second baseman outperform the outfielder by a remotely similar margin (Julian Javier *vs.* Walt Williams, and Tony Taylor *vs.* Dan Meyer).

If you're looking for a way around the study, you could argue that what we had here was a problem with a very subtle type of quality leakage, caused by second basemen having seasons which did not truly represent their abilities. Dick Green may have hit as well as Don Baylor as a rookie, you might argue, but that doesn't mean that he was as good a hitter as Baylor at that time. He just had a good year.

That's possible. Baylor certainly did have a much better minor-league hitting record than did Green. On the other hand, Jim Lefebvre not only had a better minor-

league hitting record than Reggie Smith, but hit better than Smith in his second year in the majors. It seems unlikely to me that the difference would be caused by quality leakage, for this reason. The outfielders might have been better *hitters* than the second basemen (which is the group characteristic, and might leak into the study despite the control), but if so the second basemen would have more defensive value (also a group characteristic). What happens here is that they not only are lesser hitters, but have shorter careers—indicating that the hitting strength is not being offset by defensive value. But I don't really know, and it would be inappropriate for me to pretend that the study was perfect, because it surely isn't.

Several of the other position comparisons suggested the same thing. *When second basemen were compared to similar shortstops (good hitters),* the shortstops played 25% more games and hit almost three times as many homers; however, that was a group of just seven comparisons, and one of the comparable shortstops was Ernie Banks, who hit more homers than all seven second basemen combined.

When second basemen were compared to similar shortstops (both creating fewer than 4.25 runs per 25 outs), the shortstops played 24% more games and hit 36% more career home runs. There were 38 players in each group.

When second basemen were compared to similar-hitting catchers (light hitters), the catchers played 32% more games.

However, *when second basemen were compared to first basemen with similar batting records,* the second basemen, though hitting somewhat less in future years, had longer careers, both for light hitters and for good hitters. *When second basemen were compared to third basemen, there was little difference noted.*

On the whole, the pattern of the evidence would indicate that second basemen lose almost as much of their offensive potential as do catchers.

Other Positions

Among the other positions, the biggest surprise was the poor development of third basemen as hitters. In some studies, third basemen performed almost as poorly relative to their rookie seasons as did second basemen and catchers, although perhaps for a different reason.

Up until about 1935, third base was a "glove" position; third basemen were simply not expected to hit, just as shortstops and second basemen and sometimes catchers are not expected to hit. Since 1935 there have been a good number of exceptional third basemen, like Brooks Robinson, Ron Santo, Mike Schmidt, George Brett, George Kell, Buddy Bell, Ken Boyer, Graig Nettles, Wade Boggs, Bill Madlock, and Eddie Mathews, who were both good glove men and exceptional hitters, or in some cases glove wizards and very good hitters. There have been so many of these players that teams feel that they *need* to have a power hitter at third base, and they have repeatedly tried to force-feed power hitters onto the position. As a result, somewhat unrealistic expectations of what a third baseman should be have developed. They are often expected to be fourth- or fifth-place hitters and glove wizards as well.

Because of these unrealistic expectations, there is a large number of third basemen in the study who came up and hit fairly well, yet washed out of the majors because their defense was felt to be inadequate or because their managers wanted more power at the spot. In addition, third basemen in the study seemed to be injury-prone in ways that are not obviously related to their position; they were always getting hammered in the head by pitched balls, ruining their backs, getting fat in mid-career and contracting strange diseases. A few of these who would fit in one class or another include Jim Ray Hart, Joe Foy, Pete Ward, Bill Melton, Max Alvis, Rich Rollins, Dave Roberts, Al Rosen, Billy Grabarkewitz, Jim Finigan, Gene Freese, and Randy Jackson. All of these seemed, as young players, destined for a greater stardom than actually awaited them. In the end, although it was clear that the rookie third basemen in the study did show markedly substandard development as hitters, it was not at all clear to me why this had happened or what conclusions could be drawn from it.

The other positions reflect the standard defensive spectrum reading, from left to right, first base, left field, right field, third base, second base, center field, and shortstop. As a player ages, he tends to lose defensive skills, and consequently to slide leftward along the scale. As a result of this common pattern, first basemen are expected to hit more than shortstops, because there are more candidates around to fill the position.

For this reason, as I would have expected, the players who begin their careers at the right end of the defensive spectrum have markedly longer careers than comparable hitters who begin their careers at the left end of the spectrum. A rookie center fielder who can hit will play about 15–20% longer in the major leagues than a right or left fielder of the same offensive ability, and nearly 40% longer than a first baseman.

As the level of the offensive contribution increases, the importance of position along the defensive spectrum decreases. If you create seven runs a game, the quality of your defensive contribution is less important than if you create four or five runs per game (per 25 or 27 outs). Still, first basemen do not play as long in the majors as outfielders of the same ability as hitters, no matter how well they hit. And shortstops who can hit, though few in number, tend to have tremendously long major league careers.

Because of the complex nature of the interrelationships, it is not possible to state ratios representing the career expectation for each position, as was done for different ages.

Comparable Players on Good Teams and Poor Teams

One issue in which I have had a long-term interest is the question of whether or not there is a difference between the developmental tendencies of young players on good teams, and on poor teams. That is, if you have two young players who are the same age, play the same position and have the same batting statistics, but one of whom plays for a good team and the other of whom plays for a poor team, will the one who plays for a good team have more of a tendency to develop in future years?

It has always seemed to me—always, ever since I was a Kansas City A's fan as a kid, and they had a long series of rookies who never developed—that promising players on bad teams don't tend to make as much progress from the point at which they enter the league. A poor team tends to put more pressure on a young player, regarding him either as a potential savior or as the reason the team isn't doing better, or in some cases as both. At the same time, the good team has more to offer a young player in the way of assistance—better coaching, better instruction, and, most importantly, the example of successful players going about their business. The Kansas City A's (an extreme case of a bad team, no doubt) would hail some AAA player as a superstar, slap him in the lineup and expect him to turn the team around. When they and their fans discovered him to be an ordinary talent, they would talk about his failures and shortcomings. The Yankees and later Orioles would just ease the player into a job, try to teach him how to do things, find out what he could do and couldn't do, assign him to do the things he was capable of doing, and watch him develop.

In this study, I looked for comparability in all aspects of play, age and position, but selected only "matches" in which there was a minimum difference of .140 in the won-lost records of the two teams. If one rookie's team had a winning percentage of .420 (65–89 in 154 games, 68–94 in 162) the other rookie's team had to be *at least* .560 (86–68 in 154 games, 91–71 in 162).

In this study, I allowed duplications on good teams but not on poor teams, and used a relatively low standard of similarity, thus selecting a huge field (112 sets of similar rookies). A few of those comps:

The 1967 Kansas City A's had a rookie center fielder named Rick Monday who hit .251 with 14 homers and 58 RBI. The 1961 Los Angeles Dodgers had a rookie center fielder named Willie Davis who hit .254 with 12 homers and 45 RBI in a little less playing time. Both players were 21. The A's were 62–99, a last-place team. The Dodgers finished second at 89–65.

Both players went on to have fine careers.

The 1966 Chicago Cubs had a rookie outfielder named Adolpho Phillips, who hit .260 with 16 homers and 36 RBI. The 1958 San Francisco Giants, who finished a little over .500, had a rookie outfielder named Willie Kirkland, who hit .258 with 14 homers and 56 RBI. Both players were 24.

Neither player went on to have a distinguished career, but Kirkland was somewhat more successful, outhomering Phillips 148–59 in their careers.

A rookie shortstop for the 1959 Philadelphia Phillies (64–90) hit .261 with 7 homers and 28 RBI. His name was Joe Koppe, and he was 28 years old. A rookie second baseman for the Chicago White Sox in 1964 (98–64) hit .262 with 4 homers and 30 RBI. His name was Don Buford, and he was 27 years old.

Buford went on to become a significantly better player.

A rookie first baseman for the San Diego Padres in 1969 hit .255 with 24 homers and 66 RBI. That was Nate Colbert, and he was 23, and the Padres were 52–110. A rookie outfielder for the Los Angeles Dodgers in 1960 hit .268 with 23 homers and 77 RBI. That was Frank Howard, also 23, and the Dodgers were 82–72.

In the long run, Howard had a much better career. I find this comparison particularly intriguing, because Colbert was much more successful in the short run, being the Padres biggest star in their first four years, while Howard struggled for nearly eight years before learning to control his ability. I always wonder what Colbert would have done had there been a Willie McCovey or a Bobby Grich or a Bob Gibson around to teach him how to deal with his success.

A few more comps, taking it from the top of the alphabet and listing the player with the bad team first: Joe Adcock and Dan Driessen, Hank Allen and Sandy Valdespino, Rob Andrews and Bobby Valentine, Loren Babe and Ted Uhlaender, Gus Bell and Henry Aaron, Buddy Bradford and Rod Gaspar, George Brett and Tony Kubek, Jim Finigan and Thurman Munson, Tito Francona and Jim Lefebvre, Owen Friend and Dave Johnson, and Pedro Garcia and Davey Williams.

As a group, the rookies who played on good teams did go on to have distinctly, it not dramatically, better careers. The 112 rookies who played for poor teams played 105,179 major league games. The rookies who played for good teams played 133,271—27% more. The rookies who played on good teams eventually hit 33% more home runs (11,842–8,886), had 33% more hits and did almost everything else 33% more times.

In this study there could be a serious problem with quality leakage. The players who played on good teams could very well have been better players or better prospects in ways too subtle for the similarity method to pick up. Nonetheless, the way that the method looks at players is not that different from the way that you and I look at rookies, and it seems like a worthwhile thing to keep in mind when considering who to draft in your rotisserie league or your Strat-O-Matic league.

"Young Player's Skills" and "Old Player's Skills"

I have speculated a number of times, most recently in the Minnesota Twins comment on page 88 of the 1986 *Abstract,* that players who have "old player's skills" should tend to peak earlier and have shorter careers than those who have "young player's skills."

As a player ages, his skills undergo certain predictable changes. All players lose speed as they age; thus, speed-related skills are young player's skills.

As a player ages, power increases as a percentage of value, not in every case but in most. Thus, power is an old player's skill.

As a player ages, he will tend in most cases to draw more walks. Thus, drawing walks is an old player's skill.

As a player ages, his batting average will almost always decrease. Thus, hitting for average is a young player's skill.

As a player ages, he tends to drivein more runs and score fewer. Thus, runs scored are a young player's skill, and RBI are an old player's skill.

All players tend to follow this pattern to one degree or another, and all players are finished when they reach the point at which the gains in power and strike zone judgment can no longer offset the losses in speed and batting average. It makes sense, then, that the further along in this progression the player is (regardless of age), the closer he is to the end of his career (or, conversely, the earlier he is in this progression, the longer he can be expected to play).

But a lot of things that make sense nonetheless are not true. To study this issue, I eliminated the ordinary method of calculating similarity scores, and based similarity strictly on age, position on the field, runs created, and runs created per out. In forming the two comparison groups for this study:

In every case, the two rookies were the same age.

In every case, the rookie with young skills scored more runs.

In every case, the rookie with old skills drove in more runs.

In every case, the rookie with young skills hit for a higher batting average.

In every case, the rookie with old skills hit more home runs.

In every case, the rookie with young skills hit more triples.

In every case, the rookie with young skills stole more bases.

In every case, the rookie with old skills drew more walks.

From there, I selected for the closest possible matches in runs created, runs created per game and position on the field.

There were 36 "matches" selected for this study.

Pete Rose, a 22-year-old rookie in 1963, created 77 runs (4.23 per game) with young player's skills. Jim Lefebvre, a 22-year-old rookie in 1965, created 68 runs (4.15 per game) with old player's skills. Rose, obviously, had a longer career.

Tommie Agee, 23 years old in 1966, created 89 runs (4.89 per game) with young player's skills. Willie Montanez, 23 in 1971, created 93 runs (5.22 per game) with skills characteristic of an older player. Nonetheless, Montanez played much longer in the major leagues.

Ernie Banks, 23 years old in 1954, created 81 runs (4.72 per game) with young player's skills. Bill Melton, 23 years old in 1969, created 78 runs (4.71 per game) with old player's skills.

Lou Brock, 23 years old in 1962, created 57 runs (4.44 per game) in 1961 with young player's skills. Jim Pagliaroni, 23 years old in 1961, created 53 runs (4.64 per game) with old player's skills.

A few others: George Brett and Roy Howell, Roberto Clemente and Boog Powell, Alvin Dark and Joe Ferguson, Tommy Harper and John Milner, Randy Jackson and Norm Zauchin, Sonny Jackson and Sixto Lezcano, Eddie Kasko and Bob Boone, Wally Moon and Rich Rollins, Manny Sanguillen and Bill Serena, Jose Tartabull and Mike Schmidt, Harvey Kuenn and Ron Hansen.

As you can probably gather from the list of players, the players with young player's skills did, in fact, last longer and perform better over a period of time. It's not a dramatic difference; there are players like Mike Schmidt, who begin with low batting averages and power, raise the batting average over time, and show terrific development. Still, the players with young player's skills did play 33% more games in their careers (48,583 to 36,530). The player with young player's skills played more major league games than the comparison player in 23 of the 36 cases.

I did two studies of the issue, of which the one described here is the second. The first one showed a 21% advantage for the player's with young player's skills, but I was afraid that that had resulted from a position bias (that is, the players with young player's skills played longer because they tended to be able to play more demanding defensive positions). So I redefined similarity so that it placed much tighter demands on playing the same or a similar defensive position. To my surprise, the second study *increased* the advantage of the players with young player's skills.

Comparisons Based on Differences in Speed Categories

A related study focused only upon differences in the speed categories of triples and stolen bases. In this study, players who hit triples and stole bases were compared to other players who had similar batting statistics at similar ages, but with fewer triples and stolen bases. For example, Tommie Agee in 1966 is compared to Bobby Murcer in 1969:

		Areas of Similarity			Areas of Contrast	
	Age	HR	RBI	Avg.	3B	SB
T. Agee	23	22	86	.273	8	44
B. Murcer	23	26	82	.259	4	7

Bobby Grich, 1972, was comparable to Dan Ford, 1975, except faster:

	Age	HR	RBI	Avg.	3B	SB
B. Grich	23	12	50	.278	3	13
D. Ford	23	15	59	.280	1	6

Hansome Ransom Jackson was comparable, as a rookie, to Rip Repulski, except faster:

	Age	HR	RBI	Avg.	3B	SB
R. Jackson	25	16	76	.275	6	14
R. Repulski	25	15	66	.275	4	3

Julian Javier was comparable, as a rookie, to Bobby Wine, only faster:

	Age	HR	RBI	Avg.	3B	SB
J. Javier	23	4	21	.237	8	19
B. Wine	23	4	25	.244	0	2

Roger Metzger was comparable, as a rookie, to Mike Tyson, except faster:

	Age	HR	RBI	Avg.	3B	SB
R. Metzger	23	0	26	.235	11	15
M. Tyson	23	1	33	.243	4	2

One doesn't ordinarily think about catchers as having speed, but John Roseboro as a catcher was faster than Johnny Orsino:

	Age	HR	RBI	Avg.	3B	SB
Roseboro	25	14	43	.271	9	11
Orsino	25	19	56	.272	1	2

A few others: Jake Wood and Davey Williams, Cesar Tovar and Glenn Beckert, Wally Moon and Rich Rollins, and Tony Taylor and Jack Brohamer.

There were 40 such comparisons. The fast players did, in fact, play 43% more major league games, 55,757–39,066. In this particular study, the advantage in home runs was smaller than the advantage in any other category (38%), reversing the usual pattern. But the advantage in runs scored was 76%, the advantage in triples was exactly 100% (1624–812) and the advantage in stolen bases was about 400% (5771–1169), proving that if you start out stealing more bases you will continue to do so.

Many players, perhaps most players, are driven out of the major leagues indirectly because they lose their speed. If you can create seven runs a game it doesn't matter how fast you are; you can play first base or DH. But as a player loses speed as he ages, he loses the ability to play the positions (center field, shortstop, second base) at which offensive ability is scarce, and thus loses the ability to stay in the majors *without* creating seven runs a game. That's another reason that catchers who don't hit play longer than players at any other position who don't hit—nobody cares when they lose their speed. So there is no doubt that speed is the key to the advantage of the players who have young player's skills.

Strikout-to-Walk Ratio as an Indicator of Potential Growth

Strikeout-to-walk ratio holds a particular fascination in trying to ascertain how players develop because, among all categories, strikeouts and walks would appear to bear the closest relationship to learning. All skills, to one degree or another, are learned, and thus the ability to do anything is learned and is, to one degree or another, however slight, a testimony to a player's ability to learn.

Ordinarily the learning process is shaded beneath the veil of physical abilities; Don Baylor can learn to hit home runs a lot more easily than Willie Randolph because he's just a lot stronger than Willie Randolph. Rickey Henderson can learn to steal bases more easily than Ossie Virgil because . . . why am I expanding upon this concept? Anyway, the fascination of strikeout-to-walk ratios is that the veil seems thinner, and the ability to learn more visible. If Willie Randolph has command of the strike zone and Damaso Garcia doesn't, this doesn't have anything to do with their strength or speed and very little to do with their reflexes; it has to do with their command of a fundamental. Our language reflects that; we say that Willie Randolph *knows* the strike zone, or that Don Baylor *muscles* a pitch out of the park.

Many of us believe, then, that when a young player has a poor strikeout-to-walk ratio, that this may be an indication of an inability or unwillingness to get on top of the fundamentals of hitting. It could well be, on the other hand, that a poor K/W ratio indicates a potential area of improvement, and thus could actually be a positive when considering future production. "If Cory Snyder can hit like he does swinging at almost anything," this argument would go, "imagine what he will be capable of *once he learns the strike zone.*"

To study this issue, I identified 47 matched sets of

players, with one player in every case having more strike-outs and fewer walks (hence, a worse strikeout to walk ratio) than the other. Five quick comparisons:

	Areas of Similarity				Areas of Contrast	
	Age	HR	RBI	Avg.	SO	BB
D. Williams	24	13	55	.254	48	63
P. Garcia	23	15	54	.245	40	119
B. Bell	20	9	36	.255	34	29
C. Flood	20	10	41	.261	31	56
E. Charles	27	17	74	.288	54	70
P. Herrara	27	17	71	.281	51	136
S. Braun	23	5	35	.254	48	50
C. James	23	4	44	.255	15	59
R. Hansen	22	22	86	.255	69	94
R. Jackson	22	29	74	.250	50	171

Strikeout to walk ratio is apparently not an indicator of potential growth or development for a rookie. The 47 rookies in the study who had good strikeout-to-walk ratios played (or are expected to play) 50,969 major league games; the 47 rookies who had poor strikeout-to-walk ratios played 53,401. The difference, slightly less than 5%, is too small to justify any conclusion.

The rookies with poor K/W ratios had better subsequent careers in 25 of 47 cases—meaning essentially nothing. Although the hitters with poor K/W ratios continued to strike out more often and walk less often, they showed slightly more development of power (5,336 home runs as opposed to 4,686) at a very minimal cost in batting average (.264–.262).

Eddie Epstein argues that what is significant about strikeout-to-walk ratios is how they change over a period of years; if a player, after being in the league a few years, not only fails to improve in this area but actually goes backward, that may be a signal that something is amiss in his development as a hitter. That may well be, but that's another study. Looking just at a rookie, strikeouts and walks give no significant information about future development.

Growth Rates of Comparable Black Players and White Players

Let me say, before I start this, that nobody likes to write about race. We would all prefer to be colorblind. I was doing these studies, and I had a code in it for the player's race, and while I was studying how one group of players developed over time compared to another group, I thought I would do a run of black players against white players, fully expecting that it would show nothing in particular or nothing beyond the outside range of chance, and I would file it away and never mention that I had looked at the issue at all.

In the black/white study, there were 54 players in each group—54 non-duplicating white rookies, and in each case the one black player who was most similar. The results were astonishing.

In 44 of the 54 cases, the black player went on have a better major-league career. In only 10 cases of the 54,

or 18%, did the white player play more major-league games or surpass his black counterpart in most of the major categories.

The white players played 53,524 major-league games. The black players played 79,461 major-league games— 48% more.

The black players had 66% more major-league hits.

The black players hit 71% more major-league doubles.

The black players hit 93% more triples.

The black players hit 66% more home runs.

The black players scored 69% more runs.

The black players stole almost 400% more bases.

Forty-four of fifty-four—82%.

Many of the differences were dramatic.

As rookies, Rob Andrews and Al Cowens had similar batting records.

As rookies, Gus Bell and Henry Aaron had similar batting records.

As rookies, Buddy Blatnik and Chuck Hinton had similar batting records.

As rookies, Kent Hadley and Don Baylor had similar batting records.

As rookies, Dalton Jones and Paul Blair had similar batting records.

As rookies, Syd O'Brien and Willie Stargell had similar batting records.

As rookies, Johnny Orsino and John Rosenboro had similar batting records.

As rookies, Charley Smith and George Foster had similar batting records.

As rookies, Jim Lefebvre and Reggie Smith had similar batting records.

In all of these cases, the black player showed dramatic development as a hitter, and as a result would play more than a thousand more major league games than his white counterpart.

In only two cases within the study did a white player play a thousand games more than his black counterpart. (Ron Cey vs. Al Lewis, and Bobby Grich vs. Dan Ford.)

If you throw these eleven cases out of the study, the remaining black players still played almost 15,000 more major league games than the comparable white players.

I had studied maybe a dozen other issues, in general finding nothing where I had expected to find a little something, finding something where I had expected to find something else, but often finding solid evidence where I had expected to find solid evidence. But not evidence this solid.

The difference between the development of a black player and the development of a white player was greater than the development as hitters of an outfielder and a catcher.

The difference between the career expectation of a black player and a white player was greater than the difference between that of a slow player and a fast player, or between a player who had young player's skills and one who had old player's skills.

The difference between the development of a black player and a white player was greater than the difference between a player on a poor team and a comparable player on a good team.

The only greater difference that I could find would be between a player who came up at 20 and one who came up three or four years later.

How could it be?

How could a group of players, who as rookies were the same age and hit for the same average, with the same power stats and more or less the same everything else, divide from that point onward into almost distinct camps, the black players going on to outperform their white counterparts by a huge margin? It just doesn't make sense.

One must, in writing about sensitive issues, exercise unusual care to make sure that one is not writing about some sort of illusion, that what you are seeing is real.

I decided on a second study. I tinkered with the similarity scores method a little bit to emphasize runs created per game, triples, stolen bases, and defensive positions, helping to guard against quality leakage and speed leakage, and also providing some alternative selections in cases where a player was about as similar to one player as to another. Then I ran the study the other way, allowing duplications among the whites but no duplications among the blacks, and selecting the one white rookie most comparable to each black rookie. After making this second set of selections, I then eliminated from the second study any pairings which repeated the first study, substituting the second-best comparison for each black rookie whenever there was a second acceptable comparison. This gave me a group of 49 black/white comparisons, none of which repeated the earlier study.

The difference between the races in the second study was less dramatic, but only slightly. In 35 of the 49 cases, the black player in the second study played more major-league games. The black players in the second study played 44% more games, hit 48% more home runs, scored 65% more runs, drove in 55% more runs and stole 4.6 times as many bases.

As rookies, Ernie Banks and Bernie Allen had similar batting records. Each player was 23 years old. Both were middle infielders. The two players were about the same height and weight. Allen hit .269 with 46 extra base hits (27-7-12). Banks hit .275 with 45 extra base hits (19-7-19).

There was nothing similar about what they did in subsequent years.

As rookies, Tommy Davis and Jim King had similar records. Davis was 21, King 22. Davis hit .276 with 11 homers and 44 RBI; King hit .256 with 11 homers and 45 RBI.

Davis became an outstanding hitter. King didn't.

As rookies, Gary Mathews and Jackie Brandt had similar records. Each player was 22. They played the same position, left field. Mathews hit .300 with 12 homers and 58 RBI. Brandt hit .298 with 12 homers and 50 RBI.

Mathews became a much better hitter.

As rookies, Don Ruford and Ron Theobald had similar records.

As rookies, Gene Freese and Willie Davis had similar records.

As rookies, Tommy Harper and Tito Francona had similar records.

I pondered the possibility that the results of the study could have been caused by "speed leakage"—that is, that the black players, despite the similarity controls, ran faster than the white players, and so showed better durability and development because of this. It seems enormously unlikely that the effects of speed leakage in a study could be larger than the effects of speed if measured directly. Still, there was no question that the black rookies in the database did run much better than the white rookies, and upon examination I concluded that there was, indeed, some speed leakage into the study.

I ran a version of the study which put extremely tight controls on the speed-related categories. It made no difference; the black players still played 46% more major league games.

I ran a special study which was carefully "speed balanced" so that the white rookies selected hit as many triples and stole as many bases as the black players. There were 20 players in each group. The black players played 34% more major league games, hit 45% more home runs—and, in the long run, hit 44% more triples and stole 3.4 times as many bases.

I ran a special study that focused only on players who had very little speed. The black players who had limited speed, like Lee May, Willie Stargell, Al Oliver, Chris Chambliss, Bill Robinson, George Scott, Willie Horton, Jim Ray Hart, and Nate Colbert still, as a group, showed dramatically better development than did similar white players.

I wracked my little brain looking for possible biases in the study. Realizing that catchers don't last as long as players at other positions, and that there are few black catchers, I considered the possibility that the split in the data was caused by a position bias. Since the separation in the data is larger than it would be if all of the blacks were center fielders or shortstops (the best positions at which to start out) and all of the whites were catchers, the position bias obviously could not create the effects observed. Still, I selected a subgroup of the earlier studies in which all of the players played the same defensive position, 41 players.

It made no difference. The advantage for the black players was just as large in these 41 pairings as it was in the other 62.

I realized that, as time passed in the study period, the number of black players increased and the average length of a major league career also increased. This created the possibility of a "timeline bias," since the black players were thus "selected" from the period in which the longest careers occured.

I ran three studies to examine the possibility. In the first, I selected a subgroup of the matches in the earlier studies which included all cases in which the two players came to the major leagues within six years of one another, then checked to make sure that there was no timeline difference within this grouping. There were 27 sets of players in the time-line balanced study. The black players played 55% more major league games, hit 67% more home runs, stole 4.2 times as many bases, etc.

In the second, I considered the year in which the player came up to be an element of similarity, and thus adjusted for it. The advantage of the black players remained the same.

In the third, now beating a dead horse, I selected random sets of similar players emerging at least 12 years apart (without regard to race). The players who came up later in the period had only a 4% advantage in games played, thus eliminating timeline bias as a possible source of the difference. It is, in fact, much more likely that the increased number of black players in the game created the increase in the number of players having long careers, rather than the other way around.

Combining the two basic studies, there are 103 matched sets of players, consisting of about 70 distinct black players and 75 distinct white players. In 79 of the 103 pairings, or 77%, the black player went on to play more major league games. Comparing home runs, runs scored, RBI, or stolen bases, the black player held the advantage over 80% of the time.

And I could identify absolutely no bias to help explain why this should happen.

Comparisons to Latin Players

When I directly compared white players to Latin players, the Latin players appeared to show superior development and durability resulting in 7–12% greater career length. However, when I compared the black players to similar Latin players, the blacks dominated the comparable Latins as much as or possibly more than they did the whites, leaving some doubt as to whether the "Latin advantage" was real. It probably is; the Latin/black comparisons are based on relatively small data samples (15 players in one study, 26 in another). In the 26-player sample, which contains duplications among the black players but not among the Latins, the black players played 62% more games, hit 192% more home runs, drove in 125% more runs and stole 36% more bases than Latin players with similar batting records as rookies. The black player was more successful than his Latin counterpart in 19 of the 26 matches.

Why?

As to why this advantage should exist, it would be wise not to speculate too freely in an area that is so sensitive, but what the hell; I've been called a lot of things but "wise" isn't one of the top ten. Let's think about it for a second. It is obvious that in our society black athletes succeed in numbers which are greatly disproportionate to their percentage of the population. There are two possibilities—that blacks are better athletes because they are born better athletes, which is to say that it is genetic, or that they are born equal and become better athletes. If you asked a hundred people who are knowledgeable about genetics and a hundred athletes, I doubt that you would find more than a handful in either group who felt it likely that the advantage was genetic.

Let's assume that it isn't genetic, that we are born equal and that blacks succeed because *beginning from that equal point, they show superior growth and development as athletes*. If you think about it in that way, it is perhaps not so surprising that, given that blacks and whites leap off of some other equal platform, the blacks would once again leap higher. A major league rookie can be seen, in

a sense, as the athletic equivalent of a baby, an unformed collection of skills and potential, waiting to acquire shape.

Is it not tragically true, in our society, that black people have fewer options for success than do white people? No one would disagree with that, would they? Is it not inevitable that the fewer options a group of people have, the more energy and ability they will focus on those which are available to them? That is what is meant by the expression "backed up against a wall." Any animal, when cornered *and left no option but to fight,* will fight with more vigor and enthusiasm than in any other situation. Black athletes are, in a sense, up against a wall, often (though certainly not always) facing a desperate and very visible future should they fail as athletes.

In baseball, what we mean by saying that a group of players focuses more energy and ability on becoming ballplayers is that they display greater *determination* to succeed. The two expressions mean exactly the same thing, except that the one attaches a moral quality to the statement and the other does not. Facing a career crisis, the white player—we exaggerate, but you know what we mean—the white player wonders whether he should stick it out in baseball or whether perhaps he should go into the lumber business with Dad or the real-estate racket with Freddie. Probably he will choose to stay in baseball as long as he can—but the mere fact that he has options, and that he knows he has options, lessens his anxiety, and lessens the ferociousness with which he attacks the task of succeeding in the game. The black player, facing a career crisis, may know that should he not succeed in baseball he will return to a bleak and unpromising world, wondering whether his children will go to bed hungry. The data is, I say, perhaps less surprising when you think more about it.

Returning to the specific comparisons, the thing that strikes me about the comparable players is this: that it sure seems to me that the white players lose their speed a lot quicker than the comparable black players. In one study, you may remember that we controlled the speed categories when the players were rookies, but as time passed the black players still stole far, far more bases. If you look at some of the comparisons, you'll see a black player that you think is a much faster runner than the comparable white player. But if you look back to the point at which they entered the league, the difference in speed is not so apparent. Look at Tommie Harper and Tito Francona. Harper, 22 years old, hit 3 triples and stole 12 bases in 129 games. Francona, also 22, hit 4 triples and stole 11 bases in 139 games. As an outfielder, Francona's range factor was a little bit better, 2.05 to 1.96. Francona was 11 for 16 as a base stealer and grounded into 6 double plays. Harper was 12 for 13 but grounded into 10 double plays. Nothing that you can see about them as rookies indicates that Harper was any faster.

But if you look at them three years later, Harper has a definite speed advantage. Francona, having his first big year with the bat, had 2 triples and 2 stolen bases. Harper, having a fair year, had 5 triples and 29 stolen bases.

If you come back to them three years later, Francona had been moved to first base, though he hit 5 triples and stole three bases. Harper, playing third base for Seattle, stole 73 bases.

Come back to them four years later and you'll find Francona, a pinch hitter for the Cardinals, with one triple and nary a stolen base. At the same age, Harper is leading the American League in stolen bases with 54.

Another one is Gus Bell and Henry Aaron. As rookies, Bell hit .282 and slugged .443; Aaron hit .280 and slugged .447. Bell at that point seemed to have better speed; he hit 12 triples to Aaron's 6 and stole four bases to Aaron's two. The next year Bell led the league in triples. When Cincinnati acquired Bell they moved him to center field, and for four years he was a terrific player, hitting .300 with 25–30 home runs and 100 RBI and doing a good job in center field. He played in four All-Star games, competing for the job with people like Willie Mays, Duke Snider, and Richie Ashburn.

Yet if you check in on them at 29, Henry Aaron is stealing 31 bases in 36 attempts. Bell, fighting for playing time, hits two triples and steals two bases. Five years later, and Aaron is still stealing bases, 28 in 33 tries. Bell is out of the game.

Although Reggie Jackson and Bob Allison don't come out as most-similar players in any of my studies (primarily because Allison was two years older in his rookie season), there are important similarities between them. As rookies, these are their records:

	G	AB	R	H	2B	3B	HR	RBI	SB	Avg.
Allison	150	570	83	149	18	9	30	85	13	.261
Reggie	154	553	82	138	13	6	29	74	14	.250

Just real similar, I'd say. Another similarity is that both Allison and Jackson were star football players in college, Allison as a running back and Jackson as a defensive back. This points up the fact that both possessed outstanding speed; Allison as a rookie led the American League in triples and, unlike Jackson, played center field. He wasn't a bad center fielder.

From 1961 through 1964, Allison had seasons which would be entirely consistent with Reggie Jackson's accomplishments. In 1961 he hit .245 with 29 homers and 102 RBI. In 1962 he hit .266 with 29 homers and 102 RBI. In 1963 he hit .271 with 35 homers and 91 RBI. In 1964 he hit .287 with 32 homers and 86 RBI. Those are fine years—Reggie Jackson years, in essence. They wouldn't be Reggie's best years, but they'd fit in.

But, like Gus Bell, Allison never went any further than that. He lost his speed; by 1965 he had gone from center field to right field to left field and was putting in time at first base.

Reading Reggie's autobiography to check out Reggie's football career (I always thought he was a running back, also), I come upon this quote, describing Rick Monday as a 19-year-old superstar at Arizona State:

"He was 6′3″ and 190 pounds; he could run the 100 in about 9.7; he had an arm like a cannon . . . he was a big league ballplayer when he was nineteen years old, and he knew it."

Monday was a fine player—but he never really used that phenomenal speed as a major league player. By 30, he had lost his speed. Picking a few numbers out of the air, at 20 Rick Monday was probably 95% as fast as Willie Mays. At 25, he might have been 80% as fast. At 30, there was no comparison. After his 30th birthday, Rick Monday stole 13 bases in his career. At 40, Mays stole 23 bases.

Wally Moon was fast when he came up. Fred Lynn had excellent speed as a young player. So did Bobby Grich. So did Roger Maris, and Dale Murphy. I've got a method to analyze this now and I guess that's what I should do, but it sure does seem that the white players have more trouble retaining their speed.

APPENDIX

How Star Value Is Calculated

To calculate a player's star value, you begin awarding points for each time he does any of the following things:

Wins an MVP Award (5 Points).

Leads League in Home Runs, Runs Scored, RBI, or batting average (3 points).

Hits 40 home runs/not leading league (3 points).

Drives in or scores 100 runs/not leading league (2 points).

Has 200 hits (2 points).

Hits 30–39 home runs/not leading league (2 points).

Leads league in doubles, triples, walks, stolen bases or hits with less than 200 (1 point).

To the points awarded for any of these accomplishments, you add 1 point for each 100 games played in excess of 1,000, and 1 point for each 100 games played in excess of 900 at catcher, second base or shortstop.

Adding up all of the points awarded by these rules, you class the player according to the following scale:

76 or higher	5 (All-Time Great)
46–75	4 (Major Star)
26–45	3 (Marginal Hall of Famer)
11–25	2 (Minor Star)
1–10	1 (Good Ballplayer)

There is also a special rule that all Hall of Famers are considered to be at least "threes."

The point awards for pitchers are as follows:

Wins MVP or Cy Young Award (5 points).

Leads league in Wins, Winning Percentage, Strikeouts or ERA (3 points).

Saves 30 or more games (3 points).

Wins 18 or more games/not leading league (2 points).

Has 200 strikeouts (2 points).

Saves 20–29 games (2 points).

Leads leagues in Games, Innings Pitched, Shutouts, Complete Games, or saves with a total of 10–19 (1 point).

In addition, pitchers get 1 point for each 10 wins above 80 and 1 point for each 10 saves above 130.

The scale by which these are changed to a "star ranking" is the same as for non-pitchers.

The ten highest totals for players coming up since 1900, if you're curious, belong to Babe Ruth (159), Walter Johnson (152), Stan Musial (145), Ty Cobb (142), Henry Aaron (137), Lou Gehrig (132), Willie Mays (117), Ted Williams (116), Lefty Grove (115), and Rogers Hornsby (113). Ruth had 147 as a hitter, making him the highest-ranking non-pitcher of all time, and also had 12 as a pitcher, which would classify him as a minor star on that level. He was the only player to earn points both as a hitter and as a pitcher.

How Similarity Scores Are Figured

To figure the "degree of similarity" between two players, you start by recording (or reading in) for each player his games played, at bats, runs, hits, doubles, triples, home runs, runs batted in, walks drawn, strikeouts, stolen bases, age, and defensive position.

From this basic data, you should calculate batting average, slugging percentage, runs created, and runs created per 25 outs.

If the two players were identical in every respect, their similarity score would be 1,000. For each difference between them, you deduct a penalty. There is a penalty for each 5 difference in games played, so if one player plays 145 games and the other 135, that's a 2-point penalty. All penalties have a minus sign, so that if one player has 20 more at bats than another (−1) but the second player has five more hits (−1), the sum is −2; the two do *NOT* cancel each other out. Exactly what these penalties are must be adjusted to the needs of the study, but as a general rule I use penalties something like this:

1 point for each 5 games played.

1 point for each 20 at bats.

1 point for each 3 runs scored.

1 point for each 5 hits.

1 point for each 1.5 doubles (or 2 points for 3 doubles).

1 point for each triple.

2 points for each home run.

1 point for each 3 RBI.

1 point for each 8 walks.

1 point for each 20 strikeouts.

1 point for each 4 stolen bases.

1 point for each .001 difference in batting average.

1 point for each .002 difference in slugging percentage.

14 points for each year of difference in age.

1 point for each 3 run difference in runs created.

1 point for each .05 difference in runs created per game.

To allow for differing defensive positions, what I do is assign "position values" which go Catcher—10; Shortstop—8, Second Base—7; Center Field—5; Third Base—4; Right Field—3; Left Field—2; First Base—1; Designated Hitter—0; and then subtract 3 points for each point of difference in position value. If you're comparing a first baseman to a left fielder, that's a 3-point penalty, which is not too significant, but if you're comparing a first basemen to a center fielder, that's a 12-point penalty, which is tremendously significant when selecting comparisons in which the sum of all differences usually can be no larger than 30 to 50. Catchers are closest to shortstops (−6) and second basemen (−9), but since catchers almost never have batting records similar to those of shortstops and second basemen (they are usually more similar to first basemen and left fielders as hitters if they can hit), this in effect causes catchers to stand out by themselves, rarely being compared to anybody except other catchers.

These values have to be tinkered with constantly, for many reasons. If you're trying to compare catchers as hitters with shortstops—since shortstops tend to be much faster than catchers—you might need to increase the penalties for triples and stolen bases to keep speed differences from leaking into the study. If you're comparing first basemen to shortstops, then—because first basemen tend to be much better hitters than shortstops—you might need to increase the penalties for home runs, slugging percentage, runs created and runs created per game to keep the difference in power from leaking into the study.

If you're comparing players with good and poor strikeout-to-walk ratios, then—in addition to reversing the signs for strikeouts and walks, counting differences here to be positives rather than negatives—you might want to increase slightly the weight given to these, so as to cause the separation in strikeouts and walks to be larger.

In many cases a difference in age or defensive position may be completely irrelevant to what you are studying, so you would just block those penalties out. In what I am studying here—growth and development of groups of hitters—age is tremendously important, so there is a huge penalty for differences in age, which causes most of the players selected as similar to be the same age, and almost all of those who are of different ages to be different by only one year. For most other studies you wouldn't use such a heavy penalty for age differences.

When you make one factor more important, you are in effect making all the other elements of similarity less important. Since there are precious few identical twins playing in the majors, you have to search for the *most* similar you can find in a limited data set. Demanding more similarity in one respect means accepting less in all other respects.

The degree of similarity that you can get depends heavily on how large the data sample is. If you have 100 players in a group, you have 5,050 potential comparisons. With almost 500 players in our data base, we have over 100,000 potential comparisons, but how many of those will be useful depends on how many ways the pie has to be sliced. When studying something like black/white differences, the pie only has to be sliced 3 ways, so we have over 300 white regulars and over a hundred black regulars. Three hundred times a hundred is 30,000, so we have comfortably more than 30,000 comparisons, and we only have to use the very best of those comparisons, maybe one-third of one percent, to get the sample size that we need. That being the case, you can set the similarity standard up at 960 or something, and get very comparable players. But if you have to slice the pie ten ways—studying defensive positions, for example—then you might be comparing 50 players with 50 players, which means only 2,500 possible "matches," which means that you need to use 2% of them to make your study, which means that you have to set the similarity standard maybe as low as 925.

It's not a magic method, but a utilitarian method. You do what works, and exercise care to see that it is working.

How the "Age Lines" Are Derived

The 61% home run advantage for 20-year-olds as compared to 21-year-olds is derived in this way. First, the 20-year-olds are compared to the 21-year-olds, the 22-year-olds, the 23-year-olds, etc. The 20-year-olds hit 66% more homers than the 21-year-olds, who I am from now on going to call "the 21s." The 20s hit 94% more homers than the 22s, 139% more home runs than the 23s, 174% more than the 24s, 493% more than the 25s, etc.

Second, these figures are expressed along a single line, which states the full home run potential of a 20-year-old as "1,000" and everything else as a percentage thereof. This creates a "home run ratio line", which looks like this:

20	21	22	23	24	25
1,000	601	516	419	365	169

and which states the relationships explained before.

In this way, we can use the comparisons to the 20-year-olds not only to compare the 20s to the other ages, but also to compare, for example, 23 to 24. That is, since 20-year-olds hit 174% more homers than comparable 24-year-olds, but only

139% more than the 23-year-olds, we can estimate in this way that the 23-year-olds have 15% greater career development than comparable 24-year-olds. This, of course, is only one of many comparisons between the 23- and 24-year-olds.

Then the same thing is done with the comparisons based on 21-year-olds. That is, 21-year-olds are compared not only to 20-year-olds but also to 22s, 23s, 24s, etc. This time we state those relationships on the basis of the 21-year-olds being assumed to be 1,000:

20	21	22	23	24	25
1664	1000	756	710	470	349

This line is then adjusted to reduce the 20s back down to the level of a thousand, so that the estimates which are derived from the various ages can be easily combined. This creates:

20	21	22	23	24	25
1000	601	454	426	282	210

By combining the line estimates from age 20, age 21, etc., we have a whole series of estimates of how much difference there is between the development potential of comparable players at each age. In adding them together, we naturally and appropriately weight each of those estimates evenly except that the direct comparison counts twice as much as the others.

I hope you understand that; maybe sometime you can explain it to me. Anyway, the estimate that 20-year-olds will go on to hit 61% more homers than comparable 21-year-olds is based upon comparisons not only of 20 to 21, but of players at each age to players at every other age within the range of the study (20 through 28. There aren't enough players to go any further).

List of Rookies with Comparable Records at Different Ages

20 and 22: Ron Fairly and Elliott Maddox, Curt Flood and Tommy Harper, Joe Torre and Chris Chambliss, Willie Mays and Billy Conigliaro, Eddie Mathews and Ron Hansen, Boog Powell and John Milner

20 and 23: Hank Aaron and Al Oliver, Buddy Bell and Dave Johnson, Rick Manning and Tommy Umphlett, Eddie Mathews and Bobby Murcer, Johnny Bench and Ernie Banks, Tony Kubek and Rick Burleson

20 and 24: Johnny Bench and Bill Virdon, Roberto Clemente and Leon Roberts, Buddy Bell and Jerry Adair, Boog Powell and Harry Agganis, Rick Manning and Jim Busby, Curt Flood and Jim Davenport

20 and 26: Boog Powell and Leroy Stanton, Frank Robinson and Al Rosen, Joe Torre and Hank Bauer

20 and 27: Willie Mays and Don Lenhardt, Roberto Clemente and Johnny Blatnik, Rick Manning and Dave Lopes

20 and 28: Curt Flood and Cal Neeman, Roberto Clemente and Pete Castiglione, Rick Manning and Solly Hemus

21 and 22: Jose Cardenal and Jim Lefebvre, Dan Driessen and Paul Smith, Gene Freese and Gary Maddox, Larry Parrish and Ron Hunt, Darrell Porter and Danny Walton

21 and 23: Gus Bell and Lee Walls, Bill Buckner and Rick Burleson, Tommy Davis and Sammy White, Bill Freehan and Don Young, Roy Howell and Owen Friend, Richie Hebner and Thurman Munson

21 and 24: Curt Blefary and Roy Foster, George Brett and Jerry Coleman, Gary Carter and Bill Virdon, Jim Spencer and Paul

Casanova, Willie Davis and Willie Kirkland, Whitey Lockman and Tom Tresh

21 and 25: Rod Carew and Jim Finigan, Bob Coluccio and Bill Serena, Tim McCarver and Clint Courtney, Richie Hebner and Manny Sanguillen, Greg Luzinski and Bob Nieman, Carlos May and Johnny Orsino, Carl Yastrzemski and Rip Repulski

21 and 26: José Cardenal and Willie Tasby, Gary Carter and Joe Hague, Dwight Evans and Jim Marshall, Bill Freehan and Leroy Stanton, Rick Monday and Bob Oliver

21 and 27: Curt Blefray and Don Lenhardt, Whitey Lockman and Ed Charles, Roy Howell and Chuck Hinton

21 and 28: George Brett and Solly Hemus, Bill Buckner and Ken Retzer, Roy Howell and Cal Neeman, Jim Spencer and Joe Koppe

22 and 23: Luis Aparicio and Ted Sizemore, Chico Carrasquel and Albie Pearson, Bucky Dent and Hal Jeffcoat, Ron Hansen and Bill Melton, Mike Ivie and Charley Smith, Jim King and Don Baylor, Elliott Maddox and Don Young, John Milner and Jim Pagliaroni, Paul Smith and Rick Burleson, Reggie Smith and Pedro Garcia, Bill White and Nate Colbert

22 and 24: Milt Bolling and Alan Gallagher, Barry Foote and Ramon Webster, Tito Francona and Leon Roberts, Mike Ivie and Frank House, Jim King and Kent Hadley, Garry Maddox and Lee May, Jim Lefebvre and Gil Hodges, Ron Hunt and George Vico

22 and 25: Billy Conigliaro and Harry Anderson, Bucky Dent and Eddie Kasko, Tito Francona and Chuck Harrison, Tommy Harper and Ted Savage, Mike Hershberger and Cesar Tovar, Mike Ivie and Leo Posada, Hector Lopez and Gene Green, Roger Maris and Bill Wilson

22 and 26: Luis Aparicio and Marv Breeding, Don Buddin and Tom Hutton, Tommy Harper and Gail Hopkins, Mike Hershberger and Ron Theobald, Alan Gallagher and Joe Amalfitano, Bob Skinner and Willie Tasby

22 and 27: Mike Hershberger and Don Buford, Tommy Harper and Chuck Hinton, Barry Foote and Johnny Blatnik

22 and 28: Tommy Harper and Joe Koppe, Joe Adcock and Ken Retzer, Milt Bolling and Ed McGhee

23 and 24: Don Baylor and Ramon Webster, Brian Downing and Mike Epstein, Dick Green and Jerry Adair, Hal Jeffcoat and Jerry Coleman, Nippy Jones and Harry Agganis, Gil McDougald and Larry Doby, Tony Perez and Andre Thornton, Charley Smith and Gil Hodges

23 and 25: Ernie Banks and Randy Jackson, Rick Burleson and Sammy White, Dan Ford and Gene Green, Jerry Adair and Bob Boone, Thurman Munson and Jim Finigan, Al Oliver and Bob Nieman, Jim Pagliaroni and Bob Schmidt, Jim Sundberg and Jimmy Stewart

23 and 26: Steve Braun and Tom Hutton, Nate Colbert and Ken Hunt, Dick Green and Leroy Stanton, Ted Sizemore and Marv Breeding, Charley Smith and George Altman, Bill Sudakis and Willie Tasby, Jose Tarbabull and Don Landrum

23 and 27: Albie Pearson and Dave Lopes, Billy Williams and Don Lenhardt, Lou Brock and Johnny Blatnik, Steve Braun and Don Buford

23 and 28: Steve Braun and Alex Grammas, Lou Brock and Joe Koppe, Rick Burleson and Toby Atwell, Dave Johnson and Pete Castiglione

24 and 25: Roy Foster and Sam Bowens, Frank House and Leo Posada, Randy Hundley and Billy Cowan, Leon Roberts and Chuck Harrison, Tom Tresh and Jim Greengrass, George Vico and Bob Boone, Bill Virdon and Randy Jackson, Ramon Webster and Bob Schmidt

24 and 26: Harry Agganis and George Altman, Paul Casanova and Bob Oliver, John Donaldson and Joe Amalfitano, Mike Epstein and Jim Marshall, Joe Ginsberg and Gail Hopkins, Gil Hodges and Willie Tasby, Leon Roberts and Leroy Stanton, Bill Virdon and Pancho Herrera

24 and 27: Joe Ginsburgh and Chuck Hinton, Billy Grabarkewitz and Ed Charles, Syd O'Brien and Joe Collins, Paul Casanova and Johnny Blatnik

24 and 28: Steve Boros and Pete Castiglione, Ed Fitzgerald and Ed McGhee, Pat Kelly and Joe Koppe, Leon Roberts and Cal Neeman

25 and 26: Lenny Green and Jim Marshall, Tommie Helms and Billy Klaus, Jim Hickman and George Altman, Bob Nieman and Pancho Herrera, Ted Savage and Gail Hopkins

25 and 27: Ted Savage and Chuck Hinton, Cesar Tovar and Don Buford, Jim Greengrass and Ed Charles

25 and 28: Chuck Harrison and Cal Neeman, Clint Courtney and Toby Atwell, Eddie Kasko and Alex Grammas

26 and 27: Pancho Herrera and Ed Charles, Tom Hutton and Don Buford, Jim Marshall and Joe Collins

SECTION
II

TEAM COMMENTS

INTRODUCTION TO TEAM COMMENTS

In the second part of this book, there are comments about each team, and then there's some data. In writing the team comments this year, I decided to do something different, which was to actually write about the team. Most of the time, as I've said, I discuss issues; the team comment about the San Francisco Giants usually is actually a discussion about some issue which relates in some way to the San Francisco Giants. This year, I decided to write a two-page (2000- to 2200-word) comment about each team that would explore some of the fundamental questions about the team: If they were successful in 1986, why were they successful? If they were unsuccessful, why were they unsuccessful? What were the key decisions that gave shape to the season? What are their chances of winning the division in 1986? What did the manager contribute? How was the infield? How was the outfield? At what part of the year were they successful? When did they play themselves out of or into the race? In what respects were they outstanding, and in what respects must they improve?

It is normal for a sports publication to deal with those sorts of questions, and I guess that's why I don't ordinarily do it. It is my belief that it's impossible to write about the same things that everybody else is writing about without winding up saying the same things that everybody else is saying. The other side of that is that the tools of sabermetrics, which are developed to analyze success and failure in baseball, are not of any use unless you actually try to analyze the success or failure of a team. I probably won't do it again, but I thought just this once I would apply some of the tools of sabermetrics and some of my own dimsights and reflections to the fundamental questions about each team.

In addition, in some cases (about half, I think) I wrote other pieces that sort of relate to the team, like the team comments that I usually write, and ran them after the stat-work. Well, enough about the comments; you can read.

There are three kinds of reference material which pollute the pages of the second section of this book, the three kinds being the division sheets, the player data boxes, and the pitcher data boxes.

DIVISION SHEETS

The division sheets, which appear at the start of each division, contain six charts. The first chart breaks down the team's won-lost record into ten components—the won-lost record the first half and second half of the season, the won-lost record against right-handed and left-handed

pitching, the won-lost record at home and on the road, the won-lost record on grass fields and on artificial turf, and the won-lost record in day games and at night.

The second chart gives the team's complete batting record, while the third gives the batting records of their opponents. The elements of the batting record, for those of you who are comparatively new to this, are Games Played (G), At Bats (AB), Runs Scored (Run), Hits (Hit), Total Bases (TB), Doubles (2B), Triples (3B), Home Runs (HR), Runs Batted In (RBI), Game-Winning RBI (GW), Sacrifice Hits (SH), Sacrifice Flies (SF), Hit By Pitch (HB), Walks Drawn (TBB, for Total Bases on Balls), Intentional Walks (IBB), Strikeouts (SO), Stolen Bases (SB), Caught Stealing (CS), Double Plays (DP), Runners Left On Base (LOB), Shutouts (ShO), Batting Average (Avg.), Slugging Percentage (Slug), and On Base Percentage (OBP).

The fourth chart gives the team's complete pitching record, and the fifth gives the pitching records of the team's opponents. The categories of the pitching record are Wins (W), Losses (L), Earned Run Average (ERA), Games (G), Complete Games (CG), Shutouts (ShO), Saves (SV), Innings Pitched (IP), Hits Allowed (Hit), Total Batters Faced (TBF), Runs Allowed (Run), Earned Runs Allowed (ER), Home Runs Allowed (HR), Sacrifice Hits Allowed (SH), Sacrifice Flies Allowed (SF), Hit Batsmen (HB), Walks (TBB), Intentional Walks (IBB), Strikeouts (SO), Wild Pitches (WP), and Balks (BK).

Of course, on these four charts a good deal of data is presented twice. Sometimes the same data will be on club batting and opposition pitching. The Mets had 1,462 hits, which means that opposing pitchers *allowed* 1,462 hits. Sometimes the same data will show up on club pitching and opposition pitching. The Mets pitchers won 108 games, which means that opposition pitchers lost 108 games. Altogether I think there are 22 pieces of information which are duplicated on two of these charts.

I think it's a useful form in which to present the info, anyway, for two reasons. First, there's a certain amount of batting data that doesn't show up in the hitting record, but that does show up in the record of opposition pitchers, and there's a certain amount of pitching data that doesn't show up in the pitching record, but does show up in the opposition batting. The Cardinals benefitted from 41 opposition balks. This will probably be the only place you can go to find that out.

Second, it's very useful to learn to think of a team's batting record as being the record of opposition pitchers (which it is) or the record of pitchers as being the same as the record of the opposing batters. An understanding of the circular nature of baseball statistics is the key that makes it possible to use baseball statistics to understand baseball itself. I've written about it a million times, but it's something a lot of people still don't *know;* they read it, and they think they understand it, but then they forget that it is at the heart of understanding anything else, so that you still get people saying that baseball is 75% pitching, which is like saying that when you clap your hands the right hand makes 75% of the noise, or you still get people insisting that the players of the thirties were better players than those of the fifties because they hit for higher averages, because they haven't really understood that wins and losses and therefore winning and losing are exactly the same thing, merely looked at from a different point of view, and that hitting and pitching are the same thing, merely looked at differently. It is the fusion of these efforts into a single act which creates their existence. It is batting which distinguishes pitching from merely throwing a baseball, just as it is the g which makes gout out of out.

So anyway, presenting the records in this form is just another way to help people learn to see baseball statistics for what they are. The sixth and final chart is a chart of fielding records. The elements of the fielding record are Games Played (G), Putouts (PO), Assists (A), Errors (E), Total Chances (TC), Double Plays (DP), Triple Plays (TP), Opposition Stolen Bases (OSB), Opposition Caught Stealing (OCS), Opposition Stolen Base Percentage (OSB%), Outfield Assists (OA), Sacrifice Flies Allowed (SFA), Fielding Percentage (Pct), Defensive Efficiency Record (DER), and Opposition Runs (OR).

PLAYER DATA BOXES

For ten players on each team, there is a box of data. The top line in the chart presents the player's career record in seasonal notation. Let's take Gary Carter, since he's the first player listed. The first thing it says there is "10.43 years." Gary Carter has played 1,689 major league games, which is the same as playing a 162-game schedule 10.43 times—hence, 10.43 years.

The rest of the stats given are Gary Carter's performance totals *per 162 games*. Gary Carter has batted 6,063 times in 1,689 games, which is 582 at bats per 162 games.

Per 162 games, he has had 158 hits including 28 doubles, 2 triples and 26 homers. Per 162 games he has scored 81 runs and driven in 96. Per 162 games, he has drawn 65 walks, struck out 73 times, stolen 3 bases and been nabbed for burglary 3 times. His career batting average is .271.

On the line that comes next is the 1986 contribution to these career accomplishments. Below that, the box tells what the player did in the first half and second half of the season, what he has done against right-handed and left-handed pitchers, what he has done at home and on the road, and what he has hit on grass fields and on artificial turf.

PITCHER DATA BOXES

The top three lines of a pitcher data box give three pieces of miscellaneous data relating to the starts a pitcher has made. Those are:

1) The number of runs scored in the games which the pitcher has started. Ron Darling in 1985 made 35 starts, in which the Mets scored 144 runs, or 4.11 per game. In 1986 he made 34 starts, in which the Mets scored 167 runs. In his career he has made 107 starts, in which the Mets have scored 470 runs, or 4.39 per game.

The purpose of figuring this stuff is to enable the reader to evaluate the offensive impact on the won/lost record. Danny Jackson went just 11–12, and with his offensive help, Dwight Gooden would have gone 11–12, too.

2) The number of double plays turned in the games the pitcher has started.

3) The number of bases stolen in the games the pitcher has started.

With the development of *Project Scoresheet,* better information about these issues is becoming available, and it's about time for me to stop carrying it. This book shows that in the 34 games Ron Darling started, Met opponents stole 33 bases. The *Great American Baseball Stat Book* shows that *while Darling was actually pitching,* opponents stole 24 bases and were caught stealing 15 times, which is much better information. So obviously, I should phase out the old form.

The bottom nine lines of the pitchers box (in the National League) present breakdowns of the last two seasons, which you can figure out for yourself. The American League data is different this year, but it, too, is pretty self-explanatory.

NATIONAL LEAGUE EAST
DIVISION SHEET

	1st	2nd	RHP	LHP	Home	Road	Grass	Turf	Day	Night	Total	Pct
New York	59-25	49-29	62-32	46-22	55-26	53-28	77-37	31-17	42-19	66-35	108-54	.667
Philadelphia	42-43	44-32	59-54	27-21	49-31	37-44	18-24	68-51	27-28	59-47	86-75	.534
St. Louis	36-50	43-32	53-52	26-30	42-39	37-43	15-26	64-56	26-30	53-52	79-82	.491
Montreal	46-38	32-45	56-51	22-32	36-44	42-39	20-22	58-61	25-28	53-55	78-83	.484
Chicago	36-48	34-42	48-71	22-19	42-38	28-52	54-59	16-31	52-55	18-35	70-90	.438
Pittsburgh	35-50	29-48	41-60	23-38	31-50	33-48	16-26	48-72	20-28	44-70	64-98	.395

CLUB BATTING

	G	AB	Run	Hit	TB	2B	3B	HR	RBI	GW	SH	SF	HP	TBB	IB	SO	SB	CS	DP	LOB	SHO	Avg	Slug	OBP
New York	162	5558	783	1462	2229	261	31	148	730	102	75	53	31	631	68	968	118	48	122	1192	4	.263	.401	.339
Philadelphia	161	5483	739	1386	2192	266	39	154	696	82	66	51	40	589	70	1154	153	59	98	1151	7	.253	.400	.327
St. Louis	161	5378	601	1270	1756	216	48	58	550	69	108	46	20	568	69	905	262	78	83	1129	13	.236	.327	.309
Montreal	161	5508	637	1401	2086	255	50	110	602	73	53	42	33	537	72	1016	193	95	113	1137	11	.254	.379	.322
Chicago	160	5499	680	1409	2186	258	27	155	638	64	54	51	15	508	56	966	132	62	113	1087	10	.256	.398	.318
Pittsburgh	162	5456	663	1366	2038	273	33	111	618	59	68	44	20	569	55	929	152	84	132	1100	10	.250	.374	.321

OPPOSITION BATTING

	G	AB	Run	Hit	TB	2B	3B	HR	RBI	GW	SH	SF	HB	TBB	IB	SO	SB	CS	DP	LOB	SHO	Avg	Slug	OBP
New York	162	5519	578	1304	1884	215	28	103	535	51	62	43	31	509	29	1083	159	56	110	1135	11	.236	.341	.302
Philadelphia	161	5562	713	1473	2198	267	34	130	659	68	58	47	22	553	71	874	216	70	119	1176	11	.265	.395	.331
St. Louis	161	5446	611	1364	2105	278	29	135	568	77	53	54	22	485	73	761	91	59	141	1051	4	.250	.387	.311
Montreal	161	5487	688	1350	2032	253	36	119	639	76	80	38	33	566	61	1051	200	54	100	1121	9	.246	.370	.318
Chicago	160	5551	781	1546	2348	295	39	143	732	87	76	45	19	557	78	962	132	102	111	1132	6	.279	.423	.344
Pittsburgh	162	5479	700	1397	2155	268	38	138	646	87	66	46	37	570	55	924	137	79	109	1149	9	.255	.393	.327

CLUB PITCHING

	W	L	ERA	G	CG	SHO	SV	IP	Hit	TBF	Run	ER	HR	SH	SF	HB	TBB	IB	SO	WP	BK
New York	108	54	3.11	162	27	11	46	1484.0	1304	6165	578	513	103	62	43	31	509	29	1083	40	16
Philadelphia	86	75	3.85	161	22	11	39	1451.2	1473	6244	713	621	130	58	47	22	553	71	874	45	17
St. Louis	79	82	3.37	161	17	4	46	1466.1	1364	6061	611	549	135	53	54	22	485	73	761	38	13
Montreal	78	83	3.78	161	15	9	50	1466.1	1350	6208	688	616	119	80	38	33	566	61	1051	49	20
Chicago	70	90	4.49	160	11	6	42	1445.0	1546	6248	781	721	143	76	45	19	557	78	962	55	20
Pittsburgh	64	98	3.90	162	17	9	30	1450.2	1397	6201	700	629	138	66	46	37	570	55	924	59	20

OPPOSITION PITCHING

	W	L	ERA	G	CG	SHO	SV	IP	Hit	TBF	Run	ER	HR	SH	SF	HB	TBB	IB	SO	WP	BK
New York	54	108	4.28	162	14	4	23	1458.0	1462	6349	783	693	148	75	53	31	631	68	968	44	8
Philadelphia	75	86	4.13	161	22	7	39	1446.1	1386	6229	739	663	154	66	51	40	589	70	1154	42	16
St. Louis	82	79	3.26	161	23	13	44	1464.0	1270	6122	601	530	58	108	46	20	568	69	905	40	41
Montreal	83	78	3.52	161	17	11	38	1466.2	1401	6174	637	574	110	53	42	33	537	72	1016	39	10
Chicago	90	70	3.85	160	19	10	36	1453.1	1409	6127	680	622	155	54	51	15	508	56	966	49	14
Pittsburgh	98	64	3.62	162	18	10	55	1467.0	1366	6164	663	590	111	68	44	20	569	55	929	49	9

CLUB FIELDING

Club	G	PO	A	E	TC	DP	TP	OSB	OCS	OSB%	OA/SFA	Pct	DER	OR
New York	162	4452	1781	138	6371	145	0	159	56	.740	34/43	.978	.707	578
Philadelphia	161	4355	1761	137	6253	157	0	216	70	.755	45/47	.978	.691	713
St. Louis	161	4399	1804	123	6326	178	0	91	59	.607	45/54	.981	.718	611
Montreal	161	4399	1787	133	6319	132	0	200	54	.787	41/38	.979	.702	688
Chicago	160	4335	1784	124	6243	147	1	132	102	.564	30/45	.980	.674	781
Pittsburgh	162	4352	1918	143	6413	134	0	137	79	.634	33/46	.978	.703	.700

NEW YORK METS

The New York Mets in 1986 had the talent and handled the pressure. Since leaping into contention in 1984—Dave Johnson's first season as manager—the Mets have consolidated their strengths and whittled away on their weaknesses. They opened the 1986 season as solid favorites to win the NL East, and broke away from the pack in the opening weeks of the campaign. By the end of May they had been virtually conceded the championship by fans, press, and opposition managers—at a point when they still had to go out and win another 60 or more games to convert that paper pennant into silk. Withering every challenge in its seminal stages, they managed gracefully the tricky task of *not losing* a race to which they had been granted premature title, so gracefully that the question of the tiger getting out of the cage never really came up. They were, in short, a great ballclub, and a beautiful demonstration of what talent can do when assembled with planning and guided by intelligence.

Where were the 1986 Mets so superior to the rest of the league? Of their four big stars (Hernandez, Carter, Gooden, and Strawberry) not one had a season that was 1% better than his normal effort, and as a group they were unmistakeably, if only slightly, below their expectations. No Met was a legitimate MVP candidate.

Yet if the Mets were conspicuously without a superstar, they were even more conspicuously without a weakness. Probably no team in the history of baseball has been above average at every position—but the Mets were as close as any team has come in maybe twenty years. They were below average only at shortstop and possibly in left field. The fourth starter was almost as good as the first, and the fifth not much worse than the fourth. The bullpen was strong on the left and ready on the right. Their strength was not the flashy front-line strength of a single talent in abundance, such as the speed of the 1985 Cardinals, nor the strength of a single player head and shoulders above the league, as the Cubs had in 1984. It was the gridlock, perfectly engineered, top-to-bottom strength of an organization that had tightened every bolt and welded every seam before the season began, building a machine capable of withstanding the tremendous pressure of a nation waiting for them to lose and a league that was doing everything possible to help them lose.

When did the Mets win? Whenever and wherever they took the field. They won at home and on the road with almost equal ease. They beat left-handers and right-handers at almost the same rate. They won on grass as easily as on turf, and on turf as easily as on grass. They won day games as often as at night. Like most good teams, they were markedly less effective in one-run games (just 29–20), but grew increasingly deadly as the margin widened.

In what areas of play were they outstanding? They led the league in both ERA and runs scored. If you focus on the offense, they led the league in two of the three most important basic categories (batting average and walks drawn) and missed by only a few of leading in the third (home runs). They led the league in both on-base percentage and slugging percentage. They out-hit their opponents .263–.236. They out-homered their opponents 148–103. They bested their opponents in doubles (261–215), triples (31–28), walks drawn (631–509), and positive strikeouts (1,083–968). Though they did not use the stolen base much and were vulnerable from a defensive standpoint (their opponents stole 159 bases to the Mets' 118), it could not be said that they lacked speed, in that all three outfielders and one infielder ran very well. There may never have been a pennant winner which had such an extraordinary balance of hitting and pitching.

The Mets were an unremarkable defensive team. Early in the season, with Carter not throwing well, Kevin Mitchell and Howard Johnson playing shortstop, and George Foster in left field, the Met defense was considered suspect. The Mets were outstanding defensively at only one position, first base, and suspect at three. With a big lead, Johnson switched to Santana full time at shortstop, a pennant race equivalent of the offense-for-defense switch that managers often make when leading in a game. The release of George Foster and the switch to Dykstra in center with Heep and Wilson in left further solidified the defense. In sum, the Mets fielded .978, exactly the league average, and turned 145 double plays, exactly the league average but a good total in view of the fact that the Mets had comparatively few opponents on base.

While the Mets had been a very good team, a 98-win team, in 1985, the 1986 Mets were not better merely by luck and maturity. The acquisition of 18-game winner Bob Ojeda from Boston for a package of farmhands is justly cited as a coup, but there were other important improvements. The addition of rookie Kevin Mitchell and the development of second-year player Lenny Dykstra into one of the best in the league at his position were of tremendous value. The trade for the much-maligned Tim Teufel was a necessary and productive move, not only because Teufel played well but because his platoon mate Wally Backman is a true platoon player. Backman plays so much on intensity and enthusiasm that the everyday grind has proven in the past to rob him of his most precious resource. In addition, he simply doesn't handle left-handers. With Teufel to share the load, Backman had his finest season.

The Met bench, with a combination of Heep, Hearn, Mitchell, Wilson, Teufel, and Johnson, was always loaded if not especially productive when called on to pinch hit. The availability of these players—more "alternatives" than "substitutes"—combined with the top-to-bottom strength of the lineup to spread the load and keep the pressure off of any one pair of shoulders. Whereas an injury to Strawberry had been deadly in 1985, the 1986 crew could absorb the loss of Strawberry or Carter or a slump by Hernandez or Gooden like a Mercedes running over a paper clip. They were, like a Mercedes, a tribute to their engineers.

The superior acumen of the Met management can be seen most clearly in the development of the infield. With the exception of Keith Hernandez, who has not been considered expendable since early 1983, all of the regular Met infielders have been considered expendable by somebody within the last three years. Second baseman Wally Backman had been returned to the minor leagues despite playing fairly well for the Mets in 1982; the previous Met management had focused on and exaggerated his field weaknesses. Shortstop Rafael Santana was released by the Cardinals in January of 1984. Third baseman Knight was acquired two years ago when his career seemed almost over. The Mets used these players to piece together not an impressive infield, but an intelligent and reliable infield where another organization might have had a glaring, gap-toothed mess.

But the most important acquisitions in the construction of the Met power machine have not been those which took advantage of the available talent, but those which took advantage of situations which were created by the internal dynamics of other organizations. While many baseball executives have fulminated about how difficult it is to make trades in the 1980s, the Mets have focused on exploiting those situations in which talented players became available because of personality clashes, financial pressures, disappointed owners and questionable talent judgments. It is these trades which are the backbone of the best team in baseball in 1986. A quick review:

June 15, 1983: Keith Hernandez became available from the Cardinals because Whitey Herzog thought he had lost his desire to excel and could be a liability in the battle against drugs. Mets liberated him in exchange for a couple of modest talents.

December 8, 1983: As Vin Scully tells it now, the Dodgers had to part with **Sid Fernandez** because they were desperate for a left-handed reliever. What was reported at the time was that the Dodgers thought Fernandez had gotten literally and figuratively too big for his britches, was hard to manage and was fooling minor leaguers by changing speeds and throwing slop, but wouldn't be anything special in the majors.

December 7, 1984: Howard Johnson became available from the Tigers because Sparky Anderson didn't like him and didn't think he would develop as a third baseman.

December 10, 1984: Gary Carter became available from the Expos because his salary was painful to the front office of a bitterly disappointed team, a team with more holes than a porcupine's underwear. The Mets put together a talent package to relieve the Expos of Carter's salary.

January 16, 1986: The Twins were anxious to get rid of **Tim Teufel** because Ray Miller didn't feel he was aggres-

sive enough or quick enough on the double play. The Mets agreed to accept him in exchange for token players.

All of these players were perceived by the managers who had them as *problems;* the Mets knew that they were the kind of problems that would solve themselves if the team won. Picking up the best of the "free talents," the Mets expand their talent base and are in a position to trade a package of players for a star when the opportunity arises. This off-season the Mets have also plucked Kevin Mc-Reynolds from San Diego, which would be precisely the same type of move.

In one case (George Foster, 1982) the Mets "took advantage" of a situation and got taken; in two others (Ron Darling and Bobby Ojeda) they made traditional good trades, just doing a better job of judging and projecting the talent than did the people with whom they were dealing. Several important farm system products have supplemented this run of good planning and provided additional trade fodder, but in the main the Mets have built themselves up simply by acting *logically* in situations in which other organizations were acting *emotionally.* Their winning edge is the advantage of being the only adult in the game.

Or perhaps the only Vulcan, the only computer. There are important parallels between the 1986 Mets and the best of the bad-boy Raider teams. Those teams were portrayed, as were the Mets, as driven by arrogance and bad manners. They were in fact merely supremely talented, their arrogance and bad manners being not accidental (for this is clearly a part of the pattern by which they were assembled), not incidental (for the team would lack definition without these features), but simply irrelevant once the game begins.

As magnificent as they are, the Mets may not find it easy to repeat in 1987, and then again they might. As often noted, there have been few repeaters in the eighties, but then it has escaped notice that the Mets are already the first team in the eighties to win 90 or more games in three straight seasons. (There were nine such streaks in the seventies, by Boston, the Yankees, Kansas City, Oakland, Los Angeles, Philadelphia, Pittsburgh, and the Orioles twice.) The only other team heading into 1987 with two straight is the Angels, who have just skimmed over 90 both times and have little chance of making it three.

The addition of Kevin McReynolds should help them repeat easily in 1987. If, on the other hand, they lose Danny Heep to free agency, if Howard Johnson doesn't continue to play well, if Gary Carter's bad knee explodes on him, if Sid Fernandez continues to put on weight and Bob Ojeda returns to a more normal 14–11 level . . . well, they'll survive any one of these, but they obviously couldn't survive too many of them. The Mets may not win the World Series in 1987, and they may not even win the division. But they deserve to be a heavy favorite. I would not be surprised if they were to lose in a close race, and I would not be surprised if the race was once again over by July.

Gary CARTER, Catcher

	G	AB	Hit	2B	3B	HR	Run	RBI	TBB	SO	SB	CS	Avg
10.43 years		582	158	28	2	26	81	96	65	73	3	3	.271
1986	132	490	125	14	2	24	81	105	62	63	1	0	.255
First Half	75	274	70	7	0	16	51	65	41	35	1		.255
Second Half	57	216	55	7	2	8	30	40	21	28	0		.255
Vs. RHP		319	78	9	2	14		72	25	47		0	.245
Vs. LHP		171	47	5	0	10		33	37	16		0	.275
Home		228	61	5	2	13		51	33	28		0	.268
Road		262	64	9	0	11		54	29	35		0	.244
Grass		312	82	7	2	19		73	41	41		0	.263
Turf		178	43	7	0	5		32	21	22		0	.242

Darryl STRAWBERRY, Right Field

	G	AB	Hit	2B	3B	HR	Run	RBI	TBB	SO	SB	CS	Avg
3.19 years		568	148	26	6	34	92	108	84	156	31	12	.260
1986	136	475	123	27	5	27	76	93	72	141	28	12	.259
First Half	73	255	76	22	2	13	47	46	44	69	20	6	.298
Second Half	63	220	47	5	3	14	29	47	28	72	8	6	.214
Vs. RHP		288	84	19	3	22		66	51	77			.292
Vs. LHP		187	39	8	2	5		27	21	64			.209
Home		211	48	11	1	11		33	30	68			.227
Road		264	75	16	4	16		60	42	73			.284
Grass		309	82	18	1	18		60	46	93			.265
Turf		166	41	9	4	9		33	26	48			.247

Keith HERNANDEZ, First Base

	G	AB	Hit	2B	3B	HR	Run	RBI	TBB	SO	SB	CS	Avg
10.62 years		573	173	35	5	12	91	85	86	75	9	5	.302
1986	149	551	171	34	1	13	94	83	94	69	2	1	.310
First Half	81	306	87	16	1	6	47	38	42	36	1	0	.284
Second Half	68	245	84	18	0	7	47	45	52	33	1	1	.343
Vs. RHP		333	103	22	1	9		57	62	38			.309
Vs. LHP		218	68	12	0	4		26	32	31			.312
Home		239	74	9	1	6		36	46	31			.310
Road		312	97	25	0	7		47	48	38			.311
Grass		372	119	19	1	11		62	66	49			.320
Turf		179	52	15	0	2		21	28	20			.291

Rafael SANTANA, Shortstop

	G	AB	Hit	2B	3B	HR	Run	RBI	TBB	SO	SB	CS	Avg
2.29 years		476	117	18	1	1	41	31	33	51	0	2	.245
1986	139	394	86	11	0	1	38	28	36	43	0	0	.218
First Half	69	183	30	4	0	0	16	9	16	26	0	0	.164
Second Half	70	211	56	7	0	1	22	19	20	17	0	0	.265
Vs. RHP		231	46	7	0	0		14	16	24			.199
Vs. LHP		163	40	4	0	1		14	20	19			.245
Home		191	36	6	0	0		15	21	25			.188
Road		203	50	5	0	1		13	15	18			.246
Grass		271	59	9	0	1		22	26	30			.218
Turf		123	27	2	0	0		6	10	13			.220

Wally BACKMAN, Second Base

	G	AB	Hit	2B	3B	HR	Run	RBI	TBB	SO	SB	CS	Avg
3.53 years		503	143	22	4	2	77	35	55	69	24	11	.285
1986	124	387	124	18	2	1	67	27	36	32	13	7	.320
First Half	58	203	67	11	1	0	39	11	17	13	8	5	.330
Second Half	66	184	57	7	1	1	28	16	19	19	5	2	.310
Vs. RHP		335	113	17	1	1		19	30	22			.337
Vs. LHP		52	11	1	1	0		8	6	10			.212
Home		179	56	6	1	1		9	19	12			.313
Road		208	68	12	1	0		18	17	20			.327
Grass		260	80	10	1	1		16	26	20			.308
Turf		127	44	8	1	0		11	10	12			.346

Mookie WILSON, Left Field

	G	AB	Hit	2B	3B	HR	Run	RBI	TBB	SO	SB	CS	Avg
4.94 years		611	169	25	10	8	91	50	34	101	48	15	.277
1986	123	381	110	17	5	9	61	45	32	72	25	7	.289
First Half	56	174	49	9	2	5	29	16	12	35	13	1	.282
Second Half	67	207	61	8	3	4	32	29	20	37	12	6	.295
Vs. RHP		185	53	11	0	6		22	16	35			.286
Vs. LHP		196	57	6	5	3		23	16	37			.291
Home		173	50	9	1	4		17	17	32			.289
Road		208	60	8	4	5		28	15	40			.288
Grass		262	82	11	4	6		35	23	43			.313
Turf		119	28	6	1	3		10	9	29			.235

Ray KNIGHT, Third Base

	G	AB	Hit	2B	3B	HR	Run	RBI	TBB	SO	SB	CS	Avg
7.65 years		518	144	30	3	9	54	65	37	60	2	3	.278
1986	137	486	145	24	2	11	51	76	40	63	2	1	.298
First Half	74	268	78	13	2	9	31	43	24	42	1	1	.291
Second Half	63	218	67	11	0	2	20	33	16	21	1	0	.307
Vs. RHP		288	69	9	1	2		40	29	46			.240
Vs. LHP		198	76	15	1	9		36	11	17			.384
Home		228	66	12	2	7		35	22	34			.289
Road		258	79	12	0	4		41	18	29			.306
Grass		326	98	18	2	7		50	32	47			.301
Turf		160	47	6	0	4		26	8	16			.294

Kevin MITCHELL, Utility

	G	AB	Hit	2B	3B	HR	Run	RBI	TBB	SO	SB	CS	Avg
0.71 years		482	132	31	3	17	72	62	46	90	4	6	.275
1986	108	328	91	22	2	12	51	43	33	61	3	3	.277
First Half	52	146	50	16	0	5	26	21	16	24	3	1	.342
Second Half	56	182	41	6	2	7	25	22	17	37	0	2	.225
Vs. RHP		129	30	6	1	5		16	17	32			.233
Vs. LHP		199	61	16	1	7		27	16	29			.307
Home		162	49	15	1	4		24	18	30			.302
Road		166	42	7	1	8		19	15	31			.253
Grass		234	66	17	1	7		30	25	48			.282
Turf		94	25	5	1	5		13	8	13			.266

Lenny DYKSTRA, Center Field

	G	AB	Hit	2B	3B	HR	Run	RBI	TBB	SO	SB	CS	Avg
1.42 years		470	132	25	7	6	82	45	62	56	32	6	.280
1986	147	431	127	27	7	8	77	45	58	55	31	7	.295
First Half	77	212	74	16	5	4	40	24	27	26	18	5	.349
Second Half	70	219	53	11	2	4	37	21	31	29	13	2	.242
Vs. RHP		328	103	21	7	8		36	40	35			.314
Vs. LHP		103	24	6	0	0		9	18	20			.233
Home		211	68	16	4	4		24	27	25			.322
Road		220	59	11	3	4		21	31	30			.268
Grass		301	93	22	5	4		29	37	38			.309
Turf		130	34	5	2	4		16	21	17			.262

Tim TEUFEL, Second Base

	G	AB	Hit	2B	3B	HR	Run	RBI	TBB	SO	SB	CS	Avg
2.52 years		538	141	32	3	12	71	59	63	76	2	3	.261
1986	93	279	69	20	1	4	35	31	32	42	1	2	.247
First Half	50	145	33	9	1	2	15	20	13	23	0	1	.228
Second Half	43	134	36	11	0	2	20	11	19	19	1	1	.269
Vs. RHP		83	21	6	0	1		9	10	20			.253
Vs. LHP		196	48	14	1	3		22	22	22			.245
Home		140	33	10	0	2		17	16	27			.236
Road		139	36	10	1	2		14	16	15			.259
Grass		194	47	11	0	3		22	24	34			.242
Turf		85	22	9	1	1		9	8	8			.259

Ron DARLING

	(W–L)	GS	Run	Avg	DP	Avg	SB	Avg
1985	(16-6)	35	144	4.11	34	.97	26	.74
1986	(15-6)	34	167	4.91	36	1.06	33	.97
1983-1986		107	470	4.39	101	.94	92	.86

	G	IP	W	L	Pct	ER	BB	SO	ERA
1985 HOME	21	148.3	9	5	.643	51	56	107	3.09
1986 HOME	16	118.3	10	2	.833	31	30	95	2.36
1985 Road	15	99.7	7	1	.875	29	58	60	2.62
1986 Road	18	118.7	5	4	.556	43	51	89	3.26
1985 Grass	29	196.7	13	6	.684	67	88	139	3.07
1986 Grass	23	162.7	12	3	.800	50	51	127	2.77
1985 Turf	7	51.3	3	0	1.000	13	26	28	2.28
1986 Turf	11	74.3	3	3	.500	24	30	57	2.91
1986 Total	34	237.0	15	6	.714	74	81	184	2.81

Bob OJEDA

	(W–L)	GS	Run	Avg	DP	Avg	SB	Avg
1985	(9-11)	22	84	3.82	23	1.05	8	.36
1985	(18-5)	30	145	4.83	32	1.07	37	1.23
1980-1986		143	671	4.69	153	1.07	107	.75

	G	IP	W	L	Pct	ER	BB	SO	ERA
1985 Home	21	97.7	4	7	.364	36	27	74	3.32
1986 Home	15	107.0	9	2	.818	34	23	81	2.86
1985 Road	18	60.0	5	4	.556	34	21	28	5.10
1986 Road	17	110.3	9	3	.750	28	29	67	2.28
1985 Grass	33	139.0	7	11	.389	62	43	95	4.01
1986 Grass	19	136.0	12	2	.857	42	32	101	2.78
1985 Turf	6	18.7	2	0	1.000	8	5	7	3.86
1986 Turf	13	81.3	6	3	.667	20	20	47	2.21
1986 Total	32	217.3	18	5	.783	62	52	148	2.57

Dwight GOODEN

	(W–L)	GS	Run	Avg	DP	Avg	SB	Avg
1985	(24-4)	35	171	4.89	33	.94	25	.71
1986	(17-6)	33	153	4.64	23	.70	34	1.03
1984-1986		99	439	4.43	68	.69	113	1.14

	G	IP	W	L	Pct	ER	BB	SO	ERA
1985 Home	18	144.0	13	2	.867	24	31	143	1.50
1986 Home	16	123.0	9	3	.750	30	42	103	2.20
1985 Road	17	132.7	11	2	.846	23	38	125	1.56
1986 Road	17	127.0	8	3	.727	49	38	97	3.47
1984 Grass	23	164.3	15	6	.714	47	58	215	2.57
1985 Grass	24	183.7	12	4	.750	53	60	152	2.60
1984 Turf	8	53.7	2	3	.400	16	15	61	2.68
1985 Turf	9	66.3	5	2	.714	26	20	48	3.53
1986 Total	33	250.0	17	6	.739	79	80	200	2.84

Rick AGUILERA

	(W–L)	GS	Run	Avg	DP	Avg	SB	Avg
1985	(10-7)	19	66	3.47	13	.68	10	.53
1986	(10-7)	20	100	5.00	18	.90	8	.40
1985-1986		39	166	4.26	31	.79	18	.46

	G	IP	W	L	Pct	ER	BB	SO	ERA
1985 Home	8	46.3	3	2	.600	11	12	35	2.14
1986 Home	15	67.7	5	2	.714	28	17	52	3.72
1985 Road	13	76.0	7	5	.583	33	25	39	3.91
1986 Road	13	73.7	5	5	.500	33	19	52	4.03
1985 Grass	12	70.0	5	2	.714	15	18	48	1.93
1986 Grass	21	104.0	7	5	.583	45	20	75	3.89
1985 Turf	9	52.3	5	5	.500	29	19	26	4.99
1986 Turf	7	37.3	3	2	.600	16	16	29	3.86
1986 Total	28	141.3	10	7	.588	61	36	104	3.88

Sid FERNANDEZ

	(W–L)	GS	Run	Avg	DP	Avg	SB	Avg
1985	(9-9)	26	105	4.04	23	.88	31	1.19
1986	(16-6)	31	160	5.16	23	.74	32	1.03
1984-1986		72	331	4.60	60	.83	84	1.17

	G	IP	W	L	Pct	ER	BB	SO	ERA
1985 Home	11	70.7	5	4	.556	21	34	90	2.67
1986 Home	16	107.7	8	3	.727	26	45	109	2.17
1985 Road	15	99.7	4	5	.444	32	46	90	2.89
1986 Road	16	96.7	8	3	.727	54	46	91	5.03
1985 Grass	18	115.3	7	5	.583	34	60	127	2.65
1986 Grass	22	143.3	10	5	.667	54	61	139	3.39
1985 Turf	8	55.0	2	4	.333	19	20	53	3.11
1986 Turf	10	61.0	6	1	.857	26	30	61	3.84
1986 Total	32	204.3	16	6	.727	80	91	200	3.52

OTHERS

	(W–L)	GS	Run	Avg	DP	Avg	SB	Avg
Berenyi	(2-2)	7	32	4.57	5	.71	10	1.43
Anderson	(2-1)	5	16	3.20	4	.80	3	.60
Mitchell	(0-1)	1	1	1.00	2	2.00	0	0.00
Niemann	(2-3)	1	9	9.00	2	2.00	0	0.00

RECORDS WITH DIFFERENT STARTING CATCHERS

Catcher	Inn	ER	W–L	ERA	GS	SB	Avg
Carter	1091.0	371	77-42	3.06	119	115	.97
Hearn	328.0	130	24-12	3.57	36	33	.92
Gibbons	47.0	11	5-0	2.11	5	5	1.00
Lyons	18.0	1	2-0	.50	2	6	3.00

RUNS CREATED AND OPPOSITION RUNS CREATED

Something that I usually do somewhere in the book is present the runs created estimates for each major league team. The logic of the runs created method is that runs scored tend to be a relatively predictable outcome of individual acts such as singles, doubles, and walks. The generic formula for runs created is (Times on Base) Times (Advancement Bases) Divided by (Opportunity) Equals Runs. However, for the runs created formulas to have credibility, it is essential that they work, and that the reader have a fair opportunity to make his own judgment about how well they work. To accomplish that, I usually run the runs created formula (which is in the appendix), and the complete statistics for each team (which are on the division sheets), and the runs created estimates for each team in comparison with their actual runs scored, which I will do now.

This time, I'm going to run them in order of the disparity between runs created and actual runs.

	Runs Created	Actual Runs	
Oakland	700	731	+31
White Sox	614	644	+30
San Francisco	674	698	+24
California	765	786	+21
Cincinnati	712	732	+20
St. Louis	584	601	+17
Toronto	796	809	+13
Seattle	706	718	+12
Mets	773	783	+10
Pittsburgh	654	663	+9
Texas	762	771	+9
Cleveland	822	831	+9
Boston	792	794	+2
Baltimore	708	708	0
Philadelphia	739	739	0
Los Angeles	639	638	−1
Houston	668	654	−14
Minnesota	756	741	−15
Milwaukee	682	667	−15
San Diego	671	656	−15
Detroit	814	798	−16
Cubs	697	680	−17
Kansas City	683	654	−29
Atlanta	646	615	−31
Montreal	676	637	−39
Yankees	843	797	−46

I think you can see that there's obviously a very strong correlation between runs scored and runs created by a team. Of the 26 runs created estimates, 11 are within 2% of the actual runs, 19 are within 3%, and 23 within 5%. The largest percentage discrepancy is for Montreal, which would have been expected to score 676 runs, but actually scored only 637 because they were using the best leadoff hitter in the history of the National League as a third-place hitter. That, of course, is speculative.

The average error of the 26 estimates is 17; the standard error is 20.6, as contrasted with a standard deviation for runs scored of 68.

There were a total of 18,545 runs scored in the majors in 1986. The total of the team estimates is 18,576, a net discrepancy of 31, or one-sixth of one percent. The gross discrepancy is 445, or two and a half percent. This is a fairly normal performance for the runs created method.

There are many things which can create a discrepancy between expected runs by the run created method and actual runs scored. The primary things that I could identify would include:

1) Exceptionally poor or exceptionally good hitting with runners on base and in scoring position.

2) Baserunning errors or effective baserunning.

3) Exceptionally poor or exceptionally good lineup design.

4) An unusual number of opponent's errors.

5) Doing a particularly good or a particularly poor job of advancing runners with outs.

6) Luck, which would usually be expressed as unusual performance in one of the previous five areas.

We expect, with *Project Scoresheet,* to learn to distinguish among these various effects, and thus to develop runs-created methods which will reduce the standard error to almost nothing. However, it is important to note that 1) all of these factors, taken together, do not create huge discrepancies from the current estimates; and 2) to the extent that teams do exceed (or fall short of) runs created estimates in one year, they tend to relapse (or improve) in the next year. Although the A's may have scored 31 runs more than one would expect in view of their hitter's individual accomplishments in 1986, it is not likely that they will do the same in 1987. The tendency usually does not carry over from season to season, as it would if it were created by a skill, but tends to disappear, as it would if it were primarily created by luck.

I once believed, and wrote, that the primary cause of deviations from expected runs was opposition errors. I now realize that this is not correct, that opposition errors are one factor but no more than that. The Kansas City Royals did score 29 runs fewer than expected in part because their opponents committed only 117 errors, the fewest of any American League team. However, the Orioles benefitted from the most opposition errors, 180, and did not exceed their expected runs.

In line with the comments in the introduction to this section about the circular nature of baseball statistics, it occurred to me that I should run the runs created estimated for team defenses, too—that is, for opposition batting records. There is no obvious reason that the same formula shouldn't work for opponents batting records as well as for batting records, inasmuch as it's the same thing seen from a different standpoint, but one could make up a reason why it might not work and I've never really checked to see that it did.

It does. The chart to the right compares the runs created by each team's opponents with the runs allowed by the team.

For 1986, at least, the runs created formula actually worked better from a defensive standpoint than from an offensive standpoint. While the standard deviation of runs allowed was a little higher (70 as opposed to 68), the average error for opposition runs created was less than 15, and the standard error was 18.7.

It is interesting to note that the Red Sox allowed 37 runs fewer than one would expect in view of their hits and walks allowed. This might suggest that the Red Sox were somewhat lucky from a defensive standpoint, and that they might have a tough time keeping their ERA down in 1987. Since we know that deviations from offensive runs created tend to wash out from year to year, we would expect that deviations from defensive runs created would do the same. However, this has not been proven.

	Runs Created	Actual Runs	
California	636	684	+48
San Francisco	594	618	+24
Oakland	740	760	+20
Atlanta	704	719	+15
Montreal	676	688	+12
Cleveland	831	841	+10
Kansas City	664	673	+9
Milwaukee	725	734	+9
Los Angeles	671	679	+8
Cincinnati	711	717	+6
White Sox	694	699	+5
Texas	739	743	+4
Yankees	735	738	+3
Baltimore	759	760	+1
Houston	569	569	0
Toronto	736	733	−3
Mets	586	578	−8
Pittsburgh	711	700	−11
San Diego	738	723	−15
Detroit	729	714	−15
Cubs	797	781	−16
Seattle	853	835	−18
Minnesota	865	839	−26
St. Louis	640	611	−29
Philadelphia	743	713	−30
Boston	733	696	−37

PHILADELPHIA PHILLIES

Runners on Base:	2.015
Opponents on base:	2.048
Net Disadvantage:	−33
Won/Lost Record:	86−75

One could get the impression that the Philadelphia Phillies were the world's biggest believers in the concept of secondary average. I'm not suggesting that they use the *term* secondary average, nor that they are believers in the precise definition or statistical method that I employ to arrive at what I call secondary average: after all, I just made that stuff up a year ago, and the Phillies have been building this way for three or four years. But the Phillies for the last 14 seasons have been the beneficiaries of the remarkable talents of one Michael Jack Schmidt, a man who, despite a career batting average of just .268, has buried his once-numerous critics under an avalanche of accomplishments, becoming generally recognized as the greatest third baseman ever to play the game.

Perhaps as a consequence, an idea seems to have taken root in the Philadelphia front office that you can build a powerful offense and a solid defense out of players that another organization might not regard as talented, if you will just accept a low batting average and concentrate on the other things that cause runs to pop up on the scoreboard. The Phillies in 1986 hit just .253 as a team (eighth in the league), yet they scored 739 runs (second in the league) because their players get so many extra base hits, draw so many walks and steal so many bases (with few enough caught stealing) that they are able to get runs across the plate without many hits. A few examples, remembering that secondary averages have the same "center" as batting averages.

First baseman Von Hayes hit .305, but also hit for power (46 doubles and 19 homers), drew walks (74, ninth in the league) and stole 24 bases. Secondary average: .336.

Second baseman Juan Samuel hits just .266, but with over 40% of his hits for extra bases and 42 stolen bases. Secondary average: .298.

Third baseman Mike Schmidt hit .290 and loaded the average with 37 homers and 89 walks. Secondary average: .420.

Shortstop Steve Jeltz hit just .219, but contributed offensively with 65 walks. His secondary average of .205 is decent for a shortstop (consider Garry Templeton, .149, Craig Reynolds, .174, Rafael Santana, .124, Rafael Ramirez, .177, and Kurt Stillwell, .159).

Left fielder Gary Redus, who walks, has power and steals bases, had a secondary average of .397.

Outfielder Ron Roenicke, a tremendously disciplined hitter with a little power and a little speed, had a secondary average of .338.

And catcher Darren Daulton, who draws an obscene number of walks, went out in June with a secondary average of .493.

The Phillies team secondary average was .282, the highest in the league; the league secondary average was .255, two points higher than the league batting average.

Because of the walks, the Phillies were eighth in the league in batting average, but second in the number of runners on base. Because of the power and speed, the percentage of Philadelphia runners who scored was also the second-highest in the league (36.7%), and narrowly missed being the highest in the league (the Mets scored 36.9% of their baserunners).

From this combination, the Phillies won an unusual number of games in which they were out-hit, some in which they were out-hit badly. The Phils won 38 games in which they were either out-hit (21 games) or got no more hits than their opponents (17 games). On April 29 they were out-hit 14–11 by Houston, but won in a rout, 12–4. On June 4 they were out-hit by the Dodgers 15–7, but won the game. On July 3 they were out-hit 12–8 by Cincinnati and on July 7 they were out-hit 11–8 by Atlanta; they won both games by the same 7–3 score. On August 26 they were out-hit 14–9, but won 6–4. By contrast, there were only nine games in which the Phillies out-hit their opponents but lost, and eleven more in which they lost despite breaking even in ties.

By scoring a high percentage of their runners, the Phillies were the only team in the league to post a winning record despite having fewer runners on base than their opposition.

From an offensive standpoint, the 1986 Phillies had no tremendous weaknesses, with shortstop and center field being the weakest positions. From a defensive standpoint, the picture was, and is, improving but less rosy. When Darren Daulton's knee was destroyed in a home-plate collision with Mike Heath (June 21), John Russell wound up doing OJT at catcher. As a defense against the running game, Russell was as effective as a pea shooter in West Beirut. Philadelphia opponents stole 216 bases, the highest total I've ever seen. The defensive infield, however, was much, much better than it had been in 1985, and the outfield had one dependable strength in Glenn Wilson. Center field, historically he Phillies defensive strongpoint from Roy Thomas to Dode Paskert to Richie Ashburn to Gary Maddox, was a 1986 sore spot shared by five or more players, of whom Milt Thompson and a surprising Jeff Stone seemed to have the best chance to develop into fixtures.

The Phillies broke poorly from the gate, and were in

last place on May 25 with a 15–24 record. Erupting for a stunning seven-game streak, with all of the seven games featuring either impressive hitting or impressive pitching, they were never again in contention for either last or first place; still, in the context of expectations it must be regarded as a largely successful season.

In trying to focus on the key decisions that led to that season, one must begin by pointing to the systematic acquisition of, and patience with, developing players with subtle offensive skills. The Phillies have walked the full mile with Steve Jeltz, giving him every chance to mature into a major league shortstop despite his low average. The front office made a gutsy move in trading two veteran catchers to rest their fate with the young Daulton—and at least broke even there despite Daulton's injury, inasmuch as former number one man Virgil played worse for Atlanta than Russell did for Philly. Supplemented by marginal pickups like Redus, Roenicke and Thompson, these players complete an effective offense around the framework of Schmidt, Hayes, Wilson, and Samuel.

In putting these players together in the form of a ballclub, John Felske was both decisive and imaginative. When the trades for Redus and Thompson were announced at the winter meetings in 1985, Felske stated that one of the new outfielders would play center, Hayes would shift from center field to first base, and Schmidt would return to third base. I, for one, thought that was a silly idea. I figured that that would leave the Phillies without a quality center fielder, waste Hayes's speed and throwing arm by placing him at the position where they would be least in demand, return Schmidt to a position that he could no longer play, and push Rick Schu out of a job, probably ending his development. Only the first point proved to be true. Hayes played reasonably well at first base and had his best year with the bat, and Schmidt proved more than up to the return to third base. There was clearly a net defensive gain on the shifts. Rich Schu also seemed to regard his battle for playing time as more of a challenge than an obstacle; he had a good year with the bat in a limited role, and is probably more valuable now than he was a year ago.

At the time of Daulton's injury, Felske evaluated his options and *did not* do what most major-league managers would have done in the same circumstances, which is to look around for some 30-year-old journeyman with a decent glove to get them through the year. Instead, he used it as an opportunity to get John Russell some playing time. Russell, who doesn't hit quite often enough or run quite well enough to be a hot prospect as an outfielder, did the best he could as a catcher, which wasn't too good. But just as excessive base stealing does not guarantee success from the standpoint of the offense, so it does not guarantee failure from the standpoint of the defense; the Phillies were able to accept it as given that any time a base stealer got on first he would take second, and still win. The excessive base stealing probably cost them a little less than 15 runs, while Russell, with good power, drove in 60 runs in 93 games. (Each stolen base gives the offense, and costs the defense, about two-tenths of a run. The other 11 NL teams allowed an average of 148 stolen bases, 68 fewer than the Phillies, while catching about as many runners stealing as

did the Phillies. The net loss to the team from substandard defense against the stolen base was about 14 runs.)

Felske did what a manager is supposed to do—he knew his personnel, he knew what they could do, and he figured out how to use them to derive the maximum benefit from those skills.

Looking at the long-term future, the Phillies position appears good, with the lack of a superstar looming as the most serious need. Schmidt is 37 and talking about retiring. While good management and strong instruction can insure a flow of talent from the minor leagues, and the Phillies have had that, in the development of a superstar there is a lot of just random luck. You can do things to improve your chances, but there is no way to guarantee that you're going to come up with one of those five or six players a generation who can be the gem in the jewelry. The Phillies traded five players to Cleveland in the hope that Von Hayes would be that kind of player, and while he's a very good player, he's not quite in that class. Thus, the failure of Juan Samuel to develop as an offensive player is justifiably disappointing to the Philly faithful—and, while Samuel has improved mightily as a defensive player, I still believe that the Phillies made a costly mistake in not moving him to center field, where he would be able to make better use of his speed and would probably show better development as a hitter and better durability over time.

Looking at the near-term future, there are four key unknowns. The first is whether or not the Mets will play at a level that makes it possible for ordinary, good-quality teams to contend. The second unknown, at this writing, is Daulton's ability to come back from his injury.

But with Russell catching, the Phillies played well from August 1 to the end of the season (37–25), which does tend to indicate probable improvement in the following season (see Houston comment in 1986 *Abstract*). The other two unknowns are players who were vital to that strong finish, and are the keys to sustaining it in 1986: Bruce Ruffin and Don Carman. Since the decline of Steve Carlton, the Phillies have had no anchor to their starting rotation. They haven't had a pitcher who won 16 games in a season since John Denny in 1983. Ruffin, called up when Carlton was cut adrift, certainly appears to be capable of filling that role. Carman, converted to relief at the AA level, moved back into a starting role at the All-Star break and posted one strong start after another, compiling a 6–3 record and 2.57 ERA in 88 innings in the second half. The starting candidates also include Marvin Freeman, who did well in three starts at the end of the year.

The Phillies should score runs. With four proven hitters complemented by a group of effective role players, the Phillies have essentially an Earl-Weaver offense, except that the role players have more speed and less power than if selected by Weaver. The bullpen is deep and talented. Even with Kevin Gross and Shane Rawley still on hand, the starting corp is more of an unknown, but might develop into one of the best in the league. If it does, and if the Mets don't win 110 games, the Phillies will be in the pennant race in 1987.

John RUSSELL, Catcher

	G	AB	Hit	2B	3B	HR	Run	RBI	TBB	SO	SB	CS	Avg
1.31 years		479	115	31	2	18	52	71	42	158	2	2	.240
1986	93	315	76	21	2	13	35	60	25	103	0	1	.241
First Half	46	150	39	13	0	7	19	30	13	58	0	0	.260
Second Half	47	165	37	8	2	6	16	30	12	45	0	1	.224
Vs. RHP		193	45	11	1	9		41	12	65			.233
Vs. LHP		122	31	10	1	4		19	13	38			.254
Home		159	45	12	2	8		35	11	49			.283
Road		156	31	9	0	5		25	14	54			.199
Grass		61	14	4	0	3		9	10	20			.230
Turf		254	62	17	2	10		51	15	83			.244

Von HAYES, First Base

	G	AB	Hit	2B	3B	HR	Run	RBI	TBB	SO	SB	CS	Avg
4.81 years		567	157	30	5	14	83	76	59	81	32	12	.276
1986	158	610	186	46	2	19	107	98	74	77	24	12	.305
First Half	83	315	90	25	0	5	51	42	44	50	13	7	.286
Second Half	75	295	96	21	2	14	56	56	30	27	11	5	.325
Vs. RHP		414	140	36	2	15		64	55	50			.338
Vs. LHP		196	46	10	0	4		34	19	27			.235
Home		296	93	19	2	11		53	38	36			.314
Road		314	93	27	0	8		45	36	41			.296
Grass		170	59	15	0	6		27	14	23			.347
Turf		440	127	31	2	13		71	60	54			.289

Juan SAMUEL, Second Base

	G	AB	Hit	2B	3B	HR	Run	RBI	TBB	SO	SB	CS	Avg
2.99 years		676	181	35	15	17	104	76	30	156	57	17	.268
1986	145	591	157	36	12	16	90	78	26	142	42	14	.266
First Half	70	290	76	17	8	7	44	42	13	72	25	7	.262
Second Half	75	301	81	19	4	9	46	36	13	70	17	7	.269
Vs. RHP		407	110	23	8	11		51	21	95			.270
Vs. LHP		184	47	13	4	5		27	5	47			.255
Home		286	76	19	7	10		45	18	71			.266
Road		305	81	17	5	6		33	8	71			.266
Grass		156	46	7	0	4		15	5	39			.295
Turf		435	111	29	12	12		63	21	103			.255

Mike SCHMIDT, Third Base

	G	AB	Hit	2B	3B	HR	Run	RBI	TBB	SO	SB	CS	Avg
13.01 years		561	150	27	4	38	104	107	104	134	13	7	.268
1986	160	552	160	29	1	37	97	119	89	84	1	1	.290
First Half	85	302	86	16	1	19	51	66	37	47	0	1	.285
Second Half	75	250	74	13	0	18	46	53	52	37	1	1	.296
Vs. RHP		394	104	19	1	22		77	56	73			.264
Vs. LHP		158	56	10	0	15		42	33	11			.354
Home		258	77	17	0	20		63	46	43			.298
Road		294	83	12	1	17		56	43	41			.282
Grass		150	43	4	0	7		28	21	22			.287
Turf		402	117	25	1	30		91	68	62			.291

Steve JELTZ, Shortstop

	G	AB	Hit	2B	3B	HR	Run	RBI	TBB	SO	SB	CS	Avg
1.70 years		419	87	9	4	1	40	33	58	97	5	3	.208
1986	145	439	96	11	4	0	44	36	65	97	6	3	.219
First Half	77	231	56	7	2	0	30	23	44	45	4	2	.242
Second Half	68	28	40	4	2	0	14	13	21	52	2	1	.192
Vs. RHP		299	65	8	3	0		28	46	61			.217
Vs. LHP		140	31	3	1	0		8	19	36			.221
Home		226	49	8	3	0		21	28	53			.217
Road		213	47	3	1	0		15	37	44			.221
Grass		119	27	2	0	0		9	14	22			.227
Turf		320	69	9	4	0		27	51	75			.216

Gary REDUS, Left Field

	G	AB	Hit	2B	3B	HR	Run	RBI	TBB	SO	SB	CS	Avg
2.83 years		535	133	28	8	15	100	50	77	118	60	16	.248
1986	90	340	84	22	4	11	62	33	47	78	25	7	.247
First Half	26	102	27	11	0	3	19	10	15	22	11	2	.265
Second Half	64	238	57	11	4	8	43	23	32	56	14	5	.239
Vs. RHP		231	57	15	3	9		23	20	52			.247
Vs. LHP		109	27	7	1	2		10	27	26			.248
Home		170	49	15	3	8		23	22	40			.288
Road		170	35	7	1	3		10	25	38			.206
Grass		71	15	3	0	1		6	12	18			.211
Turf		269	69	19	4	10		27	35	60			.257

Milt THOMPSON, Outfield

	G	AB	Hit	2B	3B	HR	Run	RBI	TBB	SO	SB	CS	Avg
1.20 years		484	134	13	3	7	59	28	37	91	35	8	.276
1986	96	299	75	7	1	6	38	23	26	62	19	4	.251
First Half	49	156	30	3	0	3	17	10			9		.192
Second Half	47	143	45	4	1	3	21	13			10		.315
Vs. RHP		249	64	6	1	6		21	23	49			.257
Vs. LHP		50	11	1	0	0		2	3	13			.220
Home		154	42	4	1	4		13	14	33			.273
Road		145	33	3	0	2		10	12	29			.228
Grass		85	19	2	0	2		6	6	19			.224
Turf		214	56	5	1	4		17	20	43			.262

Glenn WILSON, Right Field

	G	AB	Hit	2B	3B	HR	Run	RBI	TBB	SO	SB	CS	Avg
4.17 years		565	152	31	5	14	64	76	32	94	5	2	.270
1986	155	584	158	30	4	15	70	84	42	91	5	1	.271
First Half	84	311	75	16	0	7	36	41	27	50	2	0	.241
Second Half	71	273	83	14	4	8	34	43	15	41	3	1	.304
Vs. RHP		397	116	20	4	11		63	30	66			.292
Vs. LHP		187	42	10	0	4		21	12	25			.225
Home		285	86	22	2	7		40	24	41			.302
Road		299	72	8	2	8		44	18	50			.241
Grass		163	36	5	2	2		20	5	25			.221
Turf		421	122	25	2	13		64	37	66			.290

Jeff STONE, Outfield

	G	AB	Hit	2B	3B	HR	Run	RBI	TBB	SO	SB	CS	Avg
1.42 years		494	147	10	11	4	68	34	31	91	46	11	.298
1986	82	249	69	6	4	6	32	19	20	52	19	6	.277
First Half	41	126	33	2	1	3	15	10	11	27	11	3	.262
Second Half	41	123	36	4	3	3	17	9	9	25	8	3	.293
Vs. RHP		186	49	4	3	4		17	15	42			.263
Vs. LHP		63	20	2	1	2		2	5	10			.317
Home		113	36	2	2	4		11	7	21			.319
Road		136	33	4	2	2		8	13	31			.243
Grass		77	19	3	0	2		4	5	20			.247
Turf		172	50	3	4	4		15	15	32			.291

Ron ROENICKE, Outfield

	G	AB	Hit	2B	3B	HR	Run	RBI	TBB	SO	SB	CS	Avg
2.78 years		346	86	17	1	6	46	37	62	62	8	3	.249
1986	102	275	69	13	1	5	42	42	61	52	2	2	.251
First Half	53	180	49	10	1	4	26	30	31	31	2	0	.272
Second Half	49	95	20	3	0	1	16	12	30	21	0	2	.211
Vs. RHP		168	35	8	1	2		25	34	29			.208
Vs. LHP		107	34	5	0	3		17	27	23			.318
Home		142	39	8	1	4		23	40	33			.275
Road		133	30	5	0	1		19	21	19			.226
Grass		70	17	3	0	0		9	10	13			.243
Turf		205	52	10	1	5		33	51	39			.254

Kevin GROSS

	(W–L)	GS	Run	Avg	DP	Avg	SB	Avg
1985	(15-13)	31	104	3.35	25	.81	35	1.13
1986	(12-12)	36	162	4.50	37	1.03	45	1.25
1983-1986		98	387	3.95	90	.92	123	1.26

	G	IP	W	L	Pct	ER	BB	SO	ERA
1985 Home	18	96.3	8	4	.667	32	33	79	2.99
1986 Home	20	134.0	7	7	.500	35	22	36	2.35
1985 Road	20	109.3	7	9	.438	46	48	72	3.79
1986 Road	17	107.7	5	5	.500	73	72	118	6.10
1985 Grass	10	49.3	3	6	.333	31	22	39	5.66
1986 Grass	10	68.7	3	3	.500	39	30	36	5.11
1985 Turf	28	156.3	12	7	.632	47	59	112	2.71
1986 Turf	27	173.0	9	9	.500	69	64	118	3.59
1985 Total	37	241.7	12	12	.500	108	94	154	4.02

Shane RAWLEY

	(W–L)	GS	Run	Avg	DP	Avg	SB	Avg
1985	(13-8)	31	142	4.58	30	.97	32	1.03
1986	(11-7)	23	130	5.65	24	1.04	31	1.35
1978-1986		137	619	4.52	134	.98	102	.74

	G	IP	W	L	Pct	ER	BB	SO	ERA
1985 Home	18	99.3	6	6	.500	38	46	51	3.44
1986 Home	11	69.0	7	3	.700	30	29	31	3.91
1985 Road	18	99.3	7	2	.778	35	35	55	3.17
1986 Road	12	88.7	4	4	.500	32	21	42	3.25
1985 Grass	10	58.0	2	2	.500	23	20	32	3.57
1986 Grass	4	27.7	1	2	.333	16	3	15	5.20
1985 Turf	26	140.7	11	6	.647	50	61	74	3.20
1986 Turf	19	130.0	10	5	.667	46	47	58	3.18
1986 Total	23	157.7	11	7	.611	62	50	73	3.54

Charles HUDSON

	(W–L)	GS	Run	Avg	DP	Avg	SB	Avg
1985	(8-13)	26	127	4.88	13	.50	25	.96
1986	(7-10)	23	91	3.96	19	.83	30	1.30
1983-1986		105	470	4.48	66	.63	122	1.16

	G	IP	W	L	Pct	ER	BB	SO	ERA
1985 Home	18	93.3	3	5	.375	40	28	56	3.86
1986 Home	17	69.7	3	5	.375	35	22	36	4.52
1985 Road	20	99.7	5	8	.385	41	46	66	3.70
1986 Road	16	74.3	4	5	.444	44	36	46	5.33
1985 Grass	10	46.0	1	4	.200	24	21	25	4.70
1986 Grass	7	28.3	1	2	.333	21	13	25	6.67
1985 Turf	28	147.0	7	9	.438	57	53	97	3.49
1986 Turf	26	115.7	6	8	.429	58	45	57	4.51
1986 Total	33	144.0	7	10	.412	79	58	82	4.94

Bruce RUFFIN

	(W–L)	GS	Run	Avg	DP	Avg	SB	Avg
1986	(9-4)	21	101	4.81	23	1.10	28	1.33

	G	IP	W	L	Pct	ER	BB	SO	ERA
1986 Home	12	87.7	6	2	.750	21	25	36	2.16
1986 Road	9	58.7	3	2	.600	19	19	34	2.91
1986 Grass	5	37.0	3	1	.750	5	8	18	1.22
1986 Turf	16	109.3	6	3	.667	35	36	52	2.88
1986 Total	21	146.3	9	4	.692	40	44	70	2.46

OTHERS

	(W–L)	GS	Run	Avg	DP	Avg	SB	Avg
Carlton	(4-8)	16	78	4.88	20	1.25	15	.94
Maddux	(3-7)	16	67	4.19	12	.75	31	1.94
Carman	(10-5)	14	48	3.43	11	.79	17	1.21
Toliver	(0-2)	5	20	4.00	6	1.20	12	2.40
Bittiger	(1-1)	3	15	5.00	2	.67	4	1.33
Freeman	(2-0)	3	21	7.00	3	1.00	3	1.00
Hume	(4-1)	1	6	6.00	0	0.00	0	0.00

RECORDS WITH DIFFERENT STARTING CATCHERS

Catcher	Inn	ER	W–L	ERA	GS	SB	Avg
Russell	749.1	322	44-37	3.87	81	115	1.42
Daulton	397.1	187	22-23	4.24	45	54	1.20
Reynolds	305.0	112	20-15	3.30	35	47	1.34

ST. LOUIS CARDINALS

Runners on Base:	1.858
Opponents on Base:	1.871
Net Disadvantage:	−13
Won/Lost Record:	79−82

In a decade in which first-place teams have found it difficult to repeat, the Cardinals in 1986 performed one of the most sudden champions-into-chumps transitions. Whitey Herzog has had a brilliant managerial career by developing teams strong in speed, defense, and pitching—particularly the bullpen. Emphasizing those features in the context of a complete team has served him well, but in 1986 he had the fastest team in baseball, one of the best defensive teams in baseball, and one of the better pitching staffs in the league topped by the best reliever in the league—and still finished under .500.

On the field, the difference between the 1985 and 1986 Cardinals can be easily isolated: The 1985 Cardinals got people on base and the 1986 Cardinals didn't. The pitching wasn't much different: They dropped from second to fourth in ERA. Relative to the league they lost 22 runs, being 86 runs better-than-league in 1985, 64 runs in 1986. The defense, which Herzog proclaimed in preseason possibly the greatest in the history of baseball, was good. The Cards led the league in fielding percentage, could turn a double play and had an excellent .718 defensive effeciency record, meaning that the Cardinals converted 71.8% of balls in play into outs.

The Cardinals' base running did not decline: their stolen base percentage was up, and their stolen bases as a percentage of runners on base were almost the same. But in 1985 St. Louis led the league in batting average, at .264. In 1986 they finished last at .236. In 1985 they led the league in walks, with 586. In 1986, with the number of walks up around the league, they dipped to fifth at 568. The dismal .309 team on-base percentage ended the innings before the big payoffs were reached. The Cardinals in 1985 had 186 multiple-run innings, in which they scored 514 runs. In 1986 they had 139 multiple-run innings, accounting for 368 runs. *The drop in on-base percentage is the only important statistical indicator of the difference between the two teams.*

That imposing decline involved most of the lineup, although Van Slyke and Ozzie had good years and Pendleton was no worse than 1985. Lead-off man Vince Coleman dropped from a poor .320 on-base percentage to an inadequate .301. Willie McGee dropped from an excellent .384 to .309. Tommie Herr dropped from .379 to .342, and Jack Clark dropped from .393 out of the lineup with an injury. Nobody picked up the slack.

Whenever this happens, the mind will not accept that there may be no original force behind it, that it may simply be a series of random misfortunes. There was, then, no shortage of explanations, most of which turned around the performance of the Cardinals in the 1985 World Series. Tim McCarver compared the decline of the 1986 Cardinals to that of 1969, after the Cards also blew a 3–1 lead in the 1968 Series. Others saw in the season a return to normal of players who were having career seasons in 1985.

The McCarver explanation seems reasonably credible to me, and will become immensely popular this summer if the Red Sox also crumble. I'm not an advocate of the "career years" explanation of how teams win pennants, and I don't think that the 1985 Cardinals were much over their heads as a group, but certainly it is true that those who were over their heads came crashing to earth like flies under a bug light.

The normal problem that organizations have after winning is freezing up, brushing over the weaknesses of marginal players by tying their skills to the team's success ("We won with him last year, didn't we?"). The Royals stuck with Lynn Jones and Greg Pryor, who had done nothing in 1985 or would do less in 1986. Herzog, as in 1983, instead used the championship as an opportunity to gamble. To Herzog, winning gives the manager the elbow room to assert himself. If the manager makes some moves after he wins and they don't all work, he won't be fired for a year or two; there's a grace period. If he doesn't do anything after winning the team will get complacent; in a couple of years when he does shake things up, then if the moves don't work right away he'll be out of a job.

So the 1985 Cardinals won, but with a lot of veterans in marginal roles. Herzog and Maxvill decided to shake the branches. Joacquin Andujar was exchanged for a new catcher. The bench in 1985 had Steve Braun, Mike Jorgensen, Brian Harper, and Ivan DeJesus, as well as Cesar Cedeno and Darrell Porter, who were regulars for brief periods. None of these players were back in 1986; in their places were José Oguendo, Steve Lake, Tom Lawless, Alan Knicely, Clint Hurdle, and Curtis Ford. Starting in place of Andujar was Tim Conroy.

Herzog was a student of Casey Stengel's, and it was Casey's belief that the way to keep a team on top was to keep the ordinary players fighting for their jobs. I was in St. Louis in May, and Jose Oguendo was playing second base instead of Tommie Herr. A reporter told me that Whitey had told him "I'm worried about Tommie. He's hitting .140, but he's not doing anything extra to get himself going. He's doing his work, but he's just doing what he has to." Whitey's frankness was surprising, as always, but that's just Herzog: He didn't want it to be any secret that he wasn't happy with Herr's play or effort, that if Herr didn't get it going, then 110 RBI last year or no, the other guy was gonna play.

Herr eventually did get started, but the Cardinals were 24–35, 19 games out by mid-June, before an injury to Jack Clark put the pennant chase out of its misery. I make no claims to understanding the psychology of why teams flourish and decline, but if you combine the McCarver explanation and Herzog's attack-your-problems-before-you-lose philosophy into one idea, the synthesis suggests that Herzog's dump-the-veterans approach may not have been exactly the right thing for this team at that moment, given that they were carrying a seed of self-doubt from the previous October. I question in particular the decision to let Darrell Porter go and acquire Mike Heath. Porter isn't as old as people think; he just came up young and has had so many ups and downs that he seems old. Even hitting .221 in 1985, Porter was an effective player, a capable handler of pitchers with an excellent secondary average. Mike Heath is only three years younger, is suspect as a handler of pitchers, has never hit well on artificial turf and doesn't match Porter in power or strike zone judgment. Granted, Heath throws well, but to make this switch, you're going to give up a 20-game winner? I believe the change from Porter to Heath exacerbated the Cardinal problems.

At the same time, I liked Tim Conroy, and I thought he would pitch well for the Cardinals. He didn't.

I see five critical factors in the Cardinal demise: the 1985 World Series failure, the switch from Porter to Heath, the injuries to Clark and McGee, and the white-hot start of the Mets, which put pressure on the Cardinals at a moment when they may have been suffering self-doubts, and perhaps precipitated an early-season panic. Herzog was criticized for throwing in the towel early, but the effect of his concession (and probably its purpose) was to take the pressure off the players. They played much better for the balance of the season, shooting past .500 before dropping back just under.

Many times a .500 team will have about the same totals as their opponents—for example, the Expos hit 110 home runs to their opponents 119, stole 193 bases and allowed 200, drew 537 walks and issued 566, hit 255 doubles and allowed 253. They mirrored the characteristics of the league. The Cardinals seemed to be drafting their athletes from a different species than anybody else. Not only were the Cardinals tremendous base stealers, swiping 262, but with Heath and Lavalliere Cardinal opponents stole only 91 bases, giving the Cards almost a 3–1 advantage. The Cardinals picked up another 41 bases from opposition balks (up from 23 opposition balks in 1985), while Cardinal pitchers committed only 13 balks, giving them another 3–1 advantage.

While Cardinal batters grounded into only 83 double plays, tied for the fewest in the league, Ozzie Smith and company turned 178 double plays, second-most in the league. While Cardinal batters drew 568 walks, Cardinal pitchers issued only 485 walks, fewest in the league—another 83 bases (and baserunners) for the Cardinals. The Cardinals hit 66% more triples than their opponents (48–29), another 57-base advantage.

But the Cardinals were out-homered by a ridiculous margin, 58–135 (27–63 in Busch Stadium, 31–72 on the road). The Cardinals lost the home run battle by 77: the second-worst performance in the majors was by Milwau-kee, which was out-homered by 31. That's a 308-base advantage for the opposition, which wipes out most of the positives. The Cardinals were also out-doubled 216 to 278. Lacking power and lacking men on base, the Cardinals were unable to compete in the grass/power parks, posting a 15–26 record on grass fields, worst in the league.

Reacting to his emaciated offense, Herzog ordered 108 sacrifice bunts, up more than 50% from 1985. Cardinal opponents bunted only 53 times; I'm not sure whether that's a positive or a negative, but it's certainly a difference. All added up, the Cardinals almost broke even, scoring 601 runs to their opponents 611.

Can the Cardinals win in 1987? An oddity of conventional baseball analysis is that whenever a team steals bases and is successful, people point to the base-stealing as the key to the success—ignoring the fact that the relationship between success and base-stealing is weaker than the relationship between success and outstanding performance in any other area of the game. The purpose of base-stealing is to increase a base runner's chance of scoring, yet the Cardinals scored only 32.3% of their baserunners, nearly the lowest percentage in the majors (Atlanta scored 32.2%).

The same applies to the Cardinals other most-visible strength, the bullpen; it is a cliche of the eighties that you can't win a pennant without a strong bullpen, never mind the fact that teams do win titles almost every year without strong bullpens. These strengths mean something in the 1987 outlook, but I wouldn't put too much emphasis on them.

The Cardinals remain a young team, with the lineup averaging 27.4 birthdays, the relief ace a rookie and one rookie starter. The defense is great, and the pitching has as good a chance of being championship quality as anybody else's.

But if the offense is there, I don't see it. Another problem with building around speed is that speed is the one talent which depreciates the most rapidly. Three years from now, Darryl Strawberry or Ryne Sandberg probably is going to be as good a hitter as he is now, maybe better—but over a three-year period, any player will lose some portion of his foot speed. A team that builds on speed has to continually renew that resource, while still patching holes like any other team.

Some will argue that if the Cardinals can go from 101 wins to 79 in one season, it must be possible for them to get back to 101 in one more season. Maybe, but if a man is thrown from a horse in a half-second, does that mean that he must be able to get back on in another? If you wrap your car around a tree, can you put it back together as quickly? It is a rule of nature that the processes of destruction, such as fire and violence, act more quickly than the processes of growth and development. In the course of a decade there are more teams that improve from season to season than there are that decline, which means that the declines are larger than the improvements, which implies that the same rule applies to baseball teams. While it certainly is *possible* for all of Herzog's horses and all of his men to get the Cardinals back together for 1987, it seems more likely that it will be two or three years before the Cardinals again emerge as serious contenders.

Mike LAVALLIERE, Catcher

	G	AB	Hit	2B	3B	HR	Run	RBI	TBB	SO	SB	CS	Avg
0.79 years		435	96	14	3	4	25	46	57	53	0	1	.221
1986	110	303	71	10	2	3	18	30	36	37	0	1	.234
First Half	49	117	31	2	1	1	5	14	16	14	0	0	.265
Second Half	61	186	40	8	1	2	13	16	20	23	0	1	.215
Vs. RHP		246	59	6	2	2		21	31	25			.240
Vs. LHP		57	12	4	0	1		9	5	12			.211
Home		150	33	4	1	1		13	18	17			.220
Road		153	38	6	1	2		17	18	20			.248
Grass		67	16	3	1	0		8	10	9			.239
Turf		236	55	7	1	3		22	26	28			.233

Vince COLEMAN, Left Field

	G	AB	Hit	2B	3B	HR	Run	RBI	TBB	SO	SB	CS	Avg
1.88 years		656	164	18	10	1	107	37	58	113	115	21	.250
1986	154	600	139	13	8	0	94	29	60	98	107	14	.232
First Half	81	319	80	7	7	0	47	19	36	52	58	7	.251
Second Half	73	281	59	6	1	0	47	10	24	46	49	7	.210
Vs. RHP		371	84	8	5	0		17	29	67			.226
Vs. LHP		229	55	5	3	0		12	31	31			.240
Home		320	86	5	5	0		13	36	56			.269
Road		280	53	8	3	0		16	24	42			.189
Grass		139	22	2	1	0		8	14	21			.158
Turf		461	117	11	7	0		21	46	77			.254

Jack CLARK, First Base

	G	AB	Hit	2B	3B	HR	Run	RBI	TBB	SO	SB	CS	Avg
7.62 years		578	159	31	5	25	92	92	82	92	8	6	.275
1986	65	232	55	12	2	9	34	23	45	61	1	1	.237
First Half	65	232	55	12	2	9	34	23	45	61	1	1	.237
Second Half													
Vs. RHP		143	28	6	1	3		10	29	41			.196
Vs. LHP		89	27	6	1	6		13	16	20			.303
Home		117	32	7	1	4		12	23	32			.274
Road		115	23	5	1	5		11	22	29			.200
Grass		55	9	1	0	0		1	9	13			.164
Turf		177	46	11	2	9		22	36	48			.260

Willie McGEE, Center Field

	G	AB	Hit	2B	3B	HR	Run	RBI	TBB	SO	SB	CS	Avg
4.27 years		634	189	24	12	8	89	73	32	95	42	15	.298
1986	124	497	127	22	7	7	65	48	37	82	19	16	.256
First Half	84	345	83	7	5	3	40	33	24	60	12	10	.241
Second Half	40	152	44	15	2	4	25	15	13	22	7	6	.289
Vs. RHP		298	78	15	4	2		27	21	42			.262
Vs. LHP		199	49	7	3	5		21	16	40			.246
Home		264	74	15	6	7		29	17	47			.280
Road		233	53	7	1	0		19	20	35			.227
Grass		127	26	3	0	0		6	7	13			.205
Turf		370	101	19	7	7		42	30	69			.273

Tommy HERR, Second Base

	G	AB	Hit	2B	3B	HR	Run	RBI	TBB	SO	SB	CS	Avg
5.39 years		587	162	28	6	3	78	65	67	60	24	9	.276
1986	152	559	141	30	4	2	48	61	73	75	22	8	.252
First Half	79	293	64	11	1	2	20	23	35	45	10	5	.218
Second Half	73	266	77	19	3	0	28	38	38	30	12	3	.289
Vs. RHP		338	72	16	3	1		39	42	51			.213
Vs. LHP		221	69	14	1	1		22	31	24			.312
Home		273	71	10	2	1		38	44	36			.260
Road		286	70	20	2	1		23	29	39			.245
Grass		146	30	9	1	1		8	10	21			.205
Turf		413	111	21	3	1		53	63	54			.269

Andy VAN SLYKE, Outfield-First Base

	G	AB	Hit	2B	3B	HR	Run	RBI	TBB	SO	SB	CS	Avg
3.22 years		470	122	25	7	13	64	63	63	85	32	8	.259
1986	137	418	113	23	7	13	48	61	47	85	21	8	.270
First Half	73	211	50	7	3	4	21	26	25	43	11	4	.237
Second Half	64	207	63	16	4	9	27	35	22	42	10	4	.304
Vs. RHP		302	89	17	3	12		48	33	59			.295
Vs. LHP		116	24	6	4	1		13	14	26			.207
Home		211	59	11	6	6		39	30	39			.280
Road		207	54	12	1	7		22	17	46			.261
Grass		112	29	5	1	3		8	10	25			.259
Turf		306	84	18	6	10		53	37	60			.275

Terry PENDLETON, Third Base

	G	AB	Hit	2B	3B	HR	Run	RBI	TBB	SO	SB	CS	Avg
2.31 years		604	154	25	5	3	64	70	38	72	26	10	.255
1986	159	578	138	26	5	1	56	59	34	59	24	6	.239
First Half	86	306	66	16	0	0	30	21	23	43	15	3	.216
Second Half	73	272	72	10	5	1	26	38	11	16	9	3	.265
Vs. RHP		369	80	14	2	1		32	18	43			.217
Vs. LHP		209	58	12	3	0		27	16	16			.278
Home		286	73	15	4	0		28	17	26			.255
Road		292	65	11	1	1		31	17	33			.223
Grass		135	25	3	0	1		8	11	16			.185
Turf		443	113	23	5	0		51	23	43			.255

Curt FORD, Outfield

	G	AB	Hit	2B	3B	HR	Run	RBI	TBB	SO	SB	CS	Avg
0.59 years		381	100	29	3	3	54	54	46	51	24	8	.261
1986	85	214	53	15	2	2	30	29	23	29	13	5	.248
First Half	29	82	22	7	1	1	13	6	8	11	5	3	.268
Second Half	56	132	31	8	1	1	17	23	15	18	8	2	.235
Vs. RHP		185	47	13	2	2		25	20	22			.254
Vs. LHP		29	6	2	0	0		4	3	7			.207
Home		94	26	11	1	0		18	12	13			.277
Road		120	27	4	1	2		11	11	16			.225
Grass		49	6	1	0	0		3	3	8			.122
Turf		165	47	14	2	2		26	20	21			.285

Ozzie SMITH, Shortstop

	G	AB	Hit	2B	3B	HR	Run	RBI	TBB	SO	SB	CS	Avg
8.13 years		583	144	22	5	2	72	46	65	38	37	10	.247
1986	153	514	144	19	4	0	67	54	79	27	31	7	.280
First Half	81	282	79	11	3	0	32	27	40	13	18	3	.280
Second Half	72	232	65	8	1	0	35	27	39	14	13	4	.280
Vs. RHP		310	87	11	4	0		40	48	18			.281
Vs. LHP		204	57	8	0	0		14	31	9			.279
Home		254	73	13	1	0		31	47	16			.287
Road		260	71	6	3	0		23	32	11			.273
Grass		126	28	3	2	0		10	14	6			.222
Turf		388	116	16	2	0		44	65	21			.299

Mike HEATH, Catcher

	G	AB	Hit	2B	3B	HR	Run	RBI	TBB	SO	SB	CS	Avg
5.27 years		535	133	21	4	10	60	62	36	71	7	5	.248
1986	95	288	65	11	1	8	30	36	27	53	6	4	.226
First Half	59	174	34	8	1	4	18	25	20	30	2	3	.195
Second Half	36	114	31	3	0	4	12	11	7	23	4	1	.272
Vs. RHP		110	21	3	0	2		10	11	22			.191
Vs. LHP		178	44	8	1	6		26	16	31			.247
Home		159	39	5	1	4		15	14	26			.245
Road		129	26	6	0	4		21	13	27			.202
Grass		129	30	4	0	5		15	10	29			.233
Turf		159	35	7	1	3		21	17	24			.220

Bob FORSCH

	(W–L)	GS	Run	Avg	DP	Avg	SB	Avg
1985	(9-6)	19	90	4.74	25	1.32	10	.53
1986	(14-10)	33	142	4.30	42	1.27	19	.58
1976-1986		311	1362	4.38	325	1.05	212	.68

	G	IP	W	L	Pct	ER	BB	SO	ERA
1985 Home	19	73.7	5	3	.625	29	21	22	3.54
1986 Home	17	125.0	8	4	.667	37	28	49	2.66
1985 Road	17	62.3	4	3	.571	30	26	26	4.33
1986 Road	16	105.0	6	6	.500	46	40	55	3.94
1985 Grass	10	34.7	3	1	.750	14	15	12	3.63
1986 Grass	8	51.0	2	4	.333	21	22	26	3.71
1985 Turf	26	101.3	6	5	.545	45	32	36	4.00
1986 Turf	25	179.0	12	6	.667	62	46	78	3.12
1986 Total	33	230.0	14	10	.583	83	68	104	3.25

Danny COX

	(W–L)	GS	Run	Avg	DP	Avg	SB	Avg
1985	(18-9)	35	150	4.29	30	.86	13	.37
1986	(12-13)	32	110	3.44	32	1.00	21	.66
1983-1986		106	397	3.75	119	1.12	56	.53

	G	IP	W	L	Pct	ER	BB	SO	ERA
1985 Home	19	133.0	10	5	.667	38	28	72	2.57
1986 Home	17	124.3	6	6	.500	40	31	52	2.90
1985 Road	16	108.0	8	4	.667	39	36	59	3.25
1986 Road	15	95.7	6	7	.462	31	29	56	2.92
1985 Grass	7	46.7	4	2	.667	17	16	23	3.28
1986 Grass	6	39.7	2	4	.333	10	15	26	2.27
1985 Turf	28	194.3	14	7	.667	60	48	108	2.78
1986 Turf	26	180.3	10	9	.526	61	45	82	3.04
1986 Total	32	220.0	12	13	.480	71	60	108	2.90

John TUDOR

	(W–L)	GS	Run	Avg	DP	Avg	SB	Avg
1985	(21-8)	36	160	4.44	25	.69	16	.44
1986	(13-7)	30	117	3.90	34	1.13	10	.33
1979-1986		192	800	4.17	180	.94	105	.55

	G	IP	W	L	Pct	ER	BB	SO	ERA
1985 Home	20	161.3	15	2	.882	25	21	102	1.39
1986 Home	17	127.0	9	2	.818	35	27	60	2.48
1985 Road	16	113.7	6	6	.500	34	28	67	2.69
1986 Road	13	92.0	4	5	.444	36	26	47	3.52
1985 Grass	8	57.3	3	4	.429	15	11	37	2.35
1986 Grass	7	48.7	1	4	.200	19	16	24	3.51
1985 Turf	28	217.7	18	4	.818	44	38	132	1.82
1986 Turf	23	170.3	12	3	.800	52	37	83	2.75
1986 Total	30	219.0	13	7	.650	71	53	107	2.92

Greg MATHEWS

	(W–L)	GS	Run	Avg	DP	Avg	SB	Avg
1986	(11-8)	22	76	3.45	22	1.00	12	.55

	G	IP	W	L	Pct	ER	BB	SO	ERA
1986 Home	8	53.7	5	2	.714	19	13	24	3.19
1986 Road	15	91.7	6	6	.500	40	31	43	3.93
1986 Grass	6	36.7	2	2	.500	14	12	15	3.44
1986 Turf	17	108.7	9	6	.600	45	32	52	3.73
1986 Total	23	145.3	11	8	.579	59	44	67	3.65

Tim CONROY

	(W–L)	GS	Run	Avg	DP	Avg	SB	Avg
1985	(0-1)	2	6	3.00	5	2.50	1	.50
1986	(5-11)	21	78	3.71	20	.95	18	.86
1978-1986		62	235	3.79	55	.89	50	.81

	G	IP	W	L	Pct	ER	BB	SO	ERA
1985 Home	8	13.0	0	1	0.000	7	8	2	4.85
1986 Home	14	63.7	2	7	.222	38	31	32	5.37
1985 Road	8	12.3	0	0	0.000	5	7	6	3.65
1986 Road	11	51.7	3	4	.429	29	25	47	5.05
1985 Grass	12	22.0	0	1	0.000	12	13	6	4.91
1986 Grass	4	22.3	1	2	.333	11	9	21	4.43
1985 Turf	4	3.3	0	0	0.000	0	2	2	0.00
1986 Turf	21	93.0	4	9	.308	56	47	58	5.42
1986 Total	25	115.3	5	11	.312	67	56	79	5.23

OTHERS

	(W–L)	GS	Run	Avg	DP	Avg	SB	Avg
Burris	(4-5)	10	42	4.20	10	1.00	3	.30
Horton	(4-3)	9	25	2.78	11	1.22	5	.56
Kepshire	(0-1)	1	2	2.00	1	1.00	1	1.00
Ownbey	(1-3)	3	9	3.00	3	.67	1	.33

RECORDS WITH DIFFERENT STARTING CATCHERS

Catcher	Inn	ER	W–L	ERA	GS	SB	Avg
LaValliere	838.0	289	50-43	3.10	93	50	.54
Heath	478.2	195	21-30	3.67	51	35	.69
Lake	121.2	56	7-7	4.14	14	4	.29
Hurdle	28.0	9	1-2	2.89	3	3	1.00

THE FASTEST PLAYER IN BASEBALL

It being observed last summer that Willie Wilson didn't seem to run quite as well as he used to, Wilson replied that yes, he did think he had lost a stride but that he didn't think anyone except him could tell the difference. First of all, this isn't true (anyone can see the difference), but this comment struck me because the evidence of Wilson's loss of speed is all over the statistics. Wilson, who used to steal 80 bases a year, now steals 30 or 40. Whereas he once stole successfully in almost 90% of his attempts, now he's in the range of 80%. Whereas he once went to the plate over 700 times and grounded into only one double play, he now grounds into one a month or so. Whereas he used to hit several inside-the-park homers a year, he hit none in 1986. Whereas he once scored 133 runs in a season, he scored only 77 in 1986. Whereas he once made 3.4 plays a game in the outfield, last year he made 2.66. Whereas he used to hit at least twelve triples a year, he hit only 7 in 1986. How could anyone not "see" that he had lost a step?

This got me to thinking that because speed is, as Whitey Herzog says, the only thing you can use both on offense and defense, it is probably the only characteristic of a player that you can evaluate by looking at so many different areas of play. Then I got to thinking that since we can and it's a question of considerable interest—who are the fastest players in the game, and who are the slowest—why don't we?

You could make dozens of valid speed-related generalizations about baseball. Young players tend to run better than old players. Fast players probably hit more doubles than slow players. Fast players may not draw as many walks as slower players, because there is more emphasis on keeping them off base. Fast players probably hit for a higher average, as a group, than slow players. Those generalizations and many like them; while true, are probably not consistently enough true in specific cases that they can be used to evaluate speed.

I based the evaluation on six basic categories: stolen bases, stolen base percentage, triples, runs scored as a percentage of times on base, grounded into double plays, and range factor. No one of these is a pure indicator of speed; for example, the frequency of grounding into double plays is effected by where you hit in the batting order, whether you bat right-handed or left-handed, how often you are called on to bunt, how hard you hit the ball, and whether you play on a grass field or on artificial turf, among other things. Some of the outside influences you can adjust for, and some you can't. I set up a system to adjust for some of the outside influences, and then looked at the six categories as a whole.

I decided to rate speed on a 10-point scale. I had originally intended to make 5.0 the average, but as it turned out 5.0 represents somewhat above-average speed. The player is rated from 0 to 10 on his accomplishments in each of those six areas, and the average of the six scores is his "Speed Score."

It is theoretically possible to score "10." To score a perfect 10, you'd have to be a 90% base stealer, you'd have to try to steal at least 50% of the time when you were on base, you'd have to break into double figures in triples and score 100 or more runs, you couldn't ground into any double plays and you'd have to have an extremely high range factor at a tough defensive position. It is not theoretically possible to score "0," but you could score as low as 0.2. The grimy details of the system are in the appendix.

I ran the system through for all National Leaguers playing a hundred or more games, and for selected American League regulars who I thought might be among the fastest or slowest around, plus Gary Redus, who just missed the hundred games. If the system is right, the fastest player in baseball in 1986 was Vince Coleman. The top ten:

1.	Vince Coleman	8.75
2.	Rickey Henderson	7.93
3.	Eric Davis	7.83
4.	Gary Redus	7.79
5.	Juan Samuel	7.76
6.	Gary Pettis	7.65
	Tim Raines	7.65
8.	Lenny Dykstra	7.56
9.	Barry Bonds	7.48
10.	Mookie Wilson	7.39

Basically, as far as speed goes, Vince Coleman is in a class by himself at this moment. The players behind him are very close to one another, but not at all close to Coleman. Coleman's six scores are 9.19 (stolen base percentage), 10.0 (stolen base frequency), 9.96 (triples), 9.19 (runs scored), 7.86 (grounding into double plays), and 6.28 (defensive position and range.) He beats Rickey Henderson in five out of the six categories, and Rickey is in second place. (Henderson's only edge is in defensive position and range. Although Henderson scored 130 runs and Coleman only 94, Coleman rates the edge in runs scored with adjustments for home runs and times on base.)

As to the slowest players in baseball, Alan Ashby, a 35-year-old catcher, rates the nod. The bottom ten:

1.	Alan Ashby	1.66
2.	Steve Garvey	1.69
3.	Bob Horner	1.77
4.	Ron Hassey	1.79
5.	Terry Harper	1.82
6.	Cecil Cooper	1.90
7.	Carlton Fisk	1.93
8.	Ozzie Virgil	1.95
9.	Greg Brock	2.03
10.	Steve Balboni	2.05

Actually, Butch Wynegar, who didn't play a hundred games in 1986, scored at only 1.48. Wynegar or Hassey may actually be the slowest player in baseball, although none of those guys is going to break open the 40/40 class.

There are two players in this class who have been regarded as having decent speed. Carlton Fisk stole 17 bases in 1985, but Carlton's 39 years old now and has gotten up to about 240 pounds, at a guess, so that's no real surprise. (The surprise was that he stole 17 bases.) Terry Harper steals a base now and then so I didn't expect to see him on this list, but then maybe he only looks reasonably fast among the Braves. Anyway, in 1986 he was 3-for-9 as a base stealer, grounded into an awful number of double plays and didn't hit a triple.

So far I've been presenting the speed scores with two decimals, but that's just to clear up the lists; the scores surely aren't *that* accurate, so I'll switch to one decimal. It's a first effort, but I'm quite pleased with the accuracy of the method. The first question is, do the people who score high actually run well? Obviously, they do; there can't be any question that any of the people who make up the "top ten" list could outrun any of the people who make up the "bottom ten" list by a mile. There's a lot of question, of course, about whether all of the people who score at 1.7 are actually any slower than the people who score at 1.9, but that's asking a lot. After all, it is extremely questionable that a pitcher who has an ERA of 2.70 is actually a better pitcher than somebody with an ERA of 2.90. There is not only a positive correlation between speed scores and actual speed, but a very strong correlation. We can't be too concerned that it's not a perfect correlation.

Probably the biggest improvement in the method would be to use two-year totals, which is what I originally intended to do. Some of the indicators, such as triples and double-play rates, would benefit from the stability of the larger data sample. Another problem could be that it is hard to get a read on the speed of players who don't steal bases, and sometimes a player could be rated too low just because he doesn't run much. It could be said, in a sense, that the method attempts to distill pure speed out of an amalgam representing the ability to use speed within the form of a baseball game, and that the purification process can never be perfected.

Players used to stage footraces before the games sometimes. There used to be a popular promotion called the "field day" on which the players would race and throw the javelin and stuff. That was back in the days of Max Carey and Sam Rice. They stopped doing it, which is too bad, so we have to guess at and argue about who is faster than who. This is just a part of the argument.

The fastest in the National League, by position, were:

Catcher	Bob Brenly	3.3
First	Sid Bream	4.6
Second	Juan Samuel	7.8
Third	Terry Pendleton	5.9
Short	Ozzie Smith	6.2
Left	Vince Coleman	8.7
Center	Len Dykstra	7.6
Right	Joe Orsulak	7.4

One thing to note here is that *left* field, rather than center, has become the speed position in the National League. The three fastest players, and five of the top ten, are primarily left fielders, although all of them have played some center. Other players who scored at 6.5 or higher, alphabetically: Billy Hatcher, 7.2; Willie McGee, 6.8; Eddie Milner, 7.3; Omar Moreno, 7.0; Darryl Strawberry, 6.6; Andy Van Slyke, 6.7; and Mitch Webster, 7.2.

A few other National League selections:

Fastest infielder:	Juan Samuel
Fastest outfielder:	Vince Coleman
Fastest player over 30:	Mookie Wilson
Fastest player over 35:	Phil Garner (4.6)
Fastest white player:	Len Dykstra

Dave Lopes didn't play a hundred games, or he would presumably have been the fastest player over 35. An All-Slow team:

Catcher	Alan Ashby	1.7
First	Steve Garvey	1.7
Second	Johnny Ray	2.8
Third	Graig Nettles	2.1
Short	Rafael Santana	2.5
Left	Carmello Martinez	2.2
Center	Jerry Mumphrey	4.1
Right	Terry Harper	1.8

The biggest surprise on the All-Slow team is that Johnny Ray edged out Tim Flannery at second base.

The Cardinals, of course, were the fastest *team* in the major leagues. The team speed scores for the fastest and slowest major league teams:

1.	St. Louis	6.19
2.	Montreal	5.58
	Cleveland	5.58
4.	Philadelphia	5.56
5.	Cincinnati	5.47
22.	Minnesota	4.41
23.	San Diego	4.38
24.	Atlanta	4.22
25.	Boston	3.82
26.	Baltimore	3.72

I didn't have time to do much with speed scores of players from the past, so I can't really tell you who the fastest players of all time were, or how Willie Mays or Mackey Mantle would size up or even if the system works well over time. I would bet that Ernie Lombardi would score as the slowest ever and probably would be below 1.00 several years, but I haven't run the numbers.

The highest score I've seen was Willie Wilson in his first two years as a regular, 9.23 in each season. Wilson in 1979 maxed out on three charts (stolen base frequency, triples hit and runs per time on base). In 1980 Wilson's scores were 9.1, 9.1, 10, 9.95, 8.1, and 9.2—all higher than Coleman's except for the two stolen base indicators. Since then Wilson has declined to 7.9 in 1981, then to 7.8, 8.8, 8.4, 8.2, and 7.3, the lowest of his career, in 1986. He's still faster than anyone else in his age group other than Mookie Wilson.

Tim Raines dropped in 1986 to 7.7, matching the lowest of his career; he's been in the eights, too, but was apparently never as fast as Coleman. His scores beginning in 1981: 8.0, 7.7, 8.1, 8.2, 8.0, and 7.7.

Coleman's 1985 score, 8.69, was almost the same as in 1986. Willie McGee, nursing injuries, dropped sharply in 1986 after scoring at 7.8, 7.8, and 8.3 the previous three years.

The only two players out of the past that I figured were Willie Davis and Maury Wills, 1961–1965. Wills in 1962 scored at 8.94, the highest I've found other than Willie Wilson. In addition to his historic stolen base totals, Wills scored 9.9 on triples and 9.7 on runs scored. With the exception of that one year, both Wills and Willie Davis scored consistently in the sevens.

Between the extremes, a scale representing the players speed as an announcer would probably describe it would read something like this:

7.0   One of the fastest in the league
6.5   Outstanding speed
6.0   Very fast
5.5   Fast
5.0   Runs well
4.5   Runs fairly well
4.0   Has average or above speed
3.5   Speed is about average
3.0   Not a threat to steal
2.5   Below-average speed
2.0   Does not run well

While I've been treating this thing basically as a toy, just running numbers to see who looks better than who, there are some substantial sabermetric questions for which it would be handy. Obviously, all players lose speed as they age, but if you studied that loss of speed over time so as to learn what the normal pattern is, the knowledge could be used in several ways. It would help an organization to project what a player's skills would be. How fast do you usually have to be to play center field, and how long will it be before Willie Wilson passes that point? At what age does the loss in speed accelerate? Is Von Hayes losing his speed faster than normal? How much faster do catchers lose their speed than outfielders? Do white players actually lose their speed more rapidly than black players? All of those questions could be studied.

MONTREAL EXPOS

Runners on Base:	1,971
Opponents on Base:	1,949
Net Advantage:	+22
Won/Lost Record:	78–83

For a while, the Montreal Expos made a good show out of it. Picked by most to finish near the bottom of the National League East, the Expos stumbled through the cold of April as if going nowhere in particular; they were 3–6 on April 19. Tim Raines, though reaching base in every game, had not scored a run. Then they won a couple and they lost a couple and they won a couple and they lost one and they won a couple and they lost one more; the team had reached .500 for a day before dropping back to 9–10. There were some good signs. Andre Dawson homered in four straight games. Jay Tibbs won his first three decisions, including a shutout. Tim Raines had a hitting streak going, and had still reached base in every game.

On the third of May in Montreal, Nolan Ryan held a 5–1 lead in the early innings. Rallying for a run here and there, the Expos won the game 6–5 on a tenth-inning triple by Hubie Brooks. The next day the Expos came from behind to win again, and the day after that they did it again. The rallies ignited a thrilling streak that pushed the Expos into second place, hard behind the Mets, a position that they would not relinquish until the end of July. When Tim Raines gunned down Steve Sax at the plate in the ninth inning on May 11, the streak had reached eight games and the Expos were 17–10, four games behind the Mets.

If you're going to have a streak like that you might as well enjoy it, and in the giddy, heady days of the early May, the Expos drank deeply of the excitement. Third baseman Tim Wallach opined that "We have more quality pitching than any other team in our division, and that includes the Mets." General Manager Murray Cook described the Expo offense, which had a slugging percentage during the eight-game streak of .496, as "intimidating." Bryn Smith said that he, Hesketh, Tibbs, and Youmans were capable of winning 15 games apiece. It was observed by all that the attitude in the clubhouse was the best it had ever been, and Wallach thought that the Expos would win a hundred games.

It would soon become apparent that the Expos would not win a hundred games, but they continued to play well; this was one bubble that was destined never to break, but to shrink slowly into nothingness. With two outfielders in their option years, the Expos were the beneficiaries of some outstanding early performances. Rookie Andres Gallaraga hit .415 in April with 3 homers and 8 RBI. In early June Andre Dawson was hitting .300 with 12 homers, though his RBI count was disappointing, and Tim Raines was turning in about one incredible game a week without any bad ones. He had a 17-game hitting streak.

His string of reaching in every game reached 42 straight in the last week of May before a stomach virus forced him to leave the lineup in the middle of a game. In the 42 games he had 54 hits and 30 walks; in one two-week stretch his box score lines included 5340, 4320, 4321, and 5334. In one game he doubled left-handed and right-handed in the same inning.

But even the brilliant Raines was forced to take a back seat to the remarkable performance by Hubie Brooks. I have, in the past, not been kind to Hubie, and I don't think I owe him any apologies. As an error-prone third baseman with a secondary average below .200 and a batting average that came and went, Brooks was about as close as you can come to a worthless player. By dint of hard work, he has become a respectable, if unimpressive, defensive shortstop. But for the third straight year in 1986, Hubie pushed himself to a new offensive level. On June 5, Brooks was hitting .327 with 12 homers and 40 RBI in 41 games, incredible offensive production for a shortstop. When a finger injury shortly after that eliminated his power, he stopped pulling the ball and drove his batting average to .340. Hubie was clearly the Most Valuable Player in the National League before the All-Star break. With the help of Webster, Wallach, Gallaraga, Dawson, Fitzgerald, and Raines, the Expo offense was leading the league in homers, and battling for the lead in all the other important categories.

A few things were beginning to go wrong. Hubie Brooks missed six games with the finger injury, which apparently was caused by slamming the top hand into the bottom hand at the conclusion of his swing. In early June, Andre Dawson's knees finally forced him to go on the disabled list for the first time in his career.

On June 8, Larry Bearnarth persuaded a struggling Floyd Youmans, with a 5.91 ERA, to try a one-game experiment of junking his curve ball and working with his fastball and change; Youmans pitched a one-hitter, and was one of the best pitchers in the league the rest of the year. But the rest of the pitchers were not keeping pace. On June 17, Joe Hesketh's ERA was 7.14, and the scouts all know it is bad luck to have the ERA of a jetliner.

Gradually the dream was slipping away. On May 18 the Expos were 24–16, in second place and four games back. Two weeks later they were 28–24, still in second place but nine games back. Despite beating the Mets two out of three, they arrived at the next two-week marker (June 16) at 36–29, still in second place but ten games back. Despite again beating the Mets two out of three, they arrived at the next two-week interval (June 30) eleven and a half back at 44–34. Andres Gallaraga was side-lined after being beaned by Jeff Dedmon in Atlanta on July 6. When Hubie Brooks hand was placed in a cast on July 20, the race was over.

From that point on, the Expo offense deteriorated so rapidly and so severely that it seemed impossible that for half a season it had been regarded as a strong offense. The injuries are too numerous to list. Gallaraga, described by Rodgers in early June as the second-best first baseman in the league, required surgery on a torn cartilage in his right knee, and limped to an unimpressive season. Mike Fitzgerald, hitting .282, fractured a finger trying to stop a wild pitch in early August. Joe Hesketh went on the disabled list in July with "extreme muscle discomfort beneath his shoulder." "Extreme muscle discomfort" is usually called pain, and the part of your body beneath your shoulder is usually called your arm. Tim Wallace dropped from .269 with 14 homers and 51 RBI at the All-Star break to the disappointing totals of .233, 18 and 71. Not one Expo starter won 15 games. Only Raines and Webster continued to hit until the final bell. With the exception of those two and Floyd Youmans, the Expo collapse was complete.

In some ways, the Expos by the end of the season were a team that was not as good as its statistics. The Expos' team totals were those of a team which would expect to score 676 runs. The Expos actually scored only 637 runs—the largest deviation from runs created for any National League team. It is hard to isolate the cause of the inefficiency, because the Expos hit reasonably well with men in scoring position, but certainly moving Tim Raines into the third spot had something to do with it. Anyway, because of this offensive inefficiency, the Expos had a losing record despite getting more men on base than their opponents—the only National League team to do that, although the distinction is pretty technical. The Expos had only 1% more men on base than their opponents, and finished just two and a half games under .500.

To any team, the rash of injuries that the Expos suffered would have been damaging; to another team, it might not have been fatal. The Expos had no bench—nothing. Expo pinch hitters hit just .188 with 2 homers in 240 at bats, but the failure to win the game off the bench wasn't the biggest problem. Several Expos may have aggravated their injuries by trying to stay in the lineup, and when the injuries finally won the struggle, the players who had to go in and play were awful. Non-pitchers hitting less than .220 had 1,046 at bats for the Expos, more than for any other NL team (such players had 165 at bats for the Giants and 158 for the Dodgers). I observed in a midsummer newsletter that the difference between the frontline starters and the bench players was larger for the Expos than for any other team, and when the yannigans had to go in and play, the results were predictable.

Let's take a hit-and-run look at some of the strengths and weaknesses of the Expo play, without commenting on the sources for these:

The Expos bunted only 53 times, tying the Astros for the fewest bunts in the league.

The Expos were the victims of 200 stolen bases, eleven more than they allowed in 1985, which was then the highest total in the major leagues. The Phillies relieved them of that distinction in 1986.

As mentioned in the Cardinal comment, most of the Expos' final totals simply reflected their opposition; in sum they were a .500 team that did everything about as badly as they did well.

The Expos played well against right-handed pitchers (56–51), but had trouble against left-handers (22–32). The .393 pct against lefties was third-worst in the league. With Brooks and Dawson being right-handed hitters and Raines a switch hitter, there is no obvious reason for this.

The Expos had good team speed, but did not make effective use of it. They led the major leagues in triples with 50. They were second in the league in stolen bases, with 193, but were not really effective base stealers, having 95 runners caught stealing. Whereas the Cardinals had a net gain of about 23 runs on their stolen base attempts, the Expos, while stealing 74% as many bases, had a probable gain of only 10 runs—not even allowing for the fact that the Expos actually scored 39 runs fewer than would have been expected, which is to say that they scored 49 runs fewer than we would have expected had they not attempted to steal any bases. Like the Cardinals, the Expos scored only 32.3% of their runners reaching base, just missing the lowest percentage in the league, despite a decent team batting average (.254). The only real benefit from the running game was from Tim Raines, who stole 70 bases in 79 attempts, adding about 10 runs to the team total; the rest of the team was 125 for 209, meaning that they added nothing to the offense of the team, and indeed would probably have been better off had they just held first.

As to what the 1987 season might hold in store, there is little reason to be optimistic. While the Expos were a comparatively young team, with the eight regulars averaging just 27.4 years of age and only one key pitcher (Reardon) being a true veteran, that factor would appear to be outweighed by others. As mentioned elsewhere, the performance of the team late in the season is a proven indicator of the probable movement of the team in future years, and the Expos would appear to be a classic example of why. Their pitching staff at year's end was in shambles. With the exception of Randy St. Claire, a relief pitcher, there appears to be almost nothing in the farm system to help. Bryn Smith could return and help stabilize the rotation, but then Raines and Dawson may not return. Unless the irrepressible Hubie Brooks has a triple crown season, it is hard to see how the Expos can compete in 1987.

The 1987 season will begin the acid test for Murray Cook as a general manager. Cook as GM has received generally kind reviews for picking up players like Mitch Webster, Tom Foley, and Andy McGaffigan without giving up much or by having them included as extras in trades for bigger stars. But the effect of these moves has been only to forestall disaster in the face of the breakup of the Dick Williams team, with Gary Carter having to be traded, Steve Rogers losing effectiveness, and players like Al Oliver, Warren Cromartie, Charlie Lea, and Scott Sanderson outliving their usefulness. With Dawson and Raines becoming eligible for free agency, that era is over and the period in which Cook can be evaluated by specific moves has ended with it. He's on the same ground as anybody else now: If the team wins he's successful and if they lose he isn't. The future is dim now; if Raines and Dawson are lost to free agency, it will be dark.

Mike FITZGERALD, Catcher

	G	AB	Hit	2B	3B	HR	Run	RBI	TBB	SO	SB	CS	Avg
1.86 years		476	112	19	2	8	36	57	50	89	5	3	.236
1986	73	209	59	13	1	6	20	37	27	34	3	2	.282
First Half	63	182	51	11	1	6	19	36	26	30	3	2	.280
Second Half	10	27	8	2	0	0	1	1	1	4	0	0	.296
Vs. RHP		143	44	9	1	5		29	18	27			.308
Vs. LHP		66	15	4	0	1		8	9	7			.227
Home		97	27	2	1	1		13	12	21			.278
Road		112	32	11	0	5		24	15	13			.286
Grass		63	19	8	0	3		16	8	5			.302
Turf		146	40	5	1	3		21	19	29			.274

Tim WALLACH, Third Base

	G	AB	Hit	2B	3B	HR	Run	RBI	TBB	SO	SB	CS	Avg
5.18 years		585	149	30	3	21	65	78	46	91	5	5	.254
1986	134	480	112	22	1	18	50	71	44	72	8	4	.233
First Half	84	297	80	18	1	14	37	51	32	48	4	1	.269
Second Half	50	183	32	4	0	4	13	20	12	24	4	3	.175
Vs. RHP		345	84	13	1	15		17	56	27	53			.243
Vs. LHP		135	28	9	0	3		33	15	17	19			.207
Home		229	51	7	1	6		33	21	34			.223
Road		251	61	15	0	12		38	23	38			.243
Grass		136	27	7	0	6		18	15	27			.199
Turf		344	85	15	1	12		53	29	45			.247

Andres GALARRAGA, First Base

	G	AB	Hit	2B	3B	HR	Run	RBI	TBB	SO	SB	CS	Avg
0.80 years		497	127	18	0	15	60	58	41	122	9	9	.255
1986	105	321	87	13	0	10	39	42	30	79	6	5	.271
First Half	76	220	55	7	0	8	28	26	20	54	6	3	.250
Second Half	29	101	32	6	0	2	11	16	10	25	0	2	.317
Vs. RHP		201	47	8	0	6		28	17	56			.234
Vs. LHP		120	40	5	0	4		14	13	23			.333
Home		161	46	8	0	4		21	15	39			.286
Road		160	41	5	0	6		21	15	40			.256
Grass		86	20	3	0	3		13	8	20			.233
Turf		235	67	10	0	7		29	22	59			.285

Mitch WEBSTER, Center Field

	G	AB	Hit	2B	3B	HR	Run	RBI	TBB	SO	SB	CS	Avg
1.62 years		508	143	25	10	12	82	51	49	74	32	15	.283
1986	151	576	167	31	13	8	89	49	57	78	36	15	.290
First Half	78	289	78	19	2	5	44	26	37	36	22	9	.270
Second Half	73	287	89	12	11	3	45	23	20	42	14	6	.310
Vs. RHP		376	99	15	11	3		29	45	55			.263
Vs. LHP		200	68	16	2	5		20	12	23			.340
Home		283	75	15	8	2		24	28	34			.265
Road		293	92	16	5	6		25	29	44			.314
Grass		148	52	10	0	3		12	13	21			.351
Turf		428	115	21	13	5		37	44	57			.269

Hubie BROOKS, Shortstop

	G	AB	Hit	2B	3B	HR	Run	RBI	TBB	SO	SB	CS	Avg
4.86 years		608	169	28	5	11	64	78	38	96	8	6	.278
1986	80	306	104	18	5	14	50	58	25	60	4	2	.340
First Half	75	288	96	16	5	14	47	54	24	59	4	2	.333
Second Half	5	18	8	2	0	0	3	4	1	1	0	0	.444
Vs. RHP		221	73	12	2	9		41	12	47			.330
Vs. LHP		85	31	6	3	5		17	13	13			.365
Home		137	48	8	2	3		26	14	24			.350
Road		169	56	10	3	11		32	11	36			.331
Grass		103	34	8	0	8		21	6	24			.330
Turf		203	70	10	5	6		37	19	36			.345

Andre DAWSON, Right Field

	G	AB	Hit	2B	3B	HR	Run	RBI	TBB	SO	SB	CS	Avg
8.91 years		632	177	33	8	25	93	94	40	101	28	10	.280
1986	130	496	141	32	2	20	65	78	37	79	18	12	.284
First Half	58	222	61	12	2	14	33	31	18	39	9	5	.275
Second Half	72	274	80	20	0	6	32	47	19	40	9	7	.292
Vs. RHP		335	88	20	1	9		53	23	59			.263
Vs. LHP		161	53	12	1	11		25	14	20			.329
Home		243	72	11	0	11		32	19	39			.296
Road		253	69	21	2	9		46	18	40			.273
Grass		143	42	10	1	4		23	10	25			.294
Turf		353	99	22	1	16		55	27	54			.280

Tim RAINES, Left Field

	G	AB	Hit	2B	3B	HR	Run	RBI	TBB	SO	SB	CS	Avg
5.44 years		619	189	33	10	9	111	58	86	69	85	13	.305
1986	151	580	194	35	10	9	91	62	78	60	70	9	.334
First Half	75	312	104	21	6	6	51	33	41	36	41	4	.333
Second Half	76	268	90	14	4	3	40	29	37	24	29	5	.336
Vs. RHP		397	137	26	8	5		34	58	43			.345
Vs. LHP		183	57	9	2	4		28	20	17			.311
Home		282	92	17	3	4		36	39	28			.326
Road		298	102	18	7	5		26	39	32			.342
Grass		155	52	9	1	2		13	25	16			.335
Turf		425	142	26	9	7		49	53	44			.334

Tom FOLEY, Shortstop

	G	AB	Hit	2B	3B	HR	Run	RBI	TBB	SO	SB	CS	Avg
2.26 years		393	97	18	4	4	37	36	38	55	7	4	.248
1986	103	263	70	15	3	1	26	23	30	37	10	3	.266
First Half	35	57	15	2	1	0	7	4	10	11	2	0	.263
Second Half	68	206	55	13	2	1	19	19	20	26	8	3	.267
Vs. RHP		232	61	14	3	1		19	27	29			.263
Vs. LHP		31	9	1	0	0		4	3	8			.290
Home		120	29	5	1	1		10	18	21			.242
Road		143	41	10	2	0		13	12	16			.287
Grass		66	21	4	2	0		6	5	5			.318
Turf		197	49	11	1	1		17	25	32			.249

Vance LAW, Second Base

	G	AB	Hit	2B	3B	HR	Run	RBI	TBB	SO	SB	CS	Avg
4.47 years		507	127	24	4	9	62	58	55	81	5	3	.250
1986	112	360	81	17	2	5	37	44	37	66	3	5	.225
First Half	74	251	52	10	2	3	26	29	28	51	3	2	.207
Second Half	38	109	29	7	0	2	11	15	9	15	0	3	.266
Vs. RHP		233	49	10	1	1		33	23	26	46			.210
Vs. LHP		127	32	7	1	4		4	21	11	20			.252
Home		177	46	11	1	3		28	20	25			.260
Road		183	35	6	1	2		16	17	41			.191
Grass		105	16	5	0	1		9	7	23			.152
Turf		255	65	12	2	4		35	30	43			.255

Wayne KRENCHICKI, Infield

	G	AB	Hit	2B	3B	HR	Run	RBI	TBB	SO	SB	CS	Avg
3.40 years		313	83	13	1	4	32	31	31	42	2	2	.266
1986	101	221	53	6	2	2	21	23	22	32	2	4	.240
First Half	55	95	24	3	1	2	7	11	9	15	0	0	.253
Second Half	46	126	29	3	1	0	14	12	13	17	2	4	.230
Vs. RHP		214	53	6	2	2		23	22	28			.248
Vs. LHP		7	0	0	0	0		0	0	4			.000
Home		91	21	1	2	1		10	17	17			.231
Road		130	32	5	0	1		13	5	15			.246
Grass		70	18	3	0	1		11	5	10			.257
Turf		151	35	3	2	1		12	17	22			.232

Floyd YOUMANS

	(W–L)	GS	Run	Avg	DP	Avg	SB	Avg
1985	(4-3)	12	50	4.17	9	.75	27	2.25
1986	(13-12)	32	129	4.03	18	.56	61	1.91
1985-1986		44	179	4.07	27	.61	88	2.00

	G	IP	W	L	Pct	ER	BB	SO	ERA
1985 Home	6	34.0	0	2	0.000	9	21	24	2.38
1986 Home	17	112.7	6	9	.400	52	66	109	4.15
1985 Road	8	43.0	4	1	.800	12	28	30	2.51
1986 Road	16	106.3	7	3	.700	34	52	93	2.88
1985 Grass	3	21.0	2	1	.667	6	13	11	2.57
1986 Grass	8	54.7	4	1	.800	18	31	39	2.96
1985 Turf	11	56.0	2	2	.500	15	36	43	2.41
1986 Road	25	164.3	9	11	.450	68	87	163	3.72
1986 Total	33	219.0	13	12	.520	86	118	202	3.53

Bryn SMITH

	(W–L)	GS	Run	Avg	DP	Avg	SB	Avg
1985	(18-5)	32	174	5.44	32	1.00	28	.88
1986	(10-8)	30	136	4.53	27	.90	33	1.10
1979-1986		102	454	4.45	100	.98	87	.85

	G	IP	W	L	Pct	ER	BB	SO	ERA
1985 Home	15	112.3	11	2	.846	29	25	62	2.32
1986 Home	13	86.3	5	3	.625	36	28	52	3.75
1985 Road	17	110.0	7	3	.700	43	16	65	3.52
1986 Road	17	101.0	5	5	.500	46	35	53	4.10
1985 Grass	12	78.0	6	3	.667	28	13	46	3.23
1986 Grass	11	64.3	2	5	.286	34	27	26	4.76
1985 Turf	20	144.3	12	2	.857	44	28	81	2.74
1986 Turf	19	123.0	8	3	.727	48	36	79	3.51
1985 Total	30	187.3	10	8	.556	82	63	105	3.94

Jay TIBBS

	(W–L)	GS	Run	Avg	DP	Avg	SB	Avg
1985	(10-16)	34	140	4.12	38	1.12	16	.47
1986	(7-9)	31	112	3.61	27	.87	24	.77
1984-1986		79	313	3.96	85	1.08	51	.65

	G	IP	W	L	Pct	ER	BB	SO	ERA
1985 Home	17	108.3	5	7	.417	44	3	51	3.66
1986 Home	20	115.7	3	6	.333	51	42	68	3.97
1985 Road	18	109.7	5	9	.357	51	46	47	4.19
1986 Road	15	74.7	4	3	.571	33	28	49	3.98
1985 Grass	10	59.0	0	7	0.000	33	24	26	5.03
1986 Grass	7	29.7	1	2	.333	15	16	12	4.55
1985 Turf	25	159.0	10	9	.526	62	59	72	3.51
1986 Turf	28	160.7	6	7	.462	69	54	105	3.87
1985 Total	35	190.3	7	9	.438	84	70	117	3.97

OTHERS

	(W–L)	GS	Run	Avg	DP	Avg	SB	Avg
Hesketh	(6-5)	15	59	3.93	10	.67	19	1.27
Martinez	(3-6)	15	45	3.00	14	.93	19	1.27
McGaffigan	(10-5)	14	70	5.00	12	.86	12	.86
Sebra	(5-5)	13	46	3.54	6	.46	18	1.38
Valdez	(0-4)	5	11	2.20	6	1.20	7	1.40
Owchinko	(1-0)	3	15	5.00	4	1.33	4	1.33
Burke	(9-7)	2	7	3.50	3	1.50	1	.50
Schatzeder	(6-5)	1	7	7.00	2	2.00	3	3.00

RECORDS WITH DIFFERENT STARTING CATCHERS

Catcher	Inn	ER	W–L	ERA	GS	SB	Avg
Fitzgerald	546.0	226	37-24	3.73	61	82	1.34
Bilardello	493.1	216	22-31	3.94	53	49	.92
Nieto	182.2	83	8-12	4.09	20	35	1.75
Hunt	163.1	57	8-10	3.14	18	19	1.06
Tejada	81.0	34	3-6	3.78	9	14	1.56

CHICAGO CUBS

Runners on Base:	1,932
Opponents on Base:	2,122
Net Disadvantage:	– 190
Won-Lost Record:	70–90

The Chicago Cubs opened the 1986 season expecting to contend for the National-League title. Those expectations were unrealistic, founded in the fantasy that an injury-prone pitching staff would somehow spring to health and be able to keep the opposition from abusing the friendly fences of Wrigley, and shingled over by the sheepish logic that what we did once, in 1984, we can do again in 1986. The season was a long, hard lesson that miracles cannot be repeated on demand, that the 1984 pennant resulted in part from a unique set of circumstances at a moment that came and went. The harsh summer split the Cub organization into bitter splinter groups which attacked one another in a season-long party game of Pin-the-Blame-on-the-Donkey. It was not a pretty time in baseball's prettiest park.

Let's start by looking at the talent on the team. The Cubs' double-play combination rivals the Tigers' as the best in baseball. Ryne Sandberg is as good a second baseman as there is, and as valuable year in and year out as any offensive and defensive package in the league. Shawon Dunston is a tremendous shortstop, a diving acrobat with a phenomenal arm, whose occasional misplays are fairly trivial in the context of his contributions: As a hitter he is developing.

That's the good news. No other Cub regular, including Moreland, Davis and Durham, is significantly more than an expansion type of player. To a degree, Wrigley Field disguises this, inflating these players' statistics so that people think that they are productive hitters. Because they think these men are productive hitters, nothing is done about replacing them or supplementing them to make them into viable platoon players. They are allowed to continue in their jobs, and they simply are not championship quality regulars.

The Cub outfield was easily the worst in baseball. I mean, you'd think that any team could come up with *one* outfielder who was *either* a good hitter *or* a good fielder. Among the Cub outfielders, all were below average both offensively and defensively. The best Cub outfielder was Keith Moreland—the best, on the basis of the fact that he does have some offensive strengths and some defensive strengths. To be honest, he's pretty terrible. In road games last year Moreland hit .249 with 4 homers and 34 RBI. In a normal park he'd probably come home and hit about .260, .270 with another 4 homers (exactly 50% of home runs are hit by the home team) and 35, 40 RBI—a total of .255 with 8 homers and 74 RBI, which anybody would immediately see was inadequate for a right fielder with his

defensive skills. This was not an atypical year for him: In road games in 1985 he hit .272 with 3 homers and 43 RBI, and in road games in 1985 he hit .295 but with 3 homers and 30 RBI. Absolutely the only reason he continues to play is that he gets enough fly balls up on the windy days at Wrigley that people think he has some power. As an outfielder he has a fine arm, gives a good effort and moves around better than the Ayatollah Khomeini.

Moreland, however, was the *best* of the Cub outfielders. In left field was Gary Matthews, an alleged power hitter who is 36 years old and drove in 46 runs, which is 6 more than the year before. As an outfielder, Matthews makes Keith Moreland look like Gary Pettis. In fact, Matthews would probably make the Ayatollah look like a good outfielder. It gets worse. In center field was Jerry Mumphrey, who (like Matthews) was once a pretty good player and remains a decent enough singles hitter, but who has a secondary average below .200, limited range and no throwing arm. Before Mumphrey came they had Bob Dernier out there, who is a good center fielder by the standards of the rest of the team and is a good hitter by the standards of people past retirement age. He is a fine base stealer.

Why Jim Frey chose to play these people is something that I am sure he will elucidate for us on the Cub radio broadcasts, but for now it's a mystery. Brian Dayett, who is probably a better player than any of these men, hit .383 in spring training and was told that he had a job, but when he went hitless in the first two games of the season Jim Frey put him back on the bench and then shipped him out. Perhaps even more puzzling is Frey's inability to write the name "Thad Bosley" on a lineup card. Bosley is a line-drive hitter, a disciplined hitter, a fine runner, and a graceful outfielder: he has done an excellent job as the Cubs' top pinch hitter for the last four years. In addition, he is a left-handed hitter, which the Cubs desperately need: they were over .500 against left-handed pitchers, but with every regular except Durham and the switch-hitting Mumphrey being right-handed, had the worst record in the league against right-handed pitchers (48–71).

Like most of us, Bosley would like to think that bigger and better things might eventually be in store for him. Frey seemed to consider the very idea to be repulsive, and flatly refused, no matter how desperate his options, to let Bosley play.

Well, enough about the outfield: To give you an idea of how bad they were, Chico Walker was called up in September and was regarded as a godsend. The pitching staff was just as bad as the outfield, but whereas Wrigley Field makes the outfielders stats look decent, it makes the pitcher's stats look even worse. The Cub Earned Run Average (4.49) was half a run a game worse than that of any other team in the league. The last team to have an ERA that much worse than any competitor was in 1975, when the Cubs had a 4.57 ERA as opposed to 4.05 for the second-worst team.

The league batting average in 1986 was .253. Against no other club was the batting average higher than .266. Against the Cubs, it was .279.

The league slugging percentage in 1986 was .380. Against no other club was it higher than .395. Against the Cubs, the league slugging percentage was a rather remarkable .423.

Lee Smith had another fine year, with 31 saves giving him 126 over the last four seasons; with the decline of Quisenberry he is perhaps the most consistent year-in, year-out reliever in the game. Ed Lynch pitched well after joining the team in the mid-summer, buttressing the supposition that the key to winning in a big hitter's park is not to walk anybody. The rest of the staff shall remain nameless at their own request.

Other than Sandberg and Lee Smith, the Cubs best player was catcher Jody Davis. Davis did a tremendous job of controlling the running game, with the Cubs officially throwing out 102 opponents stealing, easily the most in the league (the Giants were second with 87), while allowing only 132 stolen bases, the third-fewest in the league. Those of you who watch the Cubs on cable know that Davis has come a long way defensively: A player who three years ago had trouble throwing has learned to get out of the crouch and fire as well as any catcher in baseball. John Dewan's *Chicago Baseball Report* reports that runners who attempted to steal with Davis catching were successful just 97 times in 184 tries, which becomes 97 for 201 if you count 8 times runners were picked off base by pitchers and 9 times when they were picked off by Davis. Clearly, opposition managers would have been better off to have instructed their runners to hang close at first and forget about stealing, which partially explains why the Cubs were able to beat the Cardinals more times than they beat anybody else (they were 10–7 *vs.* the Cards.)

As a hitter Davis has power, enough to hit 12–18 homers a year in another park, although his average would probably hang in the .230–.240 range. He's a decent player, but he'd be a better player if they'd get him some help instead of asking him to catch 145 games a year. First baseman Leon Durham would be a good platoon player; he's a disciplined hitter with a little power and a C+ first baseman. He doesn't hit left-handers, and over the Cubs' last 162 road games he's hit .237 with 13 homers and 47 RBI, so he isn't any budding Mike Schmidt, either.

Because of the power of their double-play combination, and because they play in Wrigley Field, the Cubs did lead the league in home runs, out-homering their opponents by twelve (155–143). But they finished tenth in on-base percentage, so that they derived minimal value from those homers and finished fourth in the league in runs scored. In Wrigley Field, that ain't good enough. The Cubs are not likely to win anything unless they lead the league in runs scored.

As this collection of non-talent wound its way toward a thoroughly unsurprising fifth-place finish, the games became a sideshow to the ongoing weirdness of an organization in turmoil. General Manager Dallas Green was unhappy with the effort given, which brings up a question: If Dallas Green thinks that lousy players are lousy players because they don't try hard enough, how does he explain his own career? On May 15, Green was quoted as saying that Jim Frey must learn to criticize his players sometimes, holding them accountable for their performance. On May 17, seven Cubs became ill with food poisoning apparently contracted through room service in a Houston hotel. On June 5, Jim Frey tried out Green's advice on Steve Trout, remarking that "In my opinion (his problem) is definitely not physical. So we know what's left." Apparently this carping came as too little too late, because on June 12, with the Cubs having won 23 games out of 56 games and being only sixteen and a half behind the Mets, Frey was fired and replaced by Gene Michael.

The Cubs continued to lose. In July, ballgirl Marla Collins was fired for showing off some of her secret recipes in *Better Homes and Gardens*. Or was it *Redbook* . . . whatever; I didn't see them but I guess they were pretty exciting. I used to read those magazines but after a while all the recipes started to look alike. In August, George Frazier and his 5.40 ERA were traded to the Twins; Frazier alleged that the problem with the Cubs was that Harry Carey and Steve Stone created a negative atmosphere among the fans. Harry Carey said that Frazier was inept. The Cubs were mathematically eliminated on September first. Gene Michael spent most of September denying reports that he would not return as Cub manager.

Why he wants to, I'm not sure. There is little reason to think that 1987 will be much better. The Cubs played almost .500 ball on grass fields, but were 16–31 on artificial turf. The Cubs are slow and weak defensively in the outfield. How are they going to repair this?

The 1986 season was such a disappointment that it surely marks the end of an era and the beginning of a rebuilding period, but there is little on hand to rebuild with. The "kids" who were called up from the Cub farm system in September were Greg Maddux, Chico Walker, Brian Dayett, Dave Martinez, and Rafael Palmeiro. Maddux and Martinez were up last year and were awful. Walker and Dayett are probably better than what the Cubs have, but are both older than Alan Trammell and haven't yet established themselves in the majors. Only Palmeiro seems to have any real chance to make an impact.

Jody DAVIS, Catcher

	G	AB	Hit	2B	3B	HR	Run	RBI	TBB	SO	SB	CS	Avg
4.80 years		551	140	29	2	20	57	80	47	105	1	2	.254
1986	148	528	132	27	2	21	61	74	41	110	0	1	.250
First Half	82	300	74	13	2	11	30	38	22	69	0	1	.247
Second Half	66	228	58	14	0	10	31	36	19	41	0	0	.254
Vs. RHP		393	101	20	2	18	44	62	30	93	0		.257
Vs. LHP		135	31	7	0	3	17	12	11	17	0		.230
Home		262	70	12	1	14		49	20	57	0		.267
Road		266	62	15	1	7		25	21	53	0		.233
Grass		377	90	18	1	16		56	32	80	0		.239
Turf		151	42	9	1	5		18	9	30	0		.278

Gary MATTHEWS, Left Field

	G	AB	Hit	2B	3B	HR	Run	RBI	TBB	SO	SB	CS	Avg
12.00 years		582	164	26	4	19	89	80	77	91	15	6	.282
1986	123	370	96	16	1	21	49	46	60	59	3	2	.259
First Half	68	191	45	9	1	10	25	23	37	29	2	1	.235
Second Half	55	179	51	7	0	11	24	23	23	30	1	1	.285
Vs. RHP		265	59	10	0	15	33	31	37	50			.223
Vs. LHP		105	37	6	1	6	16	15	23	9			.352
Home		185	51	7	1	11		28	30	31			.276
Road		185	45	9	0	10		18	30	28			.243
Grass		274	75	11	1	18		40	43	43			.274
Turf		96	21	5	0	3		6	17	16			.219

Leon DURHAM, First Base

	G	AB	Hit	2B	3B	HR	Run	RBI	TBB	SO	SB	CS	Avg
5.32 years		565	159	30	7	22	82	86	71	104	20	11	.281
1986	141	484	127	18	7	20	66	65	67	98	8	7	.262
First Half	75	268	66	5	3	10	31	39	37	79	5	5	.246
Second Half	66	216	61	13	4	10	35	26	30	19	3	2	.282
Vs. RHP		353	98	15	4	17	55	50	57	69			.278
Vs. LHP		131	29	3	3	3	11	15	10	29			.221
Home		279	79	13	5	13		43	35	48			.283
Road		205	48	5	2	7		22	32	50			.234
Grass		349	98	14	6	15		52	40	61			.281
Turf		135	29	4	1	5		13	27	37			.215

Bob DERNIER, Center Field

	G	AB	Hit	2B	3B	HR	Run	RBI	TBB	SO	SB	CS	Avg
3.93 years		492	125	20	3	3	74	28	46	60	47	12	.254
1986	108	324	73	14	1	4	32	18	22	41	27	2	.225
First Half	54	168	29	6	0	1	13	9	14	25	7	1	.173
Second Half	54	156	44	8	1	3	19	9	8	16	20	1	.282
Vs. RHP		219	41	7	1	2	19	8	13	36			.187
Vs. LHP		105	32	7	0	2	13	10	9	5			.305
Home		157	40	7	1	2		9	10	14			.255
Road		167	33	7	0	2		9	12	27			.198
Grass		214	53	10	1	4		15	14	26			.248
Turf		110	20	4	0	0		3	8	15			.182

Ryne SANDBERG, Second Base

	G	AB	Hit	2B	3B	HR	Run	RBI	TBB	SO	SB	CS	Avg
4.88 years		645	185	31	8	15	101	71	50	92	39	11	.287
1986	154	627	178	28	5	14	68	76	46	79	34	11	.284
First Half	83	338	92	17	3	8	33	45	25	40	11	4	.272
Second Half	71	289	86	11	2	6	35	31	21	39	23	7	.298
Vs. RHP		463	134	24	3	10	54	55	34	63			.289
Vs. LHP		164	44	4	2	4	14	21	12	16			.268
Home		321	97	18	2	8		41	23	42			.302
Road		306	81	10	3	6		35	23	37			.265
Grass		445	125	22	2	11		51	35	59			.281
Turf		182	53	6	3	3		25	11	20			.291

Keith MORELAND, Right Field

	G	AB	Hit	2B	3B	HR	Run	RBI	TBB	SO	SB	CS	Avg
5.48 years		563	161	26	2	15	66	87	54	64	4	5	.286
1986	156	586	159	30	0	12	72	79	53	48	3	6	.271
First Half	84	319	87	16	0	7	41	46	34	27	2	5	.273
Second Half	72	267	72	14	0	5	31	33	19	21	1	1	.270
Vs. RHP		434	111	23	0	7	43	62	28	41			.256
Vs. LHP		152	48	7	0	5	29	17	25	7			.316
Home		297	87	19	0	8		45	22	24			.293
Road		289	72	11	0	4		34	31	24			.249
Grass		417	120	24	0	10		58	38	38			.288
Turf		169	39	6	0	2		21	15	10			.231

Ron CEY, Third Base

	G	AB	Hit	2B	3B	HR	Run	RBI	TBB	SO	SB	CS	Avg
12.52 years		564	147	26	2	25	77	90	79	96	2	2	.261
1986	97	256	70	21	0	13	42	36	44	66	0	0	.273
First Half	53	149	41	15	0	7	24	20	21	38	0	0	.275
Second Half	44	107	29	6	0	6	18	16	23	28	0	0	.271
Vs. RHP		176	44	11	0	8	21	22	26	47	0	0	.250
Vs. LHP		80	26	10	0	5	21	14	18	19	0	0	.325
Home		137	33	10	0	4		18	23	43	0	0	.241
Road		119	37	11	0	9		18	21	23	0	0	.311
Grass		192	51	16	0	9		27	31	54	0	0	.266
Turf		64	19	5	0	4		9	13	12	0	0	.297

Jerry MUMPHREY, Center Field

	G	AB	Hit	2B	3B	HR	Run	RBI	TBB	SO	SB	CS	Avg
8.67 years		533	153	23	6	7	71	60	50	72	20	9	.288
1986	111	309	94	11	2	5	37	32	26	45	2	3	.304
First Half	66	194	52	7	0	2	23	13	21	29	2	1	.268
Second Half	45	115	42	4	2	3	14	19	5	16	0	2	.365
Vs. RHP		247	82	10	2	5	33	30	19	36			.332
Vs. LHP		62	12	1	0	0	4	2	7	9			.194
Home		147	53	7	2	4		22	15	19			.361
Road		162	41	4	0	1		10	11	26			.253
Grass		235	77	9	2	5		25	23	36			.328
Turf		74	17	2	0	0		7	3	9			.230

Shawon DUNSTON, Shortstop

	G	AB	Hit	2B	3B	HR	Run	RBI	TBB	SO	SB	CS	Avg
1.38 years		601	152	35	5	15	77	62	29	113	17	10	.253
1986	150	581	145	37	3	17	66	68	21	114	13	11	.250
First Half	83	328	91	22	2	9	40	34	15	56	10	9	.277
Second Half	67	253	54	15	1	8	26	34	6	58	3	2	.213
Vs. RHP		422	109	27	2	11	46	43	17	86			.258
Vs. LHP		159	36	10	1	6	20	25	4	28			.226
Home		305	80	24	1	10		38	9	61			.262
Road		276	65	13	2	7		30	12	53			.236
Grass		427	111	29	3	13		53	13	78			.260
Turf		154	34	8	0	4		15	8	36			.221

Chris SPEIER, Infield

	G	AB	Hit	2B	3B	HR	Run	RBI	TBB	SO	SB	CS	Avg
12.59 years		527	130	22	4	8	55	53	62	71	3	3	.246
1986	95	155	44	8	0	6	21	23	15	32	2	2	.284
First Half	47	68	15	0	0	4	9	11	8	15	0	1	.221
Second Half	48	87	29	8	0	2	12	12	7	17	2	1	.333
Vs. RHP		110	33	5	0	4	17	16	11	24			.300
Vs. LHP		45	11	3	0	2	4	7	4	8			.244
Home		68	21	3	0	2		6	9	18			.309
Road		87	23	5	0	4		17	6	14			.264
Grass		99	28	3	0	3		9	12	24			.283
Turf		56	16	5	0	3		14	3	8			.286

Dennis ECKERSLEY

	(W–L)	GS	Run	Avg	DP	Avg	SB	Avg
1985	(11-7)	25	101	4.04	11	.44	19	.76
1986	(6-11)	32	129	4.03	19	.59	24	.75
1976-1986		335	1443	4.31	227	.68	348	1.04

	G	IP	W	L	Pct	ER	BB	SO	ERA
1985 Home	10	70.3	5	2	.714	27	7	64	3.45
1986 Home	13	83.3	4	5	.444	48	20	59	5.18
1985 Road	15	99.0	6	5	.545	31	12	53	2.82
1986 Road	20	117.7	2	6	.250	54	23	78	4.13
1985 Grass	14	94.3	5	4	.556	34	11	76	3.24
1986 Grass	23	144.3	6	8	.429	76	28	107	4.74
1985 Turf	11	75.0	6	3	.667	24	8	41	2.88
1986 Turf	10	56.7	0	3	0.000	26	15	30	4.13
1986 Total	33	201.0	6	11	.353	102	43	137	4.57

Steve TROUT

	(W–L)	GS	Run	Avg	DP	Avg	SB	Avg
1985	(9-7)	24	115	4.79	29	1.21	16	.67
1986	(5-7)	25	131	5.24	21	.84	17	.68
1978-1986		181	841	4.65	201	1.11	117	.65

	G	IP	W	L	Pct	ER	BB	SO	ERA
1985 Home	13	79.7	6	2	.750	30	38	24	3.39
1986 Home	20	82.0	3	2	.600	46	39	36	5.05
1985 Road	11	61.0	3	5	.375	23	25	20	3.39
1986 Road	17	79.0	2	5	.286	39	39	33	4.44
1985 Grass	18	106.0	7	4	.636	42	48	29	3.57
1986 Grass	26	111.0	3	4	.429	59	61	54	4.78
1985 Turf	6	34.7	2	3	.400	11	15	15	2.86
1986 Turf	11	50.0	2	3	.400	26	17	15	4.68
1986 Total	37	161.0	5	7	.417	85	78	69	4.75

Scott SANDERSON

	(W–L)	GS	Run	Avg	DP	Avg	SB	Avg
1985	(5-6)	19	83	4.37	13	.68	14	.74
1986	(9-11)	28	107	3.82	23	.82	16	.57
1978-1986		212	855	4.03	144	.68	146	.69

	G	IP	W	L	Pct	ER	BB	SO	ERA
1985 Home	11	69.3	3	3	.500	25	17	50	3.25
1986 Home	19	94.0	7	5	.583	37	22	70	3.54
1985 Road	8	51.7	2	3	.400	17	10	30	2.96
1986 Road	18	75.7	2	6	.250	42	15	54	5.00
1985 Grass	15	94.7	4	4	.500	27	23	69	2.57
1986 Grass	27	137.7	9	9	.500	61	30	104	3.99
1985 Turf	4	26.3	1	2	.333	15	8	15	5.13
1986 Turf	10	32.0	0	2	0.000	18	7	20	5.06
1986 Total	37	169.7	9	11	.450	79	37	124	4.19

OTHERS

	(W–L)	GS	Run	Avg	DP	Avg	SB	Avg
Hall	(1-2)	4	20	5.00	4	1.00	0	0.00
Hoffman	(6-2)	8	40	5.00	11	1.38	6	.75
Keough	(5-4)	2	4	2.00	4	2.00	0	0.00
Lynch	(7-5)	13	58	4.46	16	1.23	8	.62
Maddux	(2-4)	5	26	5.20	6	1.20	5	1.00
Moyer	(7-4)	16	77	4.81	21	1.31	21	1.31

RECORDS WITH DIFFERENT STARTING CATCHERS

Catcher	Inn	ER	W–L	ERA	GS	SB	Avg
Davis	1274.0	636	59-82	4.49	142	98	.69
Moreland	90.0	38	6-4	3.80	10	13	1.30
Lake	37.0	27	3-1	6.57	4	8	2.00
Martin	35.0	16	2-2	4.11	4	10	2.50
Christmas	9.0	4	0-1	4.00	1	3	3.00

Rick SUTCLIFFE

	(W–L)	GS	Run	Avg	DP	Avg	SB	Avg
1985	(8-8)	20	74	3.70	20	1.00	20	1.00
1986	(5-14)	27	88	3.26	23	.85	33	1.22
1976-1986		191	875	4.58	162	.85	174	.91

	G	IP	W	L	Pct	ER	BB	SO	ERA
1985 Home	8	55.0	4	2	.667	21	21	37	3.44
1986 Home	16	99.3	3	6	.333	48	58	73	4.35
1985 Road	12	75.0	4	6	.400	25	23	65	3.00
1986 Road	12	77.3	2	8	.200	43	38	49	5.00
1985 Grass	14	89.7	7	4	.636	31	34	65	3.11
1986 Grass	20	130.3	3	9	.250	61	71	93	4.21
1985 Turf	6	40.3	1	4	.200	15	10	37	.335
1986 Turf	8	46.3	2	5	.286	30	25	29	5.83
1986 Total	28	176.7	5	14	.263	91	96	122	4.64

SCHMIDT VS. THE CUBS?

If Mike Schmidt hit against the Cubs all the time, what would he hit?

I have a method to answer that question. I've had the method since the late seventies, but haven't written anything about it in the *Abstract* since 1981 and even then only explained part of the method. I'm not going to explain it here, either, inasmuch as that would require a long and not particularly interesting article. I only invented half of it; Dallas Adams invented the rest. It's an important piece of work because what we did, between us, was to develop a method that applies not only to this question but to literally millions of other questions, many of them non-baseball related. We've written about it in the *Baseball Analyst* and will get around to writing about it in the *Abstract* sometime.

Suppose that you start with the simplest question, which is suppose that a team with a won-lost record of 80–50 is playing a team with a won-lost record of 70–60. How often will the first team win?

The formula that will figure this is $(80 \times 60) / ((80 \times 60) + (50 \times 70))$, which will tell you that the 80-win team should win 57.8% of the time. There was a long logical progression which led up to the conclusion that this method should work, and it has been shown that it does work, but it's just too long to explain right now.

Anyway, I found that method, but it only applies to won-lost records in a .500 league. Dallas Adams figured out a way to divorce the method from a .500 league and make it apply to the same sort of questions where the norm was .255 or something instead of .500. If a hitter hitting .272 faces a pitcher against whom the league hits .204 in a league in which the league batting average is .255, what will the hitter probably hit?

If you're trying to construct a computer simulation of a baseball game, it is essential to have a good method to answer that question, and there is no standard method available, so a lot of people make very bad decisions about how to do this. Some people, for example, will base the outcome average on just the average of the confronting figures. This is terrible. I mean, suppose that a .300 hitter is facing a pitcher against whom the league average is also .300 in a league in which the batting average is .250? What will the player hit?

Well, the player hits .300 against a league in which the average pitcher allows a .250 average. That means that, facing a pitcher who allows a .250 average, he should hit .300. So when he goes up against a pitcher who *allows* a .300 average, he sure as hell has got to hit a lot more than just .300. If *both* the hitter and the pitcher are driving the batting average up, it's got to be way up.

Or look at it this way: Suppose that both averages are .260. If the league average is .250, both factors are driving that average up, so the outcome average has to be *over* to .260. If the league is .270, both factors are driving the

outcome average down, so it has to be *under* .260. So to calculate the outcome average, you have to know the league context.

Anyway, suppose Mike Schmidt was hitting all year against the Cubs. Against the National League, an average hitter hits .253. Against the Cubs, an average hitter hits .279 (see division sheet) with a considerable increase in power. So if Mike Schmidt was hitting all year against the Cubs, he'd have to hit quite a bit better than his usual miserable .290 with 37 homers and 119 RBI. But how large is the effect? How much does a given hitter gain?

Not allowing for platoon factors, I ran estimates of what ten National League hitters would hit against the Cubs and against the Mets. I chose the Cubs because they would have the largest impact on the players record, and I chose the Mets because they were the best contrast to the Cubs. An added bonus is that the Mets were weak in the one area in which the Cubs were strong—preventing the running game. Here are my estimates:

MIKE SCHMIDT

	G	AB	Run	Hit	2B	3B	HR	RBI	BB	SO	SB	CS	Avg
Against Cubs	160	551	112	175	34	2	41	138	90	82	1	2	.318
Against League	160	552	97	160	29	1	37	119	89	84	1	2	.290
Against Mets	160	557	83	151	26	1	30	101	84	94	1	2	.270

The batting average may not be precise because I figured these before rounding them off. I should figure out Schmidt's career record against the Cubbies; it might be even better than projected. Of course, Schmidt's famous for Bear-Battering. More:

DALE MURPHY

	G	AB	Run	Hit	2B	3B	HR	RBI	BB	SO	SB	CS	Avg
Against Cubs	160	613	103	179	34	8	32	96	76	138	5	9	.292
Against League	160	614	89	163	29	7	29	83	75	141	7	7	.265
Against Mets	160	619	76	153	26	6	24	71	70	156	8	6	.248

TIM RAINES

	G	AB	Run	Hit	2B	3B	HR	RBI	BB	SO	SB	CS	Avg
Against Cubs	151	581	105	212	41	11	10	72	77	59	65	14	.364
Against League	151	580	91	194	35	10	9	62	78	60	70	9	.334
Against Mets	151	584	78	183	30	8	7	53	74	68	72	7	.314

BARRY BONDS

	G	AB	Run	Hit	2B	3B	HR	RBI	BB	SO	SB	CS	Avg
Against Cubs	113	411	83	102	30	4	18	56	67	100	33	10	.247
Against League	113	413	72	92	26	3	16	48	65	102	36	7	.223
Against Mets	113	417	62	86	23	3	13	41	61	113	37	6	.207

TERRY PENDLETON

	G	AB	Run	Hit	2B	3B	HR	RBI	BB	SO	SB	CS	Avg
Against Cubs	159	579	65	152	30	6	1	69	35	58	21	9	.262
Against League	159	578	56	138	26	5	1	59	34	59	24	6	.239
Against Mets	159	581	48	130	22	4	1	50	31	67	25	5	.223

DARRYL STRAWBERRY

	G	AB	Run	Hit	2B	3B	HR	RBI	BB	SO	SB	CS	Avg
Against Cubs	136	474	88	135	32	6	30	108	73	138	23	17	.286
Against League	136	475	76	123	27	5	27	93	72	141	28	12	.259
Against Mets	136	479	65	116	24	4	22	79	68	155	30	10	.241

ERIC DAVIS

	G	AB	Run	Hit	2B	3B	HR	RBI	BB	SO	SB	CS	Avg
Against Cubs	132	414	112	126	18	4	30	83	69	98	74	17	.305
Against League	132	415	97	115	15	3	27	71	68	100	80	11	.277
Against Mets	132	419	83	108	13	3	22	60	64	111	82	9	.258

JOSE URIBE

	G	AB	Run	Hit	2B	3B	HR	RBI	BB	SO	SB	CS	Avg
Against Cubs	157	452	53	112	17	1	3	50	62	74	18	15	.247
Against League	157	453	46	101	15	1	3	43	61	76	22	11	.223
Against Mets	157	457	39	95	13	1	2	37	57	85	24	9	.207

MARIANO DUNCAN

	G	AB	Run	Hit	2B	3B	HR	RBI	BB	SO	SB	CS	Avg
Against Cubs	109	407	54	102	8	0	9	35	30	76	42	19	.252
Against League	109	407	47	93	7	0	8	30	30	78	48	13	.229
Against Mets	109	409	40	87	6	0	6	25	28	87	51	10	.213

KEVIN BASS

	G	AB	Run	Hit	2B	3B	HR	RBI	BB	SO	SB	CS	Avg
Against Cubs	157	590	96	201	38	6	22	92	39	70	18	17	.339
Against League	157	591	83	184	33	5	20	79	38	72	22	13	.311
Against Mets	157	594	71	174	29	4	16	67	35	81	24	11	.292

PITTSBURGH PIRATES

Runners on Base:	1,955
Opponents on Base:	2,004
Net Disadvantage:	−49
Won-Lost Record:	64−98

There are two primary points to be made about the Pirates at the outset. One is that they are on the very brink of being a much better team than they have been. The other is that, because they do have a few pieces missing, they have been forced to ask some players to do things that they're not really capable of doing. Once the point is reached at which they can stop doing this, those individuals will probably play better, and the team may improve quickly.

As to the 1985 season itself, there is not a great deal to discuss: The Pirates played .500 ball in April, began losing in May and continued to lose until early October. With the Cardinals playing as badly as they were it took until mid-June for the Pirates to claim last place, and even then the Cubs threatened to challenge for the position, but an 11–22 record from September 1 to season's end put the pretenders away.

With the possible exception of Tony Pena and team MVP Rick Rhoden, the Pirates had no legitimate stars, but they also did not have a great many weaknesses. Once a lifetime .300 hitter, Pena's batting average had dropped sharply in recent years as word got around the league that he would swing at anything. At the All-Star break last year Pena was hitting just .241, but he appeared to discover the concept of plate discipline at that point, and rallied strongly to finish with a .288 average (.345 the second half) and a career-high 53 walks. At five of the other seven spots, the Pirates had solid players—Bream at first, Ray at second, Morrison at third, Reynolds in left and Barry Bonds in center. Bream, Ray, Morrison, and Reynolds are decent but have little star potential, but Barry Bonds was an impressive rookie despite his .223 average, playing a good center field and compiling a secondary average over .400. Barry keeps saying that sooner or later people will realize that he is not his father, but people would realize it a lot quicker if he'd stop *playing* like his father.

Anyway, the point was that the Pirates don't have a generally weak lineup. Whereas a lot of bad teams, like the Cubs, are just sort of puny all over, the Pirates have a solid lineup with two outstanding weaknesses (shortstop and right field) and no outstanding strengths. That's a much stronger position. If Belliard should develop as a shortstop, if Mike Diaz or Mike Brown should develop into a slugging outfielder, the Pirates would have no outstanding weaknesses among the everyday players. If Barry Bonds should develop as expected or if Bream should surprise, the Pirates lineup could be excellent.

The pitching may have further to go. The Pirates best pitcher, and arguably as good a starting pitcher as there was in the league, was Rick Rhoden. It was Rhoden's fifth consecutive 200-inning season after battling his way back from a rotator cuff injury, an amazing accomplishment. Three of his last four seasons in Pittsburgh were outstanding. At 33, Rhoden struck out a career-high 159 batters. Unfortunately, there was a perception that his contract status required that he be traded. His staff-stabilizing effectiveness will be sorely missed. For Rhoden, the Pirates got what looks like a promising collection of arms from the Yankees, and Pirate fans can take some solace in remembering that the Bill Madlock deal was similar at the time it was made. But at this point, who will be the ace of the Pirate staff or the ace of the bullpen in 1987 is anybody's guess. Rick Reuschel has the most proven value, and Bob Kipper appears to have outstanding potential, as does Doug Drabek.

The bullpen has been awful since 1983, and it is not immediately apparent when or how this will change. Perhaps the next major test for Jim Leyland will be his ability to identify a potential relief ace. There are some managers, like Whitey Herzog, Bill Virdon, and Gene Mauch, who have a proven ability to look over the pitchers in camp in spring training, evaluate their stuff, evaluate their makeup, and pick the guy who can cut it as a relief ace. Other managers will just try anybody out there and see who gets hot, an approach that probably works 10% of the time. It's important that Leyland tackle the problem head-on.

Other than the bullpen, probably the most urgent need is for a cleanup hitter to come forward. Barry Bonds could be the man if he raises his average, or Sid Bream perhaps or Mike Diaz. But the Pirates led the league in grounding into double plays, and it seems to me that the reason for this, more than a lack of speed, is that the Pirates were forced to use players in the middle of the order who aren't true power hitters and don't uppercut, don't strike out a lot and don't hit a lot of fly balls to the outfield. In the middle of the order, those players wind up hitting into double plays. Pena and Ray, neither of whom is exceptionally slow, tied for the league lead in grounding into double plays with Gary Carter, all three players having 21. At any rate, the Pirates need to increase their power from spots three through five in the order.

No team is ever certain to improve, but if there is one team in 1987 that is most *nearly* certain to improve, it would have to be the Pirates. The fact that a team is on the very brink of becoming a good club does not necessarily mean that they will go *over* the brink; it merely means that there is a certain statistical probability of it. Sometimes, like a car at the end of an overpass in the movies, the team reaches the brink and goes back.

But the Pirates should be better because the talent on the 1986 team was far better than the won-lost record would indicate. It is a proven principle of sabermetrics that when a team wins significantly more or significantly fewer games than would be predicted by their runs scored and runs allowed, that team will tend in the next season to move in the direction of what their indicated won-lost record should have been (that is, if a team actually wins only 70 games, but could have been expected to win 80 based on the number of runs they scored and the number they allowed, that team will have a strong tendency to improve in the following season). This principle, which is known as the Johnson effect, was discovered during investigations based upon the thesis that deviations from expected wins and losses as projected from runs and runs allowed are principly the result of random luck, and thus tend not to repeat themselves from season to season.

The Pirates in 1986 scored 663 runs while allowing 700; as such they would ordinarily be expected to win about 77 games. They actually won only 64—a deviation of 13 games. That's an enormous, an unusual, deviation, the largest in the major leagues in 1986 and in fact larger than the combined deviations for any other two teams. While no other team in the league was more than 10 games under .500 in one-run games, the Pirates were 21 games under at 16–37; which of course is the cause of the deviation. Anyway, the Johnson effect would thus predict the Pirates to improve markedly in 1987, based on the fact that teams that snow this characteristic almost always do improve. It may sound complicated, but what I'm really saying is that the Pirates will probably improve because their individual abilities are better than have so far been reflected in the won-lost record.

The Pirates should be better in 1987 because they are a young team, and while it is true that the problem with young players is that sometimes they go backward instead of forward, it is also true that young *teams* tend to move forward much more often than they move backward. The Pirates eight most-regular starters in 1986 averaged 25.6 years of age, giving the Pirates the youngest starting lineup in baseball.

Opposition relievers posted 55 saves against the Pirates, the most against any major-league team. Whereas a poor team generally will force comparatively few opposition saves as a percentage of losses—because they will lose games by wider margins than a good team—saves by relief pitchers accounted for 56% of the Pirate losses, as opposed to a league average of 49%, and as contrasted to 40% for the Cubs (36 of 90), or 40% for the Mariners (38 of 95). The point is, again, that the Pirates were very close to winning a lot more games than they actually won.

As a backdrop to the season, the Pirates provided baseball fans with an intriguing moral, legal, and ethical controversy when they filed suit on April 21 seeking to wipe out multimillion-dollar future payments to former Pi-

rate Dave Parker. Surprisingly, the nation's press corp, after railing against drug use for three years and after abusing Parker on any available pretext for six years, reacted unsympathetically to the lawsuit, resting their case heavily on the fact that not only were the new Pirate owners seeking to alter a contract to which they were not originally a party, but were seeking to alter it on the basis of things that happened before they arrived. While that's a legitimate point, it should not obscure the fact that there's a lot of money involved ($5.3 million), and the Pirates' legal position is strong. Blowing aside the smokescreens, the central legal issue appears to be whether or not Parker fulfilled his contract; to get the money, Parker's attorneys must convince the jury that Parker fulfilled the contract to the best of his ability. Remembering the kind of shape that Parker was in at that time, and remembering his own comments at the time of Curtis Strong's trial, it's going to require a hell of an argument.

The reaction of the press may have been based upon the fact that the Pirate owners are the new kids on the block, and a lot of established people wonder whether or not they know what they're doing. My sense of it is that if the 1985–86 free-agent lockup continues, and the owners regain control of the players' movement, then the Pirates may win the gamble. If, on the other hand, free agents resume moving from team to team, the Pirates may have shot themselves in the foot. After the Parker suit, they're going to have to pay for everything up front, because no one is going to trust them to hold the money. It's not simply that they won't be able to compete for free agents, although that too could be costly, but that they may lose their own players because of a lack of confidence in the clubs willingness to fulfill the contract. If there is unrestricted free-agent movement this winter, the Pirates might be well advised to settle the suit.

In seeking to focus on the essential decision that made the 1986 season what it was, one is struck by the fact that this was, after all, the *first season* of a rebuilding period. The Pirates were favored by many to win the NL East as recently as 1984, and when they actually did lead the league in ERA in 1984, though finishing last at 75–87, it was natural for them to hope that the promise of 1984 would bloom a year late in 1985. When it didn't, the Pirates traded Bill Madlock to the Dodgers for three players and John Candelaria and George Hendrick to the Angels for a couple more players, fired Chuck and hired a real manager, and began rebuilding their team—August, 1985. While there is certainly a lot of work to be done, to have come as far as they have as quickly as they have must be considered a very solid piece of work.

And while I like the Pirate team, there is virtually no chance that they will win the division in 1987. They finished 44 games out last year, and I seriously doubt that any team since 1910 has won the pennant the year after finishing 44 games out. A rebuilding period normally takes a lot longer than two years. If the Pirates are in position to contend by 1989, that would be an excellent performance.

Tony PENA, Catcher

	G	AB	Hit	2B	3B	HR	Run	RBI	TBB	SO	SB	CS	Avg
4.94 years		581	166	28	3	13	62	69	35	75	8	8	.286
1986	144	510	147	26	2	10	56	52	53	69	9	10	.288
First Half	77	278	67	16	1	7	35	29	30	45	2	5	.241
Second Half	67	232	80	10	1	3	21	23	23	24	7	5	.345
Vs. RHP		336	89	18	0	6		37	33	51			.265
Vs. LHP		174	58	8	2	4		15	20	18			.333
Home		255	76	12	0	5		25	35	29			.298
Road		255	71	14	2	5		27	18	40			.278
Grass		137	35	5	0	2		14	12	21			.255
Turf		373	112	21	2	8		38	41	48			.300

R. J. REYNOLDS, Left Field

	G	AB	Hit	2B	3B	HR	Run	RBI	TBB	SO	SB	CS	Avg
1.97 years		525	141	29	6	8	69	63	40	89	23	10	.269
1986	118	402	108	30	2	9	63	48	40	78	16	9	.269
First Half	76	273	78	23	1	7	46	31	29	57	11	7	.286
Second Half	42	129	30	7	1	2	17	17	11	21	5	2	.233
Vs. RHP		297	85	25	1	9		37	31	57			.286
Vs. LHP		105	23	5	1	0		11	9	21			.219
Home		198	56	18	2	6		29	24	34			.283
Road		204	52	12	0	3		19	16	44			.255
Grass		114	35	5	0	3		12	11	26			.307
Turf		288	73	25	2	6		36	29	52			.253

Sid BREAM, First Base

	G	AB	Hit	2B	3B	HR	Run	RBI	TBB	SO	SB	CS	Avg
1.52 years		481	122	31	3	14	61	70	57	71	9	6	.253
1986	154	522	140	37	5	16	73	77	60	73	13	7	.268
First Half	81	270	74	20	3	11	41	40	40	41	7	6	.274
Second Half	73	252	66	17	2	5	32	37	20	32	6	1	.262
Vs. RHP		370	106	26	4	14		56	49	50			.286
Vs. LHP		152	34	11	1	2		21	11	23			.224
Home		262	74	23	3	5		33	27	34			.282
Road		260	66	14	2	11		44	33	39			.254
Grass		136	32	7	1	5		21	14	23			.235
Turf		386	108	30	4	11		56	46	50			.280

Joe ORSULAK, Outfield

	G	AB	Hit	2B	3B	HR	Run	RBI	TBB	SO	SB	CS	Avg
1.84 years		476	129	18	8	1	68	24	30	40	28	13	.272
1986	138	401	100	19	6	2	60	19	28	38	24	11	.249
First Half	79	250	71	15	3	2	41	18	21	21	16	9	.284
Second Half	59	151	29	4	3	0	19	1	7	17	8	2	.192
Vs. RHP		351	87	18	5	2		18	26	33			.248
Vs. LHP		50	13	1	1	0		1	2	5			.260
Home		183	41	8	3	0		4	16	15			.224
Road		218	59	11	3	2		15	12	23			.271
Grass		110	37	7	2	2		10	6	11			.336
Turf		291	63	12	4	0		9	22	27			.216

Johnny RAY, Second Base

	G	AB	Hit	2B	3B	HR	Run	RBI	TBB	SO	SB	CS	Avg
4.99 years		612	176	37	5	6	73	68	44	34	13	8	.288
1986	155	579	174	33	0	7	67	78	58	47	6	9	.301
First Half	82	302	89	20	0	3	33	47	34	31	4	5	.295
Second Half	73	277	85	13	0	4	34	31	24	16	2	4	.307
Vs. RHP		357	116	25	0	6		52	39	29			.325
Vs. LHP		222	58	8	0	1		26	19	18			.261
Home		298	85	18	0	2		36	33	28			.285
Road		281	89	15	0	5		42	25	19			.317
Grass		146	45	7	0	2		21	14	12			.308
Turf		433	129	26	0	5		57	44	35			.298

Mike BROWN, Right Field

	G	AB	Hit	2B	3B	HR	Run	RBI	TBB	SO	SB	CS	Avg
1.83 years		465	124	26	4	13	55	60	41	67	3	5	.267
1986	87	243	53	7	0	4	18	26	27	32	2	3	.218
First Half	69	203	48	7	0	4	17	26	22	28	2	3	.236
Second Half	18	40	5	0	0	0	1	0	5	4	0	0	.125
Vs. RHP		126	30	5	0	3		17	10	19			.238
Vs. LHP		117	23	2	0	1		9	17	13			.197
Home		130	27	3	0	1		15	10	14			.208
Road		113	26	4	0	3		11	17	18			.230
Grass		74	18	3	0	2		7	15	9			.243
Turf		169	35	4	0	2		19	12	23			.207

Jim MORRISON, Third Base

	G	AB	Hit	2B	3B	HR	Run	RBI	TBB	SO	SB	CS	Avg
5.46 years		503	134	26	3	18	55	64	32	75	7	5	.266
1986	154	537	147	35	4	23	58	88	47	88	9	8	.274
First Half	81	278	66	12	2	11	27	41	30	55	6	3	.237
Second Half	73	259	81	23	2	12	31	47	17	33	3	5	.313
Vs. RHP		345	96	22	3	17		62	27	64			.278
Vs. LHP		192	51	13	1	6		26	20	24			.266
Home		269	80	15	4	11		50	30	46			.297
Road		268	67	20	0	12		38	17	42			.250
Grass		142	42	9	0	8		22	9	25			.296
Turf		395	105	26	4	15		66	38	63			.266

Barry BONDS, Second Base

	G	AB	Hit	2B	3B	HR	Run	RBI	TBB	SO	SB	CS	Avg
0.70 years		592	132	37	4	23	103	69	93	146	52	10	.223
1986	113	413	92	26	3	16	72	48	65	102	36	7	.223
First Half	40	151	35	13	1	7	27	17	29	45	15	3	.232
Second Half	73	262	57	13	2	9	45	31	36	57	21	4	.218
Vs. RHP		262	59	16	1	13		34	36	63			.225
Vs. LHP		151	33	10	2	3		14	29	39			.219
Home		211	51	17	2	9		26	36	56			.242
Road		202	41	9	1	7		22	29	46			.203
Grass		94	22	5	0	4		11	13	29			.234
Turf		319	70	21	3	12		37	52	73			.219

Rafael BELLIARD, Shortstop

	G	AB	Hit	2B	3B	HR	Run	RBI	TBB	SO	SB	CS	Avg
1.03 years		343	80	5	2	0	40	31	25	59	16	3	.232
1986	117	309	72	5	2	0	33	31	26	54	12	5	.233
First Half	64	165	41	2	2	0	19	23	12	31	10	1	.248
Second Half	53	144	31	3	0	0	14	8	14	23	2	1	.215
Vs. RHP		187	42	5	2	0		20	17	37			.225
Vs. LHP		122	30	0	0	0		11	9	17			.246
Home		144	30	2	1	0		16	12	18			.208
Road		165	42	3	1	0		15	14	36			.255
Grass		95	29	2	1	0		10	6	23			.305
Turf		214	43	3	1	0		21	20	31			.201

Bobby BONILLA, Outfield

	G	AB	Hit	2B	3B	HR	Run	RBI	TBB	SO	SB	CS	Avg
0.85 years		500	128	19	5	4	65	50	73	103	9	6	.256
1986	138	426	109	16	4	3	55	43	62	88	8	5	.256
First Half	68	213	55	9	2	2	25	24	32	43	4	1	.258
Second Half	70	213	54	7	2	1	30	19	30	45	4	4	.254
Vs. RHP		244	60	7	3	3		24	39	63			.246
Vs. LHP		182	49	9	1	0		19	23	25			.269
Home		200	54	7	3	2		31	29	37			.270
Road		226	55	9	1	1		12	33	51			.243
Grass		238	70	8	2	3		27	35	43			.294
Turf		188	39	8	2	0		16	27	45			.207

Rick RHODEN

	(W–L)	GS	Run	Avg	DP	Avg	SB	Avg
1985	(10-15)	35	128	3.66	19	.54	23	.66
1986	(15-12)	34	151	4.44	27	.79	23	.68
1976-1986		293	1235	4.22	259	.88	191	.65

	G	IP	W	L	Pct	ER	BB	SO	ERA
1985 Home	19	118.0	7	9	.438	58	38	66	4.42
1986 Home	19	140.0	9	6	.600	43	42	93	2.76
1985 Road	16	95.3	3	6	.333	48	31	62	4.53
1986 Road	15	113.7	6	6	.500	37	34	66	2.93
1985 Grass	9	58.0	2	4	.333	25	17	35	3.88
1986 Grass	8	56.7	2	3	.400	18	19	31	2.86
1985 Turf	26	155.3	8	11	.421	81	52	93	4.69
1986 Turf	26	197.0	13	9	.591	62	57	128	2.83
1986 Total	34	253.7	15	12	.556	80	76	159	2.84

Mike BIELECKI

	(W–L)	GS	Run	Avg	DP	Avg	SB	Avg
1985	(2-3)	7	18	2.57	5	.71	1	.14
1986	(6-11)	27	120	4.44	20	.74	25	.93
1985-1986		34	138	4.06	25	.74	26	.76

	G	IP	W	L	Pct	ER	BB	SO	ERA
1985 Home	4	20.3	1	2	.333	15	17	11	6.64
1986 Home	14	77.7	2	6	.250	40	44	46	4.64
1985 Road	3	25.0	1	1	.500	8	14	11	2.88
1986 Road	17	71.0	4	5	.444	37	39	37	4.69
1985 Grass	2	15.7	0	1	.000	6	8	7	3.45
1986 Grass	9	40.7	4	1	.800	18	19	20	3.98
1985 Turf	5	30.0	2	2	.500	17	23	15	5.10
1986 Turf	22	108.0	2	10	.167	59	64	63	4.92
1986 Total	31	148.7	6	11	.353	77	83	83	4.66

Rick REUSCHEL

	(W–L)	GS	Run	Avg	DP	Avg	SB	Avg
1985	(14-8)	26	96	3.69	25	.96	14	.54
1986	(9-16)	34	142	4.18	21	.62	26	.76
1977-1986		274	1096	4.00	216	.79	175	.64

	G	IP	W	L	Pct	ER	BB	SO	ERA
1985 Home	16	104.3	12	3	.800	26	25	76	2.24
1986 Home	17	104.3	5	8	.385	38	32	60	3.28
1985 Road	15	89.7	2	5	.286	23	27	62	2.31
1986 Road	18	111.3	4	8	.333	57	25	65	4.61
1985 Grass	8	52.0	1	2	.333	14	15	41	2.42
1986 Grass	9	51.3	2	3	.400	34	17	29	5.96
1985 Turf	23	142.0	13	6	.684	35	37	97	2.22
1986 Turf	26	164.3	7	13	.350	61	40	96	3.34
1986 Total	35	215.7	9	16	.360	95	57	125	3.96

OTHERS

	(W–L)	GS	Run	Avg	DP	Avg	SB	Avg
Kipper	(6-8)	19	69	3.63	11	.58	17	.89
Walk	(7-8)	15	54	3.60	23	1.53	14	.93
McWilliams	(3-11)	15	70	4.67	13	.87	7	.47
Patterson	(2-3)	5	17	3.40	6	1.20	3	.60
Fansler	(0-3)	5	12	2.40	7	1.40	2	.40
Winn	(3-5)	3	9	3.00	6	2.00	11	3.67
Bauveur	(0-0)	3	15	5.00	2	.67	4	1.33
DeLeon	(1-3)	1	4	4.00	0	0.00	4	4.00
Pena	(0-3)	1	0	0.00	0	0.00	1	1.00

RECORDS WITH DIFFERENT STARTING CATCHERS

Catcher	Inn	ER	W–L	ERA	GS	SB	Avg
Pena	1181.0	512	52-80	3.90	132	108	.82
Ortiz	261.2	109	12-17	3.75	29	28	.97
Rodriguez	8.0	8	0-1	9.00	1	1	1.00

RUSHING 'EM

Force-feeding of young players, rushing them to the major leagues after serving a brief apprenticeship in the minors, has led to a decline in the quality of baseball at its highest level, most everyone agrees.... While players today may be stronger, faster and better-conditioned, their shortcomings in fundamentals soon become apparent.

—Stan Isle
The Sporting News
August 11, 1986

Almost everybody, perhaps. Tom Grieve has been quoted as saying that players in the past have been kept in the minors when they really didn't need to be, and Hal Lanier was quoted to the effect that the players of today, because of the impact of college ball, arrive more quickly than they did a generation ago. What I was wondering, though, is how large of an effect are we talking about here? How long does the average player spend in the minor leagues now, as opposed to a few years ago? How rapidly is it changing? How old are most players when they arrive at a major-league job? How many players are there around who have very little minor-league experience? How does this compare to 1960?

To study those issues, I looked at the minor-league records of all major-league players playing 100 or more games in 1940, 1960, 1970, 1980, and 1986, and also formed a subgroup of the 1986 class defined as those players playing 100 or more games for the first or second time in their careers. This gave us six groups of major-league regulars, pretty thoroughly covering the last half-century of major-league play. Altogether, there were 966 players in the six studies.

For each player, I recorded two pieces of information: the total number of minor-league games played (up to and including the season of the study) and his age as of June 30 in the first season in which he played a hundred or more games. Several people helped me do this. Due to limitations of my library, I wrote a note in the *Baseball Analyst* requesting help in locating some data about the older players minor-league records, and I received the kind assistance of Mark Endoh, Dallas Adams, Edward Smith, Jerry Lansche, and Larry Kempster.

There has not been, either in the last few years or over the last ten years, any dramatic change in the length of time players spend in the minor leagues or in the age at which players reach the majors. The average number of minor-league games played by major-league regulars has been remarkably consistent at about 450 ever since 1940, and is not dropping at this time.

In 1940 the average major-league regular had played 456 minor-league games, and was 23.7 years old at the time that he played 100 major-league games for the first time. This was based on 130 players.

In 1960 the average number of minor-league games

had gone up to 468, and the average age of reaching the majors was up to 24.1. This was based on 140 players.

In 1970 the average number of minor-league games had edged up to 471, but the average age of reaching the majors had dropped to 23.6. Because of expansion, the number of players playing 100 or more games was up to 213.

Between 1970 and 1980 the average number of minor-league games played did decline to 434, an 8% drop from the previous decade. However, apparently because of more players coming into the game out of college, the average age at which players played 100 games for the first time was almost unchanged, at 23.7. There were 245 players studied.

Between 1980 and 1986 the average number of minor-league games turned back up to 438, with the average age of first regular season going up to 24.0. There were 238 players studied.

And in the subgroup of 1986 study which focused on the *new* regulars, the players who were playing 100 games for the first or second time, the average number of minor-league games played was 468—virtually as high as at any point in the study—and the average age of attaining regular status was 24.4 years, the oldest of any group. There were 70 such players.

None of the figures derived from this study, including the drop from 471 games to 434 during the 1970s, is statistically significant.

While the average number of minor-league games played has not declined significantly, it would nonetheless be possible that *the number of players playing very few minor-league games* could have increased, thus fulfilling Isle's condition. It hasn't.

In 1986 there were three major-league regulars who had no minor-league experience (Winfield, Horner, and Incaviglia). In 1960 there were four such players (Al Kaline, Dick Groat, Ed Yost, and Ernie Banks). In 1986 that was three out of 238, or 1.3%. In 1960 it was four out of 140, or 3.5%. In 1986 all three of those players had played college ball. In 1960 two of the four (Kaline and Yost) came to the majors straight out of high school.

In 1960 there were six major-league players who had less than 100 games of major-league experience, or 4.3%. In 1986 there were eight such regulars, or 3.4%.

In 1960 there were 14 regulars who had less than 200 games of minor-league experience, or 10%. In 1986 there were 22 such players, or 9.3%.

There *aren't* more players who come to the majors with little minor-league experience than there used to be. There are fewer. The decline in the average number of minor-league games played during the period 1960–1986, slight as it is (from 468 to 438) is entirely due to the virtual disappearance of the long-term minor leaguer. In 1960 there were eleven players who had played 800 minor-league games, and five who had played a thousand minor-league games (Jim Gentile, Billy Gardner, Walt Moryn, Norm Larker, and Maury Wills). In 1986, despite a field that was 70% larger, there were only two regulars who had played a thousand minor-league games (Mike Easler and Jerry Hairston), and only six who had played 800 or more, the others being Pat Tabler, Gary Ward, Mitch Webster, and Rafael Santana. With the exception of those players, the average was actually *higher* in 1986 than in 1960, 425–408.

Focusing on the "new regulars," the players who were playing 100 or more games for the first or second time in 1986, we get the same pattern only more so. There are 70 such players. One of those players, Pete Incaviglia, played no minor-league ball, and two more (Oddibe McDowell and Will Clark) had played less than a hundred minor-league games. That percentage—3 out of 70 players with very little experience—is historically normal. When you consider that all three of those players had played four years of college ball and that two of them played on the Olympic team, their quick appearance in the major leagues can hardly be shocking when compared with that of Dick Groat or Sam Chapman or Ed Yost. And when you're talking about players being rushed to the majors and not being fundamentally sound, I know for sure you ain't talking about Oddibe McDowell.

Of the 70 new regulars, only two others (Cory Snyder and Barry Bonds) played less than 200 minor-league games. Again, that percentage of players with very little minor-league experience is not high. Five out of 70 is 7%, as opposed to 10% in 1960 (14 of 140), and 13% in 1940 (17 of 130). If you want to go to 300 games, the picture doesn't change. Only 10 of the 70 new regulars have played less than 300 minor-league games, with the 200–299 group including Andy Allanson, Kurt Stillwell, Mariano Duncan, Terry Pendleton, and Robby Thompson. Ten out of 70 is 14%, as opposed to 21% in 1960 (31 of 140).

While there were these ten players who had less than 300 games of minor-league experience, there is a tendency to focus on those few players as if they were representative of the way things are done now. Look at the other end of the spectrum. Tim Hulett played 634 minor-league games. Rob Deer played 795. Joel Skinner played 602. Buddy Biancalana played 682. Jim Presley, Danny Tartabull and Ken Phelps of Seattle all played over 600. Terry Harper played 693. Mitch Webster, Andres Gallaraga, and Tom Foley of Montreal all played over 600. Rafael Santana and Ron Roenicke played over 600 games in the minors. So while there is a tail on both ends, as always, the distribution curve breaks about where it always has: about 450 games.

Enough percentages: Let's talk specifics. Doing the

study, one thing that I noted was that the average number of minor-league games played by a team was inversely related to how good a team they were. The better the team, the fewer minor-league games they had played on the average. The 1960 Yankees, for example, had no regulars who took longer than about three-and-a-half years to get through the minors, with the most minor-league games being 517 by Roger Maris. On the other hand, five of the eight 1960 Kansas City A's regulars had played 517 or more games. The reason for this is fairly obvious: The better players spend less time in the minor leagues. Yogi Berra went through the minors in 188 games, Mickey Mantle in 266, Willie Mays in 116, Roberto Clemente in 87 and Hank Aaron in 224. The same pattern seemed to apply to leagues. In 1940, when the American League was the dominant league, the AL average was 420 minor-league games, and the NL average 492. By 1960 this had about evened out, 466 for the American and 471 for the National. By 1970, when the National League had become dominant, the National League average was much lower, 456–486. By 1986 this was almost even again, 434–442 (NL lower).

Anyway, there are two points: One, that there have always been players who went through the minor leagues quickly, and there are fewer now then there were a generation ago; and two, that since good players usually go through the minor more quickly than poor players, it would be very strange to infer than an increase in the number of players going quickly through the minors was leading to a decline in the quality of play.

Even if such an increase were occurring, which it isn't. The reality is that the teams of today are showing *more* restraint about pushing young players than has ever been the case. Two times last summer, I heard announcers use Shawon Dunston as an example of one of these young players nowadays who was rushed through the minors too fast. Well, look at Shawon Dunston. Here is a kid who has got all the tools. He runs. His throwing arm is incredible. He's agile. He's got a quick bat with some pop in it. In spite of these things, the Cubs made Shawon Dunston play 377 minor-league games.

That, gentlemen, is extraordinary. For a team to keep an offensive and defensive shortstop prospect of Dunston's calibre in the minor leagues for 377 games . . . well, look up the outstanding shortstops and the outstanding short-stop *prospects* of any generation, and you won't find five who played 377 minor-league games. Look at the top shortstops who came up in the seventies. Ozzie Smith played only 68 minor-league games, Robin Yount only 64. Garry Templeton played 271 minor-league games. Bill Russell, Chris Speier, and Roy Smalley didn't play 377 minor-league games. Larry Bowa did, but barely (409). Dave Concepcion played 258 minor-league games, and Alan Trammell 196.

Go back to the shortstops of the sixties—Luis Aparicio played 244 minor-league games, Jim Fregosi 326, Don Kessinger 123. Bert Campaneris played 245 minor-league games. The outstanding shortstops of the fifties included Tony Kubek (368), Dick Groat (0), and Ernie Banks (0). The outstanding shortstops of the thirties included Dick Bartell (148), Joe Cronin (239), Luke Appling (104), Arky Vaughan (132). The outstanding shortstops of the forties included Lou Boudreau (175) and Pee Wee Reese (287) (don't have data for Phil Rizzuto). Honus Wagner and Rabbit Maranville made the majors quicker than Shawon Dunston. So if Dunston was "rushed" to the majors, I've got to say he was rushed slower than anybody in the history of baseball.

If you want me to say that Dunston is a polished shortstop, I can't. But I remember when Campy Campaneris came up, people said the same thing about him. Shawon Dunston is a hell-of-a-lot-better shortstop than anybody else the Cubs have—and that's the only comparison that counts, because that's the reason he's the Cub shortstop. And that explains why the average number of minor-league games played has hardly moved in the last 50 years and probably won't move in the next 50. The rule is exactly what it has always been: The minute a young player is better than the guy ahead of him, he gets the job, polished or not polished.

And as to the thesis that the quality of play is being dragged down by force-feeding of young players, it simply isn't happening.

NATIONAL LEAGUE WEST
DIVISION SHEET

	1st	2nd	RHP	LHP	Home	Road	Grass	Turf	Day	Night	TOTAL	Pct
Houston	47-41	49-25	65-39	31-27	52-29	44-37	23-25	73-41	32-22	64-44	96-66	.593
Cincinnati	40-44	46-32	59-58	27-18	43-38	43-38	25-23	61-53	27-31	59-45	86-76	.531
San Francisco	48-40	35-39	64-50	19-29	46-35	37-44	65-55	18-24	40-37	43-42	83-79	.512
San Diego	45-43	29-45	45-59	29-29	43-38	31-50	56-64	18-24	25-31	49-57	74-88	.457
Los Angeles	40-48	33-41	44-58	29-31	46-35	27-54	58-62	15-27	24-27	49-62	73-89	.451
Atlanta	42-46	30-43	51-62	21-27	41-40	31-49	58-62	14-27	21-25	51-64	72-89	.447

CLUB BATTING

	G	AB	Run	Hit	TB	2B	3B	HR	RBI	GW	SH	SF	HB	TBB	IB	SO	SB	CS	DP	LOB	SHO	Avg	Slug	OBP
Houston	162	5441	654	1388	2071	244	32	125	613	78	53	41	24	536	90	916	163	75	126	1113	6	.255	.381	.322
Cincinnati	162	5536	732	1404	2143	237	35	144	670	79	65	41	18	586	55	920	177	53	127	1129	7	.254	.387	.325
San Francisco	162	5501	698	1394	2063	269	29	114	637	77	101	34	37	536	86	1087	148	93	83	1132	12	.253	.375	.322
San Diego	162	5515	656	1442	2139	239	25	136	629	72	66	35	18	484	74	917	96	68	130	1099	9	.261	.388	.321
Los Angeles	162	5471	638	1373	2023	232	14	130	599	68	81	39	32	478	58	966	155	67	109	1083	14	.251	.370	.313
Atlanta	161	5384	615	1348	2051	241	24	138	575	66	79	42	24	538	62	904	93	76	124	1145	10	.250	.381	.319

OPPOSITION BATTING

	G	AB	Run	Hit	TB	2B	3B	HR	RBI	GW	SH	SF	HB	TBB	IB	SO	SB	CS	DP	LOB	SHO	Avg	Slug	OBP
Houston	162	5339	569	1203	1844	233	30	116	532	60	82	42	23	523	60	1160	176	62	78	1115	19	.225	.345	.295
Cincinnati	162	5550	717	1465	2186	255	29	136	680	71	86	60	17	524	81	924	135	69	128	1119	8	.264	.394	.326
San Francisco	162	5350	618	1264	1881	192	31	121	587	76	79	44	29	591	78	992	137	87	119	1094	10	.236	.352	.313
San Diego	162	5459	723	1406	2155	239	30	150	675	82	82	36	27	607	75	934	159	64	100	1116	7	.258	.395	.333
Los Angeles	162	5569	679	1428	2089	252	32	115	627	83	75	30	26	499	79	1051	123	74	88	1157	14	.256	.375	.319
Atlanta	161	5419	719	1443	2100	244	31	117	677	83	70	34	26	576	63	932	177	82	157	1132	5	.266	.388	.338

CLUB PITCHING

	W	L	ERA	G	CG	SHO	SV	IP	Hit	TBF	Run	ER	HR	SH	SF	HB	TBB	IB	SO	WP	BK
Houston	96	66	3.15	162	18	19	51	1456.1	1203	6010	569	509	116	82	42	23	523	60	1160	50	11
Cincinnati	86	76	3.91	162	14	8	45	1468.0	1465	6240	717	638	136	86	60	17	524	81	924	39	5
San Francisco	83	79	3.33	162	18	10	35	1460.1	1264	6093	618	541	121	79	44	29	591	78	992	58	15
San Diego	74	88	3.99	162	13	7	32	1443.1	1406	6212	723	640	150	82	36	27	607	75	934	38	18
Los Angeles	73	89	3.76	162	35	14	25	1454.1	1428	6199	679	608	115	75	30	26	499	79	1051	51	10
Atlanta	72	89	3.97	161	17	5	39	1424.2	1443	6125	719	629	117	70	34	26	576	63	932	44	11

OPPOSITION PITCHING

	W	L	ERA	G	CG	SHO	SV	IP	Hit	TBF	Run	ER	HR	SH	SF	HB	TBB	IB	SO	WP	BK
Houston	66	96	3.63	162	20	6	27	1442.2	1388	6095	654	582	125	53	41	24	536	78	916	47	13
Cincinnati	76	86	3.89	162	13	7	39	1461.2	1404	6246	732	632	144	65	41	18	586	55	920	50	14
San Francisco	79	83	3.72	162	18	12	44	1460.2	1394	6212	698	604	114	101	34	37	536	86	1087	55	12
San Diego	88	74	3.44	162	22	9	46	1454.1	1442	6118	656	556	136	66	35	18	484	74	917	51	9
Los Angeles	89	73	3.54	162	19	14	38	1460.0	1373	6101	638	574	130	81	39	32	478	58	966	44	13
Atlanta	89	72	3.41	161	19	10	51	1436.1	1348	6069	615	544	138	79	42	24	538	62	904	56	17

CLUB FIELDING

Club	G	PO	A	E	TC	DP	TP	OSB	OCS	OSB%	OA/SFA	Pct	DER	OR
Houston	162	4369	1565	130	6064	108	0	176	62	.739	29/42	.979	.718	569
Cincinnati	162	4404	1809	140	6353	160	0	135	69	.662	21/60	.978	.693	717
San Francisco	162	4381	1794	143	6318	149	0	137	87	.612	36/44	.977	.715	618
San Diego	162	4330	1629	137	6096	135	0	157	64	.710	40/36	.978	.700	723
Los Angeles	162	4363	1801	181	6345	118	0	123	74	.594	37/30	.971	.687	679
Atlanta	161	4274	2026	141	6441	181	1	177	82	.683	23/34	.978	.681	719

HOUSTON ASTROS

Runners on Base:	1,948
Opponents on Base:	1,749
Net Advantage:	+199
Won-Lost Record:	96-66

For the Houston Astros, all the elements came together in 1986. With a combination of youth and experience, pitching and power, talent and management, the Astros outclassed their division and coasted to an easy victory that might, with better luck, have been capped by even greater success in October.

As interpreted by a great portion of the nation's media, the key to the Astros' success was their ability to move baserunners. From the first day of spring training (this must be a direct quote from *somebody*, although I don't know who), Lanier had the Astros working on hitting behind the runners, making contact, moving baserunners along even with their outs. This theme was hammered upon by writers and broadcasters until by sheer repetition it became the accepted version of "How Hal Lanier Made the Astros a Winning Ballclub."

My own opinion is that the crap about moving the baserunners is at least 98% hokum. I intended to get out the Astros scoresheets from *Project Scoresheet* and do a count of how many times they did move runners along with outs, but I didn't do it. I apologize, because it's really not good to speculate about issues on which objective knowledge could be located with enough work. But I have reasons for what I think, which are at least as good as a lot of other people's, so here goes.

If the Astros were, in fact, exceptionally talented at advancing runners with outs, then that should cause them to score more runs than would be projected by the runs created formula. Shouldn't it? I mean, if you have a skill that "doesn't show up in the box scores," then that means you have a better team than the box scores are telling you, which means that you'll score more runs than another team would with the same combination of singles, doubles, triples, etc.

The Astros *didn't* score more runs than another team would have with the same combination of singles, doubles, triples, etc. They scored fewer. By the technical version of the runs created formula, one would expect a team with the Astros' category totals to score 668 runs. The Astros scored only 654. That's a normal deviation; there's nothing surprising about it *unless one asserts that the Astros had some additional advantage which is not reflected in the statistics*. But if the Astros *were* exceptionally good at moving runners with outs, then they must have been exceptionally poor in some other "intangible" area, such as hitting with runners in scoring position, or they would have scored many more runs than they did.

If the Astros were particularly good at moving baserunners, and if this was the key to their success, then one would expect them to score a higher-than-normal percentage of their runners on base. They didn't. The Astros scored 33.6% of their runners, whereas the league average was 34.4%.

If the Astros were adept at moving baserunners with outs, then one would expect them to be successful at avoiding the double play. In fact, the Astros grounded into 126 double plays, an above-average total. Indeed, the Astros lost 10% of their runners on first base to ground-ball double plays, 126 of 1,256, the *highest* percentage in the division, although the Reds and Padres grounded into slightly more total double plays.

To tell you the truth, I don't even think that Hal Lanier believes this stuff. Whenever I saw him interviewed, he never attributed the success of the Astros to moving baserunners. He stressed that the most important thing that Whitey Herzog taught him was how to handle the pitching staff. If you don't understand why a change takes place, if you just glance at the statistics and nothing jumps out at you, it is easy to attribute that change to something that is "beyond the statistics," something too subtle for the statistics to pick up. It's a way of having an explanation for something that you don't really understand. The problem with such "greater essence" explanations is that, like divine intervention and conspiracy theories, they can be manipulated to explain *everything*, and thus are ultimately unsatisfying as an explanation for anything. Unsatisfying and, in this case, false.

My opinion is that, *as an offensive manager*, Hal Lanier did a very poor job. The Astros in 1986 had a lot of things going for them. Kevin Bass developed as a hitter from .269 with 16 homers to .311 with 20 homers. Glenn Davis got in his first full year, and had the best season by an Astros power hitter in over a decade. Denny Walling had a potent season with the bat, an unexpected bonus. In spite of these advantages, and *in spite of the fact that the number of runs scored was up around the rest of the league*, the Astros dropped from 693 runs scored to 654. You're going to have a hell of a time convincing me that that's a good offensive performance. I think the offense declined in large part because Lanier tangled up the machine by using Billy Hatcher as the leadoff man and number two hitter.

But while Lanier did a very poor job with the offense, he did an excellent job with the pitching staff. As Whitey Herzog has done throughout his career, Lanier moved DeShaies, Ryan, Darwin, Keough, Madden, and others in and out so that the people he figured would win the pennant for him, Scott and Knepper, could keep working on regular rotation and keep piling up the wins. He used his bullpen well, he used his marginal starters well, and his big men came through for him. He took chances on a couple of unproven pitchers, DeShaies and Kerfeld, and his judgment of them proved sound.

To support the pitchers, Lanier made one major defensive switch, trading Jerry Mumphrey for Hatcher and putting Hatcher in center field, thus settling Kevin Bass in right field and Terry Puhl on the bench. There is no doubt that this improved the defense and made the pitchers better. My comment about Hatcher was not that he shouldn't play, but that Lanier assigned a major offensive role to a player with minor offensive skills.

With a strikeout staff and solid interior and exterior defense, the Astros allowed their opponents only 1,203 hits, 61 fewer than allowed by any other team, and the lowest total in the major leagues in a complete season since the Orioles allowed 1,194 in 1969. The batting average of Houston opponents was .225, eleven points lower than the batting average against any other team. Astro pitchers struck out 1,160 men—remarkably, having almost as many strikeouts as hits allowed. The 1,160 strikeouts were also the most since 1969, when the Astros struck out 1,221. The on-base percentage of Astros opponents was .295, the lowest in baseball.

The Astros threw 19 shutouts, 5 more than any other National League team.

Backing this superb pitching staff was a mobile, aggressive defense. The Astros' defensive efficiency record was .718, tying the Cardinals' as the best in the league. That measures the collective range of the fielders, which was unquestionably good, but there were holes in the defense, most notably at catcher. The Houston defense against the running game was the weakest in the division, with opponents stealing 176 bases in 238 attempts (Atlanta opponents stole 177 bases, but in 259 attempts. The stolen-base percentage against the Astros was easily the worst in the division, .739, and the stolen-base total missed by only one of being the worst).

The Astros turned only 108 double plays, fewest in the major leagues, which is also caused in part by the poor prevention of the stolen base. Other contributing factors include the low number of opponents on base and the high number of strikeouts.

The Astros' infield was strong both offensively and defensively, with Davis and Doran being outstanding young players, and player combinations doing a fine job at the other two spots (Walling and Garner at third, Reynolds and Thon at shortstop). Bill Doran had perhaps the poorest offensive and defensive season of his career, but began to receive some overdue recognition because of the success of the team. The outfield was improved defensively with the addition of Hatcher and improved offensively with the development of Bass, although the off year or decline of José Cruz may have offset that. The catching was not improved, as young Mark Bailey was sent out after he put on weight and stopped hitting, leaving Ageless Alan Ashby sharing the job with John Mizerock.

Alternating players at shortstop, third base, catcher, and center field also gave the Astros a stronger bench, and Lanier likes to use his bench. Astro pinch hitters hit a league-leading .280 (67 for 239). The leading individual pinch hitters were Craig Reynolds (9 for 22, .409), Denny Walling (12 for 31, .387), Terry Puhl (8 for 28, .286), and Jim Pankovits (11 for 38, .289).

Although the offense was unspectacular, the Astros were shut out only six times, fewest in the division.

While the Astros over a period of years have had a huge home-park advantage (that is to say, they played far better in Houston than on the road), this Astro edition had merely the normal eight-game home-park edge, playing quite well (44-37) on the road. Only the Mets had a better road record among National League teams.

There was a perception around the league that the Astros were weaker against left-handed pitchers. The Astros had 58 decisions against lefties, well above average, and were just 31–27 (.535) against them, whereas they were 65–39 (.625) against right-handers. Probably the biggest reason for this is that the lefties take Walling out of the lineup, but Kevin Bass, Glenn Davis, and Bill Doran would seem to pick up most of the slack (see breakdowns for hitters).

From what little I can see, neither the short-term nor the mid-term future appears exceptionally bright for the Astros. The Astros have several brilliant young talents, notably Kevin Bass, Bill Doran, and Glenn Davis. But in view of the number of players having career years and considering the age of several key performers, I see little likelihood that the Astros starting eight will play at the same level next year. Despite their success in 1986, about half of the Astros pitchers were fat. That's going to take a toll within a couple of years. Mike Scott was not fat, but it's an open question as to whether the complete framework of the man (the arm, the body, the mind, the will, the psyche) will support the role into which his newfound command of his "split-fingered fastball" has projected him.

There are several reasons that teams may have had trouble repeating championship seasons in the eighties, but one of them is that it has become so common for contending teams that are in a position to win to load up with veteran players near their last payday to push them over the top. The Astros did this, adding Lopes, Driessen, Aurelio Lopez, and Danny Darwin. Of the four, only Darwin seems a good bet to contribute in 1987, and by the time the Astros know for sure who will have to be replaced, they may be ten games behind. That, at least, is what has happened to several other champions of the eighties.

The Astros should face stiffer competition from Cincinnati and Los Angeles than they did last year. Within a couple of years, if not this year, the Astros bullpen will have to be rebuilt. The keys to coming out ahead of the challenge of 1987 may lie with Jim DeShaies and Danny Darwin, the only two Astro pitchers who have a good chance of contributing significantly more in 1987 than they did in 1986. The Astros have half-a-dozen fair outfield prospects (Eric Bullock, Ty Gainey, Tony Walker, Louie Meadows), one of whom may move into an outfield job, but I can't foresee any of them making a big impact. The failure of Robby Wine to develop as a hitter leaves the organization exposed at catcher.

Looking at the longer term, I think the Astros talent will probably break up simply because General Manager Dick Wagner is such an odious person that over time he will drive away the talented people who work beneath him, just as he did in Cincinnati. I foresee a difficult two- or three-year period ahead for the Astros. If they can come through that with their talent corps intact, then the future should be brighter.

Alan ASHBY, Catcher

	G	AB	Hit	2B	3B	HR	Run	RBI	TBB	SO	SB	CS	Avg
7.10 years		486	118	22	2	10	45	58	53	74	1	1	.242
1986	120	315	81	15	0	7	24	38	39	56	1	0	.257
First Half	53	102	23	3	0	3	8	9	0	0	0	0	.225
Second Half	67	213	58	12	0	4	16	29	39	56	1	0	.272
Vs. RHP		199	49	8	0	5		25	31	40		0	.246
Vs. LHP		116	32	7	0	2		13	8	16		0	.276
Home		155	39	7	0	1		18	18	25		0	.252
Road		160	42	8	0	6		20	21	31		0	.263
Grass		94	23	3	0	3		9	13	25		0	.245
Turf		221	58	12	0	4		29	26	31		0	.262

José CRUZ, Left Field

	G	AB	Hit	2B	3B	HR	Run	RBI	TBB	SO	SB	CS	Avg
13.51 years		553	159	28	7	11	73	76	63	71	23	10	.287
1986	141	479	133	22	4	10	48	72	55	86	3	4	.278
First Half	75	249	62	9	3	1	22	31	27	47	1	3	.249
Second Half	66	230	71	13	1	9	26	41	28	39	2	1	.309
Vs. RHP		285	78	15	0	8		44	43	45			.274
Vs. LHP		194	55	7	4	2		28	12	41			.284
Home		245	73	10	2	5		44	32	46			.298
Road		234	60	12	2	5		28	23	40			.256
Grass		141	31	6	0	2		14	14	28			.220
Turf		338	102	16	4	8		58	41	58			.302

Glenn DAVIS, First Base

	G	AB	Hit	2B	3B	HR	Run	RBI	TBB	SO	SB	CS	Avg
1.70 years		578	153	28	2	31	87	102	56	89	2	1	.264
1986	158	574	152	32	3	31	91	101	64	72	3	1	.265
First Half	87	325	88	18	2	20	48	60	0	0	2	0	.271
Second Half	71	249	64	14	1	11	43	41	64	72	1	1	.257
Vs. RHP		362	94	18	2	19		58	36	49			.260
Vs. LHP		212	58	14	1	12		43	28	23			.274
Home		285	85	16	2	17		58	32	30			.298
Road		289	67	16	1	14		43	32	42			.232
Grass		169	39	10	0	6		18	15	26			.231
Turf		405	113	22	3	25		83	49	46			.279

Billy HATCHER, Center Field

	G	AB	Hit	2B	3B	HR	Run	RBI	TBB	SO	SB	CS	Avg
1.16 years		509	128	23	4	7	69	40	27	55	36	16	.252
1986	127	419	108	15	4	6	55	36	22	52	38	14	.258
First Half	62	166	42	6	1	1	23	11	5	26	21	6	.253
Second Half	65	253	66	9	3	5	32	25	17	26	17	8	.261
Vs. RHP		209	48	10	0	3		15	9	29			.230
Vs. LHP		210	60	5	4	3		21	13	23			.286
Home		218	56	8	2	2		16	10	23			.257
Road		201	52	7	2	4		20	12	29			.259
Grass		124	31	3	2	3		15	10	18			.250
Turf		295	77	12	2	3		21	12	34			.261

Bill DORAN, Second Base

	G	AB	Hit	2B	3B	HR	Run	RBI	TBB	SO	SB	CS	Avg
3.83 years		603	165	24	7	8	91	48	80	71	27	15	.274
1986	145	550	152	29	3	6	92	37	81	57	42	19	.276
First Half	84	321	89	14	2	5	50	22	51	31	31	1	.277
Second Half	61	229	63	15	1	1	42	15	30	26	11	18	.275
Vs. RHP		336	87	16	3	3		18	56	39			.259
Vs. LHP		214	65	13	0	3		19	25	18			.304
Home		270	74	18	0	3		20	44	24			.274
Road		280	78	11	3	3		17	37	33			.279
Grass		171	42	8	2	3		10	21	23			.246
Turf		379	110	21	1	3		27	60	34			.290

Kevin BASS, Right Field

	G	AB	Hit	2B	3B	HR	Run	RBI	TBB	SO	SB	CS	Avg
3.37 years		501	137	25	5	12	65	58	24	68	14	8	.274
1986	157	591	184	33	5	20	83	79	38	72	22	13	.311
First Half	87	322	98	16	2	13	43	36	25	42	14	10	.304
Second Half	70	269	86	17	3	7	40	43	13	30	8	3	.320
Vs. RHP		343	104	15	5	8		37	31	41			.303
Vs. LHP		248	80	18	0	12		42	7	31			.323
Home		296	93	14	2	5		36	18	37			.314
Road		295	91	19	3	15		43	20	35			.308
Grass		170	51	11	3	10		26	9	20			.300
Turf		421	133	22	2	10		53	29	52			.316

Denny WALLING, Third Base

	G	AB	Hit	2B	3B	HR	Run	RBI	TBB	SO	SB	CS	Avg
5.57 years		383	107	17	4	7	51	53	41	39	7	3	.278
1986	130	382	119	23	1	13	54	58	36	31	1	1	.312
First Half	70	184	57	12	0	5	28	27	21	13	1	1	.310
Second Half	60	198	62	11	1	8	26	31	15	18	0	0	.313
Vs. RHP		324	108	22	1	13		51	30	25			.333
Vs. LHP		58	11	1	0	0		7	6	6			.190
Home		190	56	10	0	5		28	17	13			.295
Road		192	63	13	1	8		30	19	18			.328
Grass		110	38	7	1	5		18	10	14			.345
Turf		272	81	16	0	8		40	26	17			.298

Phil GARNER, Third Base

	G	AB	Hit	2B	3B	HR	Run	RBI	TBB	SO	SB	CS	Avg
10.69 years		550	144	27	8	10	70	67	50	74	20	7	.262
1986	107	313	83	14	3	9	43	41	30	45	12	6	.265
First Half	68	203	54	10	2	8	35	31	23	27	10	4	.266
Second Half	39	110	29	4	1	1	8	10	7	18	2	2	.264
Vs. RHP		121	27	4	0	3		12	10	23			.223
Vs. LHP		192	56	10	3	6		29	20	22			.292
Home		151	40	5	2	7		19	16	20			.265
Road		162	43	9	1	7		22	14	25			.265
Grass		92	25	4	1	4		14	11	14			.272
Turf		221	58	10	2	5		27	19	31			.262

Craig REYNOLDS, Shortstop

	G	AB	Hit	2B	3B	HR	Run	RBI	TBB	SO	SB	CS	Avg
7.27 years		515	133	16	9	5	56	44	23	44	7	4	.259
1986	114	313	78	7	3	6	32	41	12	31	3	1	.249
First Half	59	163	42	3	2	3	19	23	5	14	3	0	.258
Second Half	55	150	36	4	1	3	13	18	7	17	0	1	.240
Vs. RHP		278	73	6	3	6		40	12	24			.263
Vs. LHP		35	5	1	0	0		1	0	7			.143
Home		144	46	3	1	4		21	5	14			.319
Road		169	32	4	2	2		20	7	17			.189
Grass		110	22	4	0	1		15	3	14			.200
Turf		203	56	3	3	5		26	9	17			.276

Dickie THON, Shortstop

	G	AB	Hit	2B	3B	HR	Run	RBI	TBB	SO	SB	CS	Avg
4.01 years		519	141	25	6	8	64	48	40	69	24	10	.272
1986	106	278	69	13	1	3	24	21	29	49	6	5	.248
First Half	52	156	37	10	1	1	8	11	14	26	2	1	.237
Second Half	54	122	32	3	0	2	16	10	15	23	4	4	.262
Vs. RHP		101	26	7	0	2		11	9	23			.257
Vs. LHP		177	43	6	1	1		10	20	26			.243
Home		148	37	9	1	0		9	16	26			.250
Road		130	32	4	0	3		12	13	23			.246
Grass		69	14	0	0	2		6	8	17			.203
Turf		209	55	13	1	1		15	21	32			.263

Bob KNEPPER

	(W–L)	GS	Run	Avg	DP	Avg	SB	Avg
1985	(15-13)	37	150	4.05	44	1.19	15	.41
1986	(17-12)	38	158	4.16	35	.92	23	.61
1977-1986		318	1059	3.33	311	.98	267	.84

	G	IP	W	L	Pct	ER	BB	SO	ERA
1985 Home	19	123.0	5	8	.385	48	22	64	3.51
1986 Home	20	131.7	9	6	.600	53	24	77	3.62
1985 Road	18	118.0	10	5	.667	47	32	67	3.58
1986 Road	20	126.3	8	6	.571	37	38	66	2.64
1985 Grass	9	61.7	6	1	.857	19	16	33	2.77
1986 Grass	13	82.7	4	4	.500	25	21	44	2.72
1985 Turf	28	179.3	9	12	.429	76	38	98	3.81
1986 Turf	27	175.3	13	8	.619	65	41	99	3.34
1986 Total	40	258.0	17	12	.586	90	62	143	3.14

Mike SCOTT

	(W–L)	GS	Run	Avg	DP	Avg	SB	Avg
1985	(18-8)	35	176	5.03	38	1.09	24	.69
1986	(18-10)	37	145	3.92	17	.46	50	1.35
1979-1986		185	783	4.23	161	.87	185	1.00

	G	IP	W	L	Pct	ER	BB	SO	ERA
1985 Home	17	120.0	11	2	.846	29	35	74	2.17
1986 Home	20	151.3	10	8	.556	37	28	155	2.20
1985 Road	19	101.7	7	6	.538	52	45	63	4.60
1986 Road	17	124.0	8	2	.800	31	44	151	2.25
1985 Grass	11	65.0	4	3	.571	25	25	41	3.46
1986 Grass	8	59.0	3	1	.750	13	18	77	1.98
1985 Turf	25	156.7	14	5	.737	56	55	96	3.22
1986 Turf	29	216.3	15	9	.625	55	54	229	2.29
1986 Total	37	275.3	18	10	.643	68	72	306	2.22

Nolan RYAN

	(W–L)	GS	Run	Avg	DP	Avg	SB	Avg
1985	(10-12)	35	135	3.86	29	.83	36	1.03
1986	(12-8)	30	113	3.77	16	.53	38	1.27
1977-1986		356	1371	3.85	276	.78	418	1.17

	G	IP	W	L	Pct	ER	BB	SO	ERA
1985 Home	19	134.7	7	3	.700	47	43	118	3.14
1986 Home	17	109.0	9	4	.692	31	49	122	2.56
1985 Road	16	97.3	3	9	.250	51	52	91	4.72
1986 Road	13	69.0	3	4	.429	35	33	72	4.57
1985 Grass	9	52.0	3	4	.429	32	24	45	5.54
1986 Grass	7	39.7	1	2	.333	17	15	38	3.86
1985 Turf	26	180.0	7	8	.467	66	71	164	3.30
1986 Turf	23	138.3	11	6	.647	49	67	156	3.19
1986 Total	30	178.0	12	8	.600	66	82	194	3.34

Jim DESHAIES

	(W–L)	GS	Run	Avg	DP	Avg	SB	Avg
1986	(12-5)	26	110	4.23	15	.58	23	.88
1984-1986		28	118	4.21	18	.64	24	.86

	G	IP	W	L	Pct	ER	BB	SO	ERA
1985 Home	1	1.3	0	0	0.000	0	0	1	0.00
1986 Home	15	85.0	6	3	.667	32	30	71	3.39
1985 Road	1	1.7	0	0	0.000	0	0	1	0.00
1986 Road	11	59.0	6	2	.750	20	29	57	3.05
1985 Grass	0	0.0	0	0	0.000	0	0	0	0.00
1986 Grass	5	27.0	2	1	.667	11	8	29	3.67
1985 Turf	2	3.0	0	0	0.000	0	0	2	0.00
1986 Turf	21	117.0	10	4	.714	41	51	99	3.15
1986 Total	26	144.0	12	5	.706	52	59	128	3.25

OTHERS

	(W–L)	GS	Run	Avg	DP	Avg	SB	Avg
Darwin	(5-2)	8	37	4.62	3	.38	8	1.00
Knudson	(1-5)	7	30	4.29	6	.86	13	1.86
Madden	(1-2)	6	23	3.83	10	1.67	14	2.33
Keough	(5-4)	5	27	5.40	4	.80	3	.60
Hernandez	(2-3)	4	10	2.50	1	.25	4	1.00
Solano	(3-1)	1	1	1.00	1	1.00	0	0.00

RECORDS WITH DIFFERENT STARTING CATCHERS

Catcher	Inn	ER	W–L	ERA	GS	SB	Avg
Ashby	785.0	270	60-27	3.10	87	94	1.08
Bailey	396.2	133	22-22	3.02	44	50	1.14
Mizerock	265.2	106	13-17	3.59	30	28	.93
Wine	9.0	0	1-0		1	2	2.00

INDICATED ERA

I have a new freak-show stat here, if you're in the mood for one. A pitcher's record, as I wrote in *Meaningful and Meaningless Records,* generally gives a more accurate quick reading of the player's ability than does a hitting record, but the frustrating thing about a pitcher's record is that so much of it is seen through the veil of the team. A "pitcher's" wins and losses are, of course, really the wins and losses of the team for which he plays, and his ERA, his saves, his hits-per-nine-innings, and runs-per-nine-innings are also to a considerable extent a creation of the defense behind him. How can you get a reading on a pitcher's effectiveness without being so dependent on the team?

There are two elements of a pitcher's record that are independent of the team. Those are his walks and his home runs allowed. Those are the two elements on which, as the announcer says, the defense can't help you; if you don't throw strikes or the ball leaves the park there is nothing Willie Mays or Ozzie Smith can do about it.

I was wondering, then, if there was some simple way to combine these two categories into a meaningful indicator of the pitcher's self-destructive tendencies. What I came up with was indicated ERA, the formula for which is (HRA $\times$ TBB $\times$ 100) $\div$ Innings Pitched^2. Let's take Ricky Horton of St. Louis, since he pitched 100.1 innings, which we can round off to a hundred without doing too much damage. Horton's a good, little-known pitcher, what they call a Baltimore draft, a pitcher who moves the ball in and out and changes speeds, thus being effective without much of a fastball. In his 100 innings he gave up 7 home runs and walked only 26 men, both good figures. Seven times 26 is 182, times 100 is 18,200. A hundred squared is 10,000, so his indicated ERA is 18,200 divided by 10,000, which is 1.82. His actual ERA: 2.24.

Indicated ERA is like secondary average in several respects, but unlike it in a couple of key respects:

1) The formulas are simple. These are handy ways of expressing an idea, not the tools of technical analysis.

2) Secondary averages are devised in such a way that the league averages are almost the same as the league batting average, thus making the outcomes meaningful to the reader without his having to learn a new scale. In the same way, league indicated ERAs are in the same range as league ERAs.

3) As is true of secondary average, while the center is about the same, individual marks are more extreme. While the league batting and secondary averages are both about .260, almost all batting averages are in the range of .200 to .350, but secondary averages run from .100 to .500. Indicated ERAs, too, range all the way from 1.00 to 7.00. And occasionally beyond.

4) Some of the same elements comprise the two statistics, but from the opposite point of view. Indicated ERA is composed of power and walks; secondary average is composed of power, walks, and speed. A pitcher who has

a low indicated ERA would be a pitcher against whom opposition hitters would have a low secondary average.

However, the relationship that the new stat bears to the traditional one is wholly different. Secondary average focuses on abilities which are *not* reflected in batting average, and thus it is a very valid defense for Gary Redus to say that although he hit just .247, his secondary average was .397. What you're saying is that despite the low average, he was an effective offensive player. But indicated ERA focuses on particular accomplishments which *are* part of the pitcher's primary ERA, and thus it's not really a defense of any pitcher to say that he had a bad ERA but a good indicated ERA. If his indicated ERA is good, then he must have had a weakness somewhere else that caused him to fail. If you consider batting average to be a house, then secondary average is a neighboring house. If you consider ERA to be a house, then indicated ERA is a wing of that house, a couple of rooms or a floor—but not a separate house.

For a group of pitchers who have an ERA around 4.00, the indicated ERA will also be about 4.00. As the ERA moves lower or higher, the indicated ERA will decentralize, becoming disproportionately lower or higher. In the National League in 1986, the league ERA was 3.72. The indicated ERA was 3.27. Most successful pitchers will be successful at either throwing strikes or not allowing home runs, or both, and thus will have indicated ERAs in the twos. Ferguson Jenkins, for example, gave up almost 500 homers in his career, but had superb control and thus an indicated ERA of 2.39. Bert Blyleven, a similar pitcher with respect to strikeouts, walks, and home runs allowed, had an indicated ERA below 2.00 for his career until his historic 50-homer season in 1986. Nolan Ryan, on the other hand, has walked more people than anybody else in history, but allows very few homers (228 in 4,131 innings), and thus has a career indicated ERA of 3.03.

Generally speaking, a low indicated ERA will go with a low ERA, and thus it "indicates" a quality pitcher. A few career figures, with the actual ERA in parentheses: Whitey Ford, 3.24 (2.75), Hoyt Wilhelm, 2.30 (2.52), Elroy Face, 2.70 (3.48), Sandy Koufax, 3.01 (2.76), Jim Bunning, 2.60 (3.27), Don Drysdale, 2.03 (2.95), Bob Gibson, 2.27 (2.91), Jim Kaat, 2.09 (3.45), Juan Marichal, 1.84 (2.89), Gaylord Perry, 1.92 (3.10), Luis Tiant, 3.15 (3.30), Jim Palmer, 2.55 (2.86), and Rollie Fingers, 1.99 (2.90).

There are some pitchers, however, whose particular specialties are throwing strikes and throwing ground balls for strikes, and those pitchers will have unrealistically low indicated ERAs, being consistently in the ones. Those pitchers are usually somewhat weaker in other areas; they don't strike out a lot of people and they give up a lot of well-hit ground balls and line drives. As such they are very dependent on the teams for which they pitch; with a good team, they'll win big, but with a poorer team they may lose big. Tommy John was the prototype of this group; he has always had good control and has never allowed more than 20 homers in a season. As a rookie in 1964 his indicated ERA (3.96) was almost the same as his actual ERA (3.93), but between 1964 and 1985 he never had an indicated ERA higher than 2.68. In his best years, his indicated ERAs have been exceptionally low. In 1966, when he went 14–11 with a 2.62 ERA, he allowed only 13 homers and walked only 57 men in 223 innings (both excellent figures) for an indicated ERA of 1.49. In 1968, when he had an actual ERA of 1.98, his indicated ERA was 1.56.

In 1974, when John was 13–3 when his arm fell off in mid-season, Tommy allowed only 4 homers and walked only 42 men in 153 innings, for an indicated ERA of 0.72. By his mid-thirties, John had refined his style to where he was able to virtually extinguish both opposition homers and walks, and that was the beginning of a string of extraordinary indicated ERAs. Upon his return in 1976, his first indicated ERA (in 207 innings) was 1.00. In 1977 it was 1.24. In 1978 it was 1.29. In 1979, when John was 21–9 with a 2.97 ERA despite giving up about one hit per nine innings, he allowed only 9 homers and walked only 65 men. Indicated ERA: 0.77. In 1980, when he was 22–9, his indicated ERA was 1.04. Among pitchers who have pitched 2,000 innings or more, John may be the all-time leader in indicated ERA, with a remarkable career figure of 1.71.

The 1986 leader was a similar pitcher, a pitcher I have described many times as being a member of the Tommy John family. Rick Honeycutt of the Dodgers issued only 45 walks and was hit for only 9 homers in 171 innings, an indicated ERA of 1.39 (1.385, actually). The third digit is necessary because his teammate Bob Welch was only .001 higher, at 1.386. Welch suffered awful offensive and defensive support, and thus wound up 7–13. In general, though, the league leaders in indicated ERA and the league leaders in actual ERA were closely related:

	INDICATED ERA		ACTUAL ERA	
1.	Honeycutt	1.39	Scott	2.22
2.	Welch	1.39	Ojeda	2.57
3.	Scott	1.61	Darling	2.81
4.	Ojeda	1.65	Rhoden	2.84
5.	Cox	1.74	Gooden	2.84
6.	Rhoden	2.01	Cox	2.90
7.	Z. Smith	2.01	Tudor	2.92
8.	Knepper	2.05	Krukow	3.05
9.	Hershiser	2.09	Garrelts	3.11
10.	Valenzuela	2.11	Knepper	3.14
11.	Gooden	2.18	Valenzuela	3.14
12.	Krukow	2.20	Forsch	3.25
13.	Eckersley	2.24	Welch	3.28
14.	Tibbs	2.32	Honeycutt	3.32

Eleven pitchers are on both lists, with two of the three exceptions being the last two men on the indicated ERA list.

No American Leaguer had an indicated ERA below 2.00, with the top five men being Mark Gubicza (2.06), Charlie Leibrandt (2.12), Roger Clemens (2.18), Mike Witt (2.22), and Curt Young (2.76). The worst indicated ERAs were by Rick Sutcliffe in the National League (96

walks and 18 homers in 177 innings for a 5.54 indicated ERA) and José Rijo in the American League (108 walks and 24 homers in 194 innings for 6.91).

As a team, the Mets led the National League in indicated ERA (2.38) as well as in actual ERA (3.11). The figures for all major league teams:

NL	Indicated	Actual	AL	Indicated	Actual
Mets	2.38	3.11	KC	2.79	3.82
LA	2.71	3.76	Cal	3.45	3.84
Hous	2.86	3.15	Tor	3.67	4.08
StL	3.05	3.37	Mil	3.81	4.02
Mon	3.13	3.78	Chi	3.85	3.94
Cin	3.31	3.91	Bos	3.87	3.93
Atl	3.32	3.97	NY	4.13	4.11
SF	3.35	3.33	Bal	4.59	4.30
Phil	3.41	3.85	Cle	4.82	4.58
Pitt	3.74	3.90	Sea	4.83	4.65
Chi	3.81	4.49	Minn	4.90	4.77
SD	4.37	3.99	Det	5.01	4.02
			Tex	5.07	4.11
			Oak	5.39	4.31

The American League indicated ERA was 4.30; the actual ERA, 4.18.

As I said, this thing is basically a freak-show stat, not possessing a great deal of analytical value. However, I think it would be fair to suggest on the basis of these charts that in the case of Oakland, the defense is probably good enough to do the job if the pitchers would stop walking so many people and throwing so many gopher balls. They had an indicated ERA of 5.39 on the things that the pitchers did without help; the fielders cut it to 4.31. The same applies to Texas (5.07/4.11). On the other hand, there are some teams (such as the Cubs) whose pure pitching stats are made worse by the lack of a defense behind them.

I did a study to see whether indicated ERA had any predictive value—that is, if you take two pitchers who have about the same ERA but very different indicated ERAs, is there any evidence that the "indicated" ERA is a leading indicator of future performance. To report on the study in full would take several boring pages, so let's just say that, in the rare case where there is a tremendous disparity between the indicated and the actual ERA, there is some reason to look at it, but that unless the gap is tremendous it probably doesn't tell you anything. It's probably a fair generalization that if a pitcher shows a very low indicated ERA but isn't effective while working for a poor team, he probably would be much more effective for a good team, whereas if he has an indicated ERA of 5.00 he probably would not be very useful to anybody. But I haven't done any studies to evaluate that notion.

A few other pitchers who have had extremely low indicated ERAs: Ken Holtzman, Fritz Peterson, Bob Moose, Steve Rogers, Geoff Zahn, and Randy Jones. Jones in 1978 had an indicated ERA of 0.60, with an actual of 2.88. In order to be effective most of those pitchers need to have indicated ERAs below 2.00.

The king of indicated ERA, however, is a relief pitcher who never pitches enough innings to qualify for league leadership, but who nonetheless has clearly established a combination of phenomenal control—possibly the greatest in the history of the game—and an ability to keep the ball in the park. After he came up in mid-season in 1979, Dan Quisenberry pitched 40 innings and walked only 7 men, but gave up 5 home runs for an indicated ERA of a very respectable 2.19. Since then, however, Quisenberry's indicated ERA has never been as high as 1.00! His indicated ERAs, beginning in 1980: 0.82, 0.39, 0.77, 0.34, 0.72, 0.77, and 0.73. That's what once made Quisenberry the most effective reliever in the American League and, in my opinion, would make him a tremendously effective starting pitcher as well. In 1983, when Quiz saved 45 games, he pitched 139 innings (half as many as a hard-working starter) while walking only 11 men—yet at the same time allowing only six home runs. His career indicated ERA: 0.85.

CINCINNATI REDS

Runners on Base:	2,008
Opponents on Base:	2,006
Net Advantage:	+2
Won-Lost Record:	86-76

For the Cincinnati Reds, the 1986 season was a consolidation year in which the team, after struggling through the early part of the campaign, cemented the gains of 1985 and prepared to do combat in 1987 upon a solid foundation. While it may have been regarded as a disappointing season by some, who were so optimistic as to think that the progress of 1985 could be carried even further in 1986, in my estimation it was an extremely successful season for the Reds, a season in which they won more games than there was any reason to expect them to win, and at the same time accomplished much of the tricky work of bridging the gap between past and future.

To summarize the 1985 Reds quickly, the offense was championship quality but the pitching and defense weren't. The Reds scored 732 runs, 34 more than any other team in the division. Both elements of the Cincinnati offense, their ability to get men on base and their ability to score those who reached, were fairly strong, the latter being somewhat stronger. The Reds scored 36.5% of their runners on base, the highest percentage in the division.

The strikeout-to-walk ratio of Reds hitters, 1.57-1, was the best in the league except for the Mets.

Opposing pitchers were able to complete only 13 games, the lowest in the major leagues.

The Reds secondary average, .271, was the best in the division.

The Reds scored 20 runs more than one would have expected them to score by the runs created method (732-712).

The three players who keyed this offensive performance, in order of how surprising they were, were (1) Eric Davis, who exploded from perennial disappointment to one of the outstanding offensive players in the league, (2) Buddy Bell, who recovered from a substandard 1985 season and a slow start in 1986 with a blistering August streak that gave him one of his best seasons, and (3) Dave Parker, who nearly duplicated his MVP-candidate comeback season of the previous year. With the exception of these three men, the Cincinnati offense was ordinary, or even rather poor.

The Cincinnati defense for most of the season was not good. First basemen Rose, Esasky, and Perez had limited range even for first basemen, and defense at that position was a problem. There were also defensive problems in the outfield. The Cincinnati outfielders do not throw well. Cincinnati opponents had 60 sacrifice flies, tying Cleveland for the most in the major leagues, while their outfielders threw out only 21 runners during the year, the fewest

of any team in the league. Though no one seems to want to talk about it, Dave Parker in right field has become a defensive liability. Parker was always error-prone, and at 35 he simply is so slow, or more accurately he takes so long to accelerate, that his range is severely limited and his fine throwing arm somewhat negated because he is not in position to throw. People can and do go first-to-third on him and take extra bases on him. When Parker was combined with the inexperienced Eric Davis in center and Nick Esasky in left, the exterior defense was a problem. With the 37- or 38-year-old Dave Concepcion playing shortstop and Mario Soto getting hammered, the Reds were allowing so many runs that they were often not able to stay in the game.

So it was that on June 30 the Reds had a 31–41 record and an ERA of almost 4.00. They were losing with an old team. The Reds most-regular starting lineup in 1986 was the oldest in the National League, with only two regulars (Eric Davis and Nick Esasky) being younger than 30. At what could have been the watershed of his managerial career, Pete Rose began restructuring the team, attempting the dicey task of rebuilding the Reds without dropping out of contention. By year's end the Reds were playing Kurt Stillwell and Barry Larkin at shortstop rather than Concepcion, while rookie outfielder Kal Daniels was playing more in the outfield, with Esasky shifting to first and Rose and Perez hardly playing. Still, the Reds in 1987 will have anything but a young team; Dave Parker and Buddy Bell will turn 36 during the season, Bo Diaz is 34, and Oester will be 31 in May.

Cincinnati opponents had 1,465 hits, most in the division, and scored 717 runs, which is not the most in the division but is too many for a contender. The most bitter disappointment of the Reds 1986 season was the wipeout of Mario Soto. The brilliant right-hander, one of the finest starting pitchers in baseball during the Cincinnati down period of the early eighties, remained unable to share in the Reds revival, finishing 5–10 with a 4.71 ERA. Tom Browning, a 20-game winner as a rookie in 1985, also dropped to 14–13 with a 3.81 ERA, but at least Browning remained healthy and preserved the hope that he will have a better year next year. Soto's performance left Reds fans with a sickening feeling that Soto may have wasted his good years on a team that wasn't worthy of him.

Failure, however, creates opportunity. Ted Power, the Reds' bullpen stopper in 1985, lost his effectiveness in 1986, which was no surprise to you or me, and his place was taken by rookie Rob Murphy, 6–0 with an 0.72 ERA in 34 outings. Then, when John Denny went out for the year in August, Rose shifted Power to the starting rotation, with outstanding success. After a couple of tentative outings, Power closed the year with one fine performance after another. Thus, the Reds apparently wound up the year with four starters ready to do in 1987—Gullickson, Browning, Denny, and Power—and a well-stocked bullpen of Franco, Murphy, and Russell. With Larkin playing extremely well at shortstop, Ron Oester playing the best defense of his career at second base and Kal Daniels in the outfield, the Reds finished the season very strong. Sitting with a record of 47–52 on August 1, they went 39–24 the rest of the way to close with a respectable 86–76 record.

Pete Rose, in short, did one hell of a job of trimming the veterans, sorting out the rookies, and getting the Reds ready to contend. The controversy over whether Rose should retire has largely obscured the fact that, as a manager, Rose is one of the most intriguing and impressive in the league. Rose's managerial style is not easy to characterize; he shows no strong predisposition either to play for the big inning or to go for one run, either to go with youth or stick with veterans, either to rely on his starters or to rush to the bullpen, either to platoon or go with a set eight. In each area, he seems to make sensible, middle-of-the-road decisions based on the particulars of the situation. Most managers can be classified either as tacticians or emotional leaders. None of the National League's emotional leaders, such as Lasorda and Tanner, has the impact on his team's outlook that Pete does. Rose's teams know that they are expected to hustle, and hustle they do. That's the most that leadership can hope to accomplish.

Yet, while he certainly is not an intellectual, Rose is just as much a tactician as he is an emotional leader. As he was modest enough to say of himself when he was hired, Pete probably knows the game, knows the details of how to play the game, better than any other manager. Watching him manage, watching his teams play, you believe that he does. You may not say, "Gee, that's clever" as you would at something Gene Mauch does, but you never really have any doubt that he knows what he is doing and why he is doing it.

With regard to young players like Stillwell, Davis, Daniels, and Larkin, Rose doesn't do what Dick Williams might do, which is to stick them in the lineup and tell them not to blow it—yet neither does he do what so many managers do, which is to bury them and try to ride the veterans till they drop. He gives the kids a chance to show something, with an understanding that they are expected to show him something.

Rose is not a "platoon manager," like Bobby Cox or Earl Weaver, yet he did platoon at several positions, with Kal Daniels having 82% of his at bats against right-handers, Eddie Milner 87% of his at bats against right-handers, Max Venable 89% against righties, and Rose himself 91%, while Tony Perez had 57% of his at bats against lefties and Tracy Jones had 73%. Jones, doing his

best to avoid getting a label pasted on his forehead, hit .435 in his limited work against right-handers (10-for-23). The Reds were markedly more effective against left-handers (27–18) than right-handers (59–58). Eric Davis, a right-handed hitter, battered left-handers for a .317 average, 61 points better than he hit against right-handers (.256). That would probably explain most of the difference. Eric Davis is a super offensive player if he hits .256; if he hits .317 the opposition is in real trouble. Eleven of Davis' 46 hits against left-handers were home runs. Veteran left-handed hitter Dave Parker also hit .305 against left-handers, 50 points higher than he hit against right-handers (.255).

Is Rose a "big-inning" manager, like Weaver, or a "little-ball" manager like Mauch? Well, the Reds invested only 118 outs in first-run strategies, the lowest total of any National League team except the Cubs (116), so that he would appear to manage for the big inning from an offensive standpoint. The Reds invested 142 outs in first-run strategies in 1985, which was still below average, and cut it last year by bunting slightly less and stealing bases more successfully. On the other hand, Cincinnati pitchers issued 81 intentional walks, the most of any major-league team. This would be characteristic of a defensive manager who was more concerned about the first run in the inning rather than the big inning. It could well be that he doesn't bunt much simply because he doesn't have to with the talent he has.

How will the Reds do in '87? I have a series of "indicators" of the likely movement of a team in the following season. The indicators show the Reds as likely to decline in 1987, based on three facts: (1) the age of their starting lineup, (2) they scored slightly more runs than expected by the runs created method, and (3) they won slightly more games than would be expected in view of the number of runs scored.

My feeling is that the indicators series is wrong, that the Reds will not decline in 1987 but will in fact improve by the crucial 5–7 games that would put them in the low nineties. On the basis of the facts available in mid-December, 1986, I pick the Reds to win this division in 1987. The Reds have tremendous young talent. The outfield of Daniels, Davis, and Parker should be the best in the National League. The infield is solid except at first base. The bullpen is excellent and the starting rotation fairly sound. The catching is OK. The manager is a definite plus.

The biggest problem that I see is the lack of a rotation anchor. With the injury to Soto, the Reds don't have, or don't figure to have, any one starting pitcher who can match up against Mike Scott or Fernando. It's real tough to win a pennant with four guys who go 16–11; that just doesn't happen very often. If Mario Soto were to come back and pitch the way he once did, the Reds would blow the division away. Even without him, they are the solidest team in the National League West.

Bo DIAZ, Catcher

	G	AB	Hit	2B	3B	HR	Run	RBI	TBB	SO	SB	CS	Avg
4.43 years		526	136	27	1	14	56	74	37	69	2	3	.259
1986	134	474	129	21	0	10	50	56	40	52	1	1	.272
First Half	71	238	62	11	0	3	18	25	22	33	1	0	.261
Second Half	63	236	67	10	0	7	32	31	18	19	0	1	.284
Vs. RHP		339	93	13	0	7		38	26	40			.274
Vs. LHP		135	36	8	0	3		18	14	12			.267
Home		220	63	12	0	8		30	17	27			.286
Road		254	66	9	0	2		26	23	25			.260
Grass		168	52	6	0	2		20	12	13			.310
Turf		306	77	15	0	8		36	28	39			.252

Eric DAVIS, Left Field

	G	AB	Hit	2B	3B	HR	Run	RBI	TBB	SO	SB	CS	Avg
1.51 years		470	122	19	5	30	103	79	65	124	70	11	.259
1986	132	415	115	15	3	27	97	71	68	100	80	11	.277
First Half	67	196	56	6	2	12	49	31	30	51	42	5	.286
Second Half	65	219	59	9	1	15	48	40	38	49	38	6	.269
Vs. RHP		269	67	11	2	16		42	40	75			.249
Vs. LHP		146	48	4	1	11		29	28	25			.329
Home		198	52	6	2	12		33	32	42			.263
Road		217	63	9	1	15		38	36	58			.290
Grass		130	37	4	1	5		14	16	29			.285
Turf		285	78	11	2	22		57	52	71			.274

Nick ESASKY, First Base

	G	AB	Hit	2B	3B	HR	Run	RBI	TBB	SO	SB	CS	Avg
2.62 years		521	124	22	3	21	64	64	64	153	4	4	.238
1986	102	330	76	17	2	12	35	41	47	97	0	2	.230
First Half	41	143	32	8	1	6	19	16	24	37	0	0	.224
Second Half	61	187	44	9	1	6	16	25	23	60	0	2	.235
Vs. RHP		211	48	8	1	7		30	29	66	0		.227
Vs. LHP		119	28	9	1	5		11	18	31	0		.235
Home		158	36	10	0	9		23	19	55	0		.228
Road		172	40	7	2	3		18	28	42	0		.233
Grass		97	24	5	1	1		12	19	26	0		.247
Turf		233	52	12	1	11		29	28	71	0		.223

Eddie MILNER, Center Field

	G	AB	Hit	2B	3B	HR	Run	RBI	TBB	SO	SB	CS	Avg
4.20 years		507	130	23	7	9	80	41	61	57	32	12	.255
1986	145	424	110	22	6	15	70	47	36	56	18	11	.259
First Half	77	244	57	12	4	6	41	22	21	26	8	7	.234
Second Half	68	180	53	10	2	9	29	25	15	30	10	4	.294
Vs. RHP		366	97	19	6	15		43	33	46			.265
Vs. LHP		58	13	3	0	0		4	3	10			.224
Home		208	60	11	3	8		25	19	27			.288
Road		216	50	11	3	7		22	17	29			.231
Grass		133	36	6	2	5		11	10	19			.271
Turf		291	74	16	4	10		36	26	37			.254

Ron OESTER, Second Base

	G	AB	Hit	2B	3B	HR	Run	RBI	TBB	SO	SB	CS	Avg
6.05 years		557	148	25	4	6	62	47	49	88	6	3	.266
1986	153	523	135	23	2	8	52	44	52	84	9	2	.258
First Half	82	279	71	14	0	5	24	29	28	46	4	2	.254
Second Half	71	244	64	9	2	3	28	15	24	38	5	0	.262
Vs. RHP		385	110	18	2	7		35	37	62			.286
Vs. LHP		138	25	5	0	1		9	15	22			.181
Home		261	73	14	1	6		22	27	43			.280
Road		262	62	9	1	2		22	25	41			.237
Grass		151	37	6	1	1		9	13	26			.245
Turf		372	98	17	1	7		35	39	58			.263

Dave PARKER, Right Field

	G	AB	Hit	2B	3B	HR	Run	RBI	TBB	SO	SB	CS	Avg
10.98 years		613	184	36	6	22	89	100	45	98	13	9	.301
1986	162	637	174	31	3	31	89	116	56	126	1	6	.273
First Half	84	335	94	17	0	16	46	55	32	65	0	5	.281
Second Half	78	302	80	14	3	15	43	61	24	61	1	1	.265
Vs. RHP		404	104	18	0	21		67	47	77			.257
Vs. LHP		233	70	13	3	10		49	9	49			.300
Home		313	84	19	2	17		57	28	59			.268
Road		324	90	12	1	14		59	28	67			.278
Grass		190	54	5	1	9		34	19	40			.284
Turf		447	120	26	2	22		82	37	86			.268

Buddy BELL, Third Base

	G	AB	Hit	2B	3B	HR	Run	RBI	TBB	SO	SB	CS	Avg
13.17 years		613	173	30	4	13	79	75	56	53	4	6	.282
1986	155	568	158	29	3	20	89	75	73	49	2	8	.278
First Half	79	273	66	14	1	5	30	29	29	24	0	5	.242
Second Half	76	295	92	15	2	15	59	46	44	25	2	3	.312
Vs. RHP		391	111	20	2	12		50	51	33			.284
Vs. LHP		177	47	9	1	8		25	22	16			.266
Home		277	85	12	3	14		45	34	19			.307
Road		291	73	17	0	6		30	39	30			.251
Grass		176	44	11	0	4		21	23	20			.250
Turf		392	114	18	3	16		54	50	29			.291

Kurt STILLWELL, Shortstop

	G	AB	Hit	2B	3B	HR	Run	RBI	TBB	SO	SB	CS	Avg
0.64 years		435	100	9	2	0	48	41	47	73	9	3	.229
1986	104	279	64	6	1	0	31	26	30	47	6	2	.229
First Half	46	112	20	1	1	0	9	7	16	29	2	0	.179
Second Half	58	167	44	5	0	0	22	19	14	18	4	2	.263
Vs. RHP		193	43	3	1	0		19	14	33			.223
Vs. LHP		86	21	3	0	0		7	16	14			.244
Home		151	33	4	0	0		12	15	29			.219
Road		128	31	2	1	0		14	15	18			.242
Grass		99	21	1	0	0		9	11	12			.212
Turf		180	43	5	1	0		17	19	35			.239

Dave CONCEPCION, Shortstop

	G	AB	Hit	2B	3B	HR	Run	RBI	TBB	SO	SB	CS	Avg
14.20 years		581	155	26	3	7	67	64	49	80	22	7	.267
1986	90	311	81	13	2	3	42	30	26	43	13	2	.260
First Half	72	270	69	11	2	2	36	26	22	37	12	2	.256
Second Half	18	41	12	2	0	1	6	4	4	6	1	0	.293
Vs. RHP		210	47	4	2	2		23	17	33			.224
Vs. LHP		101	34	9	0	1		7	9	10			.337
Home		135	37	6	2	0		13	12	16			.274
Road		176	44	7	0	3		17	14	27			.250
Grass		102	28	2	0	3		12	6	14			.275
Turf		209	53	11	2	0		18	20	29			.254

Pete ROSE, First Base

	G	AB	Hit	2B	3B	HR	Run	RBI	TBB	SO	SB	CS	Avg
21.99 years		639	194	34	6	7	98	60	71	52	9	7	.303
1986	72	237	52	8	2	0	15	25	30	31	3	0	.219
First Half	53	191	40	7	1	0	12	19	25	23	2	0	.209
Second Half	19	46	12	1	1	0	3	6	5	8	1	0	.261
Vs. RHP		215	46	8	1	0		23	29	27			.214
Vs. LHP		22	6	0	1	0		2	1	4			.273
Home		121	31	6	1	0		13	12	17			.256
Road		116	21	2	1	0		12	18	14			.181
Grass		65	15	1	1	0		9	8	7			.231
Turf		172	37	7	1	0		16	22	24			.215

Tom BROWNING

	(W–L)	GS	Run	Avg	DP	Avg	SB	Avg
1985	(20-9)	38	182	4.79	35	.92	20	.53
1986	(14-13)	39	184	4.72	33	.85	29	.74
1984-1986		80	375	4.69	71	.89	50	.62

	G	IP	W	L	Pct	ER	BB	SO	ERA
1985 Home	19	131.3	10	6	.625	60	38	70	4.11
1986 Home	17	106.7	7	6	.538	45	38	59	3.80
1985 Road	19	130.0	10	3	.769	43	35	85	2.98
1986 Road	22	136.7	7	7	.500	58	32	88	3.82
1985 Grass	12	80.7	4	2	.667	29	26	53	3.24
1986 Grass	13	90.0	5	3	.625	35	14	57	3.50
1985 Turf	26	180.7	16	7	.696	74	47	102	3.69
1986 Turf	26	153.3	9	10	.474	68	56	90	3.99
1986 Total	39	243.3	14	13	.519	103	70	147	3.81

Chris WELSH

	(W–L)	GS	Run	Avg	DP	Avg	SB	Avg
1985	(2-5)	6	20	3.33	3	.50	1	.17
1986	(6-9)	24	116	4.83	33	1.38	25	1.04
1981-1986		75	323	4.31	84	1.12	54	.72

	G	IP	W	L	Pct	ER	BB	SO	ERA
1985 Home	11	34.0	2	1	.667	13	9	11	3.44
1986 Home	13	78.0	3	6	.333	41	24	8	4.73
1985 Road	14	42.3	0	4	0.000	22	16	20	4.68
1986 Road	11	61.3	3	3	.500	33	16	32	4.84
1985 Grass	20	60.0	2	3	.400	27	19	25	4.05
1986 Grass	5	23.0	2	0	1.000	11	3	5	4.30
1985 Turf	5	16.3	0	2	0.000	8	6	6	4.41
1986 Turf	19	116.3	4	9	.308	63	37	35	4.87
1985 Total	24	139.3	6	9	.400	74	40	40	4.78

Bill GULLICKSON

	(W–L)	GS	Run	Avg	DP	Avg	SB	Avg
1985	(14-12)	29	103	3.55	26	.90	37	1.28
1986	(15-12)	37	157	4.24	32	.86	32	.86
1980-1986		207	866	4.18	160	.77	162	.78

	G	IP	W	L	Pct	ER	BB	SO	ERA
1985 Home	14	98.3	10	2	.833	18	22	40	1.65
1986 Home	18	115.0	9	6	.600	47	28	71	3.68
1985 Road	15	83.0	4	10	.286	53	25	28	5.75
1986 Road	19	129.7	6	6	.500	45	32	50	3.12
1985 Grass	8	45.0	2	6	.250	29	12	13	5.80
1986 Grass	12	72.3	2	5	.286	32	19	29	3.98
1985 Turf	21	136.3	12	6	.667	42	35	55	2.77
1986 Turf	25	172.3	13	7	.650	60	41	92	3.13
1986 Total	37	244.7	15	12	.556	92	60	121	3.38

OTHERS

	(W–L)	GS	Run	Avg	DP	Avg	SB	Avg
Soto	(5-10)	19	69	3.63	14	.74	21	1.11
Power	(10-6)	10	59	5.90	14	1.40	5	.50
Terry	(1-2)	3	18	6.00	6	2.00	3	1.00
Price	(1-2)	2	11	5.50	1	.50	3	1.50
Smith	(0-0)	1	9	9.00	1	1.00	1	1.00

RECORDS WITH DIFFERENT STARTING CATCHERS

Catcher	Inn	ER	W–L	ERA	GS	SB	Avg
Diaz	1152.0	513	65-62	4.01	127	103	.81
Butera	298.0	119	20-13	3.59	33	30	.91
Van Gorder	18.0	6	1-1	3.00	2	2	1.00

John DENNY

	(W–L)	GS	Run	Avg	DP	Avg	SB	Avg
1985	(11-14)	33	149	4.52	38	1.15	38	1.15
1986	(11-10)	27	109	4.04	27	1.00	16	.59
1976-1986		298	1328	4.46	316	1.06	195	.65

	G	IP	W	L	Pct	ER	BB	SO	ERA
1985 Home	18	123.0	4	10	.286	55	42	59	4.02
1986 Home	14	89.3	6	5	.545	44	27	53	4.43
1985 Road	15	107.7	7	4	.636	43	41	64	3.59
1986 road	13	82.0	5	5	.500	36	29	63	3.95
1985 Grass	9	65.3	4	2	.667	22	22	40	3.03
1986 Grass	7	46.7	3	2	.600	17	15	38	3.28
1985 Turf	24	165.3	7	12	.368	76	61	83	4.14
1986 Turf	20	124.7	8	8	.500	63	41	78	4.55
1986 Total	27	171.3	11	10	.524	80	56	116	4.20

SPLITS

The Cincinnati comment in the 1986 *Abstract* concerned the significance of splits in team records. I looked at the records of all major-league teams in games at home and on the road, in daylight and at night, on artificial turf and on grass fields, in one-run games and in other games, and against left-handed and right-handed pitchers. At that time I concluded that, while of course many of the splits in team records occurred because of real differences in ability, none was statistically significant at the 99% confidence level. That is, the 1985 Cincinnati Reds were 39–18 in one-run games, but 50–54 in all other games. There is a 3% chance that such a split *might* happen by random chance.

I listed the eleven *most significant* splits in team records in 1985. A year later, I thought I should look in again on those eleven splits, to see which ones repeated in 1986.

Only six of the eleven most-significant splits of 1985 were repeated in 1986 at any level, again suggesting that such splits may not mean a hell of a lot. The No. 1 most significant split of the 1985 season did not repeat in 1986. The Yankees in 1985 were 58–22 at home in Yankee Stadium, but just 39–42 on the road. But in 1986 the Yankees had the best road record in the American League (49–33), but lost the pennant in Yankee Stadium. The change could be explained by changes in the personnel.

There were two strong splits of 1985 that repeated in 1986 with comparable force. The Minnesota Twins in 1985 were 49–35 at home, but 28–50 in road games, one of the largest home-park differentials in baseball. In 1986 the Twins continued to play well at home (43–38), but poorly on the road (28–53). The California Angels in 1985 had a tremendous 30–13 record in one-run games, which was the basis of my major comment about the team. In 1986 they continued to do very well in one-run games, at 28–16.

There were four other splits of 1985 that repeated in 1986 with much less emphasis.

The Oakland A's in 1985 played much better in day games than at night. In 1986 they still played quite a bit better in day games (35–33) than at night (41–53).

The Toronto Blue Jays in 1985 played much better against right-handed pitchers than against left-handers. In 1986 they played a little better against right-handers, but the gap was narrowed to almost nothing (.534 vs. right-handers, .522 against lefties).

The Cleveland Indians in 1985 played much better in Cleveland than on the road. In 1986 they played a little bit better at home than on the road, but their home-park advantage was not large.

In 1985 the Houston Astros had a sad 2–8 record in doubleheader games. In 1986 they played only one doubleheader—but they lost both games.

The other four major splits of 1985 did not repeat in 1986:

The Cincinnati Reds in 1986 did not continue to dominate in one-run games. They were just 26–26 in one-run games, below their overall performance.

In 1985 the Reds were also 12–3 in extra-inning games, a related phenomenon. In 1986 they were just 8–10 in extra-inning games.

In 1985 the Milwaukee Brewers played much better in night games than in day games. In 1986 they played a tiny bit better in day games.

In 1985 the Kansas City Royals played dramatically better in night games (73–46) than day games (18–25). In 1986 this one turned around the other way almost as strong; the Royals were 51–67 in night games, but 25–19 in sunlight.

We should presume that part of the disappearance of these splits is due to action on the part of the teams. Teams presumably act to improve upon their weaknesses. A team that is weak against left-handers will normally attempt to improve against left-handers, and thus the disappearance of this trait does not indicate that it did not have a real origin.

But one would have a tough time tying that logic to any of the real cases under discussion. The Toronto Blue Jays *might* have done something to reduce their vulnerability to left-handers, but they *didn't*. An honest comparison of the 1985 and 1986 Blue Jays would lead you to conclude that the split disappeared more or less of its own volition.

Did the Cincinnati Reds do anything deliberately to wipe out their dominance in one-run games or in extra-inning games? Of course not. Did the Royals or the Brewers do anything to cause them to play better in day games and more poorly at night? I doubt it.

The 1985 study showed that even the most extreme splits in teams' one-season records *could* have resulted from simple luck. The 1986 season suggested that many of them probably do.

SAN FRANCISCO GIANTS

Runners on Base:	1,967
Opponents on Base:	1,884
Net Advantage:	+83
Won-Lost Record:	83-79

The San Francisco Giants were one of the surprise teams of the 1986 season and, in view of the ill fortune with which they contended, may well have been the most remarkable team of the year. After losing 100 games in 1985, the Giants made no major trades and were picked by most to finish at or near the bottom of their division again in 1986. Instead, after splitting their first eight games, the Giants then won six straight games to claim a share of first place—and, to the surprise of the nation, continued to hold their ground despite a late-May slump in which they lost seven of nine, stared down their traditional June swoon with a 16–12 record in that month, and were in first place in mid-July when an undertow of injuries and a sustained hot streak by the Astros dragged them gradually out to sea.

The injuries which were eventually to take them out of the race had actually started in the first half, but at the All-Star break the Giants were in first place with a record of 48–40. At that time they were second in the league in batting average (.264), second in runs scored (398), and fourth in ERA (3.34). Individually, third baseman Chris Brown was second in the league in batting average, at .338. Jeff Leonard led the league in game-winning RBI, with 11; he was hitting .287 with 41 RBI. Right fielder Chili Davis was hitting .294 with 55 RBI. Mike Krukow was 11–5, Mike LaCoss 9–3 with a 2.76 ERA.

No reasonable person could have expected that level of performance to continue. As it is, the Giants are only the eighth team since 1900 to post a winning record following a season in which they lost a hundred games, and no such team has ever won a championship. There remains a nagging feeling that, free of injuries, the Giants would have had a heck of a shot at being the first. A four-city road trip immediately after the All-Star game badly—and as it turned out irreparably—damaged the Giants' chances of pulling off a miracle, for not only did the Giants lose 9 out of 12 games, dropping them four and a half behind the sizzling Astros, but a continuing series of injuries left them too weak to scramble back into contention. A brief and incomplete catalogue of the Giants aches and pains:

Chris Brown missed 12 games early in the season with pulled muscles in his thigh and groin.

Chili Davis bruised his left shoulder making a diving catch in center field, May 24. The shoulder gave him increasing trouble throughout the season.

Roger Mason went on the disabled list with a sore elbow following his start of May 29. The elbow effectively ended his season.

Dan Gladden jammed his right thumb diving for a ninth-inning triple in Montreal, June 3. He was out several weeks.

Will Clark hyperextended his left elbow and sprained his left wrist attempting unsuccessfully to hurdle Andres Gallaraga in the same game, June 3. He was out about six weeks.

Robby Thompson was bothered by a knee problem a good part of the season.

Chris Brown fouled a ball above his eye during batting practice, June 17, and was out briefly.

Pitcher Jim Gott was lost for almost the whole season, and had surgery to repair a torn rotator cuff on June 24.

Greg Minton suffered strained cartilage in his rib cage, mid-July.

Mike Krukow went on the 15-day disabled list after contusions in his left thigh suffered in a brawl with St. Louis, July 22.

Jeff Leonard, after hitting six homers by May 14, hit no more for the rest of the season. Leonard had a "subluxated tendon" in his wrist (God, I hope that one doesn't catch on like the rotator cuff) carried over from the previous season, and it was hoped that the winter rest would cure the problem. The loose wrist tendon bothered him when he did things like throw or swing a bat. When it began to bother him again in May, it cut off his power and caused him great pain. He finally had a steroid shot on July 3, but when that failed to alleviate the problem his season was ended by surgery on August 7.

Mike LaCoss had a painful bone chip on his right big toe, and perhaps should not have been pitching the second half of the season.

Chris Brown injured his right shoulder in a collision with Mike Heath in early July. The shoulder worsened and finally ended Brown's season in late August.

Despite all of these injuries, the Giants never collapsed; they hung tough and posted a 35–39 record after the All-Star break—far better than expectations would have been at the season's start.

The Giants were a much-improved team both offensively and defensively. Looking at the Giants' team totals, you can get very confused about whether the Giants were an average team that was lucky or a good team that was unlucky in terms of wins and losses. Let's set up the background: in 1985 the average National League team scored and allowed 658 runs. The Giants scored only 556 runs, worst in the league (−102) and allowed 674, 16 more than average.

In 1986 the league average was up to 675. The Giants scored 698, so that means that *relative to the league* they gained 125 runs offensively. The 1986 Giants allowed 618 runs, so relative to the league the Giants improved defensively by 73 runs.

This brings us to two important points: 1) that the Giants' total offensive and defensive improvement last year was massive, 198 runs, and 2) that more of the improvement was *offensive* than defensive. In other words, Roger Craig's teaching his pitchers the split-fingered fastball couldn't have been the dominant factor in the improvement of the team, since that improves the pitching and over 60% of the improvement was in the hitting.

But when you look more closely at the offense, the question of why they were 24 runs better than the league becomes a puzzle. The league batting average was .253; the Giants batting average was .253. The league on-base percentage was .322; the Giants on-base percentage was .322. The league slugging percentage was .380; the Giants slugging percentage was .375. The league stolen base average was 153 per team; the Giants stole 148 and had a poor stolen base percentage. But the average team should have scored 675 runs by the runs created method, and did; the Giants should have scored 674, but scored 698.

Some of the deviation may have been luck, but by making heavy use of first-run strategies, the Giants avoided the double play and eventually scored 35.5% of their runners. They invested 194 outs in first-run strategies, the most in the National League. The Giants bunted 101 times, second in the league behind the Cardinals, and lost 93 runners attempting to steal, second in the league behind the Expos. Possibly as a result of the bunts, the Giants received 86 intentional walks, most in the majors. Apparently, they invested the outs wisely, as they grounded into only 83 double plays, tying the Cardinals for fewest in the majors. The Giants grounded into only 68 double plays per 1,000 runners on first base (Estimated by Singles + Walks + Hit Batsmen − Stolen Base Attempts − Sacrifice Hits). Every other NL team grounded into at least 76 double plays per 1,000 runners on first base.

So if you had told me that the Giants had a good year because Roger Craig had the team moving baserunners, I'd have believed it. The media explanations of the good years for Houston and San Francisco last year were that Houston had a good year because Lanier had the team moving baserunners, and San Francisco had a good year because Craig had the Giants pitchers throwing the split-fingered fastball. The statistical evidence is completely inconsistent with both explanations—but oddly, if you just swapped them you'd have a perfect fit. The Houston pitchers had a terrific year and were striking everybody out, while the Giants apparently did an excellent job of moving baserunners.

The Giants hit only 114 home runs, fewest in the division, but hit 269 doubles, most in the division, another reason they received so many intentional walks. In any case, assuming even that the Giant offense was average, it was dramatically improved from 1985. Equally puzzling were the Giant pitching and defense. Giant pitchers allowed 591 walks, most in the league except for San Diego, and threw 58 wild pitches, most in the league except for Pittsburgh. They were only slightly better than average in home runs allowed (121 against a league average of 127).

The Giant defensive players fielded .977, second-worst in the league. They turned only 149 double plays, a fraction better than normal. Yet, again, they did best where it counts: in runs allowed. There were some positive defensive markers. The Giants allowed only 192 doubles to their opponents, by far the fewest in the league (the Mets were second, allowing 215, and the Astros third, allowing 233). Their .715 defensive efficiency record was second-best in the division.

The offense may have been lucky and the defense may have been a little lucky, but in putting the two together into wins the Giants were actually quite *un*lucky. They scored 80 more runs than they allowed, but finished just four games over .500.

If it wasn't the split-fingered fastball that was responsible for the Giants' success, what was it? I think there were four keys. One was that the Giant players, as a group, reacted to the embarrassing 1985 season with a determination to improve. Almost every Giant regular in 1986 either had a better year or was on course for a better year when stopped by injury. Second was the development of young players. The Giants had two of the best rookies in the National League, plus several other young players who contributed.

Third, I would cite the decision to hire Roger Craig. You know, this isn't the first time Roger has done this. The San Diego Padres finished 69–93 in 1977, hired Craig for 1978 and finished 84–78 before declining the following season. I think Craig did a lot of things well besides teaching the spitball, or whatever it is. Craig took a flier on Robby Thompson at second base, and that worked out great. He built up the bench and used the bench, which enabled the Giants to survive their injuries. Craig dealt good-humoredly with the early-season backbiting of players like Maldonado and Berenguer, who were unhappy with their roles on the team.

And fourth, the Giants got some career years. They got a terrific year out of Candy Maldonado, who had the best year for a pinch hitter in San Francisco history, then moved into the lineup after the injury to Leonard and continued to produce. Krukow, of course, and LaCoss during the first half were well above their norms.

As to the Giants' chances of contending in 1987, there is a titled comment included here which applies equally to Cleveland and Texas; it is to the effect that further improvement immediately is very unlikely. The fourth comment above is also a factor; Krukow and Maldonado, among others, may not repeat their 1986 season.

On the other hand, the Giants' starting lineup in 1986 averaged 25.9 years of age, making them the youngest team in the division. The fact that they won eight games fewer than projected by their runs and runs allowed is an indication that, with luck, they could have done even better last year and might do even better next year. The injury to Leonard may have been a blessing in disguise, as Maldonado may be a better hitter than Leonard, but most of the other injuries, those to Clark, Brown, Minton, etc., damaged the Giants and kept them from winning as many games as they otherwise would have won. Further improvement by the Giants in 1987 is unlikely, but it isn't impossible.

Bob BRENLY, Catcher

	G	AB	Hit	2B	3B	HR	Run	RBI	TBB	SO	SB	CS	Avg
3.80 years		507	129	23	1	18	64	66	63	76	9	8	.254
1986	149	472	116	26	0	16	60	62	74	97	10	6	.246
First Half	77	236	57	9	0	5	30	25	47	50	8	3	.242
Second Half	72	236	59	17	0	11	30	37	27	47	2	3	.250
Vs. RHP		314	74	10	0	10		38	45	65			.236
Vs. LHP		158	42	16	0	6		24	29	32			.266
Home		235	55	10	0	8		31	34	53			.234
Road		237	61	16	0	8		31	40	44			.257
Grass		354	86	18	0	12		43	57	72			.243
Turf		118	30	8	0	4		19	17	25			.254

Jeff LEONARD, Left Field

	G	AB	Hit	2B	3B	HR	Run	RBI	TBB	SO	SB	CS	Avg
5.32 years		557	152	24	6	15	71	80	42	116	23	8	.273
1986	89	341	95	11	3	6	48	42	20	62	16	3	.279
First Half	81	310	89	9	3	6	44	41	16	58	15	2	.287
Second Half	8	31	6	2	0	0	4	1	4	4	1	1	.194
Vs. RHP		222	56	8	3	3		22	16	53			.252
Vs. LHP		119	39	3	0	3		20	4	9			.328
Home		168	53	5	3	2		20	8	30			.315
Road		173	42	6	0	4		22	12	32			.243
Grass		256	78	10	3	5		34	16	48			.305
Turf		85	17	1	0	1		8	4	14			.200

Will CLARK, First Base

	G	AB	Hit	2B	3B	HR	Run	RBI	TBB	SO	SB	CS	Avg
0.69 years		595	171	39	3	16	96	60	50	111	6	10	.287
1986	111	408	117	27	2	11	66	41	34	76	4	7	.287
First Half	47	192	50	11	2	6	32	18	0	0	1	0	.260
Second Half	64	216	67	16	0	5	34	23	34	76	3	7	.310
Vs. RHP		278	77	19	2	9		27	26	49			.277
Vs. LHP		130	40	8	0	2		14	8	27			.308
Home		220	74	15	1	7		26	19	35			.336
Road		188	43	12	1	4		15	15	41			.229
Grass		311	98	21	2	9		33	31	61			.315
Turf		97	19	6	0	2		8	3	15			.196

Dan GLADDEN, Center Field

	G	AB	Hit	2B	3B	HR	Run	RBI	TBB	SO	SB	CS	Avg
2.15 years		586	164	23	5	7	91	51	54	86	44	20	.281
1986	102	351	97	16	1	4	55	29	39	59	27	10	.276
First Half	47	185	52	9	0	2	31	13	15	27	11	7	.281
Second Half	55	166	45	7	1	2	24	16	24	32	16	3	.271
Vs. RHP		228	63	10	1	4		22	20	35			.276
Vs. LHP		123	34	6	0	0		7	19	24			.276
Home		162	44	5	0	1		10	26	30			.272
Road		189	53	11	1	3		19	13	29			.280
Grass		249	64	8	0	3		17	31	42			.257
Turf		102	33	8	1	1		12	8	17			.324

Rob THOMPSON, Second Base

	G	AB	Hit	2B	3B	HR	Run	RBI	TBB	SO	SB	CS	Avg
0.92 years		597	162	29	3	8	79	51	46	122	13	16	.271
1986	149	549	149	27	3	7	73	47	42	112	12	15	.271
First Half	85	301	82	14	2	4	39	31	27	55	8	10	.272
Second Half	64	248	67	13	1	3	34	16	15	57	4	5	.270
Vs. RHP		379	101	17	2	4		32	28	78			.266
Vs. LHP		170	48	10	1	3		15	14	34			.282
Home		255	75	17	2	4		28	26	43			.294
Road		294	74	10	1	3		19	16	69			.252
Grass		395	116	22	3	7		39	38	75			.294
Turf		154	33	5	0	0		8	4	37			.214

Chili DAVIS, Outfield

	G	AB	Hit	2B	3B	HR	Run	RBI	TBB	SO	SB	CS	Avg
4.48 years		592	160	27	4	17	79	76	65	105	18	12	.270
1986	153	526	146	28	3	13	71	70	84	96	16	13	.278
First Half	84	293	86	17	3	9	45	55	42	43	10	11	.294
Second Half	69	233	60	11	0	4	26	15	42	53	6	2	.258
Vs. RHP		358	108	25	2	8		46	74	71			.302
Vs. LHP		168	38	3	1	5		24	10	25			.226
Home		258	75	14	0	7		37	43	52			.291
Road		268	71	14	3	6		33	41	44			.265
Grass		395	116	21	1	10		53	66	77			.294
Turf		131	30	7	2	3		17	18	19			.229

Chris BROWN, Third Base

	G	AB	Hit	2B	3B	HR	Run	RBI	TBB	SO	SB	CS	Avg
1.67 years		559	164	26	4	14	64	73	48	84	10	8	.293
1986	116	416	132	16	3	7	57	49	33	43	13	9	.317
First Half	73	269	91	11	2	7	36	35	28	24	11	6	.338
Second Half	43	147	41	5	1	0	21	14	5	19	2	3	.279
Vs. RHP		278	92	8	2	4		39	27	29			.331
Vs. LHP		138	40	8	1	3		10	6	14			.290
Home		228	76	7	2	3		30	23	25			.333
Road		188	56	9	1	4		19	10	18			.298
Grass		311	101	9	3	4		38	27	30			.325
Turf		105	31	7	0	3		11	6	13			.295

Candy MALDONADO, Outfield

	G	AB	Hit	2B	3B	HR	Run	RBI	TBB	SO	SB	CS	Avg
2.65 years		359	87	20	2	11	37	52	24	63	2	3	.243
1986	133	405	102	31	3	18	49	85	20	77	4	4	.252
First Half	65	166	45	14	2	6	20	34	6	30	3	2	.271
Second Half	68	239	57	17	1	12	29	51	14	47	1	2	.238
Vs. RHP		272	71	21	1	12		54	17	57			.261
Vs. LHP		133	31	10	2	6		31	3	20			.233
Home		197	45	16	1	6		42	8	38			.228
Road		208	57	15	2	12		43	12	39			.274
Grass		282	73	23	2	13		63	11	54			.259
Turf		123	29	8	1	5		22	9	23			.236

José URIBE, Shortstop

	G	AB	Hit	2B	3B	HR	Run	RBI	TBB	SO	SB	CS	Avg
1.93 years		492	113	18	3	3	50	37	47	70	16	7	.229
1986	157	453	101	15	1	3	46	43	61	76	22	11	.223
First Half	88	276	66	8	0	2	24	26	29	36	15	5	.239
Second Half	69	177	35	7	1	1	22	17	32	40	7	6	.198
Vs. RHP		307	70	8	1	0		26	46	43			.228
Vs. LHP		146	31	7	0	3		17	15	33			.212
Home		219	48	7	0	1		18	37	35			.219
Road		234	53	8	1	2		25	24	41			.226
Grass		337	79	10	0	2		34	50	53			.234
Turf		116	22	5	1	1		9	11	23			.190

Bob MELVIN, Catcher

	G	AB	Hit	2B	3B	HR	Run	RBI	TBB	SO	SB	CS	Avg
0.80 years		436	97	22	4	6	42	36	22	112	4	2	.223
1986	89	268	60	14	2	5	24	25	15	69	3	2	.224
First Half	48	152	38	9	1	1	8	10	5	39	1	1	.250
Second Half	41	116	22	5	1	4	16	15	10	30	2	1	.190
Vs. RHP		164	28	7	2	2		15	8	50			.171
Vs. LHP		104	32	7	0	3		10	7	19			.308
Home		109	24	8	0	2		8	4	28			.220
Road		159	36	6	2	3		17	11	41			.226
Grass		176	31	8	0	4		15	8	49			.176
Turf		92	29	6	2	1		10	7	20			.315

Mike KRUKOW

	(W–L)	GS	Run	Avg	DP	Avg	SB	Avg
1985	(8-11)	28	81	2.89	18	.64	29	1.04
1986	(20-9)	34	173	5.09	25	.74	25	.74
1976-1986		298	1302	4.37	233	.78	323	1.08

	G	IP	W	L	Pct	ER	BB	SO	ERA
1985 Home	15	116.3	6	5	.545	29	29	98	2.24
1986 Home	16	127.3	12	4	.750	35	17	92	2.47
1985 Road	13	78.3	2	6	.250	44	20	52	5.06
1986 Road	18	117.7	8	5	.615	48	38	86	3.67
1985 Grass	20	148.0	8	5	.615	46	36	115	2.80
1986 Grass	26	191.7	17	6	.739	68	33	138	3.19
1985 Turf	8	46.7	0	6	0.000	27	13	35	5.21
1986 Turf	8	53.3	3	3	.500	15	22	40	2.53
1986 Total	34	245.0	20	9	.690	83	55	178	3.05

Vida BLUE

	(W–L)	GS	Run	Avg	DP	Avg	SB	Avg
1985	(7-11)	20	96	4.80	14	.70	15	.75
1986	(10-10)	28	111	3.96	25	.89	27	.96
1976-1986		286	1126	3.94	203	.71	190	.66

	G	IP	W	L	Pct	ER	BB	SO	ERA
1985 Home	19	79.0	6	2	.750	39	44	56	4.44
1986 Home	16	95.7	6	6	.500	32	47	57	3.01
1985 Road	14	52.0	2	6	.250	26	3	47	4.50
1986 Road	12	61.0	4	4	.500	25	30	43	3.69
1985 Grass	29	119.7	8	6	.571	58	71	97	4.36
1986 Grass	19	110.0	7	6	.538	37	53	62	3.03
1985 Turf	4	11.3	0	2	0.000	7	9	6	5.56
1986 Turf	9	46.7	3	4	.429	20	24	38	3.86
1986 Total	28	156.7	10	10	7.000	57	77	100	3.27

Mike LACOSS

	(W–L)	GS	Run	Avg	DP	Avg	SB	Avg
1986	(10-13)	31	160	5.16	29	.94	22	.71
1978-1986		163	678	4.16	172	1.06	154	.94

	G	IP	W	L	Pct	ER	BB	SO	ERA
1985 Home	10	21.3	1	1	.500	15	15	13	6.33
1986 Home	18	108.0	7	4	.636	34	33	45	2.83
1985 Road	11	19.3	0	0	0.000	8	14	13	3.72
1986 Road	19	96.3	3	9	.250	47	37	41	4.39
1985 Grass	10	18.0	0	0	0.000	4	11	12	2.00
1986 Grass	28	149.0	9	8	.529	58	53	65	3.50
1985 Turf	11	22.7	1	1	.500	19	18	14	7.54
1986 Turf	9	55.3	1	5	.167	23	17	21	3.74
1986 Total	37	204.3	10	13	.435	81	70	86	3.57

OTHERS

	(W–L)	GS	Run	Avg	DP	Avg	SB	Avg
Garrelts	(13-9)	18	64	3.56	27	1.50	26	1.44
Downs	(4-4)	14	45	3.21	12	.86	15	1.07
Mason	(3-4)	11	43	3.91	7	.64	7	.64
Mulholland	(1-7)	10	25	2.50	10	1.00	5	.50
Carlton	(1-3)	6	33	5.50	3	.50	4	.67
Berenguer	(2-3)	4	18	4.50	4	1.00	2	.50
Davis	(5-7)	2	4	2.00	2	1.00	1	.50
Gott	(0-0)	2	14	7.00	3	1.50	1	.50
Robinson	(6-3)	1	7	7.00	0	0.00	1	1.00
Grant	(0-1)	1	1	1.00	1	1.00	0	0.00

RECORDS WITH DIFFERENT STARTING CATCHERS

Catcher	Inn	ER	W–L	ERA	GS	SB	Avg
Brenly	693.2	256	40-38	3.32	78	56	.72
Melvin	688.2	263	39-37	3.44	76	68	.89
Quellette	60.0	12	4-2	1.80	6	9	1.50
Gulden	18.0	10	0-2	5.00	2	2	1.00

WHY CLEVELAND, TEXAS AND SAN FRANCISCO SHOULDN'T BE EXPECTED TO CONTEND IN 1987

I'm going to make one comment here that applies equally to three teams, and then I'll refer to it the other two times. It's very odd to have exactly this set of circumstances occurring three times in one season, but we do; the comment applies to the Giants, Indians, and Rangers. When a team improves dramatically in one season, there is a very powerful tendency for them to relapse in the next season. When a team improves by 20 games in a season, there will always be an expectation that they will be able to make further improvements in the following season—as there was last year for the Reds, who actually had not quite improved by 20 games.

But in fact, such teams very rarely improve again in the next season; at least 80% of the time, they will decline in the following season, and many times decline seriously. The reasons for this are not that hard to diagnose, and the declines shouldn't be that unexpected. When a team improves by 20 or more games in a season, part of the reason will be that some of their players play over their heads. To name one from each team, Mike Krukow, Tony Bernazard, and Scott Fletcher all had seasons that were well above their established norms. Such players tend, in the main, to return in the direction from which they have come, dragging their teams with them. This tendency, which is called the plexiglass principle, applies to individuals as well as teams; if a man hits .240 in one season and .300 the next, the odds are strong that he will hit less than .300 in the third. If the improvement is based on rookies, some of those rookies will hit the sophomore jinx.

While 80% or more of such teams will relapse, those relapses will be more serious in some cases than in others. If the team improves by 20 games but doesn't move into contending position—that is, if they improve from 63 wins to 83 rather than from 73 to 93—then the plexiglass principle is somewhat less compelling. A team that wins 83 games will still recognize that work needs to be done and changes need to be made, while a team that wins the pennant or comes very close will be less inclined to identify and address its remaining weaknesses. Since Cleveland, Texas, and San Francisco all remain a safe distance from first place, all will likely continue to work toward further improvement.

A team that makes a great leap forward will tend to relapse in the next season whether the improvement was accomplished by the addition of young players or whether it was accomplished by veterans having exceptional seasons. However, as you might expect, the tendency to relapse is somewhat weaker if the improvement was based on young players. Since all three teams did make a substantial portion of their improvement with the addition or development of young players, all are somewhat favored in this respect.

On the other hand, sometimes a team will "improve" by 20 games because they have had an off season, as the Dodgers did in 1986, a season that is not really reflective of the strength of the organization. Those "comeback" teams have a comparatively slight tendency to relapse, nothing like 80%—but none of the three we are discussing fits that description, either.

Among the three teams, there is a good chance that *one* will continue to improve in 1987—but it is virtually certain that, as a group, they will suffer some "decline," some loss of the ground that was gained in 1986.

To guess accurately which of the three would be the one to continue to gain ground would be impossible, but there are a few points worth making. When teams improve by 20 games or more, one of the things that usually happens is that their luck improves. The most suspect portion of any team's improvement is that portion based on luck or on factors that are not apparent in the runs-scored/runs-allowed columns. Both the Indians and the Rangers were a little bit lucky in 1986; that is, they both scored a few more runs than one would expect them to score based on their other statistics, and won a few more games than one would expect them to win based on the number of runs they scored. The Giants, as discussed, were lucky in some respects but unlucky in others.

LOS ANGELES DODGERS

Runners on Base:	1,883
Opponents on Base:	1,953
Net Disadvantage:	−70
Won-Lost Record:	73-89

How serious is it? 1986 was the worst season for the Dodgers in almost 20 years. With a team that was supposed to be in the prime of its life, the Dodgers have had losing records in two of the last three seasons. Only one other time since 1938 have the Dodgers had a losing record twice in three years, and then they knew they were rebuilding. Is the Dodger dynasty moribund? Will they be back in the race in 1987? If not, when will they return?

You will learn in due time that I have no answers to these questions, so don't hold your breath. To put the Dodgers of 1986 in two sentences: The starting staff was very good, the catching was adequate, and Steve Sax was brilliant. The rest of the team was awful.

I should say right off that the Dodger team is not really as bad as it looked in 1986. It couldn't possibly be. To watch the Dodgers play last August or September, you would have thought that this team would never post a winning record again. The Dodgers combined a poor offense and a horrendous bullpen with the worst team defense that I have ever seen in the major leagues. The resulting combination would likely have reached last place if the season had gone on long enough. The last two months of the season the Dodgers won 24 and lost 37, the same as the Padres.

The Dodgers hit only 14 triples during the year, a National League record for the fewest triples by a team (it would have been a major-league record except the Orioles hit only 13).

The Dodgers were shut out 14 times, most in the majors.

Dodger relievers had 25 saves, the fewest in the league.

At times the Dodgers had Franklin Stubbs, who is not spectacularly mobile for a first baseman, in center field.

An easy way to evaluate a defense is to contrast the errors with the double plays. There are about as many double plays (positive) as there are errors (negative), although a few more double plays. National League teams that have positive ratios have winning records about 60% of the time, while teams that have negative ratios have losing records over 65% of the time, so the comparison is meaningful. The Dodgers had 118 double plays and committed 181 errors—a phenomenal −63. No other major-league team was worse than −22. This is not totally new; the Dodgers were −35 in 1985, easily the worst in the majors, and −36 in 1983.

The Dodger team defensive statistics were so bad that I thought there had to be some sort of park illusion, something having to do with the surface or officious scoring. I asked Susie to go through the box scores and count home and road errors and DPs. The park has nothing to do with it; the Dodgers committed 95 errors in road games, 86 at home: they turned only 60 double plays in road games, and only 58 at home. Their defensive stats would be as bad in any other park.

The Dodgers had only 376 extra base hits, the fewest of any team in the division.

The Dodgers had only 1,883 men on base, again the fewest of any team in the division.

The season went off course in the last days of spring training, when Pedro Guerrero changed his mind about sliding into third base and decided to destroy his knee instead. *The injury to Guerrero, absent complications, should not have been devastating to this team.* I do not recall this with pleasure, but I believed a year ago that the Dodgers were about equal to the Mets, with strong pitching and an exceptional power center. In 1985 the Dodgers scored 103 runs more than they allowed. With Madlock on hand for the full season, with the shortstop problem apparently solved by Mariano Duncan, it appeared they might be stronger in 1986. Guerrero's injury could have been expected to cost them maybe 40, 45 runs, less than half of their margin over their opponents. There was every reason to think the Dodgers could stay in contention until Guerrero returned in August.

In the early part of the season, with the fine performance of Franklin Stubbs, it appeared the direct cost of Guerrero's loss would be much less than estimated. Stubbs at mid-season seemed likely to hit 25–30 homers, possibly more. But everything in the world was going wrong, nothing directly as a result of Guerrero's injury, but everything compounding everything else from that point. The Dodger hitters, perhaps putting pressure on themselves, hit .204 as a team over the first three weeks of the season. The bullpen was awful. Niedenfuer, his confidence perhaps shaken by his historic fastball to Jack Clark, was ineffective. The Dodgers lost the first eight games in which the bullpen was used. They were losing two-thirds of their one-run games in the early part of the season.

And then the injuries started. I just ran down a list of injuries for the Giants, and I don't have the space to do that here because of the other things that I wanted to say, but the Dodger casualty list was even more formidable than that of their dear friends to the north. Summarize it this way: With the exception of Steve Sax, every Dodger regular was lost for a significant portion of the schedule with injuries. All seven of them, and most of the top reserves. At least six Dodger pitchers had serious arm injuries during the season.

Still, the Dodger starting rotation remained strong.

Fernando Valenzuela had his best year. Bob Welch and Rick Honeycutt pitched extremely well, although their won-lost records do not reflect this. Orel Hershiser didn't have as good a season as in 1986, but he was OK. Dodger pitchers walked only 499 men (second best in the league), struck out 1,051 (tied for third), and allowed only 115 home runs (second best in the league).

The defense against the running game was good, allowing only 123 stolen bases in 197 attempts. The 123 OSB was the lowest in the league except for the Cardinals, and the opposition stolen base percentage was low.

The Dodgers completed 35 games, 8 more than any other NL team; this, however, is as much a reflection of Lasorda's terror of his bullpen as it is a tribute to the starting corps.

The Dodgers declined in 1986 by 144 runs, from +103 to −41.

What was not visible in watching them play, what you had to keep in mind when studying the box scores, was that the Dodgers had a lot of resources that were not on the field. Obviously, Los Angeles is very likely to have a better year next year; there shouldn't be any question about that.

Still, one can't avoid the feeling that something may be seriously wrong with the organization. One of the historic strengths of the Dodgers has been their organizational decision-making. We were always given the impression that the Dodgers talked things over before they did them, thrashing through decisions that ordinarily would be made by a manager on the seat of his pants. In 1966 when the Dodgers picked up iron-glove slugger Dick Stuart and had him playing first in place of the light-hitting defensive wizard Wes Parker, Parker sounded off about it, saying that if the Dodgers were going to win again he would have to play. The Dodgers held a meeting, talked it out, and decided that Parker was right: Back into the lineup he went, and the Dodgers did win. The Dodgers took input not only from the manager but from the scouts, the coaches, and the front office, and were stronger because of it.

What seems to have happened since the death of Walter O'Malley in 1979 is that organizational decision-making has decayed into bureaucratic indecisiveness. The Dodgers in the eighties don't *attack* problems. Confronted with a gap in the lineup, the Dodgers go into a delay game, trying to stall until a solution materializes from the farm system.

Some of the defensive problems are the result of injuries and bad luck. But I can't avoid the feeling that most of the Dodgers' defensive problems are the result of institutional arrogance. Arrogance is thinking that you can do things that you can't really do, combined with an insufficient respect for the complexity of the world. When the Dodgers were rebuilding following the end of the Koufax/ Drysdale years, they made a number of late-in-life position switches, moving Bill Russell to shortstop after he went through the minors as an outfielder and converting Dave Lopes from a AAA outfielder to a second baseman at the age of 26. Russell and Lopes were not *good* infielders, but they were good offensive players and the Dodgers were able to win.

So the organization got the idea that they could look at a player's skills, put them on a chart, and decide what slot the player should fill. That approach makes insufficient allowances for the difficult adaptation of player to position, a process that usually takes years, requires the development of position-specific skills, and tests tiny but crucial attributes of the player which may turn out, after two or three years, to be missing. A byproduct of the belief that the organization can switch the player to wherever they have a need is that some Dodgers move into major-league jobs with little experience at the positions they are expected to man. The major leagues become a training ground where the players are expected to refine their defensive skills. The end result is the defensive nightmare that has plagued the Dodgers in three of the last four seasons.

It is curious, and troubling, that the most conspicuous failures of the Dodger organization are at the two positions where good organizations most often produce surpluses: shortstop and center field. *Most major-league players, when they enter professional baseball, are either shortstops or center fielders*. The organizations draft athletes, and start the best athletes out at those two positions. If a young player can hit but has trouble defensively, he can be shifted to a less demanding spot. But if the organization is productive, as the Mets have been in recent years, they will usually have some surplus at one position or the other.

I look over the top Dodger drafts in the years 1980 through 1984, and I see a lot of catchers, a lot of first and third basemen, oodles of pitchers, but comparatively few players at those positions that are normally priorities in the draft. Why? Why aren't the Dodgers drafting to fill these positions? José Gonzalez is their hot prospect in center. He may develop but right now he's been in organized baseball for six years and can't hit his weight.

I know they like to grow their own, but if the Dodgers are still the Dodgers, why can't they figure out a trade to fill a couple of holes? When the Dodgers started having bullpen troubles last year, I figured, "Well, you know the Dodgers will be able to come up with a young pitcher." The situation just got worse and worse; they couldn't come up with anything. Why not, with all those pitchers who have been top draft picks in recent years?

Al Campanis says that "we try to operate in eight-year cycles, because we feel that is how many good years we can expect from a player who comes out of our system." Well, fine, but where are we in the cycle? I mean, are we starting a building cycle here, or what? I figure that with Fernando (1981), Sax (1982), Howe (1980), Marshall (1982), Guerrero (1980), and Brock (1983) if you're looking for eight years a player 1986 should be about the middle of an upswing. Why isn't it? Why is the bench so weak?

Maybe I just don't understand. Anyway, if the Dodgers can stay healthy, this is bound to be a better year. They could win the division. They've got the rotation; if Marshall and Guerrero are healthy they'll score enough runs. The Dodgers are still a young team, although the average age of the 1986 starters is misleading because it doesn't include Guerrero.

But the downside is this. If they don't get it together, the 1987 season could mark the formal burial of nearly five decades of Dodgers excellence.

Mike SCIOSCIA, Catcher

	G	AB	Hit	2B	3B	HR	Run	RBI	TBB	SO	SB	CS	Avg
4.10 years		479	126	22	1	6	44	48	70	32	3	2	.264
1986	122	374	94	18	1	5	36	26	62	23	3	3	.251
First Half	54	158	43	9	0	2	15	10	33	13	1	3	.272
Second Half	68	216	51	9	1	3	21	16	29	10	2	0	.236
Vs. RHP		267	69	16	1	3		20	44	16			.258
Vs. LHP		107	25	2	0	2		6	18	7			.234
Home		170	42	7	0	2		9	25	12			.247
Road		204	52	11	1	3		17	37	11			.255
Grass		277	70	14	0	5		18	47	21			.253
Turf		97	24	4	1	0		8	15	2			.247

Reggie WILLIAMS, Left Field

	G	AB	Hit	2B	3B	HR	Run	RBI	TBB	SO	SB	CS	Avg
0.93 years		337	94	15	2	4	42	35	25	66	11	3	.279
1986	128	303	84	14	2	4	35	32	23	57	9	3	.277
First Half	60	158	48	12	1	0	15	15	8	31	5	2	.304
Second Half	68	145	36	2	1	4	20	17	15	26	4	1	.248
Vs. RHP		133	34	5	0	3		19	8	29			.256
Vs. LHP		170	50	9	2	1		13	15	28			.294
Home		151	41	7	1	1		12	12	27			.272
Road		152	43	7	1	3		20	11	30			.283
Grass		214	62	10	2	2		21	15	38			.290
Turf		89	22	4	0	2		11	8	19			.247

Greg BROCK, First Base

	G	AB	Hit	2B	3B	HR	Run	RBI	TBB	SO	SB	CS	Avg
3.06 years		492	115	17	1	23	64	72	70	83	6	3	.233
1986	115	325	76	13	0	16	33	52	37	60	2	5	.234
First Half	59	177	37	4	0	8	18	24	23	33	1	5	.209
Second Half	56	148	39	9	0	8	15	28	14	27	1	0	.264
Vs. RHP		266	70	10	0	16		51	28	37			.263
Vs. LHP		59	6	3	0	0		1	9	23			.102
Home		140	33	0	0	5		20	15	25			.236
Road		185	43	13	0	11		32	22	35			.232
Grass		239	53	5	0	8		36	33	41			.222
Turf		86	23	8	0	8		16	4	19			.267

Ken LANDREAUX, Center Field

	G	AB	Hit	2B	3B	HR	Run	RBI	TBB	SO	SB	CS	Avg
7.09 years		553	150	25	6	12	71	64	40	55	20	8	.271
1986	103	283	74	13	2	4	34	29	22	39	10	5	.261
First Half	78	233	63	11	2	3	32	26	20	32	8	5	.270
Second Half	25	50	11	2	0	1	2	3	2	7	2	0	.220
Vs. RHP		237	62	10	2	4		21	20	34			.262
Vs. LHP		46	12	3	0	0		8	2	5			.261
Home		127	30	4	0	1		14	14	14			.236
Road		156	44	9	2	3		15	8	25			.282
Grass		205	50	10	1	3		18	18	28			.244
Turf		78	24	3	1	1		11	4	11			.308

Steve SAX, Second Base

	G	AB	Hit	2B	3B	HR	Run	RBI	TBB	SO	SB	CS	Avg
4.78 years		643	183	25	5	4	88	48	57	62	44	15	.284
1986	157	633	210	43	4	6	91	56	59	58	40	17	.332
First Half	84	333	107	21	2	4	47	28	35	36	22	10	.321
Second Half	73	300	103	22	2	2	44	28	24	22	18	7	.343
Vs. RHP		407	136	23	3	3		35	41	41			.334
Vs. LHP		226	74	20	1	3		21	18	17			.327
Home		306	95	19	1	1		21	33	27			.310
Road		327	115	24	3	5		35	26	31			.352
Grass		447	138	27	4	4		36	51	43			.309
Turf		186	72	16	0	2		20	8	15			.387

Mike MARSHALL, Right Field

	G	AB	Hit	2B	3B	HR	Run	RBI	TBB	SO	SB	CS	Avg
3.55 years		543	145	25	1	25	69	81	45	134	6	6	.268
1986	103	330	77	11	0	19	47	53	27	90	4	4	.233
First Half	76	286	74	11	0	18	43	48	23	73	4	2	.259
Second Half	27	44	3	0	0	1	4	5	4	17	0	2	.068
Vs. RHP		201	45	4	0	10		32	11	56			.224
Vs. LHP		129	32	7	0	9		21	16	34			.248
Home		179	43	7	0	13		34	16	40			.240
Road		151	34	4	0	6		19	11	50			.225
Grass		261	67	9	0	18		48	22	63			.257
Turf		69	10	2	0	1		5	5	27			.145

Bill MADLOCK, Third Base

	G	AB	Hit	2B	3B	HR	Run	RBI	TBB	SO	SB	CS	Avg
10.48 years		592	182	31	3	14	82	77	54	44	16	8	.307
1986	111	379	106	17	0	10	38	60	30	43	3	3	.280
First Half	47	174	40	5	0	4	13	22	11	23	0	0	.230
Second Half	64	205	66	12	0	6	25	38	19	20	3	3	.322
Vs. RHP		238	62	11	0	4		37	18	32			.261
Vs. LHP		141	44	6	0	6		23	12	11			.312
Home		186	49	6	0	4		29	19	22			.263
Road		193	57	11	0	6		31	11	21			.295
Grass		262	74	11	0	6		37	23	26			.282
Turf		117	32	6	0	4		23	7	17			.274

Franklin STUBBS, Outfield

	G	AB	Hit	2B	3B	HR	Run	RBI	TBB	SO	SB	CS	Avg
1.41 years		457	98	9	3	22	54	54	43	122	6	2	.215
1986	132	420	95	11	1	23	55	58	37	107	7	1	.226
First Half	69	217	58	5	1	15	30	37	20	56	5	1	.267
Second Half	63	203	37	6	0	8	25	21	17	51	2	0	.182
Vs. RHP		323	73	8	1	19		48	34	91			.226
Vs. LHP		97	22	3	0	4		10	3	16			.227
Home		195	51	5	1	12		33	17	48			.262
Road		225	44	6	0	11		25	20	59			.196
Grass		296	64	7	1	15		41	27	81			.216
Turf		124	31	4	0	8		17	10	26			.250

Mariano DUNCAN, Shortstop

	G	AB	Hit	2B	3B	HR	Run	RBI	TBB	SO	SB	CS	Avg
1.55 years		625	148	20	4	9	78	45	44	123	56	14	.237
1986	109	407	93	7	0	8	47	30	30	78	48	13	.229
First Half	72	272	60	4	0	6	33	21	22	50	32	10	.221
Second Half	37	135	33	3	0	2	14	9	8	28	16	3	.244
Vs. RHP		234	48	4	0	4		14	22	50			.205
Vs. LHP		173	45	3	0	4		16	8	28			.260
Home		205	45	2	0	2		10	15	44			.220
Road		202	48	5	0	6		20	15	34			.238
Grass		334	74	6	0	6		23	25	68			.222
Turf		73	19	1	0	2		7	5	10			.260

Enos CABELL, First Base

	G	AB	Hit	2B	3B	HR	Run	RBI	TBB	SO	SB	CS	Avg
10.42 years		571	158	25	5	6	72	57	25	66	23	12	.277
1986	107	277	71	11	0	2	27	29	14	26	10	4	.256
First Half	58	151	37	6	0	0	14	16	8	14	6	1	.245
Second Half	49	126	34	5	0	2	13	13	6	12	4	3	.270
Vs. RHP		80	15	0	0	0		8	4	10			.188
Vs. LHP		197	56	11	0	2		21	10	16			.284
Home		144	39	7	0	2		22	7	13			.271
Road		133	32	4	0	0		7	7	13			.241
Grass		212	57	9	0	2		26	10	21			.269
Turf		65	14	2	0	0		3	4	5			.215

Orel HERSHISER

	(W–L)	GS	Run	Avg	DP	Avg	SB	Avg
1985	(19-3)	34	153	4.50	33	.97	36	1.06
1986	(14-14)	35	131	3.74	22	.63	31	.89
1984-1986		89	358	4.02	74	.83	79	.89

	G	IP	W	L	Pct	ER	BB	SO	ERA
1985 Home	19	133.3	11	0	1.000	16	39	96	1.08
1986 Home	18	129.0	10	5	.667	44	41	85	3.07
1985 Road	17	106.3	8	3	.727	38	29	61	3.22
1986 Road	17	102.3	4	9	.308	55	45	68	4.84
1985 Grass	28	188.7	15	2	.882	38	52	134	1.81
1986 Grass	25	173.0	12	9	.571	65	53	102	3.38
1985 Turf	8	51.0	4	1	.800	16	16	23	2.82
1986 Turf	10	58.3	2	5	.286	34	33	51	5.25
1986 Total	35	231.3	14	14	.500	99	86	153	3.85

Rick HONEYCUTT

	(W–L)	GS	Run	Avg	DP	Avg	SB	Avg
1985	(8-12)	25	93	3.72	24	.96	14	.56
1986	(11-9)	28	113	4.04	15	.54	15	.54
1981-1986		245	949	3.87	267	1.09	127	.52

	G	IP	W	L	Pct	ER	BB	SO	ERA
1985 Home	17	80.0	5	6	.455	24	22	43	2.70
1986 Home	17	97.0	6	4	.600	29	21	50	2.69
1985 Road	14	62.0	3	6	.333	30	27	24	4.35
1986 Road	15	74.0	5	5	.500	34	24	50	4.14
1985 Grass	22	103.0	6	8	.429	32	31	54	2.80
1986 Grass	26	141.0	8	7	.533	50	35	81	3.19
1985 Turf	9	39.0	2	4	.333	22	18	13	5.08
1986 Turf	6	30.0	3	2	.600	13	10	19	3.90
1986 Total	32	171.0	11	9	.550	63	45	100	3.32

Fernando VALENZUELA

	(W–L)	GS	Run	Avg	DP	Avg	SB	Avg
1985	(17-10)	35	147	4.20	24	.69	19	.54
1986	(21-11)	34	160	4.71	26	.76	21	.62
1981-1986		200	818	4.09	155	.78	161	.81

	G	IP	W	L	Pct	ER	BB	SO	ERA
1985 Home	17	133.7	7	5	.583	31	49	108	2.09
1986 Home	16	130.7	11	3	.786	32	30	121	2.20
1985 Road	18	138.7	10	5	.667	43	52	100	2.79
1986 road	18	138.7	10	8	.556	62	55	121	4.02
1985 Grass	26	201.3	12	8	.600	48	79	159	2.15
1986 Grass	24	190.3	15	7	.682	64	57	168	3.03
1985 Turf	9	71.0	5	2	.714	26	22	49	3.30
1986 Turf	10	79.0	6	4	.600	30	28	74	3.42
1986 Total	34	269.3	21	11	.656	94	85	242	3.14

OTHERS

	(W–L)	GS	Run	Avg	DP	Avg	SB	Avg
Reuss	(2-6)	13	57	4.38	11	.85	9	.69
Pena	(1-2)	10	48	4.80	10	1.00	11	1.10
Powell	(2-7)	6	15	2.50	6	1.00	7	1.17
Holton	(2-3)	3	6	2.00	2	.67	4	1.33

RECORDS WITH DIFFERENT STARTING CATCHERS

Catcher	Inn	ER	W–L	ERA	GS	SB	Avg
Scioscia	970.0	403	51-57	3.74	108	79	.73
Trevino	449.1	193	20-30	3.87	50	39	.78
Fimple	35.0	12	2-2	3.09	4	3	.75

Bob WELCH

	(W–L)	GS	Run	Avg	DP	Avg	SB	Avg
1985	(14-4)	23	107	4.65	13	.57	13	.57
1986	(7-13)	33	108	3.27	22	.67	27	.82
1979-1986		232	916	3.95	162	.70	152	.66

	G	IP	W	L	Pct	ER	BB	SO	ERA
1985 Home	13	96.7	9	3	.750	29	21	64	2.70
1986 Home	18	132.0	5	6	.455	39	30	93	2.66
1985 Road	10	70.7	5	1	.833	14	14	32	1.78
1986 Road	15	103.7	2	7	.222	47	25	90	4.08
1985 Grass	17	121.3	10	3	.769	34	26	75	2.52
1986 Grass	27	198.7	7	8	.467	65	46	151	2.94
1985 Turf	4	46.0	4	1	.800	9	9	21	1.76
1986 Turf	6	37.0	0	5	0.000	21	9	32	5.11
1986 Total	33	235.7	7	13	.350	86	55	183	3.28

YOU DON'T SAY

Probably the stupidest thing that people say regularly about baseball is that of course baseball is not basically a sport. Baseball is basically a business.

Of course baseball is not basically a business; if it were it would have gone out of existence in the 1890s. Let us suppose that the economic structure of baseball were to collapse, that the "business" of baseball were to become untenable and go the way of all dinosaurs, while the public interest in the *sport* of baseball remained alive. Would baseball then cease to exist? Of course not. New economic structures would sprout from the ground like mushrooms. New businessmen would appear, anxious to make a buck by catering to the interest in the sport. There would be new contracts, new agreements, new logos, and perhaps a few new players along with the new "businessmen"—but there would be baseball just as before, as pervasive as ever, suffering no more than the jolt of an unexpected speed bump.

Suppose, however, that the *sporting* interest in baseball, the omnipresent public interest in who is winning and who is losing and why, were somehow to vanish. Would the business of baseball then carry on as before? Why, of course it could not; lacking the public dollars that follow the public interest, the business would immediately cease to exist. The businessmen, and even the athletes, are the mere servants of the craving for the sport.

So obviously, the game is essentially a sport. It must be a sport to survive. The business will survive precisely as long as it remains a sport.

What is so curious is that otherwise intelligent men can be tricked into failing to see this, and will say with earnest faces that of course baseball is basically a business. Why do they think this? Because *Peter O'Malley* sees it basically as a business? Because *Reggie Jackson* sees it as basically a way to make a living?

But this is merely a fault of perception, a disorientation in their habits of thought that results from their peculiar relationship to the enterprise. Consider the same argument as it might apply to anything else—let us say a can of O'Malley's Beef and Beans. Obviously, to Albert O'Malley, who owns the business, it is basically a business. To Roger Jackson, who drives a truck for O'Malley, Beef and Beans is basically a way to make a living.

But to the man who buys the Beef and Beans and takes it on his picnic, what is it? It is essentially a *food,* of course. No one but a jackass would argue that because Beef and Beans is basically a business to Albert O'Malley, because it is basically a business to Roger Jackson, it therefore is basically a business.

The unique thing about sports fans is that they have so much trouble understanding this. It would be stupid for Bill James to believe that because baseball is a business to Peter O'Malley and Reggie Jackson that therefore it must be basically a business to him, too. It would be stupid for Bill James to forget that it is not he who must accommodate the businessman, but the businessman who must accommodate him. In the Beef and Bean business, even Albert O'Malley and Roger Jackson would certainly recognize this. They would remind themselves daily that what they were dealing with here was essentially a food. They would regard such daily reminders as being essential to their being able to serve the public. They would never allow themselves to lapse into thinking that what was essential to the business was their getting their dollar.

The unique arrogance of the baseball businessmen is that, seeing themselves quoted in the paper every day, seeing their own distorted perspective on the undertaking reflected in the daily press, they have allowed themselves the luxury of forgetting this.

But what is far more remarkable is that baseball fans go along with it. Baseball fans have the ultimate victim mentality: they are actually willing to treat their own perceptions as merely an illusion. Baseball fans will swear up and down that what baseball really is is not what *they* see baseball as being, but what Reggie Jackson and Peter O'Malley see it as being.

Anybody who tells you that baseball is basically a business is either badly confused or a jackass. And you can tell her I said so.

SAN DIEGO PADRES

Runners on Base:	1,944
Opponents on Base:	2,040
Net Disadvantage:	−96
Won-Lost Record:	74-88

For the San Diego Padres, 1986 was a bizarre season. The Padres misjudged their talent, mishandled their managerial situation, put pressure on their players, and sat back and watched the wheels fall off.

The April 28 edition of *The Sporting News* featured the Padres on the cover. "Team Turmoil," read the big letters, and underneath, "Their manager, Dick Williams, resigned just as spring training was to begin. Their best pitcher, LaMarr Hoyt, entered a rehabilitation clinic. But the San Diego Padres, undaunted, marched into the season with their sights set on winning the NL's West Division."

For half a season, it appeared that the Padres had overcome this most unpromising premise for a season, and would actually contend. As late as the All-Star break the Padres were 45–43, only three games behind the division-leading San Francisco Giants. LaMarr Hoyt, unavailable at the beginning of the season and floundering with a 6.36 ERA through his first 14 outings, was rounding into shape, so to speak; by mid-July he had cut his ERA to 4.97 and boosted his won-lost to 5–4. In mid-June, with all that they had overcome, I really thought that the San Diego Padres might actually win their division. Here, let me read you what I wrote in the last newsletter, which helps to explain why the Padres had played well in the first half, despite the problems, and why I thought they might be even better in the second half.

> Steve Boros's place in the managerial world appears to be that of professional antidote. Previous manager was a grump? HIRE STEVE! He's nice. He's friendly. He's intellectual. Previous manager let the speed game deteriorate? HIRE STEVE! He'll run-run-de-doo-run-run. Sometimes he'll run-run-de-doo-run-run himself right out of innings, but he's nice about it. Previous manager didn't use his bench? HIRE STEVE!

> Steve has become obsessive about using his bench; he's running people like Kruk, Wynne, Royster, Roberts, Bochy, and Iorg in and out of the game like a Chinese fire drill, but at least he is developing a bench, and it may well pay off handsomely in the stretch.

And well it might have, but what drugs and turmoil had been unable to accomplish in three months, tendinitis and terminal managerial incompetence accomplished in the next few weeks. In July, Dave Dravecky and Eric Show both started to suffer from tendinitis in their elbows, and Steve Boros's infantile fascination with the stolen base finally got the upper hand on him. The noose with which Steve Boros hanged himself was a 26-year-old outfielder named Marvell Wynne, whom Boros decided to make the foundation of his offense, based solely on the fact that Wynne is a fast runner.

The notion that this man could adequately perform the vital leadoff function is ludicrous. You have to understand, to begin with, that Wynne is not even a decent base stealer. In his three previous seasons with the Pirates, Wynne had stolen 46 bases and been caught 34 times, a nifty 58% success ratio, which is significantly worse than not stealing bases at all. But far more serious than the fact that Wynne can't steal bases is that he can't hit, either. Wynne carried a career batting average of .245 into the season. When Chuck Tanner used him as his leadoff man for the entire 1984 season, the Pirate offense was so impotent that the Pirates, picked by many to win their division, finished last despite leading the league in ERA. Wynne scored just 77 runs while batting 653 times. In addition to the fact that Wynne is a poor base stealer and a bad hitter with no power, he rarely walks and strikes out a lot. I mean, among all the outfielders in the National League, there probably are no more than a couple who would be worse leadoff men than Marvell Wynne. He's almost a perfect negative image of Tim Raines. Carmello Martinez, for Chrissakes, would score far more runs as a leadoff man.

So why did Boros make this decision? Two reasons. For one, Wynne as of July 3 was hitting .313—in 128 at bats. Of course, as any baseball fan over the age of eight could have predicted, Wynne's batting average began to dive like Mike Scott throwing a scuffed cantaloupe as soon as he got more playing time. Wynne hit .225 from July 3 to the end of the season.

And second, Boros felt that there was a compelling need to get some speed in the lineup. The Padres did, in fact, have an exceptionally slow lineup—sort of like the Red Sox. Boros argued that Wynne being on base (the people who like to make this argument just *assume* that the guy will be on base) would make the next hitter better. He would point out that in 1984, when the Padres won the pennant, the speedy Alan Wiggins was leading off and Tony Gwynn hit .351—.317 with the bases empty, but .406 with men on base. In 1985, with the Padres having slower leadoff men, Gwynn did not show the same effect, hitting .302 with the bases empty but .337 with men on base.

This, to Boros, was compelling evidence of the value of speed. To me, if Tony Gwynn hits much better with men on base than without men on base, then that provides a strong incentive to get a leadoff man *who can get on base*, thus holding the first baseman on the bag and opening up a hole. In any case, Wynne stopped hitting, and the Padre offense simply died. Between June 18 and July 20, Wynne batted leadoff in 19 games. The Padres went 6–13 in those games, and scored more than four runs only three times. After that, Wynne kept playing but moved to a spot below the power center.

What is it that makes a man an intellectual? There are a lot of things that will get that moniker hung on you, but one of the most fundamental characteristics of an intellectual is that an intellectual is a person who shakes off the truisms and faiths that others will try to nurture in him, and believes what logic and evidence tell him to believe. For Steve Boros, the sad thing is that this man, who has the manners and the reputation of an intellectual, has destroyed his managerial career by doggedly, blindly pursuing phantom payoffs from the running game, payoffs for which there is no evidence and which a modicum of intellectual skepticism should tell him not to count on.

In any case, in time John Kruk took over the main part of the third outfield job, with McReynolds returning to center. Kruk did a good job, but the Padres had dropped like a rock, and were out of contention by early August. The other big reason for the decline was injuries in the pitching staff, similar to what Oakland suffered when Boros managed them in 1983. There are baseball people who will tell you that Boros's biggest weakness is not the stolen base, but his inability to run a pitching staff.

Then things got *really* weird, with Gossage firing potshots at McDonalds and all; the Padres finished 74–88, 22 games out. Slow and with average power, the Padres were poor offensively and defensively. Offensively, they hit .261, second-best in the league, but had a secondary average of just .232, lowest in the National League, and thus scored just 656 runs, 18 below average. With Steve Garvey and Garry Templeton, notoriously selfish hitters, the Padres drew just 484 walks, second-fewest in the league.

The half of the time that Wynne wasn't playing, the Padres outfield, actually, may have been as good as any in the league. With Gwynn, McReynolds, and Kruk in the outfield the Padres had a sterling offensive unit and adequate defense. Gwynn had the finest season of his brilliant career, hitting .329, hitting with increased power, drawing 52 walks, and stealing 37 bases in 46 attempts. In the outfield he had good range and an excellent arm. McReynolds, though out of position in center field and the subject of incessant stupid criticism about what people imagine to be his potential, hit .288 with 26 homers, 96 RBI, and a secondary average of .348.

The infield, however, was terrible. Steve Garvey is an awful player, a poor defensive first baseman who doesn't hit for average, and has limited power and a secondary average below .200. Garry Templeton, his knees having ruined him as a shortstop, is kept in the lineup apparently for his bat. He scored 42 runs and drove in 44, hit 2 triples and 2 homers and drew 14 unintentional walks. Third baseman Graig Nettles hit .218 and fielded remarkably well for a man in his forties. The second base platoon was decent, but the offense had only two good offensive players, in McReynolds and Gwynn.

The pitching and defense were worse than the offense. In the two "strictly pitching" indicators, Padre pitchers were hammered for 150 home runs, the most in the National League, and walked 607 men, also the most in the National League. The mixed pitching and defense indicators are almost as poor. The Padres' defensive efficiency record, .670, was the worst in the National League, meaning that 33% of balls put into play against the Padres became hits, a consequence of the lack of speed in the outfield and the lack of range by all four infielders. The Padres fielded .978, the league average, and turned 135 double plays, ten below average.

The Padres do have some decent pitchers if they can keep them healthy and give them a little defensive support. A starting rotation of Show, Dravecky, Hawkins, and Storm Davis would be, if healthy, certainly more than adequate. We're bleeding into the question of how the team will perform in 1987, so maybe I should back up and hit it head-on.

As a managerial prospect, I like Larry Bowa a great deal. It is my belief that there are two absolute requisites for a successful manager: He must command the respect of his players, and he must communicate to each player a sense of the urgency of doing your best work. I feel certain that Bowa will meet those two challenges. He was an intense player, always in the game. That's got to rub off on his players. He was never particularly tolerant of journalists, fans, umpires, or teammates; there is no reason to think he will tolerate shoddy effort from his team. As to his knowledge of the game, Bowa played major-league ball very well for sixteen years without exceptional native ability. I never *liked* the personality that he projected, but I think he'll be an excellent manager.

But to make this team competitive quickly, he's going to have to face up to some very difficult problems, and he's going to have to catch some breaks. Somebody, sometime, has got to face up to the fact that Steve Garvey is killing the team. Somebody has got to lead this organization to face the fact that Garry Templeton is finished as a championship caliber player.

That given, enormous challenges remain. Several rookies (Benito Santiago, Stan Jefferson, Jimmy Jones, possibly Randy Asadoor) are projected in key roles. Kevin Mitchell could develop into a tremendous power-hitting third baseman, but he didn't really hit anything the second half of 1986. If the Mets thought he was destined to be a tremendous power-hitting third baseman, they wouldn't have traded him.

The pitching rotation could be excellent if the proven pitchers remain healthy and a couple of the youngsters come through, but that's what the Cubs were saying a year ago. The crisis in Hoyt's career is almost certainly a blessing to the Padres; as it was he wasn't going to do anything except once in a while pitch well enough to fool you into pitching him some more. The bullpen appears to be the deepest and strongest part of the team, despite some question about Gossage's ability to bounce back. Certainly Gossage needs a personality type like Bowa to manage him.

If enough of the rookies come through, and if Bowa does redefine the roles of Garvey and Templeton, it is not unrealistic to talk about the 1987 Padres being better than those of 1986. It is most realistic to think of 1987 as the beginning of a rebuilding period which will pay off several years down the road.

Terry KENNEDY, Catcher

	G	AB	Hit	2B	3B	HR	Run	RBI	TBB	SO	SB	CS	Avg
5.94 years		568	154	30	2	14	58	80	40	95	1	2	.272
1986	141	432	114	22	1	12	46	57	37	74	0	3	.264
First Half	81	264	72	13	1	8	31	36	25	41	0	2	.273
Second Half	60	168	42	9	0	4	15	21	12	33	0	1	.250
Vs. RHP		336	92	15	1	9		47	30	50			.274
Vs. LHP		96	22	7	0	3		10	7	24			.229
Home		214	60	9	0	7		26	19	39			.280
Road		218	54	13	1	5		31	18	35			.248
Grass		320	87	12	0	10		38	28	55			.272
Turf		112	27	10	1	2		19	9	19			.241

John KRUK, Left Field

	G	AB	Hit	2B	3B	HR	Run	RBI	TBB	SO	SB	CS	Avg
0.75 years		369	114	21	3	5	44	50	60	77	3	5	.309
1986	122	278	86	16	2	4	33	38	45	58	2	4	.309
First Half	56	81	25	6	0	1	10	10	12	17	1	2	.309
Second Half	66	197	61	10	2	3	23	28	33	41	1	2	.310
Vs RHP		199	62	13	2	4		26	32	38			.312
Vs. LHP		79	24	3	0	0		12	13	20			.304
Home		103	32	11	0	1		12	17	25			.311
Road		175	54	5	2	3		26	28	33			.309
Grass		187	55	12	0	3		24	26	44			.294
Turf		91	31	4	2	1		14	19	14			.341

Steve GARVEY, First Base

	G	AB	Hit	2B	3B	HR	Run	RBI	TBB	SO	SB	CS	Avg
14.23 years		616	182	31	3	21	80	91	34	70	6	4	.295
1986	155	557	142	22	0	21	58	81	23	72	1	2	.255
First Half	88	326	77	11	0	13	31	39	13	34	1	1	.236
Second Half	67	231	65	11	0	8	27	42	10	38	0	1	.281
Vs. RHP		372	90	13	0	9		47	15	52			.242
Vs. LHP		185	52	9	0	12		34	8	20			.281
Home		279	68	10	0	11		39	15	37			.244
Road		278	74	12	0	10		42	8	35			.266
Grass		409	100	17	0	13		53	15	51			.244
Turf		148	42	5	0	8		28	8	21			.284

Kevin McREYNOLDS, Center Field

	G	AB	Hit	2B	3B	HR	Run	RBI	TBB	SO	SB	CS	Avg
3.06 years		584	154	27	6	21	76	85	51	86	6	6	.263
1986	158	560	161	31	6	26	89	96	66	83	8	6	.288
First Half	86	311	83	17	3	13	46	47	37	50	5	4	.267
Second Half	72	249	78	14	3	13	43	49	29	33	3	2	.313
Vs. RHP		368	96	19	3	16		62	44	62			.261
Vs. LHP		192	65	12	3	10		34	22	21			.339
Home		276	81	13	3	14		45	35	46			.293
Road		284	80	18	3	12		51	31	37			.282
Grass		410	111	19	4	18		64	49	63			.271
Turf		150	50	12	2	8		32	17	20			.333

Tim FLANNERY, Second Base

	G	AB	Hit	2B	3B	HR	Run	RBI	TBB	SO	SB	CS	Avg
4.41 years		430	112	14	5	2	47	37	45	48	3	4	.260
1986	134	368	103	11	2	3	48	28	54	61	3	6	.280
First Half	76	192	51	8	2	3	22	18	30	27	1	3	.266
Second Half	58	176	52	3	0	0	26	10	24	34	2	3	.295
Vs. RHP		312	95	8	2	2		25	50	47			.304
Vs. LHP		56	8	3	0	1		3	4	14			.143
Home		183	54	4	1	1		17	27	33			.295
Road		185	49	7	1	2		11	27	28			.265
Grass		268	77	5	1	3		26	40	40			.287
Turf		100	26	6	1	0		2	14	21			.260

Tony GWYNN, Right Field

	G	AB	Hit	2B	3B	HR	Run	RBI	TBB	SO	SB	CS	Avg
3.78 years		626	204	28	7	7	93	61	51	34	26	12	.326
1986	160	642	211	33	7	14	107	59	52	35	37	9	.329
First Half	87	343	117	17	5	9	59	36	34	24	17	3	.341
Second Half	73	299	94	16	2	5	48	23	18	11	20	6	.314
Vs. RHP		406	133	20	1	6		26	31	23			.328
Vs. LHP		236	78	13	6	8		33	21	12			.331
Home		317	108	14	4	8		26	27	20			.341
Road		325	103	19	3	6		33	25	15			.317
Grass		474	158	24	6	10		40	36	29			.333
Turf		168	53	9	1	4		19	16	6			.315

Graig NETTLES, Third Base

	G	AB	Hit	2B	3B	HR	Run	RBI	TBB	SO	SB	CS	Avg
15.48 years		563	140	20	2	25	76	82	68	75	2	2	.249
1986	126	354	77	9	0	16	36	55	41	60	0	1	.218
First Half	71	203	45	2	0	12	24	33	23	36	0	1	.222
Second Half	55	151	32	7	0	4	12	22	18	26	0	0	.212
Vs. RHP		301	68	8	0	13		48	39	49	0		.226
Vs. LHP		53	9	1	0	3		7	2	13	0		.170
Home		166	44	5	0	13		38	27	36	0		.265
Road		188	33	4	0	3		17	14	26	0		.176
Grass		253	59	7	0	15		50	35	49	0		.233
Turf		101	18	2	0	1		5	6	13	0		.178

Marvell WYNNE, Center Field

	G	AB	Hit	2B	3B	HR	Run	RBI	TBB	SO	SB	CS	Avg
3.07 years		536	133	21	6	5	65	39	37	74	19	15	.248
1986	137	288	76	19	2	7	34	37	15	45	11	11	.264
First Half	77	168	50	11	1	4	22	20	6	21	8	10	.298
Second Half	60	120	26	8	1	3	12	17	9	24	3	1	.217
Vs. RHP		218	63	15	2	5		32	11	26			.289
Vs. LHP		70	13	4	0	2		5	4	19			.186
Home		177	55	13	2	5		24	5	30			.311
Road		111	21	6	0	2		13	10	15			.189
Grass		222	65	15	2	6		28	15	37			.293
Turf		66	11	4	0	1		9	0	8			.167

Garry TEMPLETON, Shortstop

	G	AB	Hit	2B	3B	HR	Run	RBI	TBB	SO	SB	CS	Avg
8.78 years		633	180	27	10	5	80	59	29	88	24	13	.284
1986	147	510	126	21	2	2	42	44	35	86	10	5	.247
First Half	84	303	68	6	1	2	24	28	21	51	7	5	.224
Second Half	63	207	58	15	1	0	18	16	14	35	3	0	.280
Vs. RHP		335	81	14	1	0		30	18	57			.242
Vs. LHP		175	45	7	1	2		14	17	29			.257
Home		269	62	10	2	1		24	21	54			.230
Road		241	64	11	0	1		20	14	32			.266
Grass		380	92	14	2	1		32	30	71			.242
Turf		130	34	7	0	1		12	5	15			.262

Jerry ROYSTER, Infield

	G	AB	Hit	2B	3B	HR	Run	RBI	TBB	SO	SB	CS	Avg
7.94 years		492	123	19	4	4	65	41	48	61	23	12	.250
1986	118	257	66	12	0	5	31	26	32	45	3	5	.257
First Half	62	137	32	9	0	1	17	10	15	21	1	2	.234
Second Half	56	120	34	3	0	4	14	16	17	24	2	3	.283
Vs. RHP		70	15	0	0	2		8	8	17			.214
Vs. LHP		187	51	12	0	3		18	24	28			.273
Home		118	29	8	0	2		12	13	18			.246
Road		139	37	4	0	3		14	19	27			.266
Grass		181	47	9	0	3		16	20	30			.260
Turf		76	19	3	0	2		10	12	15			.250

Andy HAWKINS

	(W–L)	GS	Run	Avg	DP	Avg	SB	Avg
1985	(18-8)	33	149	4.52	41	1.24	18	.55
1986	(10-8)	35	163	4.66	27	.77	34	.97
1983-1986		109	486	4.46	108	.99	83	.76

	G	IP	W	L	Pct	ER	BB	SO	ERA
1985 Home	18	126.0	10	6	.625	44	35	35	3.14
1986 Home	18	108.3	6	2	.750	37	32	54	3.07
1985 Road	15	102.7	8	2	.800	36	30	34	3.16
1986 Road	19	101.0	4	6	.400	63	43	63	5.61
1985 Grass	25	174.7	14	7	.667	61	45	49	3.14
1986 Grass	28	165.0	8	4	.667	63	46	91	3.44
1985 Turf	8	54.0	4	1	.800	19	20	20	3.17
1986 Turf	9	44.3	2	4	.333	37	29	26	7.51
1986 Total	37	209.3	10	8	.556	100	75	117	4.30

Eric SHOW

	(W–L)	GS	Run	Avg	DP	Avg	SB	Avg
1985	(12-11)	35	134	3.83	29	.83	30	.86
1986	(9-5)	22	83	3.77	16	.73	17	.77
1982-1986		136	521	3.83	106	.78	111	.82

	G	IP	W	L	Pct	ER	BB	SO	ERA
1985 Home	17	107.3	6	5	.545	42	42	69	3.52
1986 Home	13	77.7	5	3	.625	24	36	59	2.78
1985 Road	18	125.7	6	6	.500	38	45	72	2.72
1986 Road	11	58.7	4	2	.667	21	33	35	3.22
1985 Grass	25	160.0	9	8	.529	63	61	104	3.54
1986 Grass	18	103.3	6	4	.600	36	48	70	3.14
1985 Turf	10	73.0	3	3	.500	17	26	37	2.10
1986 Turf	6	33.0	3	1	.750	9	21	24	2.45
1986 Total	24	136.3	9	5	.643	45	69	94	2.97

Dave DRAVECKY

	(W–L)	GS	Run	Avg	DP	Avg	SB	Avg
1985	(13-11)	31	110	3.55	33	1.06	29	.94
1986	(9-11)	26	90	3.46	19	.73	13	.50
1982-1986		109	416	3.82	102	.94	88	.81

	G	IP	W	L	Pct	ER	BB	SO	ERA
1985 Home	14	97.0	6	3	.667	32	25	54	2.97
1986 Home	14	86.0	3	6	.333	33	27	55	3.45
1985 Road	20	117.7	7	8	.467	38	32	51	2.91
1986 Road	12	75.3	6	5	.545	22	27	32	2.63
1985 Grass	24	156.0	9	7	.562	53	40	73	3.06
1986 Grass	18	111.7	5	7	.417	35	35	64	2.82
1985 Turf	10	58.7	4	4	.500	17	17	32	2.61
1986 Turf	8	49.7	4	4	.500	20	19	23	3.62
1986 Total	26	161.3	9	11	.450	55	54	87	3.07

OTHERS

	(W–L)	GS	Run	Avg	DP	Avg	SB	Avg
Thurmond	(3-7)	15	57	3.80	15	1.00	18	1.20
Whitson	(1-7)	12	45	3.75	11	.92	13	1.08
McCullers	(10-10)	7	21	3.00	8	1.14	1	.14
Wojna	(2-2)	7	34	4.86	9	1.29	14	2.00
LaPoint	(1-4)	4	15	3.75	2	.50	1	.25
Jones	(2-0)	3	14	4.67	1	.33	2	.67
Vosberg	(0-1)	3	13	4.33	4	1.33	5	1.67
Hayward	(0-2)	3	13	4.33	3	1.00	0	0.00

RECORDS WITH DIFFERENT STARTING CATCHERS

Catcher	Inn	ER	W–L	ERA	GS	SB	Avg
Kennedy	1014.1	430	54-60	3.82	114	102	.89
Bochy	268.0	124	13-17	4.16	30	36	1.20
Santiago	134.2	74	7-8	4.95	15	11	.73
Parent	26.1	12	0-3	4.10	3	8	2.67

LaMarr HOYT

	(W–L)	GS	Run	Avg	DP	Avg	SB	Avg
1985	(16-8)	31	110	3.55	33	1.06	28	.90
1986	(8-11)	25	108	4.32	21	.84	28	1.12
1980-1986		171	765	4.47	157	.92	114	.67

	G	IP	W	L	Pct	ER	BB	SO	ERA
1985 Home	17	117.0	9	5	.643	53	12	56	4.08
1986 Home	18	86.7	4	3	.571	38	36	44	3.95
1985 Road	14	93.3	7	3	.700	28	8	27	2.70
1986 Road	17	72.3	4	8	.333	53	32	41	6.59
1985 Grass	23	158.0	11	6	.647	64	16	71	3.65
1986 Grass	27	124.7	5	9	.357	70	50	62	5.05
1985 Turf	8	52.3	5	2	.714	17	4	12	2.92
1986 Turf	8	34.3	3	2	.600	21	18	23	5.50
1986 Total	35	159.0	8	11	.421	91	68	85	5.15

WILL THE McMEETING PLEASE COME TO ORDER?

MR. BILLIARD: Thank you for coming, gentlemen. The reason I called this meeting was to discuss what our conduct should be . . . um, what our policies should be . . . with respect to winter moves designed to restructure our team, which as you know has had a somewhat disappointing season. Before we begin, Mr. Toady has some remarks that he prepared after a conversation with Mrs. Crock, and I thought you should hear them. Frank?

MR. TOADY: Yes, Sir. To be as brief as possible, Mrs. Crock and I feel that there is a need for this organization to adopt some policies to protect ourselves against possible multimillion-dollar losses on long-term contracts. We have discussed this issue at length and have come up with two essential recommendations. Number one, the team should resolve not to enter into negotiations with any player who has a history of abuse of chemical substances. And number two, the team should no longer enter into negotiations for multi-year contracts.

MR. REASONER: Excuse me?

MR. TOADY: The team should no longer enter into negotiations for multi-year contracts. We feel, Mrs. Crock and I, that we should play it one year at a time.

MR. REASONER: Do you really think, Mrs. Crock and you, that that's feasible in today's market? And if so, how did you reach the conclusion that it was?

MR. TOADY: Evidence. We had some conversations with Larry Boner of the Player Relations and In-Laws Committee, who showed us figures which project that, at the current rates of growth, by the year 2000 major-league teams will be obligated to pay $148 billion a year to players who are no longer performing. We feel that to offer long-term contracts works to the benefit of the player, but exposes the club to additional financial risk, and thus is not in the interest of the club.

MR. REASONER: *Of course* it's not in the interest of the club. And while we're on the subject, it's not in the interest of the club that we pay the players, at all; it would be in the best interest of the club if they would just play for free. It would be in the best interest of the club if the players would pay for their own transportation and their own hotel rooms while on the road, not to mention if they would buy their own uniforms. There are times that it would be in the best interest of the club for certain players to be summarily executed. That doesn't mean that we get to do it. The point is that these things are arrived at through *negotiation*, and that in negotiations the club often agrees to do things that are in the interest of the player so that the player will do things that are in the interest of the club. Maybe if you worked hard enough at it you could even explain this to Mrs. Crock.

MR. TOADY: Oh, I don't think so. Mrs. Crock and I feel that it is in the best interest of the club not to commit ourselves to more than one year at a time.

MR. REASONER: Do Mrs. Crock and you understand that if we *don't* commit ourselves to more than one year at a time, all of our best players are just going to leave? Does Mrs. Crock also feel that it is in the best interest of our club if our best players all leave us?

MR. TOADY: Well, we haven't exactly discussed that point. I mean, we're willing to sign free agents and all. We're willing to put out good money on a one-year contract. As Mrs. Crock sees it, when you sell somebody a hamburger, they're not obligated to come back and buy another hamburger. If they like the hamburger, they'll buy another one. And if we like what we get for our money, we'll sign the player for another year. What could be more fair than that?

MR. REASONER: What good does it do to say that you're willing to sign free agents if you're going to adopt a policy that will obviously preclude the possibility of signing any free agent worth putting cheese and pickles on? And by the way, I might point out that our GM, Trader Jack, has actually *saved* this organization hundreds of thousands of dollars by getting players committed to two-year and three-year contracts when they were coming off poor years and going into outstanding years. He's noted throughout baseball for his shrewd use of multi-year contracts. Does this mean anything to you?

MR. BILLIARD: I think we've discussed this issue enough; let's have a vote on it here. All in favor of adopting Frank's recommendation, say "Aye." Seven to one? Okay, that's settled; I'll tell Jack about it first thing in the morning. Now, with respect to the possibility of acquiring additional talent through the winter . . . Ted, did you have some thoughts on that issue?

MR. REASONER: Well, there's this player in the National League named Tim Raines. Maybe you've heard of him? He's probably the best player in the league at the moment, and he's expressed an interest in playing for our team. I think we should go after him.

MR. BILLIARD: Sounds good to me. Anybody else here know anything about him?

MR. TOADY: I know all about him, and frankly I have to say that he isn't the kind of player who fits our present needs.

MR. REASONER: Doesn't fit our needs? But . . . but . . . but we need a leadoff man. And he's the best leadoff man in the history of the National League. And we need a left fielder, and he's the best left fielder in the league. And we desperately need team speed, and he steals 70 bases a year. How in the world can you suggest that he doesn't fit our needs? AND HE WOULD LIKE TO PLAY FOR US!!!

MR. TOADY: Well, we feel—Mrs. Crock and I—that there's more to it than just baseball skills. We feel that this team has a need for character and leadership. This Mr. Raines, he has a history of drug abuse, doesn't he? I sure don't think that shows the kind of character that we're looking for.

MR. REASONER: Four years ago, when Tim Raines was a 22-year-old kid and *Newsweek* was putting cocaine on the cover and proclaiming it the nation's new recreational drug, Mr. Raines went through a brief period in which he abused drugs. But he got control of it—before it got control of him. He got clean, and he's been the most durable, dynamic, exciting player in the league over the last four years. You don't think that shows some character?

MR. TOADY: Well, I think what we're looking for is more in the nature of someone who has the character not to get involved with these things at all. I mean, how do we know he's not going to go back to it? We feel, Mrs. Crock and I, that for a baseball team to win, they've got to have character as well as talent.

MR. REASONER: Well, so do I. Sports *are* tests of character as well as talent, of course they are. But if you believe that sports are tests of character, then can you possibly explain how Tim Raines got to be a great player without having character? I mean, surely there's more to having character than being raised in the suburbs, isn't there? I might even suggest that I would think that Raines's experience, in that he overcame this temptation, might have a salutary effect on some of our younger players. It would make him a stronger role model. Anyway, how do we know that Terry Kennedy or Steve Garvey isn't going to start using drugs? For that matter, how do we know that you and Mrs. Crock aren't in there smoking banana peels? You've sure got to be on something . . .

MR. BILLIARD: Well, I think you've mouthed off about long enough there, Ted. Let's take a vote on the issue. Anybody else here who feels that we should make overtures toward this Raines individual? No? Well, that's closed. Any other new business, or can I go get my hair coiffed?

MR. REYNOLDS: Mr. Billiard, I had a chance meeting this week with one of the Lord's Angels—

MR. TOADY (*Intensely interested*): Oh, really. Which one?

MR. REYNOLDS: Grumpy, I think he said his name was. The Angel Grumpy.

MR. TOADY: A good man. I know him well.

MR. REYNOLDS: I'm sure you do. Anyway, this angel said that, in view of the unique relationship that our organi-

zation had with the Almighty, he had been notified about a special dispensation on our behalf. It seems that the Lord is going to allow us, as a one-time thing, to choose a player out of the past and bring him back to earth at his prime. So long as we didn't put in artificial turf, saith the Lord. Apparently, Gabriel insisted on that.

MR. BILLIARD: Gee, that sounds good. Just any player?

MR. REYNOLDS: Any player out of the past.

MR. BILLIARD: Well, um . . . Gee, that sounds great. What about Babe Ruth?

MR. TOADY: Babe Ruth? With all due respect, Mr. Billiard, I'm sure Mrs. Crock would want us to be consistent here.

MR. BILLIARD: Is there a problem?

MR. TOADY: A large one, I'm afraid. Mr. Ruth was a known abuser of illegal chemical substances. Not just on occasion, but throughout his career. Besides that, his training habits were horrific, his education was limited, and his disrespect for team authority knew no bounds. I mean, even Goose Gossage never dangled anybody out the back of a moving 747. He was entertaining, but I'm afraid Mr. Ruth's impact on the team as a whole could be catastrophic and besides, our manager doesn't think he's fast enough.

MR. BILLIARD: OK, scratch the Barnbuno. What about the . . . um, the Atlanta Peachtree, was he called?

MR. REASONER: Ty Cobb, you mean?

MR. BILLIARD: That's him. What about Ty Cobb?

MR. TOADY: Mr. Billiard, with all due respect, Mr. Cobb is, if that's possible, an even more appalling suggestion than Mr. Ruth. Cobb was . . . well, little more than a common thug, really. He was involved in constant fights with opponents, teammates, butcher's clerks, even umpires. Sometimes he carried a gun. He was incredibly greedy. Many people believe that he helped to fix a game, for heaven's sake. I hardly think he exemplifies the kind of athlete we're looking for.

MR. BILLIARD: Right. We could go for a pure hitter, instead. What about, um, this Mr. Williams, this "Freddie Ballgame"? What about him?

MR. TOADY: Mr. Williams was pretty hard to get along with, too. His attitude toward the press and public was very poor. He was quoted as saying that if you pour hot water over a sportswriter you'll have instant shit, and on one occasion he made an obscene gesture toward the fans. I think we'd better rule him out.

MR. REASONER: In my opinion, sir, I think we should go for a pitcher. What about Lefty Grove, supposed to be the greatest pitcher ever? I think we should go for him.

MR. TOADY: Another hothead, I'm afraid. A fine pitcher but an emotional adolescent, really, a guy who threw tantrums when things didn't go his way.

MR. REASONER: What about another pitcher . . . how about that guy that Reagan played in the movie . . . ?

MR. TOADY: Didn't you watch it? The man had a serious drinking problem. In the movie they made out like he got control of it, but he never really did.

MR. REASONER: Oh, right. How stupid of me . . . anybody have an interest in Mickey Mantle? He always seemed like a good guy to me.

MR. TOADY: Another overgrown adolescent. Training habits were very poor, honestly—in fact we have reports that he was hung over on the field at times. He drank more than the type of player we're looking for, which is to say that he drank more than Mrs. Crock does.

MR. REASONER: Willie Mays?

MR. TOADY: We have evidence that he missed church on a number of occasions. With no good reason, really.

MR. REASONER: How about Frank Robinson or Bob Gibson, somebody like that?

MR. TOADY: Oh, both of those guys were sheer heck to get along with, particularly after a loss. Also, wasn't Robinson involved in a DWI incident one time? Something like that.

MR. REASONER: Roberto Clemente, then?

MR. TOADY: Chronic complainer. Prone to injuries. Didn't get along well with some of his managers.

MR. REASONER: I guess outfielders are like that. What about one of those great middle infielders, like Honus Wagner or Rogers Hornsby.

MR. TOADY: Wagner was another man who enjoyed the night life, I'm afraid. Maybe it wasn't a problem, but I'm sure he could drink Mrs. Crock under the table. And Hornsby, he was a real attitude case, a guy who'd rip the front office or his own teammates if he took a

notion. Couldn't nobody get along with him. We could have another Goose Gossage on our hands.

MR. REASONER: OK, I give up. Isn't there *anybody* who is acceptable to you?

MR. TOADY: Oh, my yes; I can name a number of acceptable candidates . . . there's Amos Strunk, Tommy Thevenow, Joe Quinn. Our office has never received any negative information pertaining to any of these people. But we feel the ultimate, the perfect candidate to help our ballclub is a player of recent vintage, an infielder of the 1970s who was taken untimely away. I refer, of course, to the great Danny Thompson.

MR. REASONER: Danny Thompson? Was that the Minnesota kid who married into the Griffith family? Is that who you mean?

MR. TOADY: A fine man and a fine player. I'm sure Mrs. Crock would be very pleased by his selection.

MR. REASONER: Let me get this straight. You've got a chance to pick up any player from the history of baseball, and, on the basis of the number of good-conduct medals earned, you're going to pick DANNY THOMPSON?

MR. BILLIARD: That's enough, Ted. We don't want to get emotional about this. It sounds to me like Mr. Thompson will bring to the team exactly the attributes we're looking for. Well, if there are no more suggestions, I'm late to my appointment with my hair stylist. Shall we go with Danny Thompson, then?

MR. REYNOLDS: I'll tell Grumpy. Do you think we need to brief the media on this?

MR. BILLIARD: No, I don't think that will be necessary. Just issue him a uniform and tell him when to report to Spring Training. If he's everything Mr. Toady tells us he is, nobody will ever know he's around.

SOME RANDOM THOUGHTS
ON BASEBALL AND BALLPLAYERS
—Mike Kopf

Gossage Gets His Point Across: What is going on in San Diego? First the Goose denounces management for being more interested in personal character than in winning, and then, as if to prove it, said management suspends him for, essentially, lacking character. All very nice, except that suspending a player merely for lacking character is of dubious legality (not to mention the horrible precedent: If all teams suspend their players who lack character, we'll be down to four- or five-man rosters before we know it), and there's reason to believe Gossage could've persuaded an arbitrator of that fact. So what does he do but return to the fold, meekly, tail between his legs, pay a nominal fine and say, in effect, I was wrong; character is important. Chalk up a major victory for the Padres and decent behavior, right?

How, then, to explain the hiring of Larry Bowa as manager? Leave aside the question of inexperience, this guy lacks character like Dracula lacks a suntan. He shows them who's boss by spewing tobacco juice in the face of Pam Postema (all right, granted, gender should be irrele-

vant) and other umpires, and of course, as a player, his selflessness and warm encouragement to rookies were legendary—ask Shawon Dunston. But he has an intense desire to win. Billy Martin has a similar desire.

Which brings me back to the San Diego brass. I want to know, after the initial white heat of anger which led to Goose's suspension had cooled down, at what point did Ballard Smith et al. sit down, analyze the entire season, from the departure of Dick Williams to the hiring of Mr. Liberal Humanism, Steve Boros, through the clubhouse ban on beer to the second-half collapse amid complaints that Boros was too soft; at what point, I say, did the light bulbs flash in their minds and their fists come smashing down on the table in unison, followed by the chorus, "Goddamit, Gossage is right! The hell with character, we want to win. Where can we find a manager as rotten as Billy Martin, but who'll work cheap?" Sound absurd? Maybe, but it seems to me the only sensible explanation for the Padres' behavior. How the Goose must be chortling now.

Will the damage that the designated hitter has done to the moral fiber of baseball, not to mention that of the nation at large, never cease? Recently I phoned a friend, no admirer of baseball, to discuss theater tickets. In the course of a mercifully brief conversation—she had a cold and her voice was shot—I asked if there was anything I could do to ease her misery. "No, thanks," she rasped. "Scott is my designated chicken soup provider." It wasn't until I'd hung up that I realized what she'd said—"designated chicken soup provider." And she cares not a farthing for baseball. It then dawned on me that, probably for years, I had been listening to—and for all I know contributing to—this unspeakable linguistic perversion. And now I'm really worried, because it is one thing to have the DH in baseball, where, as with Prohibition, that other ignoble experiment, there remains hope of eventual repeal, but if indeed variations on the designated hitter theme have been subtly, remorselessly infiltrating our idioms (I now shudder with horror at the thought that the friend who prepares these manuscripts considers himself my designated typist), how will we ever cleanse the language?

I suspect this was all part of a conscious plot by the American League Maggots: to gradually pollute the language, as well as baseball, so that their deviation would take root at all levels of society, the less easily to be exterminated by baseball's aroused defenders of the Faith. How else to explain the original formulation of that repugnant term, "designated hitter," when a more accurate literal description would have been, for example, the one-dimensional player, or perhaps the perpetual pinch hitter, or how about (and this is my particular favorite) the pitcher's pimp? It's a totally accurate description of what occurs, and since pimp is a well-entrenched part of the language, there could be no sinister infestation by linguistic means— my friend would never call Scott her chicken soup pimp. Also, in baseball shorthand, pitcher's pimp would become PP, which of course is also a euphemism for human excretion, which is exactly what the designated hitter concept is. So if you want to perform a good deed that will benefit both baseball and the language, write to Peter Ueberroth and tell him that you're tired of linguistic prostitution; you want the designated hitter to be renamed the pitcher's pimp. I'm sure we'll receive the vociferous support of John Simon and William Safire in this endeavor.

On the other hand, maybe the designated hitter infiltrating the language can be turned to our advantage. Did you see where, recently, Secretary of State Shultz described National Security Advisor Poindexter as the "designted hitter" of the Administration's Iran policy? I'll wager Poindexter liked the appellation not even a little bit, but it signifies what can be done. If designated hitter must be part of the language, what's to prevent us from seeing that its use is only pejorative, à la Shultz on Poindexter? So from now on, whenever an asshole appears on TV or in the papers, make sure you describe him in conversation as somebody's designated hitter, e.g. "Jesse Helms, the tobacco lobby's designated hitter . . ." or "Pat Robertson, DHing for God . . ." Make sure to do this when discussing history, too. What was Adolf Eichmann but Hitler's designated hitter for the Final Solution, or Andrei Vishinsky Stalin's DH at the Moscow Purge Trials? Conversely, refer to all admirable personages as "pitchers who could also swing the bat," as in "Lincoln, a junk ball pitcher who thought he could finesse the proslavery lineup, ended up winning the game by swinging a terrible swift bat." Perhaps this is the way to destroy the DH after all: by making it a laughingstock. You don't see those "heartbreak of psoriasis" commercials anymore, do you? Take heart, anti-DHers, we can win this battle yet, and have some good fun doing it.

I suspect you noticed that three of the most exciting plays of the post-season were the home runs that almost weren't, when first Henderson, and later Evans and Strawberry, raced to the fence, gloved the ball at the last moment, only to unexpectedly lose it over the fence for a homer. Terrific baseball, but how many of us stopped to ask ourselves, could the same thing happen in our home park? Chances are the answer is no; it certainly is for the stadium I frequent, which is Royals, and presents an insurmountable eleven-foot fence throughout the outfield. There is no reason for this to be so; the height of the fence is not an integral part of the architecture as, for example, Wrigley Field's ivy-covered brick wall, or Fenway's Green Monster is—someone on high just decided that a ball hit for home run distance was not to be interfered with by leaping outfielders. The same silliness exists in Cleveland's Municipal Stadium, ballpark of my youth, where I once thrilled to the sight of Minnie Minoso almost routinely scaling the six-foot chain link fence to deprive enemy batters of the four-baggers. Happily still alive, Minnie is spared the annoyance of turning over in his grave at the sight of the Cleveland fence today, against which even Sir Edmund Hillary would be helpless.

Why do they do things like that to us? Is there some financial advantage in high fences that I'm not aware of? Some superstition that outfielders are more likely to injure themselves colliding with low fences? Or are the powers that be in baseball now so hopelessly enmeshed in the ever-increasing flow of dollars and the concomitant problems of negotiating local TV and radio contracts, awarding concession franchises and holding the salaries of journeyman outfielders to a sane and sensible three hundred thousand a year that they no longer have the time or inclination to contemplate such trivial matters as aesthetics, even when certan aesthetic improvements, such as lower fences, would not cost them a dollar of revenue? If so, then we can only echo the famous lament of Dickens: "It was the best of times, it was the worst of times . . ."

MACK

The Padres have a prospect named Shane Mack. He was born with the name. Not counting pitchers, there have been six players in major-league history named "Mack." Not one of them was born with that name. Connie Mack was born Cornelius McGillicuddy, and his son Earle was born Earle McGillicuddy. Denny Mack was born Dennis McGee, Joe Mack was born Joe Maciarz, Ray Mack was born Raymond Mickovsky, and Reddy Mack was born Joseph McNamara.

ATLANTA BRAVES

Runners on Base:	1,910
Opponents on Base:	2,045
Net Disadvantage:	−135
Won-Lost Record:	72-89

Lord, what an awful team. Awash in mediocrity from the top of the organization to the lowest utility infielder, the Atlanta Braves trudged blindly through another disappointing summer in 1986. At no point did they seem destined to contend. No element of the team was strong. The team was not marked by outstanding talent, outstanding enthusiasm, outstanding management, or outstanding uniforms. It seems incredible that just a few years ago baseball fans were worried about baseball splitting into camps in which the rich grew richer and the poor grew livestock for the rich.

The Braves, you see, represent the rich. Having inflated the salaries of all baseball to draw players to Atlanta, Ted Turner is now saddled with an ugly, overpaid ballclub that has no idea how to win. It must be easier for a camel to pass through the eye of a needle than it is for a rich team to win the division. If the powerhouse of the Dodgers is finished, at least it lasted almost a half-century. The dynastic ambitions of Ted Turner flowered and died in two weeks in 1982, when the Braves opened the season by winning their first 13 games. They have not been the same since. I'm not even sure what happened to all those free agents that the Braves were so excited about signing; the only people around who can actually play the game are those who have been there forever.

The 1986 Braves had three good players. Dale Murphy, even having lost some speed and perhaps out of position in center, even having a substandard hitting year by his own standards, remains one of the half-dozen best players in the league. Bob Horner remains an effective power hitter. Gene Garber, who was in the Atlanta bullpen when Sherman hit town, regained the relief ace job that he gave up in 1979 and handled it well.

The rest of the team varied from unimpressive and boring to decrepit and boring. Playing in a tremendous hitter's park, the Braves scored only 615 runs. Only the Cardinals scored fewer. They hit 138 home runs, fifth in the league. That was their strongest offensive number. In home runs hit on the road, they were a little below average. They were tenth in batting average, seventh in slugging, sixth in walks, last in stolen bases and last in stolen base percentage.

The Braves also pulled off a unique five-element accomplishment. They were ninth in the league in on-base percentage, meaning that they don't have many people on base to begin with, right? In spite of this, they laid down an above-average number of sacrifice bunts, and they had an above-average number of runners caught stealing. This

means they can't possibly have many people on base now, right?

One of the main purposes of bunting and stealing bases is supposed to be to stay away from the double play. So if you don't have many people on to begin with and you bunt a lot and lose a lot of runners stealing, at least you should be OK with regard to the double play?

No. The Braves still grounded into an above-average number of double plays. Wait, wait—I'm not finished. If you don't have many people on base to begin with, you lose an above-average number stealing and an above-average number by double plays, *at least* you won't be leaving people on base, right?

Wrong. The Braves still led the division in runners left on base, 1,145. Only the Mets and Phillies, the league's two best offenses, left more runners on base. It's kind of like . . . I remember reading about this case in Texas where a guy was found shot five times in the back and the coroner ruled it was suicide. The Braves are like that; they managed to destroy themselves in ways you'd never think possible.

Of their 1,910 runners on base, only 32.2% scored, the lowest percentage of any major league team. Not counting players who homered, the Braves scored only 26.9% of their runners, while every other major league team scored over 28% of their runners.

It is alleged that the Braves are poorly designed to fit their park. I don't buy it. The question of how you can figure your talent for your park is a question that arises *after* you have talent. If you don't have talent, it doesn't matter. The Braves don't have talent. If they played in St. Louis, they'd lose because they were too slow. If they played in Dodger Stadium, they'd lose because they wouldn't have the pitching that characterizes successful teams in Dodger Stadium. The Braves are just bad.

One particular respect in which the Braves were well suited for their park was that they have a pitching staff that throws an unusual number of ground balls, thus keeping the ball in the park. Atlanta pitchers allowed only 117 home runs, an exceptionally good total in this ballpark. The Braves led the league in double plays (181) in large part because of the ground-ball staff and the number of opponents on base. On the other hand, the advantage of ground balls is that they are usually turned into outs, yet the Braves' defensive efficiency record, .681, was very poor.

Braves announcer Ernie Johnson observed in August that "the Braves have tried a number of people in the leadoff spot, none with any great success." Well, gee, Omar Moreno hasn't hit .260 since 1981. His strikeout-to-walk ratios are terrible, and his base stealing has been declining in regular steps since 1980. We were expecting him to turn into Rickey Henderson?

It has now been four years since the Braves won the NL West title, just three years since they pushed the Dodgers to the wire in 1983. How did we get from there to here?

In the line of mistakes, the biggest was the trade of September 2, 1983, in which the Braves gave up Brett Butler and Brook Jacoby to acquire Len Barker. I've commented on this before, but that's got to be one of the worst trades ever made. Barker was paid a lot of money and was terrible, winning 10 games and losing 20 for the Braves before earning his release last spring. Butler and Jacoby not only were two good players, but were precisely the two good players that the Braves needed. Butler the lead-off man and center fielder, Jacoby the power-hitting third baseman. Jacoby would have even better stats in Atlanta than he does in Cleveland. Given back those two players, the Braves would have played .500 ball over the last two years.

There have been other moves that didn't work. The decision to spend 74% of the money in the world to sign Bruce Sutter led to the decisions to let Donnie Moore go and trade Steve Bedrosian. Moore and Bedrosian are now the relief aces of good teams, while Sutter has not been able to contribute and Ozzie Virgil, acquired for Bedrosian, hit .223 with 48 RBI and disappointing defense; still, with Gene Garber and Paul Assenmacher plugging up the bullpen, it cannot really be said that that sequence of moves explains much about why the Braves are 15 games worse than they were three years ago. The same applies to any other trade.

I would say that the three things which have most contributed to the decline of the Braves are 1) the Barker trade, 2) the failure of the farm system to produce capable replacements at key positions, and 3) the failure to identify and hire a major-league manager.

I wasn't kind to Chuck Tanner in the book a year ago, but I would never have believed what an awful job he would do as manager of the Braves. It is my belief that most people, as they age, become parodies of the things that they once believed in. I can't remember the exact quote, but Nathaniel Hawthorne said something to the effect that writers spend the last 30 years of their lives trying to figure out what it was that they did so well when they were younger. In the context of life, confronted with an overwhelming array of options about what we should be and how we should make decisions, we choose to emphasize certain attributes that we find within ourselves. We select a philosophy of life as a man drifting in an infinite ocean selects a direction in which to sail his raft, because we are desperate to escape this bewildering ocean, youth. Life in the ocean becomes so much easier when you know where you are going and that there is land ahead.

But once we reach the land, then we begin to think that we really understand life. We start to feel superior to the young and to the lost at sea, drifting with the currents. We forget that we once could see truth lying at the horizon in every direction. Surrounded by others who have landed on the same earth or rock on which we ourselves found comfort, we begin to think that this is the only land there is, that all who do not sail in our direction are doomed never to escape the sea. We assert our values without respect to the complexity of real-life problems. Old soldiers, espousing patriotism and love of country over all other political virtues, become blind to the faults of their countries. Their courage, no longer demanded from them, withers into bravado. Young people who chose books and learning to help them make sense of the overpowering world become so enamored of the books that they lose interest in the world that those books were supposed to help them understand until, if they are historians, they are writing papers on where Napoleon went to the bathroom and, if they are psychologists, they are running rats through multicolored mazes and, if they are sabermetricians, they are trying to figure out whether or not strikeout-to-walk ratio is an indicator of growth potential in a rookie.

So it is with Chuck Tanner, a parody of positive thinking, representing positive thought chopped loose from life or the understanding of life, positive thought rescued from the sea of values and hailed supreme over all others, positive thinking lying on a great pedestal as dead as a beached tuna. The problem isn't with the idea that a team will play better if they keep a positive frame of mind. The problem is that that homily is Chuck Tanner's entire concept of how to manage a baseball team. He is completely out of touch with the talent. He is so out of touch with the talent that he gave 359 at bats to a player (Omar Moreno) who has *NO* positives—a .234 hitter with no power with a 4–1 strikeout to walk ratio who is a 52% base stealer. He has no concept of how it is, exactly, that he is going to win, except that he figures if everybody has a good year we'll win.

Can the Braves bounce back in 1987? Having watched the Braves on cable for three years, I still find it hard to believe that they can't play better. Perhaps I'm hard on Tanner because there is an unshakeable feeling that any team with Dale Murphy in the outfield ought to contend.

But you'd have a heck of a time inferring that conclusion logically from any evidence I can see. The Braves are a veteran team, an old team. Among Horner, Hubbard, Ramirez, Oberkfell, Griffey, and Murphy, who is going to be any better next year or three years from now than he was in 1986? From a bench stocked with Bruce Benedict, Chris Chambliss, Ted Simmons, and Billy Sample, who is going to develop into a player who can plug a hole? There is some young talent, in players like Assenmacher and Thomas, but there's little in the majors and nothing ready to come out of the minors. It's not that the Braves are rebuilding, even; it's more like they'll start rebuilding in a year or two. In the meantime, if Dale Murphy goes out with an injury this is a team that could lose a hundred games.

Ozzie VIRGIL, Catcher

	G	AB	Hit	2B	3B	HR	Run	RBI	TBB	SO	SB	CS	Avg
3.07 years		487	117	20	2	20	57	66	57	102	1	1	.240
1986	114	359	80	9	0	15	45	48	63	73	1	0	.223
First Half	67	212	43	6	0	11	32	30	39	34	0	0	.203
Second Half	47	147	37	3	0	4	13	18	24	39	1	0	.252
Vs. RHP		251	52	5	0	13		36	38	62		0	.207
Vs. LHP		108	28	4	0	2		12	25	11		0	.259
Home		170	45	6	0	6		25	20	37		0	.265
Road		189	35	3	0	9		23	43	36		0	.185
Grass		265	62	6	0	11		34	49	59		0	.234
Turf		94	18	3	0	4		14	14	14		0	.191

Ken GRIFFEY, Left Field

	G	AB	Hit	2B	3B	HR	Run	RBI	TBB	SO	SB	CS	Avg
10.36 years		591	178	30	7	12	95	68	58	72	18	7	.300
1986	139	490	150	22	3	21	69	58	35	67	14	9	.306
First Half	73	257	77	7	1	10	36	29	17	35	7	3	.300
Second Half	66	233	73	15	2	11	33	29	18	32	7	6	.313
Vs. RHP		371	120	13	3	18		44	30	45			.323
Vs. LHP		119	30	9	0	3		14	5	22			.252
Home		245	75	14	0	14		30	20	30			.306
Road		245	75	8	3	7		28	15	37			.306
Grass		390	117	17	0	19		46	29	53			.300
Turf		100	33	5	3	2		12	6	14			.330

Bob HORNER, First Base

	G	AB	Hit	2B	3B	HR	Run	RBI	TBB	SO	SB	CS	Avg
5.93 years		603	168	27	1	36	92	110	57	83	2	3	.278
1986	141	517	141	22	0	27	70	87	52	72	1	4	.273
First Half	84	310	86	13	0	17	43	56	30	46	1	4	.277
Second Half	57	207	55	9	0	10	27	31	22	26	0	0	.266
Vs. RHP		349	89	12	0	20		61	32	53			.255
Vs. LHP		168	52	10	0	7		26	20	19			.310
Home		268	82	11	0	20		59	26	29			.306
Road		249	59	11	0	7		28	26	43			.237
Grass		405	113	17	0	23		71	37	57			.279
Turf		112	28	5	0	4		16	15	15			.250

Dale MURPHY, Center Field

	G	AB	Hit	2B	3B	HR	Run	RBI	TBB	SO	SB	CS	Avg
8.40 years		598	165	25	4	32	97	98	73	130	15	6	.279
1986	160	614	163	29	7	29	89	83	75	141	7	7	.265
First Half	87	322	88	16	2	14	57	36	51	79	4	4	.273
Second Half	73	292	75	13	5	15	32	47	24	62	3	3	.257
Vs. RHP		421	109	22	2	20		60	41	104			.259
Vs. LHP		193	54	7	5	9		23	34	37			.280
Home		298	80	11	4	17		40	44	66			.268
Road		316	83	18	3	12		43	31	75			.263
Grass		453	124	18	6	24		61	61	98			.274
Turf		161	39	11	1	5		22	14	43			.242

Glenn HUBBARD, Second Base

	G	AB	Hit	2B	3B	HR	Run	RBI	TBB	SO	SB	CS	Avg
6.51 years		549	133	25	3	9	66	56	63	79	5	5	.242
1986	143	408	94	16	1	4	42	36	66	74	3	2	.230
First Half	79	224	54	12	0	3	26	26	44	40	1	1	.241
Second Half	64	184	40	4	1	1	16	10	22	34	2	1	.217
Vs. RHP		280	66	10	1	3		24	37	51			.236
Vs. LHP		128	28	6	0	1		12	29	23			.219
Home		203	50	8	1	4		21	39	31			.246
Road		205	44	8	0	0		15	27	43			.215
Grass		304	74	11	1	4		26	53	52			.243
Turf		104	20	5	0	0		10	13	22			.192

Omar MORENO, Right Field

	G	AB	Hit	2B	3B	HR	Run	RBI	TBB	SO	SB	CS	Avg
8.53 years		585	147	20	10	4	82	45	45	104	57	21	.252
1986	118	359	84	18	6	4	46	27	21	77	17	16	.234
First Half	63	186	44	10	5	2	24	16	14	38	12	8	.237
Second Half	55	173	40	8	1	2	22	11	7	39	5	8	.231
Vs. RHP		318	78	17	5	4		25	18	60			.245
Vs. LHP		41	6	1	1	0		2	3	17			.146
Home		181	51	10	3	3		14	11	41			.282
Road		178	33	8	3	1		13	10	36			.185
Grass		282	71	17	4	4		21	17	64			.252
Turf		77	13	1	2	0		6	4	13			.169

Ken OBERKFELL, Third Base

	G	AB	Hit	2B	3B	HR	Run	RBI	TBB	SO	SB	CS	Avg
6.54 years		524	148	26	6	3	62	46	63	39	8	6	.283
1986	151	503	136	24	3	5	62	48	83	40	7	4	.270
First Half	82	273	85	13	0	5	32	33	38	20	4	3	.311
Second Half	69	230	51	11	3	0	30	15	45	20	3	1	.222
Vs. RHP		373	105	20	3	3		28	64	22			.282
Vs. LHP		130	31	4	0	2		20	19	18			.238
Home		268	76	11	2	2		25	43	19			.284
Road		235	60	13	1	3		23	40	21			.255
Grass		384	107	19	2	3		31	64	29			.279
Turf		119	29	5	1	2		17	19	11			.244

Andres THOMAS, Shortstop

	G	AB	Hit	2B	3B	HR	Run	RBI	TBB	SO	SB	CS	Avg
0.72 years		472	119	24	3	8	44	47	11	71	6	8	.252
1986	102	323	81	17	2	6	26	32	8	49	4	6	.251
First Half	51	157	48	12	1	4	18	17	3	20	2	1	.306
Second Half	51	166	33	5	1	2	8	15	5	29	2	5	.199
Vs. RHP		184	44	8	1	4		22	7	32			.239
Vs. LHP		139	37	9	1	2		10	1	17			.266
Home		135	27	5	1	1		11	6	16			.200
Road		188	54	12	1	5		21	2	33			.287
Grass		220	46	6	1	1		17	7	33			.209
Turf		103	35	11	1	5		15	1	16			.340

Rafael RAMIREZ, Shortstop

	G	AB	Hit	2B	3B	HR	Run	RBI	TBB	SO	SB	CS	Avg
5.38 years		625	164	24	4	7	68	52	31	69	16	11	.263
1986	134	496	119	21	1	8	57	33	21	60	19	8	.240
First Half	80	306	71	17	0	4	36	19	12	37	12	2	.232
Second Half	54	190	48	4	1	4	21	14	9	23	7	6	.253
Vs. RHP		316	82	17	1	6		28	14	40			.259
Vs LHP		180	37	4	0	2		5	7	20			.206
Home		238	56	13	1	1		18	15	31			.235
Road		258	63	8	0	7		15	6	29			.244
Grass		369	86	17	1	6		28	18	48			.233
Turf		127	33	4	0	2		5	3	12			.260

Terry HARPER, Outfield

	G	AB	Hit	2B	3B	HR	Run	RBI	TBB	SO	SB	CS	Avg
2.92 years		458	116	17	2	11	46	56	44	78	12	9	.254
1986	106	265	68	12	0	8	26	30	29	39	3	6	.257
First Half	72	189	42	6	0	6	18	22	21	29	2	6	.222
Second Half	34	76	26	6	0	2	8	8	8	10	1	0	.342
Vs. RHP		132	32	6	0	6		18	18	26			.242
Vs. LHP		133	36	6	0	2		12	11	13			.271
Home		110	33	9	0	3		15	15	15			.300
Road		155	35	3	0	5		15	14	24			.226
Grass		175	49	10	0	3		18	20	27			.280
Turf		90	19	2	0	5		12	9	12			.211

Rick MAHLER

	(W–L)	GS	Run	Avg	DP	Avg	SB	Avg
1985	(17-15)	39	184	4.72	50	1.28	14	.36
1986	(14-18)	39	158	4.05	37	.95	31	.79
1981-1986		154	629	4.08	157	1.02	111	.72

	G	IP	W	L	Pct	ER	BB	SO	ERA
1985 Home	19	135.0	8	5	.615	49	38	57	3.27
1986 Home	18	118.3	8	6	.571	44	56	20	3.35
1985 Road	20	131.7	9	10	.474	54	41	50	3.69
1986 Road	21	119.3	6	12	.333	85	39	117	6.41
1985 Grass	28	193.3	11	11	.500	67	60	81	3.12
1986 Grass	28	178.7	11	11	.500	84	69	92	4.23
1985 Turf	11	73.3	6	4	.600	36	19	26	4.42
1986 Turf	11	59.0	3	7	.300	45	26	45	6.86
1986 Total	39	237.7	14	18	.438	129	95	137	4.88

Zane SMITH

	(W–L)	GS	Run	Avg	DP	Avg	SB	Avg
1985	(9-10)	18	66	3.67	26	1.44	17	.94
1986	(8-16)	32	119	3.72	19	.59	24	.75
1984-1986		53	195	3.68	47	.89	45	.85

	G	IP	W	L	Pct	ER	BB	SO	ERA
1985 Home	20	72.7	2	5	.286	36	36	44	4.46
1986 Home	23	126.7	7	7	.500	48	61	91	3.41
1985 Road	22	74.3	7	5	.583	26	44	41	3.15
1986 Road	15	78.0	1	9	.100	44	44	48	5.08
1985 Grass	34	107.3	6	7	.462	43	53	57	3.61
1986 Grass	32	167.0	8	12	.400	78	84	115	4.20
1985 Turf	8	39.7	3	3	.500	19	27	28	4.31
1986 Turf	6	37.7	0	4	0.000	14	21	24	3.35
1985 Total	38	204.7	8	16	.333	92	105	139	4.05

Dave PALMER

	(W–L)	GS	Run	Avg	DP	Avg	SB	Avg
1985	(7-10)	23	77	3.35	27	1.17	33	1.43
1986	(11-10)	35	130	3.71	38	1.09	53	1.51
1984-1986		121	485	4.01	115	.95	141	1.17

	G	IP	W	L	Pct	ER	BB	SO	ERA
1985 Home	15	79.7	4	9	.308	37	40	62	4.18
1986 Home	16	102.3	5	2	.714	33	42	72	2.90
1985 Road	9	56.0	3	1	.750	19	27	44	3.05
1986 Road	19	107.3	6	8	.429	52	60	98	4.36
1985 Grass	4	26.7	0	1	0.000	8	16	23	2.70
1986 Grass	24	143.7	7	5	.583	78	84	115	4.89
1985 Turf	20	109.0	7	9	.438	48	51	83	3.96
1986 Turf	11	66.0	4	5	.444	7	18	55	.95
1986 Total	35	209.7	11	10	.524	85	102	170	3.65

OTHERS

	(W–L)	GS	Run	Avg	DP	Avg	SB	Avg
Alexander	(6-6)	17	72	4.24	17	1.00	12	.71
Johnson	(6-7)	15	65	4.33	16	1.07	9	.60
Acker	(3-8)	14	36	2.57	18	1.29	16	1.14
McMurtry	(1-6)	5	20	4.00	5	1.00	4	.80
Puleo	(1-2)	3	12	4.00	3	1.00	0	0.00
Speck	(2-1)	1	3	3.00	0	0.00	3	3.00

RECORDS WITH DIFFERENT STARTING CATCHERS

Catcher	Inn	ER	W–L	ERA	GS	SB	Avg
Virgil	953.2	407	51-56	3.84	107	137	1.28
Benedict	426.0	194	20-29	4.10	49	27	.55
Simmons	45.0	28	1-4	5.60	5	13	2.60

CHUCK TANNER'S FUNERAL HOME

Well, hello, hello and welcome, my friend, to Chuck's Happy Good-byes. Did you pet the puppy on your way in? Here, have a sunflower. Don't you look nice in dark colors?

Well, gee, I guess you probably know that most people in this line of work are just real serious and depressing most of the time, but we here at Chuck's Happy Good-byes have a philosophy. We want you to be able to say good-bye to your loved one with a smile on your face. We want you to come here and reflect on the *good* things about your loved one's life, and the great *joy* and *happiness* that Julie brought to you while she was with you. We want you to go out of here feeling that Julie is still with you, reminded that the bond between you has not been broken and will never be broken. We feel that if you take that approach you'll be better able to go on with your own life, while at the same time I'm sure that that's what Julie would have wanted had she been here and had she been in her right mind.

With that philosophy, we do a few things differently here than you might find at some of the more traditional places. For example, we don't even let the people who conduct our services mention that D-word. Instead of using a minister, we use a warm-up comedian. You might ask your friends, rather than sending flowers, to send balloons. We had an organist who liked to play kind of depressing tunes once in a while, but I had the bitch banned from the chapel.

Well, let's talk about Julie a little bit. As I understand it, she was a cooker? Oh, that's very different. Well, gee, she sure brought happiness to a lot of strangers, didn't she? I'm sure she enjoyed her work, too; we'll have Ernie talk about that, how Julie was a person who liked to reach out and touch those around her. She wasn't living at home, then? What were some of her other pleasures? I mean, was she a gun collector or did she just happen to have that one around? Were all of her clothes as pretty as the ones she was wearing when she was brought in?

Borrowed the .32 from a friend, huh. Well, ordinarily we do like to stress the idea of the person going on to a better place, particularly in the case of an individual who has made his or her own decision about when the time has come, but if you don't feel that would be appropriate in this case we'll just skip it. My, you'll be amazed by how good she looks; she certainly does take to makeup like a duck to water. We've developed this special embalming process in which the top part of the cheeks is treated with a different chemical than the bottom part, and it causes the face to freeze into a permanent smile. It's lovely; I'm sure you'll be delighted.

Tuesday at 7:05. It's not a good idea to wear your best black clothes, because some people complain about the holes that are left by the smile buttons. Just wear a sports shirt or something; that's fine. Did you meet Willie Starfellow on your way in? Isn't he just a wonderful person? I'd think anyone would be proud to have a pall-bearer like that. Wink at him on the way out and he'll give you a package of M&Ms for the road. Enjoy them. They're on the house.

AMERICAN LEAGUE EAST
DIVISION SHEET

	1st	2nd	RHP	LHP	Home	Road	Grass	Turf	Day	Night	TOTAL	Pct
Boston	56-31	39-35	68-49	27-17	51-30	44-36	82-55	13-11	29-27	66-39	95-66	.590
New York	50-39	40-33	67-39	23-33	41-39	49-33	71-65	19-7	29-29	61-43	90-72	.556
Detroit	43-44	44-31	57-49	30-26	49-32	38-43	78-60	9-15	25-23	62-52	87-75	.537
Toronto	47-43	39-33	62-54	24-22	42-39	44-37	34-29	52-47	30-32	56-44	86-76	.531
Cleveland	46-39	38-39	64-54	20-24	45-35	39-43	73-64	11-14	31-22	53-56	84-78	.519
Milwaukee	41-45	36-39	61-59	16-25	41-39	36-45	66-71	11-13	26-27	51-57	77-84	.478
Baltimore	46-41	27-48	50-67	23-22	37-42	36-47	59-78	14-11	26-23	47-66	73-89	.451

CLUB BATTING

	G	AB	Run	Hit	TB	2B	3B	HR	RBI	GW	SH	SF	HB	TBB	IB	SO	SB	CS	DP	LOB	SHO	Avg	Slug	OBP
Boston	161	5498	794	1488	2282	320	21	144	752	84	44	52	66	595	56	707	41	34	142	1213	11	.271	.415	.346
New York	162	5570	797	1512	2397	275	23	188	745	82	36	46	28	645	52	911	139	48	142	1217	9	.271	.430	.347
Detroit	162	5512	798	1447	2335	234	30	198	751	85	52	49	43	613	35	885	138	58	99	1164	5	.263	.424	.338
Toronto	163	5716	809	1540	2438	285	35	181	767	82	24	49	33	496	23	848	110	59	122	1099	6	.269	.427	.329
Cleveland	163	5702	831	1620	2451	270	45	157	775	80	56	49	24	456	26	944	141	54	129	1122	4	.284	.430	.337
Milwaukee	161	5461	667	1393	2105	255	38	127	625	71	53	53	27	530	26	986	100	50	122	1143	6	.255	.385	.321
Baltimore	162	5524	708	1425	2181	223	13	169	669	69	33	51	31	563	26	862	64	34	159	1159	13	.258	.395	.327

OPPOSITION BATTING

	G	AB	Run	Hit	TB	2B	3B	HR	RBI	GW	SH	SF	HB	TBB	IB	SO	SB	CS	DP	LOB	SHO	Avg	Slug	OBP
Boston	161	5516	696	1469	2282	248	32	167	661	61	38	48	26	474	35	1033	79	62	119	1120	6	.261	.414	.325
New York	162	5564	738	1461	2281	225	35	175	694	71	48	44	24	492	25	878	95	44	124	1105	8	.263	.410	.323
Detroit	162	5475	714	1374	2243	258	31	183	671	71	47	35	30	571	61	880	87	49	138	1113	12	.251	.410	.323
Toronto	163	5621	733	1467	2283	266	29	164	691	72	59	51	45	487	39	1002	95	45	119	1103	16	.261	.406	.322
Cleveland	163	5662	841	1548	2352	263	20	167	791	71	55	60	57	605	34	744	115	41	119	1255	7	.273	.415	.346
Milwaukee	161	5536	734	1478	2248	244	26	158	686	78	42	49	29	494	22	952	95	75	117	1132	12	.267	.406	.328
Baltimore	162	5518	760	1451	2306	238	43	177	726	82	46	43	21	535	41	954	123	58	132	1091	13	.263	.418	.328

CLUB PITCHING

	W	L	ERA	G	CG	SHO	SV	IP	Hit	TBF	Run	ER	HR	SH	SF	HB	TBB	IB	SO	WP	BK
Boston	95	66	3.93	161	36	6	41	1429.2	1469	6102	696	625	167	38	48	26	474	35	1033	55	8
New York	90	72	4.11	162	13	8	58	1443.1	1461	6173	738	659	175	48	44	24	492	25	878	40	3
Detroit	87	75	4.02	162	33	12	38	1443.2	1374	6158	714	645	183	47	35	30	571	61	880	50	8
Toronto	86	76	4.08	163	16	12	44	1476.0	1467	6264	733	669	164	59	51	45	487	39	1002	38	6
Cleveland	84	78	4.58	163	31	7	34	1447.2	1548	6439	841	736	167	55	60	57	605	34	744	63	13
Milwaukee	77	84	4.01	161	29	12	32	1431.2	1478	6150	734	638	158	42	49	29	494	22	952	57	9
Baltimore	73	89	4.30	162	17	6	39	1436.2	1451	6164	760	687	177	46	43	21	535	41	954	52	4

OPPOSITION PITCHING

	W	L	ERA	G	CG	SHO	SV	IP	Hit	TBF	Run	ER	HR	SH	SF	HB	TBB	IB	SO	WP
Boston	66	95	4.44	161	21	11	38	1416.0	1488	6255	794	699	144	44	52	66	595	56	707	63
New York	72	90	4.55	162	26	9	42	1437.0	1512	6325	797	726	188	36	46	28	645	52	911	56
Detroit	75	87	4.47	162	17	5	36	1435.2	1447	6269	798	713	198	52	49	43	613	35	885	55
Toronto	76	86	4.40	162	19	6	38	1470.0	1540	6318	809	718	181	24	49	33	496	23	848	46
Cleveland	78	84	4.62	162	18	4	37	1445.0	1620	6287	831	741	157	56	49	24	456	26	944	60
Milwaukee	84	77	3.70	161	32	6	42	1438.2	1393	6124	667	591	127	53	53	27	530	26	986	64
Baltimore	89	73	4.00	162	28	13	43	1445.1	1425	6202	708	642	169	33	51	31	563	26	862	45

CLUB FIELDING

	G	PO	A	E	TC	DP	TP	PB	OSB	OCS	OSB%	OA/SFA	Pct	DER	OR
Boston	161	4289	1602	129	6020	146	0	16	79	62	.560	38/48	.979	.684	794
New York	162	4330	1672	127	6129	153	0	17	95	44	.683	28/44	.979	.701	797
Detroit	162	4331	1707	108	6146	163	0	12	87	49	.640	28/35	.982	.715	798
Toronto	163	4428	1684	100	6212	150	0	9	95	45	.679	43/51	.984	.698	809
Cleveland	163	4343	1703	157	6203	148	0	20	115	41	.737	35/60	.975	.694	841
Milwaukee	161	4295	1522	146	5963	146	0	15	95	75	.559	32/49	.976	.684	667
Baltimore	162	4310	1651	135	6096	163	0	17	123	58	.680	23/43	.978	.695	708

BOSTON RED SOX

Runners on Base:	2,149
Opponents on Base:	1,969
Net Advantage:	+180
Won-Lost Record:	95-66

It is yet to be determined whether the Red Sox's 1986 season will be remembered as another in the Sox's long series of near misses and late flops, like 1949 and 1978, or as a flash of glory like 1967 and 1975. The Red Sox of 1986 were not expected to contend. They were picked to finish near .500, as they had in 1984 and 1985, maybe fifth in the division. Instead, the Red Sox pulled away from the division in May, and held onto first through a relentless summer of turmoil, tragedy, hot streaks, slumps, suspicion and self-doubt, and eventual, if blighted, victory.

The first noteworthy event in the Red Sox's season occurred on April 28, when Roger Clemens struck out 20 Seattle Mariners without walking anybody. (I just missed this historic performance on both ends. Clemens was to pitch in KC on April 26, but the game was rained out so he was moved back to Tuesday. Then I happened to be in Boston and saw the Red Sox play—on Wednesday, the 29th). Anyway, the point generally overlooked about Clemens's great game is that it triggered the streak that put the Red Sox in command. On the morning of the 28th they were 9–8, three games behind. Clemens struck out 20, and the Red Sox suddenly were red hot, winning 12 of 14 to push them to 20–10, a game in front.

With Clemens winning nearly every start, the Sox blistered the league for two months. After dropping briefly out of first, they won six straight to reach 27–13. On June 6 they were 37–16. At the end of June they were 49–25, eight games ahead of the Yankees. On July 10 they were 55–29, still eight ahead.

Then began the series of weird events which would shrink the Red Sox lead to two and a half games, giving the appearance that the Sox were fulfilling the masochistic fantasies of Boston fans by coming apart under pressure as so many other Red Sox teams have. On June 17, as a preamble, Wade Boggs's mother had been killed in a car accident. Boggs was hitting .380 at the time, but his batting average understandably had begun to slip. On July 10 the American League announced the pitchers selected for the All-Star game. Despite shaky credentials (he was 11–6 with a 3.71 ERA), Oil Can Boyd was certain he would hear his name. When he didn't, The Can threw a temper tantrum and left the park, for which he was suspended. As this storm was ready to pass, Boyd mixed it up with two narcs, one of whom filed a complaint alleging that the flyweight pitcher had assaulted him. That complication got infected with charges of drug use, racism, financial distress, press bias, and organizational arrogance, out of

which the only thing to emerge clearly was that Oil Can Boyd doesn't use drugs, his having passed more drug tests than a race horse (didn't you always wonder how they teach those horses to pee in a bottle?).

Anyway, by the time the Red Sox were ready to let Boyd pitch again, it was early August and the Scarlet Hose were clinging to a two-and-half game lead. The division had closed up to where the Sox, once leading by nine games, were only nine games away from last place. There was a strong feeling that the Red Sox must inevitably fold. A Baltimore sportswriter wrote that the Red Sox were choking, just as "they" had choked so many times before. (Casually linking together four decades of diverse frustrations, one is urged to conclude that the Red Sox uniforms must be too tight.) The pennant race became a deathwatch; the nation waited for the Red Sox to self-destruct. It is a tribute to them that they didn't panic and stampede for the exits under the month-long scrutiny that commenced with Boyd's suspension.

Three things happened to pull the Sox out of their funk. First, Oil Can returned on August 5, which stabilized the starting rotation. Second, Calvin Schiraldi emerged as the ace of the bullpen. After four excellent relief appearances in lost causes in late July, Schiraldi got a shot as the stopper in early August, and quickly converted a nagging weakness into a strength, at least until October.

Third, on August 6 Wade Boggs returned to the lead-off spot, with Barrett hitting second. The praise McNamara received for this recalls a Leo Durocher comment. The 1951 Giants drove to the pennant after Leo shifted outfielders Whitey Lockman and Bobby Thomson to first and third bases. "If I was such a genius," asked Leo in *Nice Guys Finish Last,* "why didn't I do it earlier? I was tripping over them all year. The truth is that I almost blew the pennant by waiting too long before, out of sheer desperation, I made those brilliant moves." I wonder how much credit is due a manager for figuring out that a fellow with a career on-base percentage of about .450 would make a good leadoff hitter. In any case Boggs pulled out of his depression—he had hit .247 in July—and ignited the offense. The Red Sox had scored 478 runs in 105 games through August 5, or 4.55 per game. Boggs reached four times and scored three runs on the sixth, and the Sox scored 316 runs in 56 games the rest of the year (5.64 per game).

Solidified by the acquisitions of Spike Owen and Dave Henderson on August 17, the Sox still arrived at September 4 only four and a half games ahead of the charging Blue Jays. That was when Bill Buckner started hitting home runs. John McNamara's managerial philosophy is "If it ain't broke, don't fix it, and if it is broke maybe it will fix itself." There is a wisdom in this. Some managers overreact to slumps and short-term failures that might correct themselves if the manager would let them. McNamara takes a long-term view of the player's productivity; he wants to see convincing evidence that that player is better than this one before he makes the change.

The problem with McNamara is that when things start to go wrong, the team can go into a free fall, dropping out of contention before the leaks are patched. That happened to the Reds in 1982 and the Angels in 1983, and it may well happen to the Red Sox in 1987. But in 1986, a less patient manager would have given up on Bill Buckner, who was a millstone to the team's efforts for four months. In addition to his normal wretched defensive performance, Buckner lugged a .243 batting average into the pennant race (August 14), with a secondary average below .200. He had scored just 47 runs while making over 350 outs. McNamara refused to replace him, and won the nongamble when Buckner had the hot streak of his career to buoy the Red Sox in September. Buckner's September stats, .340 with 8 homers, enabled him to finish the season with 18 homers and 102 RBI. This worm, too, would turn on McNamara during the World Series.

My comment on the Red Sox a year ago concerned the type of Red Sox team which historically has done well. In several respects the 1986 edition was not consistent with this mold. The previous Red Sox championship teams led the league in runs scored. The 1986 Sox were fifth. Most of the other teams led the league in runs scored at home by wide margins. The Sox were nowhere near the league lead, scoring 389 runs at home (about average). Most successful Sox teams have had earned run averages about the league norm. The 1986 Red Sox led the division in ERA, at 3.93. It was the first time since the split into divisions that the Red Sox have had the division's best ERA. It was also the first time that the division-leading ERA has been as high as 3.93. All of the other successful Sox teams since World War II have hit an above average number of home runs. The 1986 Sox didn't. For reasons that I couldn't explain, the ball did not carry well in Fenway in 1986, and that creates all of these statistical discrepancies between the 1986 Red Sox and the mold of their previous champions. Unlike some of the previous quality Sox, the 1986 team did not have a large home-field advantage.

Still, my summary of that piece was that "one can accurately generalize this far about the successful Red Sox teams: that they have had a good mix of left-handed and right-handed hitters, that they have probably had less power than most people imagine, that they have scored a great many runs by hitting for average, hitting a lot of doubles and their share of home runs, that their pitching staffs have had good to excellent control but (because of the park) have had only average earned run averages, that they have had some speed in center field but little otherwise, that they have had some left-handed pitching but not a lot." Almost all of that still holds. Offensively, the 1986 Red Sox were well above average in batting (.271 against a league average of .262), had some power but not terrific power and hit a ton of doubles (320, the most by any major league team since the Cardinals hit 332 in 1939). They had little speed, finishing last in the majors in stolen bases. They had a good mix of left-handed and right-handed batters. The 1986 pitchers did have terrific control, walking only 474 men, the lowest total in the major leagues, although they also struck out 1,033 men, second in the league behind the Rangers. Like the previous successful Sox teams, they had a little left-handed pitching but not much.

The Sox laid down 56 sacrifice bunts, more than any other team in the division. Because of the doubles and the bunts and because Jim Rice was going with the pitch instead of trying to pull everything, the 1986 Sox grounded into only 142 double plays, a big improvement on a critical shortcoming. Whereas in recent years the Red Sox had tended to score fewer runs than predicted by the runs created formula, in 1986 they scored 794 as compared to an expected 792.

The Red Sox struck out only 707 times, 141 fewer than any other major league team. Their strikeout to walk ratio, 1.18–1, was the best in the majors.

With the bullpen unreliable for much of the season, the Red Sox led the division in complete games with 36, only 10 of those by Clemens.

Offensively, the Red Sox were notably weak at only one position (shortstop), while they were strong at four— catcher, third base, left and right field. Defensively, they were weak at two positions (first base and center), but strong at three or more (sure ones are catcher, second base, and right field). Their starting pitching was outstanding and the bullpen eventually came through. The strengths outnumbered the weaknesses.

Still, I see little likelihood that the Red Sox will win again next year, and it is fairly likely that they will drop out of contention. The Red Sox are an old team, and the age is on key performers. Of the four Sox who drove in 90 runs, the youngest is Jim Rice at 34. The starting lineup just missed being the oldest in the division, averaging 31.1 years of age (Detroit's regulars averaged 31.2).

The Red Sox were 24–10 in one-run games, easily the best record in the league in one-run contests. There is in that some skill, but also some luck, which will likely not be there again in 1987. The Sox won four games more than projected by the Pythagorean method, which would tend to indicate a probable decline.

Roger Clemens is a great pitcher, but even if he stays healthy he isn't likely to go 24–4 again. Since Koufax in the mid-sixties, five pitchers have had seasons like Clemens had in 1986. While four of the five remained effective, none was nearly as effective the next year.

Tim McCarver has suggested that the confidence of the St. Louis Cardinals was shattered when they kicked away the 1985 World Series. Even if you don't buy this completely, the fact that the Red Sox kicked away the 1986 Series is a concern. Will Schiraldi be able to come back from his disappointments, or will he, like Niedenfuer, carry them over?

Considering all of those factors, I think the Sox will fall from contention in 1987.

Rich GEDMAN, Catcher

	G	AB	Hit	2B	3B	HR	Run	RBI	TBB	SO	SB	CS	Avg
4.05 years		526	144	33	3	17	60	71	37	80	1	0	.274
1986	135	462	119	29	0	16	49	65	37	61	1	0	.258
First Half	66	234	63	15	0	5	21	26	20	28	1	0	.269
Second Half	69	228	56	14	0	11	28	39	17	33	0	0	.246
Vs. RHP		344	97	25	0	11		51	34	43	1	0	.282
Vs. LHP		118	22	4	0	5		14	3	18	0	0	.186
Home	67	224	48	13	0	2	20	26	21	34	1	0	.214
Road	68	238	71	16	0	14	29	39	16	27	1	0	.298
Grass	113	388	95	22	0	12	41	55	32	48	1	0	.245
Turf	22	74	24	7	0	4	8	10	5	13	0	0	.324

Jim RICE, Left Field

	G	AB	Hit	2B	3B	HR	Run	RBI	TBB	SO	SB	CS	Avg
11.05 years		645	196	30	7	32	100	117	51	110	5	3	.303
1986	157	618	200	39	2	20	98	110	62	78	0	1	.324
First Half	80	322	108	28	1	8	53	57	29	38	0	1	.335
Second Half	77	296	92	11	1	12	45	53	33	40	0	0	.311
Vs. RHP		450	141	25	2	13		71	43	64	0	1	.313
Vs. LHP		168	59	14	0	7		39	19	14	0	0	.351
Home	81	312	105	25	2	10	50	48	28	35	0	1	.337
Road	76	306	95	14	0	10	48	62	34	43	0	0	.310
Grass	134	523	166	32	2	17	86	95	53	65	0	1	.317
Turf	23	95	34	7	0	3	12	15	9	13	0	0	.358

Bill BUCKNER, First Base

	G	AB	Hit	2B	3B	HR	Run	RBI	TBB	SO	SB	CS	Avg
13.43 years		627	183	34	3	12	75	80	30	29	13	5	.292
1986	153	629	168	39	2	18	73	102	40	25	6	4	.267
First Half	78	325	79	17	2	8	38	42	18	13	1	2	.243
Second Half	75	304	89	22	0	10	35	60	22	12	5	2	.293
Vs. RHP		427	124	32	1	14		72	32	15	5	3	.290
Vs. LHP		202	44	7	1	4		30	8	10	1	1	.218
Home	75	299	77	18	2	8	33	45	19	13	1	3	.258
Road	78	330	91	21	0	10	40	57	21	12	5	1	.276
Grass	130	538	142	35	2	16	61	89	35	19	5	4	.264
Turf	23	91	26	4	0	2	12	13	5	6	1	0	.286

Tony ARMAS, Center Field

	G	AB	Hit	2B	3B	HR	Run	RBI	TBB	SO	SB	CS	Avg
7.56 years		597	150	23	5	30	72	96	30	140	2	2	.251
1986	121	425	112	21	4	11	40	58	24	77	0	3	.264
First Half	54	181	49	9	1	4	16	16	14	41	0	3	.271
Second Half	67	244	63	12	3	7	24	42	10	36	0	0	.258
Vs. RHP		297	75	11	3	9		43	18	60	0	2	.253
Vs. LHP		128	37	10	1	2		15	6	17	0	1	.289
Home	62	210	57	14	2	5	21	36	17	31	0	1	.271
Road	59	215	55	7	2	6	19	22	7	46	0	2	.256
Grass	106	372	96	18	3	10	35	50	23	70	0	3	.258
Turf	15	53	16	3	1	1	5	8	1	7	0	0	.302

Marty BARRETT, Second Base

	G	AB	Hit	2B	3B	HR	Run	RBI	TBB	SO	SB	CS	Avg
3.05 years		556	156	29	3	4	71	53	54	35	9	5	.281
1986	158	625	179	39	4	4	94	60	65	31	15	7	.286
First Half	80	315	94	22	3	2	47	26	29	14	8	3	.298
Second Half	78	310	85	17	1	2	47	34	36	17	7	4	.274
Vs. RHP		454	124	27	2	0		37	36	24	13	6	.273
Vs. LHP		171	55	12	2	4		23	29	7	2	1	.322
Home	79	302	84	18	0	4	50	32	33	19	8	1	.278
Road	79	323	95	21	4	0	44	28	32	12	7	6	.294
Grass	134	529	152	30	3	4	87	47	54	28	13	6	.287
Turf	24	96	27	9	1	0	7	13	11	3	2	1	.281

Dwight EVANS, Right Field

	G	AB	Hit	2B	3B	HR	Run	RBI	TBB	SO	SB	CS	Avg
11.93 years		558	150	30	5	24	91	80	83	108	5	4	.268
1986	152	529	137	33	2	26	86	97	97	117	3	3	.259
First Half	77	282	70	19	2	10	41	50	49	55	3	2	.248
Second Half	75	247	67	14	0	16	45	47	48	62	0	1	.271
Vs. RHP		393	106	28	2	20		74	68	92	3	3	.270
Vs. LHP		136	31	5	0	6		23	29	25	0	0	.228
Home	74	241	61	18	1	8	38	41	51	42	2	2	.253
Road	78	288	76	15	1	18	48	56	46	75	1	1	.264
Grass	128	438	108	26	2	21	72	80	83	94	3	2	.247
Turf	24	91	29	7	0	5	14	17	14	23	0	1	.319

Wade BOGGS, Third Base

	G	AB	Hit	2B	3B	HR	Run	RBI	TBB	SO	SB	CS	Avg
4.48 years		621	219	40	4	7	106	72	93	46	2	2	.352
1986	149	580	207	47	2	8	107	71	105	44	0	4	.357
First Half	73	273	102	23	0	5	51	40	55	26	0	1	.374
Second Half	76	307	105	24	2	3	56	31	50	18	0	3	.342
Vs. RHP		398	143	35	0	5		44	83	26	0	3	.359
Vs. LHP		182	64	12	2	3		27	22	18	0	1	.352
Home	73	277	99	29	0	3	53	36	51	24	0	0	.357
Road	76	303	108	18	2	5	54	35	54	20	0	4	.356
Grass	126	488	172	42	0	8	88	63	89	40	0	3	.352
Turf	23	92	35	5	2	0	19	8	16	4	0	1	.380

Don BAYLOR, Designated Hitter

	G	AB	Hit	2B	3B	HR	Run	RBI	TBB	SO	SB	CS	Avg
12.79 years		590	155	27	2	25	89	92	57	75	22	9	.263
1986	160	585	139	23	1	31	93	94	62	111	3	5	.238
First Half	80	292	76	12	1	15	49	55	31	51	2	3	.260
Second Half	80	293	63	11	0	16	44	39	31	60	1	2	.215
Vs. RHP		433	104	16	0	26		76	38	84	3	5	.240
Vs. LHP		152	35	7	1	5		18	24	27	0	0	.230
Home	81	279	65	13	0	9	46	44	40	46	0	1	.233
Road	79	306	74	10	1	22	47	50	22	65	3	4	.242
Grass	137	491	118	20	1	26	80	83	59	89	2	5	.240
Turf	23	94	21	3	0	5	13	11	3	22	1	0	.223

Spike OWEN, Shortstop

	G	AB	Hit	2B	3B	HR	Run	RBI	TBB	SO	SB	CS	Avg
3.11 years		552	130	20	8	4	68	47	50	59	13	7	.235
1986	154	528	122	24	7	1	67	45	51	51	4	4	.231
First Half	77	275	72	17	6	0	35	21	21	29	0	3	.262
Second Half	77	253	50	7	1	1	32	24	30	22	4	1	.198
Vs. RHP		407	89	18	6	0		29	39	36	2	2	.219
Vs. LHP		121	33	6	1	1		16	12	15	2	2	.273
Home	80	268	66	17	6	0	37	28	31	28	1	2	.246
Road	74	260	56	7	1	1	30	17	20	23	3	2	.215
Grass	80	267	58	7	1	1	34	19	30	25	4	2	.217
Turf	74	261	64	17	6	0	33	26	21	26	0	2	.245

Dave HENDERSON, Center Field

	G	AB	Hit	2B	3B	HR	Run	RBI	TBB	SO	SB	CS	Avg
4.26 years		510	130	27	3	19	67	64	44	107	6	4	.255
1986	139	388	103	22	4	15	59	47	39	110	2	3	.265
First Half	78	255	65	12	2	11	36	36	27	75	1	3	.255
Second Half	61	133	38	10	2	4	23	11	12	35	1	0	.286
Vs. RHP		287	76	19	3	9		32	29	92	1	3	.265
Vs. LHP		101	27	3	1	6		15	10	18	1	0	.267
Home	71	206	59	11	3	10	35	29	18	61	2	2	.286
Road	68	182	44	11	1	5	24	18	21	49	0	1	.242
Grass	72	178	39	11	0	4	21	15	19	51	1	1	.219
Turf	67	210	64	11	4	11	38	32	20	59	1	2	.305

Roger CLEMENS

Year	(W–L)	GS	Run	Avg	DP	Avg	SB	Avg
1984	(9–4)	20	123	6.15	12	.60	23	1.15
1985	(7–5)	15	61	4.07	13	.87	24	1.60
1986	(24–4)	33	201	6.09	21	.64	11	.33
1984–1986		68	385	5.66	46	.68	58	.85

	1986 ERA	W–L	1985 ERA	W–L	1984 ERA	W–L	84–86 W–L
Total	2.48	24–4	3.29	7–5	4.32	9–4	40–13
Home	2.56	11–3	3.73	4–2	4.27	5–2	20–7
Road	2.41	13–1	2.83	3–3	4.39	4–2	20–6
East	2.61	11–1	2.91	2–1	3.88	4–2	17–4
West	2.38	13–3	3.50	5–4	4.71	5–2	23–9
1st Half	2.34	14–1	3.50	6–4	5.46	3–2	23–7
2nd Half	2.63	10–3	1.64	1–1	3.31	6–2	17–6
Turf	2.20	5–0	3.45	2–2	5.93	1–1	8–3
Grass	2.54	19–4	3.23	5–3	4.14	8–3	32–10
Day	2.00	8–0	4.04	2–3	4.08	3–1	13–4
Night	2.67	16–4	2.87	5–2	4.42	6–3	27–9
April	1.62	4–0	3.10	2–2			6–2
May	3.57	4–0	3.65	4–2	6.05	1–0	9–2
June	1.44	6–0	3.60	0–0	4.71	2–2	8–2
July	3.56	3–3	4.50	0–0	4.76	2–2	5–5
August	2.70	3–1	1.64	1–1	2.89	4–0	8–2
September	1.99	4–0					4–0

Al NIPPER

Year	(W–L)	GS	Run	Avg	DP	Avg	SB	Avg
1984	(11–6)	24	125	5.21	16	.67	16	.67
1985	(9–12)	25	102	4.08	29	1.16	8	.32
1986	(10–12)	26	126	4.85	28	1.08	6	.23
1983–1986		77	357	4.64	76	.99	33	.43

	1986 ERA	W–L	1985 ERA	W–L	1984 ERA	W–L	84–86 W–L
Total	5.38	10–12	4.06	9–12	3.89	11–6	30–30
Home	5.17	3–5	3.34	5–6	3.19	5–2	13–13
Road	5.58	7–7	5.05	4–6	4.62	6–4	17–17
East	5.98	5–5	3.76	5–4	4.38	6–2	16–11
West	4.96	5–7	4.32	4–8	3.54	5–4	14–19
1st Half	4.80	4–5	4.60	4–6	3.77	1–3	9–14
2nd Half	5.89	6–7	3.41	5–6	3.95	10–3	21–16
Turf	4.98	3–3	4.14	2–4	2.29	3–0	8–7
Grass	5.49	7–9	4.03	7–8	4.28	8–6	22–23
Day	4.98	2–8	4.84	2–2	3.69	5–2	9–12
Night	5.65	8–4	3.84	7–10	4.04	6–4	21–18
April	2.14	2–2	6.43	0–1	4.58	0–1	2–4
May	5.87	1–2	5.03	1–4	3.86	0–0	2–6
June	8.76	1–0	3.38	3–1	4.13	1–1	5–2
July	5.12	1–3	2.25	3–0	3.64	2–2	6–5
August	5.87	3–2	5.48	0–4	3.33	4–1	7–7
September	7.16	2–3	2.76	2–2	4.32	4–1	8–6

Oil Can BOYD

Year	(W–L)	GS	Run	Avg	DP	Avg	SB	Avg
1984	(12–12)	26	131	5.04	22	.85	13	.50
1985	(15–13)	35	178	5.09	27	.77	18	.51
1986	(16–10)	30	165	5.50	23	.77	19	.63
1983–1986		104	525	5.05	85	.82	60	.58

	1986 ERA	W–L	1985 ERA	1984 ERA	1983 ERA	82–86 W–L
Total	3.78	16–10	3.70	4.37	3.28	47–43
Home	3.66	9–6	3.76	4.28	2.54	28–25
Road	3.93	7–4	3.62	4.50	4.04	19–18
East	4.34	8–6	3.81	3.88	3.42	24–23
West	3.06	8–4	3.60	4.97	3.14	23–20
1st Half	3.67	10–6	3.19	4.85	5.25	23–20
2nd Half	3.93	6–4	4.30	4.06	3.01	24–23
Turf	7.50	0–1	3.64	4.94	3.21	4–3
Grass	3.67	16–9	3.71	4.29	3.30	43–40
Day	3.48	6–3	3.56	4.74	2.93	15–20
Night	3.99	10–7	3.77	4.15	3.56	32–23
April	4.66	1–2	3.58	5.21		3–5
May	2.66	5–1	1.58	11.32		8–5
June	3.46	4–2	3.99	3.33	5.25	11–8
July	6.75	1–1	4.47	5.40		6–6
August	3.98	2–3	4.84	2.76	3.29	8–9
September	3.80	3–1	3.66	4.65	2.79	11–10

Bruce HURST

Year	(W–L)	GS	Run	Avg	DP	Avg	SB	Avg
1984	(12–12)	33	160	4.85	20	.61	16	.48
1985	(11–13)	31	186	6.00	28	.90	17	.55
1986	(13–8)	25	105	4.20	21	.84	5	.20
1980–1986		152	754	4.96	143	.94	85	.56

	1986 ERA	W–L	1985 ERA	1984 ERA	1983 ERA	1982 ERA	82–86 W–L
Total	2.99	13–8	4.51	3.92	4.09	5.77	51–52
Home	2.37	8–3	4.66	4.67	3.93	5.89	29–27
Road	3.88	5–5	4.39	3.19	4.27	5.66	22–25
East	3.43	5–2	4.80	5.69	4.60	6.62	19–28
West	2.76	8–6	4.22	2.60	3.68	5.42	32–24
1st Half	2.79	5–3	5.14	2.67	4.64	4.48	27–25
2nd Half	3.15	8–5	4.06	5.49		7.86	24–27
Turf	3.46	1–1	4.78	3.12	2.30		4–5
Grass	2.96	12–7	4.47	4.03	4.35		44–40
Day	3.21	4–1	5.44	3.76	4.83	4.00	15–17
Night	2.91	9–7	3.97	3.99	3.80	6.88	36–35
April	3.78	1–2	4.96	1.95	3.34	4.05	7–6
May	2.05	4–1	8.69	1.99	4.91	4.34	10–9
June			5.86	3.79	5.40	5.10	6–10
July	8.00	0–2	2.57	3.97	3.83	6.64	9–6
August	3.73	3–2	4.02	5.84	3.38	6.43	9–10
September	1.72	5–1	4.22	6.83	4.06	10.80	10–11

Calvin SCHIRALDI

1986	G	IP	W–L	Sv	H	ER	SO	ERA
Total	25	51.0	4-2	9	36	8	55	1.41
Home	12	22.2	3-1	2	18	5	26	1.99
Road	13	28.1	1-1	7	18	3	29	.95
East	14	27.2	4-1	5	20	4	31	1.30
West	11	23.1	0-1	4	16	4	24	1.54
1st Half								
2nd Half	25	51.0	4-2	9	36	8	55	1.41
Turf	4	7.0	0-0	3	5	1	8	1.29
Grass	21	44.0	4-2	6	31	7	47	1.43
Day	9	17.2	2-0	3	13	3	23	1.53
Night	16	33.1	2-2	6	23	5	32	1.35
April								
May								
June								
July	4	12.2	0-0	0	10	1	12	.71
August	12	20.1	2-1	6	11	3	24	1.33
September	9	18.0	2-1	3	15	4	19	2.00

RECORDS WITH DIFFERENT STARTING CATCHERS

Catcher	Inn	ER	W–L	ERA	GS	SB	Avg
Gedman	1095.1	471	72-51	3.87	123	56	.46
Sullivan	315.4	148	22-14	4.21	36	22	.61
Sax	18.0	6	1-1	3.00	2	1	.50

STARTING PITCHERS' AVERAGE TIME AND ATTENDANCE RECORDS

Pitcher	Time	Attendance
Clemens	2:51	972
Boyd	2:53	809
Nipper	2:46	708
Hurst	2:45	694

OTHERS

Pitcher	(W–L)	GS	Run	Avg	DP	Avg	SB	Avg	Time	Att.
Seaver	(5-7)	16	65	4.06	20	1.25	16	1.00	2:52	532
Sellers	(3-7)	13	54	4.15	17	1.31	7	.54	2:49	348
Brown	(4-4)	10	39	3.90	11	1.10	7	.70	2:55	224
Woodward	(2-3)	6	22	3.67	4	.67	2	.33	3:05	164
Lollar	(2-0)	1	12	12.00	1	1.00	5	5.00	3:00	25
Stanley	(6-6)	1	5	5.00	0	.00	1	1.00	2:24	34

SCORE

Do you enjoy having opinions about issues that are beyond the realm of your experience? When you go to ballgames, do you like to try to anticipate whether a play will be scored a hit or an error? Do you often fantasize about being the one who gets to decide whether or not a pitcher gets to keep his no-hitter? Do people ever tell you that you look stupid and could carry a pencil behind your ear without ruining your image? Would you do *anything* to be involved in professional baseball? If so, you might have a future as an OFFICIAL SCORER in the AMERICAN LEAGUE CHAMPIONSHIP SERIES or possibly even the WORLD SERIES.

Yes, OFFICIAL SCORERS are often just ordinary, none-too-bright people such as yourself, who were caught hanging around the press box without a deadline and were put to work making vital decisions that have nothing to do with who wins or loses the game. And, best of all, with three OFFICIAL SCORERS now used for each game of postseason play, and virtually all major newspapers refusing to allow their writers to handle the task, opportunities in this exciting field are opening up at an explosive rate. If you would like to enter the glamorous, fast-paced, highly paid world of the OFFICIAL SCORER, and if you could accept being second-guessed on national TV and in publications like the *Baseball Abstract,* just fill out this examination and return it to Urbane Pickering's School of OFFICIAL SCORING, Valentine Design, and Toilet Training, P. O. Box E-5, Cotton Balls, Iowa. You could be eligible for valuable scholarship assistance while you study to become an OFFICIAL SCORER.

OFFICIAL SCORER'S APTITUDE TEST

Name _____

Address _____

Education (if any) _____

Favorite Official Scorer _____

This test will be self-scored, so we ask that you not look at the answer before making your selection.

1. In the seventh inning of the second game of the American League Playoff, the bases are loaded with one out when the batter grounds to second. The out is recorded at second, but on the relay to first Scofield's throw is about four feet wide of the bag and first baseman Wally Joyner, rather than catching the ball, attempts to keep his foot on the bag and reach. In so doing he falls down and the ball gets loose. Joyner picks up the ball but throws wildly toward home plate, 30 feet up the line, allowing a second run to score. Should you score this:

    A) An Error on Joyner,
    B) An Error on Schofield,
    C) Just One of Those Things,
    D) No Harm, No Foul, or
    E) Let's Blame It on Gene Mauch.

(The answer is B, an error on Schofield. While it is true that the rules do say that you can't assume a double play, the rules don't specifically tell you what to rule when the first baseman tries to create a double play that isn't there and compounds the consequences of this by making a bad throw to another base. We advise you to blame it all on the shortstop. As to rules 10.13 (e) and 10.14 (c), we never heard of either of them.)

2. In the sixth inning of the third game of the American League Playoff, there is a runner on first and one out. The batter hits a chopper down the third base line, and Wade Boggs has an easy play at first base. Instead, he attempts to make the play at second base, and the throw pulls the second baseman off the bag. Would you score this:

    A) An Error,
    B) A Fielder's Choice,
    C) An Infield Fly, or
    D) A Homicide.

(The correct answer is B, a fielder's choice. The fielder had an easy play, and he chose not to make it. The rules don't specify whether it's a good choice or a bad choice; they just say it's a choice.)

3. In the seventh game of the American League playoff, Gary Pettis is playing in left center field when a drive is slashed to deep right-center. Pettis runs six miles and comes within an eyelash of making the play, but the ball bounces off the tip of his glove and the batter reaches third. Should you score this:

    A) A Triple,
    B) An Error on Pettis,
    C) A Double and an Error,
    D) An Intentional Walk, or
    E) Guilty but Insane.

(The correct answer is B, an error on Pettis. The key question here is, "Ordinary effort for whom?" While it's true that there isn't a center fielder in the world today who would have made the play, Willie Mays and Tris Speaker would have had it easily if they'd been playing in straightaway center.)

4. In the seventh inning of the fifth game of the World Series, the batter hits a high pop foul within five feet of first base. Bill Buckner overruns it, tries to recover by leaning backward, loses his balance and falls down, the ball bouncing off the thumb of his glove. Would you score this:

A) An Error,
B) A Sacrifice Fly,
C) Normal for Bill Buckner, or
D) No Play.

(The correct answer is D, no play. While this of course would be an error for Dave Kingman or Steve Balboni, the key words in this case are "Bill Buckner." Playing with bad knees and cauliflower ankles, Bill Buckner has been an example of courage and determination for us all. He's good copy.)

NEW YORK YANKEES

Runners on Base:	2,185
Opponents on Base:	1,977
Net Advantage:	+208
Won-Lost Record:	90-72

For the New York Yankees, the season passed with the team in a holding pattern. At its best, the 1986 season was a consolidation year for the Yankees, one in which the gains of 1985, when the team reemerged as a contender, were solidified. At its worst, the 1986 season was a wasted year, a year in which the Yankee talent nucleus grew a year older and nothing was accomplished. Superlative years by Dave Righetti, Rickey Henderson, and Don Mattingly were undermined by a lack of starting pitching and critical failures at catcher and shortstop.

In Henderson and Mattingly, the Yankees have a magnificent foundation for the offense. In two players, they have tremendous power (59 homers in 1986) and tremendous speed (87 stolen bases). They have hitting for average (combined .310) and walks (142), giving a combined .377 on-base percentage with a remarkable total of 543 times reaching base—from two individuals. They have right-handed hitting and left-handed hitting. The two players hit 84 doubles in 1986, scored 247 runs and drove in 187. If you divide these totals by two you realize that you're talking about one incredible ballplayer—.310 with 42 doubles, 29 homers, 43 stolen bases, 71 walks, 123 runs scored, and 93 RBI. When you multiply that by two, you realize what the Yankees have. When you consider that most of these totals were actually *down* from 1985, when the two players scored 253 runs and drove in 217, then you realize that you're talking about true levels of ability, rather than just impressive one-year totals. Only a few times in history (Cobb and Crawford, Gehrig and Ruth, Aaron and Mathews) has any team had two offensive players of that ability in their prime at the same time.

I still believe, and many baseball men agree with me, that Henderson is the greater of the two, but with the two players in the same uniform it seems a silly thing to argue about. Those two players set up the Yankee offense to be above average in almost any area of measurement, and with the major tributaries of Winfield, Randolph, Pagliarulo, Pasqua, and Easler, the Yankee offense runs deep and wide. The Yankees hit .271, second in the league. They hit 188 home runs, third in the league. They stole 139 bases, second in the league, and hit 275 doubles (third). The Yankees drew 645 walks, more than any other major-league team except the Angels. The Yankees had a team secondary average of .300, highest in the major leagues.

The offense didn't work together as well as it might have. The Yankees scored 797 runs, an excellent total, but one would have expected a team with their batting stats to

score 843. The shortfall of 46 runs is the largest discrepancy in the American League, and was enough to cut the Yankees from first to third in the league in runs scored. The Yankees left 1,217 men on base, the most of any major-league team.

Still, it was a powerful offense, and Righetti was wonderful. The Yankees had 58 saves, which tied an American League record and was 14 more than any other American League team. What that leaves is pretty obvious: The starting pitching stunk.

Lou Piniella received generally kind reviews for his performance as a rookie manager, and no doubt he did many things well. A synopsis of the argument on Piniella's behalf is that he did the best he could to cope with a team that was seriously short of starting pitching. What is overlooked in this argument is that Piniella, *knowing that Britt Burns was not going to be able to pitch,* made the decision in spring training to release a pitcher who had gone 16–8 and 16–12 for the Yankees in the previous two seasons. My feeling is that if you release a 16-game winner, you deserve to come up short of starting pitching and the odds are overwhelming that you're going to get what you deserve. Like Joe Torre before him, Piniella released Phil Niekro because a) he didn't like him, and b) he was looking at his birth certificate rather than looking at the results.

The release of Niekro left the Yankees counting on a fling of young pitchers like Bob Tewksbury, Dennis Rasmussen, and Doug Drabek, backed up by an obscene number of washed-out vets like John Montefusco and Ed Whitson. The best news on the talent front was the development of Dennis Rasmussen as a starting pitcher and Dan Pasqua as an outfielder. Rasmussen is a pitcher whom I've always liked, and I thought the previous Yankee managers didn't show much confidence in him. Piniella gave him a chance to work through some rough spots, and he responded with an 18–6 record, but now I've got to take the opposite approach. Rasmussen didn't pitch nearly as well as the won-lost record indicates. The Yankees scored 5.84 runs per game for him, as opposed to 4.07 for Guidry. His ERA was 3.88, his strikeout and walk data unimpressive. He completed just 3 games and gave up 28 homers. He was all right, but there were a lot of better pitchers around the league. Pasqua, however, had a tremendous half-season, hitting for average (.293), hitting for power (16 homers in 280 at bats), drawing 47 walks, and even doing a decent job in the outfield. Yankee fans should not regret that the Yanks passed on Kirk Gibson. Gibson would have blocked the path for Pasqua, and in a couple of years Pasqua probably will be a better hitter than Gibson.

The development of Pasqua, however, was part of another problem. The Yankees had serious troubles against left-handed pitching, finishing 67–39 (.632) against right-handed pitching (easily the best in the league), but just 23–33 (.411) against left-handers (11th in the league). The reason for this was the development of several imbalanced platoon arrangements. Mike Easler hit .323 against right-handers, but only .226 (with a secondary average of .123) against left-handers. Ken Griffey and Claudell Washington hit a combined .284 against right-handers, but .229 against lefties. Mike Pagliarulo blasted 26 home runs in 341 at bats against right-handers, but hit .196 against lefties with 2 homers in 163 at bats. Pasqua hit .310 against right-handers but .216 against lefties, although he did hit with enough power against left-handers to give hope that he might develop into an everyday player. With Ron Hassey hitting only right-handers and Rickey Henderson having a subpar year against left-handers, with the right-handed platoon players like Roenicke, Kittle, Berra, and Cotto not being as effective as their left-handed counterparts, the Yankees were—and probably remain—vulnerable to left-handed pitching.

The Yankees' inability to win in their home park is more difficult to analyze. The Yankees, who in 1985 had had a huge home-park advantage, won 49 road games, five more than any other American League club, but did remarkably poorly in their home park, losing 10 straight home games from May 26 to June 29, their longest losing streak ever at Yankee Stadium. Only one other team in the league (Toronto) failed to play better at home than on the road, and in that case the home-field deficit was only two games.

In 1984–1985 Ron Guidry had a record of 21–4 in Yankee Stadium with a 2.87 ERA, whereas on the road he was 11–13 with a 4.84 ERA. Probably as a reaction to this, Piniella started Guidry 19 times in Yankee Stadium as opposed to 11 times on the road, but the strategy backfired as Guidry posted a 3.28 ERA in road games—actually his best in several seasons—but jumped to 4.39 at home. Guidry allowed 19 homers in 121 innings in Yankee Stadium, and the new fences can't be blamed for that but they didn't help, either. Other ERAs in Yankee Stadium: Brian Fisher, 5.91; Al Holland, 5.63; Tommy John, 3.76; Joe Niekro, 5.97; Scott Nielsen, 6.53; Rasmussen, 4.32; and Bob Shirley, 5.46. All of those pitchers did much better on the road. Then, for good measure, the Yankees also scored a few more runs on the road, the main reason for that being Rickey Henderson (.235 with 13 homers, 33 RBI, 35 stolen bases at home, .290 with 15 homers, 41 RBI, 52 stolen bases on the road).

There was a third split in the Yankee record. The Yankees were 19–7 on artificial turf, a winning percentage on the turf almost a hundred points better than any other major league team. On grass fields they were only 71–65, six games over .500. A 26-game sample is pretty small, so I'll limit my analysis of that one to this: On artificial turf, Rickey Henderson hit .316, slugged .653 and scored over a run a game, while Don Mattingly hit .438, slugged .723 and scored even more runs than Henderson. I wouldn't bet on these performances to repeat in 1987—nor, for that matter would I bet on any of the other splits to carry over.

The Yankees' reaction to these problems (not beating left-handers, not winning at home) was predictable: They got rid of Mike Easler. I remember I commented a couple of years ago that when a team acquires a player by trade and the player does well but the team has a disappointing season, they'll almost always pass along the player in another trade, figuring that he couldn't have helped them much or they would have had a better year. That's what the Pirates did with John Tudor a few years ago, and a lot of times, as the Yankees did with Easler, they'll make a second trade to get rid of the guy even if they don't get much for him.

But, of course, getting rid of Easler doesn't solve the real problems on the team. The Yankees were hurt last year by subpar performances at two key "up-the-middle" positions, catcher and shortstop. The catching platoon broke apart on Ron Hassey's knees and Butch Wynegar's psyche, leaving the Yankees scrambling with people like Espino and Lombardi. The play of Joel Skinner late in the year leaves the Yankees with reason for hope. Skinner, an exceptional defensive catcher, hit .305 with 13 RBI in September, raising his average as a Yankee to .259 (43 for 166). If Skinner hits anywhere near .259 he's going to be above average at a position where talent is always short, but the Yankees could use a fallback position. (I hear they're talking to Chicago about Ron Hassey.) The offensive and defensive dereliction of Bobby Meacham created another black hole in the infield, a hole that Wayne Tolleson will be able to occupy if not necessarily fill. I like Tolleson but he doesn't have a shortstop's arm. At this writing those two problems and the inability to beat left-handers still loom large over the Yankees' 1987 season.

Still, with the tremendous strengths that they have in other areas, the Yankees could win the pennant with Skinner and Tolleson in the lineup. My feeling is that the future of Lou Piniella as a major-league manager rests wholly on one issue: his ability to rebuild the starting rotation. With the acquisition of Rick Rhoden, the Yankees may have taken a giant step in that direction. I don't take Ron Guidry's 1986 "problems" to be all that serious. The big reason for the fall-off in Guidry's won-lost record was his offensive support, which plummeted from 5.39 runs per game to 4.07. When you figure that Guidry's offensive support declined by 1.32 runs, his runs allowed per nine innings increased by only .77 (3.62 to 4.39) and the league earned-run average was up by .05, then 66% of Guidry's decline was, in fact, attributable to his offensive support. Perhaps more to the point, Guidry in 1986 struck out 140 men and walked only 38. There are very few pitchers who can't win with a strikeout/walk ratio of almost 4–1. I figure Guidry will probably be all right.

No key Yankee is getting up in years except Guidry and Winfield and now Rhoden. They are a relatively young team. There are several young pitchers (Tewksbury, Nielsen) who might develop. The Yankees might be able to make a trade to strengthen themselves at shortstop or catcher. The Yankees have an excellent chance to win their division in 1987.

Joel SKINNER, Catcher

	G	AB	Hit	2B	3B	HR	Run	RBI	TBB	SO	SB	CS	Avg
1.14 years		394	95	13	2	5	33	40	25	102	2	4	.240
1986	114	315	73	9	1	5	23	37	16	83	1	4	.232
First Half	46	108	21	3	1	1	12	12	6	28	1	0	.194
Second Half	68	207	52	6	0	4	11	25	10	55	0	4	.251
Vs. RHP		171	42	7	1	4		21	9	47	1	1	.246
Vs. LHP		144	31	2	0	1		16	7	36	0	3	.215
Home	60	167	40	5	0	1	9	17	8	44	1	2	.239
Road	54	148	33	4	1	4	14	20	8	39	0	2	.222
Grass	101	276	64	9	1	3	19	33	16	71	1	3	.232
Turf	13	39	9	0	0	2	4	4	0	12	0	1	.231

Dan PASQUA, Left Field

	G	AB	Hit	2B	3B	HR	Run	RBI	TBB	SO	SB	CS	Avg
1.00 years		428	113	20	1	25	61	70	63	116	2	0	.264
1986	102	280	82	17	0	16	44	45	47	78	2	0	.293
First Half	36	92	26	4	0	6	12	13	15	26	1	0	.283
Second Half	66	188	56	13	0	10	32	32	32	52	1	0	.298
Vs. RHP		229	71	14	0	13		35	41	58	2	0	.310
Vs. LHP		51	11	3	0	3		10	6	20	0	0	.216
Home	50	140	38	10	0	9	25	24	29	37	0	0	.271
Road	52	140	44	7	0	7	19	21	18	41	2	0	.314
Grass	82	222	60	13	0	12	38	33	40	62	1	0	.270
Turf	20	58	22	4	0	4	6	12	7	16	1	0	.379

Don MATTINGLY, First Base

	G	AB	Hit	2B	3B	HR	Run	RBI	TBB	SO	SB	CS	Avg
3.53 years		630	209	45	3	26	99	114	48	40	1	1	.332
1986	162	677	238	53	2	31	117	113	53	35	0	0	.352
First Half	82	347	118	26	1	13	56	57	28	17	0	0	.340
Second Half	80	330	120	27	1	18	61	56	25	18	0	0	.364
Vs. RHP		434	151	30	1	26		72	36	22	0	0	.348
Vs. LHP		243	87	23	1	5		41	17	13	0	0	.358
Home	80	320	107	23	0	17	54	60	28	16	0	0	.334
Road	82	357	131	30	2	14	63	53	25	19	0	0	.367
Grass	136	565	189	38	1	26	89	94	46	30	0	0	.335
Turf	26	112	49	15	1	5	28	19	7	5	0	0	.438

Rickey HENDERSON, Center Field

	G	AB	Hit	2B	3B	HR	Run	RBI	TBB	SO	SB	CS	Avg
6.71 years		607	176	28	6	15	128	62	106	84	98	25	.290
1986	153	608	160	31	5	28	130	74	89	81	87	18	.263
First Half	81	330	93	22	2	15	75	46	47	49	49	12	.282
Second Half	72	278	67	9	3	13	55	28	42	32	38	6	.241
Vs. RHP		416	115	21	2	20		56	47	54	79	16	.276
Vs. LHP		192	45	10	3	8		18	42	27	8	2	.234
Home	78	298	70	16	3	13	62	33	43	38	35	7	.235
Road	75	310	90	15	2	15	68	41	46	43	52	11	.290
Grass	128	510	129	24	4	20	104	59	70	68	69	12	.253
Turf	25	98	31	7	1	8	26	15	19	13	18	6	.316

Willie RANDOLPH, Second Base

	G	AB	Hit	2B	3B	HR	Run	RBI	TBB	SO	SB	CS	Avg
9.22 years		598	164	23	6	4	97	49	95	49	25	8	.274
1986	141	492	136	15	2	5	76	50	94	49	15	2	.276
First Half	81	286	76	11	1	1	42	32	63	34	12	1	.266
Second Half	60	206	60	4	1	4	34	18	31	15	3	1	.291
Vs. RHP		309	79	8	1	1		37	69	35	13	2	.256
Vs. LHP		183	57	7	1	4		13	25	14	2	0	.311
Home	74	241	75	9	2	2	49	24	61	20	9	1	.311
Road	67	251	61	6	0	3	27	26	33	29	6	1	.243
Grass	122	418	121	14	2	4	67	43	85	40	11	2	.289
Turf	19	74	15	1	0	1	9	7	9	9	4	0	.203

Dave WINFIELD, Right Field

	G	AB	Hit	2B	3B	HR	Run	RBI	TBB	SO	SB	CS	Avg
12.12 years		601	172	29	6	25	94	102	65	86	16	6	.286
1986	154	565	148	31	5	24	90	104	77	106	6	5	.262
First Half	78	283	64	16	3	13	50	50	51	59	4	1	.226
Second Half	76	282	84	15	2	11	40	54	26	47	2	4	.298
Vs. RHP		368	97	21	2	12		63	40	77	6	5	.264
Vs. LHP		197	51	10	3	12		41	37	29	0	0	.259
Home	78	279	76	15	3	12	45	56	40	46	3	2	.272
Road	76	286	72	16	2	12	45	48	37	60	3	3	.252
Grass	131	476	126	28	5	22	78	97	68	87	3	3	.265
Turf	23	89	22	3	0	2	12	7	9	19	3	2	.247

Mike PAGLIARULO, Third Base

	G	AB	Hit	2B	3B	HR	Run	RBI	TBB	SO	SB	CS	Avg
2.19 years		497	119	25	4	25	69	76	52	115	2	0	.239
1986	149	504	120	24	3	28	71	71	54	120	4	1	.238
First Half	77	265	68	17	0	18	43	40	28	63	2	1	.257
Second Half	72	239	52	7	3	10	28	31	26	57	2	0	.218
Vs. RHP		341	88	15	3	26		60	43	66	4	1	.258
Vs. LHP		163	32	9	0	2		11	11	54	0	0	.196
Home	74	243	56	8	2	14	32	31	31	64	2	1	.230
Road	75	261	64	16	1	14	39	40	23	56	2	0	.245
Grass	127	422	99	21	2	24	61	56	51	101	4	1	.235
Turf	22	82	21	3	1	4	10	15	3	19	0	1	.256

Mike EASLER, Designated Hitter

	G	AB	Hit	2B	3B	HR	Run	RBI	TBB	SO	SB	CS	Avg
6.50 years		523	154	28	4	17	68	75	46	99	3	4	.294
1986	146	490	148	26	2	14	64	78	49	87	3	2	.302
First Half	74	268	89	17	1	6	33	43	23	40	2	1	.332
Second Half	72	222	59	9	1	8	31	35	26	47	1	1	.266
Vs. RHP		384	124	23	1	13		70	45	56	2	2	.323
Vs. LHP		106	24	3	1	1		8	4	31	1	0	.226
Home	70	233	67	16	1	6	32	37	24	42	1	1	.288
Road	76	257	81	10	1	8	32	41	25	45	2	1	.315
Grass	122	404	120	24	1	12	55	63	36	63	1	1	.297
Turf	24	86	28	2	1	2	9	15	13	24	2	1	.326

Wayne TOLLESON, Shortstop

	G	AB	Hit	2B	3B	HR	Run	RBI	TBB	SO	SB	CS	Avg
3.51 years		485	123	14	4	2	62	29	42	73	27	11	.255
1986	141	475	126	16	5	3	61	43	52	76	17	10	.265
First Half	68	224	54	6	3	3	36	23	33	37	13	6	.241
Second Half	73	251	72	10	2	0	25	20	19	39	4	4	.287
Vs. RHP		292	74	12	2	0		24	33	41	7	2	.253
Vs. LHP		183	52	4	3	3		19	19	35	10	8	.284
Home	68	230	60	8	3	1	29	24	24	33	9	5	.261
Road	73	245	66	8	2	2	32	19	28	43	8	5	.269
Grass	119	398	110	13	5	2	55	38	46	58	15	8	.276
Turf	22	77	16	3	0	1	6	5	6	18	2	2	.208

Ron KITTLE, Outfield-Designated Hitter

	G	AB	Hit	2B	3B	HR	Run	RBI	TBB	SO	SB	CS	Avg
3.31 years		535	123	18	1	35	72	90	47	151	5	4	.231
1986	116	376	82	13	0	21	42	60	35	110	4	1	.218
First Half	70	241	50	10	0	13	27	40	21	75	2	1	.207
Second Half	46	135	32	3	0	8	15	20	14	35	2	0	.237
Vs. RHP		197	51	6	0	14		40	15	50	4	1	.259
Vs. LHP		179	31	7	0	7		20	20	60	0	0	.173
Home	54	173	33	6	0	6	19	23	19	57	2	0	.191
Road	62	203	49	7	0	15	23	37	16	53	2	1	.241
Grass	99	320	64	8	0	15	32	47	29	102	3	1	.200
Turf	17	56	18	5	0	6	10	13	6	8	1	0	.321

Dennis RASMUSSEN

Year	(W–L)	GS	Run	Avg	DP	Avg	SB	Avg
1984	(9-6)	24	131	5.46	24	1.00	10	.42
1985	(3-5)	16	74	4.62	16	1.00	10	.62
1986	(18-6)	31	181	5.84	28	.90	15	.48
1983-1986		72	390	5.42	69	.96	35	.49

	1986		1985		1984		84-86
	ERA	W–L	ERA	W–L	ERA	W–L	W–L
Total	3.88	18-6	3.98	3-5	4.57	9-6	30-17
Home	4.32	8-2	5.08	2-2	4.17	5-3	15-7
Road	3.61	10-4	3.14	1-3	5.01	4-3	15-10
East	3.26	8-1	4.96	0-2	5.56	4-4	12-7
West	4.33	10-5	3.52	3-3	3.42	5-2	18-10
1st Half	3.47	9-2	3.54	3-4	6.32	1-3	13-9
2nd Half	4.35	9-4	6.11	0-1	3.75	8-3	17-8
Turf	3.72	5-1	4.09	1-2	5.04	3-1	9-4
Grass	3.92	13-5	3.95	2-3	4.45	6-5	21-13
Day	5.05	6-3	4.35	1-2	7.24	1-3	8-8
Night	3.47	12-3	3.63	2-3	3.82	8-3	22-9
April	2.41	2-0	2.84	0-1			2-1
May	4.70	3-1	3.12	2-1	4.15	1-1	6-3
June	3.56	3-1	4.68	0-2	6.97	0-2	3-5
July	1.74	4-0	5.21	1-1	3.00	4-0	9-1
August	4.71	2-2			3.20	3-1	5-3
September	5.10	4-2	6.75	0-0	6.04	1-2	5-4

Joe NIEKRO

Year	(W–L)	GS	Run	Avg	DP	Avg	SB	Avg
1984	(16-12)	38	182	4.79	39	1.03	46	1.21
1985	(13-14)	38	163	4.29	36	.95	56	1.47
1986	(9-10)	25	124	4.96	28	1.12	29	1.16
1977-1986		315	1327	4.21	293	.93	379	1.20

1986	G	IP	W–L	H	ER	SO	ERA
Total	25	125.2	9-10	139	68	59	4.87
Home	13	60.1	4-5	78	40	28	5.97
Road	12	65.1	5-5	61	28	31	3.86
East	11	48.2	3-5	58	34	22	6.29
West	14	77.0	6-5	81	34	37	3.97
1st Half	16	91.1	7-6	90	44	42	4.34
2nd Half	9	34.1	2-4	49	24	17	6.29
Turf	2	10.0	1-1	11	5	3	4.50
Grass	23	115.2	8-9	128	63	56	4.90
Day	7	35.1	0-3	44	25	9	6.37
Night	18	90.1	9-7	95	43	50	4.28
April	5	31.1	3-0	29	11	16	3.16
May	6	36.1	2-3	37	16	17	3.96
June	5	23.2	2-3	24	17	9	6.46
July	3	12.0	1-1	20	9	8	6.75
August	5	20.0	1-2	26	12	9	5.40
September	1	2.1	0-1	3	3	0	11.57

Ron GUIDRY

Year	(W–L)	GS	Run	Avg	DP	Avg	SB	Avg
1984	(10-11)	28	130	4.64	21	.75	15	.54
1985	(22-6)	33	178	5.39	38	1.15	13	.39
1986	(9-12)	30	122	4.07	21	.70	24	.80
1977-1986		295	1407	4.77	262	.89	131	.44

	1986		1985	1984	1983	1982	82-86
	ERA	W–L	ERA	ERA	ERA	ERA	W–L
Total	3.98	9-12	3.27	4.51	3.42	3.81	76-46
Home	4.39	6-8	2.82	2.93	2.34	3.57	47-19
Road	3.28	3-4	3.77	6.20	4.74	4.06	29-27
East	3.41	6-7	3.43	5.81	3.17	4.37	30-27
West	4.78	3-5	3.12	3.63	3.63	3.33	46-19
1st Half	4.05	4-8	2.69	4.24	2.96	4.00	39-25
2nd Half	3.89	5-4	3.92	5.02	3.79	3.59	37-21
Turf	4.37	1-1	3.00	7.77	5.29		8-6
Grass	3.93	8-11	3.29	4.09	2.93		54-32
Day	3.19	5-3	2.42	4.70	3.48	3.49	25-10
Night	4.53	4-9	3.63	4.42	3.41	3.93	51-36
April	2.45	3-0	4.26	3.70	4.80	2.79	9-8
May	4.25	1-4	2.41	4.03	2.43	3.21	16-7
June	5.92	0-3	2.11	4.98	2.14	4.50	12-8
July	3.00	1-1	3.83	4.01	3.82	4.56	12-7
August	5.06	1-2	2.08	4.29	5.02	2.98	12-7
September	3.12	3-2	4.76	9.26	2.56	4.81	15-9

Doug DRABEK

Year	(W–L)	GS	Run	Avg	DP	Avg	SB	Avg
1986	(7-8)	21	91	4.33	14	.67	4	.19

1986	G	IP	W–L	H	ER	SO	ERA
Total	27	131.2	7-8	126	60	76	4.10
Home	12	62.1	2-3	63	26	39	3.75
Road	15	69.1	5-5	63	34	37	4.41
East	15	69.2	3-4	60	32	39	4.13
West	12	62.0	4-4	66	28	37	4.06
1st Half	10	32.2	0-2	26	23	18	6.34
2nd Half	17	99.0	7-6	100	37	58	3.36
Turf	5	34.2	3-1	32	12	19	3.12
Grass	22	97.0	4-7	94	48	57	4.45
Day	10	44.1	1-4	51	24	24	4.87
Night	17	87.1	6-4	75	36	52	3.71
April							
May	1	4.1	0-0	1	1	4	2.08
June	7	18.1	0-1	18	16	9	7.85
July	7	34.0	2-3	35	18	14	4.76
August	6	39.1	1-3	42	16	30	3.66
September	6	35.2	4-1	30	9	19	2.27

Bob TEWKSBURY

Year	(W–L)	GS	Run	Avg	DP	Avg	SB	Avg
1986	(9-5)	20	100	5.00	21	1.05	3	.15

1986	G	IP	W–L	H	ER	SO	ERA
Total	23	130.1	9-5	144	48	49	3.31
Home	10	59.2	4-1	64	17	22	2.56
Road	13	70.2	5-4	80	31	27	3.95
East	14	84.0	5-2	86	25	28	2.68
West	9	46.1	4-3	58	23	21	4.47
1st Half	15	83.0	5-3	97	31	29	3.36
2nd Half	8	47.1	4-2	47	17	20	3.23
Turf	4	19.1	1-1	21	8	13	3.72
Grass	19	111.0	8-4	123	40	36	3.24
Day	9	51.2	4-2	55	19	20	3.31
Night	14	78.2	5-3	89	29	29	3.32
April	4	27.0	2-1	27	10	10	3.33
May	4	18.2	2-1	29	11	9	5.30
June	6	29.1	1-0	35	8	8	2.45
July	3	17.2	1-2	20	8	7	4.08
August Sept.	6	37.2	3-1	33	11	15	2.63

Dave RIGHETTI

1986	G	IP	W–L	Sv	H	ER	SO	ERA
Total	74	106.2	8-8	46	88	29	83	2.45
Home	32	49.2	5-5	18	37	11	48	1.99
Road	42	57.0	3-3	28	51	18	35	2.84
East	40	58.2	4-5	23	56	23	37	3.53
West	34	48.0	4-3	23	32	6	46	1.13
1st Half	37	47.2	6-4	18	45	20	38	3.78
2nd Half	37	59.0	2-4	28	43	9	45	1.37
Turf	15	18.2	1-1	12	17	6	11	2.89
Grass	59	88.0	7-7	34	71	23	72	2.35
Day	26	35.2	5-4	11	34	14	33	3.53
Night	48	71.0	3-4	35	54	15	50	1.90
April	9	13.2	2-1	5	15	7	11	4.61
May	13	16.0	2-1	7	10	3	16	1.69
June	13	13.1	1-2	5	17	9	7	6.08
July	10	18.0	2-0	6	12	2	16	1.00
August	13	22.0	0-3	10	15	3	17	1.23
September	16	23.2	1-1	13	19	5	16	1.90

OTHERS

Pitcher	(W–L)	GS	Run	Avg	DP	Avg	SB	Avg	Time	Att.
John	(5-3)	10	43	4.30	12	1.20	6	.60	2:40	263
Nielsen	(4-4)	9	53	5.89	11	1.22	4	.44	2:50	264
Shirley	(0-4)	6	13	2.17	5	.83	5	.83	2:55	151
Whitson	(5-2)	4	28	7.00	1	.25	1	.25	3:17	134
Pulido	(1-1)	3	17	5.67	7	2.33	3	1.00	3:16	98
Armstrong	(0-1)	1	8	8.00	0	.00	1	1.00	3:19	30
Arnsberg	(0-0)	1	5	5.00	1	1.00	0	.00	2:55	17
Holland	(1-0)	1	12	12.00	2	2.00	0	.00	3:45	45

RECORDS WITH DIFFERENT STARTING CATCHERS

Catcher	Inn	ER	W–L	ERA	GS	SB	Avg
Wynegar	465.2	225	27-25	4.35	52	35	.67
Skinner	461.1	203	28-24	3.96	52	24	.46
Hassey	428.1	191	29-19	4.01	48	30	.63
Espino	79.0	33	6-3	3.76	9	6	.67
Lombardi	9.0	7	0-1	7.00	1	0	.00

STARTING PITCHERS' AVERAGE TIME AND ATTENDANCE RECORDS

Pitcher	Time	Attendance
Rasmussen	2:48	808
Guidry	2:51	943
Niekro	3:03	712
Drabek	2:49	629
Tewksbury	2:52	544

MVP

The *Baseball Digest* used to do a player interview section which would commence with the question of who in baseball the player particularly admired. It was traditional in this context for the player to cite his manager or a favorite ex-manager. Catfish Hunter named Clyde Kluttz, the scout who had signed him. When asked who in baseball he particularly admired, Henry Aaron replied, "Well, myself, for one. I think I've accomplished a lot in this game."

Yes, Henry, you sure did. I thought of this when Aaron jumped into the middle of the pitcher-as-MVP controversy last November, filing a brief but silly position slobber on behalf of Don Mattingly as the American League's MVP. Regardless of what anyone thinks the rules *ought* to be, rules *are* that a pitcher is eligible and is supposed to win the award if he is more valuable than anybody else. The rules specify that any MVP voter who can't call it that way can't be an MVP voter. This being the case, when Don Mattingly expresses the opinion that Roger Clemens should not be allowed to win the award, this is exactly as noteworthy as it would be if Ron Kittle argued that pitchers shouldn't be allowed to throw two-strike curve balls, or if George Foster suggested that opposition runners should not be allowed to go from first to third on a single to left.

That there should be a controversy when the MVP rules are indulged and a pitcher wins the award is testimony first to the withdrawal desperation of baseball writers in November, and second to the elephantine arrogance of people like Don Mattingly, Ron Darling, and Henry Aaron. Athletes tend to assume that, since they're the ones who get all the money, the sport must be conducted for their benefit, and we ignorant fans and writers will be happy to change the rules to whatever the players want them to be if only they will speak up and educate us. There is an argument to be made that the rules should be changed, and maybe that can be done at the same time as the voting is changed to include the fans.

If the New York fans were disappointed in the failure of a Gotham star to win a major award in 1986, they had a point. Since 1969 New York teams have won 7 of the 36 league championships, but only 2 of the 36 MVP awards, a ratio that seems hardly right. In particular, the award to Clemens brought back the memory of 1978, when a Yankee pitcher, Ron Guidry, had a year comparable to Clemens in 1986 and the Yankees won the pennant, but the award nonetheless went to Sox slugger Jim Rice. No argument that one can make seems to balance the scales. If the key factor is winning the pennant, why didn't Guidry get the award in '78, when he went 25–3 and beat the Sox in the 163rd game of the season? Talk about playing a key role in a pennant race . . . If he didn't get it because he's a pitcher, then why did Clemens get it? The shoe rarely fits so well on the other foot, but the sportswriters decided not to place it there.

Turning now to the question of who was actually more valuable. Mattingly proffered the thought that a pitcher, who works every five days, can't possibly be as valuable as a player who is out there every day. This is a novel line of analysis, one never known to be adopted on any mission except to demonstrate the unsuitability of pitchers for the MVP award. A baseball roster consists of 24 players, usually 9 pitchers and 15 position players. If success in baseball is 37.5% due to pitching, then the average pitcher is exactly as valuable as the average everyday player. For Mattingly to be correct that a pitcher can't be as valuable as an everyday player, one must conclude that baseball is *much less* than 37.5% pitching. I don't think too many people are going to argue for that.

Don Mattingly faced a pitcher 742 times last year. Roger Clemens faced a batter 997 times. Couldn't you just as well argue that a hitter, involved in only 742 confrontations with a pitcher, can't possibly be as important as a pitcher who is involved in a thousand confrontations with a batter? Even if the hitter is a more important determinant of the outcome of each at bat than the pitcher, which he probably is, that only balances the scales.

In order to believe that the pitcher, working one day in five, is more valuable than the hitter working every day, all you have to accept is that the pitcher has five times as much impact on the games in which he appears. That seems, to put it mildly, most reasonable. I mean, I ain't never seen a form chart give the starting first basemen.

Let's back off a bit. What is it that defines value in a ballplayer? The value of a player is determined not by how often he plays, not by what position he plays, but by what that player does to help his team win. If winning is considered to be one diamondlike unit of an accomplishment, then only the players on the winning team are eligible, in that only they helped their team win.

The problem with this logic is that it asserts a principle that a) has never been followed with any consistency, and b) would be difficult to apply uniformly. Suppose that two teams are even through 162 games, as in 1978. If you consider the winning of the pennant to be one unitary accomplishment, the inevitable corollary is that there is no value in the first 162 games, since no pennant has been won. All of the value is contained in the 163rd game. Therefore, the MVP in 1978 wasn't Rice or Guidry, but Bucky Dent.

Reductio ad absurdum. A premise that leads to an obviously wrong conclusion must be an incorrect premise. Bucky Dent simply isn't what we mean when we say "Most Valuable Player." Besides, anyone can easily see that a pennant *isn't* a single indissolvable unit, like a diamond, but that it breaks naturally into hundreds of pieces.

The alternative supposition is that value exists not only in helping the team win the pennant, but in helping the team *toward* winning the pennant; therefore, Mattingly is eligible. But what is it that makes Mattingly valuable?

Mattingly is valuable primarily because he creates runs for the Yankees. Clemens is valuable primarily because he prevents runs for Red Sox opponents. In the simplest form, it would be accurate to say that Mattingly is more valuable than Clemens if Mattingly adds more runs to the Yankees than Clemens saves for the Sox.

So then, how many runs did Mattingly add to the Yankees? (I did this once before—in 1978, in an article entitled "Guidry/Rice." Since the methods have evolved somewhat since then, when I get done here I'll back up and run the numbers again for that one.)

QUESTION 1: How many runs did Don Mattingly create?

Using the most advanced version of the runs created method, Mattingly created an estimated 152 runs for the Yankees in 1986. Using most other methods, the estimate would be lower. Using Paul Johnson's estimated runs produced, a very accurate method, Mattingly is estimated to have added 135 runs to the scoreboard.

The runs created estimate would be too low for Mattingly if Mattingly had hit particularly well in run-production opportunities. He didn't. The *Project Scoresheet* data suggests that Mattingly's runs created estimate might be trimmed a little bit. Mattingly homered more often with the bases empty ($\frac{1}{19}$ at bats) than with men on base ($\frac{1}{27}$ at bats). With runners in scoring position he hit .309, 43 points below his overall average. That probably cost the team six or seven runs. Mattingly's RBI total, 113, is obviously a little bit low in consideration of his 388 total bases and the fact that he bats behind Rickey Henderson—in fact, I believe that no other player in baseball history ever had as few as 113 RBI with as many as 388 total bases.

Mattingly drove in 30% of the runners who were in scoring position for him, 22% of those in scoring position with two out. Those are good figures, but not excellent. Eddie Murray drove in 31% and 33% in those situations, Chris Brown of San Francisco 31% and 29%, and Gary Ward of Texas 35% and 33%.

The Yankees as a team scored 46 runs fewer than projected by the runs created method (797/843). Devaluing Mattingly's 152 runs created by the team rate, we could say that he probably created about 144 runs.

QUESTION 2: How many runs would the Yankees likely have gotten out of those outs had they not had Mattingly?

Of any question we will face here, this is perhaps the most impossible to answer with confidence. In figuring replacement level, we usually figure not the specific players who were available to the Yankees, but the league replacement level. The replacement level can be estimated as being about one run per 27 outs worse than the league average at the position.

The American League's other 13 regular first basemen, other than Mattingly, created 5.41 runs per 27 outs in 1986. One run less than that would be 4.41.

Another way to figure replacement level is to look at the three weakest regulars at the position. The three weakest first basemen in terms of runs created per 27 outs were Cecil Cooper (3.9), Bill Buckner (4.2), and Steve Balboni (4.46). That would place us in the same vicinity—about 4.25 to 4.4 runs per 27 outs.

This figure needs to be adjusted for the effect of the park on runs scored. The average Yankee game at home in 1986 saw 9.55 runs scored (764 in 80 games) whereas the average road game saw 9.21 runs scored (755 in 82 games), creating a downward park adjustment of a little less than 2% (4% for the home games, divided by two because only half the games are home games). However, the data in recent years would suggest that this was not a valid effect; more likely this was merely a 1986 data aberration in what is still a pitcher's park. It seems like the best thing to do is to make a very minor downward adjustment here, perhaps consolidating the estimates of the replacement player's productivity at 4.3 runs per 27 outs.

Mattingly in 1986 made 467 outs, so the replacement player, at 4.3 runs per 27 outs, would likely have contributed about 74 runs to the Yankee offense.

It is worth noting, although we won't adjust for it, that the replacement would not likely be so direct. Mattingly got to make 467 outs because he's a great hitter in the middle of the lineup. The marginal first baseman with whom we propose to replace him wouldn't hit third, and wouldn't make 467 outs. Everybody would move up; Winfield would probably hit third, with Easler and Pagliarulo getting a few extra at bats. In so doing, they would be assuming some of Mattingly's outs. This would, to a small degree, reduce the impact of the contemplated replacement.

QUESTION 3: How many extra runs did Mattingly add?

By this time, that one is simple: 144 − 74, or 70 runs.

QUESTION 4: What about defense?

Mattingly is a very good first baseman and has very good defensive stats at first base. It is likely that the defensive impact of a first baseman operates on a scale of plus or minus about ten runs a year, with someone like Keith Hernandez or Pete O'Brien probably saving his team about ten runs a year as compared to an average first baseman, and someone like Willie Aikens probably costing about ten a year. Mattingly, being good but not in Hernandez's class, is probably four to seven runs a year better than average. Obviously, that's pretty much of a guess, but we'll move Mattingly up to +75 runs.

QUESTION 5: What does that mean in terms of games?

An excellent rule of thumb is that each ten runs will change one full game in the win column. The Yankees in 1986 outscored their opponents by 59 runs, but finished 9 full games over .500, much better than the normal 10–1 ratio (6.6–1). It is likely that the loss of Don Mattingly would have cost the Yankees seven or eight games in the win column.

Again, this figure could be larger if Mattingly tended to produce his runs when the game was on the line, but there is no evidence that he did. Mattingly hit .351 in the late innings of close games, just one point less than his overall average, but his slugging percentage did decline a bit in those circumstances (.573 overall, .521 in the late innings of close games). Seventy-two percent of Mattingly's RBI came when the game was close (Yankees no more than 2 runs behind or no more than one ahead). That's a very normal figure. It is still likely that the loss of Don Mattingly would have cost the Yankees seven or eight wins.

Now we'll go through the same process for Clemens:
QUESTION 1: How many runs did Clemens allow?
He allowed 77 runs in 254 innings.

QUESTION 2: How many runs would a replacement-level pitcher probably have allowed in the same innings?

The average American League pitcher allowed 4.65 runs per nine innings. We would estimate the replacement level, again, as one run above that, or 5.65 runs per nine innings. Among pitchers pitching 162 or more innings, the three highest runs allowed rates were by Richard Dotson (5.71), Dave Stieb (5.62) and Juan Nieves (6.05). That would suggest a replacement level in the same vicinity. The pitchers who allowed more runs than that, like Ron Romanick and John Butcher, were replaced in mid-season.

As Yankee Stadium is traditionally a pitcher's park which wasn't in 1986, so Fenway is traditionally a hitter's park which wasn't in 1986. There were 739 runs scored in Fenway as opposed to 751 in Red Sox road games (same number of games). Again, this was probably just an aberration in what remains a hitter's park, and again we will deal with it by consolidating the estimates at 5.70.

A pitcher allowing 5.70 runs per 9 innings would allow 161 runs in 254 innings.

QUESTION 3: How many runs was Clemens better than the replacement-level pitcher?

Clemens allowed 77 runs, meaning that he saved the Red Sox about 84 runs as contrasted with a replacement-level pitcher.

QUESTION 4: How many games is that?

Eighty-four runs should mean about eight and a half games in the win column.

A partially independent way of looking at this is to extrapolate the difference in wins from the Red Sox runs scored by the Pythagorean Method. The Red Sox scored 201 runs in Clemens's 33 starts, or 6.09 per game. Scoring 6.09 runs per game with Clemens allowing 2.73 per game, one would expect them to win 80.8% of the time, or 27 of the 33 games (26.66). In fact, they did go 27–6 in those games.

Had they allowed 5.7 runs per game in those games instead of the 2.73 that Clemens was allowing, their winning percentage in those games would probably have been about .533, so that they would have won about 18 of those games (17.59). By this method, we would estimate that Clemens improved the Red Sox by 9.07 games.

QUESTION 5: What about defense?

The problem of defense is that some of the runs which we credit Clemens with having saved were, in all likelihood, actually saved by the defense behind him. This is a great problem, for, as you can see, the comparison is so close that even a few runs saved by the defense could be enough to make Mattingly the MVP.

For a pitcher, we adjust for defense by adjusting the estimated replacement level. If the Boston defense is above average, then that would mean that the replacement-level pitcher would allow fewer runs—maybe 5.4 or 5.5 runs per game instead of 5.7.

There is little evidence that the Red Sox defense was, on the whole, markedly above average. Their defensive efficiency record, .684, was poor, meaning that when a ball was in play against the Sox it was more likely to become a hit than it was against most teams. Their fielding percentage was average. Their double-play total was a little below average. They were very good at preventing the stolen base, due to Gedman, but their most positive defensive markers were those of the pitchers—1,033 strikeouts (2nd in the league) and 474 walks (best in the league). They were average in home runs allowed.

So I don't see any reasons to adjust the replacement level downward. We estimated Mattingly's value, as carefully as possible, at 72 runs. In order to reduce the estimate of Clemens's value to the same level, we would have to lower the replacement runs allowed level to 5.28. That's a pretty large drop, particularly when you look around at the Red Sox staff. Tim Lollar pitched 32 times for the Red Sox despite allowing 7.33 runs per nine innings. Rob Woodward started six times despite allowing 6.56 runs per nine innings. Jeff Sellers started 13 games despite allowing 6.15 runs per nine innings. And Al Nipper started 26 games *and a World Series game* despite allowing 6.18 runs per nine innings (he missed the 162-inning group of the worst three in the league by only three innings). That, I think, provides pretty convincing evidence that the Red Sox could *not* have replaced Clemens with a pitcher allowing as few as 5.28 runs per nine innings—and might well suggest that the real cost of losing Clemens might have been even larger than 84 runs.

Let's run the math:

	Mattingly	Clemens
Runs	144	77
Replacement Runs	74	161
Advantage	+70	−84
Defense	+5	
Total	+75	−84

Obviously, we've had to make enough estimates in doing this that a nine-run difference in the final product should not be absolutely convincing. *To the extent that the statistics tell the true story,* Roger Clemens was the American League's MVP in 1986. I could have interpreted the numbers so that Mattingly would have the edge—but I could also have interpreted them so that Clemens would have a *big* edge, much bigger than this. It wasn't my intention to interpret them so as to prove any point, but rather to allow them to tell us whatever they are trying to tell us.

Clemens had the best numbers. The Red Sox won the pennant. Mattingly won the MVP award in 1985, when the Yankees also finished second. To me, that means that Roger Clemens was the true MVP.

Clemens deserved the award.

I promised to take a second look at the 1978 race when I got to this point. At the time, I thought the award went to the right man (Rice). Let's run down the questions quickly:

1. How many runs did Rice create?

About 147, while making 490 outs. Oddly, both Rice and Mattingly had 677 at bats. Rice was the last player to have 400 total bases. Mattingly was the first player since to come close.

2. How many runs would a replacement-level left fielder likely have created?

Oddly, American League left fielders in 1978 also averaged 5.41 runs created per 27 outs, the same as 1986 first basemen. However, with an adjustment for the park, the 4.41 replacement level would be higher. A figure of 4.65 would be a better estimate, meaning that the replacement hitters could have been expected to create about 84 runs with 490 outs.

3. How many extra runs did Rice create for the Sox?
About 63.

4. How many games is that?
About six and a half.

5. What about defense?
Rice in 1978 had one of his best defensive seasons, perhaps his best. He was young and ran fairly well, but he was in his fourth season as an outfielder, so he knew the wall. His range factor was excellent, he had 13 assists in 114 games and committed only 3 errors. We'll give Rice 5 runs for defense, making him +68.

1. How many runs did Guidry allow?
He allowed 61 runs in 274 innings.

2. How many runs would a replacement-level pitcher have allowed?
The league average was 4.24 runs per game, so we'll peg a replacement-level pitcher at 5.24. However, with Yankee Stadium being a pitcher's park, a better estimate would be 5.05.

A pitcher allowing 5.05 per nine innings in 274 innings would allow 154 runs.

3. How many runs did Guidry save the Yankees?
Guidry saved the Yankees about 93 runs.

4. How many games is that?
More than nine.

5. What about defense?
A very, very tough question. The Yankee defense of 1978 was outstanding, with Munson catching and an infield of Chambliss, Randolph, Dent, and Nettles. Mickey Rivers in center field couldn't throw, but he wasn't Tony Armas. The Yankees' team fielding percentage was second in the league. Their defensive efficiency record, .718, was the best in the American League. They were effective against the running game. No Yankee pitcher with significant pitching time allowed anything like five runs a game. They couldn't find pitching time for guys like Tidrow and Beattie who were allowing not much more than 4.00 runs per nine innings (Beattie, 4.22 and Tidrow, 4.18).

Combining those facts, it is almost certain that the Yankees could have replaced Guidry (had they lost him) with a pitcher allowing very significantly less than 5.05 runs per nine innings. It is almost certain that the Yankees' replacement level pitcher would have held the opposition to somewhere between 4.10 and 4.30 runs per game.

And that is a real problem for us, because that is precisely the point at which the issue breaks. The loss of Rice would probably have cost the Red Sox about 68 runs. The point at which the loss of Guidry would cost the Yankees 68 runs is 4.24 runs—exactly the league average of runs allowed per nine innings.

So, at this point, I would just have to say that it's too close to call on that ground. Using a 4.24 estimate, the math works out like this:

	Jim Rice	Ron Guidry
Runs	147	61
Replacement Runs	84	129
Advantage	+63	−68
Defense	+5	
Total	+68	−68

What that leaves is this: Guidry won the key game. The Yankees won the pennant. On that basis, I would vote for Guidry as the 1978 MVP. But the numbers do not tell you who should have won.

One thing I note in closing. At a glance, the 1978 MVP candidates are more impressive than those of 1986. Guidry was 25–3, a 1.74 ERA; Clemens was 24–4 with a 2.48, not quite as good. Mattingly hit .352 with 31 homers and 113 RBI, while Rice hit .315 with 46 homers and 139 RBI. Rice had 406 total bases, Mattingly "only" 388.

But when you really try to calculate their value, it seems clear that the 1986 candidates were superior to their 1978 counterparts. Guidry had a 1.74 ERA—but backed by an excellent defense, in a pitcher's park in a league with a 3.77 ERA. In the context of his time and place (Fenway Park, 4.18 league ERA, unimpressive defense), Clemens really had a better season.

While Rice had more total bases, Mattingly probably created more runs while making fewer outs. Rice received a lot more help from his park than did Mattingly. You're talking about four great players here having four great seasons—but when I rank them, I get 1. Clemens, 2. Mattingly, 3. Guidry, and 4. Rice.

DOLLAR SIGNS

Eddie Epstein, of the Baltimore area, sent along this list of the American League players who had the most dollar value to their teams. Mr. Epstein writes that "the formula that generates these dollar values was developed by estimating the impact of certain team statistics on team winning percentage and then estimating the impact, on a major-league–wide level, of team winning percentage on team revenue. The part of the model that explains variations in team revenue also considers market characteristics, such as population, as well as factors like the impact of team attendance/revenue of an appearance in postseason play. The dollar value of a given player's season is based on his rate of production relative to the league, the amount of playing time, and the market characteristics of the player's home city." (Isn't it fun to watch a man try to put a book in a paragraph?) The American League leaders:

1. Mattingly $2,046,589
2. Clemens $1,809,884
3. Mark Eichorn $1,760,651
4. Rickey Henderson $1,435,536
5. Mike Witt $1,425,997
6. Boggs $1,378,161
7. Higuera $1,292,084
8. Jack Morris $1,253,975
9. Righetti $1,198,062
10. Barfield $1,108,577
11. Kirby Puckett $1,091,105
12. Kirk McCaskill $1,044,157
13. Joe Carter $1,021,664
14. Tom Candiotti $1,005,430

Eddie notes, however, that if Clemens had played in New York and had the same season (park effects aside) his value would have been about $2.2 million.

The "average" American League nonpitcher was worth $326,684 to his team; the "average" pitcher worth $308,336. The overall average was $318,737.

DETROIT TIGERS

Runners on Base:	2,103
Opponents on Base:	1,975
Net Advantage:	+128
Won-Lost Record:	87-75

The Detroit Tiger team which came together with so much promise in 1978 is now drifting toward the last act of what has been, in the main, a disappointing performance. Probably no team since the Dodgers of the fifties has had so many supremely talented performers whose careers were so perfectly aligned. The current Tigers have five players and one manager who have an excellent chance to go into the Hall of Fame—not the chance that Eric Davis has, at the start of his career when the record is yet to be written and anything is possible, but the chance that men have when they have starred for a decade or so and their records begin to resemble those of the greats at their positions. If Jack Morris had departed the Tigers last winter that period in the history of the Tigers would be over. As I write this they appear to have retained Morris and retained a shot at the division title in 1987, but there can be no doubt that time is sneaking out on what once appeared to be the nucleus of a great team.

Jack Morris, after eight straight winning seasons, is 45 games over .500, and three seasons away from serious Hall of Fame consideration. Lou Whitaker and Alan Trammell may have played together longer than any double-play combination in history. Each will soon be among the all-time leaders in games played at his position, and few of those around them were better hitters. Lance Parrish has an exceptional arm and is one of the most feared power-hitting catchers ever. All four joined the team late in 1977. The Tigers won 86 games in 1978. A few years behind them is Kirk Gibson, who has not quite been able to compile Hall of Fame numbers for an outfielder, but who has become generally regarded as the Tigers' best player.

All five of those players played very well in 1986, although two lost part of the season to injuries. In naming those five, we have not listed all of the Tigers' strengths in 1986 or over the last decade. The supporting cast of recent years has included very significant talents of lesser rank, such as Dan Petry and Chet Lemon. The stars of 1986 were supported by Darrell Evans, an aged first baseman who was good for 29 homers and 85 RBI, and Darnell Coles, who in his first season as a regular contributed 20 and 86, making the Tigers into a trivia question: What was the only team for which all four infielders hit 20 home runs?

One of my basic theories is that the biggest difference between the talent available to a good organization and that available to a poor organization *isn't* in the ability to produce players from the farm system, but in the ability to take advantage of the "free talent," the players who can

be picked up without trading somebody you're depending on at another spot. No organization in modern baseball is large enough or strong enough to produce on demand a player at a given position. Since Branch Rickey, no organization has been able to produce a third baseman whenever a third baseman was needed or a catcher whenever a catcher was needed. But there is always talent available; there are always players at each position who can be had cheap because they have not shown well in trials and have been squeezed out. The good organizations can identify those players and use them to plug gaps, sometimes turning those gaps into big plus signs. In the last generation the Orioles and Royals picked up guys like Dempsey, McGregor, Otis, Patek, McRae, Mayberry, and Cuellar because the organization that had them didn't have a place for them to play and didn't think their careers were going anywhere. That's one of the things that Stengel did so well in the fifties.

One key decision that helped the Tigers in 1985, then, was the rescue of Darnell Coles. Coles was available from Seattle because Jim Presley had pushed him out of the Mariners' plans. Installed at third base, his offensive performance was almost precisely what was projected by the majors-to-minors translation of his years in the Pacific Coast League, which is to say that it was pretty good, and his glovework wasn't bad enough to keep him out of the lineup. Coles was the best-hitting third baseman the Tigers have had since Ed Yost in 1959, and the Tiger management must be given credit for taking advantage of the free talent.

It's difficult to see how the people who made that decision could have made some of the others that guided the Tigers in 1986. Since 1981 Dave Collins has disappointed three teams, all of which had found him to be a leadoff man who doesn't score runs. Playing for New York in 1982, Toronto in 1983 and 1984, and Oakland in 1985, he had scored 41, 55, 59, and 52 runs while playing 111 to 128 games a year, most of them as a leadoff hitter. Why anyone still thought he would be a valued addition to the offense is a bafflement, but Collins played 124 games for the Tigers, batted 419 times, scored 44 runs and drove in 27. In the outfield, he threw out two of the many runners who tried to advance on him, which is a significant portion of his career assists total. That's one strike against the outfield.

After a brilliant season for Evansville in 1984, Nelson Simmons played well for the Tigers in 1985. Though Simmons hit just .239 in '85, ten homers in 251 at bats lifted his slugging percentage over .400, and his totals of 41 strikeouts and 26 walks represent an unusually good strikeout and walk combination for a rookie power hitter. He was 22 years old and a switch hitter, two more positives. I expected Simmons to grow into one of the top hitters in the American League.

What happened last year is a classic case of "There must be more to this story than we're reading in the newspapers." In spring training Sparky was unhappy because Simmons had spent the off-season lifting weights and becoming muscle-bound. Simmons was optioned out at the end of spring training, didn't take his assignment with grace and was released by the Tigers. Though he signed with Baltimore and did nothing for Rochester, suggesting that Sparky may have had some points, it remains as much a mystery as before why the Tigers would have roster space for Harry Spilman and Pat Sheridan but none for Nelson Simmons. Strike two against the outfield, both self-inflicted.

On opening day Kirk Gibson went 4-for-4 with two homers and 5 RBI. On April 22 Gibson was hitting .359 and slugging over .600 when his foot slipped off the bag in Boston and he jammed an ankle. We could call that strike three; by the time Gibson got his next hit on June 3 the Tigers were ten games behind the Red Sox. Although they were ahead of the Sox at the moment of the injury and beat them by a game and a half the rest of the way to the wire, Detroit was not able to overcome the deficit piled up while Gibson was out.

Though Gibson completed a fine season, the Tigers did not magically regenerate with his return. At the All-Star break they were 39–42, in last place. If the Tigers' outfield is entitled to a strike four, a strike five, or a strike six, they could make good use of them. Chet Lemon, nagged by injuries, had the first off-season since he emerged as a player of quality in 1976. Larry Herndon, who came up the same year and won one of the Rookie Awards, has had about seven off seasons and had another one last year, hitting .247 with unimpressive power. Pat Sheridan joined the Tigers after being released by the Royals, and made it through the season without causing *anyone* to wonder how the Royals could release this guy.

So the Tigers had an excellent infield and a horrible outfield. Their catching was probably the best in the league. After Lance Parrish caught 39 of the Tigers' first 41 games, Sparky commented that "he'll pay the price for what's happening now," a comment that a) proved prophetic, and b) leaves us to wonder who was making out the lineup cards. I mean, if Anderson even suspected that this would wipe Parrish out later in the season, then he must have perceived the alternative as being worse. What is worse than your All-Star catcher severely aggravating his back problems? In any case, Parrish, having one of his finest seasons, was unable to play after August 1 due to two vertebrae in his lower back rubbing against one another, but Dwight Lowry played very well and Mike Heath joined the Tigers and was the Jekyll Heath, having left the Hyde Heath in St. Louis. Lowry and Heath enabled the Tigers to play their best ball of the season without Parrish.

Led by the infielders, the Tigers blasted 198 home runs, the most of any major league team (102 of the 198 were hit on the road, only 96 in Detroit). Although the Tigers used no regular designated hitter, their DHs hit .275 with 28 homers, 102 RBI and 80 walks. John Grubb had a formidable season as a pinch hitter, fourth outfielder, and occasional DH. Despite the weak outfield, the Tiger offense was generally good and had good balance. They were above average in batting (.263–.262), home runs, walks (613–548), stolen bases (138–105), on base percentage (.338–.330) and slugging percentage (.424–.408). They grounded into only 99 double plays, fewest in the league. The Tigers scored 798 runs against a league average of 746.

The starting pitching was brilliant at times and weak at times. Morris recovered from a poor start to have one of his best seasons and be one of the league's best pitchers. Dan Petry, once considered the equal of Morris, had elbow surgery and faces a comeback battle. The other Tiger starters—Tanana, Terrell, and King—were not significantly above or significantly below average, although Terrell's ability to pitch well in 1987 is suspect. The Tiger bullpen was not the tower of strength that it was in 1984. Sparky ordered, or at least the Tigers issued, 61 intentional walks, 15 more than any other team in the league. Their strikeout, walk, and home run data were all below average. The Tigers allowed 183 home runs, the most of any team in the division (100 on the road, 83 in Detroit). Still, because of Morris, the pitching was above average, as they allowed only 714 runs. The staff ERA was 3.25 in Detroit, 4.84 on the road.

Can the Tigers win in 1987? The Tigers saw their 1986 season as lost to injuries. I don't. The Tigers' injuries were not abnormal in number, like those of Los Angeles, San Francisco, or Montreal, and injuries happen to a team when the key players begin to age. In the last few years, so many players have played until their late thirties that many people have developed unrealistic expectations about how long a player will last. The fact that Mike Schmidt is the NL MVP at 36 gives the impression that players now retain their peak abilities that long; one should remember that Schmidt is older than Greg Luzinski, Ross Grimsley, Manny Trillo, or Mike Hargrove. While dramatically more players in recent years have lasted until their late thirties, it should be remembered that a) the great majority of major league players are released before their thirty-fifth birthday, and b) the fact that a player who starts receiving piles of money at age 32 may keep himself in great shape until the age of 40 does not mean that a player who starts receiving piles of money at age 24 will do the same.

In addition to the increasing injuries that they will face in the next few years, the Tigers must rebuild both the starting rotation and the bullpen. Evans is playing month to month, and Parrish is a big question mark. Petry could come back but it's a longshot, and I don't think that Walt Terrell will ever win 12 in a season again. The Tigers do have some young pitchers like Eric King and Randy O'Neal, but they are counting on young pitchers to do things that they haven't done. The Tigers retain enough talent that they could win for another year or two. It isn't easy to see how the 1987 Tigers will be ten games better than they were in 1986, but it could happen.

Lance PARRISH, Catcher

	G	AB	Hit	2B	3B	HR	Run	RBI	TBB	SO	SB	CS	Avg
7.07 years		604	159	28	3	30	82	99	47	120	3	4	.263
1986	91	327	84	6	1	22	53	62	38	83	0	0	.257
First Half	76	276	70	6	1	18	45	55	34	68	0	0	.254
Second Half	15	51	14	0	0	4	8	7	4	15	0	0	.275
Vs. RHP		205	52	5	0	17		42	25	60	0	0	.254
Vs. LHP		122	32	1	1	5		20	13	23	0	0	.262
Home	45	158	39	2	0	8	22	27	20	29	0	0	.247
Road	46	169	45	4	1	14	31	35	18	54	0	0	.266
Grass	74	265	67	5	1	16	42	49	33	55	0	0	.253
Turf	17	62	17	1	0	6	11	13	5	28	0	0	.274

Dave COLLINS, Left Field

	G	AB	Hit	2B	3B	HR	Run	RBI	TBB	SO	SB	CS	Avg
8.44 years		531	146	20	6	4	72	41	50	70	44	16	.275
1986	124	419	113	18	2	1	44	27	44	49	27	12	.270
First Half	65	224	62	13	1	0	29	13	25	24	12	5	.277
Second Half	59	195	51	5	1	1	15	14	19	25	15	7	.262
Vs. RHP		311	88	11	1	0		15	40	41	12	8	.283
Vs. LHP		108	25	7	1	1		12	4	8	15	4	.231
Home	59	196	49	10	1	0	23	10	23	24	15	3	.250
Road	65	223	64	8	1	1	21	17	21	25	12	9	.287
Grass	104	350	93	15	2	0	36	20	36	38	21	10	.266
Turf	20	69	20	3	0	1	8	7	8	11	6	2	.290

Darrell EVANS, First Base

	G	AB	Hit	2B	3B	HR	Run	RBI	TBB	SO	SB	CS	Avg
14.11 years		550	138	21	2	25	83	82	98	84	6	4	.251
1986	151	507	122	15	0	29	78	85	91	105	3	2	.241
First Half	73	240	61	8	0	15	36	43	39	41	1		.254
Second Half	78	267	61	7	0	14	42	42	52	64	2	1	.228
Vs. RHP		360	82	11	0	20		53	68	66	2	2	.228
Vs. LHP		147	40	4	0	9		32	23	39	1	0	.272
Home	76	246	58	8	0	15	38	47	43	48	1	1	.236
Road	75	261	64	7	0	14	40	38	48	57	2	1	.245
Grass	129	431	104	13	0	26	68	75	75	89	3	2	.241
Turf	22	76	18	2	0	3	10	10	16	16	0	0	.237

Chet LEMON, Center Field

	G	AB	Hit	2B	3B	HR	Run	RBI	TBB	SO	SB	CS	Avg
9.06 years		569	158	33	5	18	82	74	58	82	6	7	.277
1986	126	403	101	21	3	12	45	53	39	53	2	1	.251
First Half	60	196	50	12	1	3	17	21	14	26	0	1	.255
Second Half	66	207	51	9	2	9	28	32	25	27	2	0	.246
Vs. RHP		241	55	11	1	5		32	24	36	2	1	.228
Vs. LHP		162	46	10	2	7		21	15	17	0	0	.284
Home	63	190	45	9	2	7	22	25	19	21	2	1	.237
Road	63	213	56	12	1	5	23	28	20	32	0	0	.263
Grass	111	355	87	17	3	12	40	48	30	47	2	1	.245
Turf	15	48	14	4	0	0	5	5	9	6	0	0	.292

Lou WHITAKER, Second Base

	G	AB	Hit	2B	3B	HR	Run	RBI	TBB	SO	SB	CS	Avg
7.92 years		594	167	26	6	12	91	66	73	73	12	7	.281
1986	144	584	157	26	6	20	95	73	63	70	13	8	.269
First Half	74	301	80	16	4	9	49	34	26	37	5	4	.266
Second Half	70	283	77	10	2	11	46	39	37	33	8	4	.272
Vs. RHP		421	121	22	4	17		53	48	37	12	6	.287
Vs. LHP		163	36	4	2	3		20	15	33	1	2	.221
Home	73	286	71	11	5	8	47	38	37	37	7	2	.248
Road	71	298	86	15	1	12	48	35	26	33	6	6	.289
Grass	123	499	136	22	6	14	79	62	54	59	11	6	.273
Turf	21	85	21	4	0	6	16	11	9	11	2	2	.247

Kirk GIBSON, Right Field

	G	AB	Hit	2B	3B	HR	Run	RBI	TBB	SO	SB	CS	Avg
4.72 years		577	159	24	7	27	92	89	65	126	30	9	.275
1986	119	441	118	11	2	28	84	86	68	107	34	6	.268
First Half	46	162	42	4	2	10	36	28	35	44	12	2	.259
Second Half	73	279	76	7	0	18	48	58	33	63	22	4	.272
Vs. RHP		277	75	6	2	21		57	48	63	30	4	.271
Vs. LHP		164	43	5	0	7		29	20	44	4	2	.262
Home	58	216	60	2	1	15	43	48	32	50	20	3	.278
Road	61	225	58	9	1	13	41	38	36	57	14	3	.258
Grass	105	391	104	9	1	25	76	77	60	99	31	5	.266
Turf	14	50	14	2	1	3	8	9	8	8	3	1	.280

Darnell COLES, Third Base

	G	AB	Hit	2B	3B	HR	Run	RBI	TBB	SO	SB	CS	Avg
1.51 years		541	136	29	2	15	66	68	58	92	5	5	.252
1986	142	521	142	30	2	20	67	86	45	84	6	2	.273
First Half	64	244	69	17	1	9	29	40	16	41	2	1	.283
Second Half	78	277	73	13	1	11	38	46	29	43	4	1	.264
Vs. RHP		351	94	19	2	17		58	27	64	4	2	.268
Vs. LHP		170	48	11	0	3		28	18	20	2	0	.282
Home	72	252	72	10	0	12	35	48	25	47	3	1	.286
Road	70	269	70	20	2	8	32	38	20	37	3	1	.260
Grass	120	435	119	26	1	17	55	71	38	71	5	1	.274
Turf	22	86	23	4	1	3	12	15	7	13	1	1	.267

Larry HERNDON, Left Field

	G	AB	Hit	2B	3B	HR	Run	RBI	TBB	SO	SB	CS	Avg
8.47 years		529	144	20	9	11	66	57	36	85	11	7	.273
1986	106	283	70	13	1	8	33	37	27	40	2	1	.247
First Half	58	175	44	9	1	4	17	20	12	27	0	1	.251
Second Half	48	108	26	4	0	4	16	17	15	13	2	0	.241
Vs. RHP		94	26	6	1	2		10	7	18	0	1	.277
Vs. LHP		189	44	7	0	6		27	20	22	2	0	.233
Home	50	137	32	5	0	4	15	14	11	22	2	0	.234
Road	56	146	38	8	1	4	18	23	16	18	0	1	.260
Grass	92	246	63	11	1	7	28	33	25	36	2	1	.256
Turf	14	37	7	2	0	1	5	4	2	4	0	0	.189

Alan TRAMMELL, Shortstop

	G	AB	Hit	2B	3B	HR	Run	RBI	TBB	SO	SB	CS	Avg
7.96 years		582	163	27	5	11	88	63	59	65	19	10	.281
1986	151	574	159	33	7	21	107	75	59	57	25	12	.277
First Half	76	285	71	14	3	6	35	32	20	32	9	6	.249
Second Half	75	289	88	19	4	15	72	43	39	25	16	6	.304
Vs. RHP		370	102	17	4	13		51	40	38	22	9	.276
Vs. LHP		204	57	16	3	8		24	19	19	3	3	.279
Home	76	282	74	13	3	8	53	35	28	35	12	3	.262
Road	75	292	85	20	4	13	54	40	31	22	13	9	.291
Grass	128	482	128	26	7	17	92	59	52	52	21	8	.266
Turf	23	92	31	7	0	4	15	16	7	5	4	4	.337

Tom BROOKENS, Infield

	G	AB	Hit	2B	3B	HR	Run	RBI	TBB	SO	SB	CS	Avg
5.72 years		465	115	22	5	8	57	52	31	73	13	9	.247
1986	98	281	76	11	2	3	42	25	20	42	11	8	.270
First Half	51	134	41	7	1	1	23	15	12	12	6	3	.306
Second Half	47	147	35	4	1	2	19	10	8	30	5	5	.238
Vs. RHP		110	25	2	0	1		14	10	22	8	3	.227
Vs. LHP		171	51	9	2	2		11	10	20	3	5	.298
Home	51	144	37	6	1	2	21	12	9	27	5	2	.257
Road	47	137	39	5	1	1	21	13	11	15	6	6	.285
Grass	86	236	58	8	2	3	36	23	18	36	10	6	.246
Turf	12	45	18	3	0	0	6	2	2	6	1	2	.400

Jack MORRIS

Year	(W–L)	GS	Run	Avg	DP	Avg	SB	Avg
1984	(19-11)	35	173	4.94	24	.69	24	.69
1985	(16-11)	35	162	4.63	32	.91	23	.66
1986	(21-8)	35	190	5.43	32	.91	24	.69
1977-1986		280	1240	4.43	266	.95	177	.63

	1986 ERA	W–L	1985 ERA	1984 ERA	1983 ERA	1982 ERA	82-86 W–L
Total	3.27	21-8	3.33	3.60	3.34	4.06	93-59
Home	2.76	10-3	4.49	3.81	3.44	3.45	45-25
Road	3.63	11-5	2.51	3.30	3.26	4.71	48-34
East	3.17	12-3	4.02	3.73	3.51	4.24	42-29
West	3.38	9-5	2.69	3.50	3.20	3.88	51-30
1st Half	4.23	7-6	3.23	3.08	4.23	4.37	46-33
2nd Half	2.44	14-2	3.44	4.25	2.59	3.72	47-26
Turf	2.81	4-0	1.42	3.42	3.35		14-6
Grass	3.40	17-8	3.72	3.64	3.34		62-37
Day	3.25	8-2	4.23	2.22	3.51	3.83	29-15
Night	3.28	13-6	2.93	4.24	3.27	4.11	64-44
April	5.60	3-2	2.16	1.98	6.25	2.14	17-8
May	3.06	1-2	2.34	1.79	4.66	3.91	13-11
June	4.34	3-1	5.31	5.16	2.53	8.36	14-11
July	.54	5-1	2.66	5.65	2.28	4.60	15-8
August	5.21	3-2	4.12	4.84	2.00	3.86	18-9
Sept.	2.26	6-0	3.56	3.89	3.32	3.16	16-12

Frank TANANA

Year	(W–L)	GS	Run	Avg	DP	Avg	SB	Avg
1984	(15-15)	35	155	4.43	27	.77	20	.57
1985	(12-14)	33	139	4.21	26	.79	16	.48
1986	(12-9)	31	148	4.77	32	1.03	20	.65
1976-1986		320	1385	4.33	260	.81	213	.67

	1986 ERA	W–L	1985 ERA	1984 ERA	1983 ERA	1982 ERA	82-86 W–L
Total	4.16	12-9	3.34	3.25	3.16	4.21	51-58
Home	3.87	8-6	3.58	3.75	3.01	3.99	26-32
Road	4.58	4-3	3.13	2.83	3.34	4.45	25-26
East	3.51	8-5	2.35	3.17	2.79	4.35	32-29
West	5.18	4-4	4.60	3.34	3.55	4.02	19-29
1st Half	3.99	8-4	2.57	3.03	1.84	3.68	25-23
2nd Half	4.40	4-5	3.48	3.48	3.83	4.88	26-35
Turf	8.20	0-2	5.21	4.21	3.60		3-7
Grass	3.71	12-7	3.04	3.14	3.12		41-33
Day	5.13	3-4	5.36	2.85	5.50	4.73	11-15
Night	3.78	9-5	2.51	3.36	2.87	4.11	40-43
April	3.13	3-1		4.31	.00	5.96	6-6
May	8.14	1-2		1.52	1.83	3.86	5-10
June	2.41	3-1	.00	3.33	2.05	2.78	11-5
July	5.96	1-0	3.00	2.90	4.80	2.51	8-11
August	4.31	2-2	3.48	3.65	1.77	5.31	12-11
September	3.13	2-3	4.06	3.98	4.95	6.04	9-15

Walt TERRELL

Year	(W–L)	GS	Run	Avg	DP	Avg	SB	Avg
1984	(11-12)	33	142	4.30	51	1.55	12	.36
1985	(15-10)	34	156	4.59	34	1.00	16	.47
1986	(15-12)	33	158	4.79	39	1.18	5	.15
1982-1986		123	524	4.26	147	1.20	60	.49

	1986 ERA	W–L	1985 ERA	W–L	85-86 W–L
Total	4.56	15-12	3.85	15-10	30-22
Home	3.35	10-3	2.86	9-2	19-5
Road	5.93	5-9	4.94	6-8	11-17
East	4.64	7-6	3.71	7-4	14-10
West	4.49	8-6	3.97	8-6	16-12
1st Half	4.66	7-7	3.92	9-4	16-11
2nd Half	4.44	8-5	3.78	6-6	14-11
Turf	6.91	0-3	6.21	2-3	2-6
Grass	4.20	15-9	3.39	13-7	28-16
Day	3.62	4-1	4.67	3-3	7-4
Night	4.95	11-11	3.55	12-7	23-18
April	6.08	2-1	3.86	2-0	4-1
May	3.47	4-1	3.86	4-1	8-2
June	4.75	1-4	4.11	3-2	4-6
July	3.22	2-2	4.21	1-3	3-5
August	5.85	2-3	2.91	3-1	5-4
September	4.67	4-1	4.36	2-3	6-4

Dan PETRY

Year	(W–L)	GS	Run	Avg	DP	Avg	SB	Avg
1984	(18-8)	35	184	5.26	31	.89	10	.29
1985	(15-13)	34	136	4.00	33	.97	22	.65
1986	(5-10)	20	83	4.15	20	1.00	13	.65
1979-1986		224	1040	4.64	248	1.11	117	.52

	1986 ERA	W–L	1985 ERA	1984 ERA	1983 ERA	1982 ERA	82-86 W–L
Total	4.66	5-10	3.36	3.24	3.92	3.22	72-51
Home	4.65	1-7	3.60	2.74	4.41	2.42	33-28
Road	4.67	4-3	3.05	3.78	3.55	4.01	39-23
East	4.62	1-4	2.15	2.54	4.58	4.07	32-21
West	4.68	4-6	4.69	3.76	3.17	2.50	40-30
First Half	4.96	4-5	3.29	3.06	4.15	3.33	40-27
2nd Half	4.26	1-5	3.44	3.41	3.72	3.07	32-24
Turf	1.00	1-0	2.51	4.14	3.12		8-5
Grass	4.96	4-10	3.47	3.05	4.04		49-37
Day	4.43	1-5	3.03	2.03	5.30	1.86	26-21
Night	4.79	4-5	3.54	3.93	3.24	3.73	46-30
April	6.10	1-2	2.90	2.06	2.01	3.56	13-6
May	3.15	3-2	3.45	3.82	4.66	3.96	15-8
June	.00	0-1	2.77	3.28	4.28	3.18	10-10
July			4.57	2.35	2.34	2.47	13-7
August	2.33	0-2	2.29	5.06	4.19	2.12	9-10
September	5.46	1-3	4.20	2.23	5.13	4.78	12-10

Willie HERNANDEZ

1986	G	IP	W–L	Sv	H	ER	SO	ERA
Total	64	88.2	8-7	24	87	35	77	3.55
Home	29	43.0	6-3	9	42	18	39	3.77
Road	35	45.2	2-4	15	45	17	38	3.35
East	35	46.1	4-3	14	49	20	31	3.88
West	29	42.1	4-4	10	38	15	46	3.19
1st Half	39	54.1	3-4	17	60	20	50	3.31
2nd Half	25	34.1	5-3	7	27	15	27	3.93
Turf	9	10.2	1-2	2	11	6	12	5.06
Grass	55	78.0	7-5	22	76	29	65	3.35
Day	21	27.0	3-2	8	23	9	23	3.00
Night	43	61.2	5-5	16	64	26	54	3.79
April	9	11.1	1-1	5	16	7	12	5.56
May	11	15.2	1-1	2	15	4	18	2.30
June	15	22.1	1-1	8	24	7	17	2.82
July	12	17.1	4-2	4	13	4	10	2.08
August	9	13.1	0-1	2	12	10	12	6.75
September	8	8.2	1-1	3	7	3	8	3.12

RECORDS WITH DIFFERENT STARTING CATCHERS

Catcher	Inn	ER	W–L	ERA	GS	SB	Avg
Parrish	733.1	316	45-37	3.88	82	40	.49
Lowry	402.2	190	22-23	4.25	45	30	.67
Heath	237.2	107	17-10	4.05	27	13	.48
Nokes	62.0	24	3-4	3.48	7	3	.43
Engle	8.0	8	0-1	9.00	2	1	1.00

STARTING PITCHERS' AVERAGE TIME AND ATTENDANCE RECORDS

Pitcher	Time	Attendance
Morris	2:46	837
Terrell	2:44	827
Tanana	2:51	680
Petry	2:51	397

OTHERS

Pitcher	(W–L)	GS	Run	Avg	DP	Avg	SB	Avg	Time	Att.
King	(11-4)	16	90	5.63	14	.88	12	.75	2:58	453
O'Neal	(3-7)	11	52	4.73	14	1.27	5	.45	2:48	307
LaPoint	(3-6)	8	37	4.63	4	.50	6	.75	2:51	181
Kelly	(1-2)	4	23	5.75	3	.75	2	.50	2:46	88
Thurmond	(4-1)	4	17	4.25	5	1.25	0	.00	2:30	110

TORONTO BLUE JAYS

Runners on Base:	2,069
Opponents on Base:	1,999
Net Advantage:	+70
Won-Lost Record:	86-76

And yet, they did not die. The Toronto Blue Jays in 1986 were harder to kill than Rasputin. The Blue Jays left the gate with a rookie manager, an unreliable bullpen, a starting rotation that was a shambles, and a controversy about who should be their leadoff man. Early in the season the Blue Jays buried themselves in what seemed like an impossible position, yet they were able to scramble back and give the Red Sox all they wanted in their battle to retain first place. Though it was a disappointing season for Blue Jay fans, it was a season that demanded courage, resilience, tenacity, and the sacrifice of personal goals from the Jays' players, and one in which those players answered the challenge in a style that must be admired. For the fans, there will be better years.

As early as May 27, the Blue Jays had been left for dead in the battle for the AL East. At 20–26 they were 11 games behind the Red Sox and last in the division. In this division, that is a serious position, for figuring that you're going to have to win 95 games to have a chance, that means you've got to go 75–41, which is playing awfully well for a long time. As of that date:

Tom Henke, counted on as the ace of the bullpen, had a 6.75 ERA in 16 appearances.

Jimmie Key, counted on as the top left-handed starter, had an ERA of 7.08.

Dennis Lamp, 11–0 with a 3.32 ERA in long relief in 1985, was 1–3 with an ERA of 8.25.

Damaso Garcia, hitting below .250 and being booed every time he took the field, had burned his uniform following a game.

Both catchers, Whitt and Martinez, were hitting below .200.

Reliever Gary Lavelle had been unable to pitch at all, and had elected to have a tendon transplanted into his left elbow, one of the most serious operations a pitcher can have.

Dave Stieb, the Jays' ace for many years, was 0–6 with a 6.83 ERA.

Though the failures of Key and Henke had been equally costly at least in combination, Dave Stieb is the marquee name on the Blue Jay pitching staff, and it was his shortcomings that were the center of attention. Some said that he wasn't throwing his slider like he used to, while others felt that, nursing a tender elbow, Stieb was not throwing *anything* like he had in his good years. To my untrained eye Stieb's stuff was, if not quite what it was in 1983, plenty good enough to win. Stieb was simply trying to make perfect pitches, not only trying to hit the

black but trying to hit the black with a breaking pitch. On the first pitch. If he missed the corner he was behind the hitter and if he caught the corner he'd try to do it again and make it break a little sharper. He was pitching like a rookie, pitching like Rich Gale or Tim Lollar.

My opinion, since everybody has one, is that Stieb's stuff had changed just enough that he no longer knew how to pitch within himself, no longer had a clear idea of exactly what he could do and what he couldn't do. In a notorious perfectionist, unable to accept his own failures or those of his teammates, this redefinition of ability had triggered a crisis of confidence, and Stieb was trying defiantly to prove that he could still do things that in reality he could never do consistently. In any case, after the first six trips through the starting rotation Stieb and Key did not have a win and Alexander had demanded a trade. Those are the top three starters for the defending division champions, who were now in deep wax.

And yet, the Blue Jays did not die. In spring training Jimy Williams, the rookie manager, had moved Lloyd Moseby into the leadoff spot, shifting Damaso Garcia to ninth with Fernandez second. Garcia, the former leadoff man, walks about as often as a southern sheriff wins the Nobel Peace Prize and steals bases in a way that makes you wish he really wouldn't, so everybody who knows anything pretty much agreed that this was an obvious move that needed to be made. Williams's selected this innocuous maneuver as a kind of Pawn to Queen Four to open up his managerial game. Garcia, however, was unhappy about the move, and with the Blue Jays struggling the reorganization of the daily box scores became a daily reminder of the symbolic separation between the Blue Jays and their successful 1985 campaign. Although no reasonable connection could be drawn between the switch and the slump (the Blue Jays were scoring about as many runs as anyone in the league, but were being killed by their pitching), Williams relented and returned Garcia to leadoff on May 8, remarking that "I still believe what we did in spring training was right, but our record says 'do something.'"

During this period two pitchers pitched well. Mark Eichorn, the true American League Rookie of the Year, posted an ERA of about 1.00 through the first two months, leading the staff in appearances from his long relief role and posting about three times as many strikeouts as hits allowed. Jim Clancy pitched fairly well with excellent offensive support, winning a couple of games in April and three more in May. Jimmy Key was the first of the confused pitchers to get his arm screwed on right, posting a 3–2 record and a 2.09 ERA in June. Tom Henke saved six games in June and had a 1.15 ERA.

The Blue Jays went 17–11 in June and didn't gain an inch on the front-running Sox, but it felt good to be over .500 and not looking up at all six teams. In early July, Garcia, getting in the spirit of things, reportedly went to Williams and said that he didn't care where he hit as long as Tony Fernandez was the leadoff man. Fernandez, unfortunately, responded to this unique gesture of esprit de corps by emulating Garcia. After drawing 43 walks in 1985 and 19 the first half of 1986, he decided that accepting further walks would be a sign of defective manhood.

When the Red Sox stumbled in July, the Blue Jays edged further up the list. They were 15–11 in July, and ended the month five and a half out, in a knot with four other teams such that any could swing from second to sixth in three days. The Blue Jays opened August by playing seven games against the Orioles in 13 days, games that would surely eliminate one team or the other and turn the six-team race into a five-team race. Going into those series five losses in seven would have looked like a cyanide pill, and yet the Jays lost five of the seven games and for good measure lost two out of three in an intervening trip to Texas, and did not die. Bouncing back with five straight wins over Texas and Chicago, they arrived at August 20 with a 65–56 record, six and a half behind Boston and two ahead of Baltimore. When the bottom dropped out on the Orioles and Cleveland drifted ten behind, the Blue Jays were suddenly very much alive in a four-team race.

After losing the last of the Chicago series and one to Minnesota, the Blue Jays finally had the hot streak they had been waiting four months for. They won the final two in the Metrodome and moved into third place, still six and a half behind but now positioned to pounce if the Red Sox came through on their long-promised collapse. Toronto beat the Indians three straight in Cleveland, terminating the Indians' pennant fantasies and cutting the margin to four and a half.

Coming home to face Minnesota, the Jays trailed 5–4 in the ninth, but rallied to beat the Twins and cut the margin to three and a half. Two more wins gained no more ground on Boston but cut the Yankees out of the race as the Yanks lost twice in Seattle; it was now the morning of September 1, and it was a two-team race.

Who could have known that, come September, the Red Sox would blow the race apart? The Blue Jays did not fold, or at least did not fold until it mattered little, but their nine-game streak ended on September 2 and in the first week of September the Red Sox did not lose. An eleven-game Bosox streak, a combination of dramatic rallies and blowouts, finished the Blue Jay charge and finished the pennant race. Looking over Kelly Gruber, Manny Lee, Cecil Fielder and Ron Shepherd, the Jays lost seven of their last eight and are in the books at 86–76, nine and a half behind the Sox.

They were closer than that. An 0–7 record in September ruined Jim Clancy's record, but he was better than 14–14. The Blue Jays scored 809 runs, second in the league and 15 more than Boston. They allowed 733, fifth in the league and 37 more than the Sox. They must make up 22 runs next year to catch the Sox.

Considering offense and defense, the Blue Jay outfield is one of the greatest ever. Bell and Barfield drove in 108 runs apiece, scored over a hundred apiece, hit over 30 doubles and 30 homers each and finished one and two in the league in outfield assists. Between them Lloyd Moseby was marvelous, if not quite an MVP candidate. I'll try to write a separate article on the greatest outfields ever, but this one is certainly right up there.

The Blue Jay infield, however, was not a strength in 1986. Tony Fernandez was excellent, although David Driscoll, who was the first person to tell me that Jesse Barfield would be a star, says that Fernandez doesn't play hitters well yet and still has a lot to learn about turning the double play. Anyway, Fernandez was obviously one of the best in the league at his position. No other Blue Jay infielder was. Willie Upshaw and Damaso Garcia, once young stars, did not have good seasons, with both declines continuing a three-year pattern. Both members of the Mullinorg platoon had disappointing seasons by their own standards.

The pitching, both starting and relief, was awful the first two months and pretty good the rest of the year. Toronto pitchers threw only 38 wild pitches, fewest in the league, and walked only 487 men, fourth in the league but only 13 more than Boston, the league leader.

The defense supporting these pitchers was good, the outfield defense superb and the infield above average. With the exception of the Cardinals, the Blue Jays are the best defensive team in the major leagues. Their .984 fielding percentage was the best in the majors.

My impressions of Jimy Williams as a first-year manager were excellent. I thought he did a fine job of rallying the team from a difficult position, and I can't see what he did that helped in any way to put them in that position. I didn't mention the 1985 post-season and the McCarver theory, which might explain some of the trouble getting started, but Williams's Blue Jays handled that better than Herzog's Cardinals. Williams was a big-inning manager, as the Blue Jays laid down only 24 sacrifice bunts, the fewest of any team in the division and tied for fewest in the league.

Blue Jay fans continued to pack into their cracking old wreck of a park. The Blue Jays drew 2,455,477, almost exactly the same as in 1985. They remained the top draw in the division, about 200,000 ahead of the Yankees.

Trying to look ahead to 1987, the Blue Jays' chances would seem to be as good as the Yankees' and better than anybody else's in the division. Dave Stieb could make up 22 runs by having a better April. Stieb was 5–3 with a 3.56 ERA after the All-Star break, and should be nearer himself in 1987. Joe Johnson, acquired from Atlanta for Doyle Alexander, seemed to find the American League to his liking and should, at the least, stabilize the staff. The Blue Jays' bullpen is excellent, their infield fair to good, their outfield superb, and their catching covered. A lot depends on how many starting pitchers have a good season.

Ernie WHITT, Catcher

	G	AB	Hit	2B	3B	HR	Run	RBI	TBB	SO	SB	CS	Avg
5.15 years		447	111	21	2	17	52	63	48	60	3	3	.248
1986	131	395	106	19	2	16	48	56	35	39	0	1	.268
First Half	62	180	44	7	1	8	26	26	22	11	0	1	.244
Second Half	69	215	62	12	1	8	22	30	13	28	0	0	.288
Vs. RHP		349	89	19	2	13		49	33	31	0	1	.255
Vs. LHP		46	17	0	0	3		7	2	8	0	0	.370
Home	65	189	50	12	2	7	23	27	22	21	0	0	.265
Road	66	206	56	7	0	9	25	29	13	18	0	1	.272
Grass	51	162	42	4	0	8	20	22	12	12	0	1	.259
Turf	80	233	64	15	2	8	28	34	23	27	0	0	.275

George BELL, Left Field

	G	AB	Hit	2B	3B	HR	Run	RBI	TBB	SO	SB	CS	Avg
3.54 years		601	172	32	6	26	84	90	33	80	12	5	.287
1986	159	641	198	38	6	31	101	108	41	62	7	8	.309
First Half	81	325	100	16	4	16	53	59	23	29	6	4	.308
Second Half	78	316	98	22	2	15	48	49	18	33	1	4	.310
Vs. RHP		462	139	28	6	21		81	31	44	7	8	.301
Vs. LHP		179	59	10	0	10		27	10	18	0	0	.330
Home	78	300	98	17	5	15	53	57	24	22	4	2	.327
Road	81	341	100	21	1	16	48	51	17	40	3	6	.293
Grass	63	265	78	14	0	11	34	39	13	34	2	5	.294
Turf	96	376	120	24	6	20	67	69	28	28	5	3	.319

Willie UPSHAW, First Base

	G	AB	Hit	2B	3B	HR	Run	RBI	TBB	SO	SB	CS	Avg
5.96 years		537	144	26	7	16	79	71	56	84	11	7	.268
1986	155	573	144	28	6	9	85	60	78	87	23	5	.251
First Half	77	284	74	14	3	2	50	31	45	44	14	1	.261
Second Half	78	289	70	14	3	7	35	29	33	43	9	4	.242
Vs. RHP		394	104	21	5	5		41	61	49	23	5	.264
Vs. LHP		179	40	7	1	4		19	17	38	0	0	.223
Home	76	267	66	16	3	3	45	32	43	46	12	1	.247
Road	79	306	78	12	3	6	40	28	35	41	11	4	.255
Grass	62	238	59	8	2	5	31	21	31	31	10	3	.248
Turf	93	335	85	20	4	4	54	39	47	56	13	2	.254

Lloyd MOSEBY, Center Field

	G	AB	Hit	2B	3B	HR	Run	RBI	TBB	SO	SB	CS	Avg
6.01 years		592	154	29	8	17	85	78	58	116	27	11	.261
1986	152	589	149	24	5	21	89	86	64	122	32	11	.253
First Half	80	323	92	13	3	12	49	46	40	72	19	9	.285
Second Half	72	266	57	11	2	9	40	40	24	50	13	2	.214
Vs. RHP		401	106	18	3	15		61	54	85	31	10	.264
Vs. LHP		188	43	6	2	6		25	10	37	1	1	.229
Home	79	290	72	14	0	11	51	43	38	67	22	4	.248
Road	73	299	77	10	5	10	38	43	26	55	10	7	.258
Grass	55	222	58	9	4	6	31	31	21	43	6	5	.261
Turf	97	367	91	15	1	15	58	55	43	79	26	6	.248

Damaso GARCIA, Second Base

	G	AB	Hit	2B	3B	HR	Run	RBI	TBB	SO	SB	CS	Avg
5.75 years		635	182	30	5	6	80	52	19	51	34	15	.286
1986	122	424	119	22	0	6	57	46	13	32	9	6	.281
First Half	69	242	71	17	0	2	39	27	11	17	6	2	.293
Second Half	53	182	48	5	0	4	18	19	2	15	3	4	.264
Vs. RHP		285	74	13	0	4		31	11	18	8	5	.260
Vs. LHP		139	45	9	0	2		15	2	14	1	1	.324
Home	57	174	49	10	0	3	26	27	3	17	4	0	.282
Road	65	250	70	12	0	3	31	19	10	15	5	6	.280
Grass	47	180	55	11	0	2	24	11	7	11	5	5	.306
Turf	75	244	64	11	0	4	33	35	6	21	4	1	.262

Jesse BARFIELD, Right Field

	G	AB	Hit	2B	3B	HR	Run	RBI	TBB	SO	SB	CS	Avg
4.41 years		527	144	25	4	29	85	85	54	131	10	7	.273
1986	158	589	170	35	2	40	107	108	69	146	8	8	.289
First Half	82	310	90	18	2	21	55	61	29	67	3	6	.290
Second Half	76	279	80	17	0	19	52	47	40	79	5	2	.287
Vs. RHP		441	128	26	2	31		82	42	105	8	8	.290
Vs. LHP		148	42	9	0	9		26	27	41	0	0	.284
Home	80	291	81	22	1	16	53	51	42	70	6	4	.278
Road	78	298	89	13	1	24	54	57	27	76	2	4	.299
Grass	62	235	70	11	1	16	40	43	24	59	1	2	.298
Turf	96	354	100	24	1	24	67	65	45	87	7	6	.282

Rance MULLINIKS, Third Base

	G	AB	Hit	2B	3B	HR	Run	RBI	TBB	SO	SB	CS	Avg
5.06 years		453	121	30	2	9	58	54	53	67	2	2	.268
1986	117	348	90	22	0	11	50	45	43	60	1	1	.259
First Half	75	229	62	12	0	10	34	36	29	37	1	0	.271
Second Half	42	119	28	10	0	1	16	9	14	23	0	1	.235
Vs. RHP		328	86	21	0	11		44	43	56	1	1	.262
Vs. LHP		20	4	1	0	0		1	0	4	0	0	.200
Home	58	176	50	14	0	5	27	23	23	30	0	1	.284
Road	59	172	40	8	0	6	23	22	20	30	1	0	.233
Grass	45	130	32	6	0	6	19	19	14	22	1	0	.246
Turf	72	218	58	16	0	5	31	26	29	38	0	1	.266

Cliff JOHNSON, Designated Hitter

	G	AB	Hit	2B	3B	HR	Run	RBI	TBB	SO	SB	CS	Avg
8.45 years		467	120	22	1	23	64	83	67	85	1	1	.258
1986	107	336	84	12	1	15	48	55	52	57	0	1	.250
First Half	68	220	63	10	1	11	31	41	29	40	0	1	.286
Second Half	39	116	21	2	0	4	17	14	23	17	0	0	.181
Vs. RHP		229	53	5	1	7		31	32	46	0	1	.231
Vs. LHP		107	31	7	0	8		24	20	11	0	0	.290
Home	57	174	47	6	0	11	28	34	25	28	0	1	.270
Road	50	162	37	6	1	4	20	21	27	29	0	0	.228
Grass	41	130	26	4	1	4	17	17	25	22	0	0	.200
Turf	66	206	58	8	0	11	31	38	27	35	0	1	.282

Tony FERNANDEZ, Shortstop

	G	AB	Hit	2B	3B	HR	Run	RBI	TBB	SO	SB	CS	Avg
2.64 years		576	170	27	9	6	74	52	34	42	16	10	.295
1986	163	687	213	33	9	10	91	65	27	52	25	12	.310
First Half	83	343	105	17	5	4	47	32	19	23	13	8	.306
Second Half	80	344	108	16	4	6	44	33	8	29	12	4	.314
Vs. RHP		482	148	21	7	5		35	18	31	18	7	.307
Vs. LHP		205	65	12	2	5		30	9	21	7	5	.317
Home	81	337	108	14	5	4	47	24	11	21	15	5	.320
Road	82	350	105	19	4	6	44	41	16	31	10	7	.300
Grass	64	272	80	14	2	5	31	30	13	26	8	6	.294
Turf	99	415	133	19	7	5	60	35	14	26	17	6	.320

Garth IORG, Third Base

	G	AB	Hit	2B	3B	HR	Run	RBI	TBB	SO	SB	CS	Avg
4.99 years		429	114	23	3	3	43	42	19	49	4	3	.265
1986	137	327	85	19	1	3	30	44	20	47	3	0	.260
First Half	66	138	37	2	0	2	15	20	6	26	2	0	.268
Second Half	71	189	48	17	1	1	15	24	14	21	1	0	.254
Vs. RHP		161	37	8	1	0		14	7	27	2	0	.230
Vs. LHP		166	48	11	0	3		30	13	20	1	0	.289
Home	68	167	36	10	1	1	16	18	8	29	2	0	.216
Road	69	160	49	9	0	2	14	26	12	18	1	0	.306
Grass	57	129	42	8	0	2	12	22	10	14	1	0	.326
Turf	80	198	43	11	1	1	18	22	10	33	2	0	.217

Jimmy KEY

Year	(W–L)	GS	Run	Avg	DP	Avg	SB	Avg
1985	(14-6)	32	149	4.66	43	1.34	18	.56
1986	(14-11)	35	179	5.11	31	.89	18	.51
1985-1986		67	328	4.90	74	1.10	36	.54

	1986		1985		1984		84-86
	ERA	W–L	ERA	W–L	ERA	W–L	W–L
Total	3.57	14-11	3.00	14-6	4.65	4-5	32-22
Home	4.50	7-9	2.66	10-3	5.13	1-2	18-14
Road	2.67	7-2	3.54	4-3	4.29	3-3	14-8
East	2.93	7-6	3.35	7-3	4.70	2-4	16-13
West	4.37	7-5	2.58	7-3	4.60	2-1	16-9
1st Half	4.44	7-5	2.59	7-3	4.23	2-4	16-12
2nd Half	2.87	7-6	3.45	7-3	4.98	2-1	16-10
Turf	4.76	8-9	2.62	10-3	5.93	1-2	19-14
Grass	2.04	6-2	3.75	4-3	3.41	3-3	13-8
Day	3.43	6-7		3-1	5.21	3-1	12-10
Night	3.69	8-4	2.92	11-4	4.40	1-4	20-12
April	11.85	0-1	2.41	0-2	4.63	2-1	2-4
May	5.19	3-2	2.87	3-0	4.32	0-1	6-3
June	2.09	3-2	2.17	3-0	3.52	0-2	6-4
July	3.24	3-1	3.20	3-2	13.50	0-0	6-3
August	3.51	2-3	3.93	2-2	3.14	2-1	6-6
September	2.01	3-2	3.35	3-0	2.70	0-0	6-2

Dave STIEB

Year	(W–L)	GS	Run	Avg	DP	Avg	SB	Avg
1984	(16-8)	35	156	4.46	37	1.06	13	.37
1985	(14-13)	36	160	4.44	31	.86	14	.39
1986	(7-12)	34	160	4.71	30	.88	20	.59
1979-1986		244	1064	4.36	259	1.06	116	.48

	1986		1985	1984	1983	1982	82-86
	ERA	W–L	ERA	ERA	ERA	ERA	W–L
Total	4.74	7-12	2.48	2.83	3.04	3.25	71-59
Home	3.93	5-5	2.96	2.71	2.97	3.20	41-28
Road	6.17	2-7	2.12	2.93	3.13	3.28	30-31
East	4.25	4-4	2.18	3.45	2.63	4.16	28-26
West	5.17	3-8	2.73	2.24	3.41	2.50	43-33
1st Half	5.78	2-9	1.84	2.42	2.54	3.96	37-34
2nd Half	3.56	5-3	3.16	3.27	3.62	2.59	34-25
Turf	4.14	6-7	2.68	2.42	3.47		39-29
Grass	6.57	1-5	2.22	3.42	2.20		15-16
Day	5.96	0-5	3.58	2.30	3.44	3.49	26-24
Night	4.05	7-7	1.78	3.06	2.76	3.06	45-35
April	6.75	0-3	2.93	1.88	1.58	3.82	9-9
May	5.36	1-3	1.69	2.27	1.73	3.53	16-9
June	4.97	1-2	1.51	3.02	4.46	5.03	9-13
July	5.01	1-2	2.03	2.25	4.39	3.35	12-8
August	4.96	1-0	3.80	2.25	2.19	3.00	10-8
September	2.45	3-2	3.04	5.28	4.31	1.74	15-12

Jim CLANCY

Year	(W–L)	GS	Run	Avg	DP	Avg	SB	Avg
1984	(13-15)	36	152	4.22	50	1.39	22	.61
1985	(9-6)	23	120	5.22	15	.65	12	.52
1986	(14-14)	34	159	4.68	27	.79	20	.59
1977-1986		277	1148	4.14	266	.96	135	.49

	1986		1985	1984	1983	1982	82-86
	ERA	W–L	ERA	ERA	ERA	ERA	W–L
Total	3.94	14-14	3.78	5.12	3.91	3.71	67-60
Home	5.26	5-6	2.53	5.86	4.08	4.79	31-28
Road	3.07	9-8	4.48	4.65	3.74	2.85	36-32
East	3.94	5-10	4.55	6.30	3.25	5.65	28-36
West	3.94	9-4	3.12	4.14	4.57	2.54	39-24
1st Half	4.08	8-5	4.48	5.16	3.63	3.56	33-30
2nd Half	3.81	6-9	2.68	5.08	4.15	3.90	34-30
Turf	4.72	9-7	2.67	5.27	3.88		32-24
Grass	2.93	5-7	4.87	4.96	3.98		19-22
Day	3.21	6-4	3.96	6.22	3.51	5.36	21-23
Night	4.37	8-10	3.66	4.67	4.12	3.00	46-37
April	3.00	2-1	3.60	2.55	3.32	5.93	5-6
May	4.17	3-2	5.96	5.12	4.21	4.34	14-9
June	5.86	2-2	4.19	8.53	3.30	1.27	12-11
July	1.54	5-0	2.05	5.97	2.81	5.84	14-9
August	4.42	2-2		3.49	3.26	5.23	11-8
September	4.89	0-7	3.14	6.63	6.37	1.94	11-17

John CERUTTI

Year	(W–L)	GS	Run	Avg	DP	Avg	SB	Avg
1986	(9-4)	20	114	5.70	24	1.20	14	.70

	G	IP	W–L	H	ER	SO	ERA
Total	34	145.1	9-4	150	67	89	4.15
Home	14	58.0	2-1	66	33	41	5.12
Road	20	87.1	7-3	84	34	48	3.50
East	17	82.0	7-1	81	31	47	3.40
West	17	63.1	2-3	69	36	42	5.12
1st Half	12	53.1	4-1	58	23	32	3.88
2nd Half	22	92.0	5-3	92	44	57	4.30
Turf	18	77.0	4-1	84	41	50	4.79
Grass	16	68.1	5-3	66	26	39	3.42
Day	8	37.0	3-1	27	17	23	4.14
Night	26	108.1	6-3	123	50	66	4.15
April							
May	3	17.0	1-1	11	5	12	2.65
June	8	30.2	2-0	40	15	16	4.40
July	7	30.2	2-2	31	14	14	4.11
August	10	34.1	3-0	39	20	26	5.24
September	6	32.2	1-1	29	13	21	3.58

Tom HENKE

1986	G	IP	W–L	Sv	H	ER	SO	ERA
Total	63	91.1	9-5	27	63	34	118	3.35
Home	33	42.2	5-2	12	28	15	46	3.16
Road	30	48.2	4-3	15	35	19	72	3.51
East	32	46.1	4-3	17	32	18	58	3.50
West	31	45.0	5-2	10	31	16	60	3.20
1st Half	31	43.1	6-3	12	32	19	58	3.95
2nd Half	32	48.0	3-2	15	31	15	60	2.81
Turf	38	54.1	6-4	13	36	21	64	3.48
Grass	25	37.0	3-1	14	27	13	54	3.16
Day	22	30.2	7-1	5	23	11	30	3.23
Night	41	60.2	2-4	22	40	23	88	3.41
April	6	7.0	2-1	3	8	9	13	11.57
May	11	17.1	2-2	1	12	8	27	4.15
June	11	15.2	2-0	6	12	2	14	1.15
July	11	14.2	1-0	5	6	4	19	2.45
August	10	17.1	1-0	4	13	4	20	2.08
September	14	19.1	1-2	8	12	7	25	3.26

RECORDS WITH DIFFERENT STARTING CATCHERS

Catcher	Inn	ER	W–L	ERA	GS	SB	Avg
Whitt	985.0	449	60-49	4.10	109	63	.58
Martinez	427.0	195	22-24	4.11	47	28	.60
Hearron	64.0	25	4-3	3.52	7	4	.57

STARTING PITCHERS' AVERAGE TIME AND ATTENDANCE RECORDS

Pitcher	Time	Attendance
Key	2:49	913
Stieb	2:47	910
Clancy	2:42	912
Cerutti	2:52	416

OTHERS

Pitcher	(W–L)	GS	Run	Avg	DP	Avg	SB	Avg	Time	Att.
Alexander	(5-4)	17	97	5.71	16	.94	10	.59	2:51	427
Johnson	(7-2)	15	73	4.87	16	1.07	3	.20	2:32	404
Acker	(2-4)	5	16	3.20	1	.20	8	1.60	2:50	120
Lamp	(2-6)	2	8	4.00	2	1.00	1	.50	2:44	66
Ward	(0-1)	1	3	3.00	2	2.00	1	1.00	3:09	33

THE GREATEST OUTFIELDS EVER

This was supposed to be an article about the greatest outfields ever. However, after I got the research done I didn't know which outfield was greater than which one or how to rank them, so I decided just to present some info about the greatest outfields ever and let you draw your own conclusions.

The Toronto outfield has now been together for three years, four if you count the tag end of the 1983 season, when George Bell came back up. I set three years as the minimum standard for inclusion in the study, to cut out the teams like the '62 Giants which got great one-year production out of players who were just together for a couple of years. To form the statistics of the three players into something that you can read and make sense of, I just divided the totals for the three outfielders by three, thus representing the skills of the three players as if they were one. For the Blue Jays, this creates:

Year	G	AB	R	H	2B	3B	HR	RBI	BB	SO	SB	Avg.	RC
1983	106	346	56	99	16	5	16	55	26	71	10	.287	58
1984	142	506	78	145	27	7	19	76	46	96	19	.286	84
1985	155	577	91	158	31	7	24	83	62	108	27	.274	95
1986	156	606	99	172	32	4	31	101	58	110	16	.284	106

The right-most column is basic runs created. As you can see at a glance, the Blue Jay outfield had their best year so far in 1986, and in fact has had their best year each year they were together. They'll be 27 this year—all three are within a few days of the same age—and 27 is usually the best year for any group of players, so there's a good chance they could push it one step further this time. The runs created per 25 outs of the three have been between 5.65 and 6.09 all four years.

When your *average* outfielder scores 99 runs, drives in 101, hits 30 doubles and 30 homers, and steals 16 bases, you've got a good corner on an offense, but this is certainly not the greatest offensive performance ever by a trio of outfielders. Bob Meusel, Earle Combs, and Babe Ruth were together for five years, and never failed to create over a hundred runs apiece:

Year	G	AB	R	H	2B	3B	HR	RBI	BB	SO	SB	Avg.	RC
1925	135	525	93	163	27	9	20	88	59	55	8	.310	102
1926	135	505	108	165	28	7	22	94	76	44	12	.327	113
1927	146	568	123	199	37	13	25	110	82	59	15	.350	146
1928	145	560	119	174	36	11	24	104	84	59	7	.310	122
1929	126	492	95	159	25	8	20	92	53	45	6	.322	100

This great Yankee outfield never hit less than .310, either, but then neither did the Browns outfield of the early twenties—Baby Doll Jacobson, Jack Tobin, and Ken Williams:

Year	G	AB	R	H	2B	3B	HR	RBI	BB	SO	SB	Avg.	RC
1919	104	389	52	125	21	7	5	48	29	32	8	.320	64
1920	147	574	94	193	34	12	8	85	42	29	17	.335	104
1921	149	606	112	212	33	13	12	89	50	31	12	.351	124
1922	148	588	113	192	30	12	20	108	59	30	21	.327	119
1923	148	595	91	194	33	11	17	82	50	24	11	.327	113
1924	134	515	89	161	31	8	13	76	51	15	11	.312	92
1925	107	381	70	126	24	5	14	69	30	15	9	.330	76

The batting stats are impressive, but (as always) you have to remember that the value of the stats is determined by what they mean in terms of wins and losses, and the ratio between wins and losses wasn't any better in the twenties than in any other decade. These guys were good—but never good enough to get the Browns into the World Series. Hitting .351 in 1921 is impressive, but seven American League regulars hit .351 or better than year. The averages compiled by the Pirates outfield of Stargell, Matty Alou and Roberto Clemente in the 1960s are a lot more impressive:

Year	G	AB	R	H	2B	3B	HR	RBI	BB	SO	SB	Avg.	RC
1966	145	553	92	179	26	7	21	83	39	87	11	.324	105
1967	140	532	81	173	22	8	15	70	44	83	9	.326	96
1968	135	498	63	145	20	6	14	59	42	69	8	.290	75
1969	148	576	94	189	31	8	16	77	53	76	9	.328	109
1970	133	521	77	157	20	7	15	64	37	68	7	.301	83

In 1966, when the three Pirate outfielders hit .324, only two other National League regulars hit as well. They sustained that kind of a performance for several years and played good defense as well, but on the other hand the won-lost record of the team wasn't all that good.

One outfield which did lead its team to the top was the Yankee combination of Charlie Keller, Joe DiMaggio, and Tommy Henrich:

Year	G	AB	R	H	2B	3B	HR	RBI	BB	SO	SB	Avg.	RC
1939	110	402	86	135	24	5	17	89	61	31	5	.336	93
1940	120	434	84	137	25	10	21	93	72	42	3	.317	101
1941	141	529	110	164	31	9	31	111	86	39	4	.311	125
1942	144	546	102	158	28	9	20	96	80	44	7	.290	100
1946	144	535	90	145	25	7	25	93	86	63	2	.271	96
1947	109	412	81	121	24	8	16	77	59	35	2	.293	80
1948	127	476	96	146	28	9	23	100	61	32	1	.306	101
1949	84	266	55	80	13	3	14	56	55	22	1	.302	59

Counting 1949, when DiMaggio was hurt half the year, Keller was a pinch hitter and Henrich playing quite a bit of first base, this unit was together for eight years, which is very unusual. What makes it even more unusual is that they lost three of their best years together to the war. The Yankees won five pennants in those years, and these guys contributed a bunch to it. In addition to hitting for good averages they played good defense, ran well, had incredible strikeout-to-walk ratios, and hit for power.

Between 1928 and 1932 the Philadelphia A's finished second, first, first, first, and second with an average of 101 wins a year. The three outfielders were Bing Miller, Mule Haas, and Al Simmons, and their averages were:

Year	G	AB	R	H	2B	3B	HR	RBI	BB	SO	SB	Avg.	RC
1928	116	435	65	141	29	7	10	77	27	25	4	.325	79
1929	143	572	104	193	38	11	19	111	35	34	9	.338	111
1930	141	557	111	182	37	10	16	111	43	30	8	.327	94
1931	122	496	87	164	36	8	13	87	38	30	3	.331	95
1932	131	511	92	159	24	6	16	91	43	45	4	.311	95

Bing Miller was 33 years old when he hooked up with the other two guys to form this outfield. Ty Cobb started out young and was in combination with all kinds of different people—Cobb, Crawford, and Matty McIntyre; Cobb, Crawford, and Davy Jones; Cobb, Crawford, and Veach; Cobb, Heilmann, and Veach. Detroit kept their players forever, just as they still do today, so you can make all kinds of combinations. From 1906 through 1910 they had Cobb, Crawford, Jones, and McIntyre (all four left-handed hitters). I don't know which combination was actually the best outfield, but the best numbers came after the lively ball era began in 1920:

Year	G	AB	R	H	2B	3B	HR	RBI	BB	SO	SB	Avg.	RC
1914	104	353	50	105	16	9	2	49	43	27	19	.297	54
1916	144	520	87	167	31	12	3	77	57	40	34	.321	81
1917	152	572	81	188	32	16	6	97	54	44	29	.328	92
1918	106	402	59	126	17	11	4	60	37	18	23	.314	70
1919	134	524	84	185	37	15	4	88	36	32	18	.352	102
1920	137	528	81	166	32	9	7	88	44	27	9	.315	88
1921	142	574	116	214	41	14	16	123	52	29	13	.372	123
1922	137	533	96	192	34	13	11	106	52	26	9	.360	114
1923	134	458	90	165	32	7	9	81	56	25	9	.360	107

Actually, Heilmann played first base in 1919 and 1920, but they were all with the team. Cobb's rival Tris Speaker was a member of an outfield that has long been considered perhaps the best defensive unit of all time, although their offensive totals weren't tremendous. Speaker and Harry Hooper are in the Hall of Fame; Duffy Lewis was the third Boston outfielder:

Year	G	AB	R	H	2B	3B	HR	RBI	BB	SO	SB	Avg.	RC
1910	149	554	79	164	19	10	6	53	49		28	.296	78
1911	134	501	82	158	29	8	6	67	52		25	.315	84
1912	151	584	106	177	36	11	6	84	67		30	.303	81
1913	146	552	83	174	32	15	2	67	52	43	28	.316	87
1914	148	537	79	157	35	14	2	70	64	38	28	.293	83
1915	150	557	89	157	25	11	1	65	72	38	22	.282	78

There weren't a lot of runs scored then, and the Red Sox won the pennant in 1912 and 1915 with these guys.

The Red Sox had another great outfield in the fifties, with Ted Williams, Jimmie Piersall, and Jackie Jensen:

Year	G	AB	R	H	2B	3B	HR	RBI	BB	SO	SB	Avg.	RC
1954	134	480	87	143	24	3	21	81	84	49	9	.297	94
1955	133	470	80	139	24	5	22	87	82	46	8	.297	96
1956	147	526	81	165	30	6	19	89	83	43	6	.314	109
1957	143	524	94	158	28	3	27	84	85	54	7	.302	109
1958	138	459	73	130	22	2	23	85	80	52	7	.284	88

And another one in the seventies, with Lynn, Rice, and Evans:

Year	G	AB	R	H	2B	3B	HR	RBI	BB	SO	SB	Avg.	RC
1974	57	191	24	55	8	4	4	31	16	32	1	.290	27
1975	139	501	85	154	33	6	19	88	48	91	8	.307	88
1976	144	530	71	148	30	7	17	71	44	94	9	.279	72
1977	121	457	75	134	22	7	24	75	44	80	4	.292	88
1978	153	572	90	166	27	7	31	95	66	98	6	.290	116
1979	152	546	101	171	35	3	33	103	69	84	6	.312	117
1980	127	461	73	132	30	5	18	69	51	75	8	.287	70

When they lost Lynn, the Sox struggled for a couple of years before putting Armas in center field—not as good a defensive outfielder, but sustaining an impressive level of offense for the outfield:

Year	G	AB	R	H	2B	3B	HR	RBI	BB	SO	SB	Avg.	RC
1983	142	557	80	143	25	2	32	97	50	110	1	.256	86
1984	159	642	109	180	30	7	34	116	57	124	3	.281	111
1985	134	516	82	141	22	3	26	82	61	90	3	.273	87
1986	143	524	75	150	31	3	19	88	61	91	1	.286	88

Armas was part of another outstanding outfield, in Oakland with Dwayne Murphy and Rickey Henderson:

Year	G	AB	R	H	2B	3B	HR	RBI	BB	SO	SB	Avg.	RC
1979	97	339	45	88	11	3	8	33	45	62	16	.260	44
1980	158	597	95	170	19	5	19	77	83	93	44	.285	91
1981	108	418	66	116	17	4	14	57	52	91	24	.278	60
1982	146	538	87	132	19	2	22	78	81	115	53	.246	77

An outfield that was perhaps even more outstanding defensively than it was offensively. The other top-notch outfield of the last ten years was the Cincinnati combination of Griffey, Foster, and Geronimo:

Year	G	AB	R	H	2B	3B	HR	RBI	BB	SO	SB	Avg.	RC
1973	60	150	20	37	7	1	4	19	11	30	3	.249	20
1974	115	326	43	88	15	4	5	38	35	64	7	.269	40
1975	138	476	78	136	21	6	11	59	52	79	10	.287	65
1976	147	537	85	170	24	10	12	81	57	83	24	.317	93
1977	154	564	98	171	29	5	25	86	55	93	11	.304	99
1978	146	505	72	138	25	5	18	70	56	92	12	.273	74
1979	113	392	56	113	21	4	14	56	44	67	4	.287	58
1980	131	406	61	114	18	5	13	62	50	67	9	.280	67

Enough. There have been many times in history when a team would have two outstanding outfielders for a good chunk of time, but never stabilize the third position enough that you could even really evaluate the group. A few of the most noteworthy two-man teams: Curt Flood and Lou Brock, Sam Rice and Goose Goslin, Duke Snider and Carl Furillo, Ted Williams and Dom DiMaggio, Stan Musial and Enos Slaughter, Vada Pinson and Frank Robinson, Reggie Smith and Carl Yastrzemski, Mel Ott and Joe Moore, Roger Maris and Mickey Mantle, and Tim Raines and Andre Dawson.

I'm not going to rate all of these great outfields one against another, but I did have a couple of thoughts. If forced to pick one outfield over all the others, I would probably go with one of the two great Yankee outfields, I suppose leaning toward the Meusel/Combs/Ruth trio.

I have, at times, expressed the opinion that the Toronto outfield might be the greatest of all time. I now realize that that position is premature: We simply can't evaluate them fairly yet. I think that if you judge the Toronto outfield *by the weakest member*, it is one of the greatest ever. I don't know who the weakest of the Toronto three is—Moseby, I suppose. Moseby is a hell of a player, and it would be hard to say that there has ever been an outfield that had three players of that caliber, even the '27 Yankees. In addition, there has probably never been another outfield in which all three men had the speed to play center field and all three men threw well enough to play right field—and if there has, I'll guarantee that they didn't all hit twenty homers a year.

But there have been many outfields that have had two Hall of Famers, one of whom was somebody like Babe Ruth or Ty Cobb or Ted Williams or Stan Musial. None of the Toronto outfielders is quite in that class yet. I am surprised to see how many outfields there have been which have had better combined stats than Toronto's—for example, Boston in 1984.

You can evaluate a player before his career is through, but you really can't evaluate him before you know that he has reached his peak. The Toronto outfield may not have had its best year yet. But if they're better in 1987 than they were in 1986, you'll have to say that they're as good as any outfield has ever been.

CLEVELAND INDIANS

Runners on Base:	2,100
Opponents on Base:	2,210
Net Disadvantage:	−110
Won-Lost Record:	84-78

For the fans and followers of the Cleveland Indians, the 1986 season was the brightest in many years. The Indians in '86 not only finished over .500 (after all, they finished over .500 in '81, '79, '76, and '68) but finished over .500 with exciting young players. For the first time in at least 20 years, the Indians give the strong impression that their work has been organized, the enemy has been located, the target is visible on radar. In the spirit of fair play, the nation's sports fans must hope that the target can be destroyed. It is well past Cleveland's turn.

Leading the charge in 1986 was a formidable offense; calling retreat was a primitive pitching staff. The Indians scored 831 runs, 22 more than any other major league team—yet they allowed even more than they scored, as well as more than any other major-league team. They had 1,620 hits, 80 more than any other major-league team, and the most since 1980. Their .284 team batting average was the highest in the majors since 1982. They had 2,451 total bases, most in the majors. They had 45 triples, tied for the major-league lead. The Indians scored 39.6% of their baserunners, the highest percentage of any major-league team.

Offensively the Indians in 1986 had only one pronounced weak spot, that being catcher. The Indians in the spring made the curious decision to release Jerry Willard, a 26-year-old catcher who had hit .270 for them in 1985 with good power, and rest their fate with Andy Allanson, an 220-pound 24-year-old with no experience above AA ball who had never hit a home run as a professional. Allanson was awful, hitting .225 with one homer and doing no better job of stopping the running game than Willard had done. One can't really understand the thinking here. Either there was a personality conflict, or else Corrales as a manager was looking around for a young Pat Corrales. He seems to have found one; Allanson's batting and slugging percentages were remarkably close to Corrales's career figures of .216 and .276.

Whatever the "thinking," the costs of this blunder were hidden by the offensive potency of the rest of the team. All four infielders (Tabler, Bernazard, Franco, and Jacoby) had solid to excellent seasons. Bernazard had a remarkable year, a Lou Whitaker year, and Franco hit .306 and cut his errors at shortstop in half. The infield was fair defensively but one of the best in the league at bat.

The outfielders were both abundant and effective. Brett Butler, though not having a good year, remained a valuable player capable of filling both a key defensive role (he is a fine defensive center fielder with an above average arm) and a key offensive role (he is one of the league's best leadoff men). Mel Hall and Cory Snyder had slugging percentages of .493 and .500, and the easily overlooked Carmen Castillo had his third straight good season in a limited role.

With those four players the Indians would have a good outfield. With the development of young Dave Clark, they'd have trouble deciding who to play in 1987. What made it an outstanding outfield was the magnificent performance of Joe Carter. In recent years the Indians' leadership, such as it was, was the quiet, dignified leadership of Andre Thornton or the brash, erratic leadership of Brett Butler. In 1986, in addition to having MVP numbers, Joe Carter emerged as one of those rare, aggressive on-field leaders in the mold of Kirk Gibson, George Brett, and Pete Rose. Leadership is a hard thing to define and there are people who think I am betraying sabermetrics every time I mention the word, but Carter was a player who gave the opposition *nothing*. If he hit a single and you didn't hustle in after it, he'd take second. If the team was ten runs behind, he'd try twice as hard, his theatrical hustle becoming an unmistakable message to the rest of the team that I'm not giving these bastards anything and you'd better not give them anything, either. They haven't beat us until we quit.

I saw a game in which the Yankees scored ten runs in an interminable four-pitcher inning in Cleveland. Carter came running off the field looking not like "God, I thought that would never end" but like "Man, have we got work to do." He went into the batter's box businesslike, intense, drove in a run, took an extra base—and ignited a 6-run rally. When the Blue Jays wiped the Indians out of the race in late August the Indians went into Fenway for the weekend. As if to say, "All right, that's enough of that. We've worked too hard to let this get away now," Carter went five-for-five in Fenway with three home runs—perhaps the best of the many remarkable box score lines that Carter would post during the season. Carter personified the in-your-face attitude of a player who didn't intend to accept any role except lead dog in the pack. That attitude spread to the rest of the team, and to my perception Carter was the key to the Indians playing well.

There were many things they didn't do well. Statistically, it was a case of one very powerful strength in an important area—the .284 team batting average—offsetting a lot of smaller shortcomings. The Indians drew only 456 walks, fewest in the American League, so that their team on-base percentage was fifth in the league. Their strikeout to walk ratio, 2.07–1, was the worst in the division and the worst in the league except for their twins, the Rangers. The Indians had two decent pitchers for most of the year (Candiotti and Niekro) and three late in the year (Swindell). The rest of the staff was wretched. Their 4.58 ERA was not the worst in the league (Seattle and Minnesota were worse), but the Indians allowed 105 unearned runs, more than anyone else in the league, and thus allowed more total runs, earned or unearned, than even Seattle or Minnesota. They led the league in errors (157), and were last in fielding percentage (.975). With two knuckle-ballers and a rookie catcher they were charged with 20 passed balls, second in the league.

Indian opponents hit 60 sacrifice flies, most in the American League.

Indian pitchers hit 57 opposition batters with pitches, the most of any major league team.

The Indians were the only team in this division to have more errors than double plays.

The Indians had some trouble with left-handed pitching, finishing 20–24 (.455) against left-handers, as opposed to 64–54 (.542) against right-handers.

The Indians and Rangers, two teams that have almost everything in common, were the only American League teams to post winning records despite having fewer men on base than the opposition.

The Indians won 84 games last year by overpowering those weaknesses with base hits. They won't win the pennant that way. The weaknesses will have to be eliminated.

There have been many cases in baseball history in which teams with unimpressive overall records but very strong offenses added two or three effective pitchers and took the league by storm:

• The New York Giants led the National League in runs scored in 1947 and 1948, but finished barely over .500 because their pitching and defense negated most of the advantage. When Leo Durocher took over he made a few key personnel switches, and the Giants vaulted to the status of serious contenders, winning the league in 1951.

• The Cincinnati Reds in 1959, perhaps the best parallel, led the league in runs scored with 764, but finished just 74–80, out of contention. Two years later their pitching jelled, and they pulled out a completely unexpected pennant.

• The San Francisco Giants in 1961 led the league in runs scored, but finished a poor third because of pitching and defense; they won the next year.

• The Minnesota Twins in 1964 led the American League in runs scored, but finished sixth at 79–83; the next year they won the pennant.

• The Cincinnati Reds in 1968 led the National League in runs scored, but finished just 83–79, one game worse than the Indians. Two years later, they emerged as the Big Red Machine.

• The Giants (again) in 1970 led the National League in runs scored with 831, but allowed almost as many and so finished 16 games out at 86–76. In 1971 they won their division.

• The Red Sox led the league in runs scored in 1974, but finished just 84–78; the next year they were champions.

• The Cardinals in 1980 led the National League in runs scored, but finished just 74–88 due to defensive problems. They solved those problems and had the best record in the division in 1981, winning the World Championship in 1982.

If you look at the Indians as being comparable to the Reds in 1959, the Reds had one capable starter (Bob Purkey) and came out of nowhere when they picked up another one in trade (Joey Jay) and developed a third from the system (Jim O'Toole). If you look at Candiotti as being the Indians' Bob Purkey and Swindell as being comparable to O'Toole, then one sharp trade acquisition might do it.

Maybe I'm belaboring the obvious here, but the point I was trying to make is that although the Indians were only about a .500 team and at that only a .500 team on probation, having lost 102 games a year ago, their position is stronger than that of most .500 teams in one respect, that if you have a quality offense it's a lot easier to build an average pitching staff than it is to start with an average pitching staff and build a quality offense. It can happen very quickly. If a .500 team has an outstanding offense, then the development of two or three pitchers can make a tremendous impact on the won-lost column, whereas if a .500 team is average in both respects the odds are they'll have to build up more slowly; or if they have a quality pitching staff but no offense that may be the weakest position of all, because adding two or three hitters isn't going to do much for you and pitchers are so unpredictable and injury-prone that a quality pitching staff may well fall apart in a year or two.

Should the Indians happen to win this division in 1987, that would mean that in a seven-year period all seven teams would have claimed the title, an odds-defying freak. The titlists would be New York (1981), Milwaukee (1982), Baltimore (1983), Detroit (1984), Toronto (1985), Boston (1986), and Cleveland (1987). It would also mean that the Yankees had gone longer without winning the AL East than any other team. I think that's unlikely; it is quite possible that the Yankees could win it this year, which would flip them from one end of the six to the other and keep the possibility alive for 1988, when the Indians may well be ready to go.

It usually takes longer than one year to build a pitching staff. I'm not really convinced that Pat Corrales can manage a championship team, but then maybe he's just a late bloomer. I'm not really convinced that Pat Corrales is any better as a manager than he was as a player, but it isn't his job to convince *me*. It's his players who have to believe.

It is unlikely that the Indian offense will be as effective in 1987. Of the Indians' ten regulars, seven (counting two rookies) had their best seasons. Of the other three, Jacoby's season was as good as his best, Butler hit a point above his career average, and Thornton was off some but is 37 years old. Some Cleveland fans will look ahead at 1987 and say "Wow, if we had only had Cory Snyder all year, we'd have scored even more runs." But Snyder is the *only* Indian regular who is a solid bet to contribute more in 1987 than in 1986. The Indians have a group of fine young hitters. Their starting lineup is the youngest in the division, with the starting nine averaging 27.2 years of age. But they're probably at least a year away from putting all the pieces together.

Andy ALLANSON, Catcher

	G	AB	Hit	2B	3B	HR	Run	RBI	TBB	SO	SB	CS	Avg
0.62 years		470	106	11	5	2	48	47	22	58	16	2	.225
1986	101	293	66	7	3	1	30	29	14	36	10	1	.225
First Half	58	177	46	5	3	1	21	21	8	21	6	1	.260
Second Half	43	116	20	2	0	0	9	8	6	15	4	0	.172
Vs. RHP		209	43	4	2	1		21	10	24	10	1	.206
Vs. LHP		84	23	3	1	0		8	4	12	0	0	.274
Home	53	147	35	3	2	0	13	16	6	13	7	1	.238
Road	48	146	31	4	1	1	17	13	8	23	3	0	.212
Grass	90	262	58	5	3	0	24	26	12	31	10	1	.221
Turf	11	31	8	2	0	1	6	3	2	5	0	0	.258

Pat TABLER, First Base

	G	AB	Hit	2B	3B	HR	Run	RBI	TBB	SO	SB	CS	Avg
3.55 years		554	159	28	5	8	70	71	50	85	2	4	.288
1986	130	473	154	29	2	6	61	48	29	75	3	1	.326
First Half	56	210	60	16	1	3	26	20	12	37	2	0	.286
Second Half	74	263	94	13	1	3	35	28	17	38	1	1	.357
Vs. RHP		323	104	18	2	4		33	16	57	3	0	.322
Vs. LHP		150	50	11	0	2		15	13	18	0	1	.333
Home	65	227	79	12	0	5	31	30	15	34	1	0	.348
Road	65	246	75	17	2	1	30	18	14	41	2	1	.305
Grass	112	396	137	25	0	6	53	44	26	65	3	1	.346
Turf	18	77	17	4	2	0	8	4	3	10	0	0	.221

Tony BERNAZARD, Second Base

	G	AB	Hit	2B	3B	HR	Run	RBI	TBB	SO	SB	CS	Avg
5.71 years		557	147	26	5	11	79	60	65	92	18	8	.264
1986	146	562	169	28	4	17	88	73	53	77	17	8	.301
First Half	76	269	86	15	2	7	37	34	25	36	9	3	.320
Second Half	70	293	83	13	2	10	51	39	28	41	8	5	.283
Vs. RHP		411	118	17	4	12		52	34	60	7	2	.287
Vs. LHP		151	51	11	0	5		21	19	17	10	6	.338
Home	76	286	94	12	3	9	45	40	26	37	8	6	.329
Road	70	276	75	16	1	8	43	33	27	40	9	2	.272
Grass	126	486	148	25	4	14	73	62	44	65	14	7	.305
Turf	20	76	21	3	0	3	15	11	9	12	3	1	.276

Brook JACOBY, Third Base

	G	AB	Hit	2B	3B	HR	Run	RBI	TBB	SO	SB	CS	Avg
2.84 years		580	159	26	4	15	77	73	48	118	2	2	.275
1986	158	583	168	30	4	17	83	80	56	137	2	1	.288
First Half	77	292	76	14	2	10	41	46	25	72	2	0	.260
Second Half	81	291	92	16	2	7	42	34	31	65	0	1	.316
Vs. RHP		422	126	24	3	12		56	37	103	2	1	.299
Vs. LHP		161	42	6	1	5		24	19	34	0	0	.261
Home	79	274	73	11	2	10	44	45	30	68	1	0	.266
Road	79	309	95	19	2	7	39	35	26	69	1	1	.307
Grass	135	491	142	22	3	17	72	74	48	117	2	1	.289
Turf	23	92	26	8	1	0	11	6	8	20	0	0	.283

Julio FRANCO, Shortstop

	G	AB	Hit	2B	3B	HR	Run	RBI	TBB	SO	SB	CS	Avg
3.91 years		634	183	28	6	7	84	83	40	67	19	10	.288
1986	149	599	183	30	5	10	80	74	32	66	10	7	.306
First Half	75	304	83	14	2	4	36	29	20	43	4	4	.273
Second Half	74	295	100	16	3	6	44	45	12	23	6	3	.339
Vs. RHP		435	127	18	4	4		52	24	56	9	6	.292
Vs. LHP		164	56	12	1	6		22	8	10	1	1	.341
Home	76	302	88	15	3	4	39	37	13	29	3	2	.291
Road	73	297	95	15	2	6	41	37	19	37	7	5	.320
Grass	129	525	162	29	5	9	71	66	27	53	9	7	.309
Turf	20	74	21	1	0	1	9	8	5	13	1	0	.284

Joe CARTER, Left Field

	G	AB	Hit	2B	3B	HR	Run	RBI	TBB	SO	SB	CS	Avg
2.43 years		595	166	29	5	23	86	91	28	98	23	7	.279
1986	162	663	200	36	9	29	108	121	32	95	29	7	.302
First Half	77	304	92	13	2	14	48	56	18	46	16	4	.303
Second Half	85	359	108	23	7	15	60	65	14	49	13	3	.301
Vs. RHP		482	143	26	5	22		87	20	59	28	6	.297
Vs. LHP		181	57	10	4	7		34	12	36	1	1	.315
Home	81	324	101	16	5	14	58	51	19	46	16	1	.312
Road	81	339	99	20	4	15	50	70	13	49	13	6	.292
Grass	137	556	165	29	7	24	96	96	27	81	25	5	.297
Turf	25	107	35	7	2	5	12	25	5	14	4	2	.327

Brett BUTLER, Center Field

	G	AB	Hit	2B	3B	HR	Run	RBI	TBB	SO	SB	CS	Avg
4.64 years		581	161	20	11	4	95	43	68	60	43	19	.277
1986	161	587	163	17	14	4	92	51	70	65	32	15	.278
First Half	76	283	70	11	5	1	45	23	39	27	15	7	.247
Second Half	85	304	93	6	9	3	47	28	31	38	17	8	.306
Vs. RHP		427	114	11	10	3		33	49	36	28	13	.267
Vs. LHP		160	49	6	4	1		18	21	29	4	2	.306
Home	81	276	75	4	9	0	39	14	39	34	11	7	.272
Road	80	311	88	13	5	4	53	37	31	31	21	8	.283
Grass	137	494	135	13	13	2	75	38	59	54	26	13	.273
Turf	24	93	28	4	1	2	17	13	11	11	6	2	.301

Cory SNYDER, Right Field

	G	AB	Hit	2B	3B	HR	Run	RBI	TBB	SO	SB	CS	Avg
0.64 years		654	178	33	2	38	91	109	25	193	3	5	.272
1986	103	416	113	21	1	24	58	69	16	123	2	3	.272
First Half	21	81	23	5	1	7	14	15	2	26	0	0	.284
Second Half	82	335	90	16	0	17	44	54	14	97	2	3	.269
Vs. RHP		298	75	14	1	16		46	14	92	2	1	.252
Vs. LHP		118	38	7	0	8		23	2	31	0	2	.322
Home	48	186	52	9	1	12	27	32	8	60	0	2	.280
Road	55	230	61	12	0	12	31	37	8	63	2	1	.265
Grass	84	333	94	14	1	22	51	57	16	98	1	3	.282
Turf	19	83	19	7	0	2	7	12	0	25	1	0	.229

Andre THORNTON, Designated Hitter

	G	AB	Hit	2B	3B	HR	Run	RBI	TBB	SO	SB	CS	Avg
9.44 years		552	141	26	2	27	83	94	92	88	5	4	.256
1986	120	401	92	14	0	17	49	66	65	67	4	1	.229
First Half	74	261	61	10	0	13	39	43	44	40	3	1	.234
Second Half	46	140	31	4	0	4	10	23	21	27	1	0	.221
Vs. RHP		278	63	11	0	11		45	43	45	4	1	.227
Vs. LHP		123	29	3	0	6		21	22	22	0	0	.236
Home	65	222	62	8	0	12	30	46	29	31	3	0	.279
Road	55	179	30	6	0	5	19	20	36	36	1	1	.168
Grass	106	353	84	12	0	15	43	60	60	59	4	1	.238
Turf	14	48	8	2	0	2	6	6	5	8	0	0	.167

Mel HALL, Outfield

	G	AB	Hit	2B	3B	HR	Run	RBI	TBB	SO	SB	CS	Avg
2.72 years		521	147	31	5	17	77	75	50	102	6	4	.281
1986	140	442	131	29	2	18	68	77	33	65	6	2	.296
First Half	65	210	63	15	1	14	37	45	18	35	1	2	.300
Second Half	75	232	68	14	1	4	31	32	15	30	5	0	.293
Vs. RHP		416	127	27	2	18		74	30	60	6	2	.305
Vs. LHP		26	4	2	0	0		3	3	5	0	0	.154
Home	69	206	57	13	1	8	29	33	12	25	1	1	.277
Road	71	236	74	16	1	10	39	44	21	40	5	1	.314
Grass	119	379	109	22	1	15	53	64	23	55	5	2	.288
Turf	21	63	22	7	1	3	15	13	10	10	1	0	.349

Tom CANDIOTTI

Year	(W–L)	GS	Run	Avg	DP	Avg	SB	Avg
1984	(2-2)	6	21	3.50	3	.50	4	.67
1986	(16-12)	34	177	5.21	34	1.00	31	.91
1983-1986		48	224	4.67	51	1.06	45	.94

	1986		1985		1984		84-86
	ERA	W–L	ERA	W–L	ERA	W–L	W–L
Total	3.57	16-12	5.29	2-2	3.23	4-4	22-18
Home	3.35	10-6	2.16	2-0	2.19	3-2	15-8
Road	3.82	6-6	8.62	0-2	5.30	1-2	7-10
East	3.55	5-7	4.58	1-1	4.79	2-4	8-12
West	3.58	11-5	6.39	1-1	.45	2-0	14-6
1st	3.70	7-6					7-6
2nd Half	3.46	9-6	5.29	2-2	3.23	4-4	15-12
Turf	5.52	1-3	20.25	0-1	1.23	1-0	2-4
Grass	3.15	15-9	3.94	2-1	3.54	3-4	20-14
Day	3.94	3-4	4.15	0-0	.57	2-0	5-4
Night	3.44	13-8	5.46	2-2	4.28	2-4	17-14
April	2.28	1-2					1-2
May	4.68	2-3					2-3
June	4.60	3-1					3-1
July	2.90	4-1	6.39	1-1			5-2
August	3.42	3-2			.62	3-0	6-2
September	3.34	3-3	4.58	1-1	6.08	1-4	5-8

Phil NIEKRO

Year	(W–L)	GS	Run	Avg	DP	Avg	SB	Avg
1984	(16-8)	31	163	5.26	39	1.26	12	.39
1985	(16-12)	33	155	4.70	39	1.18	27	.82
1986	(11-11)	32	159	4.97	35	1.09	17	.53
1976-1986		389	1712	4.40	330	.85	339	.87

	1986		1985		1984		84-86
	ERA	W–L	ERA	W–L	ERA	W–L	W–L
Total	4.32	11-11	4.09	16-12	3.09	16-8	43-31
Home	4.05	6-5	3.85	9-5	3.49	7-4	22-14
Road	4.55	5-6	4.34	7-7	2.70	9-4	21-17
East	4.32	6-7	5.33	4-9	2.33	7-2	17-18
West	4.33	5-4	3.03	12-3	3.71	9-6	26-13
1st Half	4.46	5-6	4.75	7-8	1.84	11-4	23-18
2nd Half	4.19	6-5	3.44	9-4	5.06	5-4	20-13
Turf	3.03	3-1	3.00	3-1	2.27	4-2	10-4
Grass	4.59	8-10	4.37	13-11	3.30	12-6	33-27
Day	4.25	5-3	4.04	7-3	2.30	5-2	17-8
Night	4.37	6-8	4.12	9-9	3.41	11-6	26-23
April	2.57	1-2	5.04	3-2	1.19	4-0	8-4
May	5.40	2-2	2.92	3-1	1.98	3-3	8-6
June	5.52	1-2	7.76	1-4	2.58	3-1	5-7
July	3.50	3-1	2.31	3-1	4.99	2-1	8-3
August	4.81	3-3	3.53	3-1	3.56	4-2	10-6
September	4.05	1-1	4.21	3-3	6.50	0-1	4-5

Ken SCHROM

Year	(W–L)	GS	Run	Avg	DP	Avg	SB	Avg
1984	(5-11)	21	81	3.86	14	.67	9	.43
1985	(9-12)	26	104	4.00	25	.96	15	.58
1986	(14-7)	33	172	5.21	28	.85	29	.88
1983-1986		108	479	4.44	88	.81	75	.69

	1986		1985	1984	1983	82-86
	ERA	W–L	ERA	ERA	ERA	W–L
Total	4.54	14-7	4.99	4.47	3.71	43-38
Home	3.88	9-4	5.42	3.86	2.77	27-19
Road	5.44	5-3	4.10	5.20	4.92	16-19
East	5.84	4-7	6.33	4.37	4.37	19-25
West	3.69	10-0	3.80	4.54	3.02	24-13
1st Half	3.97	9-2	4.96	3.86	4.34	23-16
2nd Half	5.21	5-5	5.02	4.70	3.39	20-22
Turf	3.58	3-0	5.10	4.29	2.76	24-17
Grass	4.73	11-7	4.65	4.76	5.59	19-21
Day	4.27	5-2	5.23	4.25	3.25	15-12
Night	4.73	9-5	4.90	4.58	3.88	28-26
April	3.52	3-1	6.38			4-3
May	4.84	0-1	5.72	.00	3.19	6-3
June	3.25	5-0	1.93	3.93	5.59	12-6
July	4.17	3-1	8.04	2.65	4.23	8-11
August	7.06	0-3	4.50	4.85	3.70	5-8
September	4.74	3-1	4.26	6.89	2.30	8-7

Ernie CAMACHO

1986	G	IP	W–L	Sv	H	ER	SO	ERA
Total	51	57.1	2-4	20	60	26	36	4.08
Home	24	28.2	1-0	6	36	18	16	5.65
Road	27	28.2	1-4	14	24	8	20	2.51
East	22	23.1	1-1	9	24	10	18	3.86
West	29	34.0	1-3	11	36	16	18	4.24
1st Half	22	25.1	1-1	11	24	12	20	4.26
2nd Half	29	32.0	1-3	9	36	14	16	3.94
Turf	9	9.2	0-3	4	13	6	6	5.59
Grass	42	47.2	2-1	16	47	20	30	3.78
Day	21	22.0	1-1	10	20	8	13	3.27
Night	30	35.1	1-3	10	40	18	23	4.58
April	9	11.2	0-0	6	10	4	14	3.09
May	5	5.2	1-0	0	7	4	1	6.35
June	8	8.0	0-1	5	7	4	5	4.50
July	7	8.1	0-1	2	8	2	4	2.16
August	12	11.0	1-0	4	12	5	6	4.09
September	10	12.2	0-2	3	16	7	6	4.97

OTHERS

Pitcher	(W–L)	GS	Run	Avg	DP	Avg	SB	Avg	Time	Att.
Schulze	(4-4)	13	61	4.69	8	.62	7	.54	2:58	266
Heaton	(3-6)	12	53	4.42	12	1.00	11	.92	2:56	186
Bailes	(10-10)	10	53	5.30	6	.60	3	.30	2:51	179
Swindell	(5-2)	9	58	6.44	5	.56	3	.33	2:53	147
Butcher	(1-5)	8	38	4.75	7	.88	5	.40	2:48	158
Roman	(1-2)	5	21	4.20	6	1.20	1	.20	2:53	93
Oelkers	(3-3)	4	19	4.75	4	1.00	4	1.00	2:43	107
Yett	(5-3)	3	20	6.67	3	1.00	2	.67	2:54	72

RECORDS WITH DIFFERENT STARTING CATCHERS

Catcher	Inn	ER	W–L	ERA	GS	SB	Avg
Allanson	813.1	408	49-43	4.51	92	67	.73
Bando	634.1	328	35-35	4.65	71	46	.65

STARTING PITCHERS' AVERAGE TIME AND ATTENDANCE RECORDS

Pitcher	Time	Attendance
Candiotti	2:50	685
Schrom	2:58	638
Niekro	2:44	805

INVERTED RECORDS

Everything that happens to a hitter also happens to a pitcher. A hitter's record and a pitcher's record are the same thing, just looked at in different ways. One thing that is kind of fun sometimes is to recast a hitter's record into the form of a pitching record. Most of the translation is pretty simple. Three categories (hits, strikeouts, and walks) can be moved directly onto the new record. For runs allowed we'll use runs created, but you could also use runs scored or some amalgam of runs scored and RBI. Earned runs are 90% of total runs allowed, and ERA follows from runs created.

To get the won-lost record, I compare the runs allowed to the league run average and project the probable won-lost record by using the Pythagorean Method. The categories of games, complete games, and shutouts are filled in by a kind of simple little formula that reduces the number of innings per game as ERA rises, with complete games and shutouts becoming correspondingly less likely.

Obviously, if the hitter is effective, then the pitchers facing him are not effective. If the hitter is winning, then the pitchers facing him are losing. These are the "pitcher's records" for the Indians' players:

	G	IP	W	L	Pct	H	R	ER	SO	BB	ERA	CG	ShO
Allanson	10	83.1	7	2	.778	66	22	20	36	14	2.16	5	3
Bando	9	69.1	5	3	.625	68	27	24	49	22	3.12	3	1
Bernazard	28	140.2	6	10	.375	169	96	86	77	53	5.50	3	0
Butler	26	156.1	8	9	.471	163	84	76	65	70	4.38	4	1
Carter	34	162.1	6	12	.333	200	116	104	95	32	5.77	3	0
Castillo	8	51	3	3	.500	57	28	25	48	9	4.41	1	0
Franco	23	152	9	8	.529	183	76	68	66	32	4.03	3	1
Hall	22	108	4	8	.333	131	75	68	65	33	5.67	2	0
Jacoby	26	144.1	7	9	.438	168	88	79	137	56	4.93	3	1
Nixon	4	26.1	2	1	.667	25	13	12	12	13	4.10	1	0
Snyder	17	105	6	6	.500	113	58	52	123	16	4.46	3	1
Tabler	22	111.1	5	7	.417	154	74	67	75	29	5.42	2	0
Thornton	17	109.6	6	6	.500	92	55	50	67	65	4.10	2	1

I also ran these for a few other players. The "Henderson" below is Rickey:

	G	IP	W	L	Pct	H	R	ER	SO	BB	ERA	CG	ShO
Barfield	39	147	4	12	.250	170	122	110	146	69	6.73	4	0
G Bell	34	157.1	6	11	.353	198	113	102	62	41	5.83	2	0
Boggs	57	132	3	12	.200	207	133	120	44	105	8.18	3	0
Coleman	23	162.1	10	8	.556	139	67	60	98	60	3.33	4	1
Deer	24	123	5	9	.357	108	82	74	179	72	5.41	2	0
Garvey	20	146	9	7	.563	142	59	53	72	23	3.27	4	1
Guillen	18	148.1	12	4	.750	137	43	39	52	12	2.37	8	4
Henderson	33	160	6	12	.333	160	112	101	81	89	5.68	3	0
Hernandez	33	132.1	4	11	.267	171	106	95	69	94	6.44	2	0
Hulett	18	140.2	11	5	.688	120	49	44	91	21	2.82	7	3
Reggie	20	112	5	7	.417	101	68	61	115	92	4.90	2	0
Kittle	15	104.1	7	5	.583	82	45	41	110	35	3.54	3	1
Lombardozzi	17	122.2	9	5	.643	103	50	45	76	52	3.30	3	1
Maldonado	16	107.2	6	6	.500	102	51	46	77	20	3.85	3	1
Mattingly	58	155.2	4	13	.235	238	135	122	35	53	7.81	4	0
S. Owen	19	145	11	5	.688	122	49	44	51	51	2.73	7	3
Phelps	28	89.2	2	8	.200	85	81	73	96	88	7.33	2	0
Puckett	39	161.2	5	13	.278	223	127	114	99	34	6.35	3	0
Raines	50	135	3	12	.200	194	130	117	60	78	7.80	3	0
Redus	16	89	4	6	.400	84	55	50	78	47	5.06	2	0
H Reynolds	15	124.1	11	3	.786	99	37	33	42	29	2.39	7	4
Rice	35	149	5	12	.294	200	133	104	78	62	6.28	3	0
E Romero	8	66.1	5	2	.714	49	19	17	16	18	2.31	4	2
Schmidt	42	137	3	12	.200	160	122	110	84	89	7.23	3	0
Strawberry	28	125.2	4	10	.286	123	92	83	141	72	5.94	2	0
W Wilson	24	159.2	10	8	.556	170	76	68	97	31	3.83	5	1

MILWAUKEE BREWERS

Runners on Base:	1,950
Opponents on Base:	2,001
Net Disadvantage:	−51
Won-Lost Record:	77-84

Exactly how good or how bad a season it was in Milwaukee in 1986 is a matter of some dispute. Many people saw it as being a good one. The front page article in the August 10–24 issue of *Baseball America* heralded the Brewers' "Bright Young Faces" which "have Brewers moving up again," and displayed pictures of Ted Higuera (can't argue with that one), Juan Nieves, and Billy Joe Robidoux. I personally saw the season as being disastrous for the Brewers' young talent, one in which no Brewer prospect looked anything like a major-league star of the future, although the Brewers' vets propped the team up and kept it near .500. In a year or two, I guess we'll know who saw it more clearly.

At no point in the season did the 1986 Brewers seem likely to contend. They hit last place in April, rallied to the middle of the division in May and held above .500 until the week before the All-Star game, when seven straight losses dropped them into the cellar. Though holding last place through most of July and August, the Brewers stayed near .500 and continued to lead the American League in earned run average until August 27. Beginning on August 27, the Brewers lost 7–5 and 6–2, won 3–1, lost 10–1, 6–1, 9–3, 4–0, 11–5, 15–4, 13–5, and 17–9. After two wins and two well-pitched games, they lost 11–7 and 8–0. All told, the Brewers allowed 121 runs in a 15-game stretch, including 56 in four consecutive games. That eliminated the chance of leading the league in ERA, but the Brewers stabilized and even eased out of the basement when the Orioles dropped by them in September.

For the season, the Brewers were only a little below .500, but they were not strong in any department. The Brewers scored only 667 runs, twelfth in the league and the fewest of any team in the division. The 667 runs scored was 23 fewer than they scored in 1985. They were last in the division in hits, batting average, total bases and home runs. They were first in (batter's) strikeouts, although oddly enough they did lead the league in sacrifice flies. They scored only 34.2% of their runners, the lowest percentage in the division, and just a hair ahead of the worst in the league.

Designated hitter was a particularly weak spot for the Brewers. Brewer DHs hit just .229, second-lowest in the league (Oakland was lower, but Oakland DHs led the league in homers). Brewer DHs hit only 14 homers, lowest in the league; scored just 64 runs, tied for the league low; and drove in only 73 runs, fewest in the league. Brewer DHs were 4 for 11 as base stealers, struck out 133 times, and had only 4 game-winning RBI.

Wait a minute—I'm going to get to the bad news. The bad news is that the Brewers were being kept afloat, such as they were, by their veterans. The Brewers' eight leading hitters were, in order, Robin Yount, Ben Oglivie, Paul Molitor, Jim Gantner, Charlie Moore, Rick Cerone, Cecil Cooper, and Rick Manning. Of that crew, the last to reach the majors was Paul Molitor in 1978. The Brewers' ninth leading hitter was Ernest Riles, a second-year player who hit a disappointing .252. *Then* you get to the rookies.

Yet the story of the Brewers as reported in the media was that 1986 was a successful unveiling of a crop of exciting rookies who will soon have the Brewers back in contention. An unveiling it certainly was; the Brewers featured eight rookies seeing significant action. When they started talking about how exciting the rookies were, I was mostly wondering who the hell they were talking about. With the exception of Dan Plesac, a relief pitcher, none of the Brewer rookies played well. None of them played *fairly* well. None of them looked anything like a player who would ever be any good.

Among the rookies, the leading hitter was Dale Sveum, who hit .246. Sveum, however, committed the phenomenal total of 30 errors in 91 games, including 26 in 65 games at third base—an .865 fielding percentage. Whereas every regular third baseman in the league had at least an even ratio of double plays to errors except Jacoby, who was at 24 and 25, Sveum was at 8 and 26. After a red-hot start with the bat, Sveum hit .190 in August and .158 in September. If Dale Sveum is a major league third baseman, there's hope yet for Butch Hobson.

Behind Sveum was Mike Felder, a leadoff prospect. Among the seven, Felder did the least to establish that he couldn't play major-league baseball. He hit only .239 with a .289 on-base percentage in 44 games, but he did run well and field well.

Glenn Braggs, who may be the best prospect in the group, may have been the worst of the lot in 1986 performance. He hit .237, struck out a lot without compensating in power, and, if possible, made a worse impression as a defensive player than Dale Sveum. Braggs, who seemed to be using Darryl Strawberry's neck and Rudy Law's throwing arm, committed 12 outfield errors, narrowly missing the league lead although he played only 56 outfield games.

Then there was Billy Joe Robidoux, at the age of 22 possibly the league's slowest DH, who hit .227 with no power. Robidoux played so badly that if he doesn't improve this spring he might well be released, and probably would not be re-signed by any other team.

In short, of the four rookies who got a shot at playing

every day, three were terrible and the other one didn't impress. Of the four rookie pitchers, Dan Plesac, a big left-hander, did very well in a relief role. Plesac was a starter in the minors, and probably should either go back to that role or move up to the role of bullpen ace in 1987. He is too good to use in long relief.

Bryan Clutterbuck didn't pitch enough to seriously damage his career, but was hit hard in 20 relief outings, harder than his 4.29 ERA would suggest.

Juan Nieves gave up 224 hits in 185 innings and posted a 4.92 ERA with an unusually high number of unearned runs. Nieves, at least, does have a chance—a slim chance—of developing into an effective pitcher. He struck out 116 men in the 185 innings, which is about average. If he could develop a reliable strikeout pitch and learn the hitters, he could improve.

Bill Wegman seems to have no chance at all, nothing going for him. Not only were his basic stats awful (5–12, 5.13 ERA), but his peripheral stats were those of a 37-year-old pitcher on the way out. He struck out just 82 men in 198 innings and was hammered for 32 homers.

If you look at the pitching staff as it was on August 26, before the wipeout, the picture isn't fundamentally different. Higuera was pitching great, Plesac was good, and Clear was remarkable. Tim Leary wasn't hurting the team, and everybody else was. The only difference is that before August 26 the others had ERAs about 4.75, and after they had ERAs about 5.00.

So the performance of the rookies was, as far as I can see, just nightmarish. Another question is what happened to B. J. Surhoff? A year ago Surhoff, the No. 1 draft pick in 1985, was being compared to Johnny Bench. In 1986 he became the invisible man of the Pacific Coast League, hitting .300 with no power and not being called up in September, even though the Brewers need help at catcher. On the other hand, the Brewers were justifiably proud of their cheap pickup of outfielder Rob Deer, who hit .232 but in 50 games in July and August belted 17 homers and drove in 46 runs. Deer struck out in almost 40% of his at bats, but his power is such that if he can keep his average over .210 he will play in the majors as long as Gorman Thomas has. I honestly don't think he can; I think the odds are 60–40 he'll slip back to .190 this year, but he certainly has a chance to be a player who can help them. The Brewers' other good news: Robin Yount doesn't intend to let a little thing like a shoulder injury keep him from getting his 3500 hits, and Teddy Higuera is the best left-handed starting pitcher in the league.

Another Brewer about whom we can argue all night is Jim Gantner, the second baseman. When Gantner came up I thought I was the only sportswriter in the country who realized how good he was. What they say about him now is that he just goes along and you never hear anything about him, but when you get to the end of the year you realize that he hasn't hurt you any. The problem is that when you get to the end of the year, you realize that he hasn't hurt *anybody;* he's just sort of filling the role. The Brewers turned only 146 double plays, tied for the fewest in the division. Gantner's a .275 hitter and an OK second baseman, an unusually consistent player both at bat and in the field. In the last three years he really hasn't done anything to help the team, and at age 33 his value is slipping rapidly. So a second baseman is another thing the Brewers will have to come up with before they're ready to win again.

The Brewers were over .500 (61–59) against right-handed pitching, but just 16–25 against left-handed pitching, the worst record in the league against left-handers except for Seattle. I am inclined to regard this as a fluke, inasmuch as the Brewer hitting is well balanced and their overall batting stats against right- and left-handers are virtually the same. Earnest Riles and Yount did not hit lefties well in '86, but Rob Deer slugged over .600 against them. I don't think that split will hold up this year.

The impression that the Brewers' farm system is productive has been created by *Baseball America,* which regularly raves about people like Surhoff, Sveum, Braggs, and Robidoux. *Baseball America* has a well-deserved reputation for its coverage of minor-league baseball, and there's a good chance that they know more about the Brewers' young players than I do. One of the sources of their reputation is that they had the courage and foresight to name the Mets as the outstanding organization in baseball one year when the major-league team won only 68 games. A lot of people ridiculed the selection, but it became obvious a year or two later that they knew exactly what they were talking about. These people had Roger Clemens and Calvin Schiraldi on their cover in 1983, and Barry Bonds and José Canseco in 1985, so when they start running Brewers on the cover, you pay attention. This is a very smart, well-edited, well-researched publication, rapidly gaining on *The Sporting News* as the most-read periodical of the game.

But, with all the respect in the world for *Baseball America,* if the Brewers are on the verge of reemerging as a contending ballclub, I am simply too blind to see it. The Brewers do not have a young team on the field at this time, which would be one indicator of probable improvement. They did not finish strong, which would be another. Their trade (Leary for Brock) is all right I suppose; I've certainly always felt that Brock was an effective player despite his low average, and I still do. He isn't going to repair the batting order.

Beyond Teddy Higuera, I don't see the pitching of a contending team. The Brewer pitching was thin before the Leary trade, and it's thinner now. Beyond Robin Yount and maybe Rob Deer, I don't see the hitting. I don't see the defense anywhere. It says here that the Milwaukee Brewers in 1987 will have a tough time winning as many games as they won in 1986.

Charlie MOORE, Catcher

	G	AB	Hit	2B	3B	HR	Run	RBI	TBB	SO	SB	CS	Avg
7.92 years		496	130	22	5	4	56	51	42	58	6	7	.262
1986	80	235	61	12	3	3	24	39	21	38	5	5	.260
First Half	42	128	38	5	3	2	14	25	13	21	5	3	.297
Second Half	38	107	23	7	0	1	10	14	8	17	0	2	.215
Vs. RHP		175	44	10	1	2		28	16	31	5	3	.251
Vs. LHP		60	17	2	2	1		11	5	7	0	2	.283
Home	36	112	34	6	2	2	13	23	10	12	4	3	.304
Road	44	123	27	6	1	1	11	16	11	26	1	2	.220
Grass	65	190	53	10	2	3	20	29	17	27	5	4	.279
Turf	15	45	8	2	1	0	4	10	4	11	0	1	.178

Ben OGLIVIE, Left Field

	G	AB	Hit	2B	3B	HR	Run	RBI	TBB	SO	SB	CS	Avg
10.83 years		546	149	26	3	22	72	83	52	79	8	6	.273
1986	103	346	98	20	1	5	31	53	30	33	1	2	.283
First Half	59	213	65	13	0	3	20	37	16	11	1	1	.305
Second Half	44	133	33	7	1	2	11	16	14	22	0	1	.248
Vs. RHP		283	82	14	1	5		44	26	25	1	2	.290
Vs. LHP		63	16	6	0	0		9	4	8	0	0	.254
Home	50	169	49	13	0	2	14	28	15	16	0	2	.290
Road	53	177	49	7	1	3	17	25	15	17	1	0	.277
Grass	85	280	78	20	1	3	26	42	28	27	1	2	.279
Turf	18	66	20	0	0	2	5	11	2	6	0	0	.303

Cecil COOPER, First Base

	G	AB	Hit	2B	3B	HR	Run	RBI	TBB	SO	SB	CS	Avg
11.31 years		627	188	36	4	21	87	96	38	76	8	4	.300
1986	134	542	140	24	1	12	46	75	41	87	1	2	.258
First Half	62	255	65	12	1	7	26	43	19	52	0	1	.255
Second Half	72	287	75	12	0	5	20	32	22	35	1	1	.261
Vs. RHP		405	101	23	1	9		52	30	59	1	1	.249
Vs. LHP		137	39	1	0	3		23	11	28	0	1	.285
Home	65	255	60	9	1	6	19	32	21	46	0	2	.235
Road	69	287	80	15	0	6	27	43	20	41	1	0	.279
Grass	112	460	115	21	1	11	38	67	33	76	0	2	.250
Turf	22	82	25	3	0	1	8	8	8	11	1	0	.305

Robin YOUNT, Center Field

	G	AB	Hit	2B	3B	HR	Run	RBI	TBB	SO	SB	CS	Avg
11.18 years		629	181	34	7	14	93	74	48	70	15	6	.287
1986	140	522	163	31	7	9	82	46	62	73	14	5	.312
First Half	66	242	82	17	2	3	43	20	31	34	8	3	.339
Second Half	74	280	81	14	5	6	39	26	31	39	6	2	.289
Vs. RHP		401	133	29	6	6		35	44	55	14	5	.332
Vs. LHP		121	30	2	1	3		11	18	18	0	0	.248
Home	69	259	77	12	6	4	37	22	28	37	8	2	.297
Road	71	263	86	19	1	5	45	24	34	36	6	3	.327
Grass	120	452	139	20	6	7	66	41	52	64	13	4	.308
Turf	20	70	24	11	1	2	16	5	10	9	1	1	.343

Jim GANTNER, Second Base

	G	AB	Hit	2B	3B	HR	Run	RBI	TBB	SO	SB	CS	Avg
6.91 years		560	154	22	3	6	65	53	35	47	9	7	.275
1986	139	497	136	25	1	7	58	38	26	50	13	7	.274
First Half	67	245	66	12	1	3	31	16	17	21	8	3	.269
Second Half	72	252	70	13	0	4	27	22	9	29	5	4	.278
Vs. RHP		369	108	21	1	7		31	20	38	10	7	.293
Vs. LHP		128	28	4	0	0		7	6	12	3	0	.219
Home	71	247	64	14	1	4	30	25	15	24	5	2	.259
Road	68	250	72	11	0	3	28	13	11	26	8	5	.288
Grass	118	423	114	21	1	6	52	34	25	42	11	7	.270
Turf	21	74	22	4	0	1	6	4	1	8	2	0	.297

Rob DEER, Right Field

	G	AB	Hit	2B	3B	HR	Run	RBI	TBB	SO	SB	CS	Avg
1.39 years		469	102	16	3	32	73	78	73	187	4	3	.218
1986	134	466	108	17	3	33	75	86	72	179	5	2	.232
First Half	60	205	44	5	2	13	30	35	28	83	2	0	.215
Second Half	74	261	64	12	1	20	45	51	44	96	3	2	.245
Vs. RHP		337	72	12	1	22		59	41	139	4	1	.214
Vs. LHP		129	36	5	2	11		27	31	40	1	1	.279
Home	70	238	54	7	1	19	43	49	37	91	3	0	.227
Road	64	228	54	10	2	14	32	37	35	88	2	2	.237
Grass	118	411	93	15	2	27	65	73	64	158	5	2	.226
Turf	16	55	15	2	1	6	10	13	8	21	0	0	.273

Paul MOLITOR, Third Base

	G	AB	Hit	2B	3B	HR	Run	RBI	TBB	SO	SB	CS	Avg
6.23 years		664	193	32	7	13	108	63	58	83	37	11	.291
1986	105	437	123	24	6	9	62	55	40	81	20	5	.281
First Half	31	120	34	8	2	3	23	18	19	25	3	0	.283
Second Half	74	317	89	16	4	6	39	37	21	56	17	5	.281
Vs. RHP		337	96	18	4	8		47	33	58	19	4	.285
Vs. LHP		100	27	6	2	1		8	7	23	1	1	.270
Home	51	213	64	9	4	5	29	34	16	34	14	4	.300
Road	54	224	59	15	2	4	33	21	24	47	6	1	.263
Grass	94	390	115	22	6	9	59	55	38	69	17	4	.295
Turf	11	47	8	2	0	0	3	0	2	12	3	1	.170

Dale SVEUM, Third Base

	G	AB	Hit	2B	3B	HR	Run	RBI	TBB	SO	SB	CS	Avg
0.56 years		564	135	23	4	12	62	62	57	112	4	5	.240
1986	91	317	76	13	2	7	35	35	32	63	4	3	.240
First Half	48	177	50	9	1	3	18	22	11	33	2	2	.282
Second Half	43	140	26	4	1	4	17	13	21	30	2	1	.186
Vs. RHP		221	52	5	1	5		23	18	48	1	2	.235
Vs. LHP		96	24	8	1	2		12	14	15	3	1	.250
Home	47	159	34	7	0	4	19	17	20	29	2	1	.214
Road	44	158	42	6	2	3	16	18	12	34	2	2	.266
Grass	74	256	59	9	1	7	30	26	27	52	4	3	.230
Turf	17	61	17	4	1	0	5	9	5	11	0	0	.279

Earnest RILES, Shortstop

	G	AB	Hit	2B	3B	HR	Run	RBI	TBB	SO	SB	CS	Avg
1.61 years		603	161	22	6	9	76	57	56	83	6	6	.267
1986	145	524	132	24	2	9	69	47	54	80	7	7	.252
First Half	75	286	75	11	1	5	37	26	31	41	4	4	.262
Second Half	70	238	57	13	1	4	32	21	23	39	3	3	.239
Vs. RHP		408	108	22	1	6		34	45	58	7	6	.265
Vs. LHP		116	24	2	1	3		13	9	22	0	1	.207
Home	70	246	64	9	2	2	36	18	29	31	5	3	.260
Road	75	278	68	15	0	7	33	29	25	49	2	4	.245
Grass	123	446	109	20	2	8	61	40	48	68	7	6	.244
Turf	22	78	23	4	0	1	8	7	6	12	0	1	.295

Gorman THOMAS, Designated Hitter

	G	AB	Hit	2B	3B	HR	Run	RBI	TBB	SO	SB	CS	Avg
8.86 years		528	119	24	1	30	77	88	79	151	6	5	.225
1986	101	315	59	8	1	16	45	36	58	105	3	3	.187
First Half	57	170	33	4	0	10	24	26	27	55	1	1	.194
Second Half	44	145	26	4	1	6	21	10	31	50	2	2	.179
Vs. RHP		218	42	5	1	11		26	33	79	3	2	.193
Vs. LHP		97	17	3	0	5		10	25	26	0	1	.175
Home	44	138	19	3	0	7	22	11	24	51	1	1	.138
Road	57	177	40	5	1	9	23	25	34	54	2	2	.226
Grass	60	188	38	5	1	9	30	19	43	61	2	2	.202
Turf	41	127	21	3	0	7	15	17	15	44	1	1	.165

Teddy HIGUERA

Year	(W–L)	GS	Run	Avg	DP	Avg	SB	Avg
1985	(15-8)	30	133	4.43	24	.80	16	.53
1986	(20-11)	34	135	4.19	22	.65	15	.44
1985-1986		64	268	4.19	46	.72	31	.48

	1986		1985		85-86
	ERA	W–L	ERA	W–L	W–L
Total	2.79	20-11	3.90	15-8	35-19
Home	1.79	10-3	5.44	7-4	17-7
Road	3.91	10-8	2.78	8-4	18-12
East	2.30	9-6	4.74	4-6	13-12
West	3.28	11-5	3.22	11-2	22-7
1st Half	2.57	10-6	4.75	5-5	15-11
2nd Half	3.05	10-5	3.28	10-3	20-8
Turf	5.14	3-3	2.35	4-1	7-4
Grass	2.40	17-8	4.33	11-7	28-15
Day	2.07	8-4	5.10	3-3	11-7
Night	3.35	12-7	3.48	12-5	24-12
April	2.23	3-1	6.08	0-1	3-2
May	2.60	3-3	3.57	3-2	6-5
June	2.25	4-2	7.27	1-2	5-4
July	3.52	3-1	3.89	4-1	7-2
August	3.02	4-1	3.14	4-0	8-1
September	3.30	3-3	2.49	3-2	6-5

Bill WEGMAN

Year	(W–L)	GS	Run	Avg	DP	Avg	SB	Avg
1985	(2-0)	3	23	7.67	5	1.67	2	.67
1986	(5-12)	32	129	4.03	24	.75	12	.38
1985-1986		35	152	4.34	29	.83	14	.40

	G	IP	W–L	H	ER	SO	ERA
Total	35	198.1	5-12	217	113	82	5.13
Home	19	110.1	2-5	123	62	49	5.06
Road	16	88.0	3-7	94	51	33	5.22
East	19	102.1	4-6	105	59	43	5.19
West	16	96.0	1-6	112	54	39	5.06
1st Half	17	108.1	2-7	118	62	43	5.15
2nd Half	18	90.0	3-5	99	51	39	5.10
Turf	4	22.1	1-3	27	12	11	4.84
Grass	31	176.0	4-9	190	101	71	5.16
Day	10	59.1	1-3	66	29	28	4.40
Night	25	139.0	4-9	151	84	54	5.44
April	4	24.1	0-1	26	11	6	4.07
May	7	45.1	0-4	53	25	18	4.96
June	5	33.2	2-1	34	21	18	5.61
July	5	27.2	1-3	28	17	8	5.53
August	7	43.0	1-1	45	21	21	4.40
September	7	24.1	1-2	31	18	11	6.66

Juan NIEVES

Year	(W–L)	GS	Run	Avg	DP	Avg	SB	Avg
1986	(11-12)	33	161	4.88	34	1.03	14	.42

1986	G	IP	W–L	H	ER	SO	ERA
Total	35	184.2	11-12	224	101	116	4.92
Home	17	78.0	4-6	105	55	49	6.35
Road	18	106.2	7-6	119	46	67	3.88
East	16	80.0	5-5	96	39	48	4.39
West	19	104.2	6-7	128	62	68	5.33
1st Half	17	106.0	7-2	111	46	62	3.91
2nd Half	18	78.2	4-10	113	55	54	6.29
Turf	4	22.0	2-1	27	12	17	4.91
Grass	31	162.2	9-11	197	89	99	4.92
Day	11	63.0	3-3	72	31	42	4.43
Night	24	121.2	8-9	152	70	74	5.18
April	4	23.1	0-1	23	12	19	4.63
May	7	42.0	5-0	49	22	20	4.71
June	5	31.2	1-1	34	12	15	3.41
July	6	37.0	4-2	35	13	30	3.16
August	5	19.0	0-3	39	22	11	10.42
September	8	31.2	1-5	44	20	21	5.68

Tim LEARY

Year	(W–L)	GS	Run	Avg	DP	Avg	SB	Avg
1984	(3-3)	7	23	3.29	8	1.14	9	1.29
1985	(1-4)	5	10	2.00	4	.80	5	1.00
1986	(12-12)	30	133	4.43	28	.93	27	.90
1981-1986		45	180	4.00	42	.93	45	1.00

	G	IP	W–L	H	ER	SO	ERA
Total	33	188.1	12-12	216	88	110	4.21
Home	17	96.1	5-8	103	46	57	4.30
Road	16	92.0	7-4	113	42	53	4.11
East	13	81.1	7-3	82	29	42	3.21
West	20	107.0	5-9	134	59	68	4.96
1st Half	18	113.0	6-8	127	58	73	4.62
2nd Half	15	75.1	6-4	89	30	37	3.58
Turf	6	38.1	2-2	41	19	23	4.46
Grass	27	150.0	10-10	175	69	87	4.14
Day	14	80.2	5-6	88	38	45	4.24
Night	19	107.2	7-6	128	50	65	4.18
April	4	24.0	2-1	30	12	19	4.50
May	7	38.0	1-3	50	27	25	6.39
June	6	44.2	3-3	43	15	26	3.02
July	4	20.2	1-3	24	12	9	5.23
August	6	27.1	2-1	36	11	16	3.62
September	6	33.2	3-1	33	11	15	2.94

Mark CLEAR

1986	G	IP	W–L	Sv	H	ER	SO	ERA
Total	59	73.2	5-5	16	53	18	85	2.20
Home	31	42.0	5-2	6	25	4	48	.86
Road	28	31.2	0-3	10	28	14	37	3.98
East	29	33.1	0-3	11	25	9	34	2.43
West	30	40.1	5-2	5	28	9	51	2.01
1st Half	23	29.1	2-3	5	21	6	40	1.84
2nd Half	36	44.1	3-2	11	32	12	45	2.44
Turf	8	9.0	0-1	3	12	7	11	7.00
Grass	51	64.2	5-4	13	41	11	74	1.53
Day	21	24.2	3-3	5	16	8	32	2.92
Night	38	49.0	2-2	11	37	10	53	1.84
April	6	6.1	0-1	1	6	1	9	1.42
May	9	12.1	2-1	2	8	1	20	.73
June	7	8.2	0-1	2	7	4	9	4.15
July	10	13.1	0-1	2	6	3	14	2.03
August	14	20.0	3-0	5	11	0	19	.00
September	13	13.0	0-1	4	15	9	14	6.23

RECORDS WITH DIFFERENT STARTING CATCHERS

Catcher	Inn	ER	W–L	ERA	GS	SB	Avg
Cerone	594.2	309	32-34	4.68	66	39	.59
Moore	551.1	204	33-30	3.33	63	31	.49
Schroeder	285.2	126	12-20	3.97	32	25	.78

STARTING PITCHERS' AVERAGE TIME AND ATTENDANCE RECORDS

Pitcher	Time	Attendance
Higuera	2:42	678
Nieves	2:54	600
Wegman	2:39	557
Leary	2:41	644

OTHERS

Pitcher	(W–L)	GS	Run	Avg	DP	Avg	SB	Avg	Time	Att.
Darwin	(6-8)	14	47	3.36	15	1.07	10	.71	2:41	319
Vuckovich	(2-4)	6	12	2.00	8	1.33	6	1.00	2:22	68
Birkbeck	(1-1)	4	19	4.75	7	1.75	3	.75	2:39	85
Bosio	(0-4)	4	15	3.75	5	1.25	6	1.50	2:53	74
Cocanower	(0-1)	2	9	4.50	3	1.50	2	1.00	3:02	45
Gibson	(1-2)	1	6	6.00	0	.00	0	.00	3:08	19
Knudson	(0-1)	1	1	1.00	0	.00	0	.00	2:26	27

BALTIMORE ORIOLES

Runners on Base:	2,019
Opponents on Base:	2,007
Net Advantage:	+12
Won-Lost Record:	73-89

It was an ending to the season that no one would have anticipated, and an ending to Earl Weaver's career that no one would have wanted. At the All-Star break the Orioles were 46–41, ten games behind the Red Sox. By August 5th the Orioles were 59–47 and had closed to within two and a half games of first place. At that moment any baseball fan east of Honolulu would have sworn that we were about to witness another patented Oriole charge. There could have been no doubt that the Orioles would finish at least 31–25, putting them over 90 wins for the twelfth time in Earl Weaver's 14 full seasons as a manager. Instead, to the eyes of an astonished nation, the Orioles were the worst team in all of baseball for the last two months, winning only 14 more games and dropping an incredible 22½ games behind the Red Sox—and all the way into last place. Like those of so many before him, the career of one of the game's greatest managers ended with a whimper.

Over the years, I have been one of Earl Weaver's most outspoken admirers, but the Orioles collapsed in 1986 largely because Weaver made a string of very poor decisions during a critical period. In general, I prefer a manager who attacks problems to one who waits for them to solve themselves—but in 1986, Earl Weaver attacked the Orioles' problems and made them worse, while John McNamara successfully waited out the Red Sox's problems.

And yet, Weaver was impatient in ways that he never was before. It has been Weaver's custom to study his talent in spring training, assign a role to each player and follow those plans in the face of all opposition until the talent would settle in mid-summer and explode in August with the precision and timing of a carefully balanced chemical mixture. The pitchers, used to three or four days' rest no matter what, always getting enough work to stay sharp without ever being ridden so hard that they would drop, would invariably grow stronger and sharper as the season went on. The platoon players, rested but never rusted, had every opportunity to learn the pitchers that they would be expected to hit in September. The defense, drilled in fundamentals in the spring, had the summer to learn to work together.

This is a remarkable statement that I'm about to make, but I can't find an exception. Between 1968 and 1981 there was not one time when Baltimore brought a player out of the minors in mid-season and put him in the lineup. Not once—for a move that is as routine for most managers as spitting tobacco juice at an umpire's feet. The Orioles made their talent decisions in the winter, when they could step back and evaluate the players objectively. There were a few times when they would send a role player out in April to get some at bats, and in 1982 they made the famous move of switching Ripken to shortstop and calling Glenn Gulliver up to play third base, but for fourteen years they never pulled a player out of the minors in mid-season and slapped him in the lineup. Weaver would reevaluate his pitching during the season, but he would make changes only when they *had* to be made, only when there was *clear evidence* that a pitcher who had been counted on was not going to come through.

The Earl Weaver of 1986 was as far removed from the orderly, determined Weaver of earlier years as the Pete Rose of 1986 was from the Rose of 1973. When Mike Young stopped hitting for power, Weaver first started resting him, then benched him, then sent him to Rochester. He did find his stroke at Rochester, but one can't help but wonder if he might not have found it quicker if Weaver had stuck with him to begin with.

Alan Wiggins hit .356 in May of 1986, but then relapsed into the offensive and defensive habits which have annoyed his managers for time out of memory. Acting out of pure frustration, Weaver sent Wiggins to Rochester. As frustrated as he was with Wiggins, Weaver could have found no convincing evidence that the people he would replace Wiggins with (either at second base or in the lead-off spot) would be any better.

At third base, Weaver released Wayne Gross in the spring (a defensible decision at the time, although I disagreed with it) and went with a combination of Rayford and Bonilla. Unhappy with Bonilla's bat, he switched to Rayford and Beniquez. When Rayford didn't hit and Beniquez couldn't do the job defensively, he switched to Tom O'Malley. When the Orioles headed into a slump, he benched O'Malley and tried Gutierrez, Rayford, Kelly Paris, Rickey Jones, and Larry Sheets.

But at third base Weaver was merely floundering, trying anything and everything to see what might work. The most mystifying decision was at catcher. The Orioles used two primary catchers, Rick Dempsey and John Stefero. With Dempsey as the starting catcher, the Orioles were 52–47 with an ERA of 3.82. With Stefero, they were 10–31 with a 4.96 ERA. Now, how long can it take you to figure out that this isn't working? Yet Weaver stuck Stefero in the lineup in August and rode with him right down the toilet.

At the critical moment of the race, at the time when Weaver should have evaluated all the options and known who he wanted to go with, he was experimenting at four positions and in the starting rotation. The Orioles didn't collapse because of injuries or slumps or a lack of guts. The Orioles collapsed because they didn't have any idea what they were doing. What good are the famed Oriole fundamentals to a team of strangers? If the Orioles were going to go into the pennant race like this, they might as well have skipped spring training. It's like the story about the woman rushing around madly on December 23rd buying gifts and wrapping them and searching frantically for salad recipes and trying to find a good deal on a turkey and getting the house ready for the relatives. "You poor dear," coos her neighbor sympathetically. "Didn't they tell you it was coming?" Earl Weaver acted as if he had no idea that the pennant race was coming.

And the leadoff men! Earl Weaver once wrote that "the leadoff hitter should be someone with a high on-base percentage, a guy who draws seventy or more walks and hits for a high average . . . My goal is to have as many players on base as possible when the number-four hitter comes to bat." He said not a word about speed in the lead-off spot. Yet in August of 1986, with the Orioles losing precious ground almost hourly, who was Earl Weaver using in the leadoff spot? John Shelby, Jackie Gutierrez, and Juan Bonilla! Shelby hit .228 and drew 18 walks in 135 games, giving him a .263 on-base percentage. Gutierrez hit .186 and drew 3 walks, giving him a .207 OBP. Bonilla hit .243 and drew 25 walks, giving him a .311 OBP. In several games Shelby led off although he had the lowest on-base percentage of anyone in the lineup. What the hell was Weaver thinking of?

Perhaps he was focusing on the Orioles' lack of speed. The Orioles hit only 13 triples, a major-league record for the fewest by a team in a season. To a considerable degree, this is a park effect. In road games, the Orioles hit 11 triples, the same number as Boston, Chicago and Seattle, and more than Minnesota (10) or the Yankees (9). But in Memorial Stadium in Baltimore, solid concrete outfield walls cut across both foul lines at a slant, and cause balls to ricochet toward center field, thus enabling the defense to pinch the outfielders together and virtually eliminate the gaps. Result: The Orioles hit only two triples in their home park and only 13 for the season, whereas the Twins hit 39 (29 in their home park) and the Mariners hit 41 (30 at home). In a more normal park, the Orioles would not have set this record.

While the park had a lot to do with it, the Orioles' team speed indicators were generally poor. They made only six stolen base attempts per hundred men on first, the lowest percentage in the league except for Boston, although the Os' stealing success rate was average. They hit only 223 doubles, the lowest total in the division. They grounded into 159 double plays, the most in the major leagues. They scored only 29.1% of their runners who were on base not counting home runs, the lowest percentage in the league. The Orioles scored 708 runs, exactly the number that would have been predicted by the runs created formula. Although finishing last, the Orioles had twelve more men on base than their opponents. They were the only American League team to post a losing record despite having more men on than their opponents.

Perhaps, with age and absence from the game, Weaver had lost confidence in his ability to make good decisions about players, and thus tried to cover one decision with another, experimenting with one player after another because he didn't want to face the decision. Perhaps he had lost the arrogance that once cleared his vision. He was no longer strong enough in his beliefs to say as he once would have, "Don't tell me about speed. I don't want to hear about speed. You win games by getting people on base and hitting home runs."

I don't have any inside information, but it is obvious that the Oriole organization is torn by serious internal conflicts. One possibility is that Weaver was getting so much conflicting input from the forces within the organization that he got lost trying to accommodate everybody. An equally good candidate is the possibility that Weaver received so much conflicting advice that he finally reacted by bull-headedly ignoring all of it. Earl Weaver accepted the blame for what happened, saying that he was the one who misjudged the personnel. But to me it seems clear that the confusion and disorganization with which the Orioles confronted the pennant race is an obvious reflection of the internal strife in the front office. Another contributing cause of the collapse was the Eddie Murray situation. Although we don't have the space to discuss the matter adequately, we should not forget that in the period leading up to the collapse, Eddie Murray went on the disabled list for the first time in his career, overreacted to some fairly innocuous remarks by the owner, and demanded a trade. That, no doubt, helped trigger a crisis of confidence within the organization, and thus helped trigger the slump.

Can the Orioles bounce back into contention in 1987? It's a difficult question. It has been shown that how a team plays late in the season tends to indicate how they will play in the following season, and the Orioles were awful late in the season. On the other hand, I almost get the feeling that the Orioles' late-season performance was *so* bad that the final totals are not representative of the team's ability. At the end of 1986 the Orioles had no catcher, no second baseman, no third baseman, no center fielder, and a poor starting rotation—but are they really that bad, and if they are how did they get to August 5 before they fell apart?

What the Orioles have going for them is one of the best power corps in the game. The Orioles have Eddie Murray, Cal Ripken, Larry Sheets, Mike Young, Fred Lynn, Terry Kennedy, Jim Traber, and a kid named Ken Gerhart. If five of the eight have good years the Orioles will hit close to 200 homers. The development of just one player who can play second or third or center field and get on base could put the Oriole offense back among the league's best. That being the case, the Os' lack of offense at one or two positions would not be crucial, and they could carry a glove to fill one of those spots.

But it is very, very difficult to see how the Oriole pitching and defense, once the cornerstone of their success, can be rebuilt so quickly. Three Oriole pitchers (Dixon, Boddicker, and Eric Bell) have the potential to be pretty good—but while three have the potential to be good, none of them has been. It seems to me unlikely that the Orioles can contend in 1987.

Rick DEMPSEY, Catcher

	G	AB	Hit	2B	3B	HR	Run	RBI	TBB	SO	SB	CS	Avg
8.76 years		451	107	21	1	9	50	43	53	66	2	2	.238
1986	122	327	68	15	1	13	42	29	45	78	1	0	.208
First Half	66	187	40	9	0	8	23	18	23	42	0	0	.214
Second Half	56	140	28	6	1	5	19	11	22	36	1	0	.200
Vs. RHP		189	33	7	0	7		14	23	57	1	0	.175
Vs. LHP		138	35	8	1	6		15	22	21	0	0	.254
Home	62	158	34	5	0	7	21	15	25	35	0	0	.215
Road	60	169	34	10	1	6	21	14	20	43	1	0	.201
Grass	102	261	52	10	1	11	36	24	38	60	1	0	.199
Turf	20	66	16	5	0	2	6	5	7	18	0	0	.242

Mike YOUNG, Left Field

	G	AB	Hit	2B	3B	HR	Run	RBI	TBB	SO	SB	CS	Avg
2.53 years		497	128	22	2	21	72	70	62	124	4	3	.257
1986	117	369	93	15	1	9	43	42	49	90	3	1	.252
First Half	71	226	54	11	0	5	27	28	36	61	1	0	.239
Second Half	46	143	39	4	1	4	16	14	13	29	2	1	.273
Vs. RHP		244	59	10	0	6		27	33	64	0	0	.242
Vs. LHP		125	34	5	1	3		15	16	26	3	1	.272
Home	56	167	45	9	0	5	22	16	22	35	2	1	.269
Road	61	202	48	6	1	4	21	26	27	55	1	0	.238
Grass	100	310	78	11	0	9	39	34	39	69	3	1	.252
Turf	17	59	15	4	1	0	4	8	10	21	0	0	.254

Eddie MURRAY, First Base

	G	AB	Hit	2B	3B	HR	Run	RBI	TBB	SO	SB	CS	Avg
9.25 years		608	181	32	2	30	96	110	77	83	6	2	.299
1986	137	495	151	25	1	17	61	84	78	49	3	0	.305
First Half	80	287	85	11	0	11	38	52	47	33	1	0	.296
Second Half	57	208	66	14	1	6	23	32	31	16	2	0	.317
Vs. RHP		359	110	17	1	11		61	65	36	1	0	.306
Vs. LHP		136	41	8	0	6		23	13	13	2	0	.301
Home	66	242	75	10	1	9	24	47	31	24	0	0	.310
Road	71	253	76	15	0	8	37	37	47	25	3	0	.300
Grass	117	422	130	22	1	15	53	76	71	42	2	0	.308
Turf	20	73	21	3	0	2	8	8	7	7	1	0	.288

John SHELBY, Center Field

	G	AB	Hit	2B	3B	HR	Run	RBI	TBB	SO	SB	CS	Avg
3.03 years		447	107	16	4	10	62	45	21	86	24	5	.240
1986	135	404	92	14	4	11	54	49	18	75	18	6	.228
First Half	65	201	44	6	1	5	29	22	9	42	10	4	.219
Second Half	70	203	48	8	3	6	25	27	9	33	8	2	.236
Vs. RHP		270	61	10	3	6		39	13	53	10	2	.226
Vs. LHP		134	31	4	1	5		10	5	22	8	4	.231
Home	66	186	37	6	0	5	22	17	6	39	8	2	.199
Road	69	218	55	8	4	6	32	32	12	36	10	4	.252
Grass	115	349	80	13	2	10	42	44	15	70	16	5	.229
Turf	20	55	12	1	2	1	12	5	3	5	2	1	.218

Alan WIGGINS, Second Base

	G	AB	Hit	2B	3B	HR	Run	RBI	TBB	SO	SB	CS	Avg
3.37 years		576	151	17	5	1	92	31	61	47	66	18	.263
1986	71	239	60	3	1	0	30	11	22	20	21	7	.251
First Half	60	221	56	3	1	0	28	10	22	18	20	7	.253
Second Half	11	18	4	0	0	0	2	1	0	2	1	0	.222
Vs. RHP		172	40	2	1	0		8	18	15	11	6	.233
Vs. LHP		67	20	1	0	0		3	4	5	10	1	.299
Home	37	124	34	2	1	0	19	5	14	7	13	5	.274
Road	34	115	26	1	0	0	11	6	8	13	8	2	.226
Grass	58	196	47	2	1	0	29	7	19	15	17	6	.240
Turf	13	43	13	1	0	0	1	4	3	5	4	1	.302

Lee LACY, Right Field

	G	AB	Hit	2B	3B	HR	Run	RBI	TBB	SO	SB	CS	Avg
8.86 years		484	140	22	4	9	69	49	38	69	21	9	.289
1986	130	491	141	18	0	11	77	47	37	71	4	6	.287
First Half	71	279	75	11	0	6	45	30	18	45	3	2	.269
Second Half	59	212	66	7	0	5	32	17	19	26	1	4	.311
Vs. RHP		334	97	13	0	6		33	24	57	4	5	.290
Vs. LHP		157	44	5	0	5		14	13	14	0	1	.280
Home	64	230	70	8	0	5	34	19	18	34	1	2	.304
Road	66	261	71	10	0	6	43	28	19	37	3	4	.272
Grass	107	399	117	13	0	10	60	38	29	55	4	3	.293
Turf	23	92	24	5	0	1	17	9	8	16	0	3	.261

Juan BENIQUEZ, Utility

	G	AB	Hit	2B	3B	HR	Run	RBI	TBB	SO	SB	CS	Avg
8.50 years		510	140	21	3	8	68	50	38	60	12	9	.275
1986	113	343	103	15	0	6	48	36	40	49	2	3	.300
First Half	54	169	54	6	0	4	23	16	20	22	0	1	.320
Second Half	59	174	49	9	0	2	25	20	20	27	2	2	.282
Vs. RHP		215	60	9	0	3		20	24	34	2	2	.279
Vs. LHP		128	43	6	0	3		16	16	15	0	1	.336
Home	56	154	42	2	0	4	17	19	18	24	0	1	.273
Road	57	189	61	13	0	2	31	17	22	25	2	2	.323
Grass	97	285	85	11	0	6	37	32	32	42	2	3	.298
Turf	16	58	18	4	0	0	11	4	8	7	0	0	.310

Larry SHEETS, Designated Hitter

	G	AB	Hit	2B	3B	HR	Run	RBI	TBB	SO	SB	CS	Avg
1.44 years		474	129	18	1	25	61	78	35	77	1	1	.271
1986	112	338	92	17	1	18	42	60	21	56	2	0	.272
First Half	53	164	51	9	1	9	22	37	12	23	0	0	.311
Second Half	59	174	41	8	0	9	20	23	9	33	2	0	.236
Vs. RHP		312	88	16	1	17		56	19	48	2	0	.282
Vs. LHP		26	4	1	0	1		4	2	8	0	0	.154
Home	58	181	50	10	0	10	23	34	6	31	0	0	.276
Road	54	157	42	7	1	8	19	26	15	25	2	0	.268
Grass	98	297	83	16	1	17	40	57	20	47	2	0	.279
Turf	14	41	9	1	0	1	2	3	1	9	0	0	.220

Cal RIPKEN, Shortstop

	G	AB	Hit	2B	3B	HR	Run	RBI	TBB	SO	SB	CS	Avg
5.12 years		627	181	36	4	26	103	92	61	81	2	3	.289
1986	162	627	177	35	1	25	98	81	70	60	4	2	.282
First Half	80	296	86	21	1	11	46	43	43	31	1	1	.291
Second Half	82	331	91	14	0	14	52	38	27	29	3	1	.275
Vs. RHP		463	118	18	1	13		56	50	48	4	2	.255
Vs. LHP		164	59	17	0	12		25	20	12	0	0	.360
Home	79	291	77	18	0	10	45	37	36	35	1	0	.265
Road	83	336	100	17	1	15	53	44	34	25	3	2	.298
Grass	137	524	139	27	1	18	80	60	60	51	4	2	.265
Turf	25	103	38	8	0	7	18	21	10	9	0	0	.369

Fred LYNN, Outfield

	G	AB	Hit	2B	3B	HR	Run	RBI	TBB	SO	SB	CS	Avg
9.49 years		589	172	35	4	25	95	98	75	89	7	5	.292
1986	112	397	114	13	1	23	67	67	53	59	2	2	.287
First Half	58	203	65	5	1	13	37	41	28	29	2	2	.320
Second Half	54	194	49	8	0	10	30	26	25	30	0	0	.253
Vs. RHP		301	88	10	1	16		46	46	35	2	2	.292
Vs. LHP		96	26	3	0	7		21	7	24	0	0	.271
Home	57	197	56	6	0	13	37	38	28	28	1	0	.284
Road	55	200	58	7	1	10	30	29	25	31	1	2	.290
Grass	88	304	81	10	0	15	51	48	42	46	1	1	.266
Turf	24	93	33	3	1	8	16	19	11	13	1	1	.355

Mike BODDICKER

Year	(W–L)	GS	Run	Avg	DP	Avg	SB	Avg
1984	(20-11)	34	148	4.35	33	.97	25	.74
1985	(12-17)	32	142	4.44	40	1.25	39	1.22
1986	(14-12)	33	167	5.06	27	.82	36	1.10
1980-1986		126	580	4.60	120	.95	122	.97

	1986 ERA	1986 W–L	1985 ERA	1984 ERA	1983 ERA	1982 ERA	82-86 W–L
Total	4.70	14-12	4.07	2.79	2.77	3.51	63-48
Home	4.66	7-4	3.40	2.17	2.11	2.84	32-22
Road	4.73	7-8	4.77	3.32	3.94	4.15	31-26
East	5.02	6-6	5.79	2.46	3.25	7.71	27-26
West	4.38	8-6	2.87	3.09	2.26	2.57	36-22
1st Half	4.54	10-4	4.12	2.71	4.02		33-21
2nd Half	4.86	4-8	4.00	2.86	2.23	3.51	30-27
Turf	3.14	4-2	5.20	2.51	2.49		11-5
Grass	5.15	10-10	3.89	2.82	2.81		51-43
Day	3.74	6-3	3.44	2.50	2.03	.00	23-14
Night	5.22	8-9	4.28	2.95	3.20	4.66	40-34
April	3.38	2-0	3.09	4.23			5-4
May	3.34	3-1	3.71	1.72	2.96		14-6
June	5.07	5-2	5.24	3.09	3.80		12-9
July	3.74	3-2	3.76	3.51	3.23		11-10
August	5.31	1-4	4.30	2.55	2.49	2.38	12-8
September	7.06	0-3	3.97	2.52	1.93	12.00	9-11

Ken DIXON

Year	(W–L)	GS	Run	Avg	DP	Avg	SB	Avg
1984	(0-1)	2	5	2.50	3	1.50	0	.00
1985	(8-4)	18	94	5.22	17	.94	10	.56
1986	(11-13)	33	142	4.30	31	.94	31	.94
1984-1986		53	241	4.55	51	.96	41	.77

	1986 ERA	1986 W–L	1985 ERA	1985 W–L	85-86 W–L
Total	4.58	11-13	3.67	8-4	19-17
Home	5.24	4-10	4.28	5-3	9-13
Road	3.92	7-3	2.59	3-1	10-4
East	4.30	5-8	2.70	3-1	8-9
West	4.94	6-5	4.88	5-3	11-8
1st Half	4.29	7-7	4.58	4-3	11-10
2nd Half	4.90	4-6	2.81	4-1	8-7
Turf	2.53	4-1	2.36	2-0	6-1
Grass	5.13	7-12	3.92	6-4	13-16
Day	5.40	2-3	4.91	1-3	3-6
Night	4.28	9-10	3.20	7-1	16-11
April	2.63	2-1	1.15	1-0	3-1
May	5.23	3-1	5.53	3-2	6-3
June	6.89	1-4	6.65	0-1	1-5
July	1.57	3-2	3.90	1-0	4-2
August	6.44	1-2	2.20	1-0	2-2
September	5.49	1-3	2.70	2-1	3-4

Scott McGREGOR

Year	(W–L)	GS	Run	Avg	DP	Avg	SB	Avg
1984	(15-12)	30	128	4.27	34	1.13	13	.43
1985	(14-14)	34	167	4.91	38	1.12	21	.62
1986	(11-15)	33	155	4.70	30	.91	20	.61
1977-1986		288	1260	4.38	284	.97	131	.45

	1986 ERA	1986 W–L	1985 ERA	1984 ERA	1983 ERA	1982 ERA	82-86 W–L
Total	4.52	11-15	4.81	3.94	3.18	4.61	72-60
Home	4.53	5-8	4.14	2.90	4.21	4.50	35-30
Road	4.51	6-7	5.45	5.72	2.56	4.74	37-30
East	4.32	4-9	4.49	4.50	2.93	5.15	27-34
West	4.69	7-6	5.12	3.47	3.44	4.24	45-26
1st Half	4.34	6-7	4.38	4.10	3.49	3.93	41-31
2nd Half	4.75	5-8	5.24	3.66	2.90	5.82	31-29
Turf	5.40	1-1	7.55	6.26	1.60		9-8
Grass	4.42	10-14	4.32	3.57	3.57		49-40
Day	4.58	6-4	3.04	5.50	2.72	4.75	22-13
Night	4.49	5-11	5.49	3.38	3.32	4.57	50-47
April	4.32	2-2	5.40	3.98	3.11	3.68	10-9
May	4.73	2-1	5.97	3.32	5.45	3.58	14-7
June	3.83	2-4	2.36	4.42	2.55	4.35	13-13
July	7.66	1-3	5.13	4.23	2.26	4.09	16-9
August	4.32	1-1	8.88	3.74	2.64	9.12	8-14
September	3.86	3-4	3.70		3.72	4.76	11-8

Mike FLANAGAN

Year	(W–L)	GS	Run	Avg	DP	Avg	SB	Avg
1984	(13-13)	34	146	4.29	36	1.06	17	.50
1985	(4-5)	15	60	4.00	18	1.20	11	.73
1986	(7-11)	28	114	4.07	32	1.14	12	.43
1977-1986		300	1342	4.47	340	1.13	126	.42

	1986 ERA	1986 W–L	1985 ERA	1984 ERA	1983 ERA	1982 ERA	82-86 W–L
Total	4.24	7-11	5.13	3.53	3.30	3.97	51-44
Home	3.73	5-2	6.40	2.90	3.50	3.75	32-15
Road	4.61	2-9	4.36	4.12	3.02	4.19	19-29
East	5.03	3-7	4.56	3.26	3.97	4.35	25-22
West	3.60	4-4	5.89	3.75	2.90	3.53	26-22
1st Half	4.35	2-6		3.54	2.72	3.60	22-20
2nd Half	4.13	5-5	5.13	3.52	3.73	4.34	29-24
Turf	4.58	1-4	3.86	5.00	.00		4-7
Grass	4.14	6-7	5.24	3.26	3.70		32-26
Day	5.55	2-5	6.75	2.97	5.30	3.45	18-14
Night	3.72	5-6	4.45	3.83	2.51	4.18	33-30
April	4.33	1-2		4.15	3.41	6.98	6-7
May	3.86	0-2		5.18	1.88	1.98	7-5
June	5.56	0-1		2.06		2.80	8-4
July	3.32	4-1	3.79	3.13		4.95	7-10
August	3.00	2-2	7.12	4.46	4.76	4.30	11-10
September	7.61	0-3	4.17	3.00	3.07	4.44	12-8

Storm DAVIS

Year	(W–L)	GS	Run	Avg	DP	Avg	SB	Avg
1984	(14-9)	31	132	4.26	28	.90	21	.68
1985	(10-8)	28	151	5.39	24	.86	24	.86
1986	(9-12)	25	99	3.96	30	1.20	18	.72
1982-1986		121	579	4.79	115	.95	80	.66

	1986 ERA	W–L	1985 ERA	1984 ERA	1983 ERA	1982 ERA	82-86 W–L
Total	3.62	9-12	4.53	3.12	3.59	3.49	54-40
Home	3.35	5-7	4.53	3.17	3.34	2.93	25-25
Road	3.95	4-5	4.52	3.07	3.81	4.17	29-15
East	3.13	2-5	7.85	3.89	4.06	3.67	19-23
West	3.91	7-7	2.91	2.45	3.27	3.20	35-17
1st Half	3.31	6-8	5.09	2.64	3.23	3.12	24-21
2nd Half	4.17	3-4	3.69	3.66	3.98	3.68	30-19
Turf	7.11	1-1	5.73	2.32	4.34		7-5
Grass	3.31	8-11	4.35	3.25	3.42		39-31
Day	3.90	3-3	5.63	2.43	3.80	3.86	16-12
Night	3.55	6-9	4.11	3.43	3.43	3.40	38-28
April	2.73	1-1	7.23	1.64	2.89	.00	3-1
May	4.33	3-3	3.44	1.84	3.38	1.00	12-7
June	2.82	2-4	4.93	4.62	2.80	1.59	6-12
July	5.56	1-0	4.44	2.05	3.38	4.44	13-3
August	3.63	2-4	4.15	4.19	3.69	3.91	11-11
September	6.00	0-0	3.32	4.46	5.74	3.94	9-6

Don AASE

1986	G	IP	W–L	Sv	H	ER	SO	ERA
Total	66	81.2	6-7	34	71	27	67	2.98
Home	33	46.1	5-3	15	37	15	36	2.91
Road	33	35.1	1-4	19	34	12	31	3.06
East	31	37.0	4-4	13	33	17	29	4.14
West	35	44.2	2-3	21	38	10	38	2.01
1st Half	36	43.0	3-3	22	30	8	39	1.67
2nd Half	30	38.2	3-4	12	41	19	28	4.42
Turf	10	10.2	0-0	7	10	4	8	3.38
Grass	56	71.0	6-7	27	61	23	59	2.92
Day	19	24.2	1-0	12	15	3	18	1.09
Night	47	57.0	5-7	22	56	24	49	3.79
April	10	11.0	1-2	4	6	2	7	1.64
May	12	13.0	1-0	9	10	1	12	.69
June	12	15.2	1-1	7	13	5	18	2.87
July	11	16.1	1-0	7	16	5	14	2.76
August	10	12.2	1-3	4	14	6	7	4.26
September	11	13.0	1-1	3	12	8	9	5.54

OTHERS

Pitcher	(W–L)	GS	Run	Avg	DP	Avg	SB	Avg	Time	Att.
Habyan	(1-3)	5	14	2.80	5	1.00	6	1.20	2:48	100
Bell	(1-2)	4	17	4.25	5	1.25	2	.50	3:03	63
Bordi	(6-4)	1	0	.00	1	1.00	0	.00	2:43	23

RECORDS WITH DIFFERENT STARTING CATCHERS

Catcher	Inn	ER	W–L	ERA	GS	SB	Avg
Dempsey	897.2	381	52-47	3.82	99	69	.70
Stefaro	343.0	189	10-31	4.96	41	37	.90
Pardo	118.0	67	5-8	5.11	13	8	.62
Rayford	44.0	29	4-1	5.93	5	5	1.00
Nichols	17.0	7	1-1	3.71	2	2	1.00
Sheets	17.0	13	1-1	6.88	2	2	1.00

STARTING PITCHERS' AVERAGE TIME AND ATTENDANCE RECORDS

Pitcher	Time	Attendance
Boddicker	2:44	792
McGregor	2:47	744
Dixon	2:58	792
Flanagan	2:44	675
Davis	2:45	563

AMERICAN LEAGUE WEST
DIVISION SHEET

	1st	2nd	RHP	LHP	Home	Road	Grass	Turf	Day	Night	TOTAL	Pct
California	48-39	44-31	68-47	24-23	50-32	42-38	80-58	12-12	28-23	64-47	92-70	.568
Texas	47-41	40-34	59-53	28-22	51-30	36-45	77-59	10-16	17-17	70-58	87-75	.537
Kansas City	40-48	36-38	58-57	18-29	45-36	31-50	25-37	51-49	25-19	51-67	76-86	.469
Oakland	34-56	42-30	51-57	25-29	47-36	29-50	62-75	14-11	35-33	41-53	76-86	.469
Chicago	40-46	32-44	47-62	25-28	41-40	31-50	62-73	10-17	25-24	47-66	72-90	.444
Minnesota	37-51	34-40	49-68	22-23	43-38	28-53	22-40	49-51	19-34	52-57	71-91	.438
Seattle	39-51	28-44	56-72	11-23	41-41	26-54	17-44	50-51	15-27	52-68	67-95	.414

CLUB BATTING

	G	AB	Run	Hit	TB	2B	3B	HR	RBI	GW	SH	SF	HB	TBB	IB	SO	SB	CS	DP	LOB	SHO	Avg	Slug	OBP
California	162	5433	786	1387	2196	236	36	167	743	83	91	61	40	671	45	860	109	42	134	1182	10	.255	.404	.338
Texas	162	5529	771	1479	2365	248	43	184	725	80	31	42	35	511	33	1088	103	84	133	1038	4	.267	.428	.331
Kansas City	162	5561	654	1403	2168	264	45	137	618	73	24	33	36	474	40	919	97	46	101	1142	12	.252	.390	.313
Oakland	162	5435	731	1370	2122	213	25	163	683	70	56	51	32	553	24	983	139	61	105	1087	6	.252	.390	.322
Chicago	162	5406	644	1335	1963	197	34	121	605	67	50	53	34	487	29	940	115	54	123	1036	13	.247	.363	.310
Minnesota	162	5531	741	1446	2369	257	39	196	700	64	44	38	37	501	33	977	81	61	123	1087	11	.261	.428	.325
Seattle	162	5498	718	1392	2191	243	41	158	681	65	52	29	34	572	38	1148	93	76	125	1104	13	.253	.399	.326

OPPOSITION BATTING

	G	AB	Run	Hit	TB	2B	3B	HR	RBI	GW	SH	SF	HB	TBB	IB	SO	SB	CS	DP	LOB	SHO	Avg	Slug	OBP
California	162	5476	684	1356	2107	228	32	153	652	67	41	44	27	478	19	955	61	55	129	1014	12	.248	.385	.309
Texas	162	5455	743	1356	2075	252	16	145	689	67	37	42	41	736	37	1059	165	51	130	1217	8	.249	.380	.340
Kansas City	162	5477	673	1413	2103	237	45	121	642	83	51	48	38	479	46	888	85	67	126	1098	13	.258	.384	.319
Oakland	162	5407	760	1334	2129	223	37	166	711	81	44	55	34	667	35	937	139	52	91	1149	8	.247	.394	.330
Chicago	162	5424	699	1361	2125	239	48	143	649	76	54	43	33	561	28	895	114	56	112	1082	8	.251	.392	.323
Minnesota	162	5619	839	1579	2553	310	32	200	801	88	43	50	46	503	37	937	111	42	138	1127	6	.281	.454	.342
Seattle	162	5626	835	1590	2480	293	42	171	775	88	41	44	49	585	27	944	106	63	165	1191	5	.283	.441	.353

CLUB PITCHING

	W	L	ERA	G	CG	SHO	SV	IP	Hit	TBF	Run	ER	HR	SH	SF	HB	TBB	IB	SO	WP	BK
California	92	70	3.84	162	29	12	40	1456.0	1356	6066	684	621	153	41	44	27	478	19	955	44	6
Texas	87	75	4.11	162	15	8	41	1450.1	1356	6311	743	662	145	37	42	41	736	37	1059	94	13
Kansas City	76	86	3.82	162	24	13	31	1440.2	1413	6093	673	612	121	51	48	38	479	46	888	43	6
Oakland	76	86	4.31	162	22	8	37	1433.0	1334	6208	760	686	166	44	55	34	667	35	937	62	19
Chicago	72	90	3.93	162	18	8	38	1442.1	1361	6115	699	630	143	54	43	33	561	28	895	55	3
Minnesota	71	91	4.77	162	39	6	24	1432.2	1579	6264	839	759	200	43	50	46	503	37	937	58	5
Seattle	67	95	4.65	162	33	5	27	1439.2	1590	6345	835	744	171	41	44	49	585	27	944	46	10

OPPOSITION PITCHING

	W	L	ERA	G	CG	SHO	SV	IP	Hit	TBF	Run	ER	HR	SH	SF	HB	TBB	IB	SO	WP
California	70	92	4.38	162	27	10	30	1443.0	1387	6296	786	702	167	91	61	40	671	45	860	48
Texas	75	87	4.34	162	28	4	31	1446.1	1479	6148	771	698	184	31	42	35	511	33	1088	61
Kansas City	86	76	3.71	162	33	12	32	1444.0	1403	6128	654	596	137	24	33	36	474	40	919	41
Oakland	86	76	4.00	162	26	6	43	1436.1	1370	6127	731	639	163	56	51	32	553	24	983	62
Chicago	90	72	3.61	162	29	13	34	1450.0	1335	6030	644	581	121	50	53	34	487	29	940	55
Minnesota	91	71	4.20	162	27	11	40	1441.0	1446	6151	741	673	196	43	38	37	501	33	977	54
Seattle	95	67	4.05	162	25	13	38	1455.0	1392	6185	718	654	158	52	29	34	572	38	1148	47

CLUB FIELDING

	G	PO	A	E	TC	DP	TP	PB	OSB	OCS	OSB%	OA/SFA	Pct	DER	OR
California	162	4368	1718	107	6193	156	0	12	61	55	.526	27/44	.983	.713	786
Texas	162	4351	1655	122	6128	160	0	25	165	51	.764	39/42	.980	.703	771
Kansas City	162	4322	1757	123	6202	153	0	16	85	67	.560	43/48	.980	.694	654
Oakland	162	4299	1597	135	6031	120	0	16	139	52	.728	24/55	.978	.719	731
Chicago	162	4327	1667	117	6111	142	1	14	114	56	.671	44/43	.981	.711	644
Minnesota	162	4298	1626	118	6042	168	0	12	111	42	.725	26/50	.980	.683	741
Seattle	162	4319	1837	156	6312	191	2	17	106	63	.627	45/44	.975	.668	718

CALIFORNIA ANGELS

Runners on Base:	2098
Opponents on Base:	1861
Net Advantage:	+237
Won-Lost Record:	92-70

The California Angels are the smartest baseball team I've ever seen. In the late seventies, when the Angels were trying to stop the Royals by firing free agents at them, they would patch together a lineup out of two or three free agents a year and a couple of rookies and some guy they could pick up in a trade who had flashy batting stats in Boston or some place, and when this "team" didn't win they would fire the manager. The Angels changed managers *in mid-season* in 1974, 1976, 1977, and 1978. They also changed managers several times in the seventies between seasons. With each manager trying to "motivate" and guide a team assembled and instructed by somebody else, the Angels had no concept of executing fundamentals in a prearranged way. Since almost everyone on the team was either a free agent or a trade acquisition, there couldn't have been any "organizational" way of doing anything, so each player just did his own thing. Although they could hit and they had Nolan Ryan and Frank Tanana, each Angels game revealed a series of outfield collisions, dropped double play balls, basepath mixups, missed cutoff men, botched hit and run attempts, and pop ups dropping in the middle of player triangles. When you bought a ticket to see the Angels play, you expected to see these things. It was so bad that even though I was a Royals fan and the Angels were the enemy and you wanted them to lose, it was irritating to watch a major-league team play this way. They were a team in name only, a team only in that they all wore the same uniform and got credited for driving each other in.

As a sinner becomes a saint and a radical becomes a Reaganite, with the passage of time the Angels have struggled away from that pole and reached the other. The talent on the Angels now is much less impressive (*Sports Illustrated* keeps picking them to finish fifth), but less impressive only in the sense of not being able to run as fast or throw as hard. I've never seen a team, anywhere, anytime, execute so well. Do Boone, DeCinces, and Downing ever make mistakes? Reggie is a smart player. Grich is a smart player. They make very few mistakes and turn the double play extremely well. Even the young guys are smart players. Wally Joyner plays like he taught first base at Stanford. When was the last time you saw Dick Schofield cost his team a run? The 1986 Angels were a great tribute to a great manager.

The statistical evidence of this type of excellence is abundant and varied, and we'll get to that in a moment, but it's not just the stats. If you're ever in a mood to watch a game *very carefully* the Angels are the team to watch.

They have all these plays they run—Bob Boone counts three and snaps the ball from a crouch to DeCinces, who is playing exactly as far off base as the runner is and beats him to the bag by a half step, which happens to be just when the ball is there. They line up two cutoff men so that the runner will watch the wrong one, and then when he thinks the throw has gone through they throw behind him. And they almost never throw the ball away while doing this.

They move runners. The Angels laid down 91 sacrifice bunts, eight fewer than in 1985 but still 35 more than any other American League team. They hit 61 sacrifice flies, eight more than any other American League team. They struck out only 860 times, fewest of any team in the division, with an exceptional 1.28–1 strikeout to walk ratio. The Angels scored 32.1% of their runners who were on base not counting home runs, the best percentage in the division. They scored 21 runs more than projected by the runs created method.

Though not a fast team, the Angels' 109 stolen bases were above the league average (105), and their stolen base percentage was an excellent 72.2%, best in the division. What Mauch's players say about him is that he never asks his players to do what they aren't capable of doing, and this is a classic case. Pettis and Schofield, the guys who are capable of stealing bases in a way that will help the team, will steal, and the rest of the team doesn't. Those two players had 91 stolen base attempts, and were successful over 80% of the time. The rest of the team attempted 60 stolen bases, and was successful 60% of the time.

The basis of any offense, however, is getting people on base. Whether you're going to grind the offense by speed, bunting, power, or whatever—and the Angels use all of them—it's not going to work if you don't have people on base. The Angels hit, as a team, just .255, seven points below the league average, yet they still had lots of people on base because they drew 671 walks, 26 more than any other major-league team. It was the highest walk total by any major-league team since the Big Red Machine drew 681 in 1976. That gave them an excellent .338 team on-base percentage, third in the league. Then you consider that Angel pitchers walked only 478 men, and the Angels have a whopping 193-baserunner advantage just in the walks. The 478 walks was the lowest total in the division, helped by the fact that Mauch ordered only 19 intentional walks, the fewest of any major-league team. There would be very few teams that would be so weak in other areas that they could have 193 more men on base than their opponents and not post a winning record.

The Angels had little edges all around. They hit eight doubles more than their opponents (236–228), giving them an edge of about six runs. They hit four more triples than their opponents (36–32), giving them an edge of about four runs. They out-homered their opponents 167–153, giving them an edge of about 20 runs. They had nine more singles than their opponents, giving them an edge of about four runs. They stole bases not often but effectively, while Boone and the pitchers eliminated the opposition running game, giving them another 18-run advantage (Angel opponents survived only 55 of 116 stolen base attempts). They had 40 hit batsmen while their opponents had 27, giving them about four runs. They had 91 sacrifice bunts while their opponents had only 41, the advantage of which is extremely debatable, but the point is that they were not inferior to their opponents in any category, and they have all these little edges which add up to about 56 runs. Then you get to the real meat of the Angels' superiority to their opponents: They had 193 more baserunners on walks, which means an extra 60-odd runs on the scoreboard, and the Angels are more than 100 runs better than their opponents. They did, in fact, outscore their opposition by 102 runs.

The Angels committed only 107 errors; their opponents committed 152. The Angels' pitchers threw 44 wild pitches, while their opponents committed 48. You can measure the same things in other ways. Given this broad base of superiority, you might expect the Angels to have no sharp splits in their record, and you would be mostly right. The California comment in the 1986 *Abstract* dealt with the success of Mauch's teams in one-run games. The reason for doing that study was that the 1985 Angels had a 30–13 record in one-run games. They continued to do well in that category in 1986, winning 29 of 45 one-run games (or 28 of 44, depending on what source you believe). The Angels were just 12–12 on artificial turf and did not do particularly well against left-handed pitchers, going 24–23 against lefties (.511) as opposed to 68–47 against righthanders (.591), but seem to have as many players who hit better against lefties as the other way around. The Angels hit .259 against left-handers, only .253 against northpaws.

Like most of the other champions of 1986, the Angels faced no rugged competition. The Angels played sub-.500 ball (23–25) through May, but Texas and California pulled in front of the division in June. The Rangers dogged their heels in a somewhat menacing manner into September, but the Royals never could get anything going, and few people thought the Rangers would mount a charge. The Angels had the best record in the league after August 1. The biggest difference between the first half of the season and the second was that Ron Romanick (5–8, 5.50) was pitching in the first half and John Candelaria (10–2, 2.55) in the second. Donnie Moore, troubled with a sore shoulder, also had a 2.22 ERA the second half of the season after 4.95 the first half, restoring a shaky bullpen. Don Sutton, always a strong finisher, finished strong once again.

Sutton looks like he intends to go 15–11 forever. The Angels' Most Valuable Player in 1986 was probably Mike Witt, one of the league's outstanding starting pitchers, and their biggest improvement from the year before was either at first base (Joyner was much better than Carew had been) or in the impressive development of Kirk McCaskill. Dividing the team into infield, outfield, starting rotation, and bullpen, the Angels' strongest element by far was the starting rotation of Witt, McCaskill, Sutton, and Candelaria, one of the best in baseball. Like many classic teams, the Angels got little offense up the middle but superb defense. Catcher Boone, though pushing 40, looks 30 and is probably the best defensive catcher in the league. Gary Pettis, though he turns 29 in April, looks 17 and is the best defensive center fielder in *anybody's* league. The double play combination of Schofield and Grich was better offensively and not as brilliant defensively, yet both are fine defensive players and neither is a .300 hitter or anything.

The corner men in that scheme are counted on to provide the offense, and they did. First baseman Wally Joyner, third baseman Doug DeCinces, and left fielder Brian Downing were all excellent offensive players as well as capable defenders at the less demanding positions. The three players were almost equally valuable; it would be very hard to say who contributed the most. In right field and at DH the Angels had very productive combinations, meaning that they got either championship quality offense or championship quality defense out of every position. They had no real weaknesses except at times the bullpen.

For the last two years, the Angels have been a surprise team. In 1987 more will be expected of them, and it will be difficult for them to avoid slipping markedly. At this point who will and will not return is still being sorted out, although it seems clear that many of the Angels' veterans will be gone. On the one hand, I can see the need for this. There is an inevitable end clearly in sight for players such as Boone, Grich, Jackson, and Hendrick, and even Don Sutton probably can't really go on more than another decade or so. If the Angels bank on those players, they're going to be buying into a declining market, and they could well make the coming decline phase (or rebuilding period) much deeper and darker than it needs to be. On the other hand, I get the feeling that the Angels might not clearly understand how valuable some of the old, slow .240 hitters really are. I don't understand why the Angels don't seem to want to re-sign Ruppert Jones. Jones hit just .229, but he had a secondary average close to .400, and was one of the key reasons for the Angels' big edge in walks. Devon White will contribute in other ways, but I doubt that he will contribute as much. I do understand why the Angels are letting Reggie go, but between Reggie and Ruppert the Angels will be losing 156 walks, 35 homers, and 138 runs scored. Still, age is an indicator of probable decline. The Angels are old (their starting lineup averages 32.3) and are wise to start blending in some younger people.

If the Angels can win 85 or 88 games and stay in contention, they ought to consider that a good year. I think they'll drop, but with their superb starting pitching I don't think they'll drop a lot further than that. In this division, that means they should have a chance to win.

Bob BOONE, Catcher

	G	AB	Hit	2B	3B	HR	Run	RBI	TBB	SO	SB	CS	Avg
11.38 years		526	132	22	2	8	49	62	47	44	3	4	.251
1986	144	442	98	12	2	7	48	49	43	30	1	0	.222
First Half	74	227	47	3	1	3	22	17	19	16	0	0	.207
Second Half	70	215	51	9	1	4	26	32	24	14	1	0	.237
Vs. RHP		290	65	9	2	5		32	26	21	1	0	.224
Vs. LHP		152	33	3	0	2		17	17	9	0	0	.217
Home	75	212	40	6	2	1	24	18	23	17	1	0	.189
Road	69	230	58	6	0	6	24	31	20	13	0	0	.252
Grass	125	373	84	11	2	6	45	42	39	27	1	0	.225
Turf	19	69	14	1	0	1	3	7	4	3	0	0	.203

Brian DOWNING, Left Field

	G	AB	Hit	2B	3B	HR	Run	RBI	TBB	SO	SB	CS	Avg
9.79 years		531	141	24	2	17	78	75	80	73	4	3	.266
1986	152	513	137	27	4	20	90	95	90	84	4	4	.267
First Half	77	268	76	17	3	9	48	44	45	41	4	2	.284
Second Half	75	245	61	10	1	11	42	51	45	43	0	2	.249
Vs. RHP		330	93	13	3	13		64	48	50	4	2	.282
Vs. LHP		183	44	14	1	7		31	42	34	0	2	.240
Home	78	260	72	10	3	13	42	53	47	37	3	2	.277
Road	74	253	65	17	1	7	48	42	43	47	1	2	.257
Grass	129	435	120	20	3	18	74	80	79	73	3	3	.276
Turf	23	78	17	7	1	2	16	15	11	11	1	1	.218

Wally JOYNER, First Base

	G	AB	Hit	2B	3B	HR	Run	RBI	TBB	SO	SB	CS	Avg
0.95 years		624	181	28	3	23	86	105	60	61	5	2	.290
1986	154	593	172	27	3	22	82	100	57	58	5	2	.290
First Half	80	314	94	12	1	19	50	61	24	36	1	1	.299
Second Half	74	279	78	15	2	3	32	39	33	22	4	1	.280
Vs. RHP		401	127	24	2	16		76	43	34	5	1	.317
Vs. LHP		192	45	3	1	6		24	14	24	0	1	.234
Home	80	294	82	10	1	11	41	40	33	27	2	2	.279
Road	74	299	90	17	2	11	41	60	24	31	3	0	.301
Grass	133	520	152	22	3	18	71	84	48	47	5	2	.292
Turf	21	73	20	5	0	4	11	16	9	11	0	0	.274

Gary PETTIS, Center Field

	G	AB	Hit	2B	3B	HR	Run	RBI	TBB	SO	SB	CS	Avg
2.78 years		528	133	17	8	4	89	46	71	140	58	15	.251
1986	154	539	139	23	4	5	93	58	69	132	50	13	.258
First Half	75	269	71	11	2	2	40	26	26	63	18	8	.264
Second Half	79	270	68	12	2	3	53	32	43	69	32	5	.252
Vs. RHP		363	90	17	2	3		36	55	97	33	8	.248
Vs. LHP		176	49	6	2	2		22	14	35	17	5	.278
Home	75	251	59	7	1	1	38	19	32	63	22	7	.235
Road	79	288	80	16	3	4	55	39	37	69	28	6	.278
Grass	130	458	114	18	2	5	80	48	59	113	42	10	.249
Turf	24	81	25	5	2	0	13	10	10	19	8	3	.309

Bobby GRICH, Second Base

	G	AB	Hit	2B	3B	HR	Run	RBI	TBB	SO	SB	CS	Avg
12.40 years		556	148	26	4	18	83	70	88	103	8	7	.226
1986	98	313	84	18	0	9	42	30	39	54	1	3	.268
First Half	39	128	32	4	0	4	15	13	9	18	0	1	.250
Second Half	59	185	52	14	0	5	27	17	30	36	1	2	.281
Vs. RHP		147	35	9	0	3		14	19	33	1	1	.238
Vs. LHP		166	49	9	0	6		16	20	21	0	1	.295
Home	46	135	42	10	0	5	19	17	12	18	1	1	.311
Road	52	178	42	8	0	4	23	13	27	36	0	2	.236
Grass	82	262	74	16	0	7	35	25	32	47	1	3	.282
Turf	16	51	10	2	0	2	7	5	7	7	0	0	.196

George HENDRICK, Right Field

	G	AB	Hit	2B	3B	HR	Run	RBI	TBB	SO	SB	CS	Avg
11.81 years		579	162	28	2	22	77	90	46	83	5	4	.279
1986	102	283	77	13	1	14	45	47	26	41	1	1	.272
First Half	51	153	39	5	1	7	22	21	13	27	1	1	.255
Second Half	51	130	38	8	0	7	23	26	13	14	0	0	.292
Vs. RHP		109	26	6	0	5		16	10	24	1	1	.239
Vs. LHP		174	51	7	1	9		31	16	17	0	0	.293
Home	51	135	39	6	0	8	16	26	12	19	0	1	.289
Road	51	148	38	7	1	6	29	21	14	22	1	0	.257
Grass	89	244	68	13	1	11	40	40	26	33	1	1	.279
Turf	13	39	9	0	0	3	5	7	0	8	0	0	.231

Doug DeCINCES, Third Base

	G	AB	Hit	2B	3B	HR	Run	RBI	TBB	SO	SB	CS	Avg
9.33 years		573	150	31	3	24	76	87	59	87	6	5	.261
1986	140	512	131	20	3	26	69	96	52	74	2	2	.256
First Half	69	256	62	10	1	10	30	43	27	32	0	1	.242
Second Half	71	256	69	10	2	16	39	53	25	42	2	1	.270
Vs. RHP		339	84	12	2	17		61	31	50	2	2	.248
Vs. LHP		173	47	8	1	9		35	21	24	0	0	.272
Home	72	259	68	8	0	14	35	49	25	39	1	0	.263
Road	68	253	63	12	3	12	34	47	27	35	1	2	.249
Grass	122	451	118	17	3	23	60	88	43	66	1	2	.262
Turf	18	61	13	3	0	3	9	8	9	8	1	0	.213

Reggie JACKSON, Designated Hitter

	G	AB	Hit	2B	3B	HR	Run	RBI	TBB	SO	SB	CS	Avg
16.70 years		571	150	27	3	33	90	99	80	150	14	7	.263
1986	132	419	101	12	2	18	65	58	92	115	1	1	.241
First Half	64	204	60	7	1	7	35	31	49	58	1	0	.294
Second Half	68	215	41	5	1	11	30	27	43	57	0	1	.191
Vs. RHP		348	84	9	2	18		54	81	91	1	1	.241
Vs. LHP		71	17	3	0	0		4	11	24	0	0	.239
Home	67	195	54	6	2	11	33	32	51	54	0	0	.277
Road	65	224	47	6	0	7	32	26	41	61	1	1	.210
Grass	115	360	89	9	2	15	56	48	83	98	1	1	.247
Turf	17	59	12	3	0	3	9	10	9	17	0	0	.203

Dick SCHOFIELD, Shortstop

	G	AB	Hit	2B	3B	HR	Run	RBI	TBB	SO	SB	CS	Avg
2.76 years		489	108	17	4	10	58	45	44	77	14	4	.221
1986	139	458	114	17	6	13	67	57	48	55	23	5	.249
First Half	64	207	48	9	1	6	32	24	23	25	13	1	.232
Second Half	75	251	66	8	5	7	35	33	25	30	10	4	.263
Vs. RHP		295	66	9	3	9		39	20	35	22	4	.224
Vs. LHP		163	48	8	3	4		18	28	20	1	1	.294
Home	72	226	52	5	2	7	32	28	30	32	12	4	.230
Road	67	232	62	12	4	6	35	29	18	23	11	1	.267
Grass	123	403	99	12	6	11	60	50	45	52	19	5	.246
Turf	16	55	15	5	0	2	7	7	3	3	4	0	.273

Ruppert JONES, Right Field

	G	AB	Hit	2B	3B	HR	Run	RBI	TBB	SO	SB	CS	Avg
7.69 years		549	137	27	5	18	80	72	67	101	18	11	.250
1986	126	393	90	21	3	17	73	49	64	87	10	3	.229
First Half	64	199	49	15	3	8	46	29	37	42	8	1	.246
Second Half	62	194	41	6	0	9	27	20	27	45	2	2	.211
Vs. RHP		348	82	18	3	15		42	56	77	10	3	.236
Vs. LHP		45	8	3	0	2		7	8	10	0	0	.178
Home	62	182	45	12	0	10	35	23	37	40	4	2	.247
Road	64	211	45	9	3	7	38	26	27	47	6	1	.213
Grass	108	331	76	20	2	13	59	40	57	74	8	3	.230
Turf	18	62	14	1	1	4	14	9	7	13	2	0	.226

Don SUTTON*

Year	(W–L)	GS	Run	Avg	DP	Avg	SB	Avg
1984	(14-12)	33	126	3.82	21	.64	25	.76
1985	(15-10)	34	158	4.65	24	.71	21	.62
1986	(15-11)	34	158	4.65	25	.74	17	.50
1976-1986		353	1506	4.27	240	.68	290	.82

	1986 ERA	W–L	1985 ERA	1984 ERA	1983 ERA	1982 ERA	82-86 W–L
Total	3.74	15-11	3.86	3.77	4.08	3.29	56-47
Home	3.23	10-6	3.31	4.00	3.96	2.73	30-25
Road	4.58	5-5	4.43	3.43	4.20	4.15	26-22
East	3.13	10-5	3.91	3.73	3.50	3.29	31-21
West	4.38	5-6	3.81	3.80	4.58		25-26
1st Half	4.59	7-5	4.06	3.61	3.31		27-21
2nd Half	2.97	8-6	3.64	3.95	5.05	3.29	29-26
Turf	4.68	2-2	6.21	3.92	3.94		10-9
Grass	3.56	13-9	3.34	3.73	4.11		42-37
Day	3.60	5-3	3.01	4.53	5.24	3.18	22-12
Night	3.80	10-8	4.21	3.52	3.46	3.38	34-35
April	10.31	0-2	6.38	3.23	1.74		7-7
May	4.78	2-3	6.44	3.67	5.35		5-8
June	2.84	4-0	1.62	4.02	2.76		11-6
July	2.94	3-2	3.51	3.22	5.40		12-7
August	3.38	3-2	2.47	4.05	5.35		9-9
September	2.30	3-2	4.42	4.35	4.15	3.29	12-10

* 1982 stats with Milwaukee only

Kirk McCASKILL

Year	(W–L)	GS	Run	Avg	DP	Avg	SB	Avg
1985	(12-12)	29	141	4.86	31	1.07	8	.28
1986	(17-10)	33	151	4.58	28	.85	10	.30
1985-1986		62	292	4.71	59	.95	18	.29

	1986 ERA	W–L	1985 ERA	W–L	85-86 W–L
Total	3.36	17-10	4.70	12-12	29-22
Home	2.93	6-5	4.58	7-4	13-9
Road	3.73	11-5	4.82	5-8	16-13
East	3.18	10-4	5.73	5-9	15-13
West	3.57	7-6	3.32	7-3	14-9
1st Half	3.57	9-5	4.39	4-5	13-10
2nd Half	3.15	8-5	4.93	8-7	16-12
Turf	4.88	2-1	3.00	1-1	3-2
Grass	3.17	15-9	4.91	11-11	26-20
Day	4.55	5-3	4.24	5-4	10-7
Night	2.93	12-7	4.99	7-8	19-15
April	3.13	2-1			2-1
May	4.54	2-2	6.30	0-3	2-5
June	3.38	4-2	3.60	2-2	6-4
July	1.64	4-1	4.38	4-2	8-3
August	5.08	2-1	3.52	3-2	5-3
September	2.77	3-3	6.13	3-3	6-6

Mike WITT

Year	(W–L)	GS	Run	Avg	DP	Avg	SB	Avg
1984	(15-11)	34	138	4.06	27	.79	17	.50
1985	(15-9)	35	144	4.11	44	1.26	22	.63
1986	(18-10)	34	178	5.24	44	1.29	8	.24
1981-1986		169	764	4.52	194	1.15	89	.53

	1986 ERA	W–L	1985 ERA	1984 ERA	1983 ERA	1982 ERA	82-86 W–L
Total	2.84	18-10	3.56	3.47	4.91	3.51	63-50
Home	2.62	11-5	3.38	2.69	4.93	2.59	34-28
Road	3.09	7-5	3.75	4.20	4.86	4.50	29-22
East	2.99	8-7	3.70	3.94	4.34	4.84	27-30
West	2.67	10-3	3.44	2.98	5.45	2.56	36-20
1st Half	3.27	9-6	2.96	3.78	4.32	3.59	31-27
2nd Half	2.42	9-4	4.29	3.14	5.36	3.43	32-23
Turf	2.97	1-1	3.03	4.89	4.64		7-4
Grass	2.83	17-9	3.65	3.17	4.95		48-40
Day	4.40	6-5	3.71	5.11	5.93	2.42	20-12
Night	2.06	12-5	3.50	2.66	4.81	3.95	43-38
April	2.91	2-1	3.18	3.92	4.85	2.73	9-8
May	3.43	2-3	3.48	5.93	4.66	3.18	7-11
June	3.42	4-2	2.82	2.35	3.86	3.41	13-6
July	2.59	3-1	3.26	2.51	5.25	4.13	10-7
August	0.21	5-0	2.87	4.14	4.99	2.98	16-6
September	4.21	2-3	5.51	2.82	5.59	4.65	8-12

Donnie MOORE

1986	G	IP	W–L	Sv	H	ER	SO	ERA
Total	49	72.2	4-5	21	60	24	53	2.97
Home	21	31.1	4-0	8	22	8	21	2.30
Road	28	41.1	0-5	13	38	16	32	3.48
East	24	33.1	1-4	11	29	13	21	3.51
West	25	39.1	3-1	10	31	11	32	2.52
1st Half	15	20.0	1-3	7	16	11	16	4.95
2nd Half	34	52.2	3-2	14	44	13	37	2.22
Turf	9	12.1	0-2	5	11	5	8	3.65
Grass	40	60.1	4-3	16	49	19	45	2.83
Day	21	29.0	3-2	10	23	8	24	2.48
Night	28	43.2	1-3	11	37	16	29	3.30
April	9	11.2	1-1	5	7	6	12	4.63
May	5	7.1	0-2	2	9	5	3	6.14
June	1	1.0	0-0	0	0	0	1	.00
July	9	14.0	0-0	5	11	2	9	1.29
August	13	19.2	2-2	6	15	5	17	2.29
September	12	19.0	1-0	3	18	6	11	2.84

OTHERS

Pitcher	(W–L)	GS	Run	Avg	DP	Avg	SB	Avg	Time	Att.
Romanick	(5-8)	18	87	4.83	24	1.33	4	.22	2:50	504
Candelaria	(10-2)	16	96	6.00	13	.81	5	.31	2:40	446
Slaton	(4-6)	12	56	4.67	7	.58	7	.58	2:47	288
Chadwick	(0-5)	7	24	3.43	6	.86	4	.57	2:51	174
Lugo	(1-1)	3	15	5.00	2	.67	1	.33	2:54	68
Ruhle	(1-3)	3	11	3.67	2	.67	3	1.00	2:36	87
Cook	(0-2)	1	3	3.00	2	2.00	2	2.00	2:46	28
Fraser	(0-0)	1	7	7.00	3	3.00	1	1.00		6

STARTING PITCHERS' AVERAGE TIME AND ATTENDANCE RECORDS

Pitcher	Time	Attendance
Sutton	2:42	956
Witt	2:49	964
McCaskill	2:48	868

RECORDS WITH DIFFERENT STARTING CATCHERS

Catcher	Inn	ER	W–L	ERA	GS	SB	Avg
Boone	1241.0	509	84-53	3.69	137	44	.32
Narron	190.0	96	7-15	4.55	22	13	.59
Miller	25.0	16	1-2	5.76	3	4	1.33

TEXAS RANGERS

Runners on Base:	2025
Opponents on Base:	2133
Net Advantage:	−108
Won-Lost Record:	87-75

As the California Angels in 1986 seemed an incarnation of the concept of experience, the Texas Rangers seemed to embody youth. With three young pitchers and young players at eight positions, the Rangers overpowered their own reckless mistakes with the cockiness of young men quite unaware that the world was not yet ready to step aside and watch them win.

A year ago this winter, the Rangers were blistered in the papers when they traded for Pete Incaviglia, who had refused to sign with Montreal because Montreal was going to send him to the minors. The going line about this trade was that 1) the Rangers had made it more difficult for everybody else to sign the number one draft picks, who were now liable to demand trades; and 2) Incaviglia had a big swing and wouldn't hit major-league pitching anyway. The second point proved to be false and the imminent disaster in the first has failed to materialize, so this petty controversy could well be forgotten now, were there not so much to be learned from it.

It simply is not true that every player has to go through a minor-league apprenticeship in order to play in the majors. It never has been true. There have always been some players (probably many players) for whom the minor leagues were just a nuisance from which they learned nothing and in which they lost 20–40% of their productive life as ballplayers. But the problem is that the most dangerous thing you can do in any learning process is to expose the student to a situation that he or she can't handle. If the young player gets in over his head his confidence can be destroyed, and fears can be set loose in his mind that can never be put away.

And so, understandably, major-league executives become hypercautious about bringing along their young players. It eventually reaches the rather silly point of many organizations insisting that every player stop at every level in his path to the majors, regardless of his individual needs. When they make an exception to their rule by jumping a player across one level—bringing up a rookie all the way from AA ball—they feel like they're doing something bold and innovative. And when an organization does try unsuccessfully to bring a player along quickly, as the Rangers did with Jeff Kunkel, then that organization will be the subject of harsh criticism from the press for having defied the sacred belief that every player should be nurtured slowly.

Throughout baseball history there have been repeated cycles of suddenly rediscovering this truth, rediscovering that some players are ready to play in the major leagues at a young age and without much minor-league experience, and then very gradually burying that secret again under the fear of destroying a player and the fear of criticism. When the cautious attitude is dominant, as in the eighties, then it takes a player of the brashness of Incaviglia to confront it, to say, "No, damn it, I *don't* need to go to the minor leagues. It's a waste of my time and talent." It takes an organization of the self-confidence and imagination of the Texas Rangers to provide an opportunity for him. And so, in a sense, the marriage of Incaviglia and the Rangers was inevitable, because the Rangers were the only organization that was equipped to meet Incaviglia's very legitimate needs.

And there we get to the nub of the matter—the arrogance of the young, the insufferable cockiness of young men for whom there is no place in the world but who will not accept that there is no place for them and who go about shoving rules and habits aside to make their place. There are two great lessons in the Incaviglia brouhaha. One is an important statement about the Ranger management: Tom Grieve and Bobby Valentine think for themselves. We have here clear evidence that one or both of those gentlemen possesses the creative arrogance to say "Look, I don't *care* what Tracy Ringolsby or Peter Gammons or Bill James is going to say about it. *I* think that the best thing for this organization is to get these kids up here and find out if they can play." And that, for the Ranger organization, is a very, very good sign. There are few people in any business who think for themselves and have the damnable arrogance to act on their own judgment—and whatever the business, you can find those people at the top of the form charts.

The import of this for baseball as a whole is that most people merely imitate the success of others. If the Rangers start to win big—maybe I should say *when* the Rangers start to win big, although it probably won't be this year—there is going to be a wave of the sincerest form of flattery. There are probably going to be many players jumping right out of college into starting roles in the major leagues. Some people feel that the Royals will stick Bo Jackson in the lineup this year, and Jackson is as green as a pool table.

Of course, in writing about this I'm not just talking about Incaviglia, but about Oddibe, who is younger than Incaviglia, and about Ruben Sierra, who is *three years* younger than either of them, and about Bobby Witt and others. To tell you how much I like the Ranger outfielders, I'd just say that Incaviglia has to have at least a 50%

chance of hitting 300 home runs in his career, and I don't like Incaviglia anywhere near as much as the other two guys. If Incaviglia develops as the Rangers dream he will, what would he be? Harmon Killebrew, probably, Killebrew being the greatest of the low-average, slow-moving sluggers. The downside is maybe Jeff Burroughs.

If Oddibe McDowell develops like the Rangers dream, he could be a lot better than that. If Incaviglia has a chance to develop into Killebrew, then McDowell has a chance to develop into Willie Mays. Well, maybe a center field Joe Morgan. Oddibe's a hell of a player already. At the worst, he should be at least as good as Chet Lemon.

If Ruben Sierra developed like the Rangers dream, he'd be Henry Aaron. At the bottom, he might be somebody like Claudell Washington. The odds are overwhelming that the three players are not going to develop into an outfield of Killebrew, Mays, and Aaron, and the odds are long on their developing into an outfield as good as Bell, Moseby, and Barfield. But an outfield of Burroughs, Chet Lemon, and Claudell Washington would be pretty good, and the odds are that they'll be better than that. If the Rangers can hold onto those three players, they're going to have a heck of an outfield.

There are so many other reasons that the Rangers had a good year that I feel helpless trying to understand them all. The continued development of Don Slaught, combined with the signing of Darrell Porter, strengthened the catching. The trade for Scott Fletcher improved the shortstop position tremendously; in retrospect I should have been able to see at the time what a good trade that was. The good year by Steve Buechelle helped. The comeback of Larry Parrish helped. Pete O'Brien should not be taken for granted merely because he always has a good year.

The improvement was largely offensive; not much was in the pitching. The Rangers in 1985 scored 617 runs and allowed 785. In 1986 they were up to 771 runs offensively (+154) and down to 743 allowed (−42). With an adjustment for the change in the league, the improvement was 74% offensive. The Rangers had the highest team batting average in the division (.267) and were second in the division in runs scored. The team was well above average in home runs, hitting 184.

They did have offensive weaknesses. They were, after all, only 25 runs better than an average offensive team. The strikeout to walk ratio of their hitters, 2.12–1, was the worst in the American League. They were awful base stealers, picking up 103 bases (below average) while losing 84 baserunners, the most of any team in the league. Their 55.1% stolen base percentage is not quite as bad as Seattle (55.0) or Boston (54.7), but they ran more often than those teams did. They had a net loss of about ten runs on their attempts to steal, although their other speed indicators were quite good. While they didn't lead the league in triples, they hit more triples as a percentage of balls in play than any other American League team. They had more stolen base attempts as a percentage of runners than any AL team except Oakland. The Rangers scored 38.1% of their runners, the highest percentage in the division. Again, that's a cocky young team—fast, but not knowing enough to use the speed effectively on the bases.

The youth of the Rangers was even more evident in the pitching. Though they led the league in strikeouts, Ranger pitchers passed out 736 walks, an astonishing to-

tal. It was the most walks by a major-league team since the 770 given up by Cleveland in 1971. The Rangers established a major-league record by throwing 94 wild pitches. They led the American League in passed balls, with 25, and were second in balks, with 13.

Bobby Valentine used 328 relievers, far more than any other team in the league (the White Sox were second at 297, and the average was 269).

In some ways I would say that I like the young Ranger pitchers as much as I like the outfielders, and in other ways I wouldn't say that I do. If you look at outstanding pitchers as rookies, there are two things that strike you. One is that they are virtually always power pitchers when they reach the majors. The other is that they are usually not successful before the age of 24 or 25. The reason for that is that if the player finds his control at a very young age, he will usually be worked too hard before his arm is fully mature, and will wind up like Frank Tanana if not Gary Nolan.

Correa is a very young pitcher who has a fine arm and seems to have the makeup of an outstanding pitcher. Bobby Witt has a chance to be an outstanding pitcher. These guys fit the profile of a future star much better than do players like Eric King, Scott Bankhead, Juan Nieves, Bill Wegman, Mark Portugal, Bob Tewksbury, and Doug Drabek. Correa, Witt, and Guzman all have a better chance of being big stars than almost any other American League rookie pitcher. But the policies that work with everyday players may well backfire with pitchers.

The Rangers had a 51–30 record in Texas, tying Boston for best home record in the league, but were just 36–45 on the road (don't you always sort of assume that a young team should have a large home/road differential? I should check that out.) Despite the impressive offensive stats, it was not a good year for hitters in Arlington. There were only 717 runs scored in Texas, as opposed to 797 scored in the Rangers' road games. The Rangers both scored and allowed more runs away from Texas than they did in their home park.

The Rangers drew 1,692,021 fans, up more than 50% from 1985 and the best attendance in the history of the franchise.

As to the Rangers' chances in 1987, I would ask first of all that you read the second comment listed under the San Francisco Giants, which applies to the Rangers as well. The Rangers will probably need a consolidation year before taking another step forward.

But it was generally felt that the young Rangers would fold in the pennant race. They didn't. The Angels, who had the best record in the American League after August 1, pulled a little further away from them, but the Rangers were 35–25 (.583) over the last two months, whereas they were only two games over .500 over the first four months. If Bobby Witt were to find his control, he could easily cut 50 runs off the number the Rangers allow. Ruben Sierra hit .330 with 13 extra base hits last August, and .290 with 7 homers and 23 RBI in September. Project those numbers out. What happens if Don Slaught is healthy all year? There are a lot of players here who could quickly become MVP candidates. I think the Rangers' future is very bright, and it is quite possible that that future could arrive in 1987.

Don SLAUGHT, Catcher

	G	AB	Hit	2B	3B	HR	Run	RBI	TBB	SO	SB	CS	Avg
2.76 years		528	147	29	5	10	57	58	28	70	4	2	.278
1986	95	314	83	17	1	13	39	46	16	59	3	1	.264
First Half	32	99	28	5	1	7	14	23	5	15	2	0	.283
Second Half	63	215	55	12	0	6	25	23	11	44	1	1	.256
Vs. RHP		195	47	10	0	8		27	12	35	1	1	.241
Vs. LHP		119	36	7	1	5		19	4	24	2	0	.303
Home	47	149	45	11	0	5	21	19	9	26	3	0	.302
Road	48	165	38	6	1	8	18	27	7	33	0	1	.230
Grass	81	268	72	14	1	10	34	38	13	50	3	1	.269
Turf	14	46	11	3	0	3	5	8	3	9	0	0	.239

Gary WARD, Left Field

	G	AB	Hit	2B	3B	HR	Run	RBI	TBB	SO	SB	CS	Avg
5.12 years		609	176	28	7	18	87	82	47	102	14	5	.289
1986	105	380	120	15	2	5	54	51	31	72	12	8	.316
First Half	66	241	71	12	2	4	34	37	24	44	7	8	.295
Second Half	39	139	49	3	0	1	20	14	7	28	5	0	.353
Vs. RHP		260	82	8	1	2		31	17	49	10	6	.315
Vs. LHP		120	38	7	1	3		20	14	23	2	2	.317
Home	54	193	62	8	1	3	23	24	13	34	8	4	.321
Road	51	187	58	7	1	2	31	27	18	38	4	4	.310
Grass	92	331	103	13	1	4	46	36	28	65	11	7	.311
Turf	13	49	17	2	1	1	8	15	3	7	1	1	.347

Pete O'BRIEN, First Base

	G	AB	Hit	2B	3B	HR	Run	RBI	TBB	SO	SB	CS	Avg
3.90 years		574	155	28	4	19	71	84	70	61	5	6	.269
1986	156	551	160	23	3	23	86	90	87	66	4	4	.290
First Half	76	268	79	14	2	10	45	41	35	33	1	1	.295
Second Half	80	283	81	9	1	13	41	49	52	33	3	3	.286
Vs. RHP		386	109	12	3	19		64	68	38	4	4	.282
Vs. LHP		165	51	11	0	4		26	19	28	0	0	.309
Home	78	265	71	13	0	11	38	41	37	34	2	2	.268
Road	78	286	89	10	3	12	48	49	50	32	2	2	.311
Grass	132	453	131	20	2	19	69	76	74	56	4	3	.289
Turf	24	98	29	3	1	4	17	14	13	10	0	1	.296

Oddibe McDOWELL, Center Field

	G	AB	Hit	2B	3B	HR	Run	RBI	TBB	SO	SB	CS	Avg
1.64 years		598	152	23	7	22	103	56	62	120	35	13	.255
1986	154	572	152	24	7	18	105	49	65	112	33	15	.266
First Half	76	287	76	14	4	11	53	29	34	54	14	10	.265
Second Half	78	285	76	10	3	7	52	20	31	58	19	5	.267
Vs. RHP		444	124	20	6	15		38	51	80	31	11	.279
Vs. LHP		128	28	4	1	3		11	14	32	2	4	.219
Home	78	290	81	13	5	8	57	28	27	62	18	8	.279
Road	76	282	71	11	2	10	48	21	38	50	15	7	.252
Grass	129	480	124	18	5	14	85	42	56	93	27	14	.258
Turf	25	92	28	6	2	4	20	7	9	19	6	1	.304

Toby HARRAH, Second Base

	G	AB	Hit	2B	3B	HR	Run	RBI	TBB	SO	SB	CS	Avg
13.30 years		556	147	23	3	15	84	69	87	65	18	7	.264
1986	95	289	63	18	2	7	36	41	44	53	2	5	.218
First Half	44	153	31	9	1	2	13	21	21	30	2	2	.203
Second Half	51	136	32	9	1	5	23	20	23	23	0	3	.235
Vs. RHP		186	39	9	0	5		27	18	37	1	4	.210
Vs. LHP		103	24	9	2	2		14	26	16	1	1	.233
Home	47	140	29	7	0	3	12	18	20	27	2	1	.207
Road	48	149	34	11	2	4	24	23	24	26	0	4	.228
Grass	82	249	55	16	1	6	31	37	37	46	2	5	.221
Turf	13	40	8	2	1	1	5	4	7	7	0	0	.200

Ruben SIERRA, Right Field

	G	AB	Hit	2B	3B	HR	Run	RBI	TBB	SO	SB	CS	Avg
0.70 years		548	145	19	14	23	72	79	32	93	10	11	.264
1986	113	382	101	13	10	16	50	55	22	65	7	8	.264
First Half	34	114	23	4	2	4	12	9	4	25	1	2	.202
Second Half	79	268	78	9	8	12	38	46	18	40	6	6	.291
Vs. RHP		283	76	9	9	12		40	18	54	4	6	.269
Vs. LHP		99	25	4	1	4		15	4	11	3	2	.253
Home	53	172	41	2	6	8	21	31	5	38	2	3	.238
Road	60	210	60	11	4	8	29	24	17	27	5	5	.286
Grass	92	297	74	7	8	11	35	42	16	53	5	7	.249
Turf	21	85	27	6	2	5	15	13	6	12	2	1	.318

Steve BUECHELE, Third Base

	G	AB	Hit	2B	3B	HR	Run	RBI	TBB	SO	SB	CS	Avg
1.37 years		496	117	18	4	18	55	55	36	99	6	7	.235
1986	153	461	112	19	2	18	54	54	35	98	5	8	.243
First Half	75	240	64	11	0	12	28	25	18	49	3	3	.267
Second Half	78	221	48	8	2	6	26	29	17	49	2	5	.217
Vs. RHP		322	74	12	1	13		37	19	63	3	6	.230
Vs. LHP		139	38	7	1	5		17	16	35	2	2	.273
Home	77	224	53	8	0	6	22	18	15	44	1	4	.237
Road	76	237	59	11	2	12	32	36	20	54	4	4	.249
Grass	130	379	92	12	2	14	46	44	29	78	5	6	.243
Turf	23	82	20	7	0	4	8	10	6	20	0	2	.244

Larry PARRISH, Designated Hitter

	G	AB	Hit	2B	3B	HR	Run	RBI	TBB	SO	SB	CS	Avg
9.99 years		583	155	32	3	21	74	84	45	109	3	3	.266
1986	129	464	128	22	1	28	67	94	52	114	3	1	.276
First Half	51	188	49	8	1	14	29	45	18	52	2	0	.261
Second Half	78	276	79	14	0	14	38	49	34	62	1	1	.286
Vs. RHP		334	95	16	0	17		65	32	81	2	1	.284
Vs. LHP		130	33	6	1	11		29	20	33	1	0	.254
Home	65	225	65	11	1	14	34	45	25	53	2	0	.289
Road	64	239	63	11	0	14	33	49	27	61	1	1	.264
Grass	111	396	111	19	1	24	59	77	46	96	3	1	.280
Turf	18	68	17	3	0	4	8	17	6	18	0	0	.250

Scott FLETCHER, Shortstop

	G	AB	Hit	2B	3B	HR	Run	RBI	TBB	SO	SB	CS	Avg
3.45 years		469	123	22	4	3	63	43	47	53	10	6	.263
1986	147	530	159	34	5	3	82	50	47	59	12	11	.300
First Half	72	240	73	13	5	1	39	19	23	29	4	5	.304
Second Half	75	290	86	21	0	2	43	31	24	30	8	6	.297
Vs. RHP		355	108	21	3	1		31	32	42	11	9	.304
Vs. LHP		175	51	13	2	2		19	15	17	1	2	.291
Home	72	253	78	15	3	2	46	25	19	27	4	5	.308
Road	75	277	81	19	2	1	36	25	28	32	8	6	.292
Grass	123	443	138	27	4	3	71	40	37	48	12	9	.312
Turf	24	87	21	7	1	0	11	10	10	11	0	2	.241

Pete INCAVIGLIA, Left Field

	G	AB	Hit	2B	3B	HR	Run	RBI	TBB	SO	SB	CS	Avg
0.94 years		572	143	22	2	32	87	93	58	196	3	2	.250
1986	153	540	135	21	2	30	82	88	55	185	3	2	.250
First Half	75	262	70	12	2	15	43	45	26	91	1	1	.267
Second Half	78	278	65	9	0	15	39	43	29	94	2	1	.234
Vs. RHP		380	86	14	0	18		57	37	130	3	2	.226
Vs. LHP		160	49	7	2	12		31	18	55	0	0	.306
Home	80	275	79	13	1	17	45	49	27	94	2	1	.287
Road	73	265	56	8	1	13	37	39	28	91	1	1	.211
Grass	130	461	119	19	2	27	69	81	48	154	2	2	.258
Turf	23	79	16	2	0	3	13	7	7	31	1	0	.203

Charlie HOUGH

Year	(W–L)	GS	Run	Avg	DP	Avg	SB	Avg
1984	(16-14)	36	157	4.36	33	.92	26	.72
1985	(14-16)	34	123	3.62	28	.82	23	.68
1986	(17-10)	33	165	5.00	33	1.00	26	.79
1979-1986		225	848	3.77	168	.75	144	.64

	1986 ERA	W–L	1985 ERA	1984 ERA	1983 ERA	1982 ERA	82-86 W–L
Total	3.79	17-10	3.31	3.76	3.18	3.95	78-66
Home	3.99	8-5	3.52	2.94	2.97	3.80	43-29
Road	3.62	9-5	3.13	4.52	3.48	4.15	35-37
East	6.78	3-6	2.97	4.36	4.36	4.56	33-36
West	2.44	14-4	3.78	3.21	2.11	3.43	45-30
1st Half	2.59	8-3	3.42	3.38	3.17	3.38	36-32
2nd Half	4.61	9-7	3.15	4.10	3.18	4.58	42-34
Turf	4.30	3-2	3.15	3.26	2.70		10-10
Grass	3.67	14-8	3.35	3.87	3.25		52-43
Day	5.62	3-3	3.79	2.74	2.87	4.25	14-15
Night	3.39	14-7	3.17	4.09	3.28	3.88	64-51
April			2.94	5.50	3.41	5.79	6-7
May	5.23	3-2	3.44	4.66	6.91	1.45	11-13
June	1.51	4-1	4.17	1.15	1.33	3.82	16-10
July	4.40	2-3	2.63	3.27	3.86	3.00	14-12
August	5.40	3-2	2.16	5.69	4.24	4.89	16-13
September	3.59	5-2	5.00	3.18	1.42	5.31	15-11

Bobby WITT

Year	(W–L)	GS	Run	Avg	DP	Avg	SB	Avg
1986	(11-9)	31	156	5.03	27	.87	53	1.71

	G	IP	W–L	H	ER	SO	ERA
Total	31	157.2	11-9	130	96	174	5.48
Home	16	90.0	6-3	69	40	94	4.00
Road	15	67.2	5-6	61	56	80	7.45
East	16	77.2	4-5	60	48	83	5.56
West	15	80.0	7-4	70	48	91	5.40
1st Half	17	89.0	4-7	72	59	92	5.97
2nd Half	14	68.2	7-2	58	37	82	4.85
Turf	3	17.1	1-1	12	9	19	4.67
Grass	28	140.1	10-8	118	87	155	5.58
Day	8	42.2	3-3	29	28	66	5.91
Night	23	115.0	8-6	101	68	108	5.32
April	4	21.1	2-0	11	9	27	3.80
May	6	28.2	0-4	25	24	14	7.53
June	6	31.0	2-2	31	22	37	6.39
July	4	17.0	1-3	15	16	21	8.47
August	5	25.2	2-0	23	11	34	3.86
September	6	34.0	4-0	25	14	41	3.71

Ed CORREA

Year	(W–L)	GS	Run	Avg	DP	Avg	SB	Avg
1985	(1-0)	1	3	3.00	2	2.00	0	.00
1986	(12-14)	32	125	3.91	26	.81	40	1.25
1985-1986		33	128	3.88	28	.85	40	1.21

	G	IP	W–L	H	ER	SO	ERA
Total	32	202.1	12-14	167	95	189	4.23
Home	13	83.2	6-6	64	37	89	3.98
Road	19	118.2	6-8	103	58	100	4.40
East	18	108.0	5-8	96	57	94	4.75
West	14	94.1	7-6	71	38	95	3.63
1st Half	16	109.2	6-6	85	45	101	3.69
2nd Half	16	92.2	6-8	82	50	88	4.86
Turf	6	38.1	1-4	38	21	36	4.93
Grass	26	164.0	11-10	129	74	153	4.06
Day	5	35.0	2-2	25	12	34	3.09
Night	27	167.1	10-12	142	83	155	4.46
April	4	25.1	1-2	22	13	21	4.62
May	5	37.2	2-1	23	7	37	1.67
June	6	38.2	2-3	35	24	35	5.59
July	5	25.2	1-3	27	19	29	6.66
August	5	27.0	2-2	30	20	18	6.67
September	7	48.0	4-3	30	12	49	2.25

José GUZMAN

Year	(W–L)	GS	Run	Avg	DP	Avg	SB	Avg
1985	(3-2)	5	20	4.00	5	1.00	5	1.00
1986	(9-15)	29	110	3.79	39	1.34	21	.72
1985-1986		34	130	3.82	44	1.29	26	.76

	G	IP	W–L	H	ER	SO	ERA
Total	29	172.1	9-15	199	87	87	4.54
Home	17	103.1	6-7	118	45	59	3.92
Road	12	69.0	3-8	81	42	28	5.48
East	16	89.1	4-9	114	47	47	4.74
West	13	83.0	5-6	85	40	40	4.34
1st Half	17	109.2	8-8	122	46	60	3.78
2nd Half	12	62.2	1-7	77	41	27	5.89
Turf	4	23.0	1-2	26	14	12	5.48
Grass	25	149.1	8-13	173	73	75	4.40
Day	6	32.1	1-4	40	19	23	5.29
Night	23	140.0	8-11	159	68	64	4.37
April	5	27.2	1-4	37	17	13	5.53
May	5	32.2	3-1	33	8	19	2.20
June	6	42.1	3-3	44	21	24	4.46
July	5	28.2	1-2	32	11	18	3.45
August	4	19.2	1-2	27	16	7	7.32
September	4	21.1	0-3	26	14	6	5.91

Mike MASON

Year	(W–L)	GS	Run	Avg	DP	Avg	SB	Avg
1984	(9-13)	24	82	3.42	26	1.08	13	.54
1985	(8-15)	30	121	4.03	32	1.07	21	.70
1986	(7-3)	22	134	6.09	21	.95	10	.45
1984-1986		76	337	4.43	79	1.04	44	.58

	1986		1985		1984		84-86
	ERA	W–L	ERA	W–L	ERA	W–L	W–L
Total	4.33	7-3	4.83	8-15	3.61	9-13	24-31
Home	4.02	4-1	4.99	4-6	4.04	4-6	12-13
Road	4.66	3-2	4.69	4-9	3.21	5-7	12-18
East	4.25	4-2	5.17	4-9	3.35	4-7	12-18
West	4.45	3-1	4.45	4-6	3.84	5-6	12-13
1st Half	4.44	5-2	4.98	5-8	2.91	5-6	15-16
2nd Half	4.19	2-1	4.66	3-7	4.43	4-7	9-15
Turf	7.36	1-1	4.45	1-2	1.99	4-2	6-5
Grass	3.62	6-2	4.90	7-13	4.14	5-11	18-26
Day	5.13	2-1	4.47	3-6	5.64	2-3	7-10
Night	3.99	5-2	4.97	5-9	3.21	7-10	17-21
April	4.44	1-0	4.63	2-2	1.76	1-0	4-2
May	3.89	3-2	5.18	2-2	3.06	1-3	6-7
June	9.82	0-0	4.66	1-3	2.22	3-2	4-5
July	2.45	2-1	5.45	0-3	4.18	2-4	4-8
August	5.89	0-0	4.24	0-2	4.96	1-2	1-4
September	3.80	1-0	4.53	3-3	5.63	1-2	5-5

OTHERS

Pitcher	(W–L)	GS	Run	Avg	DP	Avg	SB	Avg	Time	Att.
Loynd	(2-2)	8	45	5.63	7	.88	16	2.00	2:53	197
Mahler	(0-2)	5	25	5.00	7	1.40	3	.60	3:10	116
Wright	(1-0)	1	2	2.00	0	.00	0	.00	2:37	11
Brown	(1-0)	1	9	9.00	0	.00	2	2.00	3:06	7

RECORDS WITH DIFFERENT STARTING CATCHERS

Catcher	Inn	ER	W–L	ERA	GS	SB	Avg
Slaught	751.2	369	42-43	4.42	85	89	1.05
Mercado	284.1	100	21-10	3.17	31	25	.81
Porter	201.0	89	10-12	3.99	22	32	1.45
Petralli	195.1	93	14-8	4.28	22	18	.82
Stanley	18.0	11	0-2	5.50	2	1	.50

Greg HARRIS

1986	G	IP	W–L	Sv	H	ER	SO	ERA
Total	73	111.1	10-8	20	103	35	95	2.83
Home	40	64.2	9-4	13	60	19	50	2.64
Road	33	46.2	1-4	7	43	16	45	3.09
East	42	69.1	7-7	7	70	25	54	3.25
West	31	42.0	3-1	13	33	10	41	2.14
1st Half	37	57.0	3-7	15	58	19	47	3.00
2nd Half	36	54.1	7-1	5	45	16	48	2.65
Turf	10	13.2	0-1	2	13	4	13	2.63
Grass	63	97.2	10-7	18	90	31	82	2.86
Day	17	34.0	1-1	6	28	10	32	2.65
Night	56	77.1	9-7	14	75	25	63	2.91
April	10	16.1	2-3	2	23	11	12	6.06
May	12	22.1	1-3	5	19	4	17	1.61
June	13	15.1	0-1	7	14	4	14	2.35
July	11	18.2	2-1	1	20	5	19	2.41
August	14	22.0	3-0	0	15	5	13	2.05
September	13	16.2	2-0	5	12	6	20	3.24

STARTING PITCHERS' AVERAGE TIME AND ATTENDANCE RECORDS

Pitcher	Time	Attendance
Hough	2:41	673
Correa	2:49	676
Witt	2:56	603
Guzman	2:44	633
Mason	2:54	517

KANSAS CITY ROYALS

Runners on Base:	1913
Opponents on Base:	1930
Net Disadvantage:	– 17
Won-Lost Record:	76-86

For the Kansas City Royals, the season got lost behind the headlines. The Royals came in as defending World Champions, which means that they came off a winter of celebrating and into the season with their pictures on the front of the magazines. On April 12, Dennis Leonard, unable to pitch for two and a half years because of a serious knee injury, pitched a remarkable three-hit, 1–0 shutout over Toronto on national television, positioning him to become the comeback story of the season. On June 2, the Royals gambled a fourth-round draft pick on Bo Jackson, a move that was attacked as publicity-conscious at the time but became an inspired strategem on June 20 when Jackson, whose face seems to have an affinity for the covers of sports magazines, shocked the sports world by accepting an offer and reporting to Memphis. Just when the hugger-mugger over this good fortune was quieting down, the Royals were flattened by the terrible news that a cancer had taken root in the brain of manager Dick Howser. Underneath the news stories, the season was buried. The Royals never contended and never looked like or played like a contending team.

Although there was a perception that the Royals' pitching had let them down (August 10–24 headline from *Baseball America:* Pitching a Royal Pain, Bankhead Only Bright Spot), the Royals actually led the American League in Earned Run Average (3.82) and also allowed the fewest unearned runs (61). They led the league in shutouts (13, only two of which I can remember). Although they had a below-average complete game total, Royals' managers went to the bullpen only 230 times, fewest in the league, meaning that one reliever was usually all it took. Quisenberry didn't save many games, but then he wasn't given many opportunities.

One of the oddities of baseball statistics is that the pitcher is the only one who is held responsible for the success or failure of the team, and thus all of the successes or failures of the team show up in the pitcher's record, which is a large part of the reason that some people perceive baseball as being 75% pitching, and is a large part of why many people blamed the Royals' decline on the league's best pitching staff. The Royal offense was nearly the worst in the league. In particular, Danny Jackson had a terrific year undermined by the failure of his team to score runs. Jackson had a 3.20 ERA, which can be found among the league leaders at fifth, just ahead of Jack Morris and Kirk McCaskill and just behind Mike Witt and Bruce Hurst. He was not seen as having a good year (he was 11–12) because the Royals scored just 2.93 runs per game for him,

making him the worst-supported starting pitcher in the American League. Given average offensive support, his record should have been about 14–9 or 15–8. And Bret Saberhagen, while he had some very dry periods, allowed just 4.44 runs per nine innings, a better-than-league figure. His decline from 1985 was about half a result of not pitching as well, and half a result of the team not scoring as many runs for him.

Royals pitchers allowed 22 fewer home runs than any other American League team.

Even after the season, it continued to be a news year in Kansas City. First the Royals announced that they would not retain Mike Ferraro or Lee May as coaches for 1987, which might not be news except that May was popular and Ferraro had been the interim manager. Then the Royals failed to reach an agreement with Lonnie Smith, who apparently will not be back in 1987. Then the Royals pulled off one of the few major trades of the winter, lifting Danny Tartabull from Seattle.

As a Royals fan, obviously I like the Tartabull trade. I'm not pleased that Lonnie Smith isn't coming back, but I'm pleased that he's not going to be back in the outfield. The dismissal of Ferraro was a surprise, inasmuch as it was generally felt that Ferraro handled a difficult situation with as much grace as anyone could have. The attention given to his grace may have distracted many from the fact that he wasn't a terrific manager. If you divide managers into emotional leaders and tacticians, you'd have to say that as an emotional leader, Ferraro was strictly a tactician, and as a tactician he was mediocre. I say this with regret; I thought he would be better.

But the move that has the most potential to improve the team was the decision to make Hal McRae a designated hitter/hitting coach, and let Lee May go. May had been in KC for three years and had received good reviews, but while May was an effective hitting coach, he was not the right hitting coach for this organization. As a player, Lee May was a slow, low-average power hitter who had the worst strikeout to walk ratio of any major league player ever in 1,400 or more games, with 1,570 strikeouts and only 487 walks. (Incidentally, the player with the second-worst strikeout to walk ratio, Bill Robinson, is also now a highly respected hitting coach.) In the years that May was the KC hitting coach, the Royals drifted more and more in the direction of representing May's values as a hitter. They don't hit for average (.252, twelfth in the American League), rarely walk (thirteenth in the league) and strike out much more than they did in the Charlie Lau days.

Their team speed has declined somewhat and their use of the running game has declined dramatically, dropping from 182 stolen bases in 1983 to 97 in 1986—with almost exactly the same number of runners caught stealing. On the other hand, although they hit only 137 home runs because of the park in which they play, the Royals have good team power. They out-homered their opponents 137–121, winning the home run battle 60–46 in Royals Stadium, and 77–75 on the road.

That style of play just doesn't fit Royals Stadium, and more importantly it doesn't fit the Royals' talent. In particular, it doesn't suit Willie Wilson, who hits the ball much harder now than he did three years ago but much less effectively. I don't know whether Wilson will come back in 1987 or not, but I feel that he has a lot better chance of coming back with Hal McRae as the batting coach than he would have with May. I am also a lot happier to have McRae working with Kevin Seitzer than I would be with Lee May.

Certainly, having one Lee May in your lineup is a fine idea, and the Royals have that in Steve Balboni. Having a whole lineup that functions this way isn't so good. The idea of a Lee May–type player is that he is supposed to plate the runs, yet the Royals didn't do a good job of getting runners home.

To listen to the Kansas City fans and front office, one would think that driving runners home was the whole problem. The Royals' front office talked continually about the need to get someone who could hit behind Brett and drive in runs, a task which they accomplished magnificently with the acquisition of Tartabull. But nothing was ever said about the need to get more runners on base, and indeed the talk show people would blithely assure you that the Royals had plenty of people on base, they just needed to do a better job of driving them in. In fact, the Royal offense was very poor on both ends. The Royals had a low team batting average and drew only 474 walks, one more than in 1985 but still the fewest in the division. Their team on-base percentage, .313, was thirteenth in the league, ahead of only Chicago. But it is also true that they did do a poor job of driving in those who were on. They scored only 34.2% of their runners on base, the lowest percentage in the American League, and only 29.1% of runners on base not counting home runs, tied with Baltimore for the lowest percentage in the league. The Royals scored 29 runs fewer than would have been expected in view of their other offensive stats (654–683).

The Royals' secondary average, .240, was thirteenth in a fourteen-team league, ahead of only Chicago, and their runs scored total, 654, was thirteenth in the league, ahead of only Chicago. The Royals tied for the league lead in triples (45) and led the division in doubles (264), but those figures are both park-aided. The Royals hit just 16 triples on the road, only 5 more than Baltimore. They grounded into only 101 double plays, fewest in the division, but then you can't ground into double plays if you don't have people on base. Those figures do testify to decent team speed, despite the below-average stolen base total.

One of the highlights of the Royal season was the second-half emergence of two outfielders who excelled in areas that have not been Royal specialties. First was the July callup of Mike Kingery, a delightful player to watch, who goes to Seattle with the affection of all who saw him play. Though not considered a budding star, Kingery's talents are not trivial. He runs very well, throws quite well, and hasn't yet proven that he won't hit major-league pitching. He played some games in center field, and I honestly thought he was a better center fielder than Willie Wilson. But his specialty is hustle. Kingery made every play with maximum effort, in a way that Kansas City fans had not seen in several years and which pointed out how cautious and comfortable in their jobs the Royals' players have become. He was a lot of fun, and will be missed.

The other young Royal outfielder was Kevin Seitzer, who joined the team in late August and won a job, provoking the dismissal of Lonnie Smith. Seitzer, believe it or not Royals fans, can get on base. Seitzer hit .323 in 96 at bats, which don't mean much but it's a lot better than hitting .223, and he sure looked like a hitter. Better yet, he forced the pitchers to throw him strikes, and when they didn't he walked cheerfully to first; he wound up with a .440 on-base percentage, reaching base 51 times in 28 games. Seitzer has a good minor-league batting record. He hit .319 at Omaha with 13 homers, 74 RBI, and, while I don't have his walks total, he scored 86 runs with 432 at bats, so he must have been on base all year. That's not a good hitter's park or a good hitter's league. In 1985 Seitzer hit .314 in the Florida State League with 85 walks in 90 games (also 28 stolen bases), then moved on to Memphis where he hit .348 in 52 games. He hasn't yet impressed anybody with his glove.

The Royals' Most Valuable Player, by far, was Frank White, the veteran second baseman who had his best season. White not only had the best hitting record, but was the man who got the most big hits and the man who played the best defense. Perhaps I should say he was not the MVP, but the OVP, the Only Valuable Player. Nobody else was close, although Brett played well before injuring his shoulder diving for a ball in Seattle.

Can the Royals bounce back in 1987? We've got to give John Schuerholz credit for making two tremendous Boston Celtics moves in the last year—signing Bo Jackson, and acquiring Danny Tartabull. If he can pull off a third master stroke by picking up a quality catcher or shortstop, the Royals could win 90 or more again in 1987.

Short of that, I doubt it. The Royals' starting lineup was the oldest in the American League except for the Angels', and what is perhaps more striking is that before the acquisition of Tartabull the Royals did not have a proven player under the age of 30. Their only "regulars" under 30 were Biancalana and Kingery, both still trying to establish themselves. Even the Angels have three good players in their twenties, in Joyner, Schoefield and Pettis. Their starting pitching remains young and very good. They probably will play better than they did in 1986 simply because they are a better team than that, but I'll be surprised if the Royals can win more than 88 games.

Jim SUNDBERG, Catcher

	G	AB	Hit	2B	3B	HR	Run	RBI	TBB	SO	SB	CS	Avg
10.88 years		514	128	21	3	8	53	53	59	78	2	3	.250
1986	140	429	91	9	1	12	41	42	57	91	1	1	.212
First Half	69	225	48	7	0	3	17	19	23	41	1	1	.213
Second Half	71	204	43	2	1	9	24	23	34	50	0	0	.211
Vs. RHP		288	64	7	0	6		27	41	55	1	1	.222
Vs. LHP		141	27	2	1	6		15	16	36	0	0	.191
Home	68	209	41	4	0	5	18	24	25	47	1	0	.196
Road	72	220	50	5	1	7	23	18	32	44	0	1	.227
Grass	55	171	35	5	0	5	15	14	25	34	0	1	.205
Turf	85	258	56	4	1	7	26	28	32	57	1	0	.217

Lonnie SMITH, Left Field

	G	AB	Hit	2B	3B	HR	Run	RBI	TBB	SO	SB	CS	Avg
5.61 years		561	163	30	7	7	102	52	48	66	53	16	.291
1986	134	508	146	25	7	8	80	44	46	78	26	9	.287
First Half	58	202	52	9	4	3	37	23	26	34	12	2	.257
Second Half	76	306	94	16	3	5	43	21	20	44	14	7	.307
Vs. RHP		359	100	19	3	6	76	30	34	59	20	8	.279
Vs. LHP		149	46	6	4	2	4	14	12	19	6	1	.309
Home	65	243	77	14	4	2	48	20	24	30	14	5	.317
Road	69	265	69	11	3	6	32	24	22	48	12	4	.260
Grass	54	205	53	8	2	5	24	18	17	38	9	3	.259
Turf	80	303	93	17	5	3	56	26	29	40	17	6	.307

Steve BALBONI, First Base

	G	AB	Hit	2B	3B	HR	Run	RBI	TBB	SO	SB	CS	Avg
3.04 years		575	135	27	2	33	67	91	51	168	0	0	.235
1986	138	512	117	25	1	29	54	88	43	146	0	0	.229
First Half	80	293	65	16	0	16	30	44	27	81	0	0	.222
Second Half	58	219	52	9	1	13	24	44	16	65	0	0	.237
Vs. RHP		378	80	19	1	17		58	23	109	0	0	.212
Vs. LHP		134	37	6	0	12		30	20	37	0	0	.276
Home	71	251	51	14	1	10	21	37	23	75	0	0	.203
Road	67	261	66	11	0	19	33	51	20	71	0	0	.253
Grass	55	215	55	9	0	18	29	46	18	53	0	0	.256
Turf	83	297	62	16	1	11	25	42	25	93	0	0	.209

Willie WILSON, Center Field

	G	AB	Hit	2B	3B	HR	Run	RBI	TBB	SO	SB	CS	Avg
7.82 years		628	186	23	12	4	99	46	32	85	60	11	.297
1986	156	631	170	20	7	9	77	44	31	97	34	8	.269
First Half	80	328	83	7	5	4	46	24	20	52	18	5	.253
Second Half	76	303	87	13	2	5	31	20	11	45	16	3	.287
Vs. RHP		456	116	15	5	5		33	27	64	24	5	.254
Vs. LHP		175	54	5	2	4		11	4	33	10	3	.309
Home	78	309	82	8	6	5	39	19	20	40	22	5	.265
Road	78	322	88	12	1	4	38	25	11	57	12	3	.273
Grass	60	239	65	9	1	2	29	17	11	48	8	3	.272
Turf	96	392	105	11	6	7	48	27	20	49	26	5	.268

Frank WHITE, Second Base

	G	AB	Hit	2B	3B	HR	Run	RBI	TBB	SO	SB	CS	Avg
11.13 years		548	142	28	5	12	67	62	27	72	15	7	.260
1986	151	566	154	37	3	22	76	84	43	88	4	4	.272
First Half	77	298	84	19	2	9	35	44	17	46	2	3	.282
Second Half	74	268	70	18	1	13	41	40	26	42	2	1	.261
Vs. RHP		417	114	30	2	21		73	26	67	3	4	.273
Vs. LHP		149	40	7	1	1		11	17	21	1	0	.268
Home	76	277	78	18	2	12	36	54	21	38	2	2	.282
Road	75	289	76	19	1	10	40	30	22	50	2	2	.263
Grass	58	223	48	11	0	8	30	21	20	45	0	1	.215
Turf	93	343	106	26	3	14	46	63	23	43	4	3	.309

Rudy LAW, Right Field

	G	AB	Hit	2B	3B	HR	Run	RBI	TBB	SO	SB	CS	Avg
4.62 years		524	142	22	8	4	82	43	40	45	49	14	.271
1986	87	307	80	26	5	1	42	36	29	22	14	6	.261
First Half	66	246	65	21	4	1	35	31	24	19	12	5	.264
Second Half	21	61	15	5	1	0	7	5	5	3	2	1	.246
Vs. RHP		265	74	25	5	1		31	29	21	14	6	.279
Vs. LHP		42	6	1	0	0		5	0	1	0	0	.143
Home	43	144	40	14	2	1	27	20	16	5	7	3	.278
Road	44	163	40	12	3	0	15	16	13	17	7	3	.245
Grass	32	123	33	8	3	0	12	12	10	13	5	3	.268
Turf	55	184	47	18	2	1	30	24	19	9	9	3	.255

George BRETT, Third Base

	G	AB	Hit	2B	3B	HR	Run	RBI	TBB	SO	SB	CS	Avg
10.75 years		621	195	40	10	19	100	98	65	46	13	7	.314
1986	124	441	128	28	4	16	70	73	80	45	1	2	.290
First Half	78	268	78	16	1	8	45	40	59	25	1	2	.291
Second Half	46	173	50	12	3	8	25	33	21	20	0	0	.289
Vs. RHP		293	92	24	3	11		54	61	21	1	2	.314
Vs. LHP		148	36	4	1	5		19	19	24	0	0	.243
Home	59	205	66	16	4	8	39	41	36	15	1	2	.322
Road	65	236	62	12	0	8	31	32	44	30	0	0	.263
Grass	53	196	52	11	0	7	24	27	36	25	0	0	.265
Turf	71	245	76	17	4	9	46	46	44	20	1	2	.310

Hal McRAE, Designated Hitter

	G	AB	Hit	2B	3B	HR	Run	RBI	TBB	SO	SB	CS	Avg
12.75 years		563	163	38	5	15	73	85	50	61	9	6	.290
1986	112	278	70	14	0	7	22	37	18	39	0	0	.252
First Half	60	146	35	12	0	3	11	25	9	22	0	0	.240
Second Half	52	132	35	2	0	4	11	12	9	17	0	0	.265
Vs. RHP		125	29	4	0	2		13	5	18	0	0	.232
Vs. LHP		153	41	10	0	5		24	13	21	0	0	.268
Home	55	125	34	8	0	1	7	19	10	17	0	0	.272
Road	57	153	36	6	0	6	15	18	8	22	0	0	.235
Grass	43	118	27	3	0	6	12	14	6	17	0	0	.229
Turf	69	160	43	11	0	1	10	23	12	22	0	0	.269

Angel SALAZAR, Shortstop

	G	AB	Hit	2B	3B	HR	Run	RBI	TBB	SO	SB	CS	Avg
1.44 years		354	75	15	3	0	29	26	8	65	1	1	.212
1986	117	298	73	20	2	0	24	24	7	47	1	1	.245
First Half	69	183	45	12	1	0	14	12	5	26	1	1	.246
Second Half	48	115	28	8	1	0	10	12	2	21	0	0	.243
Vs. RHP		187	40	10	1	0		19	13	7	37	1	1	.214
Vs. LHP		111	33	10	1	0		5	11	0	10	0	0	.297
Home	58	127	30	6	1	0	10	9	1	18	1	1	.236
Road	59	171	43	14	1	0	14	15	6	29	0	0	.251
Grass	50	142	31	9	0	0	9	9	4	24	0	0	.218
Turf	67	156	42	11	2	0	15	15	3	23	1	1	.269

Jorgé ORTA, Designated Hitter

	G	AB	Hit	2B	3B	HR	Run	RBI	TBB	SO	SB	CS	Avg
10.70 years		540	150	25	6	12	68	69	46	66	7	6	.279
1986	106	336	93	14	2	9	35	46	23	34	0	3	.277
First Half	55	171	54	9	1	5	19	28	13	12	0	2	.316
Second Half	51	165	39	5	1	4	16	18	10	22	0	1	.236
Vs. RHP		317	89	14	2	9		43	22	30	0	3	.281
Vs. LHP		19	4	0	0	0		3	1	4	0	0	.211
Home	60	188	56	12	1	5	19	27	13	18	0	2	.298
Road	46	148	37	2	1	4	16	19	10	16	0	1	.250
Grass	35	109	31	1	1	3	14	16	8	6	0	1	.284
Turf	71	227	62	13	1	6	21	30	15	28	0	2	.273

Charlie LEIBRANDT

Year	(W–L)	GS	Run	Avg	DP	Avg	SB	Avg
1984	(11-7)	23	95	4.13	23	1.00	15	.65
1985	(17-9)	33	151	4.58	31	.94	21	.64
1986	(14-11)	34	156	4.59	37	1.09	8	.24
1980-1986		132	573	4.34	138	1.05	95	.72

	1986		1985		1984		84-86
	ERA	W–L	ERA	W–L	ERA	W–L	W–L
Total	4.09	14-11	2.69	17-9	3.63	11-7	42-27
Home	4.25	7-7	2.56	9-2	3.50	3-3	19-12
Road	3.94	7-4	2.79	8-7	3.73	8-4	23-15
East	4.60	5-7	2.92	10-3	3.74	4-3	19-13
West	3.67	9-4	2.44	7-6	3.57	7-4	23-14
1st Half	3.92	8-5	2.74	8-5	3.11	3-3	19-13
2nd Half	4.24	6-6	2.63	9-4	3.88	8-4	23-14
Turf	4.12	9-7	2.34	12-4	3.43	6-4	27-15
Grass	4.04	5-4	3.25	5-5	4.05	5-3	15-12
Day	3.49	7-2	1.85	3-2	3.00	2-2	12-6
Night	4.34	7-9	2.88	14-7	3.82	9-5	30-21
April	3.38	4-0	1.69	3-0			7-0
May	4.31	0-3	3.35	2-3			2-6
June	3.86	4-2	3.34	1-2	3.63	2-3	7-7
July	5.11	1-2	3.96	4-1	2.43	3-1	8-4
August	3.55	2-3	2.40	3-1	4.50	3-2	8-6
September	4.28	3-1	1.43	4-2	4.03	3-1	10-4

Danny JACKSON

Year	(W–L)	GS	Run	Avg	DP	Avg	SB	Avg
1984	(2-6)	11	40	3.64	14	1.27	4	.36
1985	(14-12)	32	121	3.78	38	1.19	12	.38
1986	(11-12)	27	79	2.93	33	1.22	10	.37
1983-1986		73	255	3.49	87	1.19	28	.38

	1986		1985		1984		84-86
	ERA	W–L	ERA	W–L	ERA	W–L	W–L
Total	3.20	11-12	3.42	14-12	4.26	2-6	27-30
Home	2.15	6-4	3.38	6-5	4.14	2-2	14-11
Road	3.99	5-8	3.46	8-7	4.38	0-4	13-19
East	3.64	6-5	3.54	7-5	4.61	0-4	13-14
West	2.89	5-7	3.26	7-7	4.07	2-2	14-16
1st Half	4.33	4-6	3.57	6-6	4.63	1-5	11-17
2nd Half	2.50	7-6	3.27	8-6	3.68	1-1	16-13
Turf	2.55	6-7	3.40	8-7	4.82	2-4	16-18
Grass	3.93	5-5	3.44	6-5	3.38	0-2	11-12
Day	3.63	2-0	4.04	3-5	5.19	0-2	5-7
Night	3.14	9-12	3.06	11-7	3.78	2-4	22-23
April	4.05	0-0	1.53	1-0	3.45	0-2	1-2
May	3.28	2-1	5.51	3-2	5.13	0-3	5-6
June	4.21	2-4	2.45	2-2	5.79	1-0	5-6
July	3.33	2-1	2.74	4-2			6-3
August	3.96	3-3	3.55	2-2			5-5
September	1.88	2-3	4.39	2-4	3.68	1-1	5-8

Dennis LEONARD

Year	(W–L)	GS	Run	Avg	DP	Avg	SB	Avg
1986	(8-13)	30	113	3.77	26	.87	22	.73
1976-1986		268	1256	4.69	221	.82	154	.57

	1986		1983		1982		82-86
	ERA	W–L	ERA	W–L	ERA	W–L	W–L
Total	4.44	8-13	3.71	6-3	5.10	10-6	24-22
Home	3.63	6-5	2.01	5-0	4.48	7-3	18-8
Road	5.61	2-8	6.75	1-3	6.14	3-3	6-14
East	4.02	5-7	3.88	5-3	5.91	5-4	15-14
West	4.96	3-6	2.45	1-0	4.51	5-2	9-8
1st Half	3.49	6-8	3.71	6-3	5.14	5-3	17-14
2nd Half	5.87	2-5			5.06	5-3	7-8
Turf	3.83	7-7	32.40	0-1			7-8
Grass	5.83	1-6	2.93	6-2			7-8
Day	2.55	3-1	32.40	0-1	7.20	2-4	5-6
Night	5.29	5-12	2.93	6-2	4.33	8-2	19-16
April	0.90	2-2	5.00	2-2	6.99	2-1	6-5
May	2.54	3-2	2.75	4-1	3.55	3-2	10-5
June	6.61	1-3					1-3
July	7.16	0-3					0-3
August	4.39	0-1			3.74	4-0	4-1
September	6.07	2-2			6.31	1-3	3-5

Bret SABERHAGEN

Year	(W–L)	GS	Run	Avg	DP	Avg	SB	Avg
1984	(10-11)	18	62	3.44	14	.78	12	.67
1985	(20-6)	32	144	4.50	30	.94	14	.44
1986	(7-12)	25	83	3.32	16	.64	17	.68
1984-1986		75	289	3.85	60	.80	43	.57

	1986		1985		1984		84-86
	ERA	W–L	ERA	W–L	ERA	W–L	W–L
Total	4.15	7-12	2.87	20-6	3.48	10-11	37-29
Home	3.67	2-5	2.80	10-3	2.20	4-5	16-13
Road	4.61	5-7	2.95	10-3	4.73	6-6	21-16
East	3.57	5-4	3.00	10-4	3.71	6-3	21-11
West	5.03	2-8	2.75	10-2	3.26	4-8	16-18
1st Half	4.51	4-10	2.91	9-4	3.05	3-7	16-21
2nd Half	3.40	3-2	2.82	11-2	4.04	7-4	21-8
Turf	4.40	3-7	3.09	11-4	2.52	4-6	18-17
Grass	3.86	4-5	2.55	9-2	4.63	6-5	19-12
Day	5.37	3-6	4.64	2-2	1.95	3-3	8-11
Night	3.45	4-6	2.48	18-4	3.95	7-8	29-18
April	4.56	1-2	3.65	2-2	2.08	1-1	4-5
May	3.21	1-3	3.41	3-1	4.85	1-3	5-7
June	4.91	2-4	2.83	2-1	2.77	0-3	4-8
July	4.71	2-1	2.05	5-1	2.48	2-1	9-3
August	6.00	0-0	2.64	4-0	6.26	3-1	7-1
September	3.27	1-2	3.05	4-1	2.63	3-2	8-5

Mark GUBICZA

Year	(W–L)	GS	Run	Avg	DP	Avg	SB	Avg
1984	(10-14)	29	115	3.97	29	1.00	24	.83
1985	(14-10)	28	128	4.57	27	.96	23	.82
1986	(12-6)	24	128	5.33	24	1.00	12	.50
1984-1986		81	371	4.58	80	.99	59	.73

	1986		1985		1984		84-86
	ERA	W–L	ERA	W–L	ERA	W–L	W–L
Total	3.64	12-6	4.06	14-10	4.05	10-14	36-30
Home	2.91	8-4	3.47	7-5	3.01	8-8	23-17
Road	5.00	4-2	4.61	7-5	6.59	2-6	13-13
East	4.21	6-6	4.41	6-5	3.92	6-5	18-16
West	2.84	6-0	3.73	8-5	4.18	4-9	18-14
1st Half	5.09	3-4	3.95	6-5	3.12	5-7	14-16
2nd Half	2.70	9-2	4.15	8-5	5.00	5-7	22-14
Turf	3.04	8-4	4.49	9-8	3.44	8-10	25-22
Grass	5.87	4-2	3.32	5-2	6.17	2-4	11-8
Day	2.88	4-2	4.37	2-3	4.68	2-3	8-8
Night	3.93	8-4	3.95	12-7	3.87	8-11	28-22
April	6.75	0-3	3.75	0-1	1.59	0-2	0-6
May	3.72	3-1	5.57	1-2	4.50	2-2	6-5
June	4.35	0-0	3.10	5-1	2.64	3-3	8-4
July	3.76	1-1	3.70	1-1	3.26	3-1	5-3
August	3.57	4-1	3.89	3-2	6.29	1-3	8-6
September	2.14	4-0	4.63	4-3	5.28	1-3	9-6

OTHERS

Pitcher	(W–L)	GS	Run	Avg	DP	Avg	SB	Avg	Time	Att.
Bankhead	(8-9)	17	77	4.53	10	.59	13	.76	2:46	459
Black	(5-10)	4	15	3.75	6	1.50	2	.50	2:32	122
Hargesheimer	(0-1)	1	9	9.00	1	1.00	1	1.00		27

RECORDS WITH DIFFERENT STARTING CATCHERS

Catcher	Inn	ER	W–L	ERA	GS	SB	Avg
Sundberg	1101.0	480	56-68	3.92	124	69	.56
Quirk	339.2	132	20-18	3.50	38	16	.42

STARTING PITCHERS' AVERAGE TIME AND ATTENDANCE RECORDS

Pitcher	Time	Attendance
Leibrandt	2:39	955
Leonard	2:45	818
Jackson	2:32	729
Saberhagen	2:34	574
Gubicza	2:44	644

Dan QUISENBERRY

1986	G	IP	W–L	Sv	H	ER	SO	ERA
Total	62	81.1	3-7	12	92	25	36	2.77
Home	27	36.2	2-3	2	36	10	15	2.45
Road	35	44.2	1-4	10	56	15	21	3.02
East	34	43.2	0-4	7	48	12	18	2.47
West	28	37.2	3-3	5	44	13	18	3.11
1st Half	30	40.1	0-2	8	50	12	20	2.68
2nd Half	32	41.0	3-5	4	42	13	16	2.85
Turf	36	48.2	3-4	5	47	14	19	2.59
Grass	26	32.2	0-3	7	45	11	17	3.03
Day	16	22.1	0-1	6	24	3	14	1.21
Night	46	59.0	3-6	6	68	22	22	3.36
April	7	9.2	0-0	3	9	0	6	.00
May	10	12.2	0-1	0	20	7	5	4.97
June	10	14.2	0-0	5	13	1	7	.61
July	11	13.2	0-3	1	20	8	4	5.27
August	11	15.0	1-1	2	10	2	8	1.20
September	13	15.2	2-2	1	20	7	6	4.02

OAKLAND ATHLETICS

Runners on Base:	1955
Opponents on Base:	2035
Net Disadvantage:	− 80
Won-Lost Record:	76-86

Since acquiring the Oakland A's in July of 1980, the members of the Levi-Strauss family have attempted to conduct their business in an intelligent, mature way. They have tried to be open with the press and responsive to the community. They have tried to deal with their players fairly and with a minimum of rancor. They have tried to be adults in a community of men who all too often react instead of thinking. They have hired decent and likeable men as managers. They have tried to assemble and make use of the best information available about the game. It has been an uphill battle for them, but in the middle of 1986 there were signs that perhaps it was, at long last, beginning to pay off.

The A's big story to start the year was the sensational young slugger José Canseco. With Canseco improving an already solid offense and trade acquisitions Andujar and Haas giving hope to a shaky staff, there was good reason to think the A's could win the West. Plan A for the pitching was that Joaquin would anchor the staff, backed up by Chris Codiroli (14–14 in 1985), Tim Birtsas (10–6), Jose Rijo (6–4, 3.53 ERA in 12 games), and steady Bill Krueger (7–6, 10–10, and 9–10 in his three years at Oakland), with All-Star reliever Jay Howell and Steve Ontiveros (1.93 ERA in 39 games) in the pen. On paper it was a good plan (or perhaps I believe this only in my own defense). If Andujar had been healthy, Rijo had pitched at 60% of his potential and Coldiroli had improved by just one or two games from 1985, their top three starters would have been as good as anybody's.

To summarize quickly what happened over the next three months, the pitching staff got hurt and the rest of the team gave up. Plan A started to go awry when Birtsas couldn't get anybody out in spring training, but the A's covered by picking up Moose Haas for a package of minor leaguers. Haas got off to a 6–0 start with an ERA in the ones, and was the first five-game winner in the majors. Jay Howell, however, was unable to throw hard due to a heel injury, and then developed tendinitis in the right elbow and forearm. With Ontiveros ineffective, that shot a giant hole in the bullpen. Bill Krueger went on the disabled list with a swollen elbow, and the starting corps was dangerously thin.

Curt Young was called up after a quick start at Tacoma, and he kept the staff rolling even when Moose Haas and Joaquin Andujar missed a start or two. The A's were winning as often as they were losing for the first couple of months. On May 23 they were 21–21, tied for first in the AL West. But Keith Atherton, Plan B for the bullpen

stopper, couldn't do the job and was donated to Minnesota, and the bullpen problem was driving the As' manager to distraction.

In retrospect, the moment at which the wheels fell off came when Jackie Moore decided to make José Rijo his relief ace. To be fair to Moore, it was late May and this was the first really stupid thing that he had done all year. After his outing of May 28, Rijo had struck out 74 men in 11 starts, with fair overall results (a 2–2 record, 4.38 ERA). Taking him out of the starting rotation further destabilized an already weakened rotation, while as a relief ace every mistake that the erratic 21-year-old made was exaggerated. In no time the bullpen problem had become a crisis and the entire pitching staff, starting and relief, looked like the aftermath of a New Year's Eve Grenade-Throwing Party. As a reliever, Rijo pitched 13 times with an 0–4 record, one save and an 8.53 ERA.

Then in June, Moose Haas went on the disabled list with a sore shoulder, while Joaquin Andujar opted for a pulled hamstring. The A's were losing about three games a week relative to the top of the division. In first place on May 23, they were seven games behind on June 8 at 25–32. By June 22 they were eleven games behind, at 28–42. The injuries were not limited to the pitching staff. Mickey Tettleton was out with an infected foot, and Dwayne Murphy went on the DL due to a disk in his back that was pinching a nerve.

By the middle of June, Moore's only notion of how to run a pitching staff was that if anybody pitched well as a starter he would try him in the bullpen and if anybody was OK in the bullpen he would try him as a starter. You probably think that I'm joking about that, but the Oakland fans know that I'm not. Oakland pitchers allowed only 1,334 hits, the lowest total in the American League, but (particularly during this period) their control was just awful. Bill Mooneyham had been pitching fairly well in middle relief, so on June 22, Moore used him as a starter. He pitched a pretty good game (two runs in five innings) so Moore promoted him to the role of relief ace.

José Canseco was hitting home runs and driving in runs at a remarkable pace, and Tony Phillips was hitting leadoff and having a fine start. We saw the A's play in Kansas City on June 23, and to be honest, I have not seen a team give such a pathetic effort since the Cardinals in early 1980. It was Rachel's first baseball game, and I remember I was focusing on Canseco all night, it being the first time I'd seen him, and thinking about how a rookie is like a baby, a mass of polymorphous potential that will be influenced by everything which happens, and thinking how sad it was that the A's were playing this way during the formative days of José Canseco's career, thinking that the A's had this wonderful gift in a rookie who could hit a baseball 500 feet, and that in two or three years he's going to assume that this is all there is to it, that you just show up for the games and put your numbers on the scoreboard and forget all that crap about hustle and team play and trying to win. Canseco was playing right field, and very badly I might add.

What I did not know, of course, was that during the game Dave Kingman had sent a rat in a pink box to a female reporter, Susan Fornoff, whose names spelled backward would be Ffonrof Nasus. This puerile act highlighted a long line of disgraceful behavior from Kingman toward Ms. Fornoff, which harassment had already become a bone of contention between the Oakland organization and the Bay Area press corps. The Oakland management had cringed at Kingman's moronic actions, but the rat incident was too much; Sandy Alderson flew to Kansas City and informed Kingman that any similar actions in the future would terminate his contract, stopping off while there to fire the manager. For a few days the As' players, rallying to Kingman's defense, stopped talking to the press. This was a new role for Kingman, team leadership. Before, Kingman has always been dismissed as merely an immature jerk. It turns out that all he needed was the right team to bring out this new side of his personality, a team full of immature jerks. The A's were able to oblige.

Jeff Newman ran the A's, so to speak, for a couple of weeks during which they won a couple of games. To go by what was written in *The Sporting News,* Newman didn't make any pretense of knowing what he was doing, which was an improvement over the previous two Oakland managers, who did pretend to know what they were doing. On July 1, Cleveland manager Pat Corrales charged the mound and tried to practice his martial arts on A's pitcher Dave Stewart, who cold-cocked him. The A's were 31–52, 14 games out, when Tony LaRussa was hired to bring some sanity out of the silliness.

Things improved quickly. Curt Young and Dave Stewart put the pitching staff on its feet. José Rijo went back to the starting rotation and pitched pretty well the rest of the way, and about half the injured pitchers got well. Mickey Tettleton and Dwayne Murphy returned and played well, which will cause some people to think that the difference between Moore's A's and LaRussa's A's was just luck, which is partly true but during the second half Canseco went through a serious slump and Tony Phillips was lost for seven weeks, but the A's continued to play well because somebody was around to contain the damage rather than magnifying it.

A few notes about the season:

The A's stole 139 bases, most of any team in the division, in 200 attempts, most in the league. But the A's had a lot of trouble against the running game, with opponents stealing 139 bases in 191 attempts. Only Texas allowed more OSB among American League teams, and only Texas and Cleveland threw out a smaller percentage of opponents who ran.

The A's had a 47–36 record in Oakland, fifth-best in the league, but were just 29–50 on the road, twelfth in the league. The 16-game home park advantage was the largest in the league.

The A's scored 31 runs more than projected by the runs created method (700–731).

Can the A's win this division in 1986? If I absolutely had to pick one team to win this division, I would pick the A's. The As' record after August 1 was 32–26. The strong play late in the year is the only proven leading indicator which would suggest that the A's will improve this year, but I believe they will. Why? Because I think the way the A's played the second half of the season is the true ability of the team. I think the talent is here to win, and the leadership is developing.

Oakland opponents saved 43 games, tied for the league high, indicating that the A's were close to winning quite a few games that they didn't win.

One of the things the A's need to do to put a contending team together in 1987 is get some run production out of the first base spot. Players who can hit but can't run or throw eventually wind up at first base and thus that is the position at which offensive talent is usually most abundant. In five of the last six years the A's haven't had a first baseman who could hit. The last three they've been playing Bruce Bochte there. Bochte hit .256 with 6 homers and 43 RBI in 407 at bats—decent stats if you're a shortstop, but a level of production for a first baseman that is damaging and unnecessary. The A's need to pick up a player out of the Ken Phelps class (Mike Stenhouse or Mike Easler or somebody) and control the damage. Despite having two players who hit 30 homers each (only two other major-league teams did) and two more players who hit 19 each, the A's were below the American League average in home runs.

One possibility is that Carney Lansford may be moved to first with Mark McGwire at third base. This only accomplishes the mission, however, if McGwire hits more than Bochte did. That seems like a good risk.

But the A's were winning the last half of last year even with Bochte out there. The most serious question is whether or not LaRussa can identify in spring training a group of pitchers who not only will pitch well for a time, but who have a shot at staying in the rotation and carrying the ball all the way. With the injuries here which have given opportunities to so many pitchers, LaRussa will have a dozen or more candidates for starting jobs, including Young, Haas, Stewart, Andujar, Codiroli, Mooneyham, Rijo, Plunk, Birtsas, Nelson, and Krueger. It's almost certain that there are five of those guys who can pitch 220 innings each and keep the team in almost every game. If LaRussa can identify those five pitchers, the A's will win this division.

Mickey TETTLETON, Catcher

	G	AB	Hit	2B	3B	HR	Run	RBI	TBB	SO	SB	CS	Avg
1.38 years		394	95	20	1	11	49	44	60	105	7	2	.242
1986	90	211	43	9	0	10	26	35	39	51	7	1	.204
First Half	33	86	17	4	0	2	10	11	11	17	4	1	.198
Second Half	57	125	26	5	0	8	16	24	28	34	3	0	.208
Vs. RHP		127	21	5	0	4		19	24	30	5	0	.165
Vs. LHP		84	22	4	0	6		16	15	21	2	1	.262
Home	47	106	21	4	0	4	11	11	20	22	5	0	.198
Road	43	105	22	5	0	6	15	24	19	29	2	1	.210
Grass	72	162	31	7	0	8	17	25	28	37	7	0	.191
Turf	18	49	12	2	0	2	9	10	11	14	0	1	.245

José CANSECO, Left Field

	G	AB	Hit	2B	3B	HR	Run	RBI	TBB	SO	SB	CS	Avg
1.15 years		606	151	28	1	33	88	113	60	179	14	7	.249
1986	157	600	144	29	1	33	85	117	65	175	15	7	.240
First Half	83	309	81	17	0	19	45	68	46	97	5	5	.262
Second Half	74	291	63	12	1	14	40	49	19	78	10	2	.216
Vs. RHP		415	92	18	1	25		82	52	131	15	4	.222
Vs. LHP		185	52	11	0	8		35	13	44	0	3	.281
Home	81	301	64	10	0	14	38	54	34	82	9	5	.213
Road	76	299	80	19	1	19	47	63	31	93	6	2	.268
Grass	133	496	113	19	1	28	68	95	57	143	12	7	.228
Turf	24	104	31	10	0	5	17	22	8	32	3	0	.298

Bruce BOCHTE, First Base

	G	AB	Hit	2B	3B	HR	Run	RBI	TBB	SO	SB	CS	Avg
9.49 years		551	155	26	2	11	68	69	69	70	5	4	.282
1986	125	407	104	13	1	6	57	43	65	68	3	2	.256
First Half	65	214	53	8	0	5	32	22	34	36	3	2	.248
Second Half	60	193	51	5	1	1	25	21	31	32	0	0	.264
Vs. RHP		358	94	13	1	6		39	60	59	3	2	.263
Vs. LHP		49	10	0	0	0		4	5	9	0	0	.204
Home	63	198	49	5	1	3	33	24	36	32	1	0	.247
Road	62	209	55	8	0	3	24	19	29	36	2	2	.263
Grass	106	347	90	10	1	5	47	37	56	55	3	2	.259
Turf	19	60	14	3	0	1	10	6	9	13	0	0	.233

Dwayne MURPHY, Center Field

	G	AB	Hit	2B	3B	HR	Run	RBI	TBB	SO	SB	CS	Avg
6.98 years		548	136	17	3	21	82	76	91	118	14	8	.248
1986	98	329	83	11	3	9	50	39	56	80	3	1	.252
First Half	29	98	24	3	1	2	17	15	19	20	2	0	.245
Second Half	69	231	59	8	2	7	33	24	37	60	1	1	.255
Vs. RHP		237	62	10	2	8		27	42	59	3	1	.262
Vs. LHP		92	21	1	1	1		12	14	21	0	0	.228
Home	51	168	43	3	2	5	26	18	32	39	1	0	.256
Road	47	161	40	8	1	4	24	21	24	41	2	1	.248
Grass	81	275	69	9	3	8	41	29	44	65	2	1	.251
Turf	17	54	14	2	0	1	9	10	12	15	1	0	.259

Tony PHILLIPS, Second Base

	G	AB	Hit	2B	3B	HR	Run	RBI	TBB	SO	SB	CS	Avg
3.10 years		499	128	21	5	5	73	48	62	96	15	8	.257
1986	118	441	113	14	5	5	76	52	76	82	15	10	.256
First Half	82	322	82	8	4	2	58	34	50	56	12	7	.255
Second Half	36	119	31	6	1	3	18	18	26	26	3	3	.261
Vs. RHP		307	70	9	3	2		34	47	60	5	6	.228
Vs. LHP		134	43	5	2	3		18	29	22	10	4	.321
Home	60	214	50	8	1	3	30	32	42	39	7	3	.234
Road	58	227	63	6	4	2	46	20	34	43	8	7	.278
Grass	96	355	88	12	3	4	57	44	60	63	14	9	.248
Turf	22	86	25	2	2	1	19	8	16	19	1	1	.291

Mike DAVIS, Right Field

	G	AB	Hit	2B	3B	HR	Run	RBI	TBB	SO	SB	CS	Avg
4.01 years		512	137	28	3	15	75	66	38	89	25	10	.268
1986	142	489	131	28	3	19	77	55	34	91	27	4	.268
First Half	71	247	59	18	0	9	32	28	19	48	11	2	.239
Second Half	71	242	72	10	3	10	45	27	15	43	16	2	.298
Vs. RHP		372	96	23	1	15		38	28	61	21	4	.258
Vs. LHP		117	35	5	2	4		17	6	30	6	0	.299
Home	76	244	65	14	2	11	43	29	28	40	14	1	.266
Road	66	245	66	14	1	8	34	26	6	51	13	3	.269
Grass	123	418	105	21	2	15	61	41	32	79	20	2	.251
Turf	19	71	26	7	1	4	16	14	2	12	7	2	.366

Carney LANSFORD, Third Base

	G	AB	Hit	2B	3B	HR	Run	RBI	TBB	SO	SB	CS	Avg
7.03 years		637	186	30	4	16	90	80	45	75	15	8	.292
1986	151	591	168	16	4	19	80	72	39	51	16	7	.284
First Half	76	296	86	8	1	7	37	29	18	23	7	2	.291
Second Half	75	295	82	8	3	12	43	43	21	28	9	5	.278
Vs. RHP		404	111	9	2	13		57	24	37	13	5	.275
Vs. LHP		187	57	7	2	6		15	15	14	3	2	.305
Home	78	298	95	11	3	10	44	48	24	20	8	4	.319
Road	73	293	73	5	1	9	36	24	15	31	8	3	.249
Grass	128	495	144	15	3	16	73	63	33	41	14	5	.291
Turf	23	96	24	1	1	3	7	9	6	10	2	2	.250

Dave KINGMAN, Designated Hitter

	G	AB	Hit	2B	3B	HR	Run	RBI	TBB	SO	SB	CS	Avg
11.98 years		557	131	20	2	37	75	101	51	152	7	4	.236
1986	144	561	118	19	0	35	70	94	33	126	3	3	.210
First Half	74	288	56	7	0	17	32	53	15	70	1	1	.194
Second Half	70	273	62	12	0	18	38	41	18	56	2	2	.227
Vs. RHP		388	80	11	0	21		63	20	82	3	1	.206
Vs. LHP		173	38	8	0	14		31	13	44	0	2	.220
Home	76	297	63	8	0	15	34	45	14	68	2	1	.212
Road	68	264	55	11	0	20	36	49	19	58	1	2	.208
Grass	123	477	95	16	0	24	53	68	28	113	3	3	.199
Turf	21	84	23	3	0	11	17	26	5	13	0	0	.274

Alfredo GRIFFIN, Shortstop

	G	AB	Hit	2B	3B	HR	Run	RBI	TBB	SO	SB	CS	Avg
7.58 years		582	149	21	8	3	66	44	26	51	18	13	.257
1986	162	594	169	23	6	4	74	51	35	52	33	16	.285
First Half	83	289	84	14	2	1	36	25	22	19	19	9	.291
Second Half	79	305	85	9	4	3	38	26	13	33	14	7	.279
Vs. RHP		389	117	16	5	4		46	27	28	20	9	.301
Vs. LHP		205	52	7	1	0		5	8	24	13	7	.254
Home	83	302	85	10	1	1	38	26	17	26	15	9	.281
Road	79	292	84	13	5	3	36	25	18	26	18	7	.288
Grass	137	497	140	19	5	3	55	45	30	44	24	14	.282
Turf	25	97	29	4	1	1	19	6	5	8	9	2	.299

Donnie HILL, Second Base

	G	AB	Hit	2B	3B	HR	Run	RBI	TBB	SO	SB	CS	Avg
2.20 years		483	132	19	2	5	56	49	25	47	7	4	.273
1986	108	339	96	16	2	4	37	29	23	38	5	2	.283
First Half	54	165	47	8	0	2	16	12	10	18	1	2	.285
Second Half	54	174	49	8	2	2	21	17	13	20	4	0	.282
Vs. RHP		201	58	8	1	3		20	13	23	1	0	.289
Vs. LHP		138	38	8	1	1		9	10	15	4	2	.275
Home	54	157	46	7	1	0	17	9	11	21	4	0	.293
Road	54	182	50	9	1	4	20	20	12	17	1	2	.275
Grass	91	280	77	13	1	2	31	21	20	31	4	1	.275
Turf	17	59	19	3	1	2	6	8	3	7	1	1	.322

Curt YOUNG

Year	(W–L)	GS	Run	Avg	DP	Avg	SB	Avg
1984	(9-4)	17	89	5.24	24	1.41	3	.18
1985	(0-4)	7	34	4.86	6	.86	1	.14
1986	(13-9)	27	114	4.22	16	.59	17	.63
1983-1986		53	250	4.72	48	.91	22	.42

	1986		1985		1984		84-86
	ERA	W–L	ERA	W–L	ERA	W–L	W–L
Total	3.45	13-9	7.24	0-4	4.06	9-4	22-17
Home	2.37	9-2	6.30	0-3	4.89	3-2	12-7
Road	5.19	4-7	9.00	0-1	3.36	6-2	10-10
East	3.43	9-2	6.46	0-0	4.69	3-3	12-5
West	3.48	4-7	7.63	0-4	3.56	6-1	10-12
1st Half	3.75	5-5	10.29	0-2	1.54	1-0	6-7
2nd Half	3.25	8-4	4.68	0-2	4.36	8-4	16-10
Turf	6.75	2-2	15.95	0-1	0.92	2-0	4-3
Grass	3.11	11-7	5.59	0-3	4.75	7-4	18-14
Day	3.35	6-3	3.86	0-3	5.81	2-2	8-8
Night	3.53	7-6	11.51	0-1	3.36	7-2	14-9
April			10.31	0-2			0-2
May	2.60	3-1					3-1
June	4.35	2-4			.00	1-0	3-4
July	3.41	2-1	4.76	0-0	2.79	2-1	4-2
August	3.32	3-2	.00	0-0	5.52	3-2	6-4
September	3.44	3-1	5.85	0-2	5.28	3-1	6-4

José RIJO

Year	(W–L)	GS	Run	Avg	DP	Avg	SB	Avg
1984	(2-8)	5	13	2.60	4	.80	8	1.60
1985	(6-4)	9	33	3.67	2	.22	6	.67
1986	(9-11)	26	124	4.77	11	.42	26	1.00
1984-1986		40	170	4.25	17	.43	40	1.00

	1986		1985		1984		84-86
	ERA	W–L	ERA	W–L	ERA	W–L	W–L
Total	4.65	9-11	3.53	6-4	4.76	2-8	17-23
Home	3.90	3-4	3.65	2-1	4.82	1-2	6-7
Road	5.30	6-7	3.46	4-3	4.74	1-6	11-16
East	4.05	4-7	3.44	3-1	5.40	2-2	9-10
West	5.38	5-4	3.64	3-3	4.43	0-6	8-13
1st Half	4.77	3-7			4.85	2-8	5-15
2nd Half	4.53	6-4	3.53	6-4	3.00	0-0	12-8
Turf	6.92	2-1	3.65	1-2	3.57	0-2	3-5
Grass	4.07	7-10	3.51	5-2	5.24	2-6	14-18
Day	3.69	4-2	5.51	3-1	6.59	0-3	7-6
Night	5.26	5-9	2.85	3-3	4.25	2-5	10-17
April	4.89	1-2			4.70	0-2	1-4
May	3.77	1-0			3.04	1-3	2-3
June	6.55	0-5			7.53	1-2	1-7
July	2.65	2-1			6.00	0-1	2-2
August	6.19	2-2	1.61	2-1			4-3
September	4.46	3-1	4.57	4-3			7-4

Joaquin ANDUJAR

Year	(W–L)	GS	Run	Avg	DP	Avg	SB	Avg
1984	(20-14)	36	158	4.39	33	.92	32	.89
1985	(21-12)	38	186	4.89	48	1.26	36	.95
1986	(12-7)	26	111	4.27	26	1.00	15	.58
1976-1986		282	1138	4.04	261	.93	241	.85

1986	G	IP	W–L	H	ER	SO	ERA
Total	28	155.1	12-7	139	66	72	3.82
Home	15	88.1	8-4	76	38	47	3.87
Road	13	67.0	4-3	63	28	25	3.76
East	13	76.2	7-2	61	22	36	2.58
West	15	78.2	5-5	78	44	36	5.03
1st Half	10	44.2	4-2	33	19	21	3.83
2nd Half	18	110.2	8-5	106	49	51	3.82
Turf	4	17.2	1-1	22	13	8	6.62
Grass	24	137.2	11-6	117	53	64	3.46
Day	13	78.1	5-3	68	33	44	3.79
Night	15	77.0	7-4	71	33	28	3.86
April	4	22.1	2-1	16	11	12	4.43
May	5	22.0	2-1	17	8	9	3.27
June	1	0.1	0-0	0	0	0	.00
July	4	19.1	2-1	19	8	9	3.72
August	8	44.1	2-3	47	21	17	4.26
September	6	47.0	4-1	40	18	25	3.45

Jay HOWELL

1986	G	IP	W–L	Sv	H	ER	SO	ERA
Total	38	53.1	3-6	16	53	20	42	3.38
Home	19	29.0	1-3	9	32	12	25	3.72
Road	19	24.1	2-3	7	21	8	17	2.96
East	15	18.2	0-5	4	30	15	13	7.23
West	23	34.2	3-1	12	23	5	29	1.30
1st Half	14	18.1	0-4	5	24	12	18	5.89
2nd Half	24	35.0	3-2	11	29	8	24	2.06
Turf	7	11.0	1-0	4	3	1	9	.82
Grass	31	42.1	2-6	12	50	19	33	4.04
Day	21	30.0	1-3	8	28	10	27	3.00
Night	17	23.1	2-3	8	25	10	15	3.86
April	10	14.2	0-2	4	17	8	15	4.91
May	4	3.2	0-2	1	7	4	3	9.82
June								
July	3	4.0	0-0	1	2	0	1	.00
August	12	17.2	2-0	7	11	1	11	.51
September	9	13.1	1-2	3	16	7	12	4.73

OTHERS

Pitcher	(W–L)	GS	Run	Avg	DP	Avg	SB	Avg	Time	Att.
Stewart	(9-5)	17	70	4.12	12	.71	20	1.18	2:54	320
Codiroli	(5-8)	16	77	4.81	14	.88	8	.50	2:52	314
Plunk	(4-7)	15	61	4.07	13	.87	10	.67	3:00	316
Haas	(7-2)	12	89	7.42	9	.75	9	.75	2:58	174
Langford	(1-10)	11	24	2.18	9	.82	9	.82	2:30	234
Mooneyham	(4-5)	6	32	5.33	5	.83	6	1.00	3:01	120
Krueger	(1-2)	3	20	6.67	2	.67	13	4.33	3:06	51
Rodriguez	(1-2)	3	9	3.00	2	.67	6	2.00	2:45	17

RECORDS WITH DIFFERENT STARTING CATCHERS

Catcher	Inn	ER	W–L	ERA	GS	SB	Avg
Tettleton	660.0	293	36-39	4.00	75	59	.79
Willard	437.2	205	29-20	4.22	49	41	.84
Bathe	335.1	188	11-27	5.05	38	39	1.03

STARTING PITCHERS' AVERAGE TIME AND ATTENDANCE RECORDS

Pitcher	Time	Attendance
Young	2:40	536
Andujar	2:46	234
Rijo	2:52	471

CHICAGO WHITE SOX

Runners on Base:	1856
Opponents on Base:	1955
Net Advantage:	− 99
Won–Lost Record:	72-90

Let us start our account of the Ken Harrelson command where he started it, by moving the fences back at Comiskey Park. Moving further away from the fences, Harrelson felt, would be more accommodating to the kind of team that he wanted to have, a fast, aggressive team with outstanding pitching. It might have occurred to a more timid director of operations that he didn't actually *have* any of these things; he merely thought that it would be neat to acquire them. What he actually had was a slow team whose pitchers had control problems, and whose biggest assets were a few players like Harold Baines, Carlton Fisk, Greg Walker, and Ron Kittle, who didn't run well but did have power.

So anyway, the ChiSox now had an outfield of Baines, Kittle, and Law, none of whom could play center field in any park, and whose defensive abilities were stretched to the limit to cover the field in Comiskey as it was, although Rudy Law does run well. In order to get the maximum benefit out of this shrewd maneuver, Harrelson a) released the fastest player on the team, Rudy Law, over the vigorous objections of his manager, who thought Law was ready to have an outstanding season; and b) shifted his catcher to the outfield.

There is some controversy about who actually was responsible for the decision to move Carlton Fisk to the outfield, and the next person to step forward and take credit for it will be the first as well as quite certainly the last. You almost had the feeling that this was one of those acts, like leaving a bomb in a suitcase at an airport, that somebody should call up the newspaper and take credit for, but since no one did the maneuver is variously attributed to Tony LaRussa, Ken Harrelson, and Dave Duncan, the ex-pitching coach who apparently thought that Fisk's pitch selection was suspect. Maybe we should divvy up the credit among the bright boy who thought up the move, the genius who okayed it, and the powerful intellect who decided that the need to make this move was so powerful that it justified ramming it down Fisk's throat. In any case, before making this move the White Sox had:

1) One of the league's best offensive and defensive catchers in Carlton Fisk, who had hit 37 homers and driven in 107 runs in 1985; and

2) A slow, slugging right-handed hitting left fielder/DH named Ron Kittle.

After making this move, the White Sox had:

1) No proven catcher;

2) Two slow, slugging right-handed hitting left fielder/DHs, and as a special bonus:

3) One very unhappy veteran player, who just coincidentally had been the team MVP in two of the previous three years.

Anytime you can make a trade like that, it's got to help you accomplish your mission.

As curious as these utilization-of-resources decisions were, what was most damaging about Harrelson's stewardship was his utter inability to evaluate talent. With the exception of the Britt Burns deal, which worked to the White Sox advantage because Burns wasn't able to pitch, every deal that Harrelson made, and he made a bunch of them, hurt the team. The fences can be moved back and Fisk can be returned to his position, but the White Sox can't get Scott Fletcher or Joel Skinner or Ron Kittle or Rudy Law or Edwin Correa back. The legacy of Ken Harrelson in Chicago is an emaciated talent base that may take several years to rebuild.

There's an old saying that you should choose your enemies carefully, because that's who you will eventually resemble. We are a strange race, in that as we move through life we tend to switch roles with people we once despised. The abused child grows up to abuse his own children. The rowdy student grows up to be a strict teacher. Ken Harrelson ran the White Sox exactly the way that Charles O. Finley ran the Kansas City A's in the sixties, when Harrelson played for KC. To a fan of those teams, each Hawk blunder seemed familiar. Finley loved to move the fences in and out. Every couple of years he would have some new idea about the kind of team that he was going to put together to win big with, and the first thing he would always do was move the fences around to accommodate his notion. *Then* he would worry about the talent. Making trades on the seat of his pants without the advice and counsel of his organization, making personnel decisions on intuition and then forcing everyone beneath him to accept them, firing managers and general managers and assistant general managers to cover his own mistakes, getting down on players who were slumping or couldn't do what he asked them to do and trading them for half what they would have brought a year earlier, falling in love with unproven players and then giving up on them when they turned out to be ordinary—these are all very typical Charlie Finley moves. They didn't work twenty years ago, and they won't work twenty years from now.

Well, I could give a lot more particulars, but at this point to say more about Harrelson's direction of the Sox would be beating a dead horse's ass, so I'll move on to the characteristics of the team, such as it remained. At what positions were the White Sox strong? The Sox were above average at only one position, two when Greg Walker was healthy. Right fielder Harold Baines was the Sox Most Valuable Player, and really their only good player.

At what point of the season did the Sox play well? Their only .500 month was June, when they went 15–13. That record was a combination of an early June streak and the traditional spurt of playing well after the manager's uniform is restuffed. For June as a whole Harold Baines hit .324 with 19 RBI; Bobby Bonilla hit .294 (there's another cute sequence of moves you can analyze some time); John Cangelosi drew 24 walks, stole 13 bases, and scored 21 runs; Julio Cruz hit .329 and scored 18 runs; Fisk drove in 23 runs; Greg Walker hit 5 homers and drove in 23 runs; Guillen hit .271 and drove in 15 runs; Ron Kittle hit 7 home runs; Hairston and Hulett both played well; and the White Sox pitching was so bad that they barely played .500 ball anyway.

For most of the season, the Sox were not busy compiling impressive offensive numbers. The White Sox hit only 121 home runs, fewest in the American League. They had only 1,963 total bases, fewest in the American League, and were the first American League team in three years to have less than 2,000 total bases.

The White Sox hit only 197 doubles, the fewest of any major-league team. They were the first major-league team to hit fewer than 200 doubles since 1983, and the first American League team with fewer than 200 doubles in a full season since 1979.

The White Sox infield was the weakest offensively in the American League. The White Sox outfield was the weakest offensively in the American League.

The White Sox team secondary average was .228, the lowest of any major-league team. The most positive thing about the Chicago White Sox in 1986 was that they didn't leave many people on base. The White Sox left on only 1,036 runners, the fewest of any major-league team. Of course, the White Sox had only 1,856 runners on base to begin with, fewest of any major-league team.

Their isolated power, .116, was lowest in the American League. The White Sox averaged only 2.17 extra base hits a game, while every other American League team averaged at least two and a half, and four teams averaged three.

On the other hand, for most of the season the Sox pitchers weren't getting hit so hard. Late in the season, although the Sox were still losing, there were some signs that Jim Fregosi was getting a pitching staff organized. A few September ERAs: Floyd Bannister, 2.53 in 46 innings; Steve Carlton, 2.45 in 40 innings; Joe Cowley, 2.00 in 54 innings; Bill Dawley, 3.24 in 7 outings; José DeLeon, 2.76 in 33 innings; Gene Nelson, 1.46 in 9 outings; Dave Schmidt, 2.53 in 9 outings; Ray Searage, 1.93 in 12 outings; and Bobby Thigpen, 2.76 in 10 outings. The Sox were 16–17 after September 1, their second-best month, and felt confident enough of their pitching to trade Gene Nelson to Oakland for Donnie Hill.

Which seems like an obviously good trade. The technical indicators series that I use to evaluate a team's chances of improving the next year paints a surprisingly positive picture of the White Sox's future. It reasons that:

1) The White Sox declined by 13 games in 1986, and teams that decline strongly in one season have a marked tendency to improve the next year.

2) Bad teams, by their nature, tend to improve.

3) The White Sox have a young starting lineup, averaging 26.4 years of age (second-lowest in the AL).

4) The White Sox should have won two games more than they did last year, indicating that their talent is slightly better than the 72–90 record indicates.

5) The White Sox played slightly better late in the year than they had earlier.

Adding it all together, the White Sox figure to have almost an 80% chance of being better next year.

If my indicators series didn't tell me this, I would never have thought it up myself. The only negative indicator is that the White Sox scored 644 runs with individual stats that would ordinarily have created only 614, so that (were it not for the tendency of bad teams to get better) they would probably score fewer runs next year, but that indicator is quite suspect in this case because the White Sox have done this consistently for several years.

I don't see the Sox as being a contender in 1987. While I'm generally impressed by Fregosi's approach to the team, the pitching is unproven and the offense, unfortunately, is proven. I would give the Sox perhaps a 3% chance of winning the division and a 25% chance of playing .500 ball, and those would be the lowest percentages for any team in the division.

And yet, you know, any team really can win, and the White Sox are one of the best illustrations of that that I've ever seen. I've said for years that if anybody ever offers you 200–1 odds on a baseball team winning its division, you should take it because no team is ever that much of a longshot. The scenario by which the Sox could contend in 1987 is extremely easy to see. The Sox have at least six young players who may be lifting weights and running windsprints even as I write this in December, and could shock the American League in 1987. Those include catcher Ron Karkovice, who has a strong arm and hit .247 with almost half of his hits for extra bases in 37 games last year; center fielder Daryl Boston, a prospect for several years who played very well the last two months of 1986; pitcher José DeLeon, who still has one of the game's best arms; outfielder Ivan Calderon, just one year ago regarded by the Seattle Mariners as a potential superstar; reliever Bobby Thigpen, who had a 1.77 ERA in 20 outings late in the year; and first baseman Russ Mormon, a strong line-drive hitter.

In addition to those players, Jim Fregosi can count on additional offensive help from Greg Walker, who missed half of the season with injuries, and newcomer Donnie Hill, who could well be a .300 hitter. Shortstop Ozzie Guillen, who had a disappointing sophomore season, may make some adjustments and come out strong in 1987. Guillen is still very young, and could grow as a hitter a great deal. Third baseman Dave Cochrane is a legitimate prospect. It doesn't all have to break right for them; if just three or four of those players come through and Fregosi makes good decisions about his starting pitchers, the Sox could surprise in 1987.

Carlton FISK, Catcher

	G	AB	Hit	2B	3B	HR	Run	RBI	TBB	SO	SB	CS	Avg
11.28 years		578	157	28	4	25	89	87	55	89	10	4	.271
1986	125	457	101	11	0	14	42	63	22	92	2	4	.221
First Half	74	283	62	8	0	7	30	45	21	67	2	4	.219
Second Half	51	174	39	3	0	7	12	18	1	25	0	0	.224
Vs. RHP		300	66	6	0	9		41	15	57	2	3	.220
Vs. LHP		157	35	5	0	5		22	7	35	0	1	.223
Home	62	232	48	4	0	5	15	27	8	43	0	2	.207
Road	63	225	53	7	0	9	27	36	14	49	2	2	.236
Grass	105	388	83	8	0	9	30	42	17	74	2	3	.214
Turf	20	69	18	3	0	5	12	21	5	18	0	2	.261

John CANGELOSI, Outfield

	G	AB	Hit	2B	3B	HR	Run	RBI	TBB	SO	SB	CS	Avg
0.88 years		502	118	18	3	2	76	37	81	71	57	19	.234
1986	137	438	103	16	3	2	65	32	71	61	50	17	.235
First Half	74	249	59	10	1	1	44	17	52	31	36	8	.237
Second Half	63	189	44	6	2	1	21	15	19	30	14	9	.233
Vs. RHP		304	74	7	2	0		21	45	40	24	9	.243
Vs. LHP		134	29	9	1	2		11	26	21	26	8	.216
Home	69	202	48	7	3	1	38	15	42	27	31	7	.238
Road	68	236	55	9	0	1	27	17	29	34	19	10	.233
Grass	117	366	81	12	3	2	54	24	65	53	42	12	.221
Turf	20	72	22	4	0	0	11	8	6	8	8	5	.306

Greg WALKER, First Base

	G	AB	Hit	2B	3B	HR	Run	RBI	TBB	SO	SB	CS	Avg
3.12 years		528	145	30	5	23	68	90	44	86	5	3	.275
1986	78	282	78	10	6	13	37	51	29	44	1	2	.277
First Half	55	196	50	9	3	10	25	37	24	36	1	2	.255
Second Half	23	86	28	1	3	3	12	14	5	8	0	0	.326
Vs. RHP		193	57	7	5	11		39	18	27	1	1	.295
Vs. LHP		89	21	3	1	2		12	11	17	0	1	.236
Home	43	151	42	8	5	6	22	27	21	22	0	1	.278
Road	35	131	36	2	1	7	15	24	8	22	1	1	.275
Grass	65	235	64	8	5	11	32	43	26	36	0	1	.272
Turf	13	47	14	2	1	2	5	8	3	8	1	1	.298

Steve LYONS, Outfield

	G	AB	Hit	2B	3B	HR	Run	RBI	TBB	SO	SB	CS	Avg
1.44 years		428	107	16	4	4	57	35	35	77	11	10	.249
1986	101	247	56	9	3	1	30	20	19	47	4	6	.227
First Half	64	137	34	7	2	1	22	15	13	28	2	4	.248
Second Half	37	110	22	2	1	0	8	5	6	19	2	2	.200
Vs. RHP		214	48	9	1	1		16	18	36	3	6	.224
Vs. LHP		33	8	0	2	0		4	1	11	1	0	.242
Home	52	124	31	3	3	1	16	13	12	16	2	4	.250
Road	49	123	25	6	0	0	14	7	7	31	2	2	.203
Grass	88	200	47	5	3	1	27	17	18	34	4	6	.235
Turf	13	47	9	4	0	0	3	3	1	13	0	0	.191

Julio CRUZ, Second Base

	G	AB	Hit	2B	3B	HR	Run	RBI	TBB	SO	SB	CS	Avg
7.14 years		541	128	16	4	3	78	39	67	71	48	11	.237
1986	81	209	45	2	0	0	38	19	42	28	7	2	.215
First Half	44	118	29	1	0	0	25	12	24	18	5	1	.246
Second Half	37	91	16	1	0	0	13	7	18	10	2	1	.176
Vs. RHP		136	29	1	0	0		12	32	16	4	2	.213
Vs. LHP		73	16	1	0	0		7	10	12	3	0	.219
Home	38	98	26	0	0	0	22	15	25	10	4	1	.265
Road	43	111	19	2	0	0	16	4	17	18	3	1	.171
Grass	67	169	35	1	0	0	32	19	37	22	4	1	.207
Turf	14	40	10	1	0	0	6	0	5	6	3	1	.250

Harold BAINES, Right Field

	G	AB	Hit	2B	3B	HR	Run	RBI	TBB	SO	SB	CS	Avg
6.12 years		613	176	30	6	23	80	96	43	88	5	3	.287
1986	145	570	169	29	2	21	72	88	38	89	2	1	.296
First Half	77	303	91	14	1	10	43	48	26	44	1	1	.300
Second Half	68	267	78	15	1	11	29	40	12	45	1	0	.292
Vs. RHP		364	115	21	1	18		70	28	51	2	1	.316
Vs. LHP		206	54	8	1	3		18	10	38	0	0	.262
Home	72	275	91	16	2	8	33	51	21	35	1	1	.331
Road	73	295	78	13	0	13	39	37	17	54	1	0	.264
Grass	126	486	147	22	2	19	64	81	35	78	1	1	.302
Turf	19	84	22	7	0	2	8	7	3	11	1	0	.262

Tim HULETT, Third Base

	G	AB	Hit	2B	3B	HR	Run	RBI	TBB	SO	SB	CS	Avg
1.88 years		492	121	19	5	12	56	43	28	93	6	3	.245
1986	150	520	120	16	5	17	53	44	21	91	4	1	.231
First Half	70	211	54	11	5	4	23	18	15	34	2	0	.256
Second Half	80	309	66	5	0	13	30	26	6	57	2	1	.214
Vs. RHP		326	71	10	3	8		28	8	57	4	1	.218
Vs. LHP		194	49	6	2	9		16	13	34	0	0	.253
Home	76	263	65	8	3	7	27	20	14	48	0	1	.247
Road	74	257	55	8	2	10	26	24	7	43	4	0	.214
Grass	126	438	103	10	5	17	48	40	18	76	3	1	.235
Turf	24	82	17	6	0	0	5	4	3	15	1	0	.207

Ron HASSEY, Catcher-Designated Hitter

	G	AB	Hit	2B	3B	HR	Run	RBI	TBB	SO	SB	CS	Avg
4.90 years		476	134	25	1	10	51	66	56	48	2	2	.282
1986	113	341	110	25	1	9	45	49	46	27	1	1	.323
First Half	53	157	49	13	0	6	20	27	20	15	1	1	.312
Second Half	60	184	61	12	1	3	25	22	26	12	0	0	.332
Vs. RHP		277	91	21	1	9		41	40	21	1	1	.329
Vs. LHP		64	19	4	0	0		8	6	6	0	0	.297
Home	58	167	55	13	1	5	23	26	26	13	0	1	.329
Road	55	174	55	12	0	4	22	23	20	14	1	0	.316
Grass	95	280	96	25	1	8	41	42	38	20	0	1	.343
Turf	18	61	14	0	0	1	4	7	8	7	1	0	.230

Ozzie GUILLEN, Shortstop

	G	AB	Hit	2B	3B	HR	Run	RBI	TBB	SO	SB	CS	Avg
1.91 years		544	142	21	7	2	68	42	13	46	8	4	.261
1986	159	547	137	19	4	2	58	47	12	52	8	4	.250
First Half	76	248	61	10	3	2	30	31	8	20	6	2	.246
Second Half	83	299	76	9	1	0	28	16	4	32	2	2	.254
Vs. RHP		380	94	15	4	1		38	6	32	7	4	.247
Vs. LHP		167	43	4	0	1		9	6	20	1	0	.257
Home	78	272	69	9	1	1	33	23	5	23	2	3	.254
Road	81	275	68	10	3	1	25	24	7	29	6	1	.247
Grass	132	455	109	15	4	1	51	37	12	47	5	4	.240
Turf	27	92	28	4	0	1	7	10	0	5	3	0	.304

Jerry HAIRSTON, Pinch Hitter-Designated Hitter

	G	AB	Hit	2B	3B	HR	Run	RBI	TBB	SO	SB	CS	Avg
4.86 years		322	84	17	1	5	42	38	53	44	1	1	.260
1986	101	225	61	15	0	5	32	26	26	26	0	0	.271
First Half	49	93	26	6	0	2	15	12	15	12	0	0	.280
Second Half	52	132	35	9	0	3	17	14	11	14	0	0	.265
Vs. RHP		166	48	12	0	3		21	23	15	0	0	.289
Vs. LHP		59	13	3	0	2		5	3	11	0	0	.220
Home	49	117	36	8	0	3	21	16	16	12	0	0	.308
Road	52	108	25	7	0	2	11	10	10	14	0	0	.231
Grass	82	177	51	11	0	5	26	22	22	20	0	0	.288
Turf	19	48	10	4	0	0	6	4	4	6	0	0	.208

Richard DOTSON

Year	(W–L)	GS	Run	Avg	DP	Avg	SB	Avg
1984	(14-15)	32	137	4.28	39	1.22	24	.75
1985	(3-4)	9	28	3.11	6	.67	5	.56
1986	(10-17)	34	131	3.85	29	.85	26	.76
1979-1986		202	939	4.65	215	1.06	171	.85

	1986 ERA	W–L	1985 ERA	1984 ERA	1983 ERA	1982 ERA	82-86 W–L
Total	5.48	10-17	4.47	3.59	3.23	3.84	60-58
Home	4.84	7-9	2.75	3.92	3.30	3.50	29-32
Road	6.23	3-8	9.69	3.20	3.15	4.18	31-26
East	5.86	5-9	4.50	3.44	3.52	3.39	30-31
West	5.00	5-8	4.41	3.71	2.91	4.23	30-27
1st Half	5.01	7-7	4.47	2.64	4.50	4.94	32-30
2nd Half	6.03	3-10		4.77	2.25	2.93	28-28
Turf	6.75	1-3	15.00	2.72	2.05		11-6
Grass	5.26	9-14	3.11	3.74	3.49		40-37
Day	4.95	4-5	3.08	2.75	3.91	3.49	22-15
Night	5.85	6-12	5.88	3.99	2.93	4.00	38-43
April	7.62	1-2	2.70	2.41	4.22	2.66	8-7
May	4.28	1-3	4.85	2.18	3.92	5.40	10-13
June	4.57	4-2	5.79	3.52	6.39	6.12	11-8
July	9.82	1-4		7.96	2.70	6.63	6-12
August	4.30	2-2		3.27	2.20	1.68	14-6
September	4.46	1-4		3.92	1.93	3.38	11-12

Joe COWLEY

Year	(W–L)	GS	Run	Avg	DP	Avg	SB	Avg
1984	(9-2)	11	76	6.91	5	.45	5	.45
1985	(12-6)	26	134	5.15	20	.77	20	.77
1986	(11-11)	27	125	4.63	21	.78	21	.78
1982-1986		72	367	5.10	54	.75	54	.75

	1986 ERA	W–L	1985 ERA	W–L	1984 ERA	W–L	84-86 W–L
Total	3.88	11-11	3.95	12-6	3.56	9-2	32-19
Home	2.37	6-5	3.25	4-2	2.32	7-1	17-8
Road	5.33	5-6	4.48	8-4	7.17	2-1	15-11
East	6.34	4-6	3.32	7-1	3.55	6-2	17-9
West	2.80	7-5	4.60	5-5	3.58	3-0	15-10
1st Half	4.17	4-4	3.42	7-3			11-7
2nd Half	3.72	7-7	4.43	5-3	3.56	9-2	21-12
Turf	3.60	2-2	7.03	2-3			4-5
Grass	3.97	9-9	3.39	10-3	3.56	9-2	28-14
Day	3.75	3-4	3.15	5-3	2.22	4-0	12-7
Night	3.94	8-7	4.55	7-3	4.12	5-2	20-12
April	19.29	0-1	4.19	0-1			0-2
May	4.50	1-1	3.41	4-1			5-2
June	3.07	3-1	3.63	2-1			5-2
July	5.40	2-3	4.39	3-1	2.92	1-1	6-5
August	5.81	2-3	4.28	1-1	3.50	4-0	7-4
September	2.00	3-2	3.86	2-1	3.86	4-1	9-4

Floyd BANNISTER

Year	(W–L)	GS	Run	Avg	DP	Avg	SB	Avg
1984	(14-11)	33	152	4.61	30	.91	14	.42
1985	(10-14)	34	155	4.56	31	.91	23	.68
1986	(10-14)	27	89	3.30	24	.89	16	.59
1977-1986		284	1192	4.20	223	.79	214	.75

	1986 ERA	W–L	1985 ERA	1984 ERA	1983 ERA	1982 ERA	82-86 W–L
Total	3.54	10-14	4.87	4.83	3.35	3.43	62-62
Home	2.84	5-6	3.61	4.47	3.09	3.75	30-27
Road	4.57	5-8	5.90	5.16	3.67	3.12	32-35
East	3.88	4-10	4.70	4.25	3.03	3.35	30-37
West	2.98	6-4	5.08	5.45	3.65	3.51	32-25
1st Half	3.03	5-4	4.75	4.74	4.76	3.15	26-31
2nd Half	3.82	5-10	4.98	4.91	2.23	3.75	36-31
Turf	3.15	3-1	5.53	4.84	3.83		11-6
Grass	3.59	7-13	4.70	4.83	3.23		39-43
Day	2.23	3-4	3.97	6.30	5.10	2.77	14-19
Night	4.02	7-10	5.12	4.22	2.61	3.60	48-43
April	3.00	1-2	6.08	5.12	5.64	3.46	7-10
May	2.70	1-2	2.75	5.73	4.08	3.30	8-13
June	6.75	1-0	6.33	4.40	4.00	1.98	7-6
July	5.61	2-4	3.79	3.77	2.56	4.19	13-9
August	3.68	3-2	5.40	4.02	2.88	4.10	15-11
September	2.53	2-4	5.80	6.32	2.14	3.61	12-13

Bob THIGPEN

1986	G	IP	W–L	Sv	H	ER	SO	ERA
Total	20	35.2	2-0	7	26	7	20	1.77
Home	10	16.2	1-0	5	10	2	10	1.08
Road	10	19.0	1-0	2	16	5	10	2.37
East	7	15.0	0-0	2	13	2	8	1.20
West	13	20.2	2-0	5	13	5	12	2.18
1st Half								
2nd Half	20	35.2	2-0	7	26	7	20	1.77
Turf	5	7.1	1-0	2	4	1	4	1.23
Grass	15	28.1	1-0	5	22	6	16	1.91
Day	6	12.0	0-0	3	9	2	7	1.50
Night	14	23.2	2-0	4	17	5	13	1.90
April								
May								
June								
July								
August	10	19.1	0-0	3	12	2	10	.93
September	10	16.1	2-0	4	14	5	10	2.76

OTHERS

Pitcher	(W–L)	GS	Run	Avg	DP	Avg	SB	Avg	Time	Att.
Davis	(4-5)	19	79	4.16	17	.89	12	.63	2:57	384
Allen	(7-2)	17	93	5.47	13	.76	6	.35	2:54	389
DeLeon	(4-5)	13	45	3.46	11	.85	10	.77	2:55	313
Seaver	(2-6)	12	37	3.08	11	.92	12	1.00	2:48	237
Carlton	(4-3)	10	40	4.00	13	1.30	10	1.00	2:34	152
Filson	(0-1)	1	2	2.00	0	.00	0	.00	2:36	10
Nelson	(6-6)	1	1	1.00	2	2.00	0	.00	2:28	11
Schmidt	(3-6)	1	2	2.00	1	1.00	2	2.00	3:17	17

STARTING PITCHERS' AVERAGE TIME AND ATTENDANCE RECORDS

Pitcher	Time	Attendance
Dotson	2:45	668
Bannister	2:34	570
Cowley	2:48	547

RECORDS WITH DIFFERENT STARTING CATCHERS

Catcher	Inn	ER	W–L	ERA	GS	SB	Avg
Fisk	569.1	247	29-35	3.90	64	54	.84
Skinner	444.1	216	21-28	4.38	49	30	.61
Karkovice	313.1	112	17-19	3.22	36	26	.72
Hassey	61.1	22	4-3	3.23	7	3	.43
Hill	54.0	34	1-5	5.67	6	2	.33

MINNESOTA TWINS

Runners on Base:	1984
Opponents on Base:	2128
Net Advantage:	−144
Won-Lost Record:	71-91

In contrast to the comic ineptitude of Hawk Harrelson, with his ridiculous clothes and mock profound pronouncements, there is something sad, something almost sinister about the ineptitude which guides the Minnesota Twins. For years, the Twins have had a collection of young power hitters that is the envy of the league. In 1986 the collection was enhanced when Kirby Puckett shocked the league with 31 homers among his 223 hits, while several other Twins had good seasons. The Twins had more homers (196) and more total bases (2,369) than any other team in the division—yet they were never in contention.

On the simplest level, the problems of the Twins are easy to pinpoint. The Twins had a 4.77 ERA, highest in the major leagues. Living in terror of their bullpen, they threw 39 complete games, most in the major leagues, and saved only 24 games, fewest of any major league team. Twin pitchers were hammered for 200 home runs, the highest total in the majors since Minnesota gave up 208 in 1982. Their opponents blasted 310 doubles as well, giving opponents 2,553 total bases and a .454 slugging percentage. All of those figures were easily the worst in baseball.

Many of you think that the poor pitching stats are a result of the park. The Twins' ERA at home was 4.67, the highest in the American League. Their staff ERA on the road was 4.92, also the highest in the American League. In 81 road games they gave up 93 home runs, the most in the league except Detroit. The park made this worse, as they allowed 107 at home.

The offense, despite the power, was mediocre. The Twins scored only 741 runs, an average number. At home the Twins scored 426 runs, the most of any American League team; on the road they scored only 315, which ranked eleventh. The team was below average in batting average (.261–.262) and walks drawn (501–548). They stole only 81 bases, fewest of any team in the division, and were abysmal percentage base stealers, losing 61 runners attempting to steal (net loss on stolen base attempts: about five runs). The worst offenders were Gaetti (14 for 29) and Gagne (12 for 22), but the Twins had no effective base stealers.

The defense was fairly good, although there were gaps. The Twins did a poor job of stopping the running game, with opponents stealing 111 bases in 153 attempts. More on that in a moment.

On a deeper level, the failure of the Twins to marshal their resources and head for the pennant race is puzzling. Ray Miller was hired because he was supposed to be knowledgeable about pitching. In 1984, Billy Gardner's last full season with the Twins, the Twins had a staff ERA of 3.85, fourth best in the American League. When the pitching went out the first couple of months of 1985, Gardner was axed and Miller was brought in to straighten it out.

In the June 2 issue of *The Sporting News*, Stan Isle said that "Ray Miller . . . is convinced that attitude is almost as important for an effective reliever as a major-league fastball. 'When I go to the pen,' said Miller, 'I want to see those doors come flying open and my pitcher storming out to the mound.'" By the end of the year, nobody had too much faith in what Ray Miller thought were the attributes of an effective reliever.

Another Miller mistake was forcing the Tim Teufel trade. Teufel isn't a great player, but he had value. He could play second or third and not hurt you, contribute to the offense. The Baltimore Orioles should do so well. But Miller didn't like Teufel, so he put the Twins in a position in which they had to trade him. The man that Miller pushed ahead of Teufel, Steve Lombardozzi, was actually a step backward, a somewhat better glove man but not a hitter.

Another curious decision was the reluctance to let Tim Laudner catch more. Laudner, now 28, is a big guy with a huge swing, but he connects often enough to justify the gamble. Over the last two seasons he's hit .241 with 17 homers in just 357 at bats. As the 1986 season wore on, his playing time didn't increase although the Twins' other catchers, Salas and Reed, weren't doing the job. Part of the reason may be a bad rap about his defense. The book *The Scouting Report: 1985* says that "until last year, he was borderline terrible, and at his best he remains below average. Laudner isn't quick behind the plate, has a so-so arm and can be run on." It's true that he isn't quick behind the plate and he may look awkward, but the rest of that just isn't right. Opponents stole .76 bases per game when Reed was catching, .75 with Salas, but only .56 with Laudner. It was the third straight season in which Laudner's opposition stolen base stats had been better than those of his teammates. The Twins were 31–26 with Laudner in the starting lineup, 20–29 with Reed, and 20–36 with Salas. They had a 4.42 ERA with Laudner, as opposed to 4.88 with Reed and 5.02 with Salas.

It was said last summer that a point was reached at which Miller was quoting Billy Gardner chapter and verse. Gardner didn't use his bench much and was never successful in developing a bullpen, so Miller had come in talking about the need to get the entire 25-man roster involved in the game, improve the Twins' defense up the middle, etc. By the middle of last summer he was frustrated about the bullpen, complaining about the lack of a bench and how the poor team speed cut off his options, sounding a lot like Billy Gardner. I had an on-air conversation with a Minnesota personality (I think it was J. G. Preston), who said that the experience of watching Miller and Gardner manage this team had led him to conclude that the manager just really didn't make much difference in the face of intractable team weaknesses. What I should have said, had I been quick enough, is that suppose you had a second baseman who couldn't hit for power and couldn't turn the double play, so you got rid of him and got another second baseman who couldn't hit for power or turn the double play either. Would you conclude from this that second basemen don't make any difference because they can't hit and don't turn the double play well?

Miller and Gardner happened to have some of the same weaknesses. There are managers who can study the options and create a bench, notwithstanding the fact that neither Miller nor Gardner was one of them. There are managers who almost never have serious bullpen problems, because they can look at the physical and mental makeup of the pitchers in camp, pick out a horse to ride and teach him what he needs to know.

The manager cannot carry all of the blame. The Twins' front office continues to display astonishingly little interest in solving their problems; it's a Minnesota tradition. They have allowed the team to go from season to season without a left-handed starting pitcher, without any speed, without a proven shortstop or catcher. When Ray Miller forced the Teufel trade, they could have used Teufel to whittle away on one of those problems. Instead, they shopped around for the best offer and did a poor job of evaluating the offers. Desperate for pitching, they told Jack Morris, "No thanks; we wouldn't want to get in trouble with Barry Rona." And then, too, there are the players. There is a perception around the league that the Twins don't hustle. A lack of hustle usually follows a lack of leadership.

The Twins' record is full of splits. They had a 43–38 record in Minnesota, but were just 28–53 on the road. The 15-game home/road differential missed by one game of being the largest in the league. The Twins were 22–40 on grass fields, but then those were all road games and they were even worse (6–13) on road turf, so that appears to be a part of the earlier effect. The Twins played somewhat better against lefties (22–23, .489) than right-handers (49–68, .418) and had all kinds of trouble in day games (19–34, .358).

As to the Twins' MVP, obviously it was Kirby Puckett, the delightful little round man with the big round face who was one of the best everyday players in the game. Hitting .328 with lots of doubles, 20 stolen bases, and a historic increase in power, Puckett had 365 total bases, a total that would ordinarily lead the league. He played his usual outstanding center field, running down 462 fly balls (Brett Butler was second in the league, with 434). He also very nearly accomplished the unique feat, for a leadoff man, of finishing the season with more homers than walks. I would guess no leadoff man has ever done that. In talking about Kirby we shouldn't forget Gary Gaetti, who hit .287, led the team in homers and RBI and was the league's outstanding defensive third baseman, starting 36 double plays. People have gotten MVP awards for less.

I thought the Twins would win this division a couple of years ago, and maybe they will put it together suddenly. But several things have changed since I had that attack, and I'm not so optimistic anymore. The Twins' young players aren't as young as they were. It's one thing to say that the Twins might win if Gary Gaetti develops. When Gary Gaetti has a tremendous season and the Twins lose 91 games, then what? The division isn't as weak as it was a couple of years ago, and it's going to be a lot stronger in another year. I doubt that the Twins can win the division with 85 wins now.

When the Griffiths sold out, there was excitement here that created an opportunity. The window has closed; the new owners seem to be not only just as bad but almost indistinguishable. They likes their ballplayers slow and white.

Who could lead the Twins out of the doldrums? Dave Righetti? Nah; if the Twins weren't losing games in the bullpen, they'd lose them somewhere else. Billy Martin? I don't know. The time has come for the Twins to forget about winning somewhere down the road, but Martin is at his best when working with guys from the wrong side of the tracks. The Twins' problem is that they're a collection of smooth-faced suburban kids with no instinct for the jugular. I'm afraid the mixture would explode, rather than percolate. Tim Raines? Raines would give the Twins a leadoff hitter and a left fielder, plus he might compile better stats than Rickey Henderson in this park, but that wouldn't do anything about the pitching and nobody can win nothing allowing 839 runs.

To win quickly, the Twins need one of two men. One is Whitey Herzog. Herzog would get the bullpen straightened out, build a bench, develop a running game, and put the fear of professional extinction into a few players who could sorely use it—in fact, doing those four things and running the pitching staff are precisely the things that Herzog does best. Whitey gets into problems when he goes too far, when he winds up with nothing but speed. The Twins certainly could stand to add a couple of guys who can scoot just for variety, and Herzog is smart enough not to try to run a speed offense in this park.

The other is Lou Gorman, the man who has done such fine work in Boston. The Twins need somebody to come in and make the little moves to finish off the team, find the left-handed starter and get him without letting go of Brunansky, make the trade for the shortstop and pick up a relief prospect at the same time. They also need someone to, as Gorman did for Boston, find subtle ways to remove the stigma of racism from the organization. I think either of those two men would have the Twins winning within a year. Third best candidate: Joe Carter.

The Twins *should* play better this year, but then they should have played better last year and the year before, too. I think they should play .500 or better ball in 1987 because there's just too much talent here to keep losing 91 games a year, but I'm not optimistic about their chances of winning.

Mark SALAS, Catcher

	G	AB	Hit	2B	3B	HR	Run	RBI	TBB	SO	SB	CS	Avg
1.39 years		459	122	20	6	12	58	54	26	52	2	1	.266
1986	91	258	60	7	4	8	28	33	18	32	3	1	.233
First Half	48	146	35	1	2	6	19	24	14	20	2	0	.240
Second Half	43	112	25	6	2	2	9	9	4	12	1	1	.223
Vs. RHP		238	53	7	3	8		27	17	29	3	1	.223
Vs. LHP		20	7	0	1	0		6	1	3	0	0	.350
Home	44	123	26	4	2	5	13	14	9	16	1	0	.211
Road	47	135	34	3	2	3	15	19	9	16	2	1	.252
Grass	38	104	26	2	0	2	13	13	9	10	2	0	.250
Turf	53	154	34	5	4	6	15	20	9	22	1	1	.221

Mickey HATCHER, Left Field

	G	AB	Hit	2B	3B	HR	Run	RBI	TBB	SO	SB	CS	Avg
4.70 years		541	152	28	3	6	57	57	25	39	2	2	.281
1986	115	317	88	13	3	3	40	32	19	26	2	1	.278
First Half	62	172	42	7	1	0	21	13	7	13	1	1	.244
Second Half	53	145	46	6	2	3	19	19	12	13	1	0	.317
Vs. RHP		177	37	3	2	1		15	8	17	1	0	.209
Vs. LHP		140	51	10	1	2		17	11	9	1	1	.364
Home	62	156	49	7	3	1	22	15	9	12	2	0	.314
Road	53	161	39	6	0	2	18	17	10	14	0	1	.242
Grass	41	124	27	5	0	2	12	12	9	11	0	1	.218
Turf	74	193	61	8	3	1	28	20	10	15	2	0	.316

Kent HRBEK, First Base

	G	AB	Hit	2B	3B	HR	Run	RBI	TBB	SO	SB	CS	Avg
4.70 years		599	173	33	3	25	86	101	68	88	2	2	.289
1986	149	550	147	27	1	29	85	91	71	81	2	2	.267
First Half	74	276	88	16	1	19	56	59	43	36	1	2	.319
Second Half	75	274	59	11	0	10	29	32	28	45	1	0	.215
Vs. RHP		398	106	22	1	25		63	57	48	2	2	.266
Vs. LHP		152	41	5	0	4		28	14	33	0	0	.270
Home	75	278	76	15	1	18	46	57	36	43	1	2	.273
Road	74	272	71	12	0	11	39	34	35	38	1	0	.261
Grass	55	197	52	11	0	9	29	27	26	26	1	0	.264
Turf	94	353	95	16	1	20	56	64	45	55	1	2	.269

Kirby PUCKETT, Center Field

	G	AB	Hit	2B	3B	HR	Run	RBI	TBB	SO	SB	CS	Avg
2.78 years		694	211	28	9	13	94	72	33	92	20	11	.304
1986	161	680	223	37	6	31	119	96	34	99	20	12	.328
First Half	81	353	120	19	2	16	62	47	16	40	8	7	.340
Second Half	80	327	103	18	4	15	57	49	18	59	12	5	.315
Vs. RHP		514	169	26	4	25		77	25	73	19	12	.329
Vs. LHP		166	54	11	2	6		19	9	26	1	0	.325
Home	81	346	127	21	6	14	72	51	16	53	13	9	.367
Road	80	334	96	16	0	17	47	45	18	46	7	3	.287
Grass	61	254	73	14	0	13	35	39	13	38	6	2	.287
Turf	100	426	150	23	6	18	84	57	21	61	14	10	.352

Steve LOMBARDOZZI, Second Base

	G	AB	Hit	2B	3B	HR	Run	RBI	TBB	SO	SB	CS	Avg
1.14 years		446	108	21	5	7	55	34	51	72	5	3	.243
1986	156	453	103	20	5	8	53	33	52	76	3	1	.227
First Half	77	240	63	12	5	7	35	25	30	38	2	0	.263
Second Half	79	213	40	8	0	1	18	8	22	38	1	1	.188
Vs. RHP		332	78	12	5	5		17	38	59	3	0	.235
Vs. LHP		121	25	8	0	3		16	14	17	0	1	.207
Home	77	235	59	14	3	6	37	23	28	37	2	0	.251
Road	79	218	44	6	2	2	16	10	24	39	1	1	.202
Grass	60	168	33	4	2	2	10	10	19	33	0	1	.196
Turf	96	285	70	16	3	6	43	23	33	43	3	0	.246

Tom BRUNANSKY, Right Field

	G	AB	Hit	2B	3B	HR	Run	RBI	TBB	SO	SB	CS	Avg
4.68 years		591	147	28	2	28	79	82	69	103	5	4	.248
1986	157	593	152	28	1	23	69	75	53	98	12	4	.256
First Half	80	324	92	16	1	17	45	48	23	55	8	1	.284
Second Half	77	269	60	12	0	6	24	27	30	43	4	3	.223
Vs. RHP		426	100	19	0	12		48	41	76	11	3	.235
Vs. LHP		167	52	9	1	11		27	12	22	1	1	.311
Home	78	296	79	16	1	15	41	45	26	43	8	3	.267
Road	79	297	73	12	0	8	28	30	27	55	4	1	.246
Grass	60	223	53	8	0	5	22	16	22	42	3	1	.238
Turf	97	370	99	20	1	18	47	59	31	56	9	3	.268

Gary GAETTI, Third Base

	G	AB	Hit	2B	3B	HR	Run	RBI	TBB	SO	SB	CS	Avg
4.88 years		587	149	31	2	22	74	82	46	105	9	6	.254
1986	157	596	171	34	1	34	91	108	52	108	14	15	.287
First Half	80	297	80	19	0	18	52	50	31	52	8	9	.269
Second Half	77	299	91	15	1	16	39	58	21	56	6	6	.304
Vs. RHP		445	119	28	1	23		76	34	86	13	9	.267
Vs. LHP		151	52	6	0	11		32	18	22	1	6	.344
Home	77	296	74	16	1	16	45	57	25	56	6	6	.250
Road	80	300	97	18	0	18	46	51	27	52	8	9	.323
Grass	61	228	83	16	0	16	40	39	22	40	8	7	.364
Turf	96	368	88	18	1	18	51	69	30	68	6	8	.239

Roy SMALLEY, Designated Hitter

	G	AB	Hit	2B	3B	HR	Run	RBI	TBB	SO	SB	CS	Avg
9.52 years		561	144	24	3	16	75	69	77	90	3	4	.256
1986	143	459	113	20	4	20	59	57	68	80	1	3	.246
First Half	71	236	62	15	3	14	34	35	29	38	0	1	.263
Second Half	72	223	51	5	1	6	25	22	39	42	1	2	.229
Vs. RHP		401	105	16	4	18		50	59	68	1	2	.262
Vs. LHP		58	8	4	0	2		7	9	12	0	1	.138
Home	70	222	59	11	3	9	29	28	36	40	0	3	.266
Road	73	237	54	9	1	11	30	29	32	40	1	0	.228
Grass	55	180	40	7	1	7	20	21	25	31	1	0	.222
Turf	88	279	73	13	3	13	39	36	43	49	0	3	.262

Greg GAGNE, Shortstop

	G	AB	Hit	2B	3B	HR	Run	RBI	TBB	SO	SB	CS	Avg
1.74 years		456	107	22	5	8	59	46	29	98	13	8	.236
1986	156	472	118	22	6	12	63	54	30	108	12	10	.250
First Half	79	251	62	10	3	4	25	23	17	59	7	6	.247
Second Half	77	221	56	12	3	8	38	31	13	49	5	4	.253
Vs. RHP		346	89	14	5	6		34	21	72	12	10	.257
Vs. LHP		126	29	8	1	6		20	9	36	0	0	.230
Home	80	238	57	10	4	10	36	31	17	52	5	2	.239
Road	76	234	61	12	2	2	27	23	13	56	7	8	.261
Grass	59	184	47	10	2	2	22	15	10	45	5	6	.255
Turf	97	288	71	12	4	10	41	39	20	63	7	4	.247

Randy BUSH, Outfield

	G	AB	Hit	2B	3B	HR	Run	RBI	TBB	SO	SB	CS	Avg
3.20 years		435	107	25	5	13	56	60	42	72	3	2	.247
1986	130	357	96	19	7	7	50	45	39	63	5	3	.269
First Half	61	177	45	9	5	6	27	29	21	29	2	1	.254
Second Half	69	180	51	10	2	1	23	16	18	34	3	2	.283
Vs. RHP		345	94	18	7	7		44	37	60	5	3	.272
Vs. LHP		12	2	1	0	0		1	2	3	0	0	.167
Home	64	181	55	12	5	6	30	33	18	29	3	1	.304
Road	66	176	41	7	2	1	20	12	21	34	2	2	.233
Grass	50	129	30	4	2	1	15	9	17	27	2	1	.233
Turf	80	228	66	15	5	6	35	36	22	36	3	2	.289

Frank VIOLA

Year	(W–L)	GS	Run	Avg	DP	Avg	SB	Avg
1984	(18-12)	35	145	4.14	31	.89	13	.37
1985	(18-14)	36	148	4.11	30	.83	12	.33
1986	(16-13)	37	181	4.89	34	.92	19	.51
1982-1986		164	721	4.40	152	.93	73	.45

	1986 ERA	W–L	1985 ERA	1984 ERA	1983 ERA	1982 ERA	82-86 W–L
Total	4.51	16-13	4.09	3.21	5.49	5.21	63-64
Home	4.58	6-6	3.68	2.40	5.09	6.25	29-31
Road	4.43	10-7	4.50	3.77	6.05	3.83	34-33
East	6.36	6-10	5.05	3.71	4.89	4.70	25-40
West	2.51	10-3	3.22	2.66	6.19	5.84	38-24
1st Half	4.76	9-6	4.44	2.94	4.75	3.83	33-24
2nd Half	4.23	7-7	3.78	3.45	6.11	5.86	30-40
Turf	4.75	8-7	4.11	2.71	5.23		33-32
Grass	4.16	8-6	4.06	3.69	6.14		26-22
Day	4.59	4-3	5.08	3.02	5.68	5.08	15-20
Night	4.48	12-10	3.73	3.35	5.42	5.28	48-44
April	2.97	3-1	3.86	3.60	5.94		7-8
May	7.93	1-4	4.73	1.64	5.31		9-8
June	3.48	4-1	3.79	4.50	4.18	5.01	13-8
July	4.76	3-2	5.49	2.15	5.52	5.18	11-12
August	4.46	2-2	3.02	3.70	5.82	4.38	11-12
September	3.91	3-3	3.86	3.88	6.32	6.34	12-16

Mike SMITHSON

Year	(W–L)	GS	Run	Avg	DP	Avg	SB	Avg
1984	(15-13)	36	145	4.03	26	.72	29	.81
1985	(15-14)	37	162	4.38	35	.95	30	.81
1986	(13-14)	33	162	4.91	35	1.06	28	.85
1982-1986		147	626	4.26	134	.91	121	.82

	1986 ERA	W–L	1985 ERA	1984 ERA	1983 ERA	1982 ERA	82-86 W–L
Total	4.77	13-14	4.34	3.68	3.91	5.01	56-59
Home	4.34	9-6	3.88	4.36	2.33		32-22
Road	5.32	4-8	4.35	3.51	3.49	6.91	24-37
East	5.63	5-7	4.22	4.00	4.32	3.38	25-26
West	4.21	8-7	4.48	3.37	3.46	5.35	31-33
1st Half	4.43	7-7	4.50	3.68	4.16		29-28
2nd Half	5.15	6-7	4.19	3.67	3.64	5.01	27-31
Turf	4.77	10-9	4.54	4.12	3.51		30-28
Grass	4.77	3-5	4.04	2.97	3.98		23-27
Day	5.19	3-5	3.26	4.21	5.18	16.20	11-21
Night	4.62	10-9	5.09	3.52	3.62	4.15	45-38
April	4.01	2-2	2.72	3.27	1.74		11-6
May	3.40	3-2	7.96	3.63	6.11		7-10
June	6.10	2-2	4.36	4.91	4.24		9-10
July	9.86	1-3	3.18	2.19	4.89		9-8
August	4.71	1-3	4.69	4.32	2.95	3.38	5-13
September	3.72	4-2	3.88	3.75	3.12	5.35	15-12

Bert BLYLEVEN

Year	(W–L)	GS	Run	Avg	DP	Avg	SB	Avg
1984	(19-7)	32	170	5.31	23	.72	19	.59
1985	(17-16)	28	150	5.36	29	1.04	35	1.25
1986	(17-14)	36	164	4.56	25	.69	28	.78
1976-1986		309	1327	4.29	275	.89	259	.84

	1986 ERA	W–L	1985 ERA	1984 ERA	1983 ERA	83-86 W–L
Total	4.01	17-14	3.16	2.87	3.91	60-47
Home	4.12	12-5	2.91	3.23	4.54	35-20
Road	3.86	5-9	3.49	2.50	3.44	25-27
East	4.13	9-9	4.12	3.42	5.14	23-28
West	3.87	8-5	2.53	2.47	2.97	37-19
1st Half	5.24	7-7	3.10	3.31	4.03	27-26
2nd Half	2.92	10-7	3.21	2.56	3.61	33-21
Turf	3.86	13-7	3.35	2.22	1.69	26-14
Grass	4.34	4-7	3.16	3.06	4.27	34-33
Day	4.15	4-4	3.01	3.09	4.62	17-18
Night	3.95	13-10	3.22	2.69	3.45	43-29
April	3.57	2-1	5.64	3.00	3.98	6-7
May	6.39	2-3	2.58	4.26	4.06	9-8
June	6.37	2-3	1.93	3.26	3.77	9-9
July	2.85	3-3	3.76	2.93	3.60	10-10
August	1.45	5-0	2.41	2.51	3.60	15-3
September	4.23	3-4	3.64	2.23	5.06	11-10

Keith ATHERTON*

1986	G	IP	W–L	Sv	H	ER	SO	ERA
Total	47	81.2	5-8	10	82	34	59	3.75
Home	27	43.1	4-2	6	41	18	34	3.74
Road	20	38.1	1-6	4	41	16	25	3.76
East	26	44.1	2-4	5	49	21	35	4.26
West	21	37.1	3-4	5	33	13	24	3.13
1st Half	20	41.1	3-1	5	32	11	29	2.40
2nd Half	27	40.1	2-7	5	50	23	30	5.13
Turf	33	57.0	4-6	6	58	25	41	3.95
Grass	14	24.2	1-2	4	24	9	18	3.28
Day	14	17.1	1-3	1	20	12	13	6.23
Night	33	64.1	4-5	9	62	22	46	3.08
April								
May	5	10.1	1-0	0	10	4	8	3.48
June	13	28.2	2-1	5	17	4	16	1.26
July	8	16.0	1-0	4	24	11	17	6.19
August	13	19.1	0-7	0	23	12	13	5.59
September	8	7.1	1-0	1	8	3	5	3.68

*Atherton's breakdowns with Minnesota only

OTHERS

Pitcher	(W–L)	GS	Run	Avg	DP	Avg	SB	Avg	Time	Att.
Heaton	(4-9)	17	53	3.12	16	.94	14	.82	2:44	266
Portugal	(6-10)	15	79	5.27	19	1.27	6	.40	2:45	273
Butcher	(0-3)	10	50	5.00	16	1.60	7	.70	2:52	149
Anderson	(3-6)	10	37	3.70	14	1.40	6	.60	3:00	166
Latham	(0-1)	2	9	4.50	6	3.00	2	1.00	2:42	13
Agosto	(1-2)	1	1	1.00	2	2.00	0	.00	2:38	33
Pastore	(3-1)	1	5	5.00	1	1.00	1	1.00	3:09	13

STARTING PITCHERS' AVERAGE TIME AND ATTENDANCE RECORDS

Pitcher	Time	Attendance
Viola	2:50	719
Blyleven	2:38	781
Smithson	2:51	574

RECORDS WITH DIFFERENT STARTING CATCHERS

Catcher	Inn	ER	W–L	ERA	GS	SB	Avg
Laudner	503.0	247	31-26	4.42	57	32	.56
Salas	489.0	273	20-36	5.02	56	42	.75
Reed	440.2	239	20-29	4.88	49	37	.76

BACK TO THE IMAGINARY FUTURE

For the last couple of years I've been running Brock6 projections for the Twins players, making an estimate of their expected remaining performance. Lest I be tempted to take these projections too seriously, last year this method projected Kirby Puckett to finish with 26 career homers. But then, Brock6 doesn't attempt to deal with individual variations—only to establish normal expectation. The 1986 career projections:

	G	AB	R	H	2B	3B	HR	RBI	BB	Avg.
Kirby Puckett	2143	8480	1390	2588	394	78	236	1123	512	.305
Kent Hrbek	1932	6824	1044	1915	353	22	292	1110	811	.281
Tom Brunansky	1881	6680	886	1676	317	22	308	991	728	.251
Gary Gaetti	1749	6072	834	1576	314	15	242	891	504	.260
Roy Smalley	1893	6167	821	1561	263	27	183	765	853	.253
Tim Teufel	1179	3569	445	912	211	17	67	365	410	.256
Mark Salas	1197	3390	389	904	140	40	100	432	239	.267
Greg Gagne	1241	3462	427	854	166	36	75	375	252	.247
Mickey Hatcher	904	2845	306	801	147	17	30	297	138	.281
Randy Bush	811	2150	280	532	116	26	61	277	218	247
Tim Laudner	823	2108	235	475	99	2	82	275	215	.225
Lombardozzi	704	1891	241	464	87	19	31	174	218	.246

Since I first did these projections two years ago, Puckett, Gaetti, and Laudner have markedly improved their career expectations. Hrbek, Brunansky, and Teufel have lost a significant portion of what was expected for them, while Hatcher and Bush are about the same.

SEATTLE MARINERS

Runners on Base:	1998
Opponents on Base:	2224
Net Advantage:	−226
Won-Lost Record:	67-95

By the middle of May, it was over. The Seattle Mariners, a team that has never played .500 ball, had dreams that their time had come in 1986. I wrote in the *1986 Abstract* that if Dick Williams were managing the Mariners, they would win their division. Instead, the Mariners came out swinging from the heels, striking out at a rate that seemed to doom every imaginable record for team strikeouts. Though their pitching in the early part of the year was decent, the Mariners hit just .201 for the month of April, winning 7 games and losing 14. When the Mariners continued to lose daily through the first week of May, dropping to 9–20, the M's decided that it was time to find out whether I was right.

Many of the moves that Dick Williams made after assuming command were obvious ones, long overdue. The releases granted to Al Cowens and Gorman Thomas should have been granted years ago. I mean, *winning* games with Milt Wilcox is futile, because you know that when the Mariners get in a pennant race Milt Wilcox isn't going to be there for them. But *losing* games with Milt Wilcox? What is the point in letting Milt Wilcox go 0–8 for you? I would have been shocked if Dick Williams had *not* released these guys.

Some of the later moves were more unexpected. Let's review the major ones:

1) Danny Tartabull was shifted from second base to right field, putting Harold Reynolds at second base. I have mixed feelings about this one. Some people told me that Tartabull looked awkward at second base; others said he needed work but thought he would have mastered the position. His defensive stats are pretty good, despite a .947 fielding percentage. If he can play second, a slugging second baseman is a valuable man, but one reason second basemen are rarely sluggers is that they get hurt so often that it interferes with their development as hitters. Reynolds is a true glove wizard, probably the best defensive second baseman in the league. I wouldn't have done it, but I wouldn't argue with it.

2) Ivan Calderon was shipped to the minors, and later traded to the White Sox for Scott Bradley. At the time of the trade, there was a tendency to regard Bradley as a nonentity, and to consider the trade as having been made to get rid of Calderon—much as the Tartabull trade was later supposed to have been made to get rid of Tartabull. Calderon was regarded as perhaps the brightest prospect in the organization, and the move was a bit of a stunner to hardcore baseball fans.

The day after Calderon was sent out somebody asked me if I had any idea why they had done this. "Sure," I said, "Dick Williams told Calderon to do something, and

he didn't do it." I was guessing, of course, but I later noticed that the May 19 issue of *The Sporting News* had carried a note that the Mariners arranged with Calderon's agent to have a meeting with him about his attitude. That's a serious step, and then you factor in that Scott Bradley is *not* a nonentity, but a .300-hitting catcher with good defensive skills, and the trade looks pretty good.

3) John Moses was recalled from Calgary to play center field and hit leadoff. The 29-year-old Moses doesn't project as a championship quality player, and the Mariners were still looking for a leadoff man and a center fielder.

4) Ken Phelps was installed as the everyday designated hitter. A tremendous move; see other article.

5) Spike Owen and Dave Henderson were traded to Boston for Rey Quinones, Mike Trujillo, Mike Brown, and a player to be named.

Again, the trade was a surprise, but the logic is not difficult to see. Although Owen has been promoted as a defensive wiz, the Mariners were not happy with his glovework, for reasons apparent to all who watched the Red Sox in post-season play. With Quinones hitting about as well as Owen, the Mariners could well regard Quinones for Owen as an even swap or better.

The rest of the trade amounts to "what can we get for Dave Henderson." Henderson, despite his good defensive reputation, is not a good outfielder and has not progressed as a hitter. Williams wanted a better glove in center field, and with Phil Bradley in left and Tartabull in right, there was no place to move him. Further, Henderson's offensive skills were just a poor duplication of things that the Mariners already had. Even giving up Tartabull, the Mariners *have* power hitters. Somebody around the table might have argued that sure, it looks nice on paper to have wall-to-wall power, but how many people win pennants that way? On paper it looks great to have Bill Cartwright *and* Patrick Ewing, but on the floor it doesn't work that well. On paper it looks great to have Tony Dorsett *and* Herschel Walker, but in practice it doesn't work that well. A successful ballclub is a blend of different skills, and after each skill is covered there is a diminishing utility to having more of it and more of it. You wind up like the Twins, with a whole bunch of guys who hit homers but don't win.

Another point about the trade is that Mike Trujillo is a neglected talent in the tradition of Ken Phelps. Trujillo lacks an outstanding fastball, but he's always been able to get people out, and there's no evidence he can't win 12 to 16 games.

After the season there was the Tartabull trade, which I'll discuss in the Tartabull comment. After making all of these moves the Mariners had only three players in the same positions as before—first baseman Alvin Davis, third baseman Jim Presley, and left fielder Phil Bradley. Over the season the Mariners' offense did pick up, and the Mariners wound up scoring 718 runs, just 28 below average; they were above average from the point at which Williams took over the team. They scored one run fewer than they had in 1985.

In 1985 the Mariners had struck out 942 times. That led the American League. Last year they raised that by over 200, to 1,148. Early in the season they were on target to strike out many more times than that, setting not only an American League record but a major-league record, and not only setting it but obliterating it. One of Williams's priorities was to get the young players to shorten their strokes with two strikes on them, and he did have some success.

The strikeouts lower the team batting average, but how damaging they really were is very questionable. The Mariners' team batting average, .253, wasn't all that bad (eleventh in the league, fourth in the division). The Mariners did hit only 29 sacrifice flies, fewest of any major-league team, and that surely is one negative consequence. But the Texas Rangers, who also struck out 1,088 times (second in the league, and 146 more than the M's league-leading total of 1985) scored more runs than anyone in the division except the Angels. The Phillies struck out more times than the Mariners did, leading the NL, but were second in the league in runs scored. The strikeouts certainly weren't a positive, but they aren't a critical failure, either.

Further confusing the issue of what kind of team plays well on artificial turf, the Mariners played almost .500 ball on artificial turf (50–51) but were a sad 17–44 (.279) on grass fields, the worst record on grass fields in the major leagues.

The critical failures were defensive. Although almost all of the moves that Williams made were intended to improve the *defense,* the Marines were not able to make progress in 1986 because they continued to allow so many runs. Mariner pitchers allowed 1,590 hits, the most of any major-league team in the last three years. Seattle opponents hit for an average of .283. Since their control was also poor, Seattle opponents had an on-base percentage of .353, the highest of any major league team. It was the pitching and defense that must improve for the Mariners to move forward in 1987.

Can the Mariners improve? Well, I'll certainly acknowledge that it is a lot easier to say that if Dick Williams was managing the Seattle Mariners they would win the West when Dick Willams is safely in San Diego than it is to say that when he has to deliver, but then you must acknowledge that the talent here is a whole lot different than it was a year ago. Some Mariners fans have been outraged at all the talent the team has given away in trades, but if those guys were all that good why did the Mariners lose 95 games? I think there was a need to realign the talent.

I still think that the Mariners could be a much better team than their record shows—and, in the main, a better team than they were before Dick Williams took over the team. When you looked at the Mariners a year ago, what you would see was an accumulation of shapeless talent. Williams has given that talent a definite shape, and while you can't like the record, there are a lot of things to like about the talent. Let's assume that Mickey Brantley will play center for the Mariners, with Mike Kingery in right. Ask a few questions:

Do the Mariners have power? In Davis, Presley and Phelps they still have a solid power corps.

Do the Mariners have speed? Greatly improved in the last year. With Kingery, Brantley, Phil Bradley, and Reynolds, the Mariners will have four players in the lineup who can steal a base.

How is the team up the middle? Defensively, they look pretty good to me. Scott Bradley is at least a decent defensive player, Reynolds is a terrific glove at second, Quinones should be pretty good at short, and center field is very much a question mark. If Brantley can do the job in center, the Mariners could be the strongest up-the-middle defense in the division.

Will the Mariners get people on base? Phil Bradley and Ken Phelps had among the highest on-base percentages in the league. Phelps and Alvin Davis both walk a lot, and both Bradleys are .300 hitters. Brantley and Kingery have been disciplined hitters in the minors. They should have more people on base than they had last year.

Will the Mariners score the people who get on base? If they have power and speed and they execute, why wouldn't they?

How is the infield defense? Again, if Quinones develops it could be among the best in the league. Presley and Reynolds are fine gloves, while Davis is a weak point.

How is the outfield defense? Bradley in left and Kingery in right are excellent. Brantley is an unknown.

Will the Mariner pitchers walk as many people next year? No way. Trujillo and Bankhead both have good control. With the pitchers they have added (Bankhead, Shields, Trujillo, Brown, and Powell) the Mariners shouldn't have to keep running out guys like Swift, Wilcox, Beattie, and Guetterman, who had a combined 2–27 record last year. Swift showed signs of finding himself late in the year and if he does that's a plus—but if he doesn't he won't pitch.

I didn't mention Mark Huisman, but I've always felt that Huisman could pitch. Huisman had 72 strikeouts and 25 walks in 97 innings—excellent data—but couldn't handle the relief ace role because of a propensity for throwing home-run pitches. But Huisman posted ERAs of 1.69 in August and 2.19 in September, 1986, and might well step forward in 1987.

The Mariners' starting lineup averaged 25.7 years of age, youngest in the American League.

Kurt Bevacqua said that playing for Dick Williams is like being Muammar Khaddafi's chef—every meal better be good. That's the most serious question hanging over the Mariners: Will they rebel against Williams? It is possible that Williams's progressive grouchiness has reached the point that he will not be able to command even a grudging respect from his players. If that happens, the Mariners could stumble through 1987 as timidly as ever. It would be crazy to pick them to win, in view of the simple fact that they finished 25 games out last year, and even miracle teams don't come from 25 out. Short of that, I see the Mariners as a much improved team, a team that should have the best record in the history of the organization.

Scott BRADLEY, Catcher

	G	AB	Hit	2B	3B	HR	Run	RBI	TBB	SO	SB	CS	Avg
0.65 years		447	123	17	6	8	42	48	23	20	2	3	.276
1986	77	220	66	8	3	5	20	28	13	7	1	2	.300
First Half	17	40	9	1	0	1	6	4	3	0	0	2	.225
Second Half	60	180	57	7	3	4	14	24	10	7	1	0	.317
Vs. RHP		206	63	8	2	5		28	13	7	1	2	.306
Vs. LHP		14	3	0	1	0		0	0	0	0	0	.214
Home	41	118	41	7	2	4	14	16	9	5	0	1	.347
Road	36	102	25	1	1	1	6	12	4	2	1	1	.245
Grass	27	85	23	0	1	1	5	10	5	1	1	1	.271
Turf	50	135	43	8	2	4	15	18	8	6	0	1	.319

Phil BRADLEY, Left Field

	G	AB	Hit	2B	3B	HR	Run	RBI	TBB	SO	SB	CS	Avg
2.77 years		561	170	27	6	14	88	60	63	119	24	11	.302
1986	143	526	163	27	4	12	88	50	77	134	21	12	.310
First Half	67	247	64	12	2	6	36	21	37	71	9	7	.259
Second Half	76	279	99	15	2	6	52	29	40	63	12	5	.355
Vs. RHP		400	122	23	3	10		41	58	109	21	11	.305
Vs. LHP		126	41	4	1	2		9	19	25	0	1	.325
Home	77	287	93	20	3	5	49	30	43	64	8	6	.324
Road	66	239	70	7	1	7	39	20	34	70	13	6	.293
Grass	51	178	47	3	1	6	27	15	30	55	9	4	.264
Turf	92	348	116	24	3	6	61	35	47	79	12	8	.333

Alvin DAVIS, First Base

	G	AB	Hit	2B	3B	HR	Run	RBI	TBB	SO	SB	CS	Avg
2.73 years		595	167	31	2	23	82	97	96	80	2	3	.281
1986	135	479	130	18	1	18	66	72	76	68	0	3	.271
First Half	67	237	67	13	1	11	36	44	48	33	0	2	.283
Second Half	68	242	63	5	0	7	30	28	28	35	0	1	.260
Vs. RHP		357	100	15	1	18		56	51	44	0	3	.280
Vs. LHP		122	30	3	0	0		16	25	24	0	0	.246
Home	69	249	70	9	1	14	42	48	40	29	0	2	.281
Road	66	230	60	9	0	4	24	24	36	39	0	1	.261
Grass	51	178	40	5	0	4	20	16	25	32	0	1	.225
Turf	84	301	90	13	1	14	46	56	51	36	0	2	.299

John MOSES, Center Field

	G	AB	Hit	2B	3B	HR	Run	RBI	TBB	SO	SB	CS	Avg
1.67 years		402	100	16	4	2	53	29	32	62	28	16	.249
1986	103	399	102	16	3	3	56	34	34	65	25	18	.256
First Half	38	151	39	4	2	1	20	18	16	21	12	8	.258
Second Half	65	248	63	12	1	2	36	16	18	44	13	10	.254
Vs. RHP		289	70	10	2	1		26	22	52	13	9	.242
Vs. LHP		110	32	6	1	2		8	12	13	12	9	.291
Home	56	220	51	8	3	2	35	17	21	37	10	7	.232
Road	47	179	51	8	0	1	21	17	13	28	15	11	.285
Grass	34	124	33	3	0	1	12	10	8	18	7	7	.266
Turf	69	275	69	13	3	2	44	24	26	47	18	11	.251

Harold REYNOLDS, Second Base

	G	AB	Hit	2B	3B	HR	Run	RBI	TBB	SO	SB	CS	Avg
1.38 years		449	94	19	4	1	52	23	35	48	25	12	.209
1986	126	445	99	19	4	1	46	24	29	42	30	12	.222
First Half	49	192	44	11	0	0	21	10	9	20	19	5	.229
Second Half	77	253	55	8	4	1	25	14	20	22	11	7	.217
Vs. RHP		328	75	14	4	0		15	23	29	19	6	.229
Vs. LHP		117	24	5	0	1		9	6	13	11	6	.205
Home	66	220	50	12	4	1	27	12	16	19	15	4	.227
Road	60	225	49	7	0	0	19	12	13	23	15	8	.218
Grass	47	174	32	4	0	0	13	6	10	20	11	6	.184
Turf	79	271	67	15	4	1	33	18	19	22	19	6	.247

Danny TARTABULL, Right Field

	G	AB	Hit	2B	3B	HR	Run	RBI	TBB	SO	SB	CS	Avg
1.02 years		578	160	32	7	27	85	107	69	170	5	8	.277
1986	137	511	138	25	6	25	76	96	61	157	4	8	.270
First Half	63	232	66	11	4	13	38	46	31	76	2	7	.284
Second Half	74	279	72	14	2	12	38	50	30	81	2	1	.258
Vs. RHP		386	100	16	5	22		80	44	120	3	8	.259
Vs. LHP		125	38	9	1	3		16	17	37	1	0	.304
Home	70	268	73	14	4	13	38	47	26	83	0	3	.272
Road	67	243	65	11	2	12	38	49	35	74	4	5	.267
Grass	49	175	48	6	2	9	27	39	26	56	2	4	.274
Turf	88	336	90	19	4	16	49	57	35	101	2	4	.268

Jim PRESLEY, Third Base

	G	AB	Hit	2B	3B	HR	Run	RBI	TBB	SO	SB	CS	Avg
2.35 years		613	161	33	3	28	77	97	35	143	1	3	.262
1986	155	616	163	33	4	27	83	107	32	172	0	4	.265
First Half	81	315	90	20	2	18	50	61	16	86	0	3	.286
Second Half	74	301	73	13	2	9	33	46	16	86	0	1	.243
Vs. RHP		458	112	24	3	21		84	21	123	0	4	.245
Vs. LHP		158	51	9	1	6		23	11	49	0	0	.323
Home	80	319	98	25	2	16	53	60	18	84	0	1	.307
Road	75	297	65	8	2	11	30	47	14	88	0	3	.219
Grass	57	220	47	5	1	11	23	37	13	60	0	2	.214
Turf	98	396	116	28	3	16	60	70	19	112	0	2	.293

Ken PHELPS, First Base-Designated Hitter

	G	AB	Hit	2B	3B	HR	Run	RBI	TBB	SO	SB	CS	Avg
2.29 years		398	93	14	3	28	65	68	82	107	3	3	.235
1986	125	344	85	16	4	24	69	64	88	96	2	3	.247
First Half	57	136	34	6	1	13	32	29	39	36	1	1	.250
Second Half	68	208	51	10	3	11	37	35	49	60	1	2	.245
Vs. RHP		285	71	12	3	23		51	78	78	2	3	.249
Vs. LHP		59	14	4	1	1		13	10	18	0	0	.237
Home	63	174	50	8	3	15	40	40	47	42	0	1	.287
Road	62	170	35	8	1	9	29	24	41	54	2	2	.206
Grass	46	135	24	3	0	6	22	12	31	43	1	1	.178
Turf	79	209	61	13	4	18	47	52	57	53	1	1	.292

Rey QUINONES, Shortstop

	G	AB	Hit	2B	3B	HR	Run	RBI	TBB	SO	SB	CS	Avg
0.60 years		516	112	26	2	3	53	36	40	94	7	5	.218
1986	98	312	68	16	1	2	32	22	24	57	4	3	.218
First Half	39	115	23	4	1	1	15	11	14	17	2	2	.200
Second Half	59	197	45	12	0	1	17	11	10	40	2	1	.228
Vs. RHP		209	46	10	1	2		15	16	35	4	3	.220
Vs. LHP		103	22	6	0	0		7	8	22	0	0	.214
Home	52	158	37	12	0	2	20	12	11	25	2	1	.234
Road	46	154	31	4	1	0	12	10	13	32	2	2	.201
Grass	66	198	51	11	1	2	25	20	19	37	3	3	.258
Turf	32	114	17	5	0	0	7	2	5	20	1	0	.149

Bob KEARNEY, Catcher

	G	AB	Hit	2B	3B	HR	Run	RBI	TBB	SO	SB	CS	Avg
2.81 years		466	110	22	1	10	45	47	23	77	3	4	.235
1986	81	204	49	10	0	6	23	25	12	35	0	2	.240
First Half	48	124	28	5	0	3	14	14	6	18	0	1	.226
Second Half	33	80	21	5	0	3	9	11	6	17	0	1	.263
Vs. RHP		129	29	4	0	4		17	10	20	0	1	.225
Vs. LHP		75	20	6	0	2		8	2	15	0	1	.267
Home	39	95	28	7	0	4	11	16	8	16	0	1	.295
Road	42	109	21	3	0	2	12	9	4	19	0	1	.193
Grass	29	73	14	2	0	1	7	4	4	10	0	1	.192
Turf	52	131	35	8	0	5	16	21	8	25	0	1	.267

Mike MOORE

Year	(W–L)	GS	Run	Avg	DP	Avg	SB	Avg
1984	(7-17)	33	127	3.85	22	.67	25	.76
1985	(17-10)	34	149	4.38	30	.88	12	.35
1986	(11-13)	37	179	4.84	43	1.16	20	.54
1982-1986		152	632	4.16	32	.87	104	.68

	1986		1985	1984	1983	1982	82-86
	ERA	W–L	ERA	ERA	ERA	ERA	W–L
Total	4.30	11-13	3.46	4.97	4.71	5.36	48-62
Home	4.18	7-4	3.18	4.55	4.98	5.15	29-26
Road	4.40	4-9	3.79	5.52	4.43	5.58	19-36
East	4.82	7-11	3.53	5.03	4.06	4.83	28-34
West	3.70	4-2	3.36	4.92	5.32	6.00	20-28
1st Half	4.80	5-7	3.70	4.18	7.11	6.41	19-27
2nd Half	3.81	6-6	3.30	5.71	4.12	4.48	29-35
Turf	4.29	8-7	3.41	4.55	5.54		28-29
Grass	4.31	3-6	3.56	6.09	3.42		13-19
Day	5.11	3-6	3.00	3.52	4.74	4.37	11-19
Night	3.97	8-7	3.69	5.79	4.71	5.55	37-43
April	2.36	1-2	8.00	2.57	7.25	9.39	5-11
May	6.87	1-4	1.74	4.50		5.65	5-10
June	5.04	2-1	2.93	6.03		4.97	6-4
July	4.98	2-3	2.55	5.92	3.34	3.45	11-11
August	2.98	3-1	2.75	5.84	4.04	4.82	9-11
September	3.99	2-2	4.09	4.97	5.08	5.72	12-15

Mike MORGAN

Year	(W–L)	GS	Run	Avg	DP	Avg	SB	Avg
1985	(1-1)	2	21	10.50	0	.00	4	2.00
1986	(11-17)	33	157	4.76	40	1.21	26	.79
1978-1986		78	324	4.15	99	1.27	60	.77

	1986		1983		1982		82-86
	ERA	W–L	ERA	W–L	ERA	W–L	W–L
Total	4.53	11-17	5.16	0-3	4.37	7-11	18-31
Home	5.11	4-10	4.66	0-2	4.54	2-6	6-18
Road	4.03	7-7	6.06	0-1	4.23	5-5	12-13
East	5.43	5-11	3.94	0-3	4.97	3-6	8-20
West	3.67	6-6	8.10	0-0	3.89	4-5	10-11
1st Half	4.02	6-7	5.40	0-3	4.24	5-4	11-14
2nd Half	4.98	5-10	4.15	0-0	4.52	2-7	7-17
Turf	4.86	8-11	4.96	0-2			8-13
Grass	3.96	3-6	5.68	0-1			3-7
Day	4.70	3-6	5.40	0-1	3.47	1-1	4-8
Night	4.48	8-11	5.06	0-2	4.54	6-10	14-23
April	2.00	1-2	5.27	0-1	3.65	0-0	3-3
May	6.67	2-4	4.34	0-2	2.25	1-1	3-7
June	3.50	2-1	4.50	0-0	5.97	1-3	3-4
July	5.65	3-3	81.00	0-0	3.62	1-1	4-4
August	4.32	1-4	4.50	0-0	3.96	1-3	2-7
September	4.76	2-3	3.38	0-0	7.47	1-3	3-6

Mark LANGSTON

Year	(W–L)	GS	Run	Avg	DP	Avg	SB	Avg
1984	(17-10)	33	126	3.82	27	.82	15	.45
1985	(7-14)	24	95	3.96	25	1.04	19	.79
1986	(12-14)	36	150	4.17	28	.78	19	.53
1984-1986		93	371	3.99	80	.86	53	.57

	1986		1985		1984		84-86
	ERA	W–L	ERA	W–L	ERA	W–L	W–L
Total	4.85	12-14	5.47	7-14	3.40	17-10	36-38
Home	5.39	5-7	5.43	4-5	2.52	10-3	19-15
Road	4.31	7-7	5.50	3-9	4.44	7-7	17-23
East	5.13	6-7	6.22	3-8	3.90	9-7	18-22
West	4.45	6-7	4.81	4-6	2.85	8-3	18-16
1st Half	4.73	9-6	3.94	5-6	3.55	6-6	20-18
2nd Half	4.97	3-8	7.04	2-8	3.26	11-4	16-20
Turf	4.94	7-7	5.12	5-7	3.16	11-5	23-19
Grass	4.72	5-7	6.02	2-7	3.89	6-5	13-19
Day	5.10	3-6	2.96	3-1	4.42	5-5	11-12
Night	4.74	9-8	6.16	4-13	2.91	12-5	25-26
April	6.20	1-2	2.75	3-2	5.32	1-2	5-6
May	4.60	3-2	4.94	2-3	4.25	1-2	6-7
June	3.35	5-1	8.31	0-1	2.63	3-2	8-4
July	5.74	0-2	5.79	0-1	2.66	4-2	4-5
August	6.14	2-3	5.61	2-4	2.20	4-1	8-8
September	4.00	1-4	9.25	0-3	4.42	4-1	5-8

Matt YOUNG

1986	G	IP	W–L	Sv	H	ER	SO	ERA
Total	65	103.2	8-6	13	108	44	82	3.82
Home	34	64.0	6-2	8	57	25	50	3.52
Road	31	39.2	2-4	5	51	19	32	4.31
East	33	53.1	3-1	8	53	14	43	2.36
West	32	50.1	5-5	5	55	30	39	5.36
1st Half	34	62.0	7-4	7	65	27	44	3.92
2nd Half	31	41.2	1-2	6	43	17	38	3.67
Turf	43	72.2	6-2	10	66	27	60	3.34
Grass	22	31.0	2-4	3	42	17	22	4.94
Day	16	28.2	2-2	4	34	13	21	4.08
Night	49	75.0	6-4	9	74	31	61	3.72
April	6	20.0	2-2	0	26	14	10	6.30
May	14	23.0	2-1	2	25	8	17	3.13
June	11	14.2	3-1	3	7	3	15	1.84
July	12	19.2	0-0	5	21	4	18	1.83
August	12	12.0	0-1	3	9	7	10	5.25
September	10	14.1	1-1	0	20	8	12	5.02

OTHERS

Pitcher	(W–L)	GS	Run	Avg	DP	Avg	SB	Avg	Time	Att.
Swift	(2-9)	17	77	4.53	26	1.53	16	.94	2:46	275
Wilcox	(0-8)	10	27	2.70	14	1.40	9	.90	2:44	186
Beattle	(0-6)	7	24	3.43	7	1.00	4	.57	2:55	79
Young	(8-6)	5	25	5.00	7	1.40	2	.40	2:41	75
Trujillo	(3-2)	4	15	3.75	7	1.75	2	.50	2:22	33
Guettermann	(0-4)	4	21	5.25	3	.75	1	.25	2:41	81
Reed	(4-0)	4	35	8.75	8	2.00	1	.25	2:54	63
Brown	(0-2)	2	0	.00	1	.50	5	2.50	2:54	52
Fireovid	(2-0)	1	2	2.00	2	2.00	0	.00		9
Nunez	(1-2)	1	3	3.00	1	1.00	0	.00	2:31	8

STARTING PITCHERS' AVERAGE TIME AND ATTENDANCE RECORDS

Pitcher	Time	Attendance
Moore	2:47	588
Langston	2:46	616
Morgan	2:48	570

RECORDS WITH DIFFERENT STARTING CATCHERS

Catcher	Inn	ER	W–L	ERA	GS	SB	Avg
Kearney	530.2	268	24-36	4.55	60	39	.65
Bradley	436.1	203	21-28	4.19	49	33	.67
Yeager	392.2	218	19-25	5.00	44	27	.61
Valle	80.0	55	3-6	6.19	9	6	.67

FOULS

Jeff Welch passed along some information about foul outs in Mariner games. His studies cover all Mariner games in 1985 and 1986, and are broken down by foul outs at home and on the road.

On the road, in 159 games over two years there were 235 foul outs. In 165 games in the Kingdome, there were 332 foul outs—about 40% more. First of all, this should destroy any notion that the Kingdome has small foul territory. It may *look* small, but in the areas where the foul balls are caught, there is plenty of room. Most of those foul balls, as you might guess, were caught by first and third basemen:

Fouls caught by:	Sea	Road	Total
Pitchers	3	2	5
Catchers	65	56	121
First Basemen	110	83	193
Second Basemen	6	11	17
Third Basemen	84	46	130
Shortstops	14	4	18
Left Fielders	33	17	50
Center Fielders	0	0	0
Right Fielders	17	16	33

The results make a lot of sense, and are pretty much what you'd expect—first basemen catch more pop fouls than anyone else, followed by third basemen and catchers.

The effects of this on the batting average in the park would appear to be detectable but pretty minor—probably about three points.

THE KEN PHELPS ALL-STAR TEAM

See, on the one hand you've got the Henry Cottos, and on the other hand, you've got your Ken Phelpses. If Henry Cotto is a major-league ballplayer, I'm an airplane. Cotto is one of those guys who runs well and throws pretty decent, and one year he hit .270-something (in less than 150 at bats, in Wrigley Field, with a secondary average of .164), so you get guys like Don Zimmer who will rave about this great young prospect and keep trading for him, so he'll get about eight chances to play in the major leagues before they figure out he can't hit. At first when he doesn't hit they'll say he just needs more playing time, and then they'll say that he needs to stop wiggling his elbows while the pitcher is in motion, and then they'll say he needs to point his lead foot and learn to keep his weight back, and then they'll say he needs to be more aggressive at the plate, and then they'll say that he needs to go back to wiggling his elbows. They always figure that if you can run and throw they'll *teach* you to hit. Of course they can't teach anybody to hit, but they always *think* they can, so they keep trying.

Then on the other hand you've got your Ken Phelpses. Ken Phelps has been a major-league ballplayer since at least 1980, when he hit .294 with 128 walks and a slugging percentage close to .600 at AAA Omaha, a tough park for a hitter. Through 1985 he had 567 at bats in the major leagues—one season's worth—with 40 home runs and 92 RBI. The Mariners still didn't want to let him play. See, the problem was that Chuck Cottier, in his day, was a Henry Cotto, a guy who could run and throw, but couldn't play baseball. Most major-league managers were those kind of guys. Ken Phelps, on the other hand, can't run particularly well (although he isn't exceptionally slow, either) and doesn't throw well, and if you're that kind of player and want to play major-league ball you'd better go 7-for-20 in your first week in the majors, or they'll decide it's time to take another look at Henry Cotto. Ken Phelps in his first two shots at major-league pitching went 3-for-26. Despite his limitations, the man is a major-league player. He's a major-league player because he plays good defense at first base and has a secondary average over .500, so that he can both drive in and score runs.

Ken Phelpses are just *available;* if you want one, all you have to do is ask. They are players whose real limitations are exaggerated by baseball insiders, players who get stuck with a label—the label of their limits, the label of the things they *can't* do—while those that they can do are overlooked.

Sometimes the Ken Phelpses of the world outlast their tribulations, and get to prove their mettle, sometimes they don't. Others who have include Mike Easler, Rance Mulliniks, Danny Walling, Gene Garber, Charlie Hough, Donnie Moore, Mitch Webster, Wally Backman, Jim Morrison, Charlie Leibrandt, Lee Lacy, Tony Armas, Andre Thornton, Phil Niekro, Joe Niekro, Tom Candiotti, Dar-nell Coles, Ben Oglivie and Joaquin Andujar. Anyway, one of the things that makes Dick Williams a successful manager is that he'll take one or two of those guys who has a label and say, "Look, I know you can play. I'll put you in the lineup, and if you bust your butt for me I'll keep you in there." Maybe the conversation doesn't take place, but that's the implied message. The player, who has been waiting for years for somebody to say that, is only too happy to go out and work his tail off. This expands the team's talent base, and at the same time puts a hustling, aggressive player on the field, which has a contagious effect on the rest of the lineup. Billy Martin does the same thing.

I thought, then, in honor of Dick Williams and Ken Phelps, that I would select the Ken Phelps All-Stars, a whole teamful of guys who are wearing labels, but who nonetheless can play major-league baseball, and will prove it if they ever get the chance. The Ken Phelps All-Stars, 1987:

FIRST BASE AND BATTING THIRD: Mike Stenhouse
LABEL: Too slow, too big a swing, minor league slugger who hasn't hit in the majors.

Stenhouse, four years younger than Phelps (the Macmillan Encyclopedia says six years), is a quite similar player; to date he has 416 major-league at bats with a batting average of .190. He's a left-handed power hitter who will get about as many walks as hits, and had a big year in the minor leagues at Wichita in 1983, where he and Phelps were teammates in 1982. (Phelps in 1982: .333 with 46 HR, 141 RBI; Stenhouse in 1983: .355 with 25 and 93 in 109 games.) As they had with Phelps, major-league executives talked a lot about the short right field fence in Wichita and the inability of AAA pitchers to control their curveballs; as had happened to Phelps, Stenhouse got his first chance to play in a big artificial turf stadium that didn't suit him.

Both Stenhouse and Phelps have college degrees, Phelps from Arizona State in PE, Stenhouse from Harvard in Economics. I thought Stenhouse would bust out a couple of years ago in Minnesota, but the team got off to a horrible start, the manager was under a lot of pressure, and it didn't work out. I still think he can hit. Compared to Phelps, Stenhouse is a little smaller, a little more mobile, would probably hit for a little better average but with less power.

SECOND BASE AND BATTING SECOND: Jack Perconte
LABEL: Doesn't turn the double play.

The other players in this group are mostly guys who haven't gotten a fair shot in the major leagues or who got their shot and didn't play well. Perconte, on the other hand, got his chance and played extremely well—but got dumped on anyway.

Now 32, Perconte got trapped in the Dodger system behind Dave Lopes; when Lopes was pushed aside the Dodgers decided to go with Steve Sax instead of Perconte. After further misadventures in Cleveland, René Lachemann gave Perconte a chance to play in Seattle in '84, and Perconte played well, reaching base 242 times, hitting .294 with 93 runs scored and a 29/35 performance as a base stealer. Seattle, losers of 102 games with Julio Cruz and Tony Bernazard in the 2B/leadoff spot the year before, improved by 14 games; nonetheless, when the Mariners relapsed in 1985 they decided to make Perconte the scapegoat and began talking a great deal about his lack of a throwing arm.

As a player, Perconte is similar to Nellie Fox. He's a small man, a singles hitter, a quick second baseman but with no arm. Nellie learned to compensate for his arm with his quickness on the pivot; Perconte isn't his equal there. He strikes out more than Fox—everybody does—but doesn't strike out much and is a better baserunner. He deserves a major-league job.

THIRD BASE AND BATTING SEVENTH: Randy Ready
LABEL: Not as good as he was supposed to be.

Randy Ready, 27, was once the shining star of the Milwaukee farm system, battering minor-league pitchers for averages of .376, .375, .329, and .308. Brewer fans waited with bated breath for his arrival in the majors, while the nation's sportsfans groaned in anticipation of the puns that *The Sporting News* headline writers were sure to make.

Randy hit .405 in 12 games in late 1983, and then a funny thing happened. Paul Molitor, the Brewers' third baseman, was seriously hurt, out for the 1984 season, while the Detroit Tigers blew the doors off in the opening days of the season; the Brewers, playing badly, were virtually eliminated by May 15. It created an absolutely perfect opportunity to let Ready get some playing time—yet Brewer manager René Lachemann, apparently regarding this as charity, flatly refused to accept it. Instead, he experimented with Ted Simmons at third base, and in early June announced that the third base job belonged to Roy Howell, a proven veteran of absolutely execrable quality.

Ready, facing serious family health problems as well as terminal managerial incompetence, has floundered over the last two years, returning to the Pacific Coast League briefly last fall. Yet, on balance, he *hasn't* played horribly in the major leagues; his major-league average is .238, with almost 40% of his hits for extra bases, a good many walks and good speed. Plus he can play third base. I'd be happy to start the 1987 season with Randy Ready in my lineup.

SHORTSTOP AND BATTING NINTH: Doug Baker
LABEL: Good field, no hit.

For the shortstop on our Ken Phelps All-Stars we have the usual selection of low-average/good-secondary-average/marginal-defensive players, such as we have selected at other positions, which would include Kelly Paris or Ron Gardenhire, or we have a Mark Belanger–type glove man. In this case, since we have a pretty good offensive team anyway but are stretching our defense to its limits, I think it would be a good idea to get a glove man to serve as a defensive anchor.

Doug Baker, 26, has been trapped in the Tiger system behind Alan Trammell. A .176 hitter in 159 major-league at bats, he would fight to clear the Mendoza line as a regular. But, like Belanger, he'll get a few walks, bunt when called on, run the bases well, and play a strong defensive shortstop. On this team, that's the type of player I'd be looking for at short.

Oh—another good Ken Phelps type is Scott Fletcher, the Ranger shortstop. He's always been a good player, and I'm proud to say I've always realized it, but it took until 1986 for him to find a manager who agreed with me. A year ago he would have been the perfect shortstop for us; now there's nobody as good unless you count José Oquendo, who deserves another shot but isn't exactly invisible with his .297 batting average.

LEFT FIELD AND LEADING OFF: LaSchelle Tarver
LABEL: No arm, no power, erratic baserunner.

LaSchelle Tarver, 28, is a Mets product who is now the property of the Boston Red Sox. Tarver is in the same general class of players as Rudy Law—a singles hitter and base stealer, no arm. He's not quite the baserunner that Law is, but the critical difference is that he's a better hitter. His minor-league batting averages, in all the places he's played 50 or more games, are .314, .308., .316, .326, .311, and .320. His major-league equivalences show that he would hit .285–.325 in the majors, plus he walks some and is a base stealer, though not a good percentage runner. With Tarver and Perconte at the top, our Ken Phelps All-Stars would have two people who can get on base and scoot.

CENTER FIELD AND BATTING FIFTH: Ron Roenicke
LABEL: Journeyman, doesn't do anything that stands out.

Ron Roenicke, 30, is one of those players who lacks any one central skill that would get attention and give him an identity. As a regular he would hit in the .250–.270 range, but . . .

A) he is an excellent outfielder, has a good arm, and compensates for his lack of exceptional speed by getting a good jump on the ball. He's an excellent right/left fielder, can get by in center.

B) He can steal a base now and then and is a good-percentage base stealer.

C) He walks a good deal—80/100 times a year as a regular.

D) He has some line-drive power, enough to hit 30 doubles and 10–12 homers a year.

No one item is that impressive, but if you add them up you've got a secondary average of .300–.360, and if you can hit .260 with a secondary average of .330 and do the job in center field, there should be a place for you to play.

RIGHT FIELD AND BATTING SIXTH: Brad Komminsk
LABEL: Can't handle the pressure.

Still only 26 years old, Brad Komminsk tore through the minor leagues like a Ferrari in a soap-box derby, and arrived in Atlanta wearing the millstone of a superstar label. Given 642 at bats by the Braves, he has simply failed to hit; his average is .216, and his power has been limited. Since I invented the majors-to-minors translation system in 1984, Komminsk is the one player who, given a full shot in the major leagues, has failed to compile major-league statistics that were comparable to his major league equivalences. Now he can't even hit minor-league pitching. But he can run and throw and play right field, and, like Bill Robinson, he'll get the bat going eventually. Or maybe he won't, but I'd love to take the chance.

OUTFIELDER/DH AND BATTING CLEANUP: Brian Dayett

RAP ON HIM: Hasn't hit in majors.

Brian Dayett could be described as Steve Balboni's minor-league twin. Like Balboni, he was born in January of 1957, Balboni on the 16th and Dayett six days later. Both were born in New England, Balboni in Massachusetts and Dayett in Connecticut. Both attended college in Florida, Balboni in St. Petersburg and Dayett in St. Leo. Both were drafted by the Yankees on June 6, 1978, and began to work their way through the Yankee chain.

Both are right-handed power hitters who will strike out a lot and won't hit for average. At Nashville in 1980, Balboni hit .301 with 34 homers and 122 RBI; at Nashville in '82 Dayett hit .280 with 34 homers and 96 RBI. In '83 they were teammates at Columbus; Balboni hit .274 with 27 homers and 81 RBI in 84 games, and Dayett hit .288 with 35 and 108 in 128 games. In 1984 Balboni hit .244 with KC; Dayett, batting 127 times for the Yankees, also hit .244 with virtually the same RBI rate.

The odd thing is that while Balboni has escaped the minor-league slugger label and become a valued player in Kansas City, Dayett is probably a better player than Balboni. Compared to Bones, Dayett will hit for a better average, will walk more and strike out less. He is more mobile and is a decent outfielder, a good left fielder who can be used in right. While he would not match Balboni homer for homer in the same park, with Balboni in KC and Dayett in Wrigley Field, he will more than match him if the Cubs give him a shot.

A long time ago the Cubs had an outfielder named Hank Sauer who got trapped in the minor leagues until liberated by the Reds at age 29. Sauer couldn't run, didn't throw exceptionally well, and struck out enough to keep his average in the .260s—but once he got the chance, he blasted 225 home runs and drove in 672 runs in his first seven years (32 homers and 96 RBI a year); he even won an MVP award. Dayett isn't likely to win an MVP award, but he's the same type of player. (If this team were assembled in practice it might be a good idea to put Dayett in the outfield and use Tarver as the DH. Another good outfielder/DH for this team would be Nelson Simmons, former Tiger prospect now the property of the Orioles.)

CATCHER: A platoon is appropriate.

It is harder to name a catcher in this category of players than it is a player at any other position. At the other positions we have players whose speed is held against them, but nobody cares if a catcher can't run. Elsewhere we have low-average/good-secondary-average players, but at catcher that is considered more the norm than the rule. Also, most teams are so desperate for catching help that they'll carry three catchers, so catchers get more chances than other players. I really don't see anybody that I'd consider a "good" all-around catcher who is available for the asking, so you'd have to piece together a catching combination from among the available parts. These include:

1) Steve Lake, 30. Tremendous defensive catcher, isn't likely to hit.

2) Alan Knicely, 31. Despite his poor offensive stats, this man can hit. Part of his problem is that he's played in all the worst parks for a player of his type—Houston, Cincinnati, St. Louis. He needs a shot with Atlanta or the Cubs or one of the American League teams with a small park. Defense is a serious problem.

3) Jamie Quirk, 32. Converted infielder, has superb arm and quick release, but other defensive skills need work. Has hit in the past.

4) Geno Petralli, 27. A switch hitter who can hit for a good average; throwing arm is all right but he's not Bob Boone.

5) Dave Engle, 30. Converted outfielder, a good right-handed bat and a surprisingly competent defensive catcher.

No one of those men could handle the catcher's job, but you could pick an arrangement of two or three, as Toronto has done, who could cover the spot and contribute.

STARTING PITCHER: Ray Fontenot
LABEL: Fair stuff, inconsistent

Ray Fontenot is a member of the Tommy John family of pitchers. The Tommy John family of pitchers share four primary characteristics that create a large number of secondary and tertiary characteristics. The primary characteristics are that they are left-handed, control-type pitchers who hold runners well and get a very high percentage of ground balls. The ground balls create a number of secondary characteristics such as few home runs allowed and many double plays behind them. These lead to important tertiary characteristics such as:

1) Tommy John family pitchers can win while allowing a very high number of hits per nine innings—sometimes 10.5 or 11. With few walks, few home runs, few stolen bases, and many double plays, these guys are not vulnerable to big innings, so it takes a lot of singles to beat them.

2) They are very dependent on the support of their teams. Whereas an ordinary pitcher might post a .450 winning percentage with a .400 team and a .550 with a .600 team, these guys will post a .380 percentage with a bad team, but .620 with a good team. Fontenot has looked bad with bad teams the last two years—but he was 16–11 with the Yankees in '83 and '84.

3) They are almost always more effective in their thirties than in their twenties. Tommy John was 95–96 in his twenties, but 142–75 in his thirties. Geoff Zahn was 6–14 in his twenties, but 105–95 in his thirties. Rick Honeycutt was 42–64 through age 28, but has been 45–41 at 29 through 32. Fontenot turns 30 this fall, and his best years are probably ahead of him.

STARTING PITCHER: Dan Schatzeder
LABEL: injury prone, bad mechanics.

Dan Schatzeder has a kind of funny-looking delivery, variously described as "slinging" or "shot-putting" the ball. He also had an arm injury and pitched very badly in 1981 and 1982. But he throws strikes, is a good fielder and an excellent hitter and has been very effective the rest of his career. Like Ken Phelps, what he needs mostly is for somebody to let him go through a few ups and downs without giving up on him.

STARTING PITCHER: Tim Conroy
LABEL: Too tense, poor control.

I thought Tim Conroy would make a breakthrough with the Cardinals in 1986. It didn't happen, and there is something to the logic that if you can't pitch for the Cardinals, you can't pitch. But Conroy is only 27 and has excellent stuff. His problems—control, command of his emotions—are the kind that a player often outgrows. If he doesn't develop a drinking problem or a rotator cuff injury, some day this kid is going to be a fine pitcher.

STARTING PITCHER: Brad Havens
LABEL: Finds a way to lose.

I'm a little more reluctant to put Brad Havens in this class than I am most of the others, because in his case I really don't understand what the problem is. Here's a guy who has a major-league fastball and a major-league curve, decent control, gets his strikeouts, yet he hasn't been effective in the major leagues. He's 27 now, and if he's going to find himself he'd better organize a search party pretty quick. But I'll list him here on the grounds that if you don't know why a pitcher can't win, that's better than having a pitcher that you do know why he can't win but can't do anything about it.

RELIEF ACE: Mark Huisman
LABEL: Popoff, attitude case.

Mark Huisman got a reputation as a loudmouth when he was in the Kansas City organization, when he pitched well in the spring of 1985, got sent to Omaha and overmatched the league, setting a league record for saves and being named American Association Pitcher of the Year. Huisman felt he should be in the majors, and at times was none too subtle about letting this be known, to the considerable irritation of the KC management. He hasn't pitched great in the major leagues, but his strikeout/walk ratios have been outstanding. He throws a hard sinking fastball, a pitch that I love in principle (it's easy to control but hard to hit, doesn't tear up the arm and gets ground balls). I think he'll be effective once he learns the hitters a little more. Also, I like his cocky attitude.

I should not leave you with the impression that this team, if assembled, would win 95 games and prepare to do battle with the Mets. As Ken Phelps and Scott Fletcher did in 1986, *some* of these players would prove themselves to be extremely valuable performers. Some of them would also prove that their labels were justified. If assembled, this team would probably win 70–80 games.

But, of course, although all of these players could be had for a song, nobody is suggesting assembling this team; that's not the point. I'm fairly sure that Randy Ready will eventually prove himself to be a major-league player; I'm also sure that I wouldn't push Jim Presley out of the way to take the chance. One assumes that any team has *some* talent, but some gaps in the talent. The point is that among the labeled there are some who can play, and who can be used to plug the gaps. There is at least one major-league player available at each position except possibly shortstop and catcher. Good managers succeed in large part because they know that they are smarter than the people who hang labels on players, so they don't study the labels. They study the players.

PLAYER COMMENTS

INTRODUCTION TO PLAYER RATINGS AND COMMENTS

The players are rated this year, as they were last year, by a poll of scorers participating in *Project Scoresheet*. The voters—there were about 140 this year—were divided into 26 precincts, one representing each major-league team. The regulars at each position were ranked 1 through 12 (one through 14 in the American League) by each voter, and then the votes for each precinct were added together to form one ballot, also ranking the players 1 through 12 or 1 through 14. The number in parentheses following the top-rated players represents the number of precincts in which the player was the top-rated regular at the spot.

The voters were asked to rank the players on the basis of *present, clearly established ability*. The voters are allowed to interpret that however they feel is appropriate, and can use any information that they possess about the players to make their ballots. There is no prohibition, for example, about ranking players based on post-season play.

I rate players by a poll for a simple reason: I honestly believe that that is the most accurate way to rate them. By polling the people we are polling, we get people who know the principles of sabermetrics, know that you can't ignore the walk column and that range factor can help you make sense of defensive work, but we're also incorporating knowledge of the players from a broader perspective. One hundred forty people know the players better than any one individual could know them.

There are cases where I disagree with the rankings, and a few cases where I strongly disagree with the rankings. But when I made out the rankings by formulas, there were a lot more cases where I strongly disagreed with the outcomes, and I used a lot of different formulas. There were even more cases than when I thought the ranking was all right but other people were appalled, people who assumed that the rankings represented my opinions.

Well, I have my opinions, and I set a certain store by them. But when I compare the ballot that I made out with the way people were ranked by the voters, I have to concede in 90% of the cases that there are awfully strong reasons why I might have been wrong.

I guess what I'm saying is that I used to make the rankings an exercise in statistical interpretation, trying to find ways to beat on the statistics until they said something that made sense. I realize now that the attempts to do this were generating inevitable, and damaging, misunderstandings. I realize now that when you set out to rate players you have to set the goal of getting accurate ratings above any other goal, or you have to expect criticism, even though it is very ill-informed criticism, when the rankings come out strange. Polling people who know the players is the surest, best way to incorporate a broad base of knowledge about the players into the rankings, and thus the most accurate way that I know of to rate players.

In the comments this year there are a large number of bits of data taken from the *Project Scoresheet* files compiled for the *Great American Baseball Stat Book*. Because of deadlines, I had to work from data that was not completely clean in making these comments, and there will be discrepancies between the figures that appear here and those that appear in the *Great American Baseball Stat Book*. In all such cases, the data in the other book will be correct, and the figure here will need to be corrected. However, since I will in all cases be discussing a statistic that makes a point about the player's performance or ability, rather than pointing to a specific data item, such discrepancies should not in any case invalidate the point that I am making. In other words, the point I am making is that Georges Jacques Danton didn't hit in the late innings, and I really don't care very much whether he hit .177 or .179, although I apologize for any confusion on the issue.

CATCHERS

American League

1. Rich Gedman, Boston (11)

Terrific player, keeps working, keeps getting better defensively . . . still doesn't hit left-handers worth a hoot . . .

2. Lance Parrish, Detroit (3)

His ability to catch in '87 is in question. Mike Heath will probably catch if Parrish can't, and will probably bounce back with the bat, but the Tigers will miss Parrish.

3. Ernie Whitt, Toronto (1)

Hit .195 when behind in the count, with no homers and 7 RBI in 77 at bats, .221 slugging percentage. When ahead in the count he hit .315 with 6 homers and .574 slugging.

4. Don Slaught, Texas

Opposition stolen base rate went up because the Rangers were using a lot of young, wild pitchers . . .

5. Bob Boone, California

I've been slow to realize the benefits this guy brings to the Angels, but I've got to say I'm really sold on him now. His defense is just tremendous. During the playoffs, they were talking a lot about his stealing pitches by the way he receives them, catching everything easy so it looks like a strike. I don't know about that, but he's just throwing tremendously well, better than he did five years ago. In the 137 games that he started, Angel opponents stole only 44 bases, or .32 per game. That was the best OSB rate in the majors. Boone loves to throw to the bases. I don't have a count of how many runners he has nailed off base, but I know it's a bunch, and he certainly shortens up the leads. To watch him play it looks like his knees are great, so apparently he's going to play until they just can't carry his bat anymore. He now has caught 1,808 games in the majors, more than any other catcher in history except Al Lopez (1,918). I've been following this for years, and he should get him this

year . . . Looking at the data over a period of years, it appears that the difference between Boone catching and Narron catching is about six-tenths of a run a game. It's probably not actually *that* large, but that's a massive difference . . .

6. Scott Bradley, Seattle

Bradley hit .335 in the International League in 1984, and was named International League player of the year. The major-league translation of those stats (printed in a Spring, 1985, newsletter) showed that performance as equivalent to an average just over .300 in the majors—exactly what he hit last year. In spite of that, the Yankees decided to let him go and rest their fate with Wynegar . . . the Mariners' catching should be offensively solid with Bradley, hitting .270–.310, and Dave Valle, who hit very well at Calgary and tremendously well with Seattle in September.

7. Mickey Tettleton, Oakland

One of the sure signs of a bad manager is overreacting to something that happens in front of his eyes and making a decision for which there isn't any evidence. The A's last year had a catcher named Bill Bathe who started spring training at the minor-league camp. In '85 he played at Tacoma, batting .279 with 6 homers and 45 RBI. At 25, with those kind of stats in the PCL and just fair defensive skills, he was no prospect, as is reflected in the fact that he wasn't invited to the major-league camp. But Tettleton had a heel injury and they needed an extra catcher in camp, so they moved over Bathe. Bathe hit .484 in 14 spring training games, so Jackie Moore took him with him to Oakland, sending Jerry Willard to Tacoma. With Tettleton out, Bathe actually started 38 games, and predictably was terrible, hitting .184 and

having trouble throwing out runners. There was no real evidence that he would be anything except terrible. The A's were 11–27 and had an ERA of 5.05 in the games that he started . . .

It's hard to guess exactly how much the loss of Tettleton in the early part of the season cost the A's. The A's traded Heath in part because they felt that Tettleton's ability to handle the staff was much stronger. They knew that their staff ERA was markedly better with Tettleton catching than Heath, both in 1984 and 1985. That did hold up in '86; for whatever reason, the staff ERA was 4.00 with Tettleton catching and over 4.50 without him. Over a three-year period the data makes a pretty convincing argument for Tettleton as a defensive catcher: 3.79 ERA in 163 games with Tettleton catching, about 4.60 without him.

His throwing is fair—C+ or B−. But as an offensive player, Tettleton is almost the new Gene Tenace. He walks as often as he hits and he hits for power, leading to a 1986 secondary average over .400. It's unlikely that had he been healthy he could have kept the A's in contention, but he would have helped, and they did start playing better when he returned.

8. Jim Sundberg, Kansas City

Does not hit well in Royals Stadium. Over last three years has excellent situational stats. He's hit only .238 overall, but .271 when leading off an inning, .267 with runners in scoring position and .291 in the late innings of close games. His average is dragged down by a .186 average in the least significant situation—no one on, outs already recorded in inning . . . Brock6 system projects him to finish his career with 1,938 games, 93 homers, .249 average. In other words, it gives him about one more full-time and a couple of half-time seasons . . .

9. Carlton Fisk, Chicago

Register of really silly personnel management ideas, 1986-Chi-24: "The reason we're losing is that Carlton Fisk doesn't call pitches well." What exactly was the evidence for this? If Fisk doesn't call pitches well, how come the Sox always have a better ERA with Fisk catching than without him . . . Brock6 system projects him to finish with 305 homers, .267 average, 1,056 career RBI. He's got a shot at the Hall of Fame, but really needs to come back and hit some this year. When he becomes eligible he's going to be fighting for attention among guys like Carew, Reggie, Rose, Seaver, and possibly Schmidt . . .

The new kid, Karkovice, looks pretty good, has a solid shot at the AL Rookie of the Year award if he's eligible. He has an excellent arm, hit .282 with 20 homers, 61 walks in 97 games at Birmingham, then continued to hit well in 97 at bats with the Sox.

10. Andy Allanson, Cleveland

As part of the rookies study, I wrote a program to compare the 1986 rookies with those in the 1948–1975 database so as to find the ten most comparable players to each of the 1986 rookies. As I wrote in the book a year ago when I introduced the similarity scores, one way to project what a player will do is to find similar players in the past and look at what they have done. Of course, the ten comparable players will subsequently diverge, some becoming much better than others, and it is quite possible that the 1986 rookie will do better or worse than any of the comparable rookies from the past, but it gives us

the *range of normal expectation* for a player of this type.

The similarity was based upon *age* and *fielding position* as well as batting statistics. In the case of the two 1986 catchers, Allanson and LaValliere, the system selects as most comparable hardly any catchers, so that the comparison group may be less useful for those two players than for any of the other 1986 rookies. The reason this happens is that Allanson's accomplishments—.225 with 1 home run, 10 stolen bases—are rather odd for a catcher, numbers far more commonly achieved by a middle infielder than by a catcher. Anyway, the player selected as most similar to Allanson was another Cleveland player, 1958 rookie Billy Moran. Moran in 1958 hit .226 with 1 homer and 18 RBI in 257 at bats—obviously very similar to Allanson's season. Both players had slugging percentages of .280. Both players were 24 years old. The largest difference is that Moran was an infielder and Allanson is a catcher. The similarity is measured at 967.

Following Moran in Allanson's parade were Teddy Martinez (965), Roger Freed (944), Rod Gaspar (939), Ted Uhlaender (939), Mike Phillips (935), Nyls Nyman (932), Ed Crosby (930), Steve Brye (926), and Mike Ryan (922). As you can see, none of the ten players who were comparable to Allanson as rookies was able to develop into a quality major-league player. By far the best of the ten was Ted Uhlaender, who played 898 major-league games, hitting .263.

To form an estimate of what might be expected of the 1986 rookie—Allanson in this case—I took a weighted average of what was done by the other ten players, with

the career performance of each one weighted by his similarity to Allanson. (That is, Moran weighted at 967, Ryan at 922, etc.) That method suggests that the career expectation for Allanson should be about 518 major league games, 1,415 at bats, 344 hits for an average of .243. We'll see how he does.

11. Charlie Moore, Milwaukee

There were only five times last year when a Milwaukee catcher started three or more straight games. Usually, Moore caught Higuera and Leary, Cerone caught Wegman and Nieves, and they alternated among those two and Schroeder when Darwin or Cocanower or somebody was working. That, of course, is why the ERA with Moore catching was so low (3.33) . . .

12. Joel Skinner, New York

Nickname should be "Mule."

13. Rick Dempsey, Baltimore

I got a really strong reaction from my readers in Baltimore about Dempsey, as if people felt it was important for me to understand that Dempsey was finished. I gather that Dempsey was one of the people held most responsible for the Orioles' collapse, which I find very curious since he wasn't really playing during the period of the collapse. Certainly Kennedy will be an offensive improvement, but the Orioles still had a 3.82 ERA when Dempsey was the starting catcher, and 5.01 when he wasn't . . . Dempsey in '86 drove in only 14 of 137 runners in scoring position for him, and only 4 of 68 with two out . . .

14. Mark Salas, Minnesota

Would you trade Mark Salas for Eddie Kazak?

National League

1. Gary Carter, New York (10)

Did you ever notice how much Carter's batting style is like Don Baylor's? The whole thing—stance, swing, follow-through, and results.

Baylor's stance is a little more closed and of course he crowds the plate more, but they're real similar. Carter also is hit by pitches quite a bit, six times every year. Actually, his HBP

totals since 1982 are 6, 7, 6, 6, and 6 . . . the National League leader usually has about ten . . .

Carter's teams have had better ERAs when Carter was catching than when he wasn't every year since I started figuring that in 1982 . . . I started rating players in 1980. Johnny Bench was the No. 1 rated catcher in 1980, with Carter second. From 1981 through 1987 he has rated first every year . . . Brock6 projection shows him finishing his career with 2,552 hits and 426 home runs. The Brock6 system doesn't have any idea how many knee operations he's had, but he's coping so far. The 426 homers would be a record for a catcher . . . The 1986 season was the most important of his career insofar as the Hall of Fame goes. Catchers don't get 3,000 hits: they need to play on winners to build their credentials . . .

2. Tony Pena, Pittsburgh

Didn't throw nearly as well last year as he had in the past . . . I think his bat will come back strong in '87.

3. Jody Davis, Chicago Cubs

Curious decisions of Jim Frey, #1,143: The decision to get rid of Steve Lake. Lake is a good defensive catcher, not much of a hitter. Frey decided to get rid of him without any kind of a backup and just more or less play Jody Davis every day . . . Davis led NL catchers in OSB rate, .69 per game started . . . over last three years has hit just .211 in the late innings of close games (56/265) . . . I'd rather have Brenly or Diaz than this guy, but I got out-voted . . .

4. Bob Brenly, San Francisco

Giants have had a better ERA with Brenly catching than without him for four straight years . . .

5. Bo Diaz, Cincinnati

Now 34 years old but still hasn't caught a lot of games. His production has never really stabilized, but he finished very strong last year . . .

6. Mike Scioscia, Los Angeles

Pretty good player; hits for average, good defense, one of the best strikeout-to-walk ratios in baseball. Has trouble hitting left-handers. Has little power to begin with and in the last three years 13 of his 17 home runs have come with the bases empty. In fact, 10 of his 17 home runs (59%) have come leading off an inning, although only 22% of his plate appearances have come leading off an inning . . .

7. Terry Kennedy, San Diego

Kennedy is now with Baltimore (boy, will that improve their team speed), and Benito Santiago has the San Diego job. Santiago will probably hit .240–.265 with 10–14 homers and no walks, so his edges on Kennedy are defense and mobility . . . Backup Bruce Bochy blasted 8 home runs and drove in 22 runs last year in just 127 at bats, terrific power rates. Over the last three years he has hit 18 homers in 331 at bats. He improved his K/W ratio last year, too . . .

8. Mike Fitzgerald, Montreal

His arm is pretty poor, but over the last two years the Expos are 92–62 with Fitzgerald catching and 70–98 without him. Pretty strange, huh? . . .

9. Mike LaValliere, St. Louis

Had fine defensive stats, cut off

the running game well and the Cardinals had a 3.10 staff ERA with him catching. On the other hand, he's 25 and he didn't hit . . . The ten most similar rookies were Loren Babe of Pisgah, Iowa (950), Frank Duffy (947), J. C. Martin (946), Roger Freed (945), Cito Gaston (939), Ted Uhlaender (938), Dick Hall (936), Lloyd Merriman (933), Tim Cullen (929), and Marv Blaylock (924). The group is similar to Allanson's comparables but a little better; the best is Cito Gaston, who had one great year as a hitter. Well, the best was probably Dick Hall, who moved to the mound and had a good career, but the best hitter was Gaston. The weighted average of the ten: 632 major-league games, 394 hits, 25 homers, 166 RBI, .240 average.

10. Alan Ashby, Houston

The Astros had a sensational 60–27 record with Ashby catching, as opposed to 22–22 with Bailey, although the staff ERA actually was better with Bailey . . .

11. Ozzie Virgil, Atlanta

Sub Bruce Benedict was throwing very well last year, with opponents stealing only 27 bases in 49 games . . . Virgil was a disaster, didn't hit, didn't do the job defensively, and has no speed . . .

12. John Russell, Philadelphia

His bat is good enough that he'll probably be around a while. He'd be better off in the American League where they don't run so much and he'd have more home run parks to play with . . .

FIRST BASEMEN

American League

1. Don Mattingly, New York (14)

At the start of a player's career anything is possible. Don's four years into his career now, and anything is still possible. The career record for RBI (which you *never* hear anybody mention) is 2,297, by Aaron. Aaron and Ruth are the only men to reach 2,000 RBI. I estimate that Mattingly has almost a 20% chance to become the third, which at this stage of his career is astonishing. And, while you can't look 15 or 17 years down the road, he hasn't yet proven that he won't threaten Aaron's mark. Maybe he'll break it the same day he breaks Rose's record for career hits . . .

1986 Power/Speed Number: 0
Career Power/Speed Number: 5.8
Extra base hits as a percentage of hits, 1986: .36
Times in Scoring Position: 86
Runs Scored as a Percentage of Times on Base: .401
Runs per Time on Base/Not Home Run: .330
Batting Average When Not Striking Out: .371
Batting Average When Not Striking Out or Homering: .339
1986 Speed Score: 3.5
1986 Secondary Average: .300
Career Secondary Average: .286
Chance of getting 2000 career hits: .84
Chance of getting 2500 career hits: .64
Chance of getting 3000 career hits: .39
Chance of getting 3500 career hits: .23
Chance of getting 4000 career hits: .12
Chance of getting 4500 career hits: .04
Chance of getting 5000 career hits:
 None Established
Chance of getting 300 career home runs: .82
Chance of getting 400 career home runs: .41
Chance of getting 500 career home runs: 19
Chance of getting 600 career home runs: .05
Chance of getting 700 career home runs:
 None Established
Chance of getting 938 career stolen bases:
 None Established
Chance of getting 1500 career runs scored: .35
Chance of getting 1750 career runs scored: .20
Chance of getting 2000 career runs scored: .10
Chance of getting 2250 career runs scored: .02
Chance of getting 2500 career runs scored:
 None Established
Chance of getting 1500 career RBI: .51
Chance of getting 1750 career RBI: .32
Chance of getting 2000 career RBI: .19
Chance of getting 2250 career RBI: .10
Chance of getting 2500 career RBI: .03
Chance of getting 2750 career RBI:
 None Established

2. Eddie Murray, Baltimore

Clutch stats over the last three years are awesome . . . When Eddie Murray was a rookie in 1977, the most-similar rookie to him in the 1948–1975 period was Jim Ray Hart. But the top ten would have included Jim Rice, Willie Horton, Billy Williams, and Willie Mays . . . Projected career totals by Brock6: 2,520 hits, 383 homers, 1,450 RBI, .293 average.

3. Pete O'Brien, Texas

Magnificent player, very similar to Keith Hernandez except he has more power.

4. Kent Hrbek, Minnesota

Had great first half using a new batting stance, faded badly in second half. I'm betting on 1987 to be his best season . . .

5. Wally Joyner, California

Of the ten players in the 1948–1975 period who were most similar to Wally Joyner as rookies, all ten had extremely disappointing careers. I mean, it's stunning. None of them fulfilled his potential. None of them fulfilled half of his potential. Only one or two could be classed as anything except a tremendous disappointment. Let's run them down:

The most similar rookie to Wally Joyner was Tom Tresh, 1962 Yankees. Age: Same. Both players were 24. Batting averages: .290 and .286. Homers: 22 and 20. RBI: 100 and 93. Walks: 57 and 67. Stolen Bases: 5 and 4. Runs: 82 and 94. Doubles: 27 and 26. The biggest difference between them is that Tresh was a shortstop, resulting in a similarity score of 943.

Tresh is a famous disappointment. He never had as good a season again, and washed out of the league after hitting .219, .195 and .211 from 1967 to 1969.

Tresh, however, was the *best* of

the ten comparables. Tresh played 1,192 major-league games and hit 153 homers. None of the other nine men reached those levels. The second most similar rookie was also in the AL in 1962, in Rich Rollins (.298, 16 homers, 96 RBI, 24 years old). Rollins never drove in more than 68 runs again, and became a bench warmer after hitting .249 with 5 homers in 1965. The third most-similar rookie was Jim Greengrass in 1953 (.285, 20 homers, 100 RBI, 25 years old). Greengrass lasted only one more season as a regular before he suddenly stopped hitting. Fourth most-similar was Pete Ward in 1963 (.295, 22 homers, 84 RBI, 23 years old). He had one more good year and stopped hitting. Fifth most-similar was Billy Grabarkewitz in 1970. Sixth was Ed Bouchee in 1957. Neither ever had another comparable season. All those guys had similarity sources of 924 or higher. Seventh was Irv Noren in 1950. Same thing. Eighth was Max Alvis in 1963. In his sophomore year he got spinal meningitis, never had as good a year again. Ninth and tenth were Bob Nieman and Randy Jackson. Neither one developed, although Nieman was arguably the best player among the ten. The weighted average of the career of the ten most-similar rookies to Wally Joyner: 897 major league games, 89 home runs, 764 hits, .262 average.

6. Alvin Davis, Seattle

According to the *Seattle Baseball Bulletin* (P.O. Box 221, Redmond, WA 98073), Alvin Davis had 49 3–0 counts in 1986, most of any Mariner. After going 3–0 he drew 30 walks and in the remaining 19 at bats had 7 hits including 3 home runs, also most among the Mariners . . . Davis had only 68 0–2 counts (Jim Presley had 144), but even down 0–2 hit .235 (16 for 68) with 3 homers and 7 walks. He was by far the Mariners' best hitter after getting down 0–2; the team average after hitters went 0–2 was .155 . . .

7. Greg Walker, Chicago

Over the last three years 76% of his RBI have come in close games . . .

8. Darrell Evans, Detroit

My, what a good player he has been for such a long time. He's almost a prototype of an unrecognized star: low average but excellent secondary average, grounds into extremely few double plays (still), was for a long time the second-best defensive third baseman in the National League. Even last year his secondary average was .387, seventh in the league . . .

9. Pat Tabler, Cleveland

Over the last three years Tabler has hit .313 on grass fields, but just .203 on artificial turf . . . Tabler gets stronger as the year goes on, and over three years has hit .320 with runners in scoring position. He has also driven in 64% of his runners on third base with less than two out (56/88), which is very good . . .

10. Steve Balboni, Kansas City

At this writing is a free agent with back trouble. Still expect him to return to KC, but he would hit better in almost any other park.

11. Bill Buckner, Boston

The Brock6 system projects him to finish his career with 2,801 career hits, including 194 homers. He's got a good chance to beat that and reach 3,000, but the Brock6 system evaluates him as no longer good enough to play everyday. I agree, but he has, over the last three years, hit .359 in the late innings of close games, and he did get red hot in the pennant race . . . Does this jerk ever stop complaining? I videotaped the playoffs and World Series and have been watching them over and over. Buckner was mad about something from beginning to end. Every single time a strike was called on him he bitched about it. One time there was a pick-off play at first, and he slapped a tag on the runner about a half-second late—not really close. He screamed at the umpire for not calling the guy out. In the eighth inning of the fourth game of the Playoff, Saturday in California, he tried to make a play on a ball back in the seats and a fan wouldn't make room for him. Buckner wanted to go into the stands and beat the guy up. I mean, the fan had as much right to the ball as Buckner did. Then after the Series he reportedly told the reporters that they were all assholes and didn't know anything about baseball. Bill Buckner, a man who knows his assholes.

12. Willie Upshaw, Toronto

A fast starter, has hit .315 and slugged .573 in April over last three years, with his second-best slugging percentage being .469 in July . . . hits much better at night (.285) than in day games (.237) . . . though occasionally platooned, he really doesn't have a platoon differential. . .

It's really strange to see Willie Upshaw, who hit 27 homers and drove in 104 runs just three years ago, playing like a leadoff man. Like a *good* leadoff man, mind you; he drew 78 walks and was 23 for 28 as a base stealer, but it's just not what you expect, his hitting 9 home runs.

A Toronto man by the name of David Driscoll does some terrific stuff analyzing the Blue Jays. About Willie Upshaw, for example, he can tell you that Upshaw batted 67 times last year with two runners in scoring position, and went just 13-for-67 (.194), which is why he drove in only 60 runs . . . He can tell you that Willie Upshaw hit .188 with a .208 slugging percentage when he was behind in the count, but .299 with .487 slugging percentage when in control of the count. He can tell you that Willie hit .288 with nobody out, but .227 with two out . . . David Driscoll, P.O. Box 6493, Station D, London, Ontario N5W 5S5.

13. Cecil Cooper, Milwaukee

Now 37, may fight Greg Brock for playing time.

14. Bruce Bochte, Oakland
Retired.

National League

1. Keith Hernandez, New York (12)

1986 Power/Speed Number: 3.5
Career Power/Speed Number: 109.7
Extra base hits as a percentage of hits, 1986: .28
Times in Scoring Position: 50
Runs Scored as a Percentage of Times on Base: .349
Runs Per Time on Base/Not Home Run: .316
Batting Average When Not Striking Out: .355
Batting Average When Not Striking Out or Homering: .337
1986 Speed Score: 3.8
1986 Secondary Average: .310
Career Secondary Average: .310
Chance of getting 2000 career hits: .97
Chance of getting 2500 career hits: .77
Chance of getting 3000 career hits: .22
Chance of getting 3500 career hits: .006
Chance of getting 4000 career hits:
    None Established
Chance of getting 300 career home runs:
    None Established
Chance of getting 938 career stolen bases:
    None Established
Chance of getting 1500 career runs scored: .31
Chance of getting 1750 career runs scored: .05
Chance of getting 2000 career runs scored:
    None Established
Chance of getting 1500 career RBI: .20
Chance of getting 1750 career RBI:
    None Established

2. Von Hayes, Philadelphia

Coming off his best season, hit .305 with 98 RBI. The Phillies will be happy if he stabilizes at 90% of his 1986 production.

3. Glenn Davis, Houston

Did you ever notice that Glenn Davis and his sort of stepbrother have the same initials and two of the same names? Storm's real name is George Earl Davis, and Glenn is Glenn Earl Davis . . . As an MVP candidate, he was one of those (like Carter) who was more a candidate because of the position he occupied in the pennant race than because of what he did. He's a fine player but I'm glad he didn't win the MVP.

4. Bob Horner, Atlanta
Dear Bill:

In *The Sporting News* 1986

Baseball Special, Chuck Tanner is quoted as saying about Bob Horner that "he protects people. He makes everybody in the lineup better." The writer then notes that last year with Horner hitting cleanup behind Dale Murphy, "Murphy hit .291 with 25 homers and 75 RBI in 471 at bats."

To look at the influence of Horner's presence on Murphy's performance, I projected Dale's statistics into a full season with and without Horner. Murphy in 1985 had 616 at bats, with 37 homers, 111 RBI and a .300 average. Projected to 616 at bats with Horner hitting behind him, he would hit .291 with 33 homers and 97 RBI. Projected without Horner, he would hit .331 with 51 homers and 152 RBI.

I'm sure there are problems with taking these projected figures too seriously, but they certainly are not consistent with Tanner's statement. It might be interesting to see if this pattern has been consistent over the years.

—Mark Redston

Dear Mark:

Obviously you haven't been reading the *Abstract* too long. In the 1984 book (page 258) we went back to Day One of Murphy's career and looked at what Murphy had hit when Horner was in the lineup, out of the lineup, hitting behind him, not hitting behind him, etc. Over the years Murphy had hit somewhat better when Horner was out of the lineup. It obviously is nonsense to say that Horner makes Murphy a better hitter, but demonstrating this didn't stop anybody from saying it. It is odd to see people quoting statistics to prove a point when obviously they tend to prove the opposite point, however.

—Bill

5. Jack Clark, St. Louis

Injury prone, needs to stay healthy for Cardinals to have a good chance to come back.

6. Sid Bream, Pittsburgh

Attended Liberty Baptist College in Lynchburg, Virginia.

7. Will Clark, San Francisco

Hit .402 (33/82) in the late innings of close games . . . Of the ten most-comparable rookies to Will Clark, most went on to have pretty good careers. The top ten in alphabetical order were Joe Adcock, Gus Bell, Jackie Brandt, Billy Conigliaro, Bobby Grich, Manny Jimenez, Ted Kluszewski, Hector Lopez, Richie Nebner, and Lee Walls. A weighted average of their career production shows 1,399 games, 1,267 hits, 165 homers, 658 RBI and a .274 average. Five of the ten players had more than 1,500 career hits, and three of the ten hit over 200 homers.

8. Leon Durham, Chicago

1986 Power/Speed Number: 11.4
Career Power/Speed Number: 109.7
Extra base hits as a percentage of hits, 1986: .35
Times in Scoring Position: 53
Runs Scored as a Percentage of Times on Base: .338
Runs Per Time on Base/Not Home Run: .263
Batting Average When Not Striking Out: .329
Batting Average When Not Striking Out or Homering: .292
1986 Speed Score: 5.1
1986 Secondary Average: .345
Career Secondary Average: .354
Chance of getting 2000 career hits: .35
Chance of getting 2500 career hits: .09
Chance of getting 3000 career hits: None Established
Chance of getting 300 career home runs: .32
Chance of getting 400 career home runs: .03
Chance of getting 500 career home runs: None Established
Chance of getting 938 career stolen bases: None Established
Chance of getting 1500 career runs scored: None Established
Chance of getting 1500 career RBI: .008
Chance of getting 1750 career RBI: None Established

9. Andres Gallaraga, Montreal

The ten most-similar rookies to Andres Gallaraga were Ramon Webster, 1967 (943), Kent Hadley, 1959 (943), Rich McKinney, 1971 (935), Joe Ginsberg, 1951 (922), Jerry Adair, 1961 (921), Alan Gallagher, 1970 (917), Tony Gonzalez, 1960 (917), Don Baylor, 1972 (914), Jim King, 1955 (911), and Tony Perez, 1965 (911) . . . There are some good ones down there at the bottom. The weighted average of the ten players' careers is 1,085 games, 919 hits, 107 homers and a .265 average—better than Wally Joyner's comps, but still not great. Still, if he develops like Baylor or Perez, that's pretty good . . .

10. Greg Brock, Los Angeles

Now with Milwaukee . . . Hit just .069 (4/58) in the late innings of close games.

11. Steve Garvey, San Diego

The Padres would do better if they'd release Garvey and play Carmello Martinez at first.

12. Nick Esasky, Cincinnati

Still searching for some consistency.

SECOND BASEMEN

National League

1. Ryne Sandberg, Chicago (7)

Has three-year averages of .234 in April, .340 in May . . . of his 59 homers in the last three years, 36 have been hit in Wrigley Field . . .

1986 Power/Speed Number: 19.8
Career Power/Speed Number: 106.4
Extra base hits as a percentage of hits, 1986: .264
Times in Scoring Position: 81
Runs Scored as a Percentage of Times on Base: .303
Runs Per Time on Base/Not Home Run: .257
Batting Average When Not Striking Out: .325
Batting Average When Not Striking Out or Homering: .307
1986 Speed Score: 6.1
1986 Secondary Average: .255
Career Secondary Average: .281
Chance of getting 2000 career hits: .83
Chance of getting 2500 career hits: .47
Chance of getting 3000 career hits: .24
Chance of getting 3500 career hits: .10
Chance of getting 4000 career hits: None established
Chance of getting 300 career home runs: .20
Chance of getting 400 career home runs: None established
Chance of getting 938 career stolen bases: None established
Chance of getting 1500 career runs scored: .26
Chance of getting 1750 career runs scored: .11
Chance of getting 2000 career runs scored: .006
Chance of getting 2250 career runs scored: None established
Chance of getting 1500 career RBI: .008
Chance of getting 1750 career RBI: None established

2. Steve Sax, Los Angeles (6)

Had a terrific season. I think I've written that winning a batting title in Dodger Stadium is probably at least 15 to 20 times as difficult as winning a batting title in a good hitter's park. Sax almost pulled it off, hitting .310 in Dodger Stadium but .352 on the road to miss the title by two points. He hit .387 on artificial turf, and .370 in the late innings of close games . . . his slugging percentage was a hundred points higher on the road than in Dodger Stadium (.489–.389), and over the last three years he has hit .265 in Dodger Stadium, but .306 on the road . . . over same three years his batting average in the late innings of close games is .322 . . .

Dear Bill:

We've heard a lot this year about Kirby Puckett's increase in home runs, but very little about Steve Sax's remarkable increase in doubles. In 1985 Steve Sax had the ridiculously low total of 8 doubles. He passed that on May 20, 1986, and went on to hit 43. This got me to wondering whether any other players had increased their doubles to such a degree. These are the largest increases in doubles following seasons of 300 or more at bats:

Player, Year	From	To	Gain
Earl Webb, 1931	30	67	+37
Billy Herman, 1935	21	57	+36
Steve Sax, 1986	8	43	+35
Gino Cimoli, 1959	6	40	+34
Gee Walker, 1936	22	55	+33
Enos Slaughter, 1939	20	52	+32
Robin Yount, 1982	15	45	+31
Walt Wilmot, 1894	14	45	+31

In addition to Sax and Cimoli, four other players went from less than ten doubles in seasons of 200–300 at bats to forty or more; those were Don Kolloway, Ethan Allen, Dick Bartell and Beau Bell.

Sincerely,
Ken Banta

3. Bill Doran, Houston (1)

Not a great baserunner—42 for 61 as a base stealer, grounded into 10 double plays, led the National League in the number of times caught stealing (19). Still, 81 walks and 42 stolen bases make him a pretty decent leadoff man. By reputation and observation he's a terrific defensive second baseman, although his defensive stats last year would not have suggested this. A pitching staff of Scott, Ryan, etc., could cut down the number of plays available for a second baseman.

4. Johnny Ray, Pittsburgh

Over last three years has hit only .282 in Three Rivers, but .313 on the road . . . has driven in 26% of his

runners in scoring position with two out, which is outstanding.

5. Juan Samuel, Philadelphia

Another thing that you could study using the speed scores would be the decline in speed by players at different positions—that is, how fast does a second baseman tend to lose his speed, as opposed to an outfielder, etc? I'm quite certain that a player who plays a position which demands speed will retain his speed much better than a player who plays a position at which speed is not used. Von Hayes, for example, will lose his speed much faster as a first baseman than he would if he were in the outfield. It's a rule of life that you tend to lose whatever skills you don't use.

6. Wally Backman, New York

His 1986 stats were almost identical to his 1985 stats *against right-handed pitching*. The top line below is his 1985 record against right-handed pitching; the bottom line is his complete 1986 record:

AB	H	2B	3B	HR	Avg.
389	126	20	5	1	.324
387	124	18	2	1	.320

The difference was that in 1985 he ruined his overall stats by batting 131 times against left-handers, hitting .122. In 1986 he had Teufel around so that he didn't have to. Still, the Mets get into post-season play and Brent Musburger goes on the air and tells the nation that for the Mets to win, they've got to get Backman and Dykstra in there every day, and he can't understand why Johnson can't see how important Backman is as a catalyst to the offense . . . Davey Johnson must want to just murder people like us.

7. Robby Thompson, San Francisco

Led National League in sacrifice bunts, with 18 . . . The ten most-similar rookies to Robby Thompson were Mike Andrews, Jim Busby, Roy Hartsfield, Tommy Helms, Albie Pearson, Bob Rodgers, Ted Sizemore, Bill Tuttle, George Vico, and Davey Williams. Four of the ten men played a thousand or more major league games, including the one most similar (Sizemore). The weighted average of their careers: 928 games, 810 hits, 35 homers and a .260 average.

8. Tommie Herr, St. Louis

Since I became a baseball fan in 1960, about a dozen men have had big RBI years without hitting for power. None of them has ever been able to sustain it for more than one year. Floyd Robinson in '62 drove in 109 runs with only 11 homers. The next year he drove in just 71. Wes Parker in 1970 drove in 111 with only 10 homers. The next year he drove in only 62. Carew in 1977 drove in a hundred runs with just 14 homers. In 1978 he drove in only 70.

Sometimes a team short of power will decide to try a singles-and-doubles hitter in the third spot in the lineup, figuring that if he hits the singles with men in scoring position and the doubles with men on first it will work out. Sometimes it will work for a year, but in effect you're expecting a player to deliver hits on demand, and it's almost impossible for a hitter to respond to that kind of pressure over a sustained period.

9. Ron Oester, Cincinnati

Over last three years has hit just .204 in April, putting him a long way behind his overall .265 average . . . consistent, unremarkable player . . .

10. Glenn Hubbard, Atlanta

I am absolutely baffled by why the Braves' managers have so much trouble seeing what a good ballplayer this guy is. I mean, I know that he's slow and doesn't hit for average, but look at the positives:

1) Excellent strike zone judgment—66 walks last year in less than 500 plate appearances.

2) Tremendous ability to turn the double play—as good as anybody in the game today.

3) A little power, enough to hit 30 doubles and 10 homers in a good year.

4) Avoids the double play, grounding into only 5 last year.

5) Tremendous hustle on defense.

6) Intelligent, heads-up baserunning.

You would think that Atlanta managers, struggling with this awful, inept, inert team, would just love to put Glenn Hubbard in the lineup and let him play, hoping that his attitude would infect some of the rest of the team. Instead, they seem determined to replace him. Last year's manager played Ken Oberkfell at second base in part or all of 41 games, playing Rafael Ramirez at third and Andres Thomas at short. I just can't understand what the thinking is. In what respect does this improve the team? What can an infield of Horner, Oberkfell, Thomas, and Ramirez do better than an infield of Horner, Hubbard, Thomas, and Oberkfell? Hit singles? Commit errors? Fall down? Fall down and commit errors?

If you watch the Braves for about two weeks, you will understand perfectly why Ted Turner would think that *Casablanca* would be a better movie in pastels. The man loves mediocrity. He worships mediocrity. He sends his announcers to mediocrity school, where they listen to tapes of Jay Randolph and Curt Gowdy 16 hours a day. He collects mediocre players and mediocre pitchers and hires mediocre managers to direct them. *Colorless* mediocre players. I mean, it's no wonder their attendance is terrible, and no reflection on the fine people of Atlanta, who are merely exercising a modicum of good taste in not taking this team to their hearts.

11. Tim Flannery, San Diego

The ten most similar rookies to Bip Roberts, surprisingly, weren't all that bad; they contained Dave Concepcion and several guys like Elliot Maddox, who at least had careers. The weighted average of the ten is 1,002 major league games, 785 hits, .258 average . . . Flannery remains a good platoon player, Royster too. Second base is a tough position to platoon at, inasmuch as it is in the absolute center of the field and thus in the middle of all defensive plays requiring teamwork (double plays, relays from the outfield, rundown plays). But it's a good platoon combination.

12. Vance Law, Montreal

He's not a bad player, actually; he just had some family things on his mind and didn't have a good year, and all twelve NL teams have decent second basemen so somebody's got to rate last. Brent MacInnes, team captain for Project Scoresheet in Montreal, does complete breakdowns of how every player did in every inning situation—for example, Vance Law batted 12 times with a runner on second and one man out, and went six-for-twelve, driving in the runner four times. Brent argues that, because Law hit well in key "run" situations, he actually helped the Expos even last year. Law hit .186 with the bases empty, but .281 with men on first and .268 with runners in scoring position. Brent has a method for evaluating these things, which I don't understand, but it does say that Tim Raines and Hubie Brooks were by far the best players on the team, so it seems reasonable. The method shows Law as adding 2.9 runs to the Expo offense—not much, but at least in the right column.

American League

1. Frank White, Kansas City (5)

1986 Power/Speed Number: 6.8
Career Power/Speed Number: 146.4
Extra base hits as a percentage of hits, 1986: .40
Times in Scoring Position: 66
Runs Scored as a Percentage of Times on Base: .382
Runs Per Time on Base/Not Home Run: .305
Batting Average When Not Striking Out: .322
Batting Average When Not Striking Out or Homering: .289
1986 Speed Score: 4.8
1986 Secondary Average: .276
Career Secondary Average: .210
Chance of getting 2000 career hits: .55
Chance of getting 2500 career hits:
    None Established
Chance of getting 300 career home runs:
    None Established
Chance of getting 938 career stolen bases:
    None Established
Chance of getting 1500 career runs scored:
    None Established
Chance of getting 1500 career RBI:
    None Established

2. Tony Bernazard, Cleveland (6)

Had his best offensive season, hitting .301 with 17 homers and 73 RBI, 53 walks and 17 stolen bases, grounded into only 6 double plays. Offensively, you know, he's only had one off season in his career, 1984. He's had five pretty good years with the bat since 1981, hits for a decent average with medium-range power, walks and steals bases. Defensively, he's not everything you might hope for.

3. Lou Whitaker, Detroit (3)

Whitaker and Trammell have now been the Tigers' regular double play combination since 1978, or for nine years. Whitaker has now played 1,264 games at second base in his career.

The top ten men in career games played at second are Eddie Collins, Joe Morgan, Nellie Fox, Charlie Gehringer, Bid McPhee, Bill Mazeroski, Nap Lajoie, Bobby Doerr, Red Schoendienst, and Billy Herman. None of those men played nine full years with the same shortstop. Charlie Gehringer and Billy Rogell—another part of the fabulous Tiger tradition of stability—played longer together than any other combination, seven full years and parts of three others. Joe Morgan and Dave Concepcion played together for eight years. Bill Mazeroski played six and a half years with Dick Groat, plus five full years and parts of three others with Gene Alley. Fox and Aparicio were together for seven years—the same years as Mazeroski and Groat (1956–1962). The others mostly played five or six years with one man, but no longer.

Tinker and Evers played together from 1902 to 1912, which is eleven years, but Tinker played only 26 games in 1902, 99 in 1905, and 46 in 1911. As to Reese and Robinson, Jackie Robinson played only 751 major league games as a second baseman.

So it seems unlikely that any double play combination before Whitaker and Trammell has ever been together for nine solid years. I don't know of any that has. If Whitaker and Trammell haven't already broken the major league record for games played as a double play combination, they probably will break it this year.

4. Marty Barrett, Boston

It will be interesting to see how he handles his newfound fame. He's been a good, quiet player for three years, but the word is out about him now.

5. Willie Randolph, New York

1986 Power/Speed Number: 7.5
Career Power/Speed Number: 66.8
Extra base hits as a percentage of hits, 1986: .16
Times in Scoring Position: 37
Runs Scored as a Percentage of Times on Base: .326
Runs Per Time on Base/Not Home Run: .311
Batting Average When Not Striking Out: .307
Batting Average When Not Striking Out or Homering: .300
1986 Speed Score: 5.4
1986 Secondary Average: .291
Career Secondary Average: .281
Chance of getting 2000 career hits: .90
Chance of getting 2500 career hits: .27
Chance of getting 3000 career hits: .01
Chance of getting 3500 career hits:
    None Established
Chance of getting 300 career home runs:
    None Established
Chance of getting 938 career stolen bases:
    None Established
Chance of getting 1500 career runs scored: .19
Chance of getting 1750 career runs scored:
    None Established
Chance of getting 1500 career RBI:
    None Established

6. Tony Phillips, Oakland

Injuries continue to dog him; played tremendously well early in the season. Was on target to draw a hundred walks and score a hundred runs when his season was ended.

7. Jim Gantner, Milwaukee

See Milwaukee team comment.

8. Damaso Garcia, Toronto

The difference between what he hits when behind in the count and what he hits when ahead in the count is smaller than it is for most players, which in part may explain why he has never regarded plate discipline as essential. He hit .243 when behind in the count last year, .308 when ahead in the count. Most of the Blue Jays were in the ones when hitting from behind . . .

9. Bobby Grich, California

Probably retiring. I will miss him; he's always been a favorite of mine.

One of the peculiar things about the American League in 1986 is that second base was the *oldest* position. The second basemen were older, on the average, than the players at any other spot except designated hitter. Usually second base is a young man's spot. Kids come up and play it for three or four years, and are gone as soon as they lose a step. The American League has had four outstanding second basemen for a decade (White, Whitaker, Randolph, and Grich), which is very unusual, and combined with Harrah they drive the average age way up. There were several other veterans at the position (Garcia, Bernazard, and Gantner).

10. Steve Lombardozzi, Minnesota

The ten most-similar rookies to Lombardozzi, alphabetically, were Ken Berry, Bobby Cox, Phil Garner, Pete Mackanin, Freddie Marsh of Valley Falls, Kansas, Jose Pagan, Virgil Stallcup, Jimmy Stewart, George Strickland, and Wayne Terwilliger. Three of the ten men played a thousand or more major-league games (Berry, Garner, and Pagan), with weighted averages of 900 games, 651 hits, 37 homers, 259 RBI and a .246 batting average. What the ten men have in common is obvious: Almost all of them stayed in baseball forever as coaches or managers or something. I think Berry is managing in the Royals' system now. So get used to hearing Lombardozzi's name, because I guess we're going to be hearing it for thirty years or so.

11. Harold Reynolds, Seattle

Glove man, not quite as bad an offensive player as his triple crown stats would suggest. The *Seattle Baseball Bulletin* says that he batted 31 times with a runner on first and nobody out, and got the man to second 16 times, which is above average. He is overmatched by some pitchers, as is reflected in the fact that he was 5-for-62 (.081) after the count started out 0–2.

12. Toby Harrah, Texas

Final stats projected by Brock6: 2,142 games, 212 home runs, 1,302 RBI, 1,302 walks . . . actually, he's a good candidate not to be back next year.

Chicago and Baltimore, Vacant

White Sox seem to have the position covered with Perconte and Donnie Hill. Baltimore has signed Burleson, who may or may not solve the problem for a couple of years.

THIRD BASEMEN

American League

1. Wade Boggs, Boston (14)

Hit .359 against right-handed pitchers, best in the league, and .352 against lefties, fourth in the league . . . Was second in the league in hitting both at home (.357, 10 points behind Puckett) and on the road (.356, 11 points behind Mattingly) . . . hit .380 on artificial turf, also second in the league behind Mattingly, and .352 on grass fields, second in the league behind Gaetti . . .

1986 Power/Speed Number: 0
Career Power/Speed Number: 14.0
Extra base hits as a percentage of hits, 1986: .28
Times in Scoring Position: 57
Runs Scored as a Percentage of Times on Base: .343
Runs Per Time on Base/Not Home Run: .326
Batting Average When Not Striking Out: .386
Batting Average When Not Striking Out or Homering: .377
1986 Speed Score: 3.6
1986 Secondary Average: .310
Career Secondary Average: .264
Chance of getting 2000 career hits: .87
Chance of getting 2500 career hits: .53
Chance of getting 3000 career hits: .27
Chance of getting 3500 career hits: .12
Chance of getting 4000 career hits: .02
Chance of getting 4500 career hits: None Established
Chance of getting 300 career home runs: None Established
Chance of getting 938 career stolen bases: None Established
Chance of getting 1500 career runs scored: .25
Chance of getting 1750 career runs scored: .11
Chance of getting 2000 career runs scored: .06
Chance of getting 2250 career runs scored: None Established
Chance of getting 1500 career RBI: None Established

2. George Brett, Kansas City

Projected career totals by Brock6:

G	AB	R	H	2B	3B	HR	RBI	BB	Avg.
2803	10180	1682	3093	641	131	331	1554	1284	.304

3. Gary Gaetti, Minnesota

Murdered left-handers in 1986, hitting .344 with .603 slugging percentage . . . was fourth in the American League in hitting in road games, at .323, and hit 18 home runs in neutral parks . . . and in the "grass" parks, he hit .364 (best in the league)

and slugged .645, with 16 homers in 228 at bats . . .

4. Doug DeCinces, California

Sometime I've got to go back and figure out Doug's career batting record in August. I remember years and years ago, before the *Abstract* was national, commenting that he always started slow but had a tremendous hitting record in August. He still does it. Last year he hit .337 in August with 9 homers and 25 RBI, whereas he hit .211 in May with 2 and 11. Over the last three years his slugging percentage is .545 in August, .356 in May . . .

5. Jim Presley, Seattle

Cut his double play balls to 18, after grounding into 29 in 1985 . . . strikeouts increased from a hundred to 172 . . . The *Seattle Baseball Bulletin* says that he had only 71 3–2 counts in 1986, which isn't many (Phil Bradley had 116, Alvin Davis 91 and Ken Phelps 106 in much less playing time). Whereas every other Mariner walked more often on a 3–2 count than he struck out except Tartabull (34–37), Presley struck out 28 times on 3–2 pitches and walked only 19 . . . the count went 0–2 on him 144 times last year, almost once a game. He hit just .176 on those at bats, and hit just one home run after the count started out 0–2 . . .

6. Brook Jacoby, Cleveland

In 1986 hit .370 in the late innings of close games.

7. Mike Pagliarulo, New York

Really hasn't hit a thing against left-handed pitchers, .201 over three years (50/249) with little power . . . has faded badly in September.

8. Paul Molitor, Milwaukee

Played well when healthy last year, hitting .281, stealing 20 bases in 25 attempts, playing a pretty good third base. The Brewers may play Sveum at third base, but I sure

wouldn't. Molitor started 25 double plays in 91 games at third base; Sveum started 8 in 65 games . . .

9. Darnell Coles, Detroit

The book on him a year ago was that he *probably* would hit, although he hadn't in 102 major-league games, but probably would not be too strong on defense. The difference now is that you can remove the "probablies" and the "althoughs." He did hit very well, 30 doubles as well as 20 homers, 86 RBI and 45 walks. As a defensive player, he didn't make anyone forget Tom Brookens . . .

10. Carney Lansford, Oakland

1986 Power/Speed Number: 17.4
Career Power/Speed Number: 110.4
Extra base hits as a percentage of hits, 1986: .23
Times in Scoring Position: 55
Runs Scored as a Percentage of Times on Base: .377
Runs Per Time on Base/Not Home Run: .316
Batting Average When Not Striking Out: .311
Batting Average When Not Striking Out or Homering: .286
1986 Speed Score: 5.1
1986 Secondary Average: .230
Career Secondary Average: .232
Chance of getting 2000 career hits: .87
Chance of getting 2500 career hits: .33
Chance of getting 3000 career hits: .09
Chance of getting 3500 career hits: None Established
Chance of getting 300 career home runs: .07
Chance of getting 400 career home runs: None Established
Chance of getting 938 career stolen bases: None Established
Chance of getting 1500 career runs scored: .02
Chance of getting 1750 career runs scored: None Established
Chance of getting 1500 career RBI: None Established

11. Rance Mulliniks, Toronto

When behind in the count, Mulliniks in 1986 hit .132 (9/68). When ahead in the count, he hit .430 (37/86) . . . with men on third base he hit .357 (10/28) . . .

12. Steve Buechele, Texas

His power was a surprise, hitting 18 homers in less than 500 plate appearances, but he is a good-sized guy

(6'2", 190 pounds). He's a real good defensive third baseman. Late in the season he was playing second base quite a bit (33 games), and he also did an excellent job there. He played both positions well in the minor leagues, so this wasn't a real surprise. He might play second or third this year, depending on how the needs of the team develop. The only thing Buechele hasn't done in the majors that he ought to do is hit with men on base.

The Rangers have good young infielders in their system, although no one of them who stands out above the others . . . Mike Stanley, a catcher/infielder, hit .294 in AA ball, with a secondary average over .300, then went to Oklahoma City (AAA) and hit OK, .366 in 56 games, with a secondary average almost .400, then got called up to the Rangers and hit .333 in 15 games with a secondary average of .333. He looks like he's going to play somewhere, and if it's

a question of forcing Don Slaught or Curtis Wilkerson out of the lineup, you know who it's going to be . . .

13. Tim Hulett, Chicago

Had among the worst situation stats in baseball, hitting .160 in the late innings of close games and .175 with runners in scoring position. He reverted to his minor-league form last year, hitting for power but with a lower average . . .

14. Baltimore (Vacant)

National League

1. Mike Schmidt, Philadelphia (12)

As an old guy, he naturally wears down as the season goes on. In the last three years he's batted 585 times after August 1, about one season's worth. His totals after August 1 are 48 homers, 128 RBI, 34 doubles, .299 average with .620 slugging percentage . . . Philadelphia writers used to claim that he hit most of his home runs in the early innings. In the three years for which we have data he has hit .306 in the late innings of close games, with 17 homers in 271 at bats . . . Hit .354 against left-handers, second-best in the league, and slugged .703 . . . Projected career stats by Brock6:

G	AB	R	H	2B	3B	HR	RBI	BB	Avg
2856	9673	1784	2573	468	64	621	1805	1719	.266

1986 Power/Speed Number: 1.9
Career Power/Speed Number: 252.0
Extra base hits as a percentage of hits, 1986: .42
Times in Scoring Position: 68
Runs Scored as a Percentage of Times on Base: .379
Runs Per Time on Base/Not Home Run: .274
Batting Average When Not Striking Out: .341
Batting Average When Not Striking Out or Homering: .285
1986 Speed Score: 3.3
1986 Secondary Average: .420
Career Secondary Average: .476
Chance of getting 2000 career hits: .99
Chance of getting 2500 career hits: .18
Chance of getting 3000 career hits: None Established
Chance of getting 500 career home runs: .996
Chance of getting 600 career home runs: .31
Chance of getting 700 career home runs: None Established
Chance of getting 938 career stolen bases: None Established
Chance of getting 1500 career runs scored: .95
Chance of getting 1750 career runs scored: .06

Chance of getting 2000 career runs scored: None Established
Chance of getting 1500 career RBI: .97
Chance of getting 1750 career RBI: .23
Chance of getting 2000 career RBI: None Established

2. Buddy Bell, Cincinnati

Projected career totals by Brock6:

G	AB	R	H	2B	3B	HR	RBI	BB	Avg
2683	9687	1284	2674	470	59	218	1179	933	.276

3. Chris Brown, San Francisco

Just 25, good defense (except when he was trying to play with a bum shoulder), has hit .300, has hit for power, improving K/W ratio, speed above average for a third baseman, complaints about his attitude diminished last year . . . if he works hard and the shoulder comes back, he should be the best in the league in a couple of years.

4. Denny Walling, Houston

Grade-A platoon player, good defense, good, consistent left-handed hitter with power. Hit .333 against right-handed pitchers, fifth-best in the league, and with a slugging percentage well over .500 (against right-handers) . . . Garner (right-handed platoon half) is still a good player, too.

5. Tim Wallach, Montreal

Over last three seasons has hit .314 in April, but only .199 in September. During same period has hit only 19 home runs in Montreal, 39 on the road . . . has no platoon differential . . . with no one on base and

two out Wallach batted 54 times and had only 5 hits, an .093 average . . .

6. Jim Morrison, Pittsburgh

Has only played regularly twice in his career and had good years with the bat both times. In 1980 he played second base for the White Sox, hit .283 with 40 doubles and 15 homers. The Sox complained about his defense a lot and he got hurt, so he went back to the bench for five years before he got another shot, then had an even better season. He's 34 and really not a very good defensive player, so time is not on his side, but you have to give credit to Jim Leyland for realizing that what he had was better than just fooling around there with minor leaguers and fringe players, like Baltimore was doing.

7. Ken Oberkfell, Atlanta

Here's another Chuck Tanner mystery for you—why on earth won't he let this guy bat leadoff? Last year Oberkfell hit his usual .270, while Omar Moreno hit .234, Andres Thomas finished at .251, and Rafael Ramirez hit .240. Oberkfell drew 83 walks, while Moreno drew 21, Thomas drew 8, and Ramirez drew 21. Oberkfell was 7 for 11 as a base stealer (64%), while Moreno was 17 for 33 (52%) and Thomas was 4 for 6 (40%), although Ramirez did have a good year running (19 for 27).

Now, one assumes that the identifying characteristics of a leadoff man are 1) hitting for average, 2) a good batting eye, and 3) successful baserunning. So why in tarnation would Chuck Tanner alternate Moreno, Ramirez and Thomas in the leadoff spot with Oberkfell hitting sixth and seventh? Quite simply, because he never really thinks about what a player can do, in concrete terms, to help put runs on the scoreboard. He manages strictly on *images,* and Oberkfell doesn't *look* like a leadoff man. That's as profound as Tanner gets.

8. Ray Knight, New York

Hit .384 against left-handers, best in the major leagues. The Mets acted wisely in letting him go. He's got maybe a 15% chance to have as good a season again. He's a smart player, though.

9. Terry Pendleton, St. Louis

Best defensive player at the position in the NL, bat may eventually come around. A lot of managers probably would have given up on him, but Whitey likes the glove.

10. Bill Madlock, Los Angeles

Projected career stats by Brock6: 2,117 games, 2,210 hits, 171 homers, 932 RBI, .299 average . . .

11. Ron Cey, Chicago

Was the Cubs' leading hitter away from Wrigley Field, .311 . . . Projected final career totals by Brock6: 2,308 games, 2,018 hits, 342 homers, 1,233 RBI and .258 average . . . Who is the Cubs' third baseman of the future? The Cubs used five third basemen in 1986: Dave Lopes (age 40), Chris Speier (36), Manny Trillo (35), Ron Cey (38), and Keith Moreland (32). Their AAA third baseman was Bob Bathe, who hit .224 . . . Lopes played 226⅓ innings at third and had the best range of any of the five players, making 2.91 plays per nine innings. There were 730 balls in play with Lopes at third, and Lopes made 73 plays on them, or 10% . . . Keith Moreland played 163⅓ innings, in which there were 548 balls in play, on which Moreland made 42 plays . . .

data courtesy of the *Chicago Baseball Report,* P.O. Box 46074, Chicago, Illinois 60646 . . .

12. Graig Nettles, San Diego

The Padres now have another San Diego native at third base, in Kevin Mitchell. The ten most-similar rookies to Mitchell include some players who went on to have pretty fair careers. He's a somewhat unique talent, and for that reason the most similar rookie is Andre Thornton, 1974, whose similarity score is just 912. Anyway, the ten most similar, alphabetically, are Harry Anderson (Phillies in 1957), Bob Chance (Indians in 1964), Mike Fiore (Royals in 1969), Willie Kirkland, Ted Kluszewski, Lee May, Tony Perez, John Roseboro, Willie Smith (Angels in '64), and Thornton. A weighted average of their major-league careers: 1,269 games, 1,114 hits, 168 homers, 654 RBI, .266 average . . . six of the ten players have played 1,000 major-league games, and five have played over 1,500 . . .

SHORTSTOPS

National League

1. Ozzie Smith, St. Louis (11)

One of the puzzling things about Ozzie is that no matter how well he hits, most people still think of him as a Mark Belanger–type shortstop. He hit .280 last year and drew 79 walks, a tremendous 79/27 K/W ratio. He's hit .272 over the last three years, .293 against left-handed pitching. He's a better offensive player than Luis Aparicio was, and might even steal more bases in his career than Aparicio did . . . over last three years has hit .310 in September . . .

1986 Power/Speed Number: 0
Career Power/Speed Number: 24.9
Extra base hits as a percentage of hits, 1986: .16
Times in Scoring Position: 54
Runs Scored as a Percentage of Times on Base: .298
Runs Per Time on Base/Not Home Run: .298
Batting Average When Not Striking Out: .296
Batting Average When Not Striking Out or Homering: .296
1986 Speed Score: 6.2
1986 Secondary Average: .267
Career Secondary Average: .237
Chance of getting 2000 career hits: .40
Chance of getting 2500 career hits: .06
Chance of getting 3000 career hits: None Established
Chance of getting 300 career home runs: None Established
Chance of getting 938 career stolen bases: None Established
Chance of getting 1500 career runs scored: None Established
Chance of getting 1500 career RBI: None Established

2. Hubie Brooks, Montreal (1)

It's very hard to say exactly where Hubie's offensive skills are at this point. Do we expect him to come out in 1987 and hit around .340 with power, like he was doing last year? Do we expect him to drive in a hundred runs like a couple of years ago? Or do we expect him to hit the way he hit three or four years ago? He has probably changed more from year to year than any other hitter of the eighties, so it's hard to guess what he's going to do in 1987 . . . Hit .361 with the bases empty, just .277 with men in scoring position . . . with the bases empty and two out, he hit .426 (20/47) . . . with runners on first and nobody out he went just 1 for 9 and grounded into five double plays . . . (credit Brent MacInnes for information) . . .

3. Shawon Dunston, Chicago

Terrific young shortstop, can make plays at short that even Ozzie couldn't make . . . led NL shortstops in putouts by 71 (320–249), in assists by 12 (465–453) and in double plays by one (96–95), so the league-leading 32 errors (7 more than second place) really are just in the context of his game. They shouldn't attract as much attention as they do. His .961 fielding percentage was better than Hubie Brooks or Kurt Stillwell as well as, of course, Rafael Ramirez . . . hit just .196 in the late innings of close games . . .

4. Craig Reynolds, Houston

1986 Power/Speed Number: 4.0
Career Power/Speed Number: 40.8
Extra base hits as a percentage of hits, 1986: .21
Times in Scoring Position: 19
Runs Scored as a Percentage of Times on Base: .356
Runs Per Time on Base/Not Home Run: .310
Batting Average When Not Striking Out: .277
Batting Average When Not Striking Out or Homering: .261
1986 Speed Score: 5.1
1986 Secondary Average: .147
Career Secondary Average: .150
Chance of getting 2000 career hits: None Established
Chance of getting 300 career home runs: None Established
Chance of getting 938 career stolen bases: None Established
Chance of getting 1500 career runs scored: None Established
Chance of getting 1500 career RBI: None Established

5. Barry Larkin, Cincinnati

Stillwell played the position most of the year, but Larkin took it over late and, obviously, impressed a lot of people as he did me. The weighted average of the ten most-comparable rookies to Stillwell: 523 major-league games, 350 hits, 10 homers, .241 ca- reer average. Stillwell is regarded as a good glove but no hitter. Larkin is regarded as a good glove who probably will hit some.

A year from now, Larkin just might be rated the number-one man at this position. At Denver he hit .329 with 31 doubles, ten triples and ten homers in 103 games. After being called up to Cincinnati he hit .283, with four more doubles, three triples and three homers and was 8 for 8 as a base stealer, in addition to making only four errors in 36 games at shortstop . . .

6. Mariano Duncan, Los Angeles

Seemed to go backward in all areas except baserunning (he was 48 for 61 as a base stealer). He still looks like he'll be a pretty good offensive shortstop, but his second-season glove problems were puzzling. . .

7. José Uribe, San Francisco

Has hit surprisingly well with men in scoring position—.283 over three years, as opposed to overall .230 average . . .

8. Steve Jeltz, Philadelphia

He's never going to be a hitter, but he drew 65 walks, grounded into only 9 double plays, was 6-for-9 as a base stealer. The Phillies can live with his not hitting too much if he just doesn't do too much damage to the offense. His .320 on-base percentage actually is quite good for a shortstop (compare to Ramirez, .273, Dunston, .278, Stillwell, .309, Reynolds, .274, Duncan, .284, Santana, .285, Belliard, .298, Templeton, .296, and Uribe, .315).

9. Garry Templeton, San Diego

Sometimes used as a leadoff man, but over the last three years has hit only .244 and has .268 on base percentage when leading off an inning . . . in 1986 he hit .336 in the late innings of close games . . .

turned only 60 double plays in 144 games . . .

10. Rafael Ramirez, Atlanta

Andres Thomas actually played more (and better) at shortstop, although Ramirez played more altogether. Thomas has a chance to be OK, but he has a lot of the same problems Ramirez has—makes errors, swings at anything, and runs the bases with his head down. He is better than Ramirez, however.

11. Rafael Santana, New York

Big question is whether Jeffries will get the job this year or next. My guess is that Johnson will make Jeffries start the year at Jackson to keep the press attention off him a little bit, playing Kevin Elster at short. Then, depending on how well Elster handles the job, he can bring Jeffries along and, if Elster proves himself as a major-league shortstop, have a valuable trade commodity for next winter. If Elster doesn't do the job, then Jeffries will get a shot in June or July. I will be extremely surprised if Johnson makes Jeffries play two more years in the minors . . . AAA shortstop was someone named Al Pedrique, who didn't get called up despite hitting .293. AA shortstop was Elster, who hit just .269 at Jackson (equivalent to .230–.240 in Shea), but did draw 61 walks and play good defense.

12. Rafael Belliard, Pittsburgh

Had some positives—26 walks, was 12-for-14 as a base stealer, fielded a solid .970, hit OK with men in scoring position. He still faces a battle to win a place in the majors, but if he maintains those strengths, he won't rate last next year . . . Hit just .167 (5/30) in the late innings of close games.

American League

1. Tony Fernandez, Toronto (8)

Like Garcia, hits almost as well when behind in the count as when ahead. Behind in the count, he hit .274. Ahead in the count, he hit .280, although with more power . . . excellent two-strike hitter, hit .275 with two strikes on him . . . Hit .477 (!) with men on third base (21 for 44, with 34 RBI). With men on third (only) he was 7 for 12, .583. With men on first and third he was 7 for 16, .438. With men on second and third he was 4 for 8, for .500. With the bases loaded he was 3 for 8, .375 . . . Last two seasons has hit .358 and .385 in the month of June . . . led AL shortstops in putouts and fielding percentage . . .

1986 Power/Speed Number: 14.3
Career Power/Speed Number: 22.2
Extra base hits as a percentage of hits, 1986: .24
Times in Scoring Position: 77
Runs Scored as a Percentage of Times on Base: .373
Runs Per Time on Base/Not Home Run: .346
Batting Average When Not Striking Out: .335
Batting Average When Not Striking Out or Homering: .325
1986 Speed Score: 6.6
1986 Secondary Average: .194
Career Secondary Average: .193
Chance of getting 2000 career hits: .63
Chance of getting 2500 career hits: .35
Chance of getting 3000 career hits: .18
Chance of getting 3500 career hits: .07
Chance of getting 4000 career hits: None Established
Chance of getting 300 career home runs: None Established
Chance of getting 938 career stolen bases: None Established
Chance of getting 1500 career runs scored: .08
Chance of getting 1750 career runs scored: None Established
Chance of getting 1500 career RBI: None Established

2. Cal Ripken, Baltimore (6)

In the last three years has hit .333 and slugged .553 in the late innings of close games . . . hits extremely well in the "turf" parks . . . I can't believe his Dad is going to move him to third base. *I* wouldn't do that to his boy; why should he? . . . am looking forward to George Will's book about him . . .

3. Julio Franco, Cleveland

Did you notice how many American League shortstops had good years with the bat? Three AL shortstops hit .300, Fernandez (.310), Franco (.306), and Fletcher (.300). The three F's . . . it wasn't a cheap .300; they averaged 185 hits apiece, with 32 doubles, 6 triples and 8 homers. Two other shortstops belted over 20 homers, Trammell and Ripken. Alfredo Griffin didn't miss .300 by much (.285), and rectified his most glaring weaknesses . . .

Franco has been noted in the past for making errors, but he cut the errors to 18 last year, not bad at all.

4. Alan Trammell, Detroit

Matched Lou Whitaker's batting stats again . . . In 1983 and 1984 he hit over .400 on artificial turf, and was back up to .337 on turf last year . . . hit just .196 with runners on first base last year (20/102).

5. Scott Fletcher, Texas

I've always liked this guy, but not because I thought he was going to hit .300. I've always liked him because I thought he was a good player if he hit .260. His plate discipline, line-drive power, and steady work at shortstop are good enough for me; the .300 average was just a bonus . . .

6. Dick Schofield, California

Cold-weather hitter, best months are April and September, although he did have a hot August last year . . . This guy really is a better offensive player than you might think. Few shortstops have secondary averages as high as their batting averages. Often, if they hit .240, they might have secondary averages of .140. Schofield hit .249 but had 68 extra bases on hits, drew 48 walks and was 23 for 28 as a base stealer, a total of 139 secondary bases, a secondary average over .300. When you factor in that he's still very young—six months younger than Eric Davis—and is a fine shortstop with a good arm . . . well, you've got a ballplayer there.

7. Alfredo Griffin, Oakland

Had a fine year with the bat; finally seems to have taken the notion of not swinging at bad pitches to heart . . . I should make up a register of his most famous base-running incidents sometime. There's no doubt that he pulls off more spectacular basepath commando raids than any player in twenty years, but there's considerable doubt about whether or not his team breaks even on the effort . . . over last three years has hit just .230 in the late innings of close games . . .

8. Earnest Riles, Milwaukee

Yount apparently will open the year at shortstop for the Brew Crew . . . Riles in his two years has hit .319 with runners on first base, but .237 with men in scoring position. . .

9. Spike Owen, Boston

According to the *Seattle Baseball Bulletin,* he was much the best of the Mariners at moving a runner over from first. He batted 29 times with men on first and nobody out, and got the man into scoring position 18 times, or 62% . . . Led American League shortstops in double plays by a huge margin (133–105), due in large part to Harold Reynolds, and led by a thin margin in total chances . . . will be interesting to see how he hits in Fenway Park. It sometimes seems to me that the people that Fenway helps most are left-handed singles hitters. Owen is a switch-hitting singles hitter . . .

10. Ozzie Guillen, Chicago

1986 Power/Speed Number: 3.2
Career Power/Speed Number: 5.0
Extra base hits as a percentage of hits, 1986: .18
Times in Scoring Position: 33
Runs Scored as a Percentage of Times on Base: .387
Runs Per Time on Base/Not Home Run: .378
Batting Average When Not Striking Out: .277
Batting Average When Not Striking Out or Homering: .274
1986 Speed Score: 4.4
1986 Secondary Average: .097
Career Secondary Average: .110
Chance of getting 2000 career hits: .21
Chance of getting 2500 career hits: .05
Chance of getting 3000 career hits:
    None Established
Chance of getting 300 career home runs:
    None Established
Chance of getting 938 career stolen bases:
    None Established
Chance of getting 1500 career runs scored:
    None Established
Chance of getting 1500 career RBI:
    None Established

11. Wayne Tolleson, New York

Now 31 years old, decent offensive player, hit .265 with a .338 on-base percentage, runs the bases well. Piniella's best option may be just to write his name in the lineup and live with his defensive shortcomings. He tries, won't give anything away.

12. Greg Gagne, Minnesota

Ten of his twelve major league homers have been hit with the bases empty . . .

13. Rey Quiñones, Seattle

Shortstop is almost certainly the biggest question mark facing the Mariners this year. Quiñones's ability to do the job either offensively or defensively is still in question, and you can't really afford to have a big zero out there at that position. Just two years ago he made 50 errors in the Carolina League . . .

14. Argenis Salazar, Kansas City

Very deliberate player, likes to take his time making plays in the field that another shortstop would rush. It saves him errors but really costs him double plays. He plays sometimes almost as if he were afraid to make a mistake, whereas Biancalana is aggressive, tries to make plays that are a little beyond his limits. I suspect Salazar was set back when the Expos tried to bring him along too fast. Maybe he should have stayed in AAA ball another year and then spent a year as a spare infielder to let him get his feet wet. But Bill Virdon misread him, as he is famous for doing . . .

LEFT FIELDERS

American League

1. George Bell, Toronto (12)

Bell hit .296 and hit 12 home runs when the Blue Jays were behind in the game, which is exceptional. Most of the other Jays had very low averages when their team was behind in the game, which I assume is normal, because usually when you're behind it's because the guy on the mound is pitching well . . . when the Blue Jays were behind, Moseby hit .214, Barfield .240, and several other Jays regulars were in the ones (credit David Driscoll, of course) . . . *George* Bell's season is oddly similar to that of *Gus* Bell in 1953. Gus's extra base hits were 37-5-30; George's, in 31 more at bats, were 38-6-31. Gus scored 102 runs and drove in 105; George scored 101 and drove in 108. Gus hit .300, George hit .309. Gus drew 48 walks, George 41 . . .

George's one weakness is that he has not hit well in September . . . other than Mattingly, he may be the best triple-crown candidate in baseball today . . .

1986 Power/Speed Number: 11.4
Career Power/Speed Number: 58.6
Extra base hits as a percentage of hits, 1986: .38
Times in Scoring Position: 82
Runs Scored as a Percentage of Times on Base: .419
Runs Per Time on Base/Not Home Run: .333
Batting Average When Not Striking Out: .342
Batting Average When Not Striking Out or Homering: .305
1986 Speed Score: 5.1
1986 Secondary Average: .298
Career Secondary Average: .277
Chance of getting 2000 career hits: .61
Chance of getting 2500 career hits: .32
Chance of getting 3000 career hits: .15
Chance of getting 3500 career hits: .04
Chance of getting 4000 career hits:
   None Established
Chance of getting 300 career home runs: .68
Chance of getting 400 career home runs: .30
Chance of getting 500 career home runs: .10
Chance of getting 600 career home runs:
   None Established
Chance of getting 938 career stolen bases:
   None Established
Chance of getting 1500 career runs scored: .15
Chance of getting 1750 career runs scored: .04
Chance of getting 2000 career runs scored:
   None Established

Chance of getting 1500 career RBI: .21
Chance of getting 1750 career RBI: .09
Chance of getting 2000 career RBI: 5.35
Chance of getting 2250 career RBI:
   None Established

2. Joe Carter, Cleveland (2)

Did you realize that the Sutcliffe-for-Carter trade was a swap of Kansas City boys? . . . 1988 American League MVP?

3. Jim Rice, Boston

Hit very well in the late innings of close games last year (.337) after doing poorly in that area the previous couple of years . . . superb September hitter . . . Final career stats projected by Brock6: 2,842 hits, 425 homers, 1,614 RBI, .299 average. . .

1986 Power/Speed Number: 0
Career Power/Speed Number: 95.1
Extra base hits as a percentage of hits, 1986: .31
Times in Scoring Position: 61
Runs Scored as a Percentage of Times on Base: .368
Runs Per Time on Base/Not Home Run: .317
Batting Average When Not Striking Out: .370
Batting Average When Not Striking Out or Homering: .346
1986 Speed Score: 2.5
1986 Secondary Average: .267
Career Secondary Average: .302
Chance of getting 2500 career hits: .95
Chance of getting 3000 career hits: .42
Chance of getting 3500 career hits: .08
Chance of getting 4000 career hits:
   None Established
Chance of getting 400 career home runs: .94
Chance of getting 500 career home runs: .17
Chance of getting 600 career home runs:
   None Established
Chance of getting 938 career stolen bases:
   None Established
Chance of getting 1500 career runs scored: .49
Chance of getting 1750 career runs scored: .11
Chance of getting 2000 career runs scored:
   None Established
Chance of getting 1500 career RBI: .94
Chance of getting 1750 career RBI: .50
Chance of getting 2000 career RBI: .15
Chance of getting 2250 career RBI:
   None Established

4. Phil Bradley, Seattle

Terrific player, very even balance of skills. Hitting over the .300 mark (for the third straight year) with 77 walks, he had a .405 on-base percentage, second-best in the league behind Wade Boggs—and in a tremendously important area of performance. He has some power, can steal a base, is a graceful outfielder with a decent arm who made only one error last year. He's going to be slow to draw attention because he plays in Seattle and he doesn't have any one central skill that you can point to and explain his value, but he's a real good one . . . The *Seattle Baseball Bulletin* reports that he batted 47 times with a man on first and nobody out, and advanced the runner 28 times, best percentage on the team except for Spike Owen . . . Whereas the team average on 3–2 pitches was just .197, Bradley hit .293 off the full count and drew 40 walks in 116 plate appearances.

5. Brian Downing, California

My favorite player . . . can't understand how anybody could watch the playoffs and still think Jim Rice was a better player than Brian Downing . . . Downing's secondary average was .368, ninth-best in the American League . . . final stats as projected by Brock6: 2,119 games, 1,788 at bats, 220 homers, 947 RBI, .263 average . . .

6. José Canseco, Oakland

What do you think of José Canseco as the new Ron Kittle? asks John Dewan, pointing to the following similarities:

1) Hits over 30 homers as a rookie.

2) Strikes out a lot.

3) Doesn't hit for average.

4) Plays left field.

5) Makes a lot of errors.

6) Same in-season pattern, started out strong and faded as the year went on.

7) Similar size (Canseco listed at 6'3", 215, Kittle at 6'4", 220).

This was one of the things that got me to thinking about isolating the most-similar rookies to each of the

1985 crop. Actually, the similarity scores method doesn't see Canseco as being particularly similar to Kittle, primarily because Kittle was 25 years old in his rookie season while Canseco was 21, turned 22 in July. That's a massive "dissimilarity," in that Canseco still has time to go through some ups and downs before reaching his peak. Canseco should confront the challenges of the next three years with a strong element of natural growth and development on his side that Kittle didn't have. It's like if you have two basketball players who have about the same skills, but one of them is a high-school senior and the other is a college senior, then they're not really similar, no matter how even they are. There are other differences—Canseco's arm is better, Canseco is faster, Canseco struck out in 29% of his at bats but walked 65 times, while Kittle struck out in 29% of his at bats but walked 39 times. The differences are subtle, but critical ones in projecting their development.

By far the most similar rookie to Canseco that I found, actually, was Pete Incaviglia. Of course, Incaviglia is of no use in projecting Canseco's expected growth, so he's not used as one of the ten most comparable, but he does lead the list. It's a real good list:

1.	Pete Incaviglia	917
2.	Reggie Jackson	893
3.	George Scott	893
4.	Eddie Mathews	891
5.	Bobby Murcer	890
6.	Willie Montanez	889
7.	Bill Melton	871
8.	Ron Hansen	860
9.	Greg Luzinski	857
10.	Dave Kingman	856
11.	Curt Blefray	854

It's important to note that the list has to go down to 854, which is a sign of a relatively unique player; he has to be compared to players who hit 22 homers and drove in 70 runs because there just aren't very many truly comparable players. Canseco's differences from these players tend to be *positive* differences: he is different from them in that he is better than they are and younger than they are. The method is more realistic when you're dealing with an ordinary talent, and thus *random* differences.

Anyway, of the ten useable comps, nine played in 1,500 or more major-league games, the exception

being Blefray, the least comparable player. Two of the comparable players hit more than 500 home runs, three hit more than 400, four hit more than 300, and six hit more than 200. The weighted average of their careers: 1,825 games, 1,661 hits, 290 home runs, 998 RBI and an average of .262.

7. Dan Pasqua, New York

If this kid keeps hitting, what an offense the Yankees will have. If you just double his stats, the three Yankee outfielders might hit as much as the three Toronto outfielders, and Toronto ain't got no Don Mattingly in the infield . . .

8. Pete Incaviglia, Texas

Most-similar rookies to Incaviglia include eight of the same players who were most similar to Canseco (Blefray, Hansen, Reggie, Eddie Mathews, Melton, Montanez, Murcer, and George Scott). Actually, they are much more similar to Incaviglia than they are to Canseco, with scores ranging as high as 940 (Murcer) and 934 (Reggie), and dropping only to 895, just above where the scores *start* for Canseco. The two substitutions to the list are Frank Howard and Willie Horton instead of Kingman and Luzinski. The weighted average of the ten: 1,823 games, 1,685 hits, 282 home runs, 982 RBI, and a .265 career average . . .

9. Mike Young, Baltimore

Probably the number one preseason candidate for comeback player of the year . . .

10. Lonnie Smith, Kansas City

You've probably heard what a bad outfielder he is, and let me tell you: They ain't lyin'. He really does fall down almost every game, so that as a Royals fan you just hope he won't do it with anybody fast on base. He can't throw and has a curious inability to position his glove on a ball hit right at him. But he is a good offensive player, and the Royals will miss his bat. My feeling was that he should have been shifted to DH. The reason Designated Hitters are usually slow is that they usually figure if you can run you can play the field. Lonnie was a unique case, a player who could run but couldn't play the field. The attempts to make him play the field just interfered with his attaining what he is capable of

with the bat. The Royals need people who can get on base, and Lonnie can do it . . . over last three years has hit just .237 with runners in scoring position, and just .238 in the late innings of close games . . . was hitting to right field much more last year than he has before, as is reflected in his .330 batting average with runners on first base only (hence, a hole on the right side) . . .

11. John Cangelosi, Chicago

The ten most-similar rookies to John Cangelosi produced an average of 646 major-league hits in 848 games, hitting 19 home runs and averaging .247. The best of the ten by a mile was Tony Taylor, who as a rookie in 1958 matched Cangelosi in batting average (.235) and was similar in age (22-23), runs scored (63–65), and RBI (27–32; Taylor's figure listed first in each case). Only one other similar rookie, Roger Metzger, went on to play a thousand major league games . . .

12. Dave Collins, Detroit

What? Is Collins still in the league?

13. Glenn Braggs, Milwaukee

Named by *Baseball America* as the outstanding prospect in the Pacific Coast League. My reaction on seeing him was that it must have been a pretty poor year in the Pacific Coast League. He didn't impress me, but the people who voted in the *Baseball America* poll have seen more of him than I have . . . he has a nice, smooth swing, which some people find to be reminiscent of Al Kaline, but in 58 major-league games he had 11 walks and 47 strikeouts and Al Kaline in the worst 58 games of his life didn't strike out 47 times . . . I guess we'll see.

14. Mickey Hatcher, Minnesota

Led the American League in batting against left-handed pitchers with a .364 average (51/140). The problem with Hatcher is that he has to hit .300, has to hit *over* .300, to help you. He doesn't run, draw walks, or hit for power. He doesn't play a key defensive position or play particularly well at the one he is assigned. He'd be all right as a platoon player, but it's really hard to respect a manager who would give a guy like this as much playing time as he had last year . . .

National League

1. Tim Raines, Montreal (11)

He would have been a deserving recipient of the National League Most Valuable Player award last year, which is not to say that Schmidt wasn't.

If you compare them offensively, Schmidt and Raines are oddly similar in dissimilar ways. They went to the plate almost the same number of times, 664 for Raines and 657 for Schmidt. Offense in baseball consists of two things: getting runners on base, and advancing runners. Raines won the batting title, and with seventy walks also led the National League in on-base percentage, at .413. Schmidt hit .290 himself and drew 89 walks besides, so that he was on base a lot, too. With adjustments for getting caught stealing and grounding into double plays (we penalize the hitter for taking other runners off base), Raines is credited by the runs created formula with being on base 259 times to Schmidt's 246. Close, but the edge to Raines.

As to advancing runners, Schmidt, because of his power, had 302 total bases, which is the largest factor in the advancement of runners. However, Raines had 54 extra base hits himself (35-10-9), and being the batting champion, he too had 276 total bases. In addition, Raines stole 70 bases, 69 more than Schmidt. Although the runs created method considers the value of this to be equivalent to only 36 batting bases, with an adjustment for stolen bases and miscellaneous stuff, Schmidt is credited with 326 "advancement bases" by the runs created method, while Raines is credited with 333. Again, it's very close, but again Raines has the edge. Raines did slightly more to advance *himself or other baserunners* than did Schmidt.

Putting the elements together, you get:

	Schmidt	Raines
On Base	246	259
Advancement Bases	326	333
Plate appearances	657	664
Runs Created	122	130

They're very similar, oddly similar in the proportions, but Raines probably created about eight more runs for his team than did Schmidt.

Then you have to put that into a context of outs. Schmidt made 392 batting outs (552 minus 160) and 19 miscellaneous outs (9 sacrifices, 2 caught stealing, and 8 double plays). Raines made 386 batting outs (580 minus 194) and also made 19 miscellaneous outs (4 sacrifices, 9 caught stealing, and 6 double plays). The totals are 411 outs for Schmidt, 405 for Raines.

Putting the runs in a 27-out context, you have 8.01 runs created per 27 outs for Schmidt, and 8.66 for Raines. They are one-two in the league, but Raines's small advantages add up to a significant edge, making him pretty clearly the best offensive player in the league.

Except, of course, that Schmidt *drove in* and *scored* more runs than did Raines. I'll finish the MVP argument for Raines, and then I'll get back to that.

1) Raines created more runs than Schmidt despite playing in a much tougher hitter's park. Raines's batting and slugging percentages were 16 and 50 points higher on the road than they were in Montreal. Schmidt's batting and slugging averages were 16 and 94 points higher in Philadelphia than on the road. With adjustments for the statistical distortions of the parks, Raines was really a much better hitter. Further, the average Phillies game had 9.0 runs, whereas the average Expos game had only 8.2 runs, so the runs that Raines created were more valuable—had more of a win impact—than the runs that Schmidt created in his inflated environment.

2) Schmidt at 36 started the season at first base, and spent most of the season at third base, where he was an ordinary defensive player at a somewhat key defensive position. Raines played left field, where he is an exceptional defensive player at what is not a key defensive position. Raines was third in the league in outfield assists, and twice ended games by throwing out the potential tying run at the plate. We can call their defense a wash.

3) Neither player's team was ultimately successful, but Raines's early season streak of reaching base in 42 straight games helped greatly to keep the Expos in the pennant race. It wasn't *ultimately* meaningful, but it was very meaningful at the time, Schmidt piled up 67 RBI over the last three months of the season, when the Phillies were already dead and buried as a team. Not wanting to seem too eager to claim advantages for Raines, we'll call that a wash, too.

4) Schmidt has been a great player, but he has won the award twice before. Raines has been a great player for six years now, and he's never won it. In the interests of fairness, 1986 would have been an opportunity to balance the scales.

OK, then we go back to the issue of actual run and RBI counts. I would say this: that if Schmidt's advantage in runs scored and RBI resulted from his superior performance in run-production situations, then it is reasonable to consider this an advantage for Schmidt. If, on the other hand, the advantage resulted from offensive context (that is, having better hitters surrounding him), then it is unfair to penalize Raines because his teammates were not as good as Schmidt's.

Quite clearly, those differences resulted primarily from offensive context, and not from individual differences. Consider:

1) Schmidt drove in 25% of the runners that he inherited in scoring position. Raines drove in 26%. The big difference in RBI was that Schmidt came to the plate with 253 runners in scoring position, and Raines came up with only 173 ducks on the pond.

2) Schmidt drove in 49% of his runners on third base with less than two out, 20 of 41. Raines drove in 58% of his, 18 of 31.

3) Another situation in which at bats have a disproportionate impact on runs resulting is the first at bat in the inning, the leadoff spot. Raines had 190 such at bats, and Schmidt 142. In that game situation, power increases for most hitters but on-base percentage decreases, as pitchers concentrate on not allowing walks.

Schmidt's slugging percentage increased only nine points in that situation, from .547 to .556, while his on base percentage plummetted (all of this data is in the *Great American Baseball Stat Book*) from .390 to

.340, 50 points. Adding the two together, he lost 41 points (+9, −50).
Raines, on the other hand, increased
his slugging percentage as a leadoff
hitter by 35 points, to .511, while his
on-base percentage dropped only to
.404, 9 points, so he showed net gain
of +26 (+35, −9). A big edge to
Raines.

In the late innings of close
games, pitchers strive to avoid the
game-breaking homer, so exactly the
opposite happens: Slugging percentages go down, while on-base percentages go up. Both players hit almost
their averages in the late innings of
close games—Schmidt .290 (+ or
− zero) and Raines .339 (up 6
points). But again, Schmidt's slugging percentage went down 31 points
while his on-base percentage went
up only 21, a net loss of 10 points.
Raines's slugging went down 24, but
his on-base percentage went up 28, a
net gain of four points. So again,
Raines exploited the positives of a
critical game situation more effectively than did Schmidt.

So it seems obvious that
Schmidt's higher run counts resulted
not from his own ability, but from the
fact that he was hitting in the middle
of Gary Redus, Von Hayes, and Juan
Samuel, while Raines did not have
comparable support. The Phillies
scored 739 runs as a team, second in
the league. The Expos scored 637,
tenth in the league. This shouldn't be
the criteria for who gets the MVP
award.

I'm not criticizing anybody for
his vote. I too thought, just looking
at the statistics, that Schmidt had had
the best year. Raines's remarkable
base stealing (70/79) is easy to over-
look, particularly when the run count
doesn't reflect the advantage. But
having looked at the issue more carefully, I now realize that Tim Raines
was, in fact, the best and most valuable player in the National League in
1986.

1986 Power/Speed Number: 15.9
Career Power/Speed Number: 86.9
Extra base hits as a percentage of hits, 1986: .28
Times in Scoring Position: 124
Runs Scored as a Percentage of Times on Base:
.332
Runs Per Time on Base/Not Home Run: .309
Batting Average When Not Striking Out: .373
Batting Average When Not Striking Out or
Homering: .362
1986 Speed Score: 7.7

1986 Secondary Average: .397
Career Secondary Average: .405
Chance of getting 2000 career hits: .86
Chance of getting 2500 career hits: .59
Chance of getting 3000 career hits: .31
Chance of getting 3500 career hits: .15
Chance of getting 4000 career hits: .04
Chance of getting 4500 career hits:
None Established
Chance of getting 300 career home runs:
None Established
Chance of getting 938 career stolen bases: .75
Chance of getting 1000 career stolen bases: .60
Chance of getting 1200 career stolen bases: .31
Chance of getting 1400 career stolen bases: .13
Chance of getting 1600 career stolen bases: .02
Chance of getting 1800 career stolen bases: None
Established
Chance of getting 1500 career runs scored: .45
Chance of getting 1750 career runs scored: .24
Chance of getting 2000 career runs scored: .11
Chance of getting 2250 career runs scored: .02
Chance of getting 2500 career runs scored:
None Established
Chance of getting 1500 career RBI:
None Established

2. Eric Davis, Cincinnati (1)
When Eric Davis leaves this game
What shall be writ beneath his name?
Shall we old men, o'er a glass of ale,
Legends tell and stats detail
Of wonders seen in the Cincy sun
Or merely the record of another one
Who had a chance and didn't take it
Made us dream, but didn't make it
Up that mountain, built of hope
(Lord, it is a treacherous slope).
When Eric's time has come and gone
Another youth will claim the dawn
But none of us will be the same,
What shall we see, beneath his
name?

1986 Power/Speed Number: 40.4
Career Power/Speed Number: 63.2
Extra base hits as a percentage of hits, 1986: .39
Times in Scoring Position: 125
Runs Scored as a Percentage of Times on Base:
.505
Runs Per Time on Base/Not Home Run: .424
Batting Average When Not Striking Out: .365
Batting Average When Not Striking Out or
Homering: .306
1986 Speed Score: 7.8
1986 Secondary Average: .602
Career Secondary Average: .537
Chance of getting 2000 career hits:
None Established
Chance of getting 300 career home runs: .17
Chance of getting 400 career home runs:
None Established
Chance of getting 938 career stolen bases: .04
Chance of getting 1000 career stolen bases: 4.70
Chance of getting 1200 career stolen bases: None
Established
Chance of getting 1500 career runs scored:
None Established
Chance of getting 1500 career RBI:
None Established

3. José Cruz, Houston
OK, I promise. No more poems.
José had a subpar season in '86, but
hit .384 with runners in scoring position . . . can you have a big comeback season at 39? If you can, he
will . . .

4. Gary Redus, Philadelphia
Almost half of his hits were for
extra bases, he grounded into only
two double plays and in 90 games he
stole 25 bases and scored 62 runs. In
the outfield he played the best ball of
his career. Some people said he was
a disappointment, but apart from the
injury it's sure hard for me to see
why.

5. Mookie Wilson, New York
I suppose I shouldn't comment
on this, but don't you reckon Mookie
Wilson and George Foster has got to
be the ugliest platoon combination in
the history of baseball? I never figured that Foster was as bad as the
New York writers would tell you, just
on the grounds that nobody could
have been that bad, but then I
wouldn't have wanted him on my
team, either. Mookie's a good player,
though, and should resurface with a
regular job somewhere in '87 . . .

6. Ken Griffey, Cincinnati
Hit .300 in both leagues and
combined for a career-high 21 home
runs, 8 more than ever before. Heck
of a season . . . here's another guy
Tanner wouldn't hit in the leadoff
spot. Too much power, I guess.

7. John Kruk, San Diego
What a wonderful, wonderful
player. I love him, like a Teddy Bear.
There hasn't been anybody like this
around since John Wockenfuss came
up. He's got a funny name, a funny
batting stance, and he's absolutely hi-
larious on the bases. He doesn't run
real fast but, boy, does he run hard.
When he gets pressed real hard, like
somebody is running up his back or
something, he sticks his arms out to
his sides and pinwheels them real fast
when he runs, sort of looking as if his
arms were attached to his body by a
rubber band that was too short, so
that the joints would go out straight
rather than relaxing into a normal position. At the same time, he puffs out
his cheeks and blows real hard while
he runs. I don't know how often he
does this, actually, but I've got it on

videotape. When he runs fast he runs kind of like a little fat three-year-old who hasn't quite figured out the motion yet . . .

Hit .490 (25/51) with runners on first base only . . . No rookie in the 1948–1975 period had a similarity score when compared to Kruk of 900 or higher. The highest was Mike Hargrove, 1974, at 898. The ten most-similar rookies to Kruk included two players who went on to play a thousand or more games, Hargrove and John Grubb, with the other eight being (alphabetically) Clint Courtney, Jim Finigan, Mike Fiore, Gene Green, Ernie Oravetz, Bill Sarni, Willie Smith, and Carl Taylor. Most of those guys hit three hundred as rookies, but then they dropped off to a career average of .273. The weighted average of their careers is 713 games, 560 hits, 41 homers, 247 RBI, 264 walks, and a .273 average. Somehow, I think Kruk will do better than that . . .

8. Candy Maldonado, San Francisco

Classic, mellifluous name. His season as a pinch hitter—17 for 40, 4 homers—is probably one of the ten best of all time. That he got a regular job and drove in 85 runs in the same season makes it a rather singular campaign . . .

9. R. J. Reynolds, Pittsburgh

Inconsistent, looked good at times. The Dodgers could sure have used him.

10. Vince Coleman, St. Louis

He's now 25 years old, and how much growth he has left as a hitter is questionable. His greatest asset is the one that diminishes the most rapidly as a player ages. He's probably the last player in baseball whom I would trade for if I were a general manager.

11. Franklin Stubbs, Los Angeles

Or Reggie Williams, with Stubbs at first base. The ten most-similar rookies to Reggie Williams include only one player who played a thousand major-league games, that being Chuck Hinton. The one most-similar rookie was Ted Savage . . .

12. Gary Matthews, Chicago

Final career stats as projected by Brock6: 2,361 hits, 304 homers, 1,201 RBI, .277 average . . .

CENTER FIELDERS

National League

1. Dale Murphy, Atlanta (11)

Has excellent situation stats, for the most part. Keep in mind that you're starting with a formidable base here, .285 average, .521 slugging percentage over the last three years. But over that time, 53 of his 102 homers have come with men on base although he has 25% more at bats with the bases empty. He's hit .298 and slugged .567 in the late innings of close games. His one poor situation stat is that he's only gotten 40% of his runners home from third base with less than two out . . . his .345 secondary average in '86 was among the NL's top ten . . .

1986 Power/Speed Number: 11.3
Career Power/Speed Number: 173.7
Extra base hits as a percentage of hits, 1986: .40
Times in Scoring Position: 72
Runs Scored as a Percentage of Times on Base: .371
Runs Per Time on Base/Not Home Run: .284
Batting Average When Not Striking Out: .345
Batting Average When Not Striking Out or Homering: .302
1986 Speed Score: 5.3
1986 Secondary Average: .345
Career Secondary Average: .363
Chance of getting 2000 career hits: .90
Chance of getting 2500 career hits: .43
Chance of getting 3000 career hits: .14
Chance of getting 3500 career hits: None Established
Chance of getting 300 career home runs: .97
Chance of getting 400 career home runs: .88
Chance of getting 500 career home runs: .34
Chance of getting 600 career home runs: .09
Chance of getting 700 career home runs: None Established
Chance of getting 938 career stolen bases: None Established
Chance of getting 1500 career runs scored: .37
Chance of getting 1750 career runs scored: .14
Chance of getting 2000 career runs scored: .003
Chance of getting 2250 career runs scored: None Established
Chance of getting 1500 career RBI: .34
Chance of getting 1750 career RBI: .12
Chance of getting 2000 career RBI: None Established

2. Kevin McReynolds, San Diego (1)

1986 Power/Speed Number: 12.2
Career Power/Speed Number: 27.0
Extra base hits as a percentage of hits, 1986: .39
Times in Scoring Position: 71
Runs Scored as a Percentage of Times on Base: .390
Runs Per Time on Base/Not Home Run: .312
Batting Average When Not Striking Out: .338
Batting Average When Not Striking Out or Homering: .299
1986 Speed Score: 5.8
1986 Secondary Average: .348
Career Secondary Average: .271
Chance of getting 2000 career hits: .32
Chance of getting 2500 career hits: .12
Chance of getting 3000 career hits: None Established
Chance of getting 300 career home runs: .26
Chance of getting 400 career home runs: .03
Chance of getting 500 career home runs: None Established
Chance of getting 938 career stolen bases: None Established
Chance of getting 1500 career runs scored: .005
Chance of getting 1750 career runs scored: None Established
Chance of getting 1500 career RBI: .08
Chance of getting 1750 career RBI: None Established

3. Len Dykstra, New York

He hasn't been around long, but then about half the National League center fielders have been up less than two years. Dykstra is the best of the new group. Despite his size he has power. His secondary average last year was .357, as he had 65 extra bases on hits, 58 walks, and 31 stolen bases, a total of 154 miscellaneous bases with just 431 at bats . . .

4. Mitch Webster, Montreal

Probably will become Montreal's leadoff man with the departure of Raines. He'll be good, hit .290 last year with 57 walks, 36 stolen bases and a league-leading 13 triples . . .

5. Barry Bonds, Pittsburgh

Secondary average, .438, was third-best in the National League . . . did you know there were 17 major-league players last year whose initials were B.B.? They were pitchers Bruce Berenyi, Bud Black, and Bert Blyleven; catchers Bruce Benedict, Bob Brenly, Bruce Bochy, Bill Bathe, and Bob Boone; first baseman Bill Buckner; third baseman Buddy Bell; shortstop Buddy Biancalana; and outfielders Bobby Bonilla, Barry Bonds, Brett Butler, Billy Beane, Barry Bonnell, and Bob Brower . . . The most-similar rookie to Bonds was Rick Monday, 1967 (900). The ten most-similar included six players who played a thousand or more major-league games: Gene Freese, Monday, Garry Maddox, Roger Maris, John Milner, and Sixto Lezcano . . . an odd mixture. A weighted average of their career produces totals that would be a mighty disappointment for Bonds: 1,111 games, 122 homers and 470 RBI . . . as a group the ten players had much less speed than Bonds and much lower secondary averages, suggesting that the comparison method was not able to find truly similar players . . .

6. Willie McGee, St. Louis

Over a period of three years has hit just .253 with runners on first base, a situation in which batting averages usually soar. The reason for that, of course, is that he has to take pitches to allow Coleman to run. Just one of the little hidden advantages of the running game . . .

7. Eddie Milner, Cincinnati

Now with San Francisco. He gives them four center fielders on their roster, all of approximately equal ability, but this is not odd for the Giants.

8. Jerry Mumphrey, Chicago

Hit .361 in Wrigley Field, just .253 on the road, with slugging percentages of .517 and .296 . . . Cub center fielders had only four assists, three by Dernier, who actually played more center field than anyone else. Mumphrey played 360 innings in center field without throwing anyone out from that position, and also played 678 innings in left field without throwing anyone out from there. The fact that he was also used in right should tell you what kind of an outfield the Cubs had . . . (Inning counts from the *Chicago Baseball Report*.)

9. Dan Gladden, San Francisco

Good outfielder, good leadoff man in two of his three big league seasons. Got a late start on his career, and will turn 30 in July . . . Hit .378 in 1986, .353 over the last three years with runners on first base . . .

10. Billy Hatcher, Houston

Improved the Astros defensively in center field, but why Lanier used him as a leadoff man is a puzzle. His on-base percentage was .302 . . . hit just .222 with runners in scoring position . . . grounded into only three double plays . . .

11. Milt Thompson, Philadelphia

Fighting for the position with

Redus, Stone, and Ron Roenicke. Thompson wasn't a disaster with the bat, batting 299 times and kicking in 6 homers, 26 walks, 19 stolen bases. Still, he's got to hit more than .251 . . .

12. Los Angeles (Vacant)

American League

1. Rickey Henderson, New York (13)

Six or eight years ago I developed something called the power/speed number. Power/speed number is a way of stating a player's combined ability to hit home runs and steal bases. The formula is $(HR \times SB \times 2)$ divided by $(HR + SB)$. It is so designed that if a player hits 30 homers and steals 30 bases, his power/speed number will be 30.0. If he hits 28 homers and steals 32 bases, it will be 29.9. If he hits 20 homers and steals 40 bases, it will be 26.7. If he hits no homers and steals 60 bases, it will be zero. A player has to do *both* things, hit homers and steal bases, to rate well, but doesn't have to do them in precisely equal ratios. It's a way of unifying all of those imaginary "clubs"—the 30/30 club, the 30/40 club, the 20/50 club, the 25/50 club . . . who can keep track of them anymore.

The all-time leaders in power/speed number, as I presented them in 1981, were:

	HR	SB	PSN
1. Bobby Bonds, 1973	39	43	40.9
2. Bobby Bonds, 1977	37	41	38.9
3. Ken Williams, 1922	39	37	38.0
4. Willie Mays, 1956	36	40	37.9
5. Joe Morgan, 1973	26	67	37.5
6. Bobby Bonds, 1969	32	45	37.4
7. Joe Morgan, 1976	27	60	37.2
8. Willie Mays, 1957	35	38	36.4
9. Hank Aaron, 1963	44	31	36.4
10. Bobby Bonds, 1978	31	43	36.0

In 1986, Rickey Henderson broke Bobby Bonds's 13-year-old record for the most impressive combination

of power and speed in the history of the game. Blasting 28 homers and stealing 87 bases, Henderson posted a power/speed number of 42.4. Incredibly enough, National Leaguer Eric Davis, not even playing regularly early in the season, also broke the 40 barrier, posting the second-highest power/speed number of the 1986 season—and the third highest of all time. The new all-time top ten:

	HR	SB	PSN
1. Rickey Henderson, 1986	28	87	42.4
2. Bobby Bonds, 1973	39	43	40.9
3. Eric Davis, 1986	27	80	40.4
4. Bobby Bonds, 1977	37	41	38.9
5. Ken Williams, 1922	39	37	38.0
6. Willie Mays, 1956	36	40	37.9
7. Joe Morgan, 1973	26	67	37.5
8. Bobby Bonds, 1969	32	45	37.4
9. Joe Morgan, 1976	27	60	37.2
10. Rickey Henderson, 1985	24	80	36.9

There are at least two other active players who could break into this list if things broke right for them, those being Kirk Gibson and Darryl Strawberry. Over the last six or seven years there have been many players who passed through a stage at which they looked like good candidates, including Dale Murphy, Andre Dawson, and Ryne Sandberg. But it is very tough to sustain that degree of excellence in either category—that is, to hit upwards of 25 homers or to steal upwards of 25 bases—and double tough to sustain that kind of excellence in both areas. Most players, as Willie Mays did, will pass quickly through the stage at which they post power/speed numbers in the thirties.

Mays's career power/speed num-

ber was 447.1, which is still the highest of all time, and is not at the present time being threatened. It's an amazing figure, when you stop to count up how few players have hit 447 career homers or stolen 447 career bases. The top five men in career power/speed number are Willie Mays, Bobby Bonds, Hank Aaron, Joe Morgan, and Reggie Jackson. Reggie is still edging upward at 320.2, but he'd need to steal another 60 or 70 bases to push Mays off the top of the list, and that doesn't seem real likely.

But in the long run, somewhere down the road, it seems likely that Rickey Henderson or Eric Davis will own that record, too. Rickey's going to steal, at a conservative guess, maybe 1200 bases in his career. That being the case, he needs to hit a little less than 300 home runs to rank as the greatest power/speed combination in the history of the game. Henderson has only 103 home runs now, but in the last four years his totals have been 9, 16, 24, and 28. Given the kind of consistent performer that he is, you know (like him or not) that he's going to hit at least 250–300 career home runs. And Eric Davis . . . well, who knows what he's going to do. He might hit 40 homers and steal 100 bases this year, which would be a Power/Speed number of 57.1. In time, Mays's career record is doomed.

1986 Power/Speed Number: 42.4
Career Power/Speed Number: 178.2
Extra base hits as a percentage of hits, 1986: .4
Times in Scoring Position: 151
Runs Scored as a Percentage of Times on Base: .518

Runs Per Time on Base/Not Home Run: .457
Batting Average When Not Striking Out: .304
Batting Average When Not Striking Out or
    Homering: .265
1986 Speed Score: 7.9
1986 Secondary Average: .495
Career Secondary Average: .477
Chance of getting 2000 career hits: .86
Chance of getting 2500 career hits: .46
Chance of getting 3000 career hits: .19
Chance of getting 3500 career hits: .04
Chance of getting 4000 career hits: None
    Established
Chance of getting 300 career home runs: .48
Chance of getting 400 career home runs: .15
Chance of getting 500 career home runs: None
    Established
Chance of getting 938 career stolen bases: .90
Chance of getting 1000 career stolen bases: .88
Chance of getting 1200 career stolen bases: .67
Chance of getting 1400 career stolen bases: .36
Chance of getting 1600 career stolen bases: .17
Chance of getting 1800 career stolen bases: .06
Chance of getting 2000 career stolen bases: None
    Established
Chance of getting 1500 career runs scored: .86
Chance of getting 1750 career runs scored: .66
Chance of getting 2000 career runs scored: .41
Chance of getting 2250 career runs scored: .24
Chance of getting 2500 career runs scored: .13
Chance of getting 2750 career runs scored: .05
Chance of getting 3000 career runs scored: None
    Established
Chance of getting 1500 career RBI: .90
Chance of getting 1750 career RBI: None
    Established

2. Kirby Puckett, Minnesota (1)

I suppose Kirby could do it too, now that I think about it. Kirby hit 31 homers and swiped 20 bases last year, so he could get up to 35.0 if he got serious about stealing bases. Lloyd Moseby, Oddibe McDowell, Mike Davis . . . any of those guys could develop into a Bobby Bonds type. But you pick any one of them and the odds are that he won't . . .

3. Lloyd Moseby, Toronto

Went 11-for-22 (.500) with runners on second and third last year . . . hit .133 when behind in the count, .276 when ahead . . . Let's see, if you ranked the 1927 Yankee outfielders among their contemporaries, where would they rank? Ruth would rank first in right field, obviously. Combs in center would rank second behind Simmons or third behind Simmons and Heinie Manush. Left fielder Meusel would probably rank second behind Goose Goslin. So the '86 Blue Jays rank 1/3/1 among 14 players, while the 1927 Yankees rank 2/2/1 among 8 players . . .

4. Oddibe McDowell, Texas

Made a little progress all around, scored a hundred runs and lifted his average 27 points. I still like him a lot.

5. Robin Yount, Milwaukee

Now playing shortstop, was sixth in the American League in hitting, coming off a shoulder operation without anyone seeming to think it was a good year for him. Late in the year his power returned, as he hit five homers in September after hitting only four through August. With his old power and his old position, will 1987 see the return of Robin Yount to the ranks of the league's best players?

6. Brett Butler, Cleveland

Led the American League in triples with 14, stole 32 bases and scored 92 runs . . . not bad for an off year . . .

7. Gary Pettis, California

World's best defensive outfielder, has secondary average over .300 and is a good bunter.

8. Fred Lynn, Baltimore

Actually, Shelby plays most of the time in center for Baltimore; I just rated Lynn because he's a better player. Shelby is a fine outfielder but apparently isn't allowed to take batting practice with the big kids. Lynn is too slow to play center field anymore and has trouble staying healthy, but remains an excellent offensive player, a disciplined hitter who hits for average and power.

9. Willie Wilson, Kansas City

1986 Power/Speed Number: 14.2
Career Power/Speed Number: 56.4
Extra base hits as a percentage of hits, 1986: .21
Times in Scoring Position: 70
Runs Scored as a Percentage of Times on Base:
    .367
Runs Per Time on Base/Not Home Run: .338
Batting Average When Not Striking Out: .318
Batting Average When Not Striking Out or
    Homering: .307
1986 Speed Score: 7.3
1986 Secondary Average: .200
Career Secondary Average: .240
Chance of getting 2000 career hits: .91
Chance of getting 2500 career hits: .47
Chance of getting 3000 career hits: .15
Chance of getting 3500 career hits: None
    Established
Chance of getting 300 career home runs: None
    Established
Chance of getting 938 career stolen bases: .002
Chance of getting 1000 career stolen bases: None
    Established

Chance of getting 1500 career runs scored: .17
Chance of getting 1750 career runs scored: None
    Established
Chance of getting 1500 career RBI: None
    Established

10. Chet Lemon, Detroit

At 32 and coming off his worst season in ten years . . . the Tigers should probably be trying to locate a backup plan. All of these guys—Lynn, Wilson, Lemon, Murphy, Armas—are going to be slower two years from now than they are now, and they're not good center fielders now . . . I should do a study sometime to see how many teams win pennants with center fielders in their thirties. That is, compare the age distribution for all center fielders with the age distribution for center fielders on championship teams. My instinct tells me that the championship pattern would be visibly tighter around age 27 . . .

11. Dwayne Murphy, Oakland

I was a big fan of Murphy's four or five years ago, but he can't stay healthy. He's still an above-average defensive center fielder who draws a ton of walks and has power . . . Stan Javier looks like he'll make it as a major league player if he hits . . .

12. Tony Armas, Boston

Dave Henderson's skills are extremely similar to Armas's—power, terrible K/W ratio, speed and throwing arm just adequate for center field. Henderson could hit a bunch of homers in this park . . . You know what I noticed about Henderson the very first time I saw him in '82? Two things: Number one, with two strikes on him he still tries to hit the ball out of the park, and number two, he is supposed to have a good arm but when he has to make a throw home the ball will tail up the third base line almost every time, usually winding up about 20 feet up the line. That was four years ago and he's still exactly the same. The thing about the throws is just comic; you can't believe that, after all these years, he hasn't *noticed* that he is throwing the ball 20 feet up the third base line, rather than at the catcher. He did it again in the World Series, two or three times. I think you can understand why Dick Williams wouldn't have a lot of patience with a player who hasn't been able to make a simple adjustment like that after years in the league. The two-strike home run swing seems to be working for him, though . . .

13. Daryl Boston, Chicago

Played well after his recall last August, at times brilliantly. Looks like he is ready to take his place among the best in the league at this position.

14. John Moses, Seattle

Mickey Brantley probably has the job and probably will hit, but has to prove he can still play center after having scar tissue removed from his shoulder . . .

RIGHT FIELDERS

American League

1. Jesse Barfield, Toronto (14)

Jesse has had 8 outfield double plays in each of the last two seasons, and has 21 in three seasons. That's an incredible total. There's no systematic data, but I would be very surprised if any player since Willie Mays has had that many outfield DPs in a three-year period. Most *teams* don't have eight outfield double plays in a season. Roberto Clemente, who annually led the league in assists, never had more than five double plays in a season or more than eight in a three-year period . . . A study of scoresheets found that most outfield double plays do *not* result from runners trying to advance on a fly, as you might suspect, but from runners being trapped off base (usually first base) when a fly is unexpectedly caught. (That is, outfield double plays tend to go 7–3 or 9–3, rather than 7–2 or 9–2). However, what is true of most outfield double plays almost certainly is not true of Barfield's double plays, which probably come on aborted sacrifice flies, and thus have an impact of one run apiece . . . Barfield's 1986 secondary average was .401, fifth-best in the American League . . .

Hit 15 two-strike homers in 1986. Hit .199 when behind in the count (27/136, with 5 homers), and .352 when ahead in the count (43/122, with 13 homers) . . . did not have a significant slump during the 1986 season . . .

1986 Power/Speed Number: 13.3
Career Power/Speed Number: 66.6
Extra base hits as a percentage of hits, 1986: .45
Times in Scoring Position: 85
Runs Scored as a Percentage of Times on Base: .433
Runs Per Time on Base/Not Home Run: .324
Batting Average When Not Striking Out: .384
Batting Average When Not Striking Out or Homering: .323
1986 Speed Score: 5.0
1986 Secondary Average: .401
Career Secondary Average: .351
Chance of getting 2000 career hits: .44
Chance of getting 2500 career hits: .18
Chance of getting 3000 career hits: .04
Chance of getting 3500 career hits:
    None Established
Chance of getting 300 career home runs: .85
Chance of getting 400 career home runs: .47
Chance of getting 500 career home runs: .24
Chance of getting 600 career home runs: .06
Chance of getting 700 career home runs:
    None Established
Chance of getting 938 career stolen bases:
    None Established
Chance of getting 1500 career runs scored: .19
Chance of getting 1750 career runs scored: .07
Chance of getting 2000 career runs scored:
    None Established
Chance of getting 1500 career RBI: .17
Chance of getting 1750 career RBI: .05
Chance of getting 2000 career RBI:
    None Established

2. Kirk Gibson, Detroit

Injuries kept him from having a career year. As he heads into his thirties (turns 30 on May 28), his stolen-base frequency and success rate are still increasing, which is certainly a good sign insofar as his durability is concerned. Despite missing 43 games he established a career high in stolen bases (34) and narrowly missed in homers (28/29) and walks (68/71) . . . secondary average, .456, was second best in the American League (behind Rickey Henderson) . . .

3. Harold Baines, Chicago

Another thing you could use similarity scores for is to measure consistency. A consistent player is one who turns in seasons which are similar to one another. Harold has got to be the most consistent player in baseball in the eighties, but I haven't done the work . . .

4. Dwight Evans, Boston

1986 secondary average was .406, fourth-best in the league. I meant to write a long article comparing the best right fielders of the eighties to the best of the post-war era, but didn't get it done. They'd stack up well. Winfield and Evans have been fine defensive players, and in their careers will drive in and score more runs than Clemente and Kaline.

5. Dave Winfield, New York

Only 51% of his RBI in 1986 came when the game was close (Yankees no more than two runs behind or one run ahead), which is a low figure relative to the league but not as low in absolute terms as a lot of people would lead you to believe . . . Mattingly drove in 71% of his runs when the game was close, Pagliarulo 52%. Winfield in '86 hit .238 in the late innings of close games, but over a three-year period has hit .272 in those situations . . . hot-weather hitter . . .

6. Cory Snyder, Cleveland

The ten most-similar rookies to Snyder are Rocky Colavito, Nate Colbert, Billy Conigliaro, Dick Gernert, Frank Howard, Ted Kluszewski, Bobby Murcer, Al Oliver, Johnny Orsino, and Danny Walton. The weighted averages aren't great (189 homers in 1,254 games, .277), but five of the ten comps were real good players.

I'm impressed with Snyder, but I'm a little more cautious than some people. Although K/W ratio isn't an indicator of growth potential in a rookie, his record of 123 strikeouts and 16 walks isn't something I regard as an asset. He doesn't have any speed and is now 24 years old. If he's going to develop into a superstar he's got to do it based on power and his famous throwing arm, so it seems to me that at the very best he'll be a player comparable to Colavito, Frank Howard, or Willie Stargell. He's a good prospect, but I don't see him as a superstar.

7. Danny Tartabull, Seattle

The most-similar rookie to him in the 1948–1975 period was the new Hall of Famer, Billy Williams (941). The top ten alphabetically were Bob Allison, Nate Colbert, Roy Foster, Willie Horton, Bill Melton, Willie Montanez, Bobby Murcer, Lee

Thomas, Pete Ward, and Williams. Eight of the ten played a thousand or more major-league games. The weighted average of the ten was 1,418 games, 200 homers, 742 RBI and a .269 average.

There was an interesting contrast in the reaction to the Tartabull trade as reported in *The Sporting News* and *Sports Illustrated*. Moss Klein in the December 15 *TSN* wrote that "Tartabull has obvious talent . . . but the Royals had better correct his attitude. He refused to make adjustments in his swing even though he had the worst strikeout ratio in the league . . . and he'll probably be a defensive liability at any position." Klein was trying to make sense of a trade that doesn't make sense on the surface by whittling away at Tartabull, but his comments are wide of the mark. I don't know what he means by saying that Tartabull "had the worst strikeout ratio in the league." Tartabull struck out in a little less than 31% of his at bats, which was about the same as Canseco (29%), Cory Snyder (30%) and teammate Jim Presley (28%) and less than Incaviglia (34%), Rob Deer (39%), and Gorman Thomas (33%). For a power-hitting rookie, there is nothing in the least remarkable about Tartabull's strikeout rate. Reggie Jackson and Mike Schmidt both struck out more often as rookies than did Tartabull, and Schmidt still struck out more in his third season in the league. If Klein meant strikeout-to-walk ratio, Tartabull wasn't one of the ten worst in the league.

As to the comment that Tartabull "refused to make adjustments in his swing" to curb the strikeouts: Tartabull struck out in 41% of his at bats in April and 36% in May, but cut it to 26% in July and 28% in September. Hell, it took Reggie five years to make that much progress in cutting his strikeouts. Most power hitters strike out much more in their first couple of years than they do later on, but Tartabull was cutting the rate down remarkably well as the season progressed. More to the point, if you were a rookie and you were hitting the way Tartabull was hitting, how anxious would you be to start fooling around with your swing? If you were a manager and you had a rookie who was hitting like Tartabull, how anx-ious would you be to have somebody else fooling around with his swing? I know I wouldn't tolerate it.

Each man is the conservator of his own talent. No one else has developed Danny Tartabull's abilities to where they are. No one else will suffer the consequences if the adjustments that he makes throw him into a tailspin. So long as the man is succeeding and contributing, I don't feel it's appropriate for anyone else to snipe at the way that he chooses to develop his skills.

As to the comment about his defense, I must say that as a Royals fan I ain't worried. In the last few years Tartabull has played third, second, short, right and left field. Of course he isn't terrific at any position, but with the native skills that he has, I see no reason to think he won't be a very fine defensive outfielder.

Peter Gammons in the December 22–29 *Sports Illustrated* took just the opposite approach to the trade, highlighting the riddle of the trade by stretching Tartabull's credentials while diminishing those of the new Mariners. Tartabull was now a "rare young right-handed slugger who knocked in 96 runs as a rookie despite a month's illness" who was handed over for "diminutive breaking ball pitcher Scott Bankhead, utility outfielder Mike Kingery and 10-year minor-league veteran pitcher Steve Shields." The "diminutive breaking ball pitcher" weighs 15 or 20 pounds more than Ron Guidry and has a good fastball, and the "utility outfielder" has never been used in a utility role, having been a regular since being called up in midsummer and having played well enough that the Royals, or at least their media, had projected him as a regular in 1987. Gammons lengthened the gap between the players traded to emphasize the point that the Mariners "were looking for cheap help . . . they got just what owner George Argyros wanted—seven players each making under $100,000 a year."

I don't know what truth there is to the allegation that the Mariner trades were economically motivated. In baseball it's not the kind of thing you say about your friends. It's an "allegation." You don't announce that you've made a trade to save money, but over the history of baseball there have been a hell of a lot of fine trades that were made with one eye on the balance sheet. The trade was made, at least in part, because Dick Williams evaluates talent differently than other people do. In my part of the country there used to be a basketball coach named Jack Hartman. He was a fine coach and his teams would win, but a lot of times his players didn't look like they were good athletes. Sportswriters talked a lot about how much Hartman did with so little talent, which was intended as a compliment but became a tiresome one after a while, and Hartman finally said, "Look, what is talent? Talent is just being where you are supposed to be and doing what you are supposed to do." What he was saying, in essence, was that you may think that talent is being able to run fast and jump high and stop and start quickly, but I think that talent is blocking out on the boards and cutting off the passing lanes and hitting your free throws. You recruit the guys that you think have talent and I'll recruit the guys that I think have talent, and we'll see who wins.

Williams is like that. He takes a somewhat different view of what constitutes talent than do most other managers. If you think that talent is being able to throw 92 miles an hour, fine; you take the guys who throw 92 miles an hour and work behind the hitters, and Dick will take the guys who throw 87 miles an hour and work ahead of the hitters. Scott Bankhead struck out 94 men and walked 37 in 1986. To Dick Williams, that's talent. Mike Kingery isn't going to drive in 96 runs this year, but he'll hit 96 cutoff men and break up a double play anytime he has a chance. You can say that's not talent if you want to. Steve Shields spent a long time in the minor leagues, but then he never gave up and hasn't had a sore arm in years.

A couple of other things that may have been factors in the trade were the development of Mickey Brantley and the fact that the Mariners, even giving up Tartabull, still have an excellent power corps. Brantley had a monster year at Calgary (probably as good a year all things considered as Tartabull had had the year before), and was called up in time to play 27 games with the Mariners. Although he hit just .196 with Seattle, his performance on closer examination wasn't all that bad. In exactly one-sixth of a schedule Brantley hit 3 homers and 2 triples, drew 10 walks, had 3 outfield assists. His secondary average was .265 and his fielding percentage, GIDP rate and strikeout frequency were all reasonably good. Dick Williams may have decided that, regardless of what anybody else thought, Brantley was a better player than Tartabull—exactly as in 1980 he decided that although Tim Raines was 1-for-20 as a major-league hitter and Ron LeFlore had just stolen 97 bases for him, Tim Raines was a better player. I don't know that that's what he's decided, but I'll tell you for sure that if that's what he's decided, you'd better not bet against him, because he's been managing a long time and it would be hard to prove that he has ever misjudged a player's abilities, other than second basemen.

The economic explanation for this trade doesn't make a lot of sense to me. If you just want cheap help, you can pick that up anywhere; you can always bring players out of the minors to play for $52,000. The trick is to find players who don't make a lot of money, and can produce. Tartabull will not be eligible for salary arbitration for two more years, and it is generally assumed, among baseball men, that the most productive phase of a ballplayer's career, dollar for dollar, is the years two through five. Rookies are paid hardly any money, but then a lot of them can't do the job, and after five years a player's salary has reached its peak, while his skills often are beginning to decline. If you were very interested in getting good value for the dollar, it seems likely to me that Tartabull would be the first player you would want to keep, rather than the one to trade.

As a Royals fan, I'm very happy to have Danny Tartabull. I'm sorry to lose Scott Bankhead, I'll miss Mike Kingery and I'm even a little sorry to lose Steve Shields, but I'm happier to have Danny Tartabull than I am sorry to lose all three of them. But I don't think the trade is necessarily lop-sided, and I think that if we look back at it a year from now there's a good chance we're going to see some reason for it having been made other than to save money.

8. Tom Brunansky, Minnesota

Had another good half-season . . .

9. Mike Davis, Oakland

Hit .171 in the late innings of close games . . .

10. Rob Deer, Milwaukee

Dear Bill:

You seem to like to see how different players' years match up statistically, and I share this perverted fascination with you. This one is real good . . .

Going into this year's spring training, the Brewers' manager, George Bamberger, was enamored of the power skills of his freshly unwrapped Rob Deer, picked up from the Giants for a pair of mittens and a kerosene heater. I saw Bamberger quoted several times as saying that he wanted to do the same thing for Deer that he did for Gorman Thomas in 1978.

I love to watch Deer hit, but I doubted that it would work. Deer swings as if his off-season hobby was killing flies with a sledgehammer, but his major-league equivalency for the 1984 season at Phoenix was unimpressive, and he had not hit well in 78 games in 1985. But there were many similarities between Thomas and Deer. They are (were) almost the same height and weight. They *look* alike (built like a bear, long hair and moustache), and they had produced in the minors but had never been given a full shot in the majors. How prophetic was Bambi?

	G	AB	R	H	2B	3B	HR	RBI	BB	SO	SB	Avg.
Thomas, 1978	137	452	70	111	24	1	32	86	73	133	3	.246
Deer, 1986	134	466	75	108	17	3	33	86	72	179	5	.232

Wow. I'm looking forward to seeing Deer lead the Brew Crew to the World Series this year. Four-man rotation and well-defined bullpen,

Mat Olkin

Deer Mat:

Thanks. I hadn't noticed that it was that close.

A lot of people now see Deer as the new Gorman Thomas, and have already written him down for a couple of 40-homer seasons and a ten-year career. I've been wrong a lot of times, but I don't see it; I still don't think Deer will connect often

enough, over a period of years, to stay in the lineup.

A few of the differences are subtle, but important. Thomas struck out in almost 30% of his at bats, which is a lot—in fact, his percentage is a major-league record for a career of 1,400 or more games. But Deer struck out in almost 40% of his at bats, which is A LOT. There have been players who have had good years striking out 30% of the time—but not 40%. At the 1986 rate, Deer would not only break the major-league strikeout record, but bury the pieces.

If you strike out in 40% of your at bats, then to hit .240 you've got to hit .400 when not striking out. The only player ever to hit .400 (lifetime) when not striking out was Babe Ruth, who hit .406 for his career when not striking out.

You say that both players had produced in the minors, but that's a loose generalization. Thomas in his last two minor-league seasons had hit .297 with 51 homers and 122 RBI, and .322 with 36 homers and a .297 average, both in the Pacific Coast League. Deer in his last two minor-league seasons had hit .217 with 35 homers and 99 RBI in the Texas League, and .227 with 31 homers and 69 RBI in the PCL. That's a big difference.

You would probably ask rhetorically what difference that makes after the player has proven that he can hit major-league pitching, and that gets us to the heart of the question. I really believe in the idea of major-league equivalencies of minor-league production, but in the past I've backed off when players came up and had a year that was above what their minor-league records suggested. Looking back on those occasions, it seems to me that the minor-league batting records remain a valuable indicator of major-league ability even after the player has played one year in the majors.

When I introduced the MLE (major-league equivalencies) in the 1985 *Abstract*, I pointed out that Bobby Meacham had hit 42 points higher as a rookie than the MLE showed, .253 vs. .211. I just figured that he had either improved as a hitter some, or else the MLE was off a little, and he was actually a better hitter than that. But in his second major-league season Meacham dropped to .218, and in his third he hit .224. So it wasn't that the MLE was off, at all, but merely that he happened to have a good year as a rookie.

When Brook Jacoby hit only seven home runs as a rookie in 1984 although his MLE for 1983 showed 18 homers in 439 at bats, some people wrote the MLE off as misguided. But in 1985 Jacoby hit 20 home runs, and in 1986 he hit 17. It wasn't that his MLE was off, at all, but merely that his performance, for one season, was a little below his norm.

When Mark Salas hit .300 in 1985 after his MLEs showed him hitting .230–.270, I just assumed that he was actually a better hitter than the translation showed—but then last year he hit only .233. It wasn't that the MLE was off, at all, but that he just happened to have a good year, like three dozen other players.

When Vince Coleman came up in 1985, his MLEs showed him as a player who would hit .235–.250 in the major leagues. As a rookie he hit .267, so I figured OK, he's actually a little better hitter than that. But then last year he hit .232, and had a season that looks for all the world like his MLE for 1984.

So this time, I'm going to be a tougher sale. Deer's MLEs show him as a player who is going to hit .170–.210 and strike out so often that he can't play. For one season, he rose above that, and you can project him on to 45 homers if you want to. I'm not saying that he hasn't improved as a hitter and won't stick around. I'm just saying that I'm not going to buy him lock, stock, and barrel on the basis of what he'd done so far. Scott Fletcher hit .300 last year, but that doesn't mean he's going to hit .310 next year. I still see Deer as a .195 hitter.

11. Ruben Sierra, Texas

If I could choose any of the fine rookies from the 1986 season to start a ballclub with, I would not hesitate for a second. I would choose Ruben Sierra. I would not trade him for José Canseco, although I think Canseco is going to be a tremendous power hitter. I would not trade him for Cory Snyder. I'm not sure if I would trade him for both of them.

Baseball America, in its September 25–October 9 edition, selected Sierra as the outstanding prospect in the American Association. "He has the tools to do everything," they quoted his manager. "He hits with power from both sides of the plate. He can run and throw, and he's only 20 years old . . . He just needs experience to be a great one."

That endorsement, glowing as it is, has almost nothing to do with why I like Sierra as much as I do. The basis of my tremendous attachment to this guy is simply this: that there are very, very few players who can hit major-league pitching with authority at the age of 20—and those few who can have a tremendously disproportionate history of developing into superstars. When you compound that with his obvious defensive skills (he can run like the wind and throw with the best of them) . . . well, you've got a package there.

Let's look briefly at the ten most-comparable rookies. The ten most-similar rookies, alphabetically, were Henry Aaron, Gus Bell, Billy Conigliaro, Willie Davis, Frank Howard, Rick Monday, Tony Perez, Darrell Porter, Joe Torre, and Denny Walton. Two of those players washed out (Conigliaro and Walton), but among the ten players, Gus Bell was eighth in career games played (1,741) and Willie Davis was eighth in career homers (182). The weighted average of the ten players: 1,922 homers, 1,869 hits, 271 homers, 1,026 RBI, and a .280 average.

But here's the kicker: Sierra has Canseco's problem. Canseco as a rookie is so good that he tends to be distinctly better than the most-comparable rookies. He is comparable to Darrell Porter in 1973, but he is a year younger (a big item, as you know from the rookies study), he hit for a better average, he has much more speed, and has an advantage (as a hitter) in that he is not a catcher. He is comparable to Willie Davis in 1961, but he is a year younger, hit for a better average (.264–.254), and has more power (.476 slugging against .451). He is very comparable to Tony Perez as a hitter, but he is three years younger and has defensive assets that Perez couldn't dream of. He is very comparable to Frank Howard as a rookie in terms of games played, batting average and slugging percentage, but he has speed, doesn't strike out as much and is three years younger.

So really, the only member of that gaudy group that Sierra isn't, on balance, ahead of in some major respect is Henry Aaron.

Now, let's look at one more thing. Called up about the first of June, Sierra hit .193 in June and .241 in July, totalling 6 homers and 15 RBI in 167 at bats. In 29 games in August, he hit .330 with 6 doubles, 4 triples and 3 homers, driving in 17 runs. In 31 games in September–October, he hit .290 with 7 homers and 23 RBI.

In his first month in the majors, Sierra struck out 25 times and walked only 4 (6.25–1). Over the last three months he struck out 40 times and walked 20.

So I say this is THE man from the 1986 rookie crop. There were probably seven rookies in 1986 who have a chance to develop into Hall of Famers, but Sierra has the best chance.

12. Lee Lacy, Baltimore

1986 season was almost a dead ringer for his career record in seasonal notation . . .

13. Ruppert Jones, California

Had only 90 hits and scored 73 runs, or .811 runs scored per hit. That just missed being the highest percentage in the league. Henderson had 160 hits and scored 130 runs, or .813 . . .

14. Mike Kingery, Kansas City

Fast, good arm, great hustle, had good plate discipline in the minors. He's a longshot, but he could come through in Seattle.

National League

1. Tony Gwynn, San Diego (10)

1986 Power/Speed Number: 20.3
Career Power/Speed Number: 42.4
Extra base hits as a percentage of hits, 1986: .26
Times in Scoring Position: 91
Runs Scored as a Percentage of Times on Base: .402
Runs Per Time on Base/Not Home Run: .369
Batting Average When Not Striking Out: .348
Batting Average When Not Striking Out or Homering: .332
1986 Speed Score: 6.4
1986 Secondary Average: .277
Career Secondary Average: .225
Chance of getting 2000 career hits: .83
Chance of getting 2500 career hits: .50
Chance of getting 3000 career hits: .28
Chance of getting 3500 career hits: .14
Chance of getting 4000 career hits: .04
Chance of getting 4500 career hits:
    None Established
Chance of getting 300 career home runs:
    None Established
Chance of getting 938 career stolen bases:
    None Established
Chance of getting 1500 career runs scored: .29
Chance of getting 1750 career runs scored: .04
Chance of getting 2000 career runs scored: .0004
Chance of getting 2250 career runs scored:
    None Established
Chance of getting 1500 career RBI:
    None Established

2. Dave Parker, Cincinnati (2)

Led National League in total bases for the second straight year, with 304 . . . over last three years has hit .329 with runners in scoring position, .326 with men on base, .322 when leading off an inning, but just .220 in the least significant category (no one on, not leading off) . . .

3. Darryl Strawberry, New York

What does this guy have to do to get some respect? During the 13 games of post-season play he just played superb defense in right field, but the announcers hardly said a word about it, just talked about his strikeouts. In the third game of the playoffs he broke a slump with a beautiful bunt, then turned the game around with a massive three-run homer the next time up to set up Dykstra's game-winning blast, but the next day it was like it all never happened. His secondary average last year was .459, second best in the National League. If you hit homers, draw walks, and steal bases the way he does, you can play for me if you hit .210.

Over the last three years Strawberry has a .232 average with the bases empty, but .292 with men on base. A beautiful, graceful athlete, he should not be judged as a player by what anybody imagines to be his potential.

4. Kevin Bass, Houston

Has taken two strong strides forward in the last two years. Another one would put him among the best players in the league.

5. Chili Davis, San Francisco

Good player, but hasn't developed. Has lost a lot of his speed and has never become consistent at the plate.

6. Andre Dawson, Montreal

Had his best all-around season since his knees began giving him trouble three years ago. Might be best for him to get in a grass park . . . wonder what he would hit in Wrigley Field . . .

7. Glenn Wilson, Philadelphia

Of his 35 homers in the last three years, 21 have been hit with men on base . . .

8. Andy Van Slyke, St. Louis

A fine player against a right-handed pitcher, a .260–.270 hitter with an excellent secondary average and excellent defense. But it just doesn't look like he's going to hit left-handers . . .

9. Mike Marshall, Los Angeles

Here's a trivia question for you: Who was the only player to win a triple crown in the major leagues as well as in the minors? Marshall won a triple crown at Albuquerque in 1981, and has zero chance to become the second. The first was Ted Williams . . .

10. Keith Moreland, Chicago

1986 Power/Speed Number: 4.8
Career Power/Speed Number: 32.3
Extra base hits as a Percentage of hits, 1986: .26
Times in Scoring Position: 45
Runs Scored as Percentage of Times on Base: .340
Runs Per Time on Base/Not Home Run: .300
Batting Average When Not Striking Out: .296
Batting Average When Not Striking Out or Homering: .279
1986 Speed Score: 2.1
1986 Secondary Average: .208
Career Secondary Average: .238
Chance of getting 2000 career hits: .20
Chance of getting 2500 career hits:
    None Established
Chance of getting 300 career home runs:
    None Established
Chance of getting 938 career stolen bases:
    None Established
Chance of getting 1500 career runs scored:
    None Established
Chance of getting 1500 career RBI:
    None Established

11. Joe Orsulak, Pittsburgh

Did you ever notice that if you say Orsulak over and over it sounds like the noise you hear inside of a train? Another one of those is Quisenberry. If you say Quisenberry over and over and tap the table with a pencil when you hit the qs and bs it sounds like windshield wipers . . . Orsulak has speed and can throw, but doesn't hit with power, so he's got to hit more than .249 or they'll put him on the first train going home . . .

12. Omar Moreno, Atlanta
Released.

DESIGNATED HITTERS

1. Larry Parrish, Texas (10)

Over last three years has hit .314 with runners in scoring position (117/373) . . .

1986 Power/Speed Number: 5.4
Career Power/Speed Number: 47.8
Extra base hits as a percentage of hits, 1986: .40
Times in Scoring Position: 54
Runs Scored as a Percentage of Times on Base: .368
Runs Per Time on Base/Not Home Run: .253
Batting Average When Not Striking Out: .366
Batting Average When Not Striking Out or Homering: .311
1986 Speed Score: 3.9
1986 Secondary Average: .351
Career Secondary Average: .256
Chance of getting 2000 career hits: .81
Chance of getting 2500 career hits: .12
Chance of getting 3000 career hits: None Established
Chance of getting 300 career home runs: .74
Chance of getting 400 career home runs: .09
Chance of getting 500 career home runs: None Established
Chance of getting 938 career stolen bases: None Established
Chance of getting 1500 career runs scored: None Established
Chance of getting 1500 career RBI: .09
Chance of getting 1750 career RBI: None Established

2. Ken Phelps, Seattle (3)

See Seattle comment.

3. Don Baylor, Boston (1)

Wonder who will hire him to manage? How about Oakland? Maybe California? . . . I think he can manage but I wouldn't hire him to do it until he spends a couple of years in the minors.

4. Mike Easler, New York

Now with Philadelphia. If the Philadelphia management knows why they got him or what they plan to do with him, they're certainly the only ones.

5. Larry Sheets, Baltimore

A platoon player in the best Earl Weaver tradition, hit 17 homers in 312 at bats against right-handed pitching . . .

6. Ron Hassey, Chicago

Godawful slow and can't catch anymore, but in his thirties he has emerged as a .300 hitter . . . his .329 average against right-handed pitchers was third best in the league behind Boggs and Mattingly.

7. Andre Thornton, Cleveland

Probably would be more effective in a platoon role, perhaps with Mel Hall. The development of Snyder crowds the picture, but Corrales may just cut Thornton loose.

8. Dave Kingman, Oakland

The thing about the Dave Kingman Hall of Fame debate is that almost nobody really thinks that he belongs in the Hall of Fame or has any real chance to get there. What he has is a chance to attain a single level of performance—500 homers—which is usually associated with the Hall of Fame. I trust the judgment of the voters enough that I'm not really worried about their selecting him.

9. Reggie Jackson, California

Over last three years has hit just .191 in the late innings of close games, with only 3 homers in 220 at bats. His batting averages—and remember that the Angels have been in the pennant race all three years—have been .195 in August and .209 in September, although he has hit with good power in September. In the last three years he has driven in only 20% of his runners in scoring position,

and only 31% (29/93) of his runners on third base with less than two out, which may be the lowest percentage in baseball . . . My guess is that the sudden increase in walks drawn in '86 indicates that the reflexes are going, and his average will drop sharply in '87. But in '86, at least, the power and walks gave him a secondary average of .389, sixth best in the league . . .

10. Roy Smalley, Jr., Minnesota

Over the last three years has hit just .183 in the late innings of close games.

11. Cliff Johnson, Toronto

Now holds the career record for pinch-hit home runs, with 20.

12. Ben Oglivie, Milwaukee

Oglivie spent 42 games as DH and didn't hit nearly as well in that role as he did in the outfield. Gorman Thomas spent 36 games as the Milwaukee DH and was in the ones. It's an area that needs improvement.

13. Jorge Orta, Kansas City

Kansas City designated hitters don't get on base very much and don't hit for power, but they're nice people.

14. Detroit (Vacant)

Sparky doesn't use a DH, but rotates people in and out of the spot. In 1986 his DHs included Brookens (34 at bats), Collins (80), Coles (26), Evans (145), Grubb (156), and Spilman (33). Last year, with Grubb having a monster year, the Tiger DHs may have been the best in the league, creating 104 runs (tied with Baltimore for the league lead) and made only 454 outs, fewest of any team's designated hitters . . .

STARTING PITCHERS

National League

1. Mike Scott, Houston (10)

Of Mike Scott's ten losses, five came in games in which he allowed three runs or less. He lost by scores of 1–0, 1–0, 2–1, 3–1, and 3–2 . . . Eight of his ten losses were by one run . . . If you get people on, you can run against him. Base stealers against him were 41 for 51, or 80% . . . remains tremendously strong in the late innings . . . last three years has record of 8–9 in April and May, 16–12 in June and July, 17–8 in August and September . . . ERA about a run lower at night than in day games . . .

One of the amazing things about baseball is that every year, a dozen things happen which have never happened before. In 1986, a 31-year-old pitcher with a career high of 137 strikeouts suddenly becomes a domineering strikeout pitcher. That's never happened before. I looked up how many pitchers there have been in history who led the league in strikeouts for the first time in their thirties. Most strikeout pitchers are strikeout pitchers from the day they come up, but there have been 17 other pitchers who have led the league in strikeouts for the first time at age 30 or later. None of those 17 pitchers, however, is a story anything like Mike Scott. Eight of the 17 pitchers were 30 or 31 years old, and led the league in strikeouts with totals of 153 or less, totals for the most part consistent with their previous careers. Bert Blyleven was 34 years old when he led the league in Ks in 1985, but his total of 206 strikeouts was just the seventh-best of his career. Bobo Newsome was 34 when he led the league in strikeouts for the first time in '42, but his total of 134 was his lowest in seven years. Several other pitchers, like Bob Gibson, Vic Raschi, and Carl Hubbell, were in their thirties the first time they led the league in strikeouts, but with totals completely consistent with their prior histories. Mickey Lolich struck out 308 for his first title in 1971, but he had struck out 271 two years before. The oldest men to claim their first strikeout titles were Phil Niekro in 1977 (38 years old, 262 strikeouts after previous high of 195, but he pitched 330 innings) and Early Wynn in 1957 (37 years old, 184 K). Probably the *most* comparable event in baseball history was the development of Dazzy Vance, a tremendous strikeout pitcher in the 1920s, who pitched only 33 major-league innings before turning 30, but really Mike Scott is a brand-new phenomenon. Nothing like this has ever happened before.

2. Fernando Valenzuela, Los Angeles (2)

Over the last two years has won 20 games on the road (20–13; also 18–8 at home) . . . The most interesting thing about him in the Project Scoresheet data is that, with his famous screwball, he does give right-handed hitters more trouble than left-handers. Over the three years lefties have hit .243 against him, right-handers just .218 . . . does an exceptional job of keeping the leadoff man off base (.201 batting average, .259 on base percentage for leadoff men) . . .

3. Dwight Gooden, New York

Last year he was a unanimous No. 1 selection. This year he received hardly any support for number one, being placed No. 1 on about ten ballots but not finishing first in any precincts.

There were reports last year that Mel Stottlemyre had persuaded Dwight Gooden to stop trying to strike out every hitter and to try to concentrate on getting more ground ball outs. His thinking was that going for strikeouts was placing a strain on Gooden's arm, and that in the long run he'd be more durable as a ground ball, control-type pitcher.

That's a common belief among baseball men, but it is dead wrong. Among all of the hundreds of issues that I have studied in the ten years I have been doing this, the *most* definitive evidence that I have ever found on any issue is the evidence that the career expectation for a strikeout pitcher is dramatically longer than it is for a control pitcher, a ground ball pitcher or any other class of pitchers. *Virtually all pitchers who are durable over a long period of time begin and become successful as strikeout pitchers*. In some cases, like Warren Spahn, they will become ground-ball pitchers as time passes, but in most cases they will remain strikeout pitchers as long as they are effective.

If you take two pitchers of the same age, same ERA, and same won-lost record, the one who strikes out more hitters will go on to have a better career almost 80% of the time. The greater the difference in strikeouts, the greater will be the difference in their future careers. The exact number of strikeouts that the pitcher gets is an excellent indicator of exactly how long he will last. Nolan Ryan and Steve Carlton, two of the greatest strikeout pitchers of all time, have also been two of the most remarkably durable pitchers of all time. Look at Walter Johnson, Tom Seaver, and Bob Gibson. Look at Marichal and Sutton and Ferguson Jenkins. Look at Blyleven. The guys who move the ball around in the strike zone, like Catfish Hunter, Randy Jones, and Mike Flanagan, will have some good years but almost never last as long as the power pitchers. Even Tommy John as a young pitcher was over the league average in strikeouts—as, of course, was Hunter.

Even Stottlemyre himself. People think that Stottlemyre was a durable pitcher, and he was, but he won only 164 major-league games and had his last good year at age 31. Stottlemyre came up in mid-season, 1964, and went 9–3 in 13 starts. Luis Tiant, one year older than Stottlemyre, also came up in mid-season, 1964, and went 9–3 in 16 starts (as well as 1–1 in relief.) It's as good a matched set as you can hope for, the difference between the two being that Stottlemyre was a ground-ball pitcher and Tiant was a strikeout pitcher. Stottlemyre won 164 games but was finished by 1973. Tiant lasted until 1979 (effectively); he made about 30% more starts, pitched 30% more innings and won almost 40% more games.

Why? Maybe for this reason: As a pitcher ages, his strikeout totals almost always decline. They go up for two or three years after entering the league, but, with the exception of an odd case like Mike Scott, then they decline. Once the pitcher is below average in strikeouts, he must be outstanding in some other respect in order to keep pitching, so that you might generalize that once a pitcher is below the league average in strikeouts, he usually has only two or three years left as an effective pitcher. If you visualize this as a line on a graph, the height at which the line starts to decline and length of time that it takes to reach the bottom are going to be very closely correlated. Stottlemyre came into the league at 4.6 strikeouts a game, and went up to 5.3 (1967), after which he began to decline. By 1973, striking out only three men a game, he was putting tremendous pressure on the other elements of his game. Tiant came into the league at seven strikeouts a game, and went up to 9.2 (1967–1968). In 1972 he was still striking out 6.2 men a game. In 1976 he was still striking out 4.2 men a game, and so he was still effective. But there just really aren't very many effective pitchers who strike out three men a game.

I've reported on the studies before and won't repeat them, but I'll say this: The separation of data on this issue is so dramatic that you can't miss it. If you study the issue, no matter how badly, no matter how carelessly, you can't possibly miss seeing that the strikeout pitchers last a lot longer than the control-type pitchers. There are a lot of factors

which will determine how long Dwight Gooden will pitch, and you have to be concerned about a pitcher who has been worked so hard at such a young age. But if Mel Stottlemyre wants Dwight Gooden to last as long as possible, he'd better stop this crap about throwing ground balls and tell him to concentrate on striking out as many batters as he can.

4. Bob Ojeda, New York

The Mets set a major-league record last year for non-Latin players with Spanish surnames. Maybe they were trying to qualify for some affirmative action money or something. Just on the pitching staff they had Bob Ojeda, who is from California, Sid Fernandez, who is Hawaiian, Rick Aguilera, who is from California, and Jesse Orosco, who is from Santa Barbara and looks Chinese.

5. Ron Darling, New York

Darling had 26 quality starts, most in the National League except for Mike Scott. The top five were Scott (32 in 37 starts), Darling (26 in 34), Mike Krukow (25 in 34), Bob Forsch (24 in 33), and Rick Rhoden (24 in 34) . . . Darling made 7 errors in '86, most by any major-league pitcher . . .

6. Rick Rhoden, Pittsburgh

Do you know what this trade means? It means that the two best-hitting pitchers in baseball (Lollar and Rhoden) are now in the American League . . . actually, I don't know that Rhoden and Lollar are any better than Schatzeder and Don Robinson, whose hitting is discussed in their respective staff comments, but they're certainly not any worse. In sharp contrast to 1985, when Rhoden got the Silver Slugger Award despite hitting .189 with no power, there were a lot of pitchers who had good years with the bat last year, including Rhoden (.278, 9 doubles and a homer), Schatzeder, Steve Carlton (.200, a homer and 8 RBI in 45 at bats), John Denny (.222), Bob Forsch (.171, but seven extra base hits and 12 RBI), Orel Hershiser (.239), Mike LaCoss (.230, 2 home runs), Sutcliffe (.208, 2 doubles and a homer), and Fernando (.220). At least four other pitchers also hit home runs . . .

7. John Tudor, St. Louis

In the last two years Tudor has pitched 288 innings in Busch Stadium with a 24–4 record and a 1.89 ERA. On the road he's pitched 206 innings and is 10–11, 3.06 ERA . . . on artificial turf he is 30–7; on grass fields 4–8 . . . Over the last three years his record is 8–13 in April and May, but 19–5 in August and September. In September he is 10–3 with a 1.99 ERA . . . has not pitched well when left in in the late innings of close games . . . Double play support, 34 in 30 starts, was third best in the NL . . . opponents stole only ten bases in his 30 starts, best in the National League . . .

8. Mike Krukow, San Francisco

Krukow in his four years with the Giants is 31–16 in Candlestick Park, but 19–27 on the road . . . in 1986 limited opponents to a .194 batting average with men on base . . .

9. Bob Knepper, Houston

Over the last two years is 18–11 in road games, just 14–14 in the Astrodome . . . It's hard to say what it is that has made Knepper so much better a pitcher today, as a somewhat fleshy, 32-year-old placement pitcher, than he was in his twenties, as a trim lefthander known for a good fastball and an outstanding curve. When Knepper came up with the Giants in 1977, he looked like he would be one of the outstanding pitchers of his generation, going 11–9 in four months in 1977, then 17–11 in his first full season in 1978—a win level that he never matched again until last season. In 1979 he had an off year, which no one took too seriously until he had another one; it became four off years in five. During a five-year stretch he won only 38 games, losing 61. He took tremendous criticism for his lack of emotional intensity on the mound; his name became synonymous with "talented but a loser." Just as suddenly and inexplicably, he turned it around in 1984 and has now had three straight good seasons, giving him a total of 114 career wins. He did improve his control in 1984, going from three walks a game (3.0 in 1982, 3.2 in 1983) to 2.1 walks a game over the last three years, but in the main it's as if he pitches under a veil, his successes and failures seeming equally, and uniformly, incomprehensible.

10. Danny Cox, St. Louis

His offensive support, 110 runs in 32 starts, was the third-worst in the National League last year.

11. Nolan Ryan, Houston

Committed two more errors last year, giving him 76 in his career. I believe the all-time record is 80 . . . last two seasons, record is 16–7 in the Astrodome, just 6–13 on the road . . . In the last three years has walked 67 leadoff men . . . 23 of the 38 homers he has allowed in the last three years have come with men on base, although only 40% of his opposition at bats have been with men on base . . .

12. Sid Fernandez, New York

Received the best offensive support among the Met starters, 5.16 runs per game. The average was third-best in the NL . . . an interesting pitcher, obviously intelligent on and off the mound but just as obviously out of shape. If his conditioning habits were better you'd be looking at him as a guy who was going to win a couple of hundred games, but with his girth, he won't be able to throw his weight forward as he strides, hence will put a lot more pressure on his shoulder.

13. Orel Hershiser, Los Angeles

Hershiser lost 6 games last year in which his team was shut out. When the Dodgers scored at least one run, he was 14–8 . . . Over last two years is 21–5 in Dodger Stadium, 12–12 on the road.

14. Dave Dravecky, San Diego

Cuts off the running game very well. Would win big if he could stay healthy and pitched for a good team . . . hit a homer and stole a base last year making him probably the only major-league pitcher whose power/speed number was not zero . . .

15. Bob Welch, Los Angeles

Dodgers scored only 108 runs for him in 33 starts, just barely missing the worst offensive support in the National League.

16. Bill Gullickson, Cincinnati

Did for the Reds about what he did for Montreal the year before. His career record in his home parks is now 55–26 (.679); on the road he is 33–48 (.407) . . . over the last two years is 4–11 on grass fields . . .

17. Floyd Youmans, Montreal

Does not pitch at all well in his home park in Montreal. On the road over the last two years he is 11–4

with a 2.76 ERA, but in Montreal he is just 6–11 with an ERA close to 4.00 . . . superb pitcher, but the end of his motion is not pretty. It looks to me like he'll hurt either his elbow or his back within two or three years . . . Incredibly easy to run on. In fact, he probably does the worst job of holding baserunners of anybody in baseball . . . I guess that high school coaches don't teach that . . .

18. Tom Browning, Cincinnati

1986 season is probably a fair representation of his ability. He shouldn't be expected to win 20 games a year . . .

19-Tie Bob Forsch, St. Louis

All four Cardinal starters (Forsch, Tudor, Cox, and Mathews) were among the NL pitchers receiving the best double play support. In the 33 games that Forsch started, the Cards turned 42 double plays, or 1.27 per game. Only Chris Welsh of Cincinnati received better DP support . . .

19-Tie Shane Rawley, Philadelphia

Over last three years has 8–0 record in August . . . Received the best offensive support of any NL pitcher last year, 5.65 runs per game . . .

American League

1. Roger Clemens, Boston (14)

In Clemens's 33 starts the Red Sox drew 972,000 fans, or 29,500 a start. The average was about 2,000 higher than when Clemens wasn't pitching . . . Has received the best offensive support of any American League pitcher for two years in a row, 6.09 last year (tying Mike Mason) and 6.15 in 1985. Mason was just catching up, having received the *worst* offensive support in the league in 1985 . . . With average offensive support Clemens would probably have finished 21–7.

2. Teddy Higuera, Milwaukee

Higuera had 26 quality starts, most in the American League. The

top five were Higuera (26 in 34 starts), Mike Witt (24 in 34), Clemens and McCaskill (each 23 in 33), and Jimmy Key (22 in 35) . . .

3. Mike Witt, California

Hot-weather pitcher, has 5-year record of 16–6 in August, 7–11 in May . . . Witt's double play support jumped so sharply in 1985 that I thought at the time it might be a fluke, maybe a lot of double plays turned after he was out of the game or something. By now, it's clear that it wasn't an aberration, but a switch in his pitching style. The Angels turned 44 double plays in his 34 starts last year (44/35 in 1985). It's a rare combination, a strikeout pitcher who

also gets over 60% of his non-strikeout outs on ground balls. Most strikeout pitchers, like Ryan, Gooden, Clemens, and Scott, pitch up in the strike zone and don't get many ground balls. An odd combination, but a deadly one.

4. Jack Morris, Detroit

Morris and Jim DeShaies of Houston won seven games each in 1986 that weren't classed as quality starts. Morris was 7–5 when not having a quality start, DeShaies 7–4. The only other major-league pitchers who had winning records with five or more wins when not having quality starts were Clemens (5–3) and Candelaria (5–2) . . . In the entire National League there were only three games in 1986 in which a starting pitcher allowed 6 runs and won the game. Morris himself had three such games, and three more in which he allowed five earned runs . . . Morris may not be the best pitcher in the majors, but he's got to be the most consistent. Last year I talked about Morris doing something every year to solidify his credentials as a potential Hall of Famer. Last year he did a couple of *major* things to solidify his credentials, winning 20 games for the second time and striking out 200 batters for the second time. He's probably three or four good years away from the Hall of Fame now. Morris and Fernando have got to be the best anchors for a starting rotation in baseball today . . .

5. Bruce Hurst, Boston

Hurst had only one game in 1986 in which he allowed more than four earned runs . . . The vagaries of public reaction, chapter 162: One thing you no doubt heard about the Sox last summer is that the suspension of Oil Can Boyd may actually have helped him in the long run, because he pitched well late in the year whereas always before he has faded in August and September. This is not true; Boyd actually has pitched well late in the season except for one year (career record of 11–10 in September), but actually it *is* true of Hurst, who in the previous four years had a record of 11–18 after August 1. Hurst missed almost two months with an injury last year and finished the season strong, but because he weighs 215 pounds and doesn't act like he's 14 years old, people just assume that he's strong and durable, so nobody looks at the record to check . . . Among the toughest pitchers in the league to run on . . .

6. Kirk McCaskill, California

Also among the toughest pitchers in the league to run on . . .

7. Charlie Hough, Texas

Five years ago Charlie Hough was 33 years old and had an established win level of 4.4 and 53 career wins, meaning that he was 33.4 years away from his 200th career win. Three years ago he was 35 years old and had an established win level of 13.5 with 84 career wins, meaning

that he was 8.6 years away from his 200th win. Now he's 38 (turned 39 this January) and has an established win level of 15.7 with 131 wins, meaning that he is just 4.4 years away from his 200th win . . .

8. Bert Blyleven, Minnesota

Of his record-setting 50 home runs allowed:
• 23 were hit with men on base, 27 with the bases empty.
• 26 were hit by left-handed hitters, 24 by right handers.
• 6 were hit in the late innings of close games.

9. Danny Jackson, Kansas City

Had 19 quality starts in 27 outings, or 70.4%. The only American League starters who did as well or better were Higuera and Mike Witt . . . one more reason I love to watch Danny pitch: His average start last year lasted just 2 hours, 32 minutes, the quickest in the American League. Of course, the fact that neither the Royals nor their opponents were scoring any runs helped to keep the game times down . . . Danny received the worst offensive support of any major-league pitcher, the Royals scoring only 79 runs for him in 27 starts (2.93 per game) . . . double play support was fourth-best in the American League, opposition stolen base rate was tenth best . . .

10. Dennis Rasmussen, New York

He was 14–0 in his quality starts. The only major-league pitcher who had ten or more quality starts and won all of them were Rasmussen and Gooden (also 14–0) . . . The Yankees scored 181 runs in his 31 starts, or 5.84 per game, the third-best average in the American League. With average offensive support he would probably have finished 14–10, which is still pretty good . . .

11. Oil Can Boyd, Boston

Also received excellent offensive support, 5.50 runs per game, but that's kind of misleading in his case because he was the starting pitcher in the 24–5 rout of Cleveland. Otherwise his average was below five, and the league average was 4.61 . . . I love to watch him. Despite his reputation as a head case, he's a durable, consistent pitcher with a winning record and a terrific K/W ratio.

12. Tom Candiotti, Cleveland

There were 31 bases stolen in the 34 games that he started, making him the seventh easiest pitcher in the league to run on, but actually that's pretty decent for a knuckleball pitcher . . . had Charlie Hough's record . . .

13. Jimmie Key, Toronto

According to David Driscoll, Key's opponents hit .306 when they were ahead in the count, but .164 when Key was in control of the count . . . with runners on third base Key held opponents to a .109 batting average (5 for 46) . . . However, 14 of his 24 home runs allowed came with men on base . . .

14. Curt Young, Oakland

Boy, this guy is a good one. I was very pleased to see the *Project Scoresheet* voters put him on their lists. He's a closer, a guy who can be effective into the late innings. He's tough to run on. As a rookie in '84 he threw a sinking fastball a lot; last year he seemed to be working up in the strike zone more, getting more fly balls, which made him more effective in Oakland, where fly balls die, but less effective on the road.

15. Don Sutton, California

It's not a typo: in each of the last two seasons Sutton has started exactly 34 games and the Angels have scored exactly 158 runs for him each year . . . last two years has had April ERAs of 6.38 and 10.31 . . . Sutton does not hold baserunners well (over 75% steal successfully against him) and should not be left in a close game in the late innings. When he has been, opponents have hit .309 and slugged .513 against him (1984–1986) . . . more effective in day games than at night . . .

16. John Candelaria, California

The Angels helped him to his 10–2 record by scoring six runs a game when he was the starting pitcher . . . he has now been over .500 five straight years and ten times in twelve major-league seasons. The two exceptions were 1980 (11–14) and 1981 (2–2), and he is now 52 games over .500 in his career . . .

17. Frank Viola, Minnesota

Viola struck out ten men in a game three times last year. All three times, the team was Texas. In the last three years Viola has beaten Texas eight times without a loss . . . Over those three years Viola has won 18, 18, and 16 games, making him one of four major-league pitchers to have won 16 games in each of the last three seasons. The four are Gooden, Morris, Blyleven, and Viola . . . The leading winners over the last three years are Morris and Gooden (58 each), Blyleven and Andujar (53 each), Viola (52), Valenzuela (50), Witt (48), Hough and Knepper (47 each), and Tudor and Boddicker (46 each) . . . In the last three years people attempting to steal bases against Viola are 24 for 55, costing themselves about eight runs . . .

18. Mark Gubicza, Kansas City

Went 12–2 after an 0–4 start to finish 12–6. Predictably, the Kansas City media named Gubicza as Royals' Pitcher of the Year, completely ignoring the fact that the Royals had helped him to that 12–6 record by scoring 5.33 runs a game for him. He's a good pitcher, but if Gubicza had had Danny Jackson's offensive support he would have finished about 7–11. If Jackson had had Gubicza's offensive support, he would have finished about 15–8. Who is the pitcher of the year shouldn't be determined by how lucky the pitchers are.

19. Mark Langston, Seattle

According to Steve Russell, Langston had the second-highest ERA ever for a pitcher with 200 strikeouts. Langston's ERA was 4.85; Bobo Newsome's in 1938 was 5.07. There have been seven pitchers who struck out 200 men and still had ERAs over 4.00, the others being Mickey Lolich (1974), Bob Feller (1938), Don Sutton (1970), Phil Niekro (1977), and Don Wilson (1969) . . . Langston's ERA was also the second-highest for a pitcher leading the league in strikeouts. Bobo Newsome in a different year, 1942, led the American League in K with an ERA of 4.93 . . . Langston also led the American League in errors, with 6 . . .

20-Tie Dave Stieb, Toronto

Hit 15 batters with pitches last year, leading the league in that category for the fourth time. The 15 was a career high . . . Left-handed hitters hit .332 against him in 1986 . . . much more effective in night games (27–20, 2.83 ERA over last three years) than in daylight (10–13, 4.05) . . .

20-Tie Bret Saberhagen, Kansas City

I'll say the same thing today I wrote about him three years ago, before he ever pitched in the majors: He's the new Gary Nolan.

PITCHING STAFFS*

National League

1. New York (12)

Mets starters had 101 quality starts, most in the major leagues (the Cardinals were second with 98). When they did have a quality start, their team record was 83–18, an .822 percentage, best in the majors, and their starters' record was 65–6 (.915), also best in the majors.

When they *didn't* have a quality start, their team record was 25–36 (.410), best in the major leagues . . .

Rick Aguilera is the toughest Met starter to run on . . . the Mets' pitchers allowed only 103 home runs, fewest in the majors, and walked only 509 men, 38 fewer than the NL average, for an indicated ERA of 2.38, by far the best in the major leagues . . . The Mets' top AAA starting pitcher was former Red Sox prospect John Mitchell, 12–9 with a 3.39 ERA

2. Houston

The Houston bullpen has a won–lost record of 30–16, best in the major leagues. Toronto (32–24) and the Cubs (32–31) had more bullpen victories, but the .652 percentage is the best . . . Houston starters had a record of 18–34 in games that weren't classed as quality starts. Both the 18 wins and the .346 percentage were major-league bests . . . DeShaies had 7 of the wins . . . Houston's top AAA starting pitcher was probably Ron Mathis, 9–8 with a 4.25 ERA . . .

3. St. Louis

The Cardinals led the NL in fewest walks allowed, 485, keeping their indicated ERA to 3.05, fourth best in the National League. Their actual ERA, 3.37, was also fourth . . . The Cardinals' top starter at Louisville was Joe Magrane, 9–6 with a 2.06

ERA in 15 starts, only 33 walks in 113 innings. He was called to Louisville in mid-season after going 8–4 with a 2.42 ERA at Arkansas. If he stays healthy he'll be with the big club in 1987, perhaps even break camp with them. A 6′6″ left-hander, he was the Cards' No. 1 draft pick in 1985, and was rated by *Baseball America* as the top pitching prospect in the American Association.

Dear Bill:

In the 1986 Abstract, commenting on Ray Burris, you wondered how many pitchers had won a hundred games with career winning percentages below .450. Actually, there have been sixteen such pitchers. They are, arranged by lowest winning percentage, Si Johnson (101–165, .380), Stump Weidman (102–156, .395), Sid Hudson (104–152, .406), Pedro Ramos (117–160, .422), Don Cardwell (102–138, .425), Long Tom Hughes (129–173, .427), Willie Sudhoff (102–135, .430), Bob Smith (106–139, .433), Ken Raffensberger (119–154, .436), Bob Harmon (103–133, .436), Ray Benge (101–130, .437), Vern Kennedy (104–132, .441), Ron Kline (114–144, .442), Jimmy Ring (118–149, .442), Win Mercer (131–164, .444), and Bob Groom (122–150, .449).

If you want the next Ray Burris, keep an eye on Floyd Bannister.

—Eric Berman
Crown Point, Indiana

Dear Eric:

Thanks. Actually, two other people also sent me this list, but I couldn't find their letters so you get sole credit. I would never have thought there were so many. Best.

4. Los Angeles

The pitcher who is hurt most by the Dodger defense is probably Rick Honeycutt. Honeycutt is a ground-ball pitcher who needs to get the double play, but the Dodgers turned only 15 DPs in his 28 starts. Honeycutt still had a good year, posting a sharp 3.32 ERA. The Dodgers' staff indicated ERA was 2.71, second best in baseball . . . The Dodgers' top AAA starting pitcher was Brian Holton, 10–10 with a 3.65 ERA. Holton was a first-round draft pick in the January, 1978 draft and has been in the Dodger system all these years despite pretty good records, having developed serious arm problems just at the point that he was ready to surface. His career minor league record: 85–58 . . .

5. Cincinnati

Ted Power had eight quality starts in ten starts. I'm really big on the move of Power to the rotation. I always thought he had starter stuff, rather than reliever stuff . . . the Reds' staff indicated ERA was 3.31, sixth in the National League. But their actual ERA was 3.91, ninth in the league . . . The Reds' top AAA starter was Derek Botelho, formerly of Kansas City and the Cubs, who was 11–7 with a 3.67 ERA. Actually, all five Denver starters were about even, the others being Hugh Kemp (10–7, 4.11), Mike Knox (9–12, 4.02), Jeff Montgomery (11–7, 4.39), and Pat Pacillo (11–6, 4.32). Pacillo may be the best prospect . . . The Reds turned 33 double plays in the 24 starts of Chris Welsh, highest DP support in the league (1.38 per game) . . .

6. San Francisco

The Giants' staff indicated ERA

---

*Although these comments contain some remarks about relief pitchers, the voters were asked to rate the effectiveness of the *starting* pitchers.

was 3.35, the actual ERA 3.33 . . . The Giants' top AAA starting pitcher was Mark Grant, 14–7 with a 4.90 ERA. He led the PCL in wins, but Terry Mulholland (8–5, 4.46) is regarded as a better prospect . . .

7. Pittsburgh

Don Robinson went 4-for-6 last year, lifting his lifetime batting average to .268 (96/359). He has gone 9 for 27 (.333) with 14 total bases since I chose him as baseball's best hitting pitcher two years ago . . . The Pirates' AAA starting pitching was the strongest part of the team, led by Bob Patterson (9–6, 3.40 ERA), Dave Johnson 8–7, 3.17), and Rich Sauveur (7–6, 3.03). Patterson led the PCL in strikeouts with 137, and is a strong candidate for the rotation in 1987 . . .

8. Montreal

Jay Tibbs has a 1–9 record on grass fields over the last two years . . . Bryn Smith over the last two years is 20–5 on artificial turf, but just 8–8 on grass. He is 16–5 in Montreal and 4–0 on road turf . . . don't know why he didn't draw some support in the ranking of the league's best pitchers . . . the Expos' top AAA starter was Rodger Cole, 12–4 with a 3.29 ERA. He is not regarded as a hot prospect . . .

9. Philadelphia

Bruce Ruffin had 16 quality starts in 21 outings, or 76%. Only Scott (87%) and Darling (77%) did better . . . Kevin Gross pitches extremely well in Philadelphia, with a 2.62 ERA there over the last two years. Gross has all kinds of trouble in the NL "grass" parks, with ERAs over 4.97 on grass for three straight years . . . Dan Schatzeder hit .385 in

1986, also drawing 5 walks and hitting 2 doubles, a triple and a homer to give him a .484 on-base percentage and a .654 slugging percentage. He was used as a pinch hitter some; he's listed in the official stats as having 14 games as a pinch hitter, but since he pitched in 55 games and played in 58, that doesn't seem quite right. Anyway, Schatzeder's lifetime batting average is now .253 (55/217), and his slugging percentage close to .400 . . . Like Quisenberry, Tekulve has an unusually large platoon differential. Lefthanders hit 40 points better off him than righthanders . . . the Phillies top AAA starting pitcher was Jeff Bittiger, 13–8 with a 4.15 ERA. He'll get a look . . .

10. Atlanta

I watch the Braves on cable some. I hate the team and am not impressed with most of the players, but they have added a couple of pitchers that I like pretty well. Dave Palmer has games when he just looks terrific. He has trouble holding baserunners, but I think he could win with a good team. Also Zane Smith is a lot better than the 8–16 won–lost record shows, throws a "heavy ball." If Smith develops his control and the Braves develop an infield, he could have a pretty good career . . . Craig McMurtry's indicated ERA, 4.74 was exactly the same as his actual ERA . . . The Braves top AAA pitcher was Charlie Puleo, 14–7 with a 3.49 ERA. Their AAA pitching, actually, was outstanding. Puleo is 32 and has a 17–25 record in the majors, but I still wouldn't bet a lot of money that he won't pitch well with the Braves in '87. Steve Shields (9–8, 2.59 ERA at Richmond) has got a good chance to surprise some people

in Seattle, and their third starter was Cliff Speck, 8–5 with a 2.77 ERA. Shields and Puleo tied for the league lead in strikeouts with 124.

11. San Diego

Andy Hawkins had a 7.51 ERA in nine starts on artificial turf . . . The Padres top AAA starting pitcher was Ed Wojna, 12–7 with a 3.59 ERA. He is 26, but is regarded as having a good chance to make a breakthrough in 1987 . . .

12. Chicago Cubs

Cub starters had only 69 quality starts, fewest in the National League. They had only 43 decisions in those 69 starts, the fewest of any major league team. When they did have a quality start and they did get a decision, their record was just 25–18, worst in the major leagues . . . There were only four major-league pitchers (20 or more starts) who posted losing records even in games in which they were credited with quality starts. Those four were Rick Reuschel (7–8, .467), Bob Welch (6–7, .462), Rick Sutcliffe (3–5, .375), and Dennis Eckersley (2–6, .250) . . . Cub relievers tied for the major-league lead in bullpen wins, with 32. Relievers replacing Steve Trout were 10–4 . . . Trout had an indicated ERA of 1.81, as opposed to an actual ERA of 4.75, perhaps the largest discrepancy in the league . . . The Cub bullpen also tied for the major-league lead in losses, with 30. Cub starters won only 38 games, fewest in the majors . . . Scott Sanderson over the last two seasons is 10–8 in Wrigley Field, but just 4–9 on the road . . . the Cubs top AAA starter was Greg Maddux, 10–1 with a 3.02 ERA.

American League

1. Boston (9)

Runners attempting to steal against Tom Seaver are successful almost 80% of the time . . . The Red Sox's top AAA starting pitcher was Mike Rochford, 11–10 with a 3.53 ERA. He is regarded as a marginal prospect . . .

2. California (5)

The Angels' top AAA pitcher

was Urbano Lugo, 8–6 with a 4.66 ERA. Lugo is only 24 and has pitched fairly well with the Angels, so he definitely has a chance to be a good one. Barry Rubinowitz says he has the best name for a pitcher since Van Lingle Mungo . . .

3. Kansas City

The Royals' top AAA starter was Al Hargesheimer, 13–6 with a 3.29

ERA. The same guy who used to pitch for the Giants, he's now 30 and has had two good years with Omaha, could probably do a passable job with a good major league team . . .

4. Detroit

If you look over the American League pitcher records against East division and West division teams over a period of years, you'll find a lot of pitchers whose records are dramatically better against the West division than against the East.

Frank Tanana, however, has pitched much better against the tough Eastern division teams—32–29 over five years, as opposed to 19–29 against the West . . . In the last four years Tanana is 3–7 on artificial turf, and has had a higher ERA on turf than on grass all four years. This may be part of the explanation for the poor record against Western division teams, since three of the four American League turf parks are in the West . . . Over the last five years Tanana is 9–15 in September . . . Over the last five years both Morris and Petry have won more games on the road than in Tiger Stadium . . . Walt Terrell has won 15 games in each of his two years in Detroit, but I really wonder if he can pitch effectively in 1987. He's an oddity, a right-handed Tommy John type, who lives by keeping the ball down and cutting off the running game. But last year he walked 98 men and gave up 30 homers, leading to a 4.56 ERA. It was getting worse toward the end of the year. I really think they're going to have to replace him. The Tigers' top AAA starter was probably Jack Lazorko, 8–6 with a 3.20 ERA, who definitely is not ready, but he led the American Association in strikeouts with 119.

5. Toronto

With 14 wins through August, Jim Clancy had claimed the Blue Jays' all-time lead in wins, leading Stieb 102–99. Then Clancy didn't win in September and Stieb won three to pull even at 102 apiece . . . It was the fifth time in Clancy's career that he had won 13 to 16 games, and with a 14–7 record by September first he seemed likely to get past that range for the first time, but couldn't . . . Clancy in '86 had a 5.26 ERA in Toronto, but 3.07 on the road . . . The Blue Jays' top AAA starting pitcher was Ron Musselman, 9–7 with a 3.03 ERA . . . Batters facing Jim Clancy hit almost as well when Clancy was in control of the count (.238) as when he was behind (.247), although that's a little misleading because he issued 29 walks when he got behind hitters early, as opposed to none when he jumped out in front . . . When Mark Eichorn was in con-

trol of the count, opposing hitters hit just .112 (18 for 161). Right-handed hitters hit only .134 against Eichorn . . . the league batting average against Joe Johnson was .237 with the bases empty, but .355 (44/124) when there were men on base . . . 20 of the 25 home runs off John Cerutti were hit with the bases empty. Batting averages against Cerutti were .364 when he was behind in the count, but .173 when he was ahead in the count . . . Against Dennis Lamp, the same figures were .375 and .250 . . . with men in scoring position, the batting average against Lamp was .434 (36/83). I guess you could say the hitters' eyes lit up? . . . Situational data courtesy of David Driscoll, P.O. Box 6493, Station D, London, Ontario, N5W 5S5.

6. Milwaukee

Did you notice Pete Vuckovich's stats in his late season return? Six starts, 3.06 ERA, only 11 walks in 32 innings . . . he was credited with four quality starts . . . Milwaukee's most effective AAA starting pitcher was perennial hopeful Bob Gibson, 10–4 with a 2.78 ERA.

7. Texas

The Rangers' top AAA starter was Don Welchel, 12–9 with a 3.99 ERA . . . Bobby Witt and Edwin Correa, the *very* young Ranger starters, were 1–2 in the league in three negative categories, walks (Witt 143, Correa 126), wild pitches (Witt 22, Correa 19) and opposition stolen base rate (53 in 31 starts for Witt, 40 in 32 for Correa.) That they managed to pitch .500 ball (23–23) despite these things, and despite the fact that Correa was one of the league's ten worst-supported starting pitchers, is remarkable . . . The Rangers turned 39 double plays in the 29 games started by José Guzman, highest DP rate in the league (1.34 per start) . . .

8. Minnesota

Neal Heaton lost five games in which his team was shut out, including two 1–0 losses and a 2–0 loss. He also had a no-decision in a 1–0 Twins loss. Heaton lost five games in which he allowed three runs or less, most in the American League . . . Heaton finished 7–15 despite having a better-than-league ERA in a hitter's park . . . Mike Smithson has a career record of 11–21 in day games, 45–38

at night. Smithson seems to be a cool-weather pitcher, pitching his best ball in April and September. He also has a career record of 32–22 (.593) in his home parks, but 24–37 (.393) on the road . . . The Twins' top AAA starter was probably Les Straker, 6–7 with a 3.44 ERA . . .

9. Chicago

Among Richard Dotson's 17 ERAs listed in the breakdowns, his best ERA was 4.28 in the month of May . . . White Sox whipping boy Floyd Bannister won 10 games last year despite miserable offensive support, 3.30 runs a game. He now has 101 major-league wins including five straight seasons of 10 or more. Bannister's a slow starter, second-half pitcher; he probably would benefit from more regular work early in the season . . . Isn't it kind of fun wondering whether Neil Allen is finally going to put it together? I've been trying to tell people since 1980 that Allen was a starting pitcher miscast in relief, but unfortunately he's spent the whole time telling people he was a reliever. He was 7–2 last year without great offensive support, but then he got hurt. The White Sox's top pitcher in AAA ball last year was Pete Filson, once of Minnesota, who was 14–3 with a 2.27 ERA. Filson was half starter and half reliever; their top pure starter was Bill Long, 9–9 with a 3.88 ERA . . . Filson, always regarded as having good stuff, led the American Association in ERA . . . Bannister, Seaver, and Dotson were all among the league's poorest-supported pitchers, all working with less than 3.9 runs a game . . .

10. New York

Scott Nielsen got credit for six quality starts in nine outings, despite generally unimpressive numbers . . . Louisiana Lightnin' was the only American League pitcher who did not have a winning record in his quality starts. He had 16 quality starts and was 6–6 . . . The average nine-inning game started by Joe Niekro lasted 3 hours, 3 minutes, longest in the American League . . . The Yankees' top AAA starter was also Nielsen, 11–7 with a 3.47 ERA . . . There were 29 bases stolen in the 25 games started by Niekro the Younger, second-highest rate in the American League . . .

11. Oakland

Oakland relievers had a won–lost record of 15–29, a .341 percentage, worst in the major leagues. The three worst were Oakland, Minnesota (15–26), and the Dodgers (17–28) . . . The A's scored 7.4 runs a start for Moose Haas, 89 in 12 games . . . Oakland's top AAA starting pitcher was probably Rick Rodriguez, 7–8, 3.95. He's a longshot . . . in addition to having an indicated ERA of 6.91, highest in baseball, José Rijo received the least double play support of any major league starter, 11 in 26 starts (.42 per game) . . .

12. Baltimore

Oriole starting pitchers had a record of 4–55 in games that weren't classed as quality starts, worst in the major leagues . . . Storm Davis had 16 quality starts in 24 outings, seventh-best in the American League. Of the top ten, all had winning percentages of at least .590 except Davis (9–12) and Danny Jackson (11–12) . . . Mike Boddicker has a career record of 14–6 in May, much better than any other month, but is 9–11 in September . . . Like many control pitchers, Scott McGregor is much more effective in day games (22–13 over the last five years) than at night (50–47). It's not really that he's more effective, but that power pitchers are more effective at night and finesse pitchers aren't, so the finesse pitchers are *relatively* more effective in day games, and thus have better won–lost records . . . Mike Flanagan over the last five years is 32–15 in Baltimore, but 19–29 on the road . . . Storm Davis has a career record of 13–3 in July . . . The average 9-inning game started by Ken Dixon lasted 2 hours, 58 minutes, tying for the second-longest in the league . . . The Orioles' top AAA starting pitchers were John Habyan (12–7, 4.29 ERA) and Bill Swaggerty (12–7, 4.25).

13. Seattle

The Mariners had only 62 quality starts, seven fewer than any other major-league team . . . one of the most intriguing Mariner pitchers is Bill Swift. Swift was brought to the majors with only seven games in the minors, and wasn't ready. His major-league record is 8–19 despite decent offensive support, but at times he looks like he can pitch. He throws a hard, sinking fastball, my favorite pitch, but doesn't have anything effective to set it up with. If he could learn to change speeds or throw a slider he'd make a sudden leap forward . . . The Mariners' top AAA starter was Bill Wilkinson, 8–8 with a 4.78 ERA . . . Mark Langston had 136 full counts in 1986, most among Mariner pitchers. Mike Moore handled full counts best, limiting opponents to a .187 batting average on the 3–2 pitches (17/91) . . . Mike Morgan had 119 full counts and walked the hitter 46 times . . . Langston got ahead of Seattle hitters 0–2 175 times, by far the most among the Mariners, and limited hitters to a .154 batting average when he did. Langston threw 4,123 pitches during the season, while Moore threw 4,057. Pete Ladd had the best ratio of balls to strikes among the M's, 696 to 368 (1.89–1). Billy Swift had the worst ratio, 1,087–809 (1.34–1) . . . data provided by Jeff Welch and the *Seattle Baseball Bulletin*, P.O. Box 221, Redmond, WA 98073.

14. Cleveland

The Indians' starters had a record of 17–40 in games that weren't quality starts, best in the American League . . . Phil Niekro over the last three years is 10–4 with a 2.75 ERA in 17 starts on artificial turf . . . The Indians' top AAA starting pitcher was probably Kevin Hagen, 8–11 with a 3.28 ERA. Their top AAA *pitcher* was reliever Doug Jones, who had a 2.09 ERA and 98 strikeouts in 116 innings. Jones pitched well in 11 games as a call-up, and is regarded as one of the keys to the team in 1987 . . .

ALL KINDS OF JUNK

MEASURING RUNS CREATED: THE VALUE ADDED APPROACH

—Gary R. Skoog

INTRODUCTION

One of the major interests of baseball research has long been the attempt to measure how many of a team's runs are created by each player. This article discusses how runs created can be measured from event data (that is, looking at each event in the context of play) rather than from cumulative data, as has been necessary in the past when only category totals were available. For all regulars from the 1986 season, we compute both proposed and older measures of runs created. This paper expands on results reported by the author at the 1986 SABR convention and presented to an American Statistical Association meeting.

With only a season's totals available for each player ("aggregate data") the subject of the proper attribution of runs created continues to receive refinement and controversy. Two methods, Bill James's runs created and Pete Palmer's linear weights, have defined the present state of the art. Both methods attempt to construct an index that measures runs created by each player using aggregate data. Both men have attempted to design runs created methods that are not situation dependent, as are runs scored and RBI counts, but the act of scoring runs itself is situation dependent, and so its removal per force creates a measure that varies from the ideal: We want a statistic that doesn't penalize a player for batting in fewer run producing situations than another, but at the same time rewards players who perform well in those situations. Our methodology cuts this Gordian knot by directly measuring the object of interest, the improvement or deterioration in the run expectation of the player's team at the moment of his contribution.

Given the precise event data, our first statistic, RC1 (read, runs created, version 1; marginal runs created) is appropriate for many comparative purposes in the same way that marginal cost is the appropriate cost measure in economics. Like Pete Palmer's linear weights, it is essentially mean-corrected, so that zero denotes average performance, and players are measured relative to the average. A second variant, RC2 (read, runs created, version 2) is presented, which is more descriptive in that it is generally non-negative and adds to the team's actual runs scored when aggregated over a season. As such, it is comparable to the James runs created, which will be referred to below as RCJ. Indeed, 94% of the variation in RC2 is explained by RCJ in the American League 1986 data, and 91% in the National League.

Although we don't emphasize it here, our approach unifies the sabermetric study at the micro, or event, level. It opens up a potentially more powerful and precise approach to the assessment of runs allowed by pitchers, runs created or lost on the bases, runs cost by errors in the field, or even runs lost by bad coaching decisions or umpires' mistakes. Of course, for starting pitchers ERA does approximately the same thing, but the biases of this statistic for relief pitchers are purged with the value added approach.

VALUE-ADDED

When a batter steps up to the plate, there may be 0, 1, or 2 outs, and any one of 8 runner on base situations. Thus there are 24 initial game states, abstracting from other characteristics such as the score, which teams are playing, who the players on base are, etc. When he finishes his turn at bat, he will have put his team in any one of 25 possible states (the extra state is "3 outs," and for our purposes here, no loss of generality is incurred in ignoring the configuration of the men left on base at the end of an inning). Let us denote the beginning and ending states by "s" and "t," respectively. For each state, from his team's and the league's data, we may accurately measure the distribution of runs scored in an inning, conditional on a team being in that state. Denote the means of these random variables (technically, stopping times on a specially constructed sigma algebra) by $E(s)$ and $E(t)$, and let R denote the runs scored during this transition. Then this at bat produced $R + E(t) - E(s) =$ actual runs scored on at bat plus expected team's runs in inning after player bats minus expected total team's runs in inning before player batted. There are refinements, some of which will be discussed below, but this is the basic idea.

In words, the RC1 in a plate appearance is positive to the extent that the batter advanced his team's cause more than an average amount, and similarly for negative contributions. It is measured in units of runs. For the general manager confronted with a -30 run player, this statistic tells him how many runs his team would improve if he could bring this position up to the league average. The extra runs then could be converted into extra wins by Pythagorean theory.

The transitions as a team bats through an inning must, as is shown below, sum to the actual number of runs scored, minus the expectation of the state which leads off each inning of .454 (see Table 1). This is due to the telescoping nature of the sum, and the fact that there is an absorbing state, "3 outs," to which almost all innings converge. An example below will make this clear. The exceptions are games won in the bottom of the last inning, and games suspended in the middle of an inning and not resumed.

Since, if a hitter does not increase the out count, his contribution must be positive (we haven't yet discussed errors) there can be at most 3 negative contributions in an inning.

We might prefer that the decrements of .454 be redistributed among the batters in the inning, so that the runs created becomes a total measure, calibrated so as to give the actual number of runs scored. We call this kind of total measure RC2, and briefly consider ways of doing this.

To fix ideas, consider an inning in which the leadoff hitter homers, and the next 3 batters make outs. Using Table 1, RC1 gives the measures 1.000, $-.205$, $-.154$, and $-.095$, summing to $1 - .454 = .546$. Suggestions to redistribute the .454 and get exactly one run produced include 3 philosophies:

1. Add .454/4 to all batters appearing in the inning.
2. Add .454/3 to those 3 batters who increased the out count, making obvious modifications for double and triple plays.
3. Add total runs scored in league/total plate appearances to each batter. For the 1986 AL this was 10449/86852 = .120308 and 8096/74006 = .1093965 in the NL in 1986.

An advantage of 1 and 3 is that they yield the same differential contributions as RC1. The leadoff home run in the example above left the team on average 1.205 ahead of where they would have been with an out, which uses up .205 run when it is the first out. This argument has much appeal. A drawback is that it gives the leadoff man more than one run created for his home run, which after all does return the team to the beginning state but with an extra run—all of which should yield precisely one run created. Another advantage is that runs created equals runs scored in every (half) inning, so a fortiori for every game, for every team-season, and for the league—the various levels of aggregation. Note that the entries of Table 1 are estimated from an entire season, and so are average in this sense. (We have not preserved the distinction between population averages, the E(s), and their sampled counterparts—a reader sophisticated enough to look for the difference will not be confused.)

The drawback above suggests 2, which redistributes the decrements among those players most likely to have negative runs created. It maintains one run for the solo home run, and implicitly suggests a non-negativity of runs created per plate appearance desideratum: Since runs are negative, why not extend this same property to runs created? This method does more to move the negatives toward zero than 1, although it can't totally succeed, without causing further difficulties. To see this, note that to bring all batters to non-negative numbers, we'd have to overcompensate by adding .205 times 3 = .615, and we'd have to take .615 − .454 = .161 off the home run—and this for a scheme which awarded .205—.095 = .110 of a run for making the final out! Another objection is that outs are already taken into consideration by RC1, so an adjustment based on them would result in "double counting." This method shares the advantage of having the runs balance out over every half-inning.

Both submethods 1 and 2 divide .454 explicitly; instead, we could use 3 above and take the total plate appearances divided into the total runs for a league season and add this to each at bat; this would give correct runs created on average, although inning totals wouldn't necessarily be correct. The argument is, there is unnecessary noise introduced by requiring them to add, along with a mixing of the level of aggregation. This is the method used below in the RC2 calculation. The author is not adamant in its use, however, and encourages discussion on this point in the sabermetric community before the next edition of this book.

From Palmer's simulations reported in The Hidden Game, we report his table giving the E(s) entries for the 24 states:

Table 1
Expected Future Runs In An Inning,
Conditional On The State

Runners		Outs				
		0		1		2
None	a	.454	b	.249	c	.095
1st	d	.783	e	.478	f	.209
2nd	g	1.068	h	.699	i	.348
3rd	j	1.277	k	.897	l	.382
1st, 2nd	m	1.380	n	.888	o	.457
1st, 3rd	p	1.639	q	1.088	r	.494
2nd, 3rd	s	1.946	t	1.371	u	.661
1st, 2nd, 3rd	v	2.254	w	1.546	x	.798

We have added the *Project Scoresheet* notation for the states. The idea of using these states, incidentally, goes back at least to the fundamental 1963 paper in Operations Research, "An Investigation of Strategies in Baseball," by George Lindsey, and is implicit in the work of anyone having done serious study in any branch of science. The RC measures proposed here are similar in spirit to the Mills's "player win average," although the measures address quite different questions.

Rather than simulate, we will in the future estimate these expectations from the $2106 \times 80 = 168,480$ or so such situations which arise over a major league season. There will be some statistical subtley here, for we are doing inference on realizations of a Markov chain with no ergodic events and with obvious statistical dependences. Variances, rather than our estimates themselves—means—will be affected by the fact that the same inning, say, with a leadoff home run, will have the 0000 or "a" state occurring at least twice, followed by the same events for the rest of the inning entering into the sample. In theory, one could estimate a Markov half inning transition matrix and derive estimates for the entries in table 1. This method has two drawbacks. First, the standard errors are very complicated functionals of the model parameters. Worse, model specification error would enter, and would be avoidable with the direct, nonparametric approach suggested above. The parameters of the transition matrix nevertheless are of independent interest, however, and will be estimated for various subsets of the data.

The measures of runs created reported below use

Table 1. We will sometimes refer to a state not by its letter but by four numbers, as the 0000 above. The first is 0, 1, or 2 and gives the outs; the next 3 are 0 or 1, depending on whether the base is unoccupied or not.

We do expect to see league differences in our estimated versions of Table 1, since pitchers bat in the National League. Consequently the relevant sample size will be smaller by roughly half. In fact, RC1 for National League pitchers have been computed (but not reported below) and are uniformly negative, as expected.

DETAILED EXAMPLE OF THE CALCULATION

A runner is on first, nobody out. The batter singles, the runner on first stopping at second. The third batter follows with an RBI single, leaving runners at first and second. The next batter grounds into a 6-4-3 double play, the runner advancing to third. A strikeout ends the inning.

The official statistics give the second batter a hit only. He didn't score the run or bat it in, yet he was as instrumental in manufacturing the run as the players who received the RBI or run scored. The value added approach (refer to Table 1 above) gives him $1.380 - .783 = .597$ runs. The leadoff hitter gets $.783 - .454 = .329$, and the third hitter gets 1 run, since the runners ended up at first and second, the same state he found them in. The double play gave the fourth batsman $.382 - 1.380 = -.998$, and the strikeout stranding the runner on third was $-.382$. The team earned 1.926 runs and lost 1.380 runs, giving a total of .546 above the initial state or league average of .454.

If the total decrements of .454 are added by redistributing them among the batters in the inning, we get an RC2 measure of exactly 1.

FURTHER DEVELOPMENTS: BATTING, RUNNING, AND FIELDING

For each transition, we know whether the batter's turn at bat terminated or not. In *Project Scoresheet* these are referred to as batting events and non-batting events, respectively. If the leadoff batter walks and steals second, (the latter is a non-batting event), then the second batter's initial state s is $0010 - 0$ outs, man on second, not the $0100 - 0$ outs, man on first—that prevailed when he came to the plate. The man who stole second earned $1.285 - .783 = .402$ of a run (RC1) for his stolen base, and baserunning runs created may be kept as a separate category in this way. Similarly, errors create runs for the opposition, and may be accounted for by introducing a fictitious state of errorless play between the events involving the error. Another example will make this clear.

Say the leadoff man reaches on an error. Just as in batting average calculation, we may act from the batter's perspective as though he had been put out. The fictitious state here is $1000 - 1$ out no one on. Now the transition 0000 to 1000, worth $.249 - .454 = -.205$ is awarded the batter, and the transition 1000 to 0100 worth $.783 - 249 = .534$ gives the runs created by the error. If the next 3 batters strike out, the team run potential is again reduced to 0, and their RC1 decrement is .783. Thus, the team has an RC1 total of $-.205 + -.783 = -.988$;

they were given .534 of a run by the opposition, bringing us back to the familiar .454. Since they scored no runs, to get an RC2 to equal zero, there were in effect 4 "outs" inflicting negative runs created, and the "gift" of the error might be redistributed along with the .454. Errors are not so treated in the results given below, although further refinements may incorporate them.

Observe that the 1000 to 0100 transition causes outs to decrease, and so is impossible according to baseball rules. Nevertheless, there is nothing stopping our evaluating this contrafactual state transition, and indeed there is a necessity to do this to properly evaluate the error.

Present *Project Scoresheet* data structures, and doubtless others as well, will make this decomposition difficult for some errors, notably errors allowing runners to advance on a play. Errors allowing the batter to reach are more adequately represented. Unfortunately, we need in both cases a set of heuristics to guess the result of errorless play. Here as in many areas, theory runs ahead of practice.

ELIMINATION OF SITUATION DEPENDENCE

Besides measuring precisely and directly our objective, the value added approach has a reasonable chance at correcting for "situation dependence." Several factors point to this conclusion, although ultimately a minor refinement may still be in order.

A player who bats with many men on base will have high E(s) values for leaving lots of men on base to subtract from the high R and E(t) values he earns. In the example, the three singles were worth .329, .597, and 1 run and not equal amounts, reflecting the obvious fact that run production is situation dependent. The batter who hit with 2 men on base also had most to lose by not producing, as the next paragraph shows.

To see the way the value added approach corrects for situation dependence while properly acknowledging it, consider a player batting with the bases loaded and 2 out. A walk credits him with an entire run, whereas a leadoff walk in an inning is only worth .299. But had he struck out with the bases loaded and 2 out, he would have cost his team $.798 - 0$ (expected runs after 3 outs!) $= .798$ of a run, whereas a leadoff strikeout costs .454—propitious situations will amass high totals of the traditional count data (runs and RBI) but these should have subtracted from them many runs destroyed from his failures.

At a higher level of sophistication, consider a hitter, say Wade Boggs (our 1986 AL RC leader), batting in the highest E(s) state, 0111, from which 2.254 runs are expected, and the lowest state, 2000, from which .095 runs are expected. We can take Boggs' season totals and make educated guesses as to the transition probabilities from these states to any other states. This would let us compute conditional runs created from each state, for both an individual player and the league average. Then, for there to be bias for Boggs, two things must be present. First, there must be variation in the conditional runs created across the states, which the paragraph above argues (but does not prove) will be minimal. Second, Boggs must find himself with a distribution of at bats among the 24 states that is significantly different from the league averages. This may happen for pinch hitters, and to a lesser extent for leadoff hitters, who start off the game in the same state. It is an empirical question how large these discrepancies are, if any. If found significant, a further correction to RC2 is in order.

REMARKS

1. A sacrifice fly is always a fly, usually an out, but hardly ever a sacrifice, and not an official at bat. Conventional treatment thus seems dubious. In our scheme, it is properly evaluated, since its effect is the same as any other occurrence which changes the state in the same way. Clearly the concept of "state" is intended to be a statistically "sufficient" description, capturing all and only what is essential for analysis. For some purposes, mentioned below, it may be advisable to add other information such as the score, but that is not necessary for the issue at hand.

2. A ground out accomplishing the same thing as a sacrifice bunt is here given the same credit, unlike in the official statistics. A sacrifice bunt effecting 0100 to 1010 is worth $-.084$, explaining why some managers use it so selectively. Since it does create an out, it would get a net positive value after an RC2 redistribution.

3. A three-run home run should be worth less than three runs to the batter, as the runners have some likelihood of being driven in by a subsequent hitter. Our state change adjusts for this. The double counting here has bedeviled other methods.

4. Pitching, especially relief pitching, may be analyzed with the obvious use of the value added method. However, since the game is so often on the line, one may prefer a score dependent version in which we evaluate not expected runs in the inning but the probability of winning the game in place of $E(s)$ and $E(t)$—the player win average.

5. Runner speed isn't properly adjusted yet: if a single sends a runner to third, the credit goes to the hitter and not the runner. With more (judgmental) data, this second order effect could be corrected.

6. Intentional walks are arguably not given special treatment. One place where this is clearly aberrant is in tie games in the bottom of the ninth inning or later, when the man being walked "means nothing." Then the run distribution is truncated, and from a different population than that used to estimate runs created. This is likely a third order correction, or higher.

EMPIRICAL RESULTS

The Tables below give (mean corrected) RC1, (total, positive) RC2 and the technical version of Bill James's runs created, listed under RCJ.

While we leave extensive comparison to another time, a few points may be made. First, our measure does not give "runs created or destroyed attempting to steal," which Bill's runs created method does allow for. A further refinement of RC1 and RC2 on this issue is obviously appropriate. This explains our understatements for Coleman, Henderson and Wilson. Second, the high percentage of explained variations of RC2 by RCJ—94% in the American League, 91% in the National League—have been noted. Third, the names of Boggs and Mattingly atop the AL and Schmidt and Raines atop the NL according to both methods is expected and reassuring. Finally, the diminution of agreement as one progresses toward lower RC2 and RCJ totals reminds us that RCJ was constructed on the basis of team aggregate data. Forcing it to apply to regular player totals—a sample of 600 or 700 plate appearances—is one thing; applying it to smaller totals requires its extrapolation outside the region in which it was fit. Statistical models always show such "out of sample" deterioration.*

*Editor's note: The runs created formula—technical version works with very small data samples, as is shown by the fact that it works well with games, and with very large ones such as leagues. I strongly suspect that the failure of agreement at low levels of plate appearances occurs because the failures of both methods are most apparent in small data sets where long-term randomizing factors have not acted to disguise them.

1986 AMERICAN LEAGUE RUNS CREATED

	RC1	RC2	RCJ		RC1	RC2	RCJ		RC1	RC2	RCJ
Allanson, Cle	−12	27	22	Boggs, Bos	+58	142	133	Canseco, Oak	+23	106	89
Armas, Bos	+14	68	49	B. Bonilla, Chi	0	32	32	Carter, Cle	+36	122	116
Baines, Chi	+29	103	87	J. Bonilla, Bal	−10	28	25	Castillo, Cle	+ 7	33	25
Baker, Oak	− 3	29	24	Boone, Cal	−20	41	39	Cerone, Mil	− 7	22	25
Balboni, KC	+ 6	73	67	Boston, Chi	− 3	24	28	Coles, Det	+ 7	78	81
Bando, Cle	− 2	32	27	P. Bradley, Sea	+26	100	99	Collins, Det	−22	36	49
Barfield, Tor	+44	125	122	Braggs, Mil	− 9	19	20	Cooper, Mil	+10	80	60
Barrett, Bos	+16	102	87	Brantley, Sea	− 7	6	9	J. Cruz, Chi	− 7	23	20
Bathe, Oak	− 8	6	7	Brett, KC	+29	92	89	A. Davis, Sea	+20	88	78
Baylor, Bos	+ 9	92	91	Brookens, Det	− 2	36	32	M. Davis, Oak	0	64	72
Beane, Minn	−13	10	12	Brunansky, Minn	− 5	74	78	DeCinces, Cal	+13	82	72
G Bell, Tor	+30	113	113	Buckner, Bos	+ 4	86	76	Deer, Mil	+18	84	82
Beniquez, Bal	+ 7	54	51	Buechele, Tex	− 7	55	54	Dempsey, Bal	−19	27	41
Bergman, Det	− 5	14	15	Burleson, Cal	+ 9	46	40	Downing, Cal	+37	113	96
Bernazard, Cle	+15	92	96	Bush, Minn	+12	61	53	Dwyer, Bal	+ 1	24	27
Berra, NY	+ 3	17	12	Butler, Cle	0	82	84	Easler, NY	+14	79	76
Biancalana, KC	− 3	22	20	Calderon, Chi	− 8	9	11	Da. Evans, Det	+12	84	85
Bochte, Oak	+14	71	52	Cangelosi, Chi	− 7	56	55	Dw. Evans, Bos	+34	111	100

	RC1	RC2	RCJ
Felder, Mil	− 8	13	17
Fernandez, Tor	+ 7	95	99
Fischlin, NY	− 5	9	6
Fisk, Chi	−10	49	39
Fletcher, Tex	+ 7	79	76
Foster, Chi	− 3	3	4
Franco, Cle	+ 4	81	76
Gaetti, Minn	+21	100	99
Gagne, Minn	+ 1	64	57
Gantner, Mil	−22	43	56
D. Garcia, Tor	− 5	49	44
Gedman, Bos	+ 2	63	59
K. Gibson, Det	+26	88	88
Grich, Cal	− 2	42	46
Griffey, NY	− 1	25	31
Griffin, Oak	− 8	70	71
Grubb, Det	+33	62	54
Gruber, Tor	+ 9	28	8
Guillen, Chi	−23	46	43
Gutierrez, Bal	−14	4	6
Hairston, Chi	+ 2	32	31
M. Hall, Cle	+24	82	75
Harrah, Tex	+ 1	42	35
Hatcher, Minn	+ 2	43	36
Heath, Det	− 2	10	12
R. Henderson, NY	− 4	80	112
Hendrick, Cal	+ 9	47	42
Herndon, Det	− 3	35	36
D. Hill, Oak	− 9	35	41
Howell, Cal	+10	31	27
Hrbek, Minn	+36	112	93
Hulett, Chi	−30	36	49
Incaviglia, Tex	+ 8	81	82
G. Iorg, Tex	+ 3	45	35
Re. Jackson, Cal	+13	75	68
Jacoby, Cle	+26	102	88
Javier, Oak	+ 8	23	11
C. Johnson, Tor	+19	66	52
R. Jones, Cal	+ 9	65	60
Joyner, Cal	+26	107	96
Kearney, Sea	− 3	24	20
Kingery, KC	− 6	21	23
Kingman, Oak	−11	62	57
Kittle, NY	− 3	37	34
Lacy, Bal	− 3	62	62
Lansford, Oak	− 1	76	80
Laudner, Minn	0	27	30

	RC1	RC2	RCJ
R. Law, KC	+ 7	48	40
R. Leach, Tor	+ 3	35	35
Lemon, Det	− 4	51	52
Lombardozzi, Minn	−15	47	50
Lowry, Det	+ 4	25	24
Lynn, Bal	+28	83	69
Lyons, Chi	− 3	14	13
Manning, Mil	+15	42	27
Martinez, Tor	− 6	16	12
Mattingly, NY	+48	137	150
McDowell, Tex	−13	64	83
McRae, KC	− 2	34	29
Meacham, NY	−13	10	13
Mercado, Tex	−11	3	7
Molitor, Mil	+13	71	65
Moore, Mil	+ 1	32	27
Morman, Chi	− 2	20	19
Moseby, Tor	+ 9	89	86
Moses, Sea	−16	37	40
Motley, KC	−14	14	16
Mulliniks, Tor	+16	63	48
Dw. Murphy, Oak	+ 4	52	51
E. Murray, Bal	+32	101	92
Nichols, Chi	+ 2	20	12
O'Brien, Tex	+42	119	98
O'Malley, Bal	+ 2	26	18
Oglivie, Mil	+ 6	52	45
Orta, KC	+ 2	45	42
S. Owen, Bos	−18	36	40
Paciorek, Tex	+ 2	28	22
Pagliarulo, NY	+ 7	75	74
Parrish, Det	+16	61	57
Parrish, Tex	+28	91	80
Pasqua, NY	+22	62	62
Petralli, Tex	+ 1	18	14
Pettis, Cal	+ 1	76	71
Phelps, Sea	+33	86	81
Phillips, Oak	+11	75	63
Porter, Tex	+11	32	30
Presley, Sea	+11	91	80
Pryor, KC	−11	3	3
Puckett, Minn	+37	124	127
Quirk, KC	− 8	21	22
Randolph, NY	+10	83	77
Rayford, Bal	−16	11	14
Reed, Minn	− 8	14	17
Reynolds, Sea	−36	22	37

	RC1	RC2	RCJ
Rice, Bos	+28	112	115
Riles, Mil	−11	60	59
Ripken, Bal	+25	110	102
Robidoux, Mil	− 5	21	19
Roenicke, NY	+ 4	24	22
Romero, Bos	− 1	31	19
Salas, Minn	− 9	25	27
Salazar, KC	− 3	35	26
Schofield, Cal	+ 4	67	63
Schroeder, Mil	− 7	22	22
Sheets, Bal	+21	65	47
Shelby, Bal	− 3	49	39
Sheridan, Det	+ 3	34	27
Sierra, Tex	−10	40	51
Slaught, Tex	+ 5	46	42
Smalley, Minn	+11	74	70
Lo. Smith, KC	+ 2	70	77
Snyder, Cle	+10	62	58
Stefero, Bal	+ 1	18	12
Sullivan, Bos	− 6	10	9
Sundberg, KC	− 7	52	44
Sveum, Mil	− 5	38	37
Tabler, Cle	+14	75	74
Tartabull, Sea	+29	99	85
Tettleton, Oak	+ 2	33	31
Thornton, Cle	+12	70	55
Tolleston, NY	− 5	32	33
Traber, Bal	+13	42	32
Trammell, Det	+17	96	95
Upshaw, Tor	+ 4	83	80
Walker, Chi	+24	62	48
Ward, Tex	+ 7	57	56
Washington, NY	− 4	13	16
Whitaker, Det	+ 4	82	82
F. White, KC	+13	88	84
Whitt, Tor	− 2	50	56
Wiggins, Bal	− 9	23	24
Wilfong, Cal	−11	28	23
Wilkerson, Tex	− 5	25	19
Willard, Oak	+ 6	29	23
W. Wilson, KC	−36	46	76
Winfield, NY	+25	104	89
G. Wright, Tex	− 7	6	7
Wynegar, NY	− 1	26	20
Yeager, Sea	− 4	13	9
M. Young, Bal	0	51	47
Yount, Mil	+26	98	94

1986 NATIONAL LEAGUE RUNS CREATED

	RC1	RC2	RCJ
Aguayo, Phi	− 3	13	13
Aldrete, SF	+ 2	30	31
Almon, Pitt	+14	39	25
Anderson, LA	− 3	23	20
Ashby, Hou	− 6	33	40
Backman, NY	− 5	43	59
Bailey, Hou	− 5	15	13
Bass, Hou	+13	83	97
Bell, Cin	+16	88	91
Belliard, Pitt	−14	25	26
Benedict, Atl	− 4	16	13
Bilardello, Mon	−12	11	13
Bochy, SD	+ 2	18	21
Bonds, Pitt	+ 5	58	64
Bonilla, Pitt	−10	15	21
Bosley, Chi	− 2	13	17

	RC1	RC2	RCJ
Bream, Pitt	+11	75	79
Brenly, SF	+ 3	64	71
Brock, LA	+ 5	45	42
Brooks, Mon	+18	55	65
Brown, SF	+18	69	65
M. Brown, Pitt	−10	20	20
Butera, Cin	+ 3	18	15
Cabell, LA	− 5	27	26
Candaele, Mon	− 8	4	6
G. Carter, NY	+15	78	72
Cey, Chi	+13	46	53
Chambliss, Atl	+10	25	20
Clark, StL	+ 2	33	38
W. Clark, SF	+ 1	51	62
Coleman, StL	−42	32	67
Concepcion, Cin	− 7	31	33

	RC1	RC2	RCJ
J. Cruz, Hou	+26	84	68
Daniels, Cin	+17	39	40
Daulton, Phi	+ 7	27	26
C. Davis, SF	+10	78	83
E. Davis, Cin	+31	84	95
G. Davis, Hou	+21	93	100
J. Davis, Chi	− 3	61	66
Dawson, Mon	− 2	58	75
Dernier, Chi	−10	29	30
B. Diaz, Cin	− 3	54	59
M. Diaz, Pitt	+ 3	28	33
Doran, Hou	−10	60	81
Duncan, LA	−34	15	38
Dunston, Chi	−16	51	64
Durham, Chi	+12	73	78
Dykstra, NY	+15	69	80

Name	RC1	RC2	RCJ
Esasky, Cin	− 4	38	44
Fitzgerald, Mon	+ 4	31	34
Flannery, SD	− 1	46	50
Ford, StL	0	26	27
Foster, NY	− 2	26	28
Francona, Chi	+ 1	16	11
Galarraga, Mon	+ 1	40	43
Garner, Hou	− 1	37	39
Garvey, SD	− 7	57	59
Gladden, SF	+ 8	52	49
Gwynn, SD	+20	97	113
J. Hamilton, LA	+ 6	23	12
T. Harper, Atl	− 5	27	30
B. Hatcher, Hou	− 6	43	47
Hayes, Phi	+36	112	111
Hearn, NY	− 5	11	16
Heath, StL	− 7	17	17
Heep, NY	+12	37	31
K. Hernandez, NY	+39	111	106
Herr, StL	−16	56	69
Horner, Atl	+22	85	79
Hubbard, Atl	− 5	48	47
Hurdle, StL	− 4	16	16
D. Iorg, SD	− 5	7	8
Jeltz, Phi	−13	43	40
H. Johnson, NY	+12	40	36
W. Johnson, Mon	− 1	13	14
Kennedy, SD	+ 2	54	54
Khalifa, Pitt	−19	0	9
Knight, NY	+18	77	70
Krenchicki, Mon	− 8	19	22
Kruk, SD	+16	52	47
Kutcher, SF	−10	12	20
Landreaux, LA	− 2	32	32
Landrum, StL	− 8	17	17
Larkin, Cin	+ 4	22	22
Lavalliere, StL	− 7	31	31
V. Law, Mon	− 4	40	34
Leonard, SF	− 2	39	44
Lopes, Hou	+12	33	34
Madlock, LA	+10	56	52
Maldonado, SF	+10	58	51

Name	RC1	RC2	RCJ
Marshall, LA	+ 9	49	42
C. Martinez, SD	− 6	25	31
D. Martinez, Chi	− 1	11	4
Matthews, Chi	+ 4	51	63
Matuszek, LA	+ 5	30	29
Mazzilli, NY	+ 4	17	13
McGee, StL	−18	41	53
McReynolds, SD	+24	94	103
Melvin, SF	−14	17	23
Milner, Cin	+ 5	55	59
K. Mitchell, NY	− 6	34	52
Moreland, Chi	−12	60	72
Moreno, Atl	−16	26	32
Morris, StL	− 3	9	8
Motley, Atl	+ 1	2	1
Mumphrey, Chi	− 2	35	45
D. Murphy, Atl	+28	104	102
Nettles, SD	+ 4	48	41
Newman, Mon	0	23	23
Oberkfell, Atl	+ 1	66	72
Oester, Cin	− 8	56	59
Oquendo, StL	+ 4	21	17
Ortiz, Pitt	+ 5	18	16
Pankovitz, Hou	− 4	10	14
Parker, Cin	+36	113	94
Pena, Pitt	− 9	52	68
Pendleton, StL	−32	37	50
Perez, Cin	+ 6	31	24
Puhl, Hou	−11	11	18
Quinones, SF	0	13	6
Raines, Mon	+24	96	130
Ramierez, Atl	−40	18	42
Ray, Pitt	+16	87	79
Redus, Phi	+ 3	46	55
C. Reynolds, Hou	− 5	31	28
R. J. Reynolds, Pi	0	50	55
Rn. Reynolds, Phi	− 9	5	9
L. Rivera, Mon	− 5	15	15
Roberts, SD	+ 1	29	20
R. Roenicke, Phi	+ 9	47	42
Rose, Cin	+ 3	33	23
Royster, SD	− 4	29	31

Name	RC1	RC2	RCJ
Russell, LA	− 4	23	21
Russell, Phi	+ 7	45	42
Sample, Atl	+ 1	25	31
Samuel, Phi	+ 3	72	80
Sandberg, Chi	+ 2	77	86
Santana, NY	−19	28	27
Sax, LA	+11	88	110
Schmidt, Phi	+47	119	122
Schu, Phi	− 1	25	32
Scioscia, LA	−10	39	49
Simmons, Atl	+ 5	21	16
O. Smith, StL	+10	77	73
Speier, Chi	+16	35	24
Stillwell, Cin	− 9	25	24
J. Stone, Phi	− 6	24	36
Strawberry, NY	+19	80	92
Stubbs, LA	− 3	48	51
Templeton, SD	−26	34	44
Teufel, NY	− 1	34	34
A. Thomas, Atl	−13	24	26
M. Thompson, Phi	− 8	28	34
R. Thompson, SF	−18	49	64
Thon, Hou	− 9	25	28
Trevino, LA	+ 1	27	28
Trillo, Chi	+12	31	21
Uribe, SF	−17	40	43
Van Slyke, StL	+16	67	68
Venable, Cin	− 2	16	15
Virgil, Atl	+ 1	48	49
C. Walker, Chi	− 8	4	14
Wallach, Mon	− 5	54	57
Walling, Hou	+19	65	67
Washington, Atl	− 6	10	18
U. Washington, Pitt	0	17	12
Webster, Mon	− 5	66	90
Williams, LA	+ 8	45	37
G. Wilson, Phi	+16	86	76
M. Wilson, NY	+ 4	50	58
Winningham, Mon	− 9	13	17
G. Wright, Mon	−11	4	8
Wynne, SD	+ 7	41	32
Youngblood, SF	+ 7	30	25

CONCLUSION

It is not surprising that a different sabermetric approach to runs created emerges when methodologies from statistics (regression, expectation, state space Markov chain framework) and economics (value-added, marginal and average) are combined with a vastly superior data base, as has been made available by *Project Scoresheet*. As is always true in science, the new builds on the old, and will in turn be refined. It is hoped that the new methodology introduced here will be developed and incorporated into mainstream sabermetric analysis.

MORE

For some of you, I suppose, this book will strain or even exhaust your interest in the analysis of baseball records. Others of you may have a deeper interest in the field, and might want to know where you can go to learn more about the subject.

The first thing that I might recommend that you do is get involved in *Project Scoresheet*. We need your help, and you'll enjoy the experience. We need people to score games. You'll enjoy being in contact with the other people in the scoring network, possibly getting to vote in the player rankings, and having access to the records of all the games.

If you're interested in more things to read, let me list a few:

The Great American Baseball Stat Book, produced by *Project Scoresheet,* is the most complete and informative book of its kind ever published. It should be available within a week of when this book is out. In bookstores everywhere.

The Baseball Analyst is a 20-page, six-times a year publication that I started four or five years ago, and which I edit. The magazine contains articles in sabermetrics, occsionally written by me but mostly by other people. The articles are photocopied and staple-bound into each issue, and to be honest the quality of the articles has been uneven. While there have always been some very interesting and informative pieces, there have been many articles that were technical, difficult to understand, and discussed issues of little importance. In recent months I have been working to improve the quality by being more active about soliciting articles and editing them once they are submitted, and I think we'll make some real progress in the next year. Write to the *Baseball Analyst,* P.O. Box 171, Winchester, Kansas 66097.

Geoff Beckman edits the *Project Scoresheet Baseball Report,* which contains articles written by Geoff and by the team captains of other people in *Project Scoresheet,* reporting on their teams. Many of these people are very fine writers, often witty and incisive, very knowledgeable about their teams (I'd mention some of the names except I'm afraid of who I would leave out). An issue runs about 18–20 pages, also photocopied but with a little more attention to design/appearance needs than the *Analyst.* I really recommend this one highly. Geoff Beckman, 2589 Norfolk Road, Cleveland Heights, Ohio 44106.

The *Sabermetric Review,* edited and mostly written by Gary Gillette, is a "Monthly Empirical Analysis of Baseball" (the quotation is from the sub-heading). In the *Sabermetric Review,* Gary often uses the tools of sabermetrics to analyze what is happening at the moment, presenting up-to-the-deadline secondary averages or basic runs created. One of the most interesting articles in an early issue focused on the 1985 performance of Willie McGee with Vince Coleman on base, with no one on base, with someone else on base, etc. Another article analyzed the moves made by Dick Williams after taking over the Mariners, while another presented charts detailing the age and how/when acquired status of all major league players. It's a professional production, typeset and all that, newsletter-style. Contact Meckler Publishing, 11 Ferry Lane West, Westport, Connecticut 06880.

Also professionally produced, newspaper-style with pictures and all, is *Innings,* a Canadian-based and Canadian-focused—but not totally—publication about baseball. Many of the articles are well written, and contain the offerings of many names familiar to *Abstract* readers, such as Stan Michna, Neil Munro, David Driscoll and Bill Deane. Contact *Innings,* 984 Eglinton Ave West, Toronto, Ontario M6C 2C5.

The *Chicago Baseball Report,* by John and Sue Dewan, Mark Podrazik, and Don Zminda, has two editions, one full of everything you could want to know about the Cubs, and one full of everything you could want to know about the White sox, plus some good analytical stuff. *Chicago Baseball Report,* P.O. Box 46074, Chicago, Illinois 60646.

A similarly fanatic publication about the Seattle Mariners is the *Seattle Baseball Bulletin,* Steve Russell, P.O. Box 221, Redmond, Washington 98073. Material from the Bulletin is cited throughout the book.

People in love with the Toronto Blue Jays should look into the *Toronto Blue Book,* by David Driscoll, whose address I can't find at the moment but I know I gave it two or three times already. Those enamored of the Boston Red Sox should consider the *Waseleski Baseball Report,* 10 Newton Street, Millers Falls, Massachusetts 01349.

A couple of quick citations of publications that I don't remember having seen, but am told are pretty good: *Dodger Dugout,* by Tot Holmes, P.O. Box 11. Gothenburg, Nebraska, 69138; *Tigers Stripes,* Todd Miller, P.O. Box 119, Northville, Michigan, 48167; and the *Christmann Baseball Report* (Yankees) Craig Christmann, 54 Old Chestnut Ridge Rd., Montvale, New Jersey 07645.

Andy ALLANSON

Year	Team / Lg		GS	OSB	Avg.	Inn	ER	W–L	ERA	(TmERA)
1986	Cle	A	92	67	.73	813.1	408	49-43	4.51	(4.58)

Alan ASHBY

Year	Team / Lg		GS	OSB	Avg.	Inn	ER	W–L	ERA	(TmERA)
1975	Cle	A	82	64	.78					
1976	Cle	A	73	75	1.03					
1977	Tor	A	121	67	.56					
1978	Tor	A	79	51	.65					
1979	Hous	N	103	70	.68					
1980	Hous	N	105	100	.95					
1981	Hous	N	74	59	.80					
1982	Hous	N	90	104	1.16	803.2	335	40-50	3.75	(3.42)
1983	Hous	N	79	82	1.04	715.0	269	39-40	3.39	(3.45)
1984	Hous	N	54	63	1.17	478.2	196	21-33	3.69	(3.32)
1985	Hous	N	55	60	1.09	500.2	191	24-31	3.44	(3.66)
1986	Hous	N	87	94	1.08	785.0	270	60-27	3.10	(3.15)
12 years			1002	889	.89	3283.0	1261	184-181	3.46	(3.38)

Mark BAILEY

Year	Team / Lg		GS	OSB	Avg.	Inn	ER	W–L	ERA	(TmERA)
1984	Hous	N	102	112	1.10	919.2	313	58-44	3.06	(3.32)
1985	Hous	N	96	70	.73	859.0	349	55-41	3.66	(3.66)
1986	Hous	N	44	50	1.14	396.2	133	22-22	3.02	(3.15)
3 years			242	232	.96	2175.1	795	135-107	3.29	(3.42)

Bill BATHE

Year	Team / Lg		GS	OSB	Avg.	Inn	ER	W–L	ERA	(TmERA)
1986	Oak	A	38	39	1.03	335.1	188	11-27	5.05	(4.31)

Chris BANDO

Year	Team / Lg		GS	OSB	Avg.	Inn	ER	W–L	ERA	(TmERA)
1981	Cle	A	8	4	.50					
1982	Cle	A	49	24	.49	436.1	217	21-28	4.48	(4.11)
1983	Cle	A	34	17	.50	302.0	160	14-20	4.77	(4.43)
1984	Cle	A	59	28	.47	528.1	230	33-26	3.92	(4.26)
1985	Cle	A	57	53	.93	495.1	297	15-42	5.40	(4.91)
1986	Cle	A	71	46	.65	634.1	328	35-35	4.65	(4.58)
6 years			278	172	.62	2396.1	1232	118-151	4.63	(4.48)

Bruce BENEDICT

Year	Team / Lg		GS	OSB	Avg.	Inn	ER	W–L	ERA	(TmERA)
1978	Atl	N	16	15	.94					
1979	Atl	N	69	64	.93					
1980	Atl	N	111	81	.73					
1981	Atl	N	86	83	.97					
1982	Atl	N	111	96	.86	1001.1	403	67-43	3.62	(3.82)
1983	Atl	N	129	128	.99	1146.0	476	70-59	3.74	(3.67)
1984	Atl	N	96	84	.88	860.2	335	44-52	3.50	(3.57)
1985	Atl	N	65	71	1.09	572.1	246	28-37	3.87	(4.19)
1986	Atl	N	49	27	.55	426.0	194	20-29	4.10	(3.97)
9 years			732	649	.89	4006.1	1654	229-220	3.72	(3.79)

Dann BILARDELLO

Year	Team / Lg		GS	OSB	Avg.	Inn	ER	W–L	ERA	(TmERA)
1983	Cin	N	88	70	.80	782.1	365	42-46	4.20	(3.98)
1984	Cin	N	51	42	.82	467.2	228	22-29	4.39	(4.16)
1985	Cin	N	30	19	.63	269.2	96	15-15	3.21	(3.71)
1986	Mon	N	53	49	.92	493.1	216	22-31	3.94	(3.78)
4 years			222	180	.81	2013.0	905	101-121	4.05	(3.94)

Bruce BOCHY

Year	Team / Lg		GS	OSB	Avg.	Inn	ER	W–L	ERA	(TmERA)
1978	Hous	N	45	46	1.02					
1979	Hous	N	37	40	1.08					
1980	Hous	N	2	1	.50					
1982	NY	N	16	16	1.00	140.1	48	5-11	3.08	(3.88)
1983	SD	N	8	4	.50	70.1	45	4-4	5.76	(3.62)
1984	SD	N	20	18	.90	185.1	67	12-8	3.25	(3.48)
1985	SD	N	27	30	1.11	244.1	97	13-14	3.58	(3.40)
1986	SD	N	30	36	1.20	268.0	124	13-17	4.16	(3.99)
8 years			185	191	1.03	908.1	381	47-54	3.78	(3.68)

Bob BOONE

Year	Team / Lg		GS	OSB	Avg.	Inn	ER	W–L	ERA	(TmERA)
1975	Phil	N	81	31	.38					
1976	Phil	N	97	79	.57					
1977	Phil	N	119	79	.56					
1978	Phil	N	117	68	.58					
1979	Phil	N	110	54	.49*					
1980	Phil	N	130	123	.95					
1981	Phil	N	64	77	1.20					
1982	Cal	A	138	48	.35*	1260.0	532	84-55	3.80	(3.82)
1983	Cal	A	135	65	.48	1222.2	587	60-75	4.32	(4.31)
1984	Cal	A	133	54	.41	1202.0	506	69-64	3.79	(3.96)
1985	Cal	A	136	57	.42*	1230.1	534	75-61	3.91	(3.91)
1986	Cal	A	137	44	.32*	1241.0	509	84-53	3.69	(3.84)
12 years			1397	779	.56	6156.0	2668	372-308	3.90	(3.97)

Scott BRADLEY

Year	Team / Lg		GS	OSB	Avg.	Inn	ER	W–L	ERA	(TmERA)
1985	NY	A	3	3	1.00	25.0	11	0-3	3.96	(3.69)
1986	Sea	A	49	33	.67	436.1	203	21-28	4.19	(4.65)
2 years			52	36	.69	461.1	214	21-31	4.17	(4.59)

Bob BRENLY

Year	Team / Lg		GS	OSB	Avg.	Inn	ER	W–L	ERA	(TmERA)
1981	SF	N	10	7	.70					
1982	SF	N	48	53	1.10	429.0	179	24-24	3.76	(3.64)
1983	SF	N	75	56	.75	657.2	262	33-42	3.59	(3.70)
1984	SF	N	114	101	.89	1030.1	486	49-66	4.25	(4.39)
1985	SF	N	102	85	.83	911.2	354	37-65	3.50	(3.61)
1986	SF	N	78	56	.72	693.2	256	40-38	3.32	(3.33)
6 years			427	358	.84	3722.1	1537	183-235	3.72	(3.79)

Sal BUTERA

Year	Team / Lg		GS	OSB	Avg.	Inn	ER	W–L	ERA	(TmERA)
1980	Minn	A	28	16	.57					
1981	Minn	A	51	23	.45					
1982	Minn	A	42	29	.69	369.1	201	12-30	4.90	(4.72)
1983	Det	A	1	1	1.00	11.0	4	1-0	3.27	(3.80)
1984	Mon	N	1	1	1.00	8.0	4	0-1	4.50	(3.31)
1985	Mon	N	40	42	1.05	351.2	164	19-21	4.20	(3.55)
1986	Cin	N	33	30	.91	298.0	119	20-13	3.59	(3.91)
7 years			196	142	.72	1038.0	492	52-65	4.27	(4.07)

Gary CARTER

Year	Team / Lg		GS	OSB	Avg.	Inn	ER	W–L	ERA	(TmERA)
1975	Mon	N	55	21	.38					
1976	Mon	N	54	27	.50					
1977	Mon	N	142	110	.77					
1978	Mon	N	147	80	.54*					
1979	Mon	N	135	75	.56					
1980	Mon	N	146	94	.64*					
1981	Mon	N	99	53	.54*					
1982	Mon	N	154	106	.69	1364.2	475	82-69	3.13	(3.31)
1983	Mon	N	140	89	.64	1273.0	492	71-69	3.48	(3.58)
1984	Mon	N	135	103	.76	1200.0	417	69-66	3.13	(3.31)
1985	NY	N	139	100	.72	1282.0	439	85-54	3.08	(3.11)
1986	NY	N	119	115	.97	1091.0	371	77-42	3.06	(3.11)
12 years			1465	973	.66	6210.2	2194	384-300	3.18	(3.29)

Steve CHRISTMAS

Year	Team / Lg		GS	OSB	Avg.	Inn	ER	W–L	ERA	(TmERA)
1983	Cin	N	4	3	.75	33.0	12	0-4	3.27	(3.98)
1986	Chi	N	1	3	3.00	9.0	4	0-1	4.00	(4.49)
2 years			5	6	1.20	42.0	16	0- 5	3.43	(4.08)

Rick CERONE

Year	Team / Lg		GS	OSB	Avg.	Inn	ER	W–L	ERA	(TmERA)
1975	Cle	A	3	2	.67					
1976	Cle	A	4	4	1.00					
1977	Tor	A	28	10	.36					
1978	Tor	A	79	48	.61					
1979	Tor	A	133	69	.52					
1980	NY	A	146	56	.38*					
1981	NY	A	65	34	.52					
1982	NY	A	86	55	.64	787.2	330	41-46	3.77	(3.99)
1983	NY	A	70	45	.67	624.0	292	38-32	4.21	(3.86)
1984	NY	A	36	16	.44	318.1	131	19-17	3.70	(3.78)
1985	Atl	N	78	64	.82	703.0	360	26-52	4.61	(4.19)
1986	Mil	A	66	39	.59	594.2	309	32-34	4.68	(4.02)
12 years			794	442	.56	3027.2	1422	156-181	4.23	(3.99)

Darren DAULTON

Year	Team / Lg		GS	OSB	Avg.	Inn	ER	W–L	ERA	(TmERA)
1983	Phil	N	1	2	2.00	9.0	1	1-0	1.00	(3.34)
1985	Phil	N	27	25	.93	238.2	120	11-16	4.53	(3.68)
1986	Phil	N	45	54	1.20	397.1	187	22-23	4.24	(3.85)
3 years			73	81	1.11	645.0	308	34-39	4.30	(3.78)

Jody DAVIS

Year	Team / Lg		GS	OSB	Avg.	Inn	ER	W–L	ERA	(TmERA)
1981	Chi	N	53	38	.72					
1982	Chi	N	120	93	.78	1074.2	489	56-64	4.10	(3.92)
1983	Chi	N	140	129	.92	1232.1	567	59-81	4.14	(4.08)
1984	Chi	N	141	119	.84	1257.2	510	88-53	3.65	(3.75)
1985	Chi	N	129	120	.93	1147.1	544	63-65	4.27	(4.16)
1986	Chi	N	142	98	.69*	1274.0	636	59-82	4.49	(4.49)
6 years			725	597	.82	5986.0	2746	325-345	4.13	(4.08)

Rick DEMPSEY

Year	Team / Lg		GS	OSB	Avg.	Inn	ER	W–L	ERA	(TmERA)
1975	NY	A	11	8	.73					
1976	NY/Bal	A	59	27	.46					
1977	Bal	A	84	30	.36					
1978	Bal	A	130	62	.48*					
1979	Bal	A	113	47	.42*					
1980	Bal	A	95	50	.53					
1981	Bal	A	72	32	.44					
1982	Bal	A	101	46	.46	914.1	389	61-40	3.83	(3.99)
1983	Bal	A	109	65	.60	980.0	383	68-41	3.52	(3.63)
1984	Bal	A	104	57	.55	918.0	379	58-46	3.72	(3.71)
1985	Bal	A	111	80	.72	985.1	498	56-55	4.55	(4.38)
1986	Bal	A	99	69	.70	897.2	381	52-47	3.82	(4.30)
12 years			1088	573	.53	4695.1	2030	295-229	3.89	(4.00)

Bo DIAZ

Year	Team / Lg		GS	OSB	Avg.	Inn	ER	W–L	ERA	(TmERA)
1978	Cle	A	39	23	.59					
1979	Cle	A	11	11	1.00					
1980	Cle	A	52	40	.77					
1981	Cle	A	42	20	.48					
1982	Phil	N	135	115	.85	1213.1	454	77-58	3.37	(3.61)
1983	Phil	N	127	110	.87	1141.1	398	73-53	3.14	(3.34)
1984	Phil	N	22	20	.91	194.1	63	13-9	2.92	(3.62)
1985	Phi/Cin	N	67	54	.85	607.0	239	34-33	3.54	(3.72)
1986	Cin	N	127	103	.81	1152.0	513	65-62	4.01	(3.91)
9 years			622	496	.80	4308.0	1667	262-215	3.48	(3.63)

Dave ENGLE

Year	Team / Lg		GS	OSB	Avg.	Inn	ER	W–L	ERA	(TmERA)
1983	Minn	A	70	43	.61	623.0	314	33-37	4.54	(4.66)
1984	Minn	A	80	50	.63	711.2	300	36-44	3.79	(3.85)
1985	Minn	A	12	5	.42	104.0	43	7-5	3.72	(4.48)
1986	Det	A	1	1	1.00	8.0	8	0-1	9.00	(4.02)
4 years			163	99	.61	1446.2	665	76-87	4.14	(4.25)

Juan ESPINO

Year	Team / Lg		GS	OSB	Avg.	Inn	ER	W–L	ERA	(TmERA)
1983	NY	A	8	5	.63	73.0	32	5-3	3.95	(3.86)
1985	NY	A	3	1	.33	26.0	9	2-1	3.12	(3.69)
1986	NY	A	9	6	.67	79.0	33	6-3	3.76	(4.11)
3 years			20	12	.60	178.0	74	13- 7	3.74	(3.95)

Jack FIMPLE

Year	Team / Lg		GS	OSB	Avg.	Inn	ER	W–L	ERA	(TmERA)
1983	LA	N	48	34	.71	429.2	149	28-19	3.12	(3.10)
1984	LA	N	7	8	1.14	63.0	22	3-4	3.14	(3.17)
1986	LA	N	4	3	.75	35.0	12	2-2	3.09	(3.76)
3 years			59	45	.76	527.2	183	33-25	3.12	(3.15)

Carlton FISK

Year	Team / Lg		GS	OSB	Avg.	Inn	ER	W–L	ERA	(TmERA)
1975	Box	A	68	34	.50					
1976	Bos	A	130	89	.68					
1977	Bos	A	149	61	.41					
1978	Bos	A	150	102	.68					
1979	Bos	A	34	24	.71					
1980	Bos	A	112	73	.65					
1981	Chi	A	89	64	.72					
1982	Chi	A	129	79	.61	1142.1	498	70-59	3.92	(3.87)
1983	Chi	A	123	73	.59	1099.1	452	78-45	3.70	(3.67)
1984	Chi	A	82	50	.61	751.1	342	36-46	4.10	(4.13)
1985	Chi	A	119	84	.71	1064.1	459	63-53	3.88	(4.07)
1986	Chi	A	64	54	.84	569.1	247	29-35	3.90	(3.94)
12 years			1249	787	.63	4626.2	1998	276-238	3.89	(3.92)

Mike FITZGERALD

Year	Team / Lg		GS	OSB	Avg.	Inn	ER	W–L	ERA	(TmERA)
1983	NY	N	7	12	1.17	61.0	20	2-5	2.95	(3.68)
1984	NY	N	101	88	.87	903.0	341	56-45	3.40	(3.60)
1985	Mon	N	93	107	1.15	853.1	281	55-38	2.96	(3.55)
1986	Mon	N	61	82	1.34	546.0	226	37-24	3.73	(3.78)
4 years			262	289	1.10	2363.1	868	150-112	3.31	(3.63)

Rich GEDMAN

Year	Team / Lg		GS	OSB	Avg.	Inn	ER	W–L	ERA	(TmERA)
1980	Bos	A	2	2	1.00					
1981	Bos	A	57	51	.89					
1982	Bos	A	74	60	.81	679.2	338	37-39	4.48	(4.03)
1983	Bos	A	52	70	1.35	463.0	240	24-28	4.67	(4.34)
1984	Bos	A	115	77	.67	1033.0	461	66-49	4.02	(4.18)
1985	Bos	A	129	67	.52	1153.1	505	67-62	3.94	(4.06)
1986	Bos	A	123	56	.46	1095.1	471	72-51	3.87	(3.93)
7 years			552	383	.69	4424.1	2015	266-229	4.10	(4.08)

John GIBBONS

Year	Team / Lg		GS	OSB	Avg.	Inn	ER	W–L	ERA	(TmERA)
1984	NY	N	9	9	1.00	77.0	46	4-5	5.38	(3.60)
1986	NY	N	5	5	1.00	47.0	11	5-0	2.11	(3.11)
2 years			14	14	1.00	124.0	57	9-5	4.14	(3.43)

Brad GULDEN

Year	Team / Lg		GS	OSB	Avg.	Inn	ER	W–L	ERA	(TmERA)
1979	NY	A	34	23	.68					
1981	Sea	A	6	3	.67					
1982	Mon	N	1	0	.00	8.0	9	0-1	10.13	(3.31)
1984	Cin	N	79	77	.97	713.2	306	42-37	3.86	(4.16)
1986	SF	N	2	2	1.00	18.0	10	0-2	5.00	(3.33)
5 years			122	105	.86	739.2	325	42-40	3.95	(4.13)

Ron HASSEY

Year	Team / Lg		GS	OSB	Avg.	Inn	ER	W–L	ERA	(TmERA)
1978	Cle	A	23	18	.78					
1979	Cle	A	61	50	.82					
1980	Cle	A	103	77	.75					
1981	Cle	A	53	23	.43					
1982	Cle	A	91	85	.93	837.1	342	49-42	3.68	(4.11)
1983	Cle	A	96	62	.66	853.2	422	40-56	4.45	(4.43)
1984	Cle/Chi	A	40	29	.73	371.1	179	14-25	4.34	(4.22)
1985	NY	A	65	51	.78	576.0	260	41-24	4.06	(3.69)
1986	NY	A	48	30	.63	428.1	191	29-19	4.01	(4.11)
1986	Chi	A	7	3	.43	61.1	22	4-3	3.23	(3.94)
9 years			587	428	.73	3128.0	1416	177-169	4.07	(4.13)

Randy HUNT

Year	Team / Lg		GS	OSB	Avg.	Inn	ER	W–L	ERA	(TmERA)
1985	StL	N	3	0	.00	26.0	12	1-2	4.15	(3.10)
1986	Mon	N	18	19	1.06	163.1	57	8-10	3.14	(3.78)
2 years			21	19	.90	189.1	69	9-12	3.28	(3.68)

Clint HURDLE

Year	Team / Lg		GS	OSB	Avg.	Inn	ER	W–L	ERA	(TmERA)
1985	NY	N	12	14	1.17	104.0	39	7-4	3.18	(3.11)
1986	StL	N	3	3	1.00	28.0	9	1-2	2.89	(3.37)
2 years			15	17	1.13	132.0	48	8-6	3.27	(3.16)

Ron KARKOVICE

Year	Team / Lg		GS	OSB	Avg.	Inn	ER	W–L	ERA	(TmERA)
1986	Chi	A	36	26	.74	313.1	112	17-19	3.22	(3.94)

Bob KEARNEY

Year	Team / Lg		GS	OSB	Avg.	Inn	ER	W–L	ERA	(TmERA)
1982	Oak	A	20	12	.60	180.2	89	8-12	4.43	(4.54)
1983	Oak	A	89	46	.52	799.0	379	41-48	4.27	(4.34)
1984	Sea	A	127	67	.53	1129.2	553	55-72	4.41	(4.31)
1985	Sea	A	94	54	.57	831.0	451	41-53	4.88	(4.68)
1986	Sea	A	60	39	.65	530.2	268	24-36	4.55	(4.65)
5 years			390	218	.56	3471.0	1740	169-221	4.51	(4.47)

Terry KENNEDY

Year	Team / Lg		GS	OSB	Avg.	Inn	ER	W–L	ERA	(TmERA)
1978	StL	N	9	5	.56					
1979	StL	N	27	21	.78					
1980	StL	N	38	50	1.32					
1981	SD	N	97	84	.87					
1982	SD	N	133	102	.77	1228.1	467	70-64	3.42	(3.52)
1983	SD	N	141	139	.99	1278.1	512	67-74	3.60	(3.62)
1984	SD	N	141	105	.74	1266.0	492	80-61	3.50	(3.48)
1985	SD	N	135	109	.81	1208.0	452	70-65	3.37	(3.40)
1986	SD	N	114	102	.89	1014.1	430	54-60	3.82	(3.99)
9 years			835	717	.86	5995.0	2353	341-324	3.53	(3.59)

Jeff HEARRON

Year	Team / Lg		GS	OSB	Avg.	Inn	ER	W–L	ERA	(TmERA)
1985	Tor	A	2	2	1.00	17.0	9	0-2	4.76	(3.31)
1986	Tor	A	7	4	.57	64.0	25	4-3	3.52	(4.08)
2 years			9	6	.67	81.0	34	4-5	3.78	(3.91)

Mike HEATH

Year	Team / Lg		GS	OSB	Avg.	Inn	ER	W–L	ERA	(TmERA)
1978	NY	A	23	12	.52					
1979	Oak	A	18	13	.72					
1980	Oak	A	43	23	.53					
1981	Oak	A	76	34	.45					
1982	Oak	A	77	37	.48	689.0	323	34-43	4.22	(4.54)
1983	Oak	A	69	43	.62	619.1	301	33-36	4.37	(4.34)
1984	Oak	A	95	54	.57	835.0	443	44-51	4.77	(4.48)
1985	Oak	A	94	44	.47	829.1	470	40-54	5.10	(4.41)
1986	StL	N	51	35	.69	478.2	195	21-30	3.67	(3.37)
1986	Det	A	27	13	.48	237.2	107	17-10	4.05	(4.02)
9 years			573	308	.54	3689.0	1839	189-224	4.49	(4.28)

Ed HEARN

Year	Team / Lg		GS	OSB	Avg.	Inn	ER	W–L	ERA	(TmERA)
1986	NY	N	36	33	.92	328.0	130	24-12	3.57	(3.11)

Marc HILL

Year	Team / Lg		GS	OSB	Avg.	Inn	ER	W–L	ERA	(TmERA)
1975	SF	N	47	31	.66					
1976	SF	N	41	27	.66					
1977	SF	N	95	84	.88					
1978	SF	N	105	90	.86					
1979	SF	N	53	42	.79					
1980	SF/Sea		33	25	.76					
1982	Chi	A	26	17	.65	233.1	91	14-12	3.51	(3.87)
1983	Chi	A	37	24	.65	328.0	144	19-18	3.95	(3.67)
1984	Chi	A	57	31	.54	501.2	250	26-31	4.49	(4.13)
1985	Chi	A	29	18	.62	255.0	138	12-17	4.87	(4.07)
1986	Chi	A	6	2	.33	54.0	34	1-5	5.67	(3.94)
11 years			529	391	.74	1372.0	657	72-83	4.31	(3.96)

Steve LAKE

Year	Team / Lg		GS	OSB	Avg.	Inn	ER	W–L	ERA	(TmERA)
1983	Chi	N	22	23	1.05	196.1	94	12-10	4.31	(4.08)
1984	Chi	N	15	10	.67	132.2	55	8-7	3.73	(3.75)
1985	Chi	N	33	17	.52	295.0	124	14-19	3.78	(4.16)
1986	Chi	N	4	8	2.00	37.0	27	3-1	6.57	(4.49)
1986	StL	N	14	4	.29	121.2	56	7-7	4.14	(3.37)
4 years			88	62	.70	782.2	356	44-44	4.09	(3.96)

Tim LAUDNER

Year	Team / Lg		GS	OSB	Avg.	Inn	ER	W–L	ERA	(TmERA)
1981	Minn	A	10	6	.60					
1982	Minn	A	89	74	.83	790.1	421	34-55	4.79	(4.72)
1983	Minn	A	47	53	1.13	415.2	236	18-29	5.11	(4.66)
1984	Minn	A	75	36	.48	665.1	284	42-33	3.84	(3.85)
1985	Minn	A	53	34	.64	466.0	240	21-32	4.64	(4.48)
1986	Minn	A	57	32	.56	503.0	247	31-26	4.42	(4.77)
6 years			331	235	.71	2840.1	1428	146-175	4.52	(4.48)

Mike LAVALLIERE

Year	Team / Lg		GS	OSB	Avg.	Inn	ER	W–L	ERA	(TmERA)
1984	Phil	N	2	0	.00	20.1	5	0-2	2.21	(3.62)
1985	StL	N	11	5	.45	96.0	34	6-5	3.19	(3.10)
1986	StL	N	93	50	.54	838.0	289	50-43	3.10	(3.37)
3 years			106	55	.52	954.1	328	56-50	3.09	(3.35)

Phil LOMBARDI

Year	Team / Lg		GS	OSB	Avg.	Inn	ER	W–L	ERA	(TmERA)
1986	NY	A	1	0	.00	9.0	7	0-1	7.00	(4.11)

Dwight LOWRY

Year	Team / Lg		GS	OSB	Avg.	Inn	ER	W–L	ERA	(TmERA)
1984	Det	A	11	8	.73	98.0	34	9-2	3.12	(3.49)
1986	Det	A	45	30	.67	402.2	190	22-23	4.25	(4.02)
2 years			56	33	.59	500.2	224	31-25	4.03	(3.92)

Barry LYONS

Year	Team / Lg		GS	OSB	Avg.	Inn	ER	W–L	ERA	(TmERA)
1986	NY	N	2	6	3.00	18.0	1	2-0	.50	(4.11)

Mike MARTIN

Year	Team / Lg		GS	OSB	Avg.	Inn	ER	W–L	ERA	(TmERA)
1986	Chi	N	4	10	2.50	35.0	16	2-2	4.11	(4.49)

Buck MARTINEZ

Year	Team / Lg		GS	OSB	Avg.	Inn	ER	W–L	ERA	(TmERA)
1975	KC	A	70	66	.94					
1976	KC	A	86	77	.90					
1977	KC	A	22	14	.64					
1978	Mil	A	85	44	.52					
1979	Mil	A	67	35	.52					
1980	Mil	A	74	37	.50					
1981	Tor	A	44	25	.57					
1982	Tor	A	80	30	.38	686.2	299	35-42	3.92	(3.95)
1983	Tor	A	67	31	.46	600.0	244	36-31	3.66	(4.12)
1984	Tor	A	65	20	.31	579.0	226	38-27	3.51	(3.86)
1985	Tor	A	32	22	.69	287.1	123	18-14	3.86	(3.31)
1986	Tor	A	47	28	.60	427.0	195	22-24	4.11	(4.08)
12 years			739	429	.58	2580.0	1087	149-138	3.79	(3.92)

Bob MELVIN

Year	Team / Lg		GS	OSB	Avg.	Inn	ER	W–L	ERA	(TmERA)
1985	Det	A	25	19	.76	226.1	83	12-13	3.30	(3.78)
1986	SF	N	76	68	.89	688.2	263	39-37	3.44	(3.33)
2 years			101	86	.85	915.0	346	51-50	3.40	(3.44)

Darrell MILLER

Year	Team / Lg		GS	OSB	Avg.	Inn	ER	W–L	ERA	(TmERA)
1986	Cal	A	3	4	1.33	25.0	16	1-2	5.76	(3.84)

Orlando MERCADO

Year	Team / Lg		GS	OSB	Avg.	Inn	ER	W–L	ERA	(TmERA)
1982	Sea	A	5	3	.60	43.0	17	3-2	3.56	(3.88)
1983	Sea	A	59	54	.92	523.1	254	23-36	4.37	(4.12)
1984	Sea	A	21	13	.62	185.1	85	9-12	4.13	(4.31)
1986	Tex	A	31	25	.81	284.1	100	21-10	3.17	(4.11)
4 years			116	95	.82	1036.0	456	56-60	3.96	(4.14)

John MIZEROCK

Year	Team / Lg		GS	OSB	Avg.	Inn	ER	W–L	ERA	(TmERA)
1983	Hous	N	30	26	.87	271.0	118	16-14	3.92	(3.45)
1985	Hous	N	11	13	1.18	98.1	54	4-7	4.95	(3.66)
1986	Hous	N	30	28	.93	265.2	106	13-17	3.59	(3.15)
3 years			71	67	.94	635.0	278	33-38	3.94	(3.36)

Keith MORELAND

Year	Team / Lg		GS	OSB	Avg.	Inn	ER	W–L	ERA	(TmERA)
1979	Phi	N	12	14	1.17					
1980	Phi	N	31	38	1.23					
1981	Phi	N	42	44	1.05					
1982	Chi	N	39	54	1.38	346.2	130	16-23	3.38	(3.92)
1984	Chi	N	2	1	.50	17.0	14	0-2	7.41	(3.75)
1986	Chi	N	10	13	1.30	90.0	38	6-4	3.80	(4.49)
6 years			136	164	1.21	453.2	182	22-29	3.61	(4.03)

Charlie MOORE

Year	Team / Lg		GS	OSB	Avg.	Inn	ER	W–L	ERA	(TmERA)
1975	Mil	A	40	29	.72					
1976	Mil	A	46	44	.96					
1977	Mil	A	118	81	.69					
1978	Mil	A	74	36	.49					
1979	Mil	A	89	61	.69					
1980	Mil	A	78	39	.50					
1981	Mil	A	29	18	.62					
1982	Mil	A	17	5	.29	139.0	61	9-6	3.95	(3.98)
1984	Mil	A	4	6	1.50	36.0	21	1-3	5.25	(4.06)
1985	Mil	A	96	58	.60	861.0	413	43-53	4.32	(4.39)
1986	Mil	A	63	31	.49	551.1	204	33-30	3.33	(4.02)
11 years			654	408	.62	1587.1	699	86-92	3.96	(4.21)

Jerry NARRON

Year	Team / Lg		GS	OSB	Avg.	Inn	ER	W–L	ERA	(TmERA)
1979	NY	A	29	18	.62					
1980	Sea	A	29	20	.69					
1981	Sea	A	58	45	.78					
1983	Cal	A	3	3	1.00	28.0	3	1-2	.96	(4.31)
1984	Cal	A	29	17	.59	256.0	135	12-17	4.75	(3.96)
1985	Cal	A	26	17	.65	227.0	99	15-11	3.93	(3.91)
1986	Cal	A	22	13	.59	190.0	96	7-15	4.55	(3.84)
7 years			196	133	.68	701.0	333	35-43	4.28	(3.92)

Carl NICHOLS

Year	Team / Lg		GS	OSB	Avg.	Inn	ER	W–L	ERA	(TmERA)
1986	Bal	A	2	2	1.00	17.0	7	1- 1	3.71	(4.30)

Tom NIETO

Year	Team / Lg		GS	OSB	Avg.	Inn	ER	W–L	ERA	(TmERA)
1984	StL	N	28	20	.71	248.1	101	12-16	3.66	(3.58)
1985	StL	N	83	58	.70	751.1	263	53-30	3.15	(3.10)
1986	Mon	N	20	35	1.75	182.2	83	8-12	4.09	(3.78)
3 years			131	113	.86	1182.1	447	73-58	3.40	(3.31)

Matt NOKES

Year	Team / Lg		GS	OSB	Avg.	Inn	ER	W–L	ERA	(TmERA)
1985	SF	N	13	21	1.62	117.1	59	4-9	4.53	(3.61)
1986	Det	A	7	3	.43	62.0	24	3-4	3.48	(4.02)
2 years			20	24	1.20	179.1	83	7-13	4.17	(4.16)

Junior ORTIZ

Year	Team / Lg		GS	OSB	Avg.	Inn	ER	W–L	ERA	(TmERA)
1982	Pitt	N	4	2	.50	38.0	15	2-2	3.55	(3.81)
1983	Pi/NY	N	58	68	1.17	520.1	226	27-31	3.91	(3.68)
1984	NY	N	25	26	1.04	226.0	77	16-9	3.07	(3.60)
1985	Pitt	N	23	19	.83	198.1	128	5-18	5.82	(3.97)
1986	Pitt	N	29	28	.97	261.2	109	12-17	3.75	(3.90)
5 years			139	143	1.03	1244.1	555	62-77	4.01	(3.76)

Phil OUELLETTE

Year	Team / Lg		GS	OSB	Avg.	Inn	ER	W–L	ERA	(TmERA)
1986	SF	N	6	9	1.50	60.0	12	4-2	1.80	(3.33)

Al PARDO

Year	Team / Lg		GS	OSB	Avg.	Inn	ER	W–L	ERA	(TmERA)
1985	Bal	A	23	30	1.30	205.2	105	12-11	4.61	(4.38)
1986	Bal	A	13	8	.62	118.0	67	5-8	5.11	(4.30)
2 years			36	38	1.06	323.2	172	17-19	4.78	(4.35)

Mark PARENT

Year	Team / Lg		GS	OSB	Avg.	Inn	ER	W–L	ERA	(TmERA)
1986	SD	N	3	8	2.67	26.1	12	0-3	4.10	(3.99)

Lance PARRISH

Year	Team / Lg		GS	OSB	Avg.	Inn	ER	W–L	ERA	(TmERA)
1978	Det	A	74	31	.42					
1979	Det	A	135	71	.53					
1980	Det	A	114	56	.49					
1981	Det	A	88	44	.50					
1982	Det	A	127	51	.40	1133.0	493	61-66	3.92	(3.80)
1983	Det	A	125	56	.45*	1112.2	480	68-57	3.88	(3.80)
1984	Det	A	124	44	.35*	1127.0	415	83-41	3.31	(3.49)
1985	Det	A	118	61	.52	1071.2	465	66-52	3.91	(3.78)
1986	Det	A	82	40	.49	733.1	316	45-37	3.88	(4.02)
9 years			987	454	.46	5177.2	2169	323-253	3.77	(3.76)

Tony PENA

Year	Team / Lg		GS	OSB	Avg.	Inn	ER	W–L	ERA	(TmERA)
1980	Pitt	N	5	6	1.20					
1981	Pitt	N	54	28	.50					
1982	Pitt	N	127	78	.61*	1143.2	501	67-59	3.94	(3.81)
1983	Pitt	N	144	116	.81	1303.1	478	80-64	3.30	(3.55)
1984	Pitt	N	139	97	.70*	1262.0	428	65-74	3.05	(3.11)
1985	Pitt	N	138	86	.62*	1247.0	510	52-86	3.68	(3.97)
1986	Pitt	N	132	108	.82	1181.0	512	52-80	3.90	(3.90)
7 years			739	519	.70	6137.0	2429	316-363	3.56	(3.66)

Geno PETRALLI

Year	Team / Lg		GS	OSB	Avg.	Inn	ER	W–L	ERA	(TmERA)
1982	Tor	A	8	6	.75	83.0	34	6-3	3.69	(3.95)
1985	Tex	A	32	32	1.00	280.2	177	8-24	5.69	(4.56)
1986	Tex	A	22	18	.82	195.1	93	14-8	4.28	(4.11)
3 years			62	56	.90	559.0	304	28-35	4.89	(4.32)

Darrell PORTER

Year	Team / Lg		GS	OSB	Avg.	Inn	ER	W–L	ERA	(TmERA)
1975	Mil	A	120	86	.72					
1976	Mil	A	105	87	.83					
1977	KC	A	121	60	.50					
1978	KC	A	141	76	.53					
1979	KC	A	141	64	.45					
1980	KC	A	80	39	.49					
1981	StL	N	51	41	.80					
1982	StL	N	108	94	.87	980.1	366	62-46	3.36	(3.37)
1983	StL	N	121	63	.62*	1093.2	476	58-63	3.92	(3.79)
1984	StL	N	116	94	.81	1045.2	429	63-53	3.69	(3.58)
1985	StL	N	65	39	.60	590.2	197	41-24	3.00	(3.10)
1986	Tex	A	22	32	1.45	201.0	89	10-12	3.99	(4.11)
12 years			1191	775	.65	3911.1	1557	234-198	3.58	(3.54)

Jamie QUIRK

Year	Team / Lg		GS	OSB	Avg.	Inn	ER	W–L	ERA	(TmERA)
1979	KC	A	2	1	.50					
1980	KC	A	11	13	1.18					
1981	KC	A	15	13	.87					
1982	KC	A	14	11	.79	125.0	62	6-8	4.46	(4.08)
1983	StL	N	16	23	1.44	142.0	66	6-10	4.18	(3.79)
1985	KC	A	15	11	.73	134.0	52	9-6	3.49	(3.49)
1986	KC	A	38	16	.42	339.2	132	20-18	3.50	(3.82)
7 years			111	88	.79	740.2	312	41-42	3.79	(3.80)

Floyd RAYFORD

Year	Team / Lg		GS	OSB	Avg.	Inn	ER	W–L	ERA	(TmERA)
1984	Bal	A	50	35	.70	453.1	178	25-25	3.53	(3.71)
1985	Bal	A	23	18	.78	201.1	76	12-11	3.40	(4.38)
1986	Bal	A	5	5	1.00	44.0	29	4-1	5.93	(4.30)
3 years			78	58	.74	698.2	283	41-37	3.65	(3.95)

Jeff REED

Year	Team / Lg		GS	OSB	Avg.	Inn	ER	W–L	ERA	(TmERA)
1984	Minn	A	7	6	.86	60.0	31	3-4	4.65	(3.85)
1985	Minn	A	2	2	1.00	17.0	3	1-1	1.59	(4.48)
1986	Minn	A	49	37	.76	440.0	239	20-29	4.88	(4.77)
3 Years			58	45	.78	517.2	273	24-34	4.75	(4.65)

Ronn REYNOLDS

Year	Team / Lg		GS	OSB	Avg.	Inn	ER	W–L	ERA	(TmERA)
1982	NY	N	2	1	.50	17.0	7	0-2	3.71	(3.88)
1983	NY	N	23	28	1.22	200.0	80	8-15	3.60	(3.68)
1985	NY	N	11	8	.73	102.0	36	7-14	3.18	(3.11)
1986	Phi	N	35	47	1.34	305.0	112	20-15	3.30	(3.85)
4 Years			71	84	1.18	624.0	235	32-36	3.39	(3.63)

Ruben RODRIGUEZ

Year	Team / Lg		GS	OSB	Avg.	Inn	ER	W–L	ERA	(TmERA)
1986	Pitt	N	1	1	1.00	8.0	8	0-1	9.00	(3.90)

John RUSSELL

Year	Team / Lg		GS	OSB	Avg.	Inn	ER	W–L	ERA	(TmERA)
1986	Phil	N	81	115	1.42	749.1	322	44-37	3.87	(3.85)

Mark SALAS

Year	Team / Lg		GS	OSB	Avg.	Inn	ER	W–L	ERA	(TmERA)
1984	StL	N	2	4	2.00	17.0	4	1-1	2.12	(3.58)
1985	Minn	A	95	58	.61	839.1	424	48-47	4.55	(4.48)
1986	Minn	A	56	42	.75	489.0	273	20-36	5.02	(4.77)
3 years			153	104	.68	1345.1	701	69-84	4.69	(4.69)

Benito SANTIAGO

Year	Team / Lg		GS	OSB	Avg.	Inn	ER	W–L	ERA	(TmERA)
1986	SD	N	15	11	.73	134.2	74	7-8	4.95	(3.99)

Dave SAX

Year	Team / Lg		GS	OSB	Avg.	Inn	ER	W–L	ERA	(TmERA)
1983	LA	N	1	4	4.00	9.0	3	0-1	3.00	(3.10)
1985	Bos	A	11	13	1.18	96.1	41	5-6	3.84	(4.06)
1986	Bos	A	2	1	.50	18.0	6	1-1	3.00	(3.93)
3 years			14	18	1.29	123.1	50	6-8	3.65	(3.97)

Bill SCHROEDER

Year	Team / Lg		GS	OSB	Avg.	Inn	ER	W–L	ERA	(TmERA)
1983	Mil	A	22	17	.77	203.0	85	15-7	3.77	(4.02)
1984	Mil	A	58	50	.86	512.1	239	26-32	4.20	(4.06)
1985	Mil	A	46	39	.85	407.0	194	19-27	4.29	(4.39)
1986	Mil	A	32	25	.78	285.2	126	12-20	3.97	(4.02)
4 years			158	131	.83	1408.0	644	72-86	4.12	(4.14)

Mike SCIOSCIA

Year	Team / Lg		GS	OSB	Avg.	Inn	ER	W–L	ERA	(TmERA)
1980	LA	N	44	49	1.11					
1981	LA	N	87	64	.74					
1982	LA	N	107	84	.79	984.0	371	57-50	3.39	(3.26)
1983	LA	N	10	3	.30	93.2	34	8-2	3.27	(3.10)
1984	LA	N	101	75	.74	914.2	300	55-46	2.95	(3.17)
1985	LA	N	130	81	.62	1178.0	380	78-52	2.90	(2.96)
1986	LA	N	108	79	.73	970.0	403	51-57	3.74	(3.76)
7 years			587	435	.74	4140.1	1488	249-207	3.23	(3.27)

Larry SHEETS

Year	Team / Lg		GS	OSB	Avg.	Inn	ER	W–L	ERA	(TmERA)
1986	Bal	A	2	2	1.00	17.0	13	1-1	6.88	(4.30)

Ted SIMMONS

Year	Team / Lg		GS	OSB	Avg.	Inn	ER	W–L	ERA	(TmERA)
1975	StL	N	148	99	.67					
1976	StL	N	107	62	.58					
1977	StL	N	139	96	.69					
1978	StL	N	119	120	1.01					
1979	StL	N	118	100	.85					
1980	StL	N	121	116	.96					
1981	Mil	A	73	47	.64					
1982	Mil	A	119	94	.79	1077.1	456	72-47	3.81	(3.98)
1983	Mil	A	84	84	1.00	749.1	321	41-43	3.86	(4.02)
1985	Mil	A	11	8	.73	100.0	57	6-5	5.13	(4.39)
1986	Atl	N	5	13	2.60	45.0	28	1-4	5.60	(3.97)
11 years			1044	839	.80	1971.2	862	120-99	3.93	(4.02)

Joel SKINNER

Year	Team / Lg		GS	OSB	Avg.	Inn	ER	W–L	ERA	(TmERA)
1983	Chi	A	2	2	1.00	18.0	0	2-0	.00	(3.67)
1984	Chi	A	23	19	.83	201.1	76	12-11	3.40	(4.13)
1985	Chi	A	15	11	.73	132.1	59	8-7	4.02	(4.07)
1986	Chi	A	49	30	.61	444.1	216	21-28	4.38	(3.94)
1986	NY	A	52	24	.46	461.1	203	28-24	3.96	(4.11)
4 years			141	86	.61	1257.1	554	71-70	3.97	(4.04)

Don SLAUGHT

Year	Team / Lg		GS	OSB	Avg.	Inn	ER	W–L	ERA	(TmERA)
1982	KC	A	31	12	.39	285.2	141	15-17	4.44	(4.08)
1983	KC	A	73	48	.66	646.1	307	37-36	4.27	(4.25)
1984	KC	A	112	65	.58	1007.2	426	60-52	3.80	(3.92)
1985	Tex	A	97	55	.57	852.1	412	38-59	4.35	(4.56)
1986	Tex	A	85	89	1.05	751.2	369	42-43	4.42	(4.11)
5 years			398	269	.68	3543.2	1655	192-207	4.20	(4.19)

Mike STANLEY

Year	Team / Lg		GS	OSB	Avg.	Inn	ER	W–L	ERA	(TmERA)
1986	Tex	A	2	1	.50	18.0	11	0-2	5.50	(4.11)

John STEFARO

Year	Team / Lg		GS	OSB	Avg.	Inn	ER	W–L	ERA	(TmERA)
1983	Bal	A	1	0	.00	9.0	8	0-1	8.00	(3.63)
1986	Bal	A	41	37	.90	343.0	189	10-31	4.96	(4.30)
2 years			42	37	.88	352.0	197	10-32	5.04	(4.28)

Marc SULLIVAN

Year	Team / Lg		GS	OSB	Avg.	Inn	ER	W–L	ERA	(TmERA)
1984	Bos	A	2	1	.50	17.0	18	1-1	9.53	(4.18)
1985	Bos	A	23	13	.57	211.2	113	9-13	4.82	(4.06)
1986	Bos	A	35	22	.61	316.1	148	22-14	4.21	(3.93)
3 years			60	36	.60	545.0	279	32-28	4.61	(3.99)

Jim SUNDBERG

Year	Team / Lg		GS	OSB	Avg.	Inn	ER	W–L	ERA	(TmERA)
1975	Tex	A	149	78	.52					
1976	Tex	A	134	98	.73					
1977	Tex	A	136	47	.35*					
1978	Tex	A	146	74	.51					
1979	Tex	A	144	74	.51					
1980	Tex	A	147	101	.69					
1981	Tex	A	97	40	.41*					
1982	Tex	A	129	74	.57	1137.2	554	49-80	4.38	(4.28)
1983	Tex	A	118	78	.66	1063.0	395	54-63	3.34	(3.31)
1984	Mil	A	99	40	.40	885.0	386	40-59	3.93	(4.06)
1985	KC	A	107	60	.56	969.1	372	61-46	3.45	(3.49)
1986	KC	A	124	69	.56	1101.0	480	56-68	3.92	(3.82)
12 years			1530	833	.54	5156.0	2187	260-316	3.82	(3.82)

Wilfredo TEJADA

Year	Team / Lg		GS	OSB	Avg.	Inn	ER	W–L	ERA	(TmERA)
1986	Mon	N	9	14	1.56	81.0	34	3-6	3.78	(3.78)

Mickey TETTLETON

Year	Team / Lg		GS	OSB	Avg.	Inn	ER	W–L	ERA	(TmERA)
1984	Oak	A	22	8	.36	198.0	86	10-12	3.91	(4.48)
1985	Oak	A	66	60	.91	601.2	236	36-30	3.53	(4.41)
1986	Oak	A	75	59	.79	660.0	293	36-39	4.00	(4.31)
3 years			163	127	.78	1459.2	615	82-81	3.79	(4.37)

Alejandro TREVINO

Year	Team / Lg		GS	OSB	Avg.	Inn	ER	W–L	ERA	(TmERA)
1978	NY	N	3	0	.00					
1979	NY	N	33	22	.67					
1980	NY	N	78	58	.74					
1981	NY	N	37	17	.46					
1982	Cin	N	104	89	.86	936.1	346	44-59	3.33	(3.66)
1983	Cin	N	51	40	.78	458.2	186	24-27	3.65	(3.98)
1984	Atl	N	65	68	1.05	577.1	238	35-30	3.71	(3.57)
1985	SF	N	47	37	.79	419.0	170	22-25	3.65	(3.61)
1986	LA	N	50	39	.78	449.1	193	20-30	3.87	(3.76)
9 years			468	370	.79	2840.2	1133	145-171	3.59	(3.70)

Dave VALLE

Year	Team / Lg		GS	OSB	Avg.	Inn	ER	W–L	ERA	(TmERA)
1984	Sea	A	7	3	.42	65.0	16	6-1	2.22	(4.31)
1985	Sea	A	19	15	.79	162.0	100	7-12	5.56	(4.68)
1986	Sea	A	9	6	.67	80.0	55	3-6	6.19	(4.65)
3 years			35	24	.69	307.0	171	16-19	5.01	(4.60)

David VAN GORDER

Year	Team / Lg		GS	OSB	Avg.	Inn	ER	W–L	ERA	(TmERA)
1982	Cin	N	44	50	1.14	397.0	181	14-31	4.10	(3.66)
1984	Cin	N	31	29	.94	271.2	136	6-25	4.51	(4.16)
1985	Cin	N	43	29	.67	379.2	172	24-18	4.08	(3.71)
1986	Cin	N	2	2	1.00	18.0	6	1-1	3.00	(3.91)
4 years			120	110	.92	1066.1	495	45-75	4.18	(3.81)

Ozzie VIRGIL

Year	Team / Lg		GS	OSB	Avg.	Inn	ER	W–L	ERA	(TmERA)
1982	Phil	N	26	32	1.23	234.0	130	11-15	5.00	(3.61)
1983	Phil	N	35	53	1.51	311.1	145	16-19	4.19	(3.34)
1984	Phil	N	124	105	.85	1108.2	452	64-60	3.67	(3.62)
1985	Phil	N	115	118	1.03	1024.1	397	57-58	3.49	(3.68)
1986	Atl	N	107	137	1.28	953.2	407	51-56	3.84	(3.97)
5 years			407	445	1.09	3632.0	1531	199-208	3.79	(3.70)

Ernie WHITT

Year	Team / Lg		GS	OSB	Avg.	Inn	ER	W–L	ERA	(TmERA)
1978	Tor	A	1	0	.00					
1979	Tor	A	92	73	.79					
1981	Tor	A	60	28	.47					
1982	Tor	A	74	43	.58	674.0	301	37-39	4.02	(3.95)
1983	Tor	A	95	51	.54	854.0	406	53-42	4.28	(4.12)
1984	Tor	A	97	51	.53	885.0	402	51-46	4.09	(3.86)
1985	Tor	A	113	55	.49	1015.2	363	73-40	3.22	(3.31)
1986	Tor	A	109	63	.58	985.0	449	60-49	4.10	(4.08)
8 years			641	364	.57	4413.2	1912	274-216	3.92	(3.85)

Jerry WILLARD

Year	Team / Lg		GS	OSB	Avg.	Inn	ER	W–L	ERA	(TmERA)
1984	Cle	A	67	45	.67	594.2	304	28-39	4.60	(4.26)
1985	Cle	A	83	66	.80	733.2	403	36-47	4.95	(4.91)
1986	Oak	A	49	41	.84	437.2	205	29-20	4.22	(4.31)
3 years			199	152	.76	1766.0	912	93-106	4.65	(4.54)

Robbie WINE

Year	Team / Lg		GS	OSB	Avg.	Inn	ER	W–L	ERA	(TmERA)
1986	Hous	N	1	2	2.00	9.0	0	1-0	0	(3.15)

Butch WYNEGAR

Year	Team / Lg		GS	OSB	Avg.	Inn	ER	W–L	ERA	(TmERA)
1976	Minn	A	133	124	.93					
1977	Minn	A	138	80	.58					
1978	Minn	A	121	72	.60					
1979	Minn	A	141	60	.43					
1980	Minn	A	133	60	.45					
1981	Minn	A	36	29	.81					
1982	Min/NYA		82	57	.70	722.1	360	40-42	4.49	(4.18)
1983	NY	A	84	59	.70	759.2	301	48-36	3.57	(3.86)
1984	NY	A	117	69	.59	1054.2	437	65-52	3.73	(3.78)
1985	NY	A	90	54	.50	813.1	310	54-36	3.43	(3.69)
1986	NY	A	52	35	.67	465.2	225	27-25	4.35	(4.11)
11 years			1127	699	.62	3815.2	1633	234-191	3.85	(3.89)

Steve YEAGER

Year	Team / Lg		GS	OSB	Avg.	Inn	ER	W–L	ERA	(TmERA)
1975	LA	N	131	50	.38					
1976	LA	N	108	51	.47*					
1977	LA	N	118	70	.59					
1978	LA	N	72	39	.54					
1979	LA	N	89	54	.61					
1980	LA	N	66	57	.86					
1981	LA	N	23	14	.61					
1982	LA	N	54	37	.69	495.1	168	31-23	3.05	(3.26)
1983	LA	N	96	67	.70	862.2	302	53-43	3.15	(3.10)
1984	LA	N	53	48	.91	471.1	189	20-33	3.61	(3.17)
1985	LA	N	32	16	.50	1178.0	380	78-52	2.90	(2.96)
1986	Sea	A	44	27	.61	392.2	218	19-25	5.00	(4.65)
12 years			886	530	.60	3400.0	1257	201-176	3.33	(3.37)

LEADING HITTERS AGAINST RIGHT-HANDED PITCHERS

AMERICAN LEAGUE

Player, Team	G	AB	Run	Hit	2B	3B	HR	RBI	SB	Avg
Boggs, Boston	126	398	94	143	35	0	5	44	0	.359
Mattingly, New York	134	434	101	151	30	1	26	72	0	.348
Hassey, Chi/N.Y.	110	277	43	91	21	1	9	41	1	.329
Puckett, Minnesota	145	514	110	169	26	4	25	77	19	.329
Easler, New York	134	384	62	124	23	1	13	70	2	.323
Tabler, Cleveland	109	323	53	104	18	2	4	33	3	.322
Joyner, California	131	401	73	127	24	2	16	76	5	.317
Baines, Chicago	116	364	66	115	21	1	18	70	2	.316
Ward, Texas	87	260	43	82	8	1	2	31	10	.315
Brett, Kansas City	101	293	60	92	24	3	11	54	1	.314

NATIONAL LEAGUE

Player, Team	AB	Run	Hit	2B	3B	HR	RBI	SB	Avg
Raines, Montreal	397		137	26	8	5	34		.345
Hayes, Philadelphia	414		140	36	2	15	64		.338
Backman, New York	335		113	17	1	1	19		.337
Sax, Los Angeles	407		136	23	3	3	35		.334
Walling, Houston	324		108	22	1	13	51		.333
Mumphrey, Chicago	247		82	10	2	5	30		.332
Brown, San Francisco	278		92	8	2	4	39		.331
Brooks, Montreal	221		73	12	2	9	41		.330
Gwynn, San Diego	406		133	20	1	6	26		.328
Ray, Pittsburgh	357		116	25	0	6	52		.325

LEADING HITTERS AGAINST LEFT-HANDED PITCHERS
(Minimum 100 At Bats)

AMERICAN LEAGUE

Player, Team	AB	Run	Hit	2B	3B	HR	RBI	SB	Avg
Hatcher, Minnesota	140	15	51	10	1	2	17	1	.364
Ripken, Baltimore	164	9	59	17	0	12	25	0	.360
Mattingly, New York	243	16	87	23	1	5	41	0	.358
Boggs, Boston	182	13	64	12	2	3	27	0	.352
Rice, Boston	168	6	59	14	0	7	39	0	.351
Gaetti, Minnesota	151	13	52	6	0	11	32	1	.344
Franco, Cleveland	164	11	56	12	1	6	22	1	.341
Bernazard, Cleveland	151	47	51	11	0	5	21	10	.338
Beniquez, Baltimore	128	10	43	6	0	3	16	0	.336
Tabler, Cleveland	150	8	50	11	0	2	15	0	.333

NATIONAL LEAGUE

Player, Team	AB	Run	Hit	2B	3B	HR	RBI	SB	Avg
Knight, New York	198		76	15	1	9	36		.384
Schmidt, Philadelphia	158		56	10	0	15	42		.354
Matthews, Chicago	105		37	6	1	6	15		.352
Webster, Montreal	200		68	16	2	5	20		.340
McReynolds, San Diego	192		65	12	3	10	34		.339
Concepcion, Cincinnati	101		34	9	0	1	7		.337
Galarraga, Montreal	120		40	5	0	4	14		.333
Pena, Pittsburgh	174		58	8	2	4	15		.333
Gwynn, San Diego	236		78	13	6	8	33		.331
Dawson, Montreal	161		52	12	1	11	25		.329
Davis, Cincinnati	146		48	4	1	11	29		.329

LEADING HITTERS AT HOME
(Minimum 200 At Bats)

AMERICAN LEAGUE

Player, Team	G	AB	Run	Hit	2B	3B	HR	RBI	SB	Avg
Puckett, Minnesota	81	346	72	127	21	6	14	51	13	.367
Boggs, Boston	73	273	53	99	29	0	3	36	0	.357
Tabler, Cleveland	65	227	31	79	12	0	5	30	1	.348
Rice, Boston	81	312	50	105	25	2	10	48	0	.337
Mattingly, New York	80	320	54	107	23	0	17	60	0	.334
Baines, Chicago	72	275	33	91	16	2	8	51	1	.331
Bernazard, Cleveland	76	286	45	94	12	3	9	40	8	.329
Bell, Toronto	78	300	53	98	17	5	15	57	4	.327
P. Bradley, Seattle	77	287	49	93	20	3	5	30	8	.324
Brett, Kansas City	59	205	39	66	16	4	8	41	1	.322

NATIONAL LEAGUE

Player, Team	AB	Run	Hit	2B	3B	HR	RBI	SB	Avg
Brooks, Montreal	137		48	8	2	3	26		.350
Gwynn, San Diego	317		108	14	4	8	26		.341
Clark, San Francisco	220		74	15	1	7	26		.336
Brown, San Francisco	228		76	7	2	3	30		.333
Raines, Montreal	282		92	17	3	4	36		.326
Dykstra, New York	211		68	16	4	4	24		.322
Reynolds, Houston	144		46	3	1	4	21		.319
Leonard, San Francisco	168		53	5	3	2	20		.315
Bass, Houston	296		93	14	2	5	36		.314
Hayes, Philadelphia	296		93	19	2	11	53		.314

LEADING HITTERS ON THE ROAD
(Minimum 200 At Bats)

AMERICAN LEAGUE

Player, Team	G	AB	Run	Hit	2B	3B	HR	RBI	SB	Avg
Mattingly, New York	82	357	63	131	30	2	14	53	0	.367
Boggs, Boston	76	303	54	108	18	2	5	35	0	.356
Yount, Milwaukee	71	263	45	86	19	1	5	24	6	.327
Gaetti, Minnesota	80	300	46	97	18	0	18	51	8	.323
Franco, Cleveland	73	297	41	95	15	2	6	37	7	.320
Easler, New York	76	257	32	81	10	1	8	41	2	.315
Hall, Cleveland	79	309	39	95	19	2	7	35	1	.314
O'Brien, Texas	78	286	48	89	10	3	12	49	2	.311
Rice, Boston	76	306	48	95	14	0	10	62	0	.310
Jacoby, Cleveland	79	309	39	95	19	2	7	35	1	.307

NATIONAL LEAGUE

Player, Team	AB	Run	Hit	2B	3B	HR	RBI	SB	Avg
Sax, Los Angeles	327		115	24	3	5	35		.352
Raines, Montreal	298		102	18	7	5	26		.342
Brooks, Montreal	169		56	10	3	11	32		.331
Walling, Houston	192		63	13	1	8	30		.328
Backman, New York	208		68	12	1	0	18		.327
Gwynn, San Diego	325		103	19	3	6	33		.317
Ray, Pittsburgh	281		89	15	0	5	42		.317
Webster, Montreal	293		92	16	5	6	25		.314
Hernandez, New York	312		97	25	0	7	47		.311
Bass, Houston	295		91	19	3	15	43		.308

LEADING HITTERS ON ARTIFICIAL TURF
(Minimum 70 At Bats)

AMERICAN LEAGUE

Player, Team	G	AB	Run	Hit	2B	3B	HR	RBI	SB	Avg
Mattingly, New York	26	112	28	49	15	1	5	19	0	.438
Boggs, Boston	23	92	19	35	5	2	0	8	0	.380
Ripken, Baltimore	25	103	18	38	8	0	7	21	0	.369
M. Davis, Oakland	19	71	16	26	7	1	4	14	7	.366
Rice, Boston	23	95	12	34	7	0	3	15	0	.358
Lynn, Baltimore	24	93	16	33	3	1	8	19	1	.355
Puckett, Minnesota	100	426	84	150	23	6	18	57	14	.352
Yount, Milwaukee	20	70	16	24	11	1	2	5	1	.343
Trammell, Detroit	23	92	15	31	7	0	4	16	4	.337
P. Bradley, Seattle	92	348	61	116	24	3	6	35	12	.333

NATIONAL LEAGUE

Player, Team	AB	Run	Hit	2B	3B	HR	RBI	SB	Avg
Sax, Los Angeles	186		72	16	0	2	20		.387
Backman, New York	127		44	8	1	0	11		.346
Brooks, Montreal	203		70	10	5	6	37		.345
Kruk, San Diego	91		31	4	2	1	14		.341
Thomas, Atlanta	103		35	11	1	5	15		.340
Raines, Montreal	425		142	26	9	7	49		.334
McReynolds, San Diego	150		50	12	2	8	32		.333
Griffey, Atlanta	100		33	5	3	2	12		.330
Bass, Houston	421		133	22	2	10	53		.316
Melvin, San Francisco	92		29	6	2	1	10		.315
Gwynn, San Francisco	168		53	9	1	4	19		.315

LEADING HITTERS ON GRASS
(Minimum 100 At-Bats)

AMERICAN LEAGUE

Player, Team	G	AB	Run	Hit	2B	3B	HR	RBI	SB	Avg
Gaetti, Minnesota	61	228	40	83	16	0	16	39	8	.364
Boggs, Boston	126	488	88	172	42	0	8	63	0	.352
Tabler, Cleveland	112	396	53	137	25	0	6	44	3	.346
Mattingly, New York	136	565	89	189	38	1	26	94	0	.335
Iorg, Toronto	57	129	12	42	8	0	2	22	1	.326
Rice, Boston	134	523	86	166	32	2	17	95	0	.317
Fletcher, Texas	123	443	71	138	27	4	3	40	12	.312
Ward, Texas	92	331	46	103	13	1	4	36	11	.311
Franco, Cleveland	129	525	71	162	29	5	9	66	9	.309
Murray, Baltimore	117	422	53	130	22	1	15	76	2	.308
Yount, Milwaukee	120	452	66	139	20	6	7	41	13	.308

NATIONAL LEAGUE

Player, Team	AB	Run	Hit	2B	3B	HR	RBI	SB	Avg
Webster, Montreal	148		52	10	0	3	12		.351
Hayes, Philadelphia	170		59	15	0	6	27		.347
Walling, Houston	110		38	7	1	5	18		.345
Orsulak, Pittsburgh	110		37	7	2	2	10		.336
Raines, Montreal	155		52	9	1	2	13		.335
Gwynn, San Diego	474		158	24	6	10	40		.333
Brooks, Montreal	103		34	8	0	8	21		.330
Mumphrey, Chicago	235		77	9	2	5	25		.328
Brown, San Francisco	311		101	9	3	4	38		.325
Hernandez, New York	372		119	19	1	11	62		.320

STARTING PITCHERS RECEIVING BEST OFFENSIVE SUPPORT
(Based on the number of runs scored in games the pitcher has started.)

NATIONAL LEAGUE

Pitcher, Team	Starts	Runs	Runs Per Start
Shane Rawley, Philadelphia	23	130	5.65
Steve Trout, Chicago	25	131	5.24
Sid Fernandez, New York	31	160	5.16
Mike LaCoss, San Francisco	31	160	5.16
Mike Krukow, San Francisco	34	173	5.09
Rick Aguilera, New York	20	100	5.00
Ron Darling, New York	34	167	4.91
Bob Ojeda, New York	30	145	4.83
Chris Welsh, Cincinnati	24	116	4.83
Bruce Ruffin, Philadelphia	21	101	4.81

AMERICAN LEAGUE

Pitcher, Team	Starts	Runs	Runs Per Start
Roger Clemens, Boston	33	201	6.09
Mike Mason, Texas	22	134	6.09
Dennis Rasmussen, New York	31	181	5.84
John Cerutti, Toronto	20	114	5.70
Oil Can Boyd, Boston	30	165	5.60
Jack Morris, Detroit	35	190	5.43
Mark Gubicza, Kansas City	24	128	5.33
Mike Witt, California	34	178	5.24
Tom Candiotti, Cleveland	34	177	5.21
Ken Schrom, Cleveland	33	172	5.21

STARTING PITCHERS RECEIVING LEAST OFFENSIVE SUPPORT

NATIONAL LEAGUE

Pitcher, Team	Starts	Runs	Runs Per Start
Rick Sutcliffe, Chicago	27	88	3.26
Bob Welch, Los Angeles	33	108	3.27
Danny Cox, St. Louis	32	110	3.44
Greg Mathews, St. Louis	22	76	3.45
Dave Dravecky, San Diego	26	90	3.46
Steve Carlton, Phil-San Francisco	22	78	3.55
Jay Tibbs, Montreal	31	112	3.61
Tim Conroy, St. Louis	21	78	3.71
Dave Palmer, Atlanta	35	130	3.71
Zane Smith, Atlanta	32	119	3.72

AMERICAN LEAGUE

Pitcher, Team	Starts	Runs	Runs Per Start
Danny Jackson, Kansas City	27	79	2.93
Floyd Bannister, Chicago	27	89	3.30
Bret Saberhagen, Kansas City	25	83	3.32
Tom Seaver, Chicago-Boston	28	102	3.64
Neal Heaton, Cleveland-Minn.	29	106	3.66
Dennis Leonard, Kansas	30	113	3.77
Jose Guzman, Texas	29	110	3.79
Richard Dotson, Chicago	34	133	3.85
Ed Correa, Texas	32	125	3.91
Storm Davis, Baltimore	25	99	3.96

HIGHEST DOUBLE PLAY SUPPORT

NATIONAL LEAGUE

Pitcher, Team	Starts	DPs	DPs Per Start
Chris Welsh, Cincinnati	24	33	1.38
Bob Forsch, St. Louis	33	42	1.27
John Tudor, St. Louis	30	34	1.13
Bruce Ruffin, Philadelphia	21	23	1.10
Dave Palmer, Atlanta	35	38	1.09
Bob Ojeda, New York	30	32	1.07
Ron Darling, New York	34	36	1.06
Shane Rawley, Philadelphia	23	24	1.04
Kevin Gross, Philadelphia	36	37	1.03
John Denny, Cincinnati	27	27	1.00
Danny Cox, St. Louis	32	32	1.00
Greg Mathews, St. Louis	22	22	1.00

AMERICAN LEAGUE

Pitcher, Team	Starts	DPs	DPs Per Start
Jose Guzman, Texas	29	39	1.34
Mike Witt, California	34	44	1.29
Danny Jackson, Kansas City	27	33	1.22
Mike Morgan, Seattle	33	40	1.21
John Cerutti, Toronto	20	24	1.20
Storm Davis, Baltimore	25	30	1.20
Walt Terrell, Detroit	33	39	1.18
Mike Moore, Seattle	37	43	1.16
Mike Flanagan, Baltimore	28	32	1.14

LEAST DOUBLE PLAY SUPPORT

NATIONAL LEAGUE

Pitcher, Team	Starts	DPs	DPs Per Start
Mike Scott, Houston	37	17	.46
Nolan Ryan, Houston	30	16	.53
Rick Honeycutt, Los Angeles	28	15	.54
Floyd Youmans, Montreal	32	18	.56
Jim DeShaies, Houston	26	15	.58
Dennis Eckersley, Chicago	32	19	.59
Zane Smith, Atlanta	32	19	.59
Rick Reuschel, Pittsburgh	34	21	.62
Orel Hershiser, Los Angeles	35	22	.63
Bob Welch, Los Angeles	33	22	.67

AMERICAN LEAGUE

Pitcher, Team	Starts	DPs	DPs Per Start
Jose Rijo, Oakland	26	11	.42
Curt Young, Oakland	27	16	.59
Roger Clemens, Boston	33	21	.64
Bret Saberhagen, Kansas City	25	16	.64
Teddy Higuera, Milwaukee	34	22	.65
Bert Blyleven, Minnesota	36	25	.69
Ron Guidry, New York	30	21	.70
Oil Can Boyd, Boston	30	23	.77
Joe Cowley, Chicago	27	21	.78
Mark Langston, Seattle	36	28	.78

TOUGHEST STARTING PITCHERS
TO RUN ON
(Based on the number of bases stolen by the opposition in this pitcher's starts.)

NATIONAL LEAGUE

Pitcher, Team	Starts	OSB	OSB Per Start
John Tudor, St. Louis	30	10	.33
Rick Aguilera, New York	20	8	.40
Dave Dravecky, San Diego	26	13	.50
Rick Honeycutt, Los Angeles	28	15	.54
Greg Mathews, St. Louis	22	12	.55
Scott Sanderson, Chicago	28	16	.57
Bob Forsch, St. Louis	33	19	.58
John Denny, Cincinnati	27	16	.59
Bob Knepper, Houston	38	23	.61
Fernando Valenzuela, Los Angeles	34	21	.62

AMERICAN LEAGUE

Pitcher, Team	Starts	OSB	OSB Per Start
Walt Terrell, Detroit	33	5	.15
Bob Tewksbury, New York	20	3	.15
Doug Drabek, New York	21	4	.19
Bruce Hurst, Boston	25	5	.20
Al Nipper, Boston	26	6	.23
Mike Witt, California	34	8	.24
Charlie Leibrandt, Kansas City	34	8	.24
Kirk McCaskill, California	33	10	.30
Roger Clemens, Boston	33	11	.33
Danny Jackson, Kansas City	27	10	.37

EASIEST STARTING PITCHERS
TO RUN ON

NATIONAL LEAGUE

Pitcher, Team	Starts	OSB	OSB Per Start
Floyd Youmans, Montreal	32	61	1.91
Dave Palmer, Atlanta	35	53	1.51
Shane Rawley, Philadelphia	23	31	1.35
Mike Scott, Houston	37	50	1.35
Bruce Ruffin, Philadelphia	21	28	1.35
Charles Hudson, Philadelphia	23	30	1.30
Nolan Ryan, Houston	30	38	1.37
Kevin Gross, Philadelphia	36	45	1.25
Bob Ojeda, New York	30	37	1.23
Rick Sutcliffe, Chicago	27	33	1.22

AMERICAN LEAGUE

Pitcher, Team	Starts	OSB	OSB Per Start
Bobby Witt, Texas	31	53	1.71
Ed Correa, Texas	32	40	1.25
Joe Niekro, New York	25	29	1.16
Mike Boddicker, Baltimore	33	36	1.10
José Rijo, Oakland	26	26	1.00
Tom Seaver, Chicago-Boston	28	28	1.00
Ken Dixon, Baltimore	33	31	.94
Tom Candiotti, Cleveland	34	31	.91
Tim Leary, Milwaukee	30	27	.90
Ken Schrom, Cleveland	33	29	.88

A GLOSSARY OF TERMS IN USE IN SABERMETRICS

Adjusted Range Factor

The number of plays made by a player per estimated nine innings of defensive play.

Approximate Value

A crude integer estimate of the value of a given season, ranging from 0 for ineffective, part-time play up to an average of 9 or 10 for a regular player, 16 to 20 for an MVP-type season.

Award Share

The total MVP Award vote drawn by a player over the course of his career, stated in constant terms with 1.00 representing the potential vote for one season. (Award Shares could also be calculated for a few other awards, such as the Cy Young.)

Base-Out Percentage

A method developed by Barry Codell for the evaluation of offensive statistics; quite similar to total average.

Brock6 System

A complex set of several hundred interlocking formulas, designed to project a player's final career totals on the basis of his performance up to a given point in time. An earlier form was Brock2.

Career Value

The value of a player to his team over the course of his entire career.

Defensive Efficiency Record

A mathematical attempt to answer this question: Of all balls put into play against this team, what percentage did the defense succeed in turning into outs?

Defensive Spectrum

An arrangement of defensive positions according to raw abilities needed to learn to play each. The spectrum has shifted at times throughout history, but generally reads "designated hitter, first base, left field, right field, third base, center field, second base, shortstop." Catcher is not a part of the spectrum.

Defensive Winning Percentage

A technique of evaluation of defensive statistics by a series of charts, resulting in a two-digit percentage estimate. An average defensive player should have a defensive winning percentage of .50.

Established Performance Levels

A player's established performance level is the level of performance in an area which the player has clearly established that he is able to maintain.

Estimated Runs Produced

A method developed by Paul Johnson to estimate the number of runs resulting from any combination of offensive incidents. Closely parallels runs created.

Expected Remaining Future Value

Also called "Trade Value."

The Favorite Toy

A method used to estimate the chance that a player, at a given point in his career, will reach some standard of career excellence (such as 3000 hits, 500 home runs).

Game Scores

A method used to evaluate each start by a pitcher, thus focusing on the pitcher's best and worst starts.

Hall of Fame Assessment System

A method used to evaluate whether a player is doing or has done the things which characterize Hall of Famers.

Indicated ERA

A method of guessing what a pitcher's ERA might be based on the two categories for which he is wholly responsible—home runs allowed and walks.

Isolated Power

The difference between batting average and slugging percentage.

Johnson Effect

The tendency of teams that exceed their Pythagorean projection for wins in one season to relapse in the following season. Parallel effects have also been established for the tendency of teams that violate the normal relationship between offensive incidents and runs resulting; these are also sometimes referred to as Johnson Effects.

Linear Weights

A common mathematical tool used to derive the value of each element within a data set, and thus produce formulas that can combine those values. Commonly used by Pete Palmer in analyzing baseball.

Major League Equivalency

The major-league performance that is equivalent to a given performance in the minor leagues.

Offensive Earned Run Average

A method developed by Thomas Cover to estimate the number of earned runs created by each player per 27 outs.

Offensive Losses

An estimate of the number of team losses that would result from a player's offensive production.

Offensive Winning Percentage

A mathematical answer to this question: If every player on a team hit the same way that this player hits, and the team allowed an average number of runs to score, what would the team's winning percentage be?

Offensive Wins

An estimate of the number of team wins that would result from a player's offensive production.

On-Base Percentage

If you don't know what on-base percentage is you shouldn't be reading this book.

Overall Winning Percentage

A combination of offensive and defensive winning percentages.

Palmer Method

The collective analytical procedures developed by Pete Palmer.

Park Adjustment

Any of a number of methods used to adjust offensive or defensive statistics for park illusions.

Park Illusion

The distortion of offensive or defensive abilities as reflected in statistics due to the characteristics of a given park.

Peak Value

The value of a player to his team at his highest clearly established level of performance.

Project Scoresheet

A volunteer organization that collects and distributes scoresheets of all major-league games for the public.

Pythagorean Method

The practical application of the Pythagorean theory to derive conclusions or state relationships.

Pythagorean Theory

The name given to a known property of any baseball team, that being that the ratio between their wins and their losses will be similar to the relationship between the square of their runs scored and the square of their runs allowed.

Quality Starts

The number of starts in which a pitcher pitches six innings or more and gives up three runs or less.

Rachel McCarthy James

One incredibly sweet baby.

Range Factor

The average number of plays per game successfully made by a fielder (that is, total chances per game minus errors per game).

RBI Importance

That portion of a player's runs batted in that is counted as victory-important.

RBI Value

A method of assessing the value of each run batted in, developed by Tim Mulligan.

Reservoir Estimation Technique

The process of comparing a team's talent resources by figuring the "trade value" of all players on the roster.

Runs Created

An estimate of the number of team runs that would result from a player's offensive statistics; can be derived by any of a number of formulas.

Sabermetrics

The search for objective knowledge about baseball.

SABR

The Society For American Baseball Research.

Secondary Average

The sum of a player's extra bases on hits, walks, and stolen bases, expressed as a percentage of at bats.

Signature Significance

The existence, rare but occasionally seen, of significant evidence about the ability of a player that can be seen in a very small sample of his work.

Similarity Scores

A method used for evaluating the "degree of resemblance" between two players or two teams.

Speed Score

A method of evaluating a player's speed on a zero to ten scale based on his performance in six speed-related categories.

Star Value

A method of counting and weighting the star-type accomplishments of a player, such as the number of times with 200 hits or 100 RBI or 20 wins as a pitcher.

Total Average

A method developed by Thomas Boswell for the evaluation of offensive statistics.

Trade Value

An estimate of the approximate value that a player will have in the rest of his career.

Victory-Important RBI (VI-RBI)

An attempt to measure the number of a player's runs batted in which are contributions to eventual victory.

APPENDIX

APPROXIMATE VALUE
AND THE
VALUE APPROXIMATION METHOD

The traditional Value Approximation Method has 13 rules for non-pitchers, 5 rules for pitchers. These are:

Non-Pitchers:

1) Award 1 point if the player has played at least 10 games, 2 if 50 games, 3 if 100 games, 4 if 130 games or more.

2) Award 1 point if the player has hit .250 or better, 2 if .275, 3 if .300 . . . 7 if .400 or better.

3) Award 1 point if the player's slugging percentage is above .300, 2 if above .400 . . . 6 if above .800.

4) Award 1 point if the player has a home run percentage (home runs divided by at bats) of 2.5 or more, 2 if 5.0 or more, 3 if 7.5 or more, 4 if 10.0 or more.

5) Award 1 point if the player walks one time for each 10 official at bats, 2 if twice for each 10 at bats, 3 if three times for each ten at bats.

6) Award 1 point if the player steals 20 bases, 2 if 50 bases, 3 if 80 bases.

7) Award 1 point if the player drives in 70 runs while slugging less than .400, 1 point if he drives in 100 runs while slugging less than .500, or 1 if he drives in 130 while slugging less than .600.

8) Award 1 point if the player's primary defensive position (the position at which he plays the most games) is second base, third base or center field, 2 if it is shortstop. For catchers, award 1 point if the player catches 10 games, 2 if he catches 80, 3 if he catches 150.

9) Award 1 point if the player's range factor is above the league average at his position. Catchers and first basemen have no range factors; first basemen get 1 point if they have 100 assists.

10) Award 1 point if the player's fielding average is above the league average at his position.

On points nine and ten, if you are figuring a player over the course of his career, you will probably want to establish period norms for fielding average and range at the position, rather than trying to figure the league average for each season separately.

11) Award 1 point to a shortstop or second baseman who participates in 90 or more double plays, 2 for 120 or more, 3 for 150 or more. Award 1 point to an outfielder who has 12 or more assists plus double plays. Award 1 to a catcher who is better than the league average in opposition stolen bases per game.

12) Award 1 point if the player has 200 hits. Award 1 point if the player leads the league in RBI.

13) Reduce all points awarded on rules one through twelve for players who have fewer than 500 at bats and fewer than 550 plate appearances. Reduce by at bats divided by 500 or plate appearances divided by 550, whichever is better for the player.

Pitchers:

1) Award 1 point if the pitcher has pitched in 30 or more games, 2 if 55 or more, 3 if 80 or more.

2) Award 1 point if the pitcher has pitched 40 innings, 2 if 90 innings, 3 if 140 innings . . . 7 if 340 innings.

3) Figure for the pitcher his total of 2 (wins + saves) minus losses. Award 1 point if the pitcher's total is 6 or more, 2 if 14 or more, 3 if 24 or more, 4 if 36 or more, 5 if 50 or more, 6 if 66 or more, and 7 if 84 or more.

4) Award 1 point if the pitcher has won 18 or more games. Award 1 point if the pitcher led the league in ERA. Award 1 point if the pitcher led the league in saves.

5) Establish a mark 1.00 run above the league ERA. Subtract the pitcher's ERA from this, and multiply that by the number of decisions that the pitcher has had. Divide by 13. (What you are doing here is giving credit for a low ERA. If the pitcher's ERA is more than a run above the league average, this will result in a negative figure, a subtraction. A pitcher's approximate value can be reduced by this factor, but no player's approximate value can be reduced below zero.

The outcome of this point-count system is called approximate value.

In parts of this book I used a new and different Value Approximation Method. The totals for a group of players if figured by this new method would be virtually identical to the old method, but individual cases would be different. The basic difference is that whereas the traditional form works by "cut-offs"—.300 is 3 points, .299 is 2 points—the new method works in some cases by division of raw totals, and thus is less susceptible to flukes of players just skimming over several boundaries. The rules:

1) Award 1 point if the player has played in 50 games, 2 if he had played 50, 3 if 100, 4 if 130, 5 if 148 or more.

2) Award points for batting average by (batting average minus .235) divided by .028.

3) Award points for slugging percentage by (slugging percentage minus .26) divided by .09.

4) Award points for home run percentage by (home runs divided by at bats) divided by .039.

5) Award points for walks by (walks divided by at bats) divided by .12.

6) Award points for stolen bases by (stolen bases minus 10) divided by 30.

7) Award 1 extra point if the player's RBI total is at least one greater than (.4 times his total bases). Award 1 extra point if the player has 200 or more hits.

8–11) Points awarded for defense are the same as in the original method.

12) Reduce all points awarded under rules one through eleven by the formula (At Bats divided by 550) or (At Bats plus Walks divided by 600), whichever is greater, and not to exceed 1.00.

Brock2 System

A full account of the Brock2 system can be found on pages 301–305 of the 1985 *Baseball Abstract*.

Defensive Efficiency Record

A Defensive Efficiency Record is a *team* statistic, intended to estimate the percentage of all balls in play that a team has turned into outs.

To figure DER, you begin by making two estimates of the number of times that a team's defense has turned a batted ball into an out. The first is:

$$PO - K - DP - 2(TP) - OCS - A \text{ (of)}$$

This assumes that a batted ball has been turned into an out every time a putout is recorded unless (1) the putout was a strikeout, (2) two or three putouts were recorded on the same play, or (3) a runner has been thrown out on the bases. OCS is opponents caught stealing, and A (of) is outfielder's assists, both of which can be found on the division sheets.

The second estimate is:

$$TBF - K - H - W - HBP - .71 \text{ Errors}$$

This assumes that every batter facing the team's pitchers has been put out by the fielders unless 1) he strikes out, 2) he gets a hit, 3) he walks, 4) he is hit by the pitch, or 5) he reaches base on an error.

These two estimates will almost always be within 1% of one another, usually within .5%. You then take the average of the two, which is called Plays Made (PM).

DER is Plays Made divided by Plays Made Plus Plays NOT Made:

$$\frac{PM}{PM + H - HR + .71 \text{ Errors}}$$

An average defensive efficiency record is about .695. Almost all successful teams will be above average.

Defensive Winning Percentage

The exact method for deriving a defensive winning percentage is explained in the appendix to the 1983 and 1984 *Baseball Abstracts*. It has not been changed since then. In fact, it hasn't even been used seen then.

Expected Remaining Approximate Value

Also known as

Trade Value

Trade Value is used to assess the size of a team's talent pool, by comparing the "apparent futures" that a team has (see Minnesota comment).

The formula for this has two stages. First of all, you find the player's "Y Score" by the formula 24 − .6 (Age):

$$Y = 24 - .6 \text{ (Age)}$$

The Y score and the player's approximate value are then put together by the following formula:

$$(AV - Y)^2 \times \frac{(Y + 1) \times AV}{190} + \frac{AV \, (Y)^2}{13}$$

I have never, in four years, been able to get this to come out right in print, so I'm going to write it all out longhand here, so if a superscript or an operand or something gets left out in production, as it has every year, you'll still be able to figure it out. The formula has three elements:

The first is (Approximate Value Minus the Y Score) squared. Let's say we're dealing with a 21-year-old player with an approximate value of 12 (Jose Canseco). At 21 the Y score is 11.4, so (AV − Y) is .6, which squared is .36.

The second element is the Y score plus one, times the approximate value and divided by 190. For Canseco, this would be (12.4 times 12), or 148.8, divided by 190, or .77.

Those two elements are multiplied together, in this particular case yielding almost nothing (.36 times .77 is .28).

The third element is the approximate value times the square of the Y score, divided by 13. The Y score is 11.4; the square of that would be 130. Twelve times 130 divided by 13 is 120.

This is added to the product of the first two, and yields

180 + .28 = 120.28, which remains 1.20. That's a very high trade value, probably one of the ten highest in baseball.

Sometime I'll explain why this thing works and why it was designed this way, but not right now.

The Favorite Toy

The Favorite Toy is a method that is used to estimate a player's chance of getting to a specific goal—let us say, 3000 hits.

Four things are considered in this matter. Those are:

1) The Need Hits—the number of hits needed to reach the goal. (This, of course, could also be "Need Home Runs" or "Need Doubles"—whatever.)

2) The Years Remaining. The number of years remaining to reach the goal is estimated by the formula 24 − .6(age). This formula assigns a 20-year-old player 12.0 remaining seasons, a 25-year-old player 9.0 remaining seasons, a 30-year-old player 6.0 remaining seasons, and a 35-year-old player 3.0 remaining seasons. Any player who is still playing regularly is assumed to have at least 1.5 seasons remaining, regardless of his age.

3) The Established Hit Level. For 1984, the established hit level would be found by adding 1982 hits, two times 1983 hits, and three times 1984 hits, and dividing by six. However, a player cannot have an established performance level that is less than three-fourths of his most recent performance—that is, a player who had 200 hits in 1984 cannot have an established hit level below 150.00.

4) The Projected Remaining Hits. This is found by multiplying the second number, the years remaining, by the third, the established hit level.

Once you get the projected remaining hits, the chance of getting to the goal is figured by (projected remaining hits) divided by (need hits), minus .5. By this method, if your "need hits" and your "projected remaining hits" are the same, your chance of reaching the goal is 50%. If your projected reamining hits are 20% more than your need hits, the chance of reaching the goal is 70%.

Two special rules:

1) A player's chances of continuing to progress toward a goal cannot exceed .97 per year. (This rule prevents a player from figuring to have a 148% chance of reaching a goal.)

2) If a player's offensive winning percentage is below season. (That is, if a below-average hitter is two years away from reaching a goal, his chance of reaching that goal cannot be shown as better than 9/16 [three-fourths times three-fourths] regardless of his age.)

Runs Created

There are three forms of the runs created formula. All three have an A factor, a B factor, and a C factor; in all cases the formula is assembled by (A times B) divided by C. These are the three versions:

1. Basic Runs Created

   A Hits Plus Walks
      (H + W)
   B Total Bases
      (TB)
   C At Bats Plus Walks
      (AB + W)

2. Stolen Base Version

   A Hits Plus Walks Minus Caught Stealing
      (H + W − CS)
   B Total Bases Plus (.55 times Stolen Bases)
      (TB + .55 SB)
   C At Bats Plus Walks
      (AB + W)

3. Technical Version

   A Hits Plus Walks and Hit Batsmen Minus Caught Stealing
      and Grounded Into Double Plays
      (H + W + HBP − CS − GIDP)

B   Total Bases Plus .26 Times Hit Batsmen and Uninten-
     tional Walks Plus .52 Times Sacrifice Hits, Sacrifice
     Flies, And Stolen Bases
     (TB + .26 (TBB − IBB + HBP) + .52 (SH + SF + SB))
C   At Bats Plus Walks Plus Hit Batsmen Plus Sacrifice Hits
     Plus Sacrifice Flies
     (AB + TBB + HBP + SH + SF)

Offensive Winning Percentage

To figure a player's offensive winning percentage:
1) Figure runs created per 27 outs.
2) Divide by the league average of runs per game.
3) Square the result.
4) Divide that figure by one plus itself.

If done for a league, this will produce a figure above .500. If
done for a player who is average in every respect, it will produce a
figure of .500. If done for a player who is above average, it will
produce a figure above .500.

Figuring Speed Scores

To figure speed scores (see St. Louis Cardinal comment), you
begin with six basic statistics: stolen base percentage, stolen bases,
caught stealing, triples, runs scored, grounded into double plays and
defensive position and range. There is a two-step process used to
convert each area of performance to a score on a zero-to-ten scale:

Stolen Base Percentage:

1. Figure stolen base percentage as (Stolen Bases + 3) divided
by (Stolen Bases plus Caught Stealing + 7). (The additional numbers are to prevent a player who steals one base and isn't caught
stealing from having a "ten" because he has a stolen base percentage
of 1.000).
2. Call that SBP. Figure score as (SBP − .4) Times 20.

Stolen Base Attempts:

1. Figure Stolen Base attempts as a percentage of times on first
base by the formula (SB + CS) divided by Singles + BB + HBP).
Remember, singles are not the same as hits.
2. Call that SBA. Convert that to a score by figuring the square
root of SBA and dividing the square root by .07.

Triples:

1. Figure triples as a percentage of balls in play by the formula
3B divided by (AB − HR − SO).
2. Call that 3BA. Convert that to a score by dividing it by
.0016.

Runs Scored:

1. Figure runs scored as a percentage of times on base by
(R − HR) divided by (H + HB + BB − HR).
2. Call that ROB. Convert that to a score by (ROB − .1) divided by .04.

Grounded into Double Plays:

1. Figure grounded into double plays as a percentage of balls
in play by GIDP divided by (R − SO − HR).
2. Call that GIDPF. Convert that to a score by
(.063 − GIDPF) divided by .007.

Defensive position and range:

1. Assign the player a "position value" which is C-1, 1B-2,
3B-4, 2B-6, LF-6, RF-6, SS-7 and CF-8.
2. Figure the player's range factor and divide it by the expected
range factor for his position. The expected range factors are
3B-2.65, 2B-4.80, L/RF-2.00, SS-4.60 and CF-2.7. Catchers and
first basemen have no range factors, so their position value is also
their speed score for this factor.
3. Call that RER (Range over expected range.) Multiply the
position value by RER to get the score.

I noticed after doing the scores that I had set the position values
and expected ranges so that it makes virtually no difference whether
you consider an outfielder to be a center fielder or a right/left fielder,
because the results will be virtually identical either way. His position value is 33% higher, but his expected range if 35% higher, so
whichever way you figure him you'll get about the same thing.

The player's speed score is the average of these six elements.

The appendix comes not only at the end of the book but at the
end of the process of writing the book, at a time when I am quite
exhausted. If the writing and proof-reading of the appendix are
sometimes not what they ought to be, I hope you'll understand.
Have a good season; good luck to your team, and I'll see you next
year. Bye. Support Project Scoresheet.